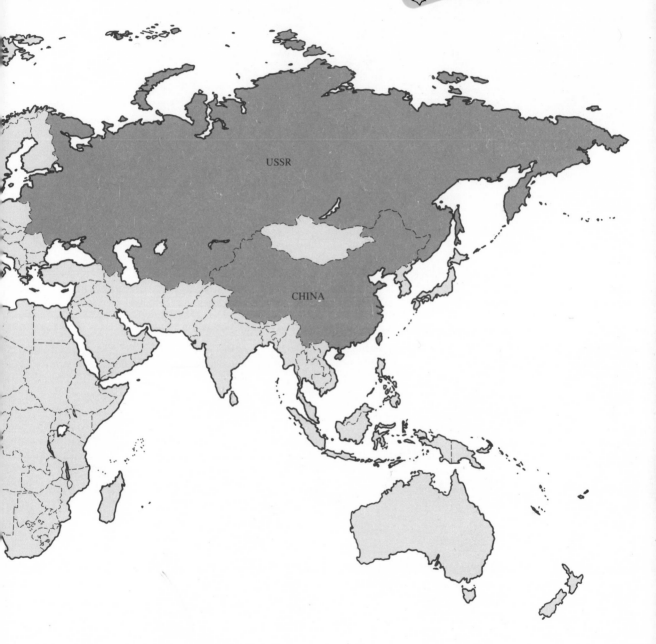

COMPARATIVE
POLITICS

COMPARATIVE POLITICS

Diverse States in an Interdependent World

David F. Roth

University of British Columbia

Paul V. Warwick

Simon Fraser University

Soviet Union sections by **David W. Paul**

HARPER & ROW, PUBLISHERS, New York
Cambridge, Philadelphia, San Francisco,
London, Mexico City, São Paulo, Singapore, Sydney

1817

Sponsoring Editor: Lauren Silverman
Project Editor: David Nickol
Cover Design: Paul Kirovac/A Good Thing, Inc.
Text Art: Fine Line Illustrations Inc.
Photo Research: Alice Lundoff
Production Manager: Willie Lane
Compositor: ComCom Division of Haddon Craftsmen, Inc.
Printer and Binder: R. R. Donnelley & Sons Company
Cover Printer: Phoenix Color

Comparative Politics: Diverse States in an Interdependent World

Library of Congress Cataloging-in-Publication Data

Roth. David F.
    Comparative politics : diverse states in an
  interdependent world / David F. Roth, Paul V. Warwick, David W. Paul.
      p.   cm.
    Includes index.
    ISBN 0-06-045626-4
    1. Comparative government.   I. Warwick, Paul.   II. Paul, David W.
  III. Title.
  JF51.R55 1989
  320.3—dc19   88-25972
                                                                     CIP

89 90 91 9 8 7 6 5 4 3 2

To Chew Chiewphin and Ping Ping,
each of whom provided valuable insights
and assistance.

D.F.R.

To B.J.C.,
who suffered silently through the preparation of this work.

P.V.W.

To my former students.

D.W.P.

Contents

A Country-by-Country Table of Contents xi
Preface xv

Introduction 1

Politics and the Political System 3
The Three Worlds 5
Organization of the Book 9

Maps 11

Part One
BACKGROUND TO POLITICS 25

1 The Historical Bases of Politics 27

Introduction 27
Britain and France: Alternative Routes to Democracy 33
The Soviet Union and China: Revolution and Development 45
Mexico and Nigeria: Colonialism and Its Aftermath 61
Conclusions 74

2 Political Frameworks 76

Introduction 76
Britain and France: Democratic Alternatives 85
The Soviet Union and China: Communist Alternatives 95
Mexico and Nigeria: Third World Political Structures 107
Conclusions 115

3   Society and Politics   118

Introduction   118
Britain and France: Cleavage Management in Liberal Democracies   129
The Soviet Union and China: Pluralist Societies Under Single-Party
    Rule   139
Mexico and Nigeria: Dimensions and Challenges of Nation Building   151
Conclusions   161

Part Two
POLITICAL ACTORS   163

4   The Citizen in Politics   165

Introduction   165
Britain and France: Citizen Roles in Liberal Democracies   173
The Soviet Union and China: Citizen Roles in Socialist Countries   184
Mexico and Nigeria: National Consciousness, Alienation, and
    Mobilization   199
Conclusions   206

5   Interest Groups and Political Parties   208

Introduction   208
Britain and France: Group Politics in Liberal Democracies   221
The Soviet Union and China: Limited Pluralism Under Single-Party
    Control   232
Mexico and Nigeria: Interest Groups and Parties in Developing
    Countries   243
Conclusions   254

6   Political Leadership, Civilian and Military   256

Introduction   256
Britain and France: Leadership in Liberal Democracies   267
Communist States: From Heroic to Institutionalized Leadership   277
Mexico and Nigeria: Toward the Institutionalization of Leadership   289
Conclusions   299

Part Three
POLITICAL PERFORMANCE 301

7 Making Public Policy: Structures and Styles 303

Introduction 303
Britain and France: Public Policy-making in Liberal Democracies 312
The Soviet Union and China: Policy-making in Communist States 321
Mexico and Nigeria: Problems of Policy-making in Developing
    Countries 333
Conclusions 341

8 The Challenges of Growth and Stagnation 343

Introduction 343
Britain and France: Managing Advanced Capitalism 353
The Soviet Union and China: Experimenting with "Market
    Socialism" 362
Mexico and Nigeria: Enduring the Setbacks in Development 375
Conclusions 387

9 The Challenge of Political Stability 389

Introduction 389
Britain and France: Political Stability in Liberal Democracies 398
Stability and Instability in the USSR and China 407
Mexico and Nigeria: The Struggle for Political Order 418
Conclusions 425

10 The Challenges of Change and the Future 427

Introduction 427
Change in Liberal Democracies 437
Change in Communist Systems 445
Change and Interdependence in the Third World 453
Reflections on Change and Interdependence 460

BIBLIOGRAPHY 463
INDEX 469

A Country-by-Country Table of Contents

Theory

1. The Historical Bases of Politics   27
2. Political Frameworks   76
3. Society and Politics   118
4. The Citizen in Politics   165
5. Interest Groups and Political Parties   208
6. Political Leadership, Civilian and Military   256
7. Making Public Policy: Structures and Styles   303
8. The Challenges of Growth and Stagnation   343
9. The Challenge of Political Stability   389
10. The Challenges of Change and the Future   427

Case Studies
Britain

1. An Evolutionary Route   34
2. Classic Parliamentarism   85
3. Conflict on Several Fronts   130
4. An Awakening Citizenry?   174
5. Collectivism in Decline   222
6. Collegial Leadership by a Civilian Elite   268
7. The Politics of "Muddling Through"   312
8. A Managed Economy   353
9. The Long Road to Stability   398
10. Coping with Lost Rank   438

France

1. A Revolutionary Route   40
2. Parliamentarism Revised   90

3. The Decline of Cleavage Conflict **136**
4. A Citizenry on Guard **179**
5. Fragmentation and Polarization **227**
6. The Consolidation of Presidentialism **273**
7. Centralized Policy-Making **317**
8. A Concerted Economy **358**
9. Stability in the Making **402**
10. Striking an Independent Course **441**

The Soviet Union

1. A Legacy of Autocracy and Revolution **47**
2. Single-Party Oligarchy **96**
3. Contained Diversity **139**
4. A Symbolically Participatory Regime **185**
5. The Party and the General Will? **233**
6. The Oligarchs **278**
7. Conservatism and Reformism **322**
8. The Ups and Downs of a Command Economy **363**
9. A Stable Oligarchy? **407**
10. The Growing Pains of a Young Superpower **446**

China

1. Revolution and Tradition **54**
2. A "People's Republic" **103**
3. Equality or Performance? **145**
4. The Ebb and Flow of Participation **192**
5. Evolving Roles for the Party and Interest Groups **238**
6. The Passing of Revolutionary Leadership **283**
7. Ideology and Policy-Making **328**
8. From Mass Mobilization to Material Incentives **369**
9. Stability Amid Revolutionary Change **412**
10. Transforming a Peasant Society **450**

Mexico

1. Toward a Modern State **62**
2. Unrestrained Presidentialism **108**
3. The Challenges of Class and Race **152**
4. Limited Participation, Limited Protest **199**
5. Interest "Sectors" and the Dominant Party **244**
6. Controlling Praetorianism **290**
7. Policy-Making under PRI Control **333**
8. Economic Development and Nationalism **375**

9. Stability Under Challenge **419**
10. The PRI Under Challenge **454**

Nigeria

1. Trials of an Emerging State **68**
2. Experimenting with Political Frameworks **111**
3. The Quest for National Unity **157**
4. Participation within Limits **203**
5. Communal Interests and Suspended Parties **249**
6. The Military in Power **295**
7. Policy-Making by a Military–Bureaucratic Elite **338**
8. Ups and Downs of a Petroeconomy **382**
9. Democratic Instability and Military Order **422**
10. The Quest for Unity and Growth **457**

Preface

The comparative approach adopted in this text takes its inspiration from the conviction that the subfield of comparative politics should be more than merely a rubric for the study of foreign political systems. For this reason, we have eschewed the "country-by-country" format more commonly found in comparative politics texts in favor of a thematic or topical mode of organization. The advantage of this approach is that it allows us to discuss in each chapter a major topic in general terms and then apply the range of considerations raised in that discussion to a diverse set of countries grouped into First, Second, and Third World categories. The range of countries we have chosen—Britain and France as liberal democracies (the First World), the Soviet Union and China as communist systems (the Second World), and Mexico and Nigeria as underdeveloped, noncommunist countries (the Third World)—is intended to enhance the generality of our presentation of topics and to facilitate explicit comparisons between liberal democratic and communist systems, developed and underdeveloped systems, and so forth.

Few comparativists would deny that a thematic approach accords better with the underlying idea of comparative politics than a country-by-country format, but most are also aware that it creates difficulties of its own. For one thing, it makes it less easy for an instructor to avoid countries with which he or she is not reasonably familiar; for another, it breaks the "flow" of the presentation of particular countries. Our conviction is that these difficulties can be overcome, and we have designed the text in a fashion that promotes this objective.

The text is constructed with maximum flexibility in mind. Although considerable efforts have been made to make each chapter comprehensible as a unit, there is no necessity that the material be approached in this fashion. Within each chapter, the sections on the liberal democratic, communist, and underdeveloped worlds are separate, and any one of them can be omitted without affecting the readability of the chapter as a whole. This means that the instructor can orient the course toward the East-West distinction by excluding the Third World sections or toward developmental processes by excluding the First World sections. More significantly, within each section the two countries involved are also covered separately, making it possible to treat Britain but not France, the Soviet Union but not China, and so on. A course covering the three worlds could be designed on the basis of Britain, the Soviet Union, and Mexico, for example, or any other of the eight possible combinations that have that format. (It is, of course, also possible to exclude just one or two countries). The instructor may prefer to bypass the other countries entirely or touch on them lightly in class and have them used as a basis for independent study or term papers by the students. Finally, the text can be used—by either the instructor or the students—in a country-by-country format; in fact, we present an alternative table of contents organized by country so that the material in the book can be approached in either fashion. The instructor is thus free to choose the combination of thematic integrity and contextual diversity that suits his or her personal and pedagogical orientations.

ACKNOWLEDGMENTS

We would like to express our appreciation to the following people who reviewed the manuscript and made numerous helpful suggestions:

Gerard Braunthal, University of Massachusetts at Amherst
Larry Elowitz, Georgia College
Michael G. Huelshoff, University of Oregon
Harvey F. Kline, University of Alabama
Lawrence Mayer, Texas Tech University
James W. Peterson, Valdosta State College
John D. Robertson, Texas A&M University
John E. Turner, University of Minnesota

We are also appreciative of the help our research assistants, Margot Beaton, Toby Hinton, and Diane Fraser, supplied at various points in the preparation of the manuscript. Finally, we would like to thank the editorial staff at Harper & Row, especially Lauren Silverman and Marianne Russell, for all their assistance and support during the long process of launching this project.

Although this book is a joint enterprise of the authors, it is appropriate to indicate the division of responsibilities that guided its realization. Concerning countries, Warwick took responsibility for Britain and France and Roth for China, Mexico, and Nigeria. David Paul contributed the Soviet Union sections.

COMPARATIVE POLITICS

Introduction

It is difficult to pass even a single day without being exposed to politics in some fashion or other. Television stations devote two or more hours of their evening programming to news reporting; newspapers and news magazines contain thousands of words on politics in each issue; even "top forty" radio stations present "news briefs" hourly or bihourly. Simple curiosity undoubtedly accounts for some of the public's interest in politics, but most people are also aware that political events, both domestic and foreign, do matter in important ways. For some issues and individuals the concern may be focused on political ideals such as democracy or human rights which they would like to see advanced in all societies, regardless of whether they or their country is affected directly. In many other cases, people appreciate that even developments in remote places can have an effect on their lives. Thus, the Iran-Iraq war, which broke out in 1979, has raised concerns in many Western countries, not so much because of the enormous human losses involved but because the war could lead to a cutting off of Persian Gulf oil exports which are essential to their economies. The overthrow of the Somoza dictatorship in Nicaragua in the same year led to fears in the United States that the tiny Central American country could fall into the orbit of the Soviet Union and become a launching pad for communist takeovers elsewhere in Latin America.

The fact that political developments in distant lands can have an impact at home means that they can easily become issues in domestic politics. Often what emerges is a complex clash involving both high-minded principles and more self-interested or nationalistic motives. The

American involvement in the Vietnam War is an excellent example. During the latter 1960s and early 1970s the American public was profoundly divided between those who believed the United States should stick to its commitment to help keep South Vietnam free of communist control, despite the enormous material and human costs that would be involved, and those who wanted the United States to end its participation in the war. Support for the U.S. presence in Vietnam was justified largely by the belief that the United States had a vital national interest in preventing the spread of communism, although, for many, an important principle was also at issue: the belief that communism is morally wrong. Opponents of U.S. involvement maintained to the contrary that the Vietnamese had a right to "national self-determination" and that it was wrong in principle for the United States to prop up a dictatorial government—but many also feared being sent there themselves.

Because political events occurring almost anywhere in the world can become matters of concern and even political debate at home, people often want to know why politics takes the forms it does in various parts of the world. Why is it, for instance, that communist movements succeeded in gaining enough support to take over governments in China and North Vietnam, whereas in countries like Britain and the United States communism has virtually no support? Why have military takeovers of civilian governments been so common in Latin America and Africa, yet so rare in other parts of the world? Why do some democratic countries, such as Italy, have eight or ten political parties when others, such as the United States and Canada, have only two or three?

The search for answers to these and many similar questions is the concern of the subfield of political science known as comparative politics. The scope of comparative politics is the entire world and, in particular, the 160-odd states that constitute the world's principal political subdivisions. Comparativists study the politics of different countries primarily with the objective of understanding how politics works in general. This is not meant to imply that politics is everywhere the same; what it means is that differences in the politics of different countries are systematic rather than accidental and in principle can be interpreted in terms of general explanations.

This orientation can be made clearer with a couple of examples. Consider the issue of democracy in the western hemisphere. The United States has had a stable democratic regime for two centuries; Mexico has had a stable (if limited) democratic regime for about half a century; many countries in Central and South America have never succeeded in establishing stable democratic regimes, despite repeated attempts to do so. A question that comparativists typically ask is, is there some factor or set of factors that accounts for the success of democratic regimes in some countries but not others? Another example involves the contrasts between communist and liberal democratic regimes. Communist regimes allow just one party, the communist party, to exercise political power and attempt to unite the whole of society behind the leadership of that party. Questions comparativists ask include: what differences in policy outputs result when power is monopolized by a communist party? How are political differences dealt with in systems that do not openly recognize their existence? Are there circumstances under which it is actually advantageous to restrict political division and discord in this fashion?

POLITICS AND THE POLITICAL SYSTEM

To be able to address questions such as these, we must first arrive at some understanding of what politics is about. Most people associate politics with the institutions and processes of government, including the ways in which government leaders are selected, laws are made and enforced, and relations between governments are conducted. Although much of what we think of as politics has to do with the activities of governments, the realm of politics actually involves a great deal more. Take political parties, for example. When party leaders occupy government positions, there is a direct connection with government, but many of the essential activities of parties take place completely outside the governmental arena. For example, parties typically hold conventions to decide on policies and choose leaders. These activities may become very important for government—especially if the party in question should happen to gain office—but they nevertheless take place separately from the governmental process. This is even more true of organized interest groups or lobbies in liberal democratic regimes. Such groups often play an important role in influencing the decisions taken by governments, but they remain private organizations that are formed and remain outside government.

As these examples illustrate, institutions, activities, and events are generally considered "political" if they have, or are intended to have, some impact on governments. Governments are concerned primarily with what political scientist David Easton once termed "the authoritative allocation of values for a society."[1] By values, Easton means anything that is valued in society, including wealth, power, prestige, and distinction. Such values, which are generally in short supply in most societies, may be allocated in a variety of ways. For example, an individual may gain distinction by performing a heroic act such as saving the life of a drowning child; alternatively, an individual may acquire great wealth by means of entrepreneurial or inventive abilities. What makes the allocations of values by governments different is that they are *authoritative;* that is, they are backed by law and ultimately by the forces at the command of governments. Thus, how much money you make may depend mainly on your own talents, but how much you are allowed to keep and enjoy will depend on how much the government chooses to tax people at

[1]D. Easton, *A Framework for Political Analysis* (Englewood Cliffs, N.J.: Prentice-Hall, 1965), p. 50.

your income level. You can try to avoid paying the taxes set by government, but if you are caught, you may lose not only the extra income but your personal freedom as well.

The fact that governments allocate values authoritatively does not mean that they do so consensually. Indeed, because values such as wealth and power are usually scarce, there will often be disagreement or conflict over how they should be allocated. In the case of taxation, a typical disagreement in liberal democracies concerns how much those with higher incomes should contribute to government revenues. Politicians and parties representing the less well-off tend to believe that the rich should be taxed at higher rates since they have gained relatively more from society and can afford it better; those representing more affluent sectors of the population counter that taking too much away from the high achievers in society will discourage them from functioning at their full potential and thereby hurt society as a whole.

In communist regimes, only one political program or ideology dominates the political arena, but it would be incorrect to assume that political competition and conflict are absent. In the Soviet Union today, for example, there are conflicts not just over who should get which jobs but also over major policy issues such as how much of the state's budget should be devoted to the military, how much competition should be allowed in a hitherto tightly controlled economy, and how free of party guidance artistic and intellectual expression should be.

The latter two issues remind us of a point noted earlier about politics: the values at stake include not just self-interested concerns but also goals and ideals to which people are committed in a principled or non-self-interested way. Many of those in the Soviet Union who oppose greater freedom of expression do so because they believe that artistic or intellectual work that does not sustain or reinforce communist ideology could hinder the task of constructing a truly communist society, which they view as a good in itself. Similarly, the requirement in the United States that the police must have a court warrant in order to search a person's home without permission was established not to help criminals, or to win their votes, but because privacy is considered a right to which everyone is entitled.

It is common for political scientists to use the term "the political system" to refer to the various institutions and actors involved in the process of allocating values authoritatively and to the ways in which these entities interact. The word "system" is employed to stress the degree of interdependence that is involved in the political process. The relationship between government leaders and top bureaucrats provides a good illustration. In principle, government leaders are supposed to make the laws and bureaucrats to administer them—a simple chain of command. In reality, their interrelations are much more complex. Bureaucrats clearly depend on government leaders to make policy decisions and allocate funding, but political leaders also depend on bureaucrats: they need the expertise and experience of bureaucrats in gathering the information required to make good decisions, in indicating where and in what respects present policies are not working well, in making informed suggestions on the best ways to improve existing policies, and in carrying out policies in a competent manner. Reciprocity also characterizes the relations of parties and governments in democratic systems. On the one hand, political parties develop policies that are intended to incorporate the demands and expectations of the portions of the citizenry they represent and convey these policies into the governmental arena; on the other hand, the policies that governments adopt and the effects they have on society influence the kinds of expectations that are formed by citizens.

It is useful to think of the political system in terms of inputs and outputs. Inputs originate in demands and expectations that people have concerning government; they may expect government to reduce unemployment or control inflation in the economy, alleviate social problems such as crime or drug abuse, and so forth. Inputs also include the degree of popular support a government or the regime itself enjoys, which in turn influences the effectiveness of the government. These orientations and attitudes about government are usually expressed organizationally through interest groups and political parties, which attempt to convey these inputs directly into the governmental arena. The output side of the political system includes the decisions that government leaders make, their application by the bureaucracy, and the effects they have on the problems or situations they are intended to address. In between are the processes of policy-making themselves: the complex ways in which legislatures, executives, bureaucracies, political parties, interest groups, and the individuals who command them interact to reach authoritative decisions. In this book, we treat all of these aspects of political systems.

THE THREE WORLDS

The complex interactions and processes that constitute politics differ enormously from one country to the next and, as we have seen, the goal of comparativists is to explain those differences. Two of the most important conditioning factors affecting political processes are already well known; they are the type of governmental system or regime a country has and its overall level of economic and political development.

There is a wide variety of regimes in the world today, but the most common types are communist regimes, military dictatorships, and liberal democratic regimes. The latter type in turn breaks down into two subtypes: presidential regimes (e.g., the United States) and parliamentary regimes (e.g., Britain). What differentiates these regimes are the specific institutions involved and the rules—both formal and informal—that govern their functioning. For example, one can readily appreciate that whether the system permits competition among political parties for power or allows only one party to rule makes a great deal of difference with respect to how the country is governed. Similarly, a parliamentary system in which the executive—the prime minister and cabinet—can be removed from power at any time by an adverse vote in the parliament functions very differently from a presidential system in which the president is elected for a fixed term and can be removed only by impeachment.

The second factor conditioning the political process is the overall level of economic and political development of the country in question. Most countries do not enjoy the high standards of living that are characteristic of the developed West. The (understandable) desire to catch up economically is very common among both the leaders and the publics of these countries, but the challenge of realizing this goal is daunting. The affluence of Western countries is the result of a centuries-long process of economic change and transformation, but for many underdeveloped countries the aim is to achieve economic development within decades rather than centuries. For new states, particularly those which emerged with the dissolution of European colonial empires after World War II, the task of economic development is complicated by low levels of political development. Political development refers to the processes of *state-building*—that is, forging a new governmental structure that can govern the country effectively and command the allegiance of its citizens—and *nation-building*—building a new national identity to offset the potential for divisiveness implicit in the presence of separate ethnic, racial, or regional loyalties in the population. No one can be certain how quickly, or even whether, these obstacles can be overcome in all new states, but it is clear that the existence of such major challenges helps to make their politics very different from politics in the developed world.

The two conditioning factors of type of regime and level of development combine to form a fundamental division of countries into the First, Second, and Third Worlds. In the First World are the liberal democracies, most notably those of Western Europe, the "Anglo-American" countries (Canada, the United States, Australia, New Zealand), and Japan. What they have in common, besides similar political institutions and ideals, are relatively high levels of political and economic development. The Second World is composed of communist countries: the Soviet Union, its East European allies, China, and a few others (Vietnam, Kampuchea, North Korea, Albania, Yugoslavia, Cuba). The criterion for membership in the Second World is clearly regime type, for the category includes countries that are relatively highly developed economically, such as the Soviet Union, countries like China and Vietnam that are still in the early stages of economic development, and countries like Yugoslavia that fall somewhere in between. The Third World is composed of all those countries that do not belong to the first two worlds.[2] Not surprisingly, it con-

---

[2]Recently, some observers have begun to refer to the poorest and most indebted of underdeveloped countries as the "Fourth World." We shall stick with the more conventional "three worlds" format here.

tains a wide variety of regime types, from dictatorships, civilian and military, to relatively open and democratic societies such as India—most of the world's countries, in fact. What gives this category its coherence is the pressing challenge of development which all its members face.

There is a natural tendency to see the First World as the United States and its allies, the Second World as the Soviet Union and its allies, and the Third World as all those countries over which the United States and the USSR compete. This, however, is misleading. The First World contains countries (e.g., Sweden and Switzerland) that are not aligned with the United States, the Second World contains countries (e.g., Yugoslavia and China) not aligned with the Soviet Union, and the Third World contains countries that clearly are aligned with either the United States (Saudi Arabia) or the Soviet Union (Angola). What defines the categories is much more complex: a varying mix of regime type and level of development such that the First World contains developed democracies, the Second World contains communist regimes at any level of development, and the Third World contains only underdeveloped noncommunist countries. The categorization is not especially logical, but it does capture a fundamental reality of global politics and economics today.

The six countries that we examine in this text were chosen to reflect this basic reality. The First World is represented by Britain and France. Both countries were at one time major world powers, with vast colonial empires that touched every corner of the globe. As a consequence, many of the world's new states are former British and French colonies, and their political development since independence has been influenced to some degree by their exposure to British and French culture, political ideals, and methods of governance. More important for our purposes, Britain and France are both very old countries whose long histories contain the origins of many of the key ideas and developments that form the context of modern politics, including nationalism, industrialism, and political democracy.

Although Britain and France share the essential First World characteristics of liberal democracy and economic development, they differ in many important respects. The British parliamentary system of government evolved gradually over several centuries and today enjoys high levels of stability and popular acceptance. France's history, in contrast, has been marked by a major revolution and several subsequent changes in regime; even after parliamentary democracy became the norm, its highly unstable functioning prevented it from attracting widespread public acceptance and respect. In the past 30 years, the French have dealt with this problem by grafting onto their parliamentary system a strong measure of presidential government, creating a quasi-presidential regime unique among the world's political systems. In the chapters that follow, it will be as much the contrasts between Britain and France as their similarities as liberal democracies that attract our attention.

The Second World is represented here by its two major powers, the

Soviet Union and the People's Republic of China. The Soviet Union, created in the aftermath of the Russian Revolution of 1917, is the world's first socialist country, and the political institutions and practices it developed set the mold for most other socialist countries, including China. The study of the Soviet Union is important not only because it is a major superpower and the chief adversary of the United States and its allies but also because its rapid rise to industrial strength and military power in the decades after 1917 has made it an important counterexample for many underdeveloped countries disillusioned with the capitalist route to development. China, the world's most populous country, is a useful foil to the Soviet Union in a number of respects. Although China has pursued economic development earnestly in the four decades since the communist takeover in 1949, it remains—unlike the Soviet Union—very much an underdeveloped country, sharing with the Third World many of its most pressing problems, including overpopulation and major developmental setbacks. China, like other socialist states, borrowed heavily from the Soviet model of government, but its politics nonetheless has followed its own unique and fascinating course since 1949. Today, both the Soviet Union and China are attempting to liberalize their highly regulated economic and political systems, but it is the Chinese who have demonstrated the greater flexibility and willingness to break with socialist traditions.

The range of countries that fall under the Third World rubric is enormous, and it is difficult to identify two that can be considered representative of the entire category. Nevertheless, our selections, Mexico and Nigeria, perform that function better than most. Mexico is one of Latin America's principal states. Like some other Latin American countries, Mexico has achieved an intermediate level of development; like them also, Mexico has met with setbacks and frustrations in its attempts to achieve full economic development. After gaining independence from Spain early in the nineteenth century, Mexico experienced a century of military dictatorships, civil wars, and repression; following its 1911 revolution, political stability was gradually consolidated through the development of strong one-party rule. Increasingly, however, demands are being heard for an evolution toward a truly competitive multiparty democracy.

Nigeria is Africa's largest and one of its most troubled countries. A former British colony which achieved independence only in 1960, Nigeria is faced with one of the most difficult problems confronting new states: the presence of rival, antagonistic ethnic groups within its borders. Ethnic tensions have been a central feature of Nigerian politics since independence, and the situation reached its most acute point in 1967, when a bloody civil war was provoked by the attempt of one ethnic group, the Ibos, to secede from the country. The influence of British traditions of democracy has been strong in Nigeria, but ethnic clashes have led the military to overthrow both the initial parliamentary regime and a subsequent presidential one. At present, Nigeria is seeking a democratic formula that will be able to withstand the pressures of ethnic antagonisms and address the problems occasioned by an underdeveloped economy, a rapidly rising population, and a huge foreign debt.

The six countries thus represent a highly diversified selection. Geographically, the selection spans most of the world's major continents and regions (Europe, Asia, Africa, and Latin America); economically, both capitalist and socialist systems as well as developed, intermediate, and underdeveloped systems are covered; politically, the range extends to liberal democratic, socialist, one-party nonsocialist, and military regimes. Through the examination of the experiences of these six countries, many of the key patterns, problems, and challenges characteristic of politics around the world will be explored.

ORGANIZATION OF THE BOOK

The book is organized into three parts, corresponding roughly to the input-output distinction discussed earlier. Part One focuses on three aspects of the background of contemporary political processes. The first chapter considers the historical evolution of each country with particular emphasis on two central aspects of political development: the establishment of modern state institutions and the emergence of cultural norms and traditions that affect the way in which politics is conducted. In Chapter 2 we look specifically at the nature and functioning of the different types of state structures present in our six countries—the products, in a sense, of the divergent courses of political development outlined in the first chapter. Chapter 3 evaluates another legacy of the past, the main divisions or cleavages within each society and the ways in which they find expression in the political arena.

Part Two stresses a more dynamic side of politics by examining the role of "political actors," that is, people in the political process. The first type of political actor is the individual citizen. Chapter 4 considers the various roles that citizens play in the different political systems and cultural traditions represented by our six cases. In Chapter 5 attention is shifted to the ways in which citizens organize themselves, or are organized, for political purposes. Two key types of politically motivated organization are of concern here: interest groups, which attempt to influence or lobby political leaders, and political parties, which seek to place their own leaders in government. In Chapter 6 we look directly at the leaders or elites who occupy high positions in government, with particular emphasis on the distinction between civilian and military rule and the circumstances that may prompt military leaders to attempt to take over political power.

The final part of the book concentrates on policy-making, the output side of government. In Chapter 7 we consider the complex processes by which policy is actually made and implemented in different regimes, including the important role that bureaucrats play and the ways in which political leaders attempt to ensure bureaucratic responsiveness to their policy directions. Chapters 8 and 9 focus on two of the most pressing challenges governments face in the policy-making field: achieving or maintaining adequate levels of economic development and prosperity and ensuring political stability. These challenges, as we shall see, are especially salient for newer, less developed countries, which often face major hurdles in both areas. Finally, we conclude our survey of comparative politics with a discussion of the challenges of the future, in particular those that are presented by the growing interdependence of the global community of states.

The issue of interdependence highlights a theme that is present throughout the book: the focus on the state. In the early chapters, our concern is with the emergence of modern state structures of different types. In the middle chapters, we look at the ways in which these structures operate and the major influences, emanating both from within and without, that condition their functioning. In the later chapters, attention is focused on the challenges of establishing and maintaining the effective operation of state structures in light of the existence of threatening social and economic conditions in some countries and of the increasing infringements on state autonomy in all countries that have accompanied the expansion of global economic and political interdependence. As things now stand, the state remains the dominant unit of political organization in the world, but there is a great deal more questioning of its ability to cope effectively with major social, economic, and political problems than there was just 20 years ago.

Maps

The United Kingdom

(Standard Statistical Regions)

ATLANTIC OCEAN

SCOTLAND

Aberdeen

Glasgow Edinburgh

North Sea

NORTHERN
IRELAND

Belfast

Newcastle

Tyne R.

NORTH

REPUBLIC
OF
IRELAND

Dublin

Irish Sea

ENGLAND

Leeds YORKSHIRE
AND
HUMBERSIDE

Liverpool Mersey R.

Manchester Sheffield

NORTH
WEST

EAST
MIDLANDS

WEST

Birmingham

EAST ANGLIA

MIDLANDS

WALES

Severn R.

Thames

Greater
London

Cardiff

Bristol

SOUTH EAST

SOUTH WEST

English Channel

FRANCE

0 ————————— 100
Scale of Miles

France
(New Regional Organization)

ENGLAND

BELGIUM

NORD

GERMANY

LUX

English Channel

Le Havre

HAUTE

PICARDIE

NORMANDIE

Seine R.

Paris

LORRAINE

ALSACE

BASSE

RÉGION PARISIENNE

Strasbourg

BRETAGNE

CHAMPAGNE

Rhine R.

PAYS DE LA LOIRE

CENTRE

BOURGOGNE

FRANCHE-COMTÉ

Nantes

Loire R.

SWITZERLAND

POITOU-CHARENTE

LIMOUSIN

Bay of Biscay

Lyon

RHÔNE-ALPES

Clermont-Ferrand

Grenoble

St. Etienne

ITALY

AUVERGNE

AQUITAINE

Bordeaux

Rhône R.

Garonne R.

MIDI-PYRÉNÉES

PROVENCE-CÔTE D'AZUR

Nice

SPAIN

Toulouse

LANGUEDOC

Marseilles
Toulon

Mediterranean Sea

CORSE

_ _ _ _ Department boundaries   _ _ _ _ Region boundaries

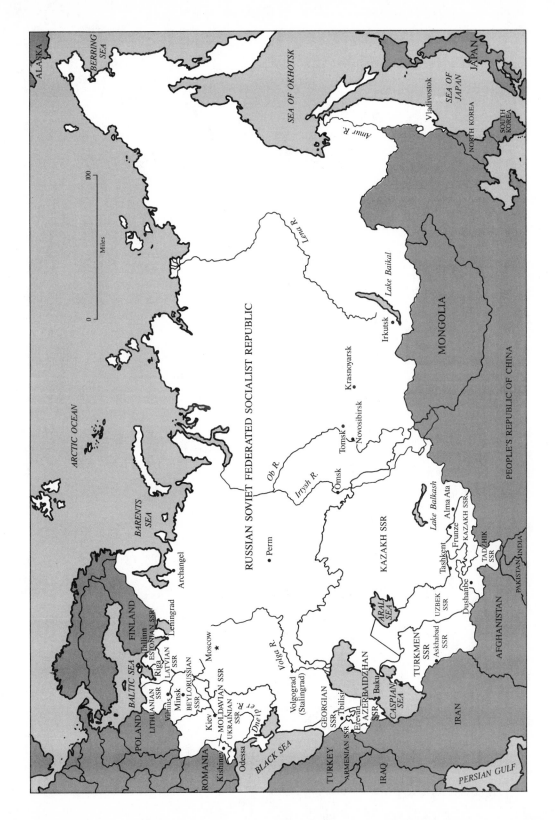

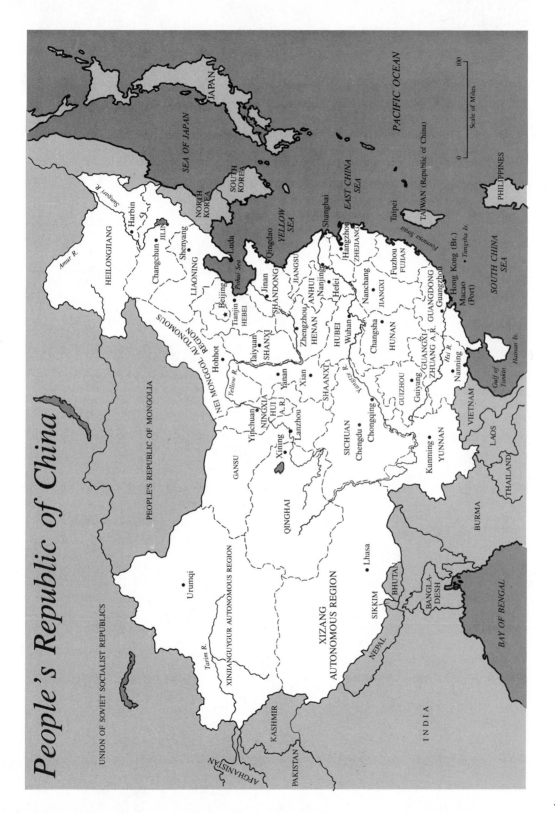

People's Republic of China

19

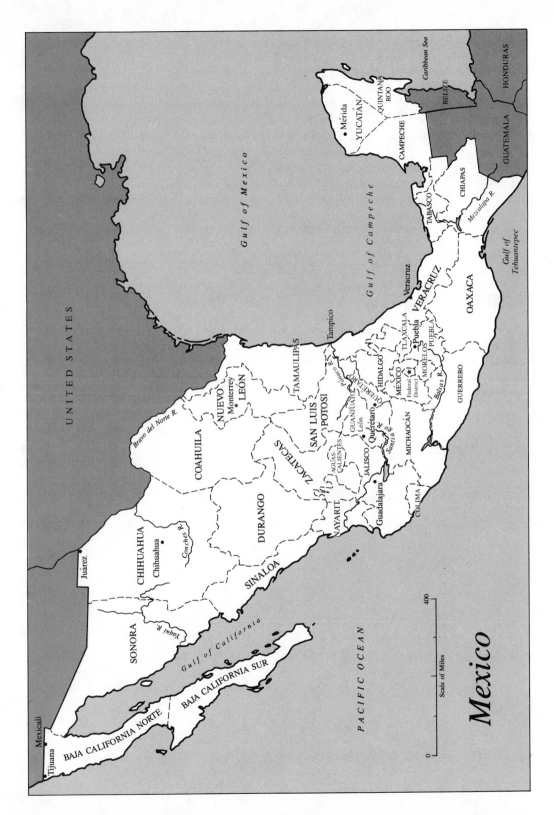

Mexico

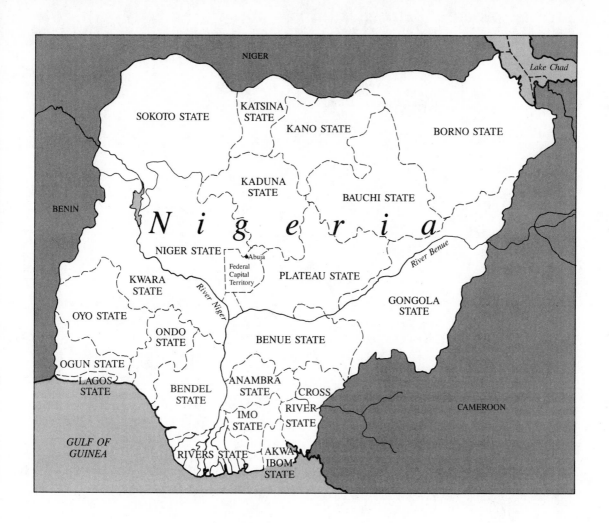

NIGER

SOKOTO STATE

KATSINA STATE

KANO STATE

BORNO STATE

Lake Chad

KADUNA STATE

BAUCHI STATE

BENIN

Nigeria

NIGER STATE

•Abuja

Federal Capital Territory

PLATEAU STATE

River Benue

KWARA STATE

GONGOLA STATE

OYO STATE

River Niger

ONDO STATE

BENUE STATE

OGUN STATE

LAGOS STATE

BENDEL STATE

ANAMBRA STATE

CROSS RIVER STATE

CAMEROON

IMO STATE

GULF OF GUINEA

RIVERS STATE

AKWA IBOM STATE

one

BACKGROUND TO POLITICS

chapter *1*

The Historical Bases of Politics

Who controls the past controls the future; who controls the present controls the past.

GEORGE ORWELL
Nineteen Eighty-Four

INTRODUCTION

In 1949 the English writer George Orwell published his famous novel *Nineteen Eighty-Four,* which portrayed a vision of the world 35 years into the future. One of the most significant characteristics of that vision was the idea that the state would engineer "correct" thinking in its citizens by manipulating the information to which they had access. In particular, the past would be constantly rewritten to accord with the evolving policies of the political leadership:

> Day by day and almost minute by minute the past was brought up to date. In this way every prediction made by the party could be shown by documentary evidence to have been correct; nor was any item of news, or any expression of opinion which conflicted with the needs of the moment ever allowed to remain on record. . . . Books also were recalled and rewritten again and again, and were invariably reissued without any admission that any alteration had been made.[1]

[1]G. Orwell, *Nineteen Eighty-Four* (New York: Harcourt, Brace & World, 1949), p. 41.

The year 1984 has come and gone without any state having realized the degree of control over people's minds that prevailed in Orwell's fictitious Oceania. Major attempts have been made, however, most notably in Hitler's Germany and in the Soviet Union under Stalin. The objective of those governments was to make the past correspond with the dictates of their ideologies so that the allegiance and the energies of their peoples could better be mobilized for the regime's benefit. Generally speaking, the more ambitious the goals of a regime, the more tempted it will be to employ elaborate means of manipulation and control over the thoughts of ordinary citizens. Nevertheless, the efforts at indoctrination under Hitler and Stalin were in reality no more than the extreme of an activity that all regimes engage in to some extent.

This basic fact often goes unnoticed because it tends to get bound up in our feelings of nationalism or patriotism. Thus, the recent efforts of the Japanese government to remove references to Japanese war crimes and war guilt from accounts of the Second World War in Japanese school texts have offended and disturbed many in the West, but far fewer are upset if the Allied firebombing of the German city of Dresden, a pointless operation which cost tens of thousands of civilian lives, is omitted from our own textbooks. It seems that most governments, and their citizens, feel the need to inculcate in the young a sense of patriotism and allegiance to their systems of government and, since few national histories are pristine, some liberties with the facts are taken with little or no dissent.

If history were no more than a convenient grab-bag of data from which governments could select favorable items with which to socialize their citizens into politically acceptable attitudes and norms, it would be a very sorry state of affairs indeed. But the impact of history on the present extends far beyond what can be taught in school texts or communicated in the mass media, however much some governments might wish it otherwise. The historical development of a society has a profound role in determining the present-day nature of its political system, its political values or culture, and its way of doing politics, both at home and abroad. To understand why a particular country has the kind of political institutions it has and how the processes of politics operate through (or around) those institutions, it is necessary to gain some grasp of the historical evolution of that society. In this chapter we shall consider some of the key developments that have molded contemporary politics—developments that no amount of historical rewriting can allay.

The Political Development of Modern States

Political scientists use the expression *political development* to refer to the processes by which modern political systems emerged from more traditional ones. The ways in which the past has molded the present are complex and often the source of considerable debate, but there is general agreement that one process is of central concern, the development of the modern state. The reason for this is that politics as we know it today exists within and among states. To have a strong, modern state is the goal of most independent societies that do not yet have one and a source of pride for most that do. *State-building* has been a major theme in the history of most developed polities and in the contemporary politics of developing ones.

States as such are not new to the world. The ancient Egyptians at the dawn of civilization had a very powerful state; so did the Romans. Much weaker states, but states nonetheless, existed in Europe during the Middle Ages. The development of states which we call "modern" essentially refers to the processes by which feudal states in medieval Europe evolved into much more powerful entities whose chief characteristic is that they possessed *sovereignty*.

The concept of sovereignty came into prominence in the sixteenth century to express the idea that the state should have exclusive control over its territory and the people who inhabit it and that it should be accountable for its actions to no other authority. This does not mean that modern states generally do whatever they like with their subjects, for another characteristic of the modern state is that it establishes and enforces a system of law to regulate both its behavior and that of its subjects. But it is the state that creates and can change the law and, in the final analysis, the subject must obey the will of the state or be punished accordingly.

These ideas seem basic to us because we live in a world of formally sovereign states. But the world was not always so. In the Middle Ages, for example, rulers in Europe faced serious challenges to their authority from above and below. Above them stood the Roman Catholic Church, which claimed ultimate authority over the whole of Western Christendom. Below them stood aristocratic or noble classes, whose obedience was often less than certain. It is true that nobles owed their monarch loyalty and a certain amount of military service in return for the land and the privileges they enjoyed, but, given the poor communications of the era and the fact that monarchs lacked standing armies of their own to enforce obedience, the temptation for nobles to go their own way was ever present. Moreover, even the theory of the time held that the authority of a monarch was limited: he was expected to interpret and enforce traditional law rather than create new law and to live off the revenues from his own estates rather than impose new taxes on his subjects.

The development of the modern state entailed the taming of challenges to state power emanating from nobles and the church, the removal of restrictions on the kinds of actions the state could undertake, and the development of institutions to enforce the will of the state. These institutions included a system of courts to apply the laws of the state throughout the realm, a bureaucracy to collect taxes and administer the state's affairs, and permanent, professional armed forces to assert the state's power against domestic and foreign opponents. In fact, it was largely the desire of rulers to increase their territory and the competition this placed them in with other rulers that provided the momentum for these developments. Rulers who were most efficient at collecting taxes and manpower and allocating those resources to military needs were obviously favored in this process. Certain "protostates" such as the duchy of Burgundy disappeared; others like its neighbor and competitor, the kingdom of France, triumphed.

The degree to which authority became concentrated in the state was conditioned by the amount of internal opposition to centralization from the aristocracy or other sources and by the degree of exposure to foreign rivals. Of the two, the second is undoubtedly the dominant factor. Resistance to the centralization of authority was generally disliked by monarchs, but what justified and stimulated the will to suppress it was the vulnerability of the country to its enemies. States without natural barriers such as mountains or seas to provide protection from powerful rivals either succumbed to their enemies or else survived by energetically, and sometimes quite ruthlessly, eradicating sources of internal disunity in order to maximize their power. In fact, the greater the exposure, the more the state came to resemble a military hierarchy, with monarch in command, aristocrats at the "officer" level, and the rest of the people forming the rank and file. One appeal of this model, which became known as "absolute monarchy" to underline the monarch's supposedly unlimited authority, was that it could be seen as a natural extension of feudalism, which had also considered king and nobles as constituting a warrior class.

The process of state-building was immensely aided in the sixteenth century by the Protestant Reformation, which shattered the unity of the Roman Catholic Church and hence its power vis-à-vis monarchs. Generally speaking, Protestantism was more successful at establishing itself in the northern tier of Europe, where the ability and the desire to escape Rome's influence were greater. But even where Catholicism survived there was still a price to be paid: the church had to align itself with the process of state-building. After all, the divisions between Protestants and Catholics had undermined the power of monarchs as well as that of the church; and the church, with its moral authority, its material wealth, and its well-developed bureaucracy, could provide valuable assistance to those monarchs who wished to consolidate and increase their power. The result was often, as in the case of France, a close church-state alliance based on the principle of a single ruler and a single religion. A similar development occurred in Russia, where the Russian Orthodox Church, lacking an international basis of support, gradually became an ally and a tool of a monarchy surrounded by foreign enemies.

Organized religion often remained subordinate to the state in Protestant countries as well; the new Church of England was even headed by the English king. But there was a crucial difference. Catholicism might be discouraged or persecuted in the Protestant lands, but toleration for Protestant sects could not so easily be denied. The result was often a greater degree of religious diversity or pluralism, and it is from the seeds of religious dissent that political dissent and political pluralism were to grow.

A very famous thesis enunciated by the sociologist Max Weber holds that the spirit of modern capitalism emerged from the work and savings ethic of Calvinists, particularly in Holland and England.[2] While the validity of the "Protestant ethic" thesis has been hotly debated, it is clear that pluralistic societies, societies that tolerate a variety of forces and opinions, have been especially conducive to the growth of capitalism. One basic reason for this is that capitalism depends on individuals being free to form their own enterprises and compete in the marketplace. It is thus an inherently pluralistic system of economic organization. The unfettered development of capitalism and the toleration of a certain pluralism in politics in turn opened the way for a peaceful evolution toward political democracy, for it, too, implies a freedom to form groups and parties in order to compete in the political arena.

Countries which took the route of absolutism were usually unable to keep up economically with their more pluralistic, less authoritarian rivals. Their economic development was hindered by a tendency in aristocratic value systems to deprecate the activities of commerce, banking, and manufacturing as beneath the dignity of gentlemen. In addition, the high costs of supporting such strong state and church structures, costs which fell largely on nonnobles, particularly businessmen and peasants, slowed economic growth. In France and Russia the eventual result was violent revolution aimed at eliminating both the monarchy and the role of organized religion in sustaining it. These revolutions did not replace authoritarian with democratic rule, however; the new leadership which emerged turned out to be just as authoritarian, but more efficient at government and more able to incorporate the people into the regime.

Incorporation of the great mass of the population into the political process is another key aspect of modern political development. It received its greatest impetus from the invention of the concept of the *nation-state.* This concept first emerged in the French Revolution of 1789, and it spread with Napoleon's conquering armies throughout Europe and eventually, via the colonial empires of European powers, throughout much of the world. Although it is not specifically a democratic concept, it does imply a union of the people (the nation) with the state. In the twentieth century it has become a particularly potent idea for arousing colonized peoples to fight for independence.

The process of awakening or creating nationalistic emotions, of mobilizing individuals to fight for, and identify with, their "nation"—a

---

[2]Max Weber, *The Protestant Ethic and the Spirit of Capitalism,* trans. T. Parsons (New York: Scribner's, 1958).

process sometimes referred to as *social mobilization*—has carried enormous problems in its wake. Today there are 160 or so sovereign states represented in the oddly, but significantly, named United Nations, but few are composed of a single nation or people. In fact, there are literally thousands of such "nations." The chief political problem of these new states is the very problem of national integration, of forging a single nation from two or more distinct peoples. It is the cause of much, if not most, of the unrest that occurs in the developing world today. For relatively homogeneous European nations like France or Germany, the ideal of one nation united under a single, powerful state has seemed an appropriate one, but for the newer additions to the world of sovereign states it is often quite unrealistic. Yet, because it connotes strength and harmony, it continues to be the focus of their aspirations. The pervasive tendency to rewrite history that was noted earlier is itself a symptom of the felt need to forge a strong sense of nationalism and to link it with loyalty to the state.

The Role of Political Culture

Understanding the different ways in which the state and society developed in different countries is central to understanding why, for example, some countries possess liberal democratic regimes while others have gone the way of more authoritarian solutions. But this is far from being the whole story. The course of political development taken in a given country also affects its values, beliefs, and norms of political life. This more subtle, more psychological side of politics is known as *political culture,* and it is often the principal vehicle by which the past continues to affect the present, long after the lessons of the history books have been forgotten.

The political culture of a country may manifest itself in a wide variety of ways; the unwritten rules that govern what one candidate may say about another in an election campaign, the degree of freedom citizens feel to communicate their political opinions to others, the sense of duty that may oblige them to report their income accurately on tax forms are common examples. But the most important aspects of political culture have to do with the ways in which political authority is perceived and exercised. The aforementioned distinction between countries which developed in a pluralistic fashion and those which pursued a more authoritarian route provides an excellent illustration. The attitudinal correlates of pluralistic societies typically include a greater tolerance for dissent and a more "bargaining," less ideological approach to political issues. This more relaxed, less dogmatic orientation is often also reflected in high degrees of what is termed "social trust," the willingness to assume that others are basically trustworthy or good unless proved otherwise. This in turn has generated a social and political climate in which it is relatively easy for parties and interest groups of all sorts to form, and the result is usually a rich associational life in society. Because of the basic tolerance for diverse opinions and the belief that these differences can be bargained out, there also tends to be a less than exalted sense of the state and its importance to society. Often the state is perceived as merely the arena in which the competitive interplay of political opinions and forces is acted out, a political marketplace whose rules ensure that the competition is fair and orderly.

Authoritarian states, in contrast, tended to repress manifestations of political pluralism and dissent; they were therefore more prone to provoke violent revolution, often leading to the emergence of new, but no less authoritarian, regimes. In these circumstances, it is much less likely that an easygoing, trustful social climate will have emerged. The tradition of authoritarianism and distrust also tends to result in a less well developed associational life within the society. Where the revolution was successful and won over or vanquished its opponents, these traits have often encouraged a high degree of submissiveness to the state, for it seems that only a powerful state can make society work. Where the revolutionary inheritance is more divided, there may be a greater ambiguity of feeling toward the state: on the one hand, a felt need for a strong state; on the other, an underlying suspiciousness of what the state or those who control it may be up to.

For newer countries, especially those whose political institutions were borrowed from foreign models, there is often an additional problem: the traditional political culture or cultures may not be suited to the institutions in question. For example, the pluralistic democracies of the West are much admired in developing countries for their ideals and their economic achievements, but where native democratic traditions are absent, Western democratic institutions may not be able to take root and survive. Given the intense hostilities that often exist between different ethnic or racial groups, which may not yet possess a strong allegiance to their new country, conformity to the norms of competitive democracy cannot always be expected. In such a situation, an authoritarian model, usually of either the one-party socialist or military government type, is often seen as more appropriate. Unfortunately, the problems of ethnic and racial divisiveness are difficult to overcome, and in the experiences of the developing countries one finds little evidence to indicate that authoritarian rule is merely a stopgap measure which will eventually give way to a loosening of the state's grip on society. In today's world, the prospects for the proliferation of liberal democracy are mixed at best.

BRITAIN AND FRANCE: ALTERNATIVE ROUTES TO DEMOCRACY

In many respects, the two liberal democracies considered in this text, Britain and France, have a great deal in common. They are both very old countries whose origins stretch back to the Middle Ages; they occupy the same regions of the world, with, for the most part, similar climates; their populations are virtually the same size, about 55 million inhabitants. More significantly, each possesses a stable and successful liberal democratic regime and a modern industrialized economy, traits which reflect the fact that both countries have been at the forefront of political and economic development for centuries. These developmental similarities are far from being circumstantial; the histories of these two countries have been linked for nearly a thousand years. In fact, the English royal family traces its roots to the conquest and subjugation of England by William of Normandy and his army of French-speaking nobles in 1066. The modern English language is largely the product of a slow merger of the Anglo-Saxon and Norman French tongues; even so famous a hero of English folklore as King Richard the Lion-Hearted (1189–1199) was more French than English and managed only the occasional visit to his English kingdom. Despite the vicissitudes of war, alliances, and dynastic succession, the cross-fertilization of languages and ideas has continued ever since.

Notwithstanding these similarities and connections, most observers are inclined to think of the two countries in terms of contrasts: after all, England staged a Protestant Reformation, France remained Catholic; England inaugurated the industrial revolution, France industrialized relatively late; England pioneered parliamentary government, France the absolute monarchy; England evolved toward full democracy in a gradual and peaceful fashion, France had to undergo a violent revolution; England has never had a written constitution, France has had more than a dozen. These contrasts can be overdrawn and frequently have been, particularly in periods when the two countries were rivals or enemies. But they do point to one basic fact: however much they influenced each other in the past and resemble each other today, the two countries essentially followed different paths to modernity. In order to understand their politics today, we must have some familiarity with the broad contours of these alternative routes.

Britain: An Evolutionary Route

The most distinctive characteristic of England[3] in the Middle Ages was its high degree of central government control. This feature is particularly noteworthy in that the normal tendency of the times was for political authority to become fragmented. In an age when standing armies were virtually unknown, it was commonplace for a king to be owed military service and loyalty from nobles whose livelihoods were provided through the possession of land and the serfs or peasants who went

---

[3]"Great Britain" was formed in 1701 when the Act of Union joined Scotland to England and Wales. Before 1701, we shall be concerned with the historical development of England, which is by far the dominant component of the union. Incidentally, the official name for the country today is "The United Kingdom of Great Britain and Northern Ireland," and it is generally referred to as either "Britain" or the "United Kingdom."

with the land. In practice, nobles typically became independent of their kings, often warring with one another or with the king in order to increase their territory and hence their wealth and power. England avoided this fate in large part because of her early vulnerability to foreign invasion. In the tenth century, the Anglo-Saxons united under a single monarch in order to expel the Danish invaders from their soil. In the eleventh century, the country was conquered and united under a single king first by the Danes (1017) and subsequently by the Normans (1066).

The Normans proved to be the last successful invaders of England, but central control did not wither away. In Normandy, the Norman nobles had had a strong tradition of obedience to their duke; in England, they had ample reason to perpetuate it, for they were vastly outnumbered by a hostile population. There were, to be sure, periods when central authority was resisted; the most famous occurred in 1215 when the incompetent and tyrannous King John (1199–1216) was forced by his barons to sign the Magna Carta or Great Charter curtailing the expansion of royal powers. But more effective monarchs imposed a degree of central control unprecedented in Europe. In the twelfth century, Henry II (1154–1189) was able to appoint and dismiss the sheriffs who controlled local government, control the administration of justice through his own royal courts, and raise taxes on noble and commoner alike—powers which his French counterparts could but envy. After a period of civil war in the fifteenth century, a similarly precocious degree of central authority was achieved by the strong Tudor monarchs, Henry VIII (1509–1547) and his daughter, Elizabeth I (1558–1603), whose reigns dominated the sixteenth century.

It was this tradition of centralized authority, and the national integration that it had fostered, that allowed Henry in 1534 to remove, by fiat and with relatively little serious opposition, the English church from the control of Rome and place it under his own command. Wars of religion between Catholics and Protestants were to ravage continental Europe for much of the century and a half after Martin Luther first challenged the Vatican in 1517, but England was scarcely touched. English national identity, which took added meaning from its opposition to the supposed evils of "popery" and to states, like Spain, which upheld papal influence, was further strengthened in the process.

The near-absolutism of Henry, epitomized by his ability to subjugate the Church of England to his authority, might suggest that England was the likeliest candidate to succeed in the development of full-blown monarchical absolutism. But such was not to be the case, for major forces had been developing in English society to counterbalance the rise of monarchical authority. As early as the thirteenth century, English landowners were beginning the long process of conversion from growing crops for subsistence to growing crops for the market. The rise of the wool trade with the European continent greatly facilitated this process, as did the relative ease with which landlords could "enclose" (fence in and take over) the common lands used by village communities and convert them to sheep pastures. By the sixteenth century, a powerful group of market-oriented landowners and their town merchant allies had come into existence. Moreover, this group was well represented in the English Parliament, an institution which had emerged in the late Middle Ages as a forum in which the crown could seek the additional revenues to finance the Hundred Years' War (1338–1452) with France.

The struggle between Parliament and the crown came to a head in the seventeenth century. The Stuart dynasty, in particular Charles I (1625–1649) and James II (1685–1688), was inspired by the model of absolute authority exemplified by Louis XIV of France. They admired the power of the French king, his ability to raise taxes, maintain a large standing army, and rule without interference from any national representative institution. Parliamentary forces, on the contrary, saw no need for a large army; since England was cut off from the major continental powers by the English Channel, the only real purpose of a large army would have been to repress opposition to the king at home. Moreover, this opposition would probably include themselves, for they regarded many of the policies of the monarchy, such as its attempts to curtail the enclosure of common lands (in order to protect the peasantry) and its propensity to sell monopoly privileges in manufacturing and trade, as unwarranted constraints on their ability to pursue profits.

In the ensuing contest, the kings' downfall can be traced in large measure to their inability to rule without the tax revenues which only Parliament could grant them. Matters reached a climax in 1649 when, following a protracted civil war between parliamentary and monarchical forces, Charles I was executed and a "Commonwealth" led by the Puritan Oliver Cromwell established in place of the monarchy. Soon after Cromwell's death, Charles II was invited from exile to assume the throne, but when his brother and successor, James II, seemed to be attempting to reimpose Catholicism, Parliament again took matters into its own hands. In the "Glorious Revolution" of 1688–1689, James was chased out of England and replaced by a Protestant monarch, William of Orange (Holland), who was willing to accept the Bill of Rights limiting royal powers.

It was through these struggles that the doctrine of parliamentary supremacy became firmly established: Parliament had assumed the right to depose monarchs who opposed its policies or its powers. Never again would the monarch set himself against the determined will of Parliament. This did not mean that democracy was just around the corner—that would have to wait more than two centuries—but it did facilitate the acceptance of political pluralism within English society. It became understood that politics was about interests, particularly material interests, and that when different interests were opposed, the issue would be decided not by repression or civil war, but by parliamentary majorities. The business of government became, increasingly, the promotion of business through the creation of appropriate laws and institutions (such as the Bank of England in 1694), the protection of trade by means of a large navy, and the acquisition of trading concessions and territories abroad. The result was rapid economic expansion in the eighteenth century, leading ultimately to industrial revolution.

Industrialization, although beneficial in many respects, is a very disruptive process. On the one hand, it creates a new industrial middle class anxious for political representation. On the other hand, it uproots many of the less well off from their tranquil villages and squeezes them into squalid slums in vast manufacturing cities, exposing them to the risks that unemployment will leave them starving or that wages will be driven below subsistence levels because of cheap child, female, and immigrant (in this case Irish) labor and stimulating in them a readily exploitable hostility to the prevailing social and political order. In Britain, the challenge came in the period from the late eighteenth century to the mid-nineteenth century. At first the governmental authorities responded with repression, especially during and after the wars with revolutionary and imperial France (1792–1815). Eventually, however, the predominantly aristocratic rulers of the country chose to give way before things got out of hand. The first breakthrough was the Reform Act of 1832, which doubled the size of the electorate (to perhaps 3 percent of the total population) and redistributed seats to accord better with the population shifts that had taken place. New industrial cities like Manchester, Leeds, and Birmingham gained representation in Parliament for the first time, and many of the "rotten boroughs" (towns whose population had declined drastically or disappeared altogether) lost theirs. The process was carried much farther in 1867 when the Second Reform Act was passed, giving the vote to all men in urban or "borough" seats who paid property taxes (this became known as the "household franchise") and lowering property qualifications for voting for all others. A further reallocation of borough seats to represent the expanding industrial cities more adequately was also enacted. In 1872 the secret ballot was introduced, making it difficult for employees or landlords to dictate the votes of their workers or tenant farmers. Reforms in 1884 and 1885 extended the household franchise to all constituencies and continued the process of reallocating seats to accord with population changes.

Why the traditional rulers of the country, the landed aristocracy, engaged in this process of gradual concession to demands for greater representation is unclear. It used to be assumed that it was an act of great political wisdom and foresight: the aristocracy saw that society had been transformed and voluntarily conceded a share of political power in order to avert revolution. More recently, it has been pointed out that each of these reforms substantially increased the number of county (rural) constituencies, which the landed aristocracy controlled, and in turn reduced the number of borough (urban) constituencies—despite the increasing urbanization of the country.[4] In fact, before 1918 Ireland, with a population of just 600,000, had more constituencies than did the seven largest

---

[4]See D. C. Moore, *The Politics of Deference* (New York: Barnes & Noble, 1976).

cities of Britain, including London. Moreover, shifting borough representation from declining towns to expanding cities had the effect of preventing suburban voters from having to vote in county constituencies, where they might have threatened aristocratic control. It thus appears that the aristocracy was more concerned to preserve and even expand its own influence in Parliament than to share it with other classes.

Even though the aristocracy's motives may have been less than noble, it certainly hit on a sensible course. By yielding to demands for a wider distribution of the franchise, the aristocracy was able to ward off radical challenges and maintain its political power, as well as its great wealth and privilege, into the present century. Not all aristocracies have been as sensible, but it must be remembered that the English aristocracy was functioning in a particularly appropriate context. Ever since the seventeenth century, politics in England had been oriented around the competition of interests: court aristocracy versus country aristocracy, landowner versus merchant, and so forth. Concomitantly, a pluralistic culture had emerged in which social trust and tolerance of dissent were widespread. As new interests emerged through the process of industrialization, it was natural that they, too, should be admitted into the political arena.

The process of opening up the political system to greater participation from below nevertheless proceeded very gradually: full democratization had to await the twentieth century. In 1911 the power of the unelected House of Lords to veto legislation was eliminated; 1918 saw the recognition of the idea that every adult male should be able to vote; surprisingly, the full realization of the principle of "one person, one vote" did not come until 1948. In part, the willingness of the public to accept the slowness of democratization derives from the past successes of British society, which were considerable. In the nineteenth century, Britain not only was able to make significant strides toward democracy without recourse to violent revolution but also managed to become for a time the world's foremost industrial economy and its dominant military power, "ruling the waves" and establishing the largest colonial empire ever known.

Underlying these successes was the early start that England had in tackling the major challenges in political development. As we have seen, English national consciousness was largely achieved by the end of the Middle Ages. The competition between church and state was resolved easily and definitely in the latter's favor in the sixteenth century. The seventeenth century saw the establishment of a framework of parliamentary government dominated by market-oriented interests, which could easily be adapted to encompass demands for greater participation that followed in the aftermath of the industrial revolution of the late eighteenth century. The cultural legacy of this gradual and largely successful developmental path included a respect for tradition and a deference to the country's rulers that allowed them sufficient leeway to move toward democracy at a measured pace. Unfortunately, this legacy can

Figure 1.1 SOME IMPORTANT EVENTS IN BRITISH HISTORY

1066	William of Normandy conquers Britain, the last successful invasion of the British Isles.
1215	King John signs the Magna Carta, limiting his authority over barons.
1265	First Parliament incorporating representation from towns meets.
1297	The principle of no taxation without consent of House of Commons is established.
1534	Henry VIII separates the Church of England from Rome's control.
1536	England and Wales are joined by the Act of Union.
1542	Henry VIII becomes king of Ireland.
1642	Civil War between parliamentary forces and supporters of Charles I breaks out.
1649	Civil war ends in execution of Charles I and establishment of the Commonwealth under Oliver Cromwell.
1660	The monarchy is restored under Charles II.
1688	The "Glorious Revolution" deposes James II for attempting to reimpose Catholicism in England.
1689	William of Orange, chosen by Parliament, becomes the king, accepts the Bill of Rights ensuring parliamentary supremacy.
1701	Act of Union joins Scotland and England, forming Great Britain.
1770's	Industrial revolution begins.
1832	First Reform Act extends the vote, eliminates "rotten boroughs."
1867	Second Reform Act lowers property qualifications for voting, introduces "household franchise" to towns.
1872	Secret ballot introduced.
1884	Third Reform Act establishes "household franchise" for all males.
1911	Power of House of Lords to veto legislation ends.
1918	Vote extended to men over 21 and most women over 30; constituencies made roughly equal.
1922	Irish Free State established; Northern Ireland remains part of the United Kingdom.
1945–1951	Postwar Labour government inaugurates the welfare state, nationalizes many industries, establishes "one person, one vote."

act as a powerful drag on change where change is most urgently needed, as it is in the troubled economy of recent years. As one author bitterly expressed it, "We lie upon our heritage like a Dunlopillo mattress, and hope, in our slumbers, those good, dead men of history will move us forward."[5]

[5]E. P. Thompson, "An Open Letter to Leszak Kolakowski," in R. Miliband and J. Saville, eds., *The Socialist Register 1973* (London: Merlin, 1974), p. 24.

A degree of manipulation may also have been involved in Britain's stability. It has been suggested that the very slowness of democratization may have made the workers so accustomed to the limitations imposed on them by the system that they simply came to accept them as a given—but not to endorse them as legitimate or morally right.[6] One can readily imagine that the world supremacy achieved by Britain in the nineteenth century would have made it difficult for the lower classes to voice criticism of the system, even if dissatisfaction or discontent had been widespread. Although this interpretation should not be taken too far—attachment to the political system in the nineteenth century was undoubtedly widespread and sincere—it may help to explain another phenomenon, the apparent change in British political culture in recent years. There is considerable evidence to suggest that the bonds of community, the political trust and deference to government and its traditional leadership, and the consensus on many basic issues may have declined relatively quickly in Britain since the 1950s.[7] Surveys show that ordinary people are no longer especially content with government or politicians and want more responsive institutions and a greater voice in public affairs. The principal political parties, Labour and Conservative, have become much more divided over a number of major issues, and the style of politics in Britain today seems less pragmatic and more ideological than it was just twenty or thirty years ago. With the appearance of nationalist parties in Scotland and Wales and violence between Protestants and Catholics in Northern Ireland (not to mention race riots in England itself), Britain now appears less a national community and more a divided multinational and multiracial one. None of this seriously threatens the stability of the political system, but it does suggest a society less certain of the old verities or of the direction it should take in the future. The comforting picture people often have of Britain—stable, contented, law-abiding, moderate—may already be out of date.

France: A Revolutionary Route

The course of France's political development over the past two centuries stands in strong contrast to Britain's gradual evolution from monarchy to democracy. Since 1789 France has experienced three monarchies, five republics, two empires, and one pseudofascist state—an average of more than one new regime every two decades. One should not overestimate the impact these changes have had on the average citizen; the laws and the state administration which governed the individual's life continued largely unchanged from one regime to the next. Nevertheless, France, which first attempted democracy in the eighteenth century, has had to

[6]H. F. Moorhouse, "The Political Incorporation of the British Working Class: An Interpretation," *Sociology* 7 (1973), pp. 341–359.

[7]A good account of these changes is given in S. Beer, *Britain Against Itself: The Political Contradictions of Collectivism* (New York: Norton, 1983).

wait well over a century and a half to see it solidly implanted as the accepted form of government for the country. The explanation for this state of affairs lies deep in French history.

The medieval kingdom of France possessed markedly less centralization of authority than did England under the Normans. Aristocrats, lacking the binding power of having conquered their lands under the command of their king, felt quite free to pursue their own interests. There is no better example of this than the behavior of the dukes of Normandy themselves. As lords of that duchy, they owed allegiance to the French king. As kings of England after 1066, they not only resisted the French kings' authority but also used their family connections with French royalty to claim the crown of France for themselves. It was the struggle over who should control France that culminated in the Hundred Years' War, which proved central to the development of the institution of the monarchy in France.

At first, when France was losing the war badly, popular forces were able to make great inroads into royal authority. Much as in England, the French crown was obliged to call an assembly representative of the different sectors or "estates" of the kingdom in order to seek financing for the war. The power of the "Estates General"—representing the three estates of nobles, clergy, and townspeople—reached its apex in 1357, when the heir to the throne accepted the supervision of a council chosen from its members. This dramatic assertion of control over the king was short-lived, however, and as France began to gain the upper hand in the struggle with England, so monarchical power grew. An important step in this process occurred in 1439, when the Estates General authorized the collection of a land tax, the *taille,* to help finance the war effort. It was largely the revenues from this tax that eventually allowed French monarchs to rule on their own—so much so that the Estates General ceased to meet at all after 1614.

The expulsion of the English from the French soil did not relieve the pressure toward greater centralization of authority. For one thing, France as a continental power was almost constantly swept up in rivalries with its powerful neighbors, Spain and the Holy Roman Empire. For another, internal disunity continued to plague the kingdom. In the second half of the sixteenth century, the country was embroiled in internal wars between Catholics and Protestants, conflicts which French monarchs were unable to control. These conflicts eventually ended in 1598, when Henry IV acceded to the throne and issued the Edict of Nantes, granting religious freedom and control of 200 fortified towns to the Protestants. But in the opinion of many, including able state-builders such as Cardinals Richelieu and Mazarin, the granting of such autonomy to Protestants only underscored the need for greater national integration and monarchical authority. Their success in enhancing monarchical authority in turn provoked regional rebellions, often led by aristocrats, in the mid-seventeenth century. These *frondes,* as they were known, were quickly repressed, but they made vivid to the young Louis XIV, who began his long reign in 1660, the need for total control. Under Louis, the "Sun King," France became the very model of absolute monarchy.

The absolutism of Louis XIV, so impressive to contemporaries for its grandeur and authority, was flawed in certain respects, however. The regime maintained the support of the aristocracy partly through its largesse and partly through its practice of exempting aristocrats from the principal tax, the *taille.* But spending lavishly and exempting the richest sector of society from the obligation of contributing to the support of the state were bound to create budgetary problems. In order to meet its financial needs, the state developed the habit of selling offices (i.e., posts) in the administration, usually honorific ones that involved no actual duties. In many cases, people bought these posts because they conferred aristocratic status and hence tax exemptions or because they provided a substantial income.

The long-term consequence of this practice was to worsen the state's financial problems, both because the number of administrative posts created was much larger than it needed to be and because the system encouraged wealthy nonnobles to abandon productive enterprise for the idle but tax-free life of an aristocrat (aristocrats were prohibited from engaging in most commercial activities). Economic development was also to suffer from Louis' decision in 1685 to revoke the Edict of Nantes, which had given Protestants their liberties. The revocation caused thousands of Protestants to flee the country for Holland or England, taking with them their considerable wealth and skills as artisans and businessmen. Central authority and religious unification were thus achieved at a high price in terms of future economic development.

France's inability to keep up with England in economic development and imperial expansion and the increasing bankruptcy of its treasury largely underlay the outbreak of revolution in 1789. For the outside world, the French Revolution marks the beginning of the modern era, as many of the values which form the context of contemporary politics, including the nation-state as the highest form of political organization and "liberty, equality, and fraternity" as its guiding principles, were developed and spread throughout Europe in its wake. Yet for France itself, the legacy of the revolution was very much a divided one. On the one hand, a quarter-century of national life without a king (1793–1815) had not convinced many to abandon their commitment to the monarchy and to the church which had sustained it. On the other hand, military defeat and the restoration of the Bourbon dynasty to the throne in 1815 left many others still faithful to the ideals of the revolution. The consequence of this bifurcation of French society was an oscillation of regime types that has lasted virtually to the present day.

The pattern of this oscillation may be described quite simply. Up until 1875, France was governed by authoritarian regimes (two monarchies and one empire), punctuated by two revolutionary outbreaks (1830,

1848–1851). After 1875 the norm was democratic government, interrupted by crises emanating from outside metropolitan France which toppled the democratic regimes. In the first such instance, the Third Republic fell as a result of the German invasion in 1940 and was followed by a brief quasi-fascist experiment under Marshal Pétain. The second instance was occasioned by a 1958 uprising of the French settlers in Algeria, supported by the army fighting the native liberation movement. It was this crisis that ended the Fourth Republic and brought into being the present regime, the Fifth Republic, headed initially by the wartime hero General Charles de Gaulle.

It has been suggested that the revolution of 1789 did more than just divide France ideologically into two opposed camps, the left (supporters of democracy) and the right (supporters of authoritarian government), making agreement on any one form of government difficult. Specifically, it is argued that the revolution also helped to divide French political culture.[8] One often-noted characteristic of that culture is the respect accorded strong authority. This trait, which probably originated during the absolute monarchy and was further reinforced during the Napoleonic Empire (1804–1815), accords the French state a great deal of leeway in running the affairs of the nation. It is reflected in a highly developed sense of the supreme role of the state in society, its privileges, its prerogatives, and the preeminence of its vision of what France should be and how that vision should be realized. But this respect for authority seems to be countered to some extent by a strong egalitarian thrust in French culture, a desire not to be subject to anyone's authority and, in particular, to resist the ultimate expression of authority, the state, at every opportunity. This presumably received expression and reinforcement during the revolution. It is exemplified in the ideas of the twentieth century philosopher Alain, who admonished the citizen to "construct every day a little barricade or, if you like, to bring every day some king before the court of the people."[9] More tellingly, it has shown itself in the weak organizational life in France and the fractious and poorly disciplined parties that until recently dominated French legislatures. At times it has almost seemed as if the elected representatives (known as "deputies") of France's parliamentary regimes failed to support cabinets in office for very long simply because they resented being subject to anyone's authority—including that of their own party leaders.

A great deal has changed since these cultural traits were identified. The notorious cabinet instability of the years between 1875 and 1958 is

---

[8]This theme was developed most eloquently by M. Crozier, *The Bureaucratic Phenomenon* (Chicago: University of Chicago Press, 1964) and *The Stalled Society* (New York: Viking, 1973), but its origins may be traced back to the great nineteenth-century sociologist Aléxis de Tocqueville in his *The Old Regime and the Revolution,* trans. S. Gilbert (New York: Doubleday Anchor, 1955).

[9]Cited in P. Williams, *Crisis and Compromise: Politics in the Fourth Republic* (Garden City, N.Y.: Doubleday, 1966), p. 5.

now virtually forgotten. In the quasi-presidential regime of today, the main parties are for the most part well organized at the grass roots level and well disciplined in the legislature. The organizational life of the society is also better developed and more positive or constructive in its aims. The so-called delinquent communities—groups in society hostile to authority, unwilling to bargain or compromise, suspicious even of their own members—are much less in evidence in social and political life now than they were just a few decades ago. Support for the present regime is well-nigh universal: even the electoral victory of the Socialists in 1981, once thought unimaginably dangerous, was accepted with little fuss.

These changes of recent years are partly the result of the modernization of French society since 1945 and partly the result of the change in regime in 1958, as we shall see. But we must be cautious in interpreting the evidence. The ability of the French to rise up spontaneously in revolt, to erect real barricades, was demonstrated as recently as 1968, when a student-worker revolt occurred of such proportions that it appeared to threaten the regime itself. Moreover, it happened at a time so apparently tranquil for France that a journalist had even declared, just weeks before the event, that France "was bored with itself." On the other hand, the continuing strong respect for the state's authority has made it difficult for the French to understand just what the Watergate scandal of 1972–1974 was all about—most assumed it was normal for a head of state to break laws if he chose. Until very recently, French television was entirely state-

Students in Paris retreat from an attack by riot police during demonstrations that paralyzed France in May and June of 1968. (Marc Riboud / Magnum)

owned and characteristically biased in favor of the government of the day in its news reporting; the notion, universally accepted in Britain, that even state-owned broadcasting should be fair to the opposition has not been an integral part of the French political scene.

Although these legacies of authoritarian government and democratic rebelliousness persist, they should not be taken to mean that France is any less a democracy than Britain. In fact, certain of France's legacies compare very favorably with those engendered by Britain's less tumultuous political development. One of these is a much stronger egalitarian thrust in French politics and culture. If democracy is about equality—and to a large extent it must be—then the French have appreciated and realized its import more clearly than have the British. The French also seem less tied to hollow traditions, more willing to question and challenge the inheritance of the past. They have also developed a much stronger, more activist state, one which is more disposed to shape the course of future change and to coerce a reluctant society to follow its lead. The traits have helped France develop economically more adeptly than Britain in the postwar years. Despite a history of political instability and economic retardation relative to Britain, it seems that France has managed in a few decades to overcome both disadvantages and is today better placed to confront the future. Perhaps the lesson here is that a troubled past is not an unpardonable offense.

THE SOVIET UNION AND CHINA: REVOLUTION AND DEVELOPMENT

It is difficult to imagine two countries more differently placed to receive the impact of the West than the Russian and the Chinese. While Russia had lived for centuries under the influence of the more technologically and intellectually advanced states of Europe, Chinese culture received a severe shock when the impact of Western power and Western ideas was first felt in full force in the nineteenth century. While Russians had struggled with a sense of inferiority of their society vis-à-vis the West since the sixteenth century, the Chinese had basked for hundreds, if not thousands, of years in the conviction that theirs was the greatest of civilizations, immeasurably superior to that of the "barbarians" from the West. Despite these very different starting points, however, the two societies shared certain features that predisposed them to a revolutionary communist solution to the challenges of modernization. First of all, both societies were confronted with the enormous task of addressing their own technological and military inferiority. The highly autocratic structures of their traditional political systems in both cases proved inadequate to the challenges they faced and were replaced by force. Finally, and perhaps most significantly, their previous traditions of authoritarian rule helped to point both societies away from a pluralist or market-oriented mode of development and toward a state-led mode. Differences in history and culture, however, have meant that while the overall

Figure 1.2 **SOME IMPORTANT EVENTS IN FRENCH HISTORY**

1338	The Hundred Years' War with England begins.
1357	The "Great Ordinance" prescribes the supervision of government by a council of the Estates General.
1439	The Estates General grants Charles VII the *taille* (a land tax) to support the struggle against the English, paving the way for the monarchy's independence.
1452	The Hundred Years' War ends.
1562	Civil wars between Protestants and Catholics begin.
1598	Henry IV issues the Edict of Nantes, granting Protestants freedom of worship and control of 200 fortified towns.
1614	Last meeting of Estates General before 1789.
1648	Aristocratic rebellions *(frondes)* against central authority break out.
1660–1714	Reign of Louis XIV, the "Sun King."
1685	Louis revokes the Edict of Nantes; Protestants flee France for England and Holland.
1789	Outbreak of the French Revolution.
1792	Monarchy abolished; the First Republic created.
1804	Napoleon Bonaparte creates the First Empire, with himself as emperor.
1815	Bourbon dynasty reestablished.
1830	The July Revolution forces abdication of Charles X and his replacement as king by Louis Philippe.
1848	Revolution removes Louis Philippe and establishes the Second Republic.
1851	Louis-Napoleon overthrows the Republic and establishes the Second Empire.
1870	Defeat of France by Prussia ends the Second Empire.
1875	The Third Republic, France's longest lasting regime since 1789, is established.
1940	German invasion ends the Third Republic and leads to the quasi-fascist Vichy regime under Marshal Pétain.
1944	Provisional government of General Charles de Gaulle is established in liberated France.
1946	Establishment of the Fourth Republic.
1958	Revolt of military and settlers in Algeria ends the Fourth Republic.
1959	De Gaulle establishes the Fifth Republic.
1968	Student-worker strikes and demonstrations paralyze France.
1981	The Socialists, led by President Mitterrand, are elected to power.

solution—communism—is the same, the politics of the two countries are far from being identical.

The Soviet Union: A Legacy of Autocracy and Revolution

The Bolshevik Revolution of October 1917 marks the beginning of communist power in the country known today as the Union of Soviet Socialist Republics. The Soviet state, however, traces its ancestry back through more than a thousand years of monarchy in the lands of Russia. Unlike their counterparts in England, the Russian monarchs, known as *tsars,* effectively resisted the nobility's attempts to limit their power. Reforms, demanded ultimately by the middle and lower classes, proved to be too little, too late, and in the midst of World War I the monarch was overthrown by violence. Unlike the revolution in France, the Russian revolution has ultimately led not to liberal democracy but to a renewed and strengthened centralism under the leadership of a single-party oligarchy.

Soviet ideology portrays the communist state as a revolutionary creation that has rejected the negative legacy of tsarism, but, objectively speaking, one would have to weigh heavily the influence of Russian history on the modern political culture. One legacy of that history is the persistence of autocracy. The best-remembered tsars—Ivan III "the Great" (1462–1505), Ivan IV "the Terrible" (1533–1584), Peter I "the Great" (1694–1725), and Catherine II "the Great" (1762–1796)—all strengthened monarchical authority at the expense of the minor princes and *boyars* (landed nobility). In the century before 1917, while much of Europe was undergoing revolutionary change, the tsars oscillated between policies of intensified repression and piecemeal reform; this only inflamed the growing opposition movements, whose leaders were attracted to the political ideas of the Western intelligentsia—liberalism, anarchism, socialism, Marxism. For example, a spontaneous revolution in 1905 prompted Nicholas II (1894–1917), the last of the tsars, to create Russia's first parliament, the Duma, but, characteristically, he refused to allow it to infringe on his powers as an absolute monarch. This obduracy served to encourage the spread of revolutionary sentiments.

Throughout the long history of autocracy, the tsar's authority was underwritten by force. Ivan the Terrible created the *Oprichnina,* a state within the state, whose agents enforced the monarch's rule by methods that included the murder of many boyars and the confiscation of their property. Nicholas I (1825–1855) created the so-called Third Section, a secret police network which infiltrated the ranks of political dissenters and sometimes provoked them into actions for which they would be arrested. Thus autocracy went hand in hand with police surveillance and arbitrary arrest—a combination familiar in recent times as well.

A second legacy is that of empire. The first Russian state, centered in Kiev, was a federation of principalities extending far to the west, north, and east; by A.D. 1050 its territories were already large by comparison to today's European countries. Later, following the rise of Muscovy (Moscow), Russia's monarchs extended their rule across increasingly distant frontiers, which by 1689 reached from the border of Poland to the Pacific Ocean and from the Caspian Sea to the Arctic. During the eighteenth and nineteenth centuries, the Russian Empire swallowed up Finland and the neighboring Baltic countries, together with nearly half of Poland, and annexed large areas of central and northeastern Asia. All these lands, except for Poland and Finland, are today incorporated into the Soviet Union—a country bigger than the United States and Canada combined, containing dozens of nations with a myriad of cultural traditions and more than 100 spoken languages. Dominating all the other peoples are the Great Russians, who constitute barely half of the total population.

A third legacy from the tsarist past is a tendency to xenophobia—a fear of things foreign—which stems from repeated conflicts with foreigners, who have many times invaded the Russian homeland. The longest period of foreign occupation was that of the Mongols (1240–1480), but costly wars have been fought on Russian soil against the medieval Teutonic Knights, against Sweden, Poland, Lithuania, and Napoleonic France. Between 1815 and 1914, while Western Europe enjoyed a century of relative peace, Russia fought three wars against Turkey, one of which (the Crimean War of 1853–1855) brought the British and French in on Turkey's side, and one against Japan. The embittering effects of these conflicts were augmented by the teachings of the Russian Orthodox Church, which considered foreign religious and philosophical ideas heretical. As for the political ideas, the tsars consistently viewed all Western "isms" with suspicion, if not outright hostility.

Over and against these xenophobic tendencies, though hardly counterbalancing them, was an admiration for Western technology and, to a degree, cultural achievements. Peter the Great, for example, encouraged the nobility to imitate Western styles of grooming and fashion, while he sought to modernize the Russian army and emulate the European bureaucratic-absolutist state structure. With the partitions of Poland (1772–1795), through which Catherine the Great collaborated with Austria and Prussia to carve up that once-powerful kingdom, Russia became a major actor in the European power system, and in their efforts to advance that role the nineteenth-century tsars looked longingly to European science, industry, and military technology. A large portion of Russia's late-blooming industry was built with foreign (mostly German) capital. Still, Russia's rulers through Nicholas II struggled to resist the social impact of the West. A similar ambivalence can be seen among the monarchy's political opponents, who often found themselves in conflict over whether or not Western answers were appropriate to Russian questions.

Another legacy is that of economic backwardness. As of 1914, about

85 percent of the population still lived in rural districts. Agricultural technology was primitive, and in years of poor harvests, famine was not uncommon. There was no tradition of an independent landholding peasantry, as serfdom had been abolished only in 1861 and progress toward an equitable redistribution of farmlands took place haltingly. Some industries developed during the late nineteenth century, primarily under the state's direction, and the pace of industrialization increased in the years leading up to 1914, but the Russian economy remained far behind that of every other major European country. By the 1920s, moreover, the new communist government had to grapple with an economy that had been further ravaged by a world war and four additional years of civil war.

The final tsarist legacy is a tradition of dissent and revolt. For centuries, isolated peasant rebellions took place in localities of central Russia; these were invariably aimed at landlords and not meant to oppose the rule of the tsar. Occasionally there occurred uprisings of the Don Cossacks, a community of peasants in the southern Ukraine who enjoyed a degree of political autonomy. In some of the empire's other peripheral lands, movements for national autonomy developed; in 1830–1831 and again in 1863, revolts in Poland were violently put down. Elsewhere during the second half of the nineteenth century, opposition movements sprouted among disaffected members of the intelligentsia. The most radical groups engaged in occasional uprisings and political terrorism; in 1881, a member of one such group, called the People's Will, assassinated Tsar Alexander II. It was from this heritage of dissent and revolt that V. I. Lenin, who led the Bolsheviks to power in 1917, emerged, and it is from this long tradition that the dissidents in the Soviet Union today have also descended.

While it is important to understand the depth of Russian political traditions, it is equally important to acknowledge the revolutionary nature of the regime that came into power in November 1917[10] and the changes Soviet society has since undergone. In place of the monarch who ruled autocratically, a mass party became supreme; today, the Communist Party of the Soviet Union (CPSU) is led by a small oligarchy which makes most major decisions, but it relies on the participation of several million party members organized in a complicated hierarchy of structures throughout the USSR. In place of Orthodox Christianity, the official creed is the secular ideology of Marxism-Leninism. In place of an archaic social structure in which distinctions of class, wealth, and privilege were stark, a far more complex society has evolved in which there is nominally only one class but effectively many layers and divisions based on occupation, income, education, ethnicity, and place of resi-

---

[10]Until 1918 Russia employed the old Julian calendar, which in this century is thirteen days behind that used in the West (the Gregorian). The Bolsheviks seized power on October 25, 1917 (Julian calendar); today, the "Great October Revolution" is celebrated on November 7.

dence. Finally, the country's economy has developed from that of a marginal European standard to one which, notwithstanding its chronic structural deficiencies, today supports one of the world's two mightiest and technologically most advanced military systems.

The Bolshevik Revolution was actually the second of two revolutions in 1917. The first, the February Revolution,[11] began as a spontaneous mass demonstration. Expressing its frustration at the food shortages and other hardships caused by the world war, the mob in the capital city of Petrograd (now called Leningrad) drew fire from the armed troops sent to quiet them. The unrest quickly spread beyond Petrograd and grew into an uprising among a wide-ranging, but unorganized and leaderless, segment of the population. Tsar Nicholas, his government weakened by wartime defeats and conflicts between the army and the bureaucracy, abdicated. Left to pick up the pieces were the leaders of the political parties constituting the Duma (which the tsar had just dissolved). The Provisional Government, which took over power, found itself confronted by a losing war effort, a state budget on the brink of collapse, a growing rebelliousness among the national minorities, and a newly unified workers' movement organized in *soviets* (factory councils). Within months, the government's position became untenable; refusing to make a capitulationist peace with Germany and unable to rescue the flagging economy, the Provisional Government lost its cohesion. In a nearly bloodless coup d'état engineered by a small circle of activists led by Lenin, the Bolsheviks seized power in the name of the soviets.

The legacy of Vladimir Ilyich Lenin is complex and controversial, but the man who masterminded the October Revolution is revered to this day as a national hero without historical or contemporary rivals. Lenin was primarily a man of action, a brilliant political strategist, yet his voluminous theoretical works are invoked in Soviet speeches and writings today as gospel. (Jokingly, it is said that Lenin, being immortal, continues to write from his mausoleum.) As a leader, he could debate a point fiercely until his view prevailed; and yet it is important to note that, in the leadership councils of the Bolshevik party, alternative strategies and tactics were vigorously discussed and decisions were taken by majority vote.[12] As the head of the ruling party after 1917, Lenin never aspired to dictatorial power but, instead, governed through the party oligarchy. It was his dream that, once Russian society had rid itself of bourgeois and aristocratic elements, the party would lead the workers to a true democracy.

Early in 1918, the new Soviet government made peace with Ger-

[11]February 22–March 2 (Julian calendar); March 7–15 (Gregorian).

[12]The name "Bolsheviks" *(Bol'sheviki),* meaning those in the majority, was adopted by Lenin's wing of the Russian Social Democratic Workers' Party in 1903, when they won a vote on the question of who should serve on the editorial board of the party's newspaper, *Iskra (The Spark).* The party's name passed through several official variations before its present form, the Communist Party of the Soviet Union, was adopted.

many in the Treaty of Brest-Litovsk. Immediately, however, there were other enemies to contend with. On the Bolsheviks' side were members and supporters of several left-wing parties; these were organized into the Red Army by Leon Trotsky. On the other side was an alliance of forces ranging from moderate socialists to monarchists; their "White" armies were led, most often, by antirevolutionary generals. Many members of national minorities joined the Whites, hoping to gain independence. Finland, Estonia, Latvia, Lithuania, and the Ukraine were already lost; Poland would gain independence at the end of the world war. The danger was that more of the peripheral territories would follow. In addition, the Red Army found itself in isolated battles against American, French, British, and Czech troops.

While contending with these hostile forces, Lenin's government instituted a series of harsh policies known as War Communism. These policies, adopted in May 1918, included the nationalization of industry, the institution of centralized economic planning, the distribution of basic goods and services free on a rationed basis, and egalitarian wages. They were accompanied by draconian measures to neutralize the opposition, including the direct application of death sentences by the *Cheka* (political police). Severe food shortages prompted the government to requisition grain and to begin a forced collectivization of farmlands. War Communism lasted from 1918 until 1921, when the civil war finally wound to a conclusion. By this time, the country's economic crisis had worsened.

The party leadership responded by enacting the New Economic Policy (NEP). The forced collectivization of farmlands was abandoned; instead, peasants were allowed to produce privately and sell their goods on the free market while being encouraged, through taxes and incentives, to join cooperatives voluntarily. Key industries remained in state hands, but small and medium-sized concerns were reprivatized. The power of the secret police was curtailed, and the arts flourished as a result of a relatively permissive censorship. For a few years, Russian intellectual life became freer than it ever had been.

Lenin died in 1924. Political life remained firmly in the hands of the party, and the programs of NEP continued until 1928. However, Lenin's policy reversals left an ambiguous legacy, which has confused party leaders ever since, and at no time was the ambiguity greater than during the succession struggle of 1924–1928. The man who emerged on top, Joseph Stalin, did so by slandering his rivals and manipulating the party leadership to exclude them from the ranks. Eventually he would have them murdered.

Stalin dominated the party and imposed his will on the country for 25 years. He inaugurated a "Third Revolution"—a revolution from above, brought about by the state—meant to catapult the USSR into the modern era as a major industrial power. The policies of NEP were discarded; all industries were again nationalized, and the peasants were compelled to join collective farms. Government-directed planning replaced the market in all respects, as economic production came under the directives of elaborate five-year plans. Workers were asked to sacrifice for society's well-being; wages were very low, indiscipline or poor performance on the job was often severely punished, and unusually high productivity was rewarded by public recognition. In the countryside, resistance to collectivization ran very high as peasants were unwilling to give up their lands; literally millions of peasants died, killed either by the state police or by famine, and many more were sent to prison camps in Siberia. Still others streamed into the cities to join the burgeoning industrial proletariat; because of inadequate housing supplies, they lived in barracks hastily set up and closely regimented. Workers, the "chosen people" of the revolution, were lionized by the state; many who recalled their miserable status before the revolution believed they were now participating in the creation of a new civilization, but many others felt only the oppression of a militarized society.

It was Stalin who brought back the reality of autocracy. Within the Communist party, he eliminated those who opposed his rule or his policies. In a series of shocking public trials, numerous onetime party leaders—men who had been close associates of Lenin and of Stalin himself—were unjustly convicted of treason and sentenced to death. Nor did the purge stop there; fueled by Stalin's fear of subversion, bordering on paranoia, his agents arrested, tortured, and prosecuted tens of thousands of communists while, through further arbitrary arrests and the recruitment of informants, they propagated a generalized terror which convinced virtually the entire population that no one was safe.

The legacy of Stalin, in contrast to that of Lenin, is largely negative. It is true that the 25 years of the dictator's rule saw some remarkable progress: the USSR was transformed into an industrial and military power second only to the United States; the country had survived World War II, despite suffering the most devastating population losses in the history of international warfare; and in the course of victory the Soviet army secured the long-vulnerable western borders by occupying nearly all the countries of Eastern Europe and, in the wake of occupation, created the basis for a postwar empire larger than that of the tsars. On the home front, however, the morale of the ruling Communist party had been seriously damaged by the purges and by Stalin's personalistic rule; literature and art had been almost destroyed by an uncompromising censorship; education and scholarship had been forced into narrow and archaic methods, their substance constricted by ideologically-dictated truths; the Russian Orthodox Church, as well as all other social institutions, had lost all effective moral influence; and even the economic system—which, on the surface, seemed to present a success story—had failed to balance the need for capital production and military hardware, on the one hand, with a modicum of comfort for consumers, on the other.

In 1956, three years after the death of Stalin, the new chief of the

CPSU, Nikita Khrushchev, denounced the excesses of the late dictator—the "crimes of the Stalin era," as they were called. Since 1953 the Soviet political system has changed substantially. Gone are the blood purges as a way of eliminating opposition within the party; gone, in general, is the ubiquitous terror by which society was kept rigidly under control. Gone, too, is one-man rule. Under Khrushchev's leadership, the party ceremoniously returned to what were called "Leninist norms," which, at the top levels of the hierarchy, meant collective decision-making.

Yet many of the systemic realities growing out of the Third Revolution have survived. Industry remains mostly state-owned, agriculture

Figure 1.3 SOME IMPORTANT EVENTS IN RUSSIAN HISTORY

c. 988	Vladmir, Prince of Kiev, converts to Christianity.
1240–1480	Russia is ruled by the Mongol "Golden Horde."
1452–1517	Rise of Muscovy under Ivan III and Vasily III.
1547	Ivan IV ("the Terrible"), crowned by the Metropolitan of the Russian Church, becomes the first prince to take the title Tsar (Caesar).
1598–1613	The "Time of Troubles"—the only period when the boyars seriously contest the Russian throne.
1618	Polish army advances to Moscow but fails to take the city.
1712	Peter the Great moves the capital to St. Petersburg.
1812	Army of Napoleon I captures Moscow but fails to conquer Russia.
1861	Alexander II emancipates the serfs.
1905	Revolution forces Nicholas II to establish the Duma.
1914	Outbreak of World War I.
1917	February Revolution brings down the monarchy and leads to the formation of the Provisional Government; eight months later, the Bolsheviks seize power in the "Great October Revolution."
1918–1921	War Communism.
1921–1928	New Economic Policy (NEP).
1924	Death of Lenin (January 21).
1928	Stalin launches "Third Revolution."
1941	Germany attacks the Soviet Union, beginning a war that claims more than 20 million Soviet lives.
1953	Death of Joseph Stalin (March 5).
1956	CPSU First Secretary N. S. Khrushchev denounces Stalin's "crimes," thereafter consolidates his own power as "first among equals" within a revived CPSU oligarchy.
1964	Khrushchev is ousted, replaced by Leonid Brezhnev as party chief and Alexei Kosygin as Premier; by about 1970 Brezhnev is clearly "first among equals."
1985	Mikhail Gorbachev becomes party chief, representing transition of Soviet leadership to a new generation.

collectivized. Open political opposition is not tolerated, and the public expression of dissent is dealt with, in individual cases, by police harassment, arrest, often incarceration, and sometimes exile. One should not accept the polemical image, widely held in the West, that the Soviet Union today is a vast prison, for the overwhelming majority of its citizens live normal lives without a sense of personal danger. But still, the ghost of Stalin lives. A dissident Soviet historian has thus evaluated the Stalinist legacy:

> The Soviet Union passed through a serious disease and lost many of its finest sons. When the cult of Stalin's personality was exposed a great step was made to recovery. But not everything connected with Stalinism is behind us, by no means everything.[13]

China: Revolution and Tradition

In China, the leaders of a billion people seek to transform fundamentally a society whose roots stretch back through three millennia of civilized life. Although the changes that have been wrought in the four decades of communist rule are highly significant, the residue of China's long and unique past still influences its present to a very considerable degree. In fact, while China has adopted a Western ideology—Marxism-Leninism— and aspires to be a modern nation-state, Chinese political behavior continues to be molded by a largely traditional political culture shaped, above all, by the teachings of Confucius.

The Confucian cultural system emerged from an institutionalized monarchy and a legal-philosophic system dating back to the Zhou dynasty, founded in 1122 B.C. In the centuries following the Zhou dynasty, feuding minikingdoms frequently plagued China. It was under the Han dynasty (206 B.C.–A.D. 222) that authority was finally centralized, slavery abolished, and the Confucian ideology established officially. According to Confucian thought, the ideal social structure is founded on a set of prescriptions for the relations of ruler and subjects, neighbor and neighbor, father and son, husband and wife, brother and brother. These regulations, based on the norms of filial piety (veneration of parents) and loyalty to the ruler, go so far as to describe the modes in which persons should walk, talk, and sit consistent with these status relationships. If the individual learns these relationships and applies them with sincerity, the result will be good government and a society in harmony with its rulers.

This outlook led logically to the creation under the Tang dynasty (A.D. 618–906) of a bureaucracy whose personnel were recruited on the basis of examinations in Confucian principles. This recruiting procedure created one of the first modern bureaucracies—that is, a bureauc-

---

[13]Roy A. Medvedev, *Let History Judge: The Origins and Consequences of Stalinism,* trans. Colleen Taylor (New York: Knopf, 1971), p. 566.

racy based on merit or achievement as opposed to favoritism or inheritance. However, by the mid-nineteenth century, the Confucian bureaucratic system had become a conservative obstacle to social change. It glorified the past and ignored the need to adapt to a rapidly changing present. The "modernity" of its method of recruiting bureaucrats was countered by its atavistic and antimodern outlook on contemporary problems.

In Confucianism, familial loyalty and private, as opposed to public, interests are emphasized. This tradition is in sharp contrast to those of many Western societies, where stress is laid on civic or community-minded values, including norms of social and political trust. According to Confucius, the individual owes loyalty first to the central authority, particularly the emperor and the bureaucrats, and then to the family, headed by the father. The family is the overwhelming focus of attention, and family interests always take precedence when they conflict with the interests of friends or acquaintances.

This family-based social structure produced behavior that hindered modernization of the Chinese economy and society. A set of landowning families dominated the civil service, enjoyed enormous privileges, refused to engage in manual labor, and became associated with many abuses: compulsory unpaid labor for landlord and state, exorbitant land rents, private armed bands, and the use of violence to control the peasants. Most significantly, the landowners who controlled political power acted to prevent the growth of an urban capitalist class that might one day have rivaled their dominant position in Chinese society.

It took the arrival of Europeans to upset this highly authoritarian social and political order. At first, Chinese treatment of foreigners was a function of their relations with neighboring Southeast Asian states, which had been allowed to trade with China provided they acknowledged Chinese superiority through tribute missions. This system disintegrated when British traders settled in Canton in the nineteenth century and built up a triangular trade between India, China, and England. The British demand was primarily for tea; the Chinese wanted raw cotton and, increasingly, opium from India. By the 1830s there were an estimated 2 million to 10 million habitual opium smokers in China, many of them government officials. When the provincial governor in Canton ordered a crackdown on the opium trade in 1939, the British responded with force, triggering the First Opium War. China's defeat in the war resulted in the first of a series of "unequal treaties" with foreign trading powers. The treaties guaranteed foreigners preferential trade conditions, fixed tariff rates on imports, and asserted the doctrine of extraterritorial rights, which, among other things, prevented the Chinese from punishing foreign merchants or sailors who committed crimes in Chinese ports.

European penetration and the Japanese defeat of China in the Sino-Japanese War (1894–1895) were a constant source of shame to the Chinese, aware of their historical greatness. In 1895, Kang Yuwei led a protest movement which advocated rejecting peace with Japan, moving the capital inland to allow for prolonged warfare, and instituting a series of reforms, including a stronger centralized government to cope with the threats from abroad, a parliament, Western dress, and even equality of the sexes. The movement's goal was a blending of East and West, with emphasis on maintaining Eastern ethics and importing Western science. Three years later, Kang gained access to Emperor Guang Xu and was able to have a number of reforms enacted during a period known as The Hundred Days. Reactionary forces led by the dowager empress soon revoked these reforms, but the need for change did not abate.

The inability of the Chinese government to resist foreign demands stimulated more opposition to the Chinese imperial tradition. After the deaths of the emperor and the dowager empress in 1908, conditions were ripe for the 1911 republican revolution. In its ultimate effort to survive, the Qing dynasty made concessions that contributed to China's readiness for revolution: students were sent abroad to study, and elections for 21 provincial assemblies were announced for 1909. Many students who returned supported the call of Sun Yatsen, a foreign-educated student himself, for the overthrow of the monarchy and the creation of a republic. Moreover, the provincial elections resulted in the accession to power of businessmen, journalists, and educators, who used the provincial assemblies not to support the regime but to overthrow it. In 1911 they declared provincial autonomy from the Qing (Manchu) dynasty. The dynasty appealed to the warlord General Yuan Shikai to restore order, but he joined the opposition instead and demanded the abdication of the remaining Qing family. The fall of the Qing dynasty lead to the creation of a republic under Sun Yatsen in 1912, but the new regime's authority was challenged by feudal military warlords, who fought among themselves and against the republicans for control of China. Only the outbreak of World War I gave China a brief respite.

With the Europeans fighting each other thousands of miles away and its own economy rapidly modernizing, Japan saw an opportunity to enhance its own economic interests in China. In 1915 the Japanese presented China with a set of 21 demands that, if accepted, would have made China a virtual colony of Japan. In addition, the Russian Revolution prompted the United States to make secret agreements with Japan recognizing Japanese interests in Shandung Province and special rights in Manchuria in exchange for Japan's invasion of Siberia. Chinese intellectuals heard of these secret treaties through the Peace Conference of Versailles in 1919, and 3000 Chinese students and intellectuals demonstrated in protest on May 4, 1919. The May Fourth Movement, as it came to be called, proposed a plan for China's development which included the adoption of Western science, technology, and political ideas such as Marxism. Thus, although nationalistic, this movement, like others, was prepared to adopt what it saw as the best from the West in order to achieve its objectives. The protest movement spread to 200 Chinese cities and towns during the following 18 months, and over 20 million participated. One of those participants was Mao Zedong, who became a leading member of a small group of Marxist intellectuals promoting a spontaneous, nationwide united front of laborers, peasants, and intellectuals.

By the 1920s, the central government was in the hands of a broad coalition consisting of the communists, including Mao, and the left and right wings of the Guomindang party under Jiang Kaishek. The communists participated under orders from Stalin, whose help Jiang Kaishek had enlisted in organizing the Guomindang party and the armed forces. Mao and the other Chinese communist leaders obeyed reluctantly, believing that they could have been better off organizing the peasants and building their own military force. This belief proved to be justified, for Jiang turned on them in April 1927. Nevertheless, Stalin continued his support of Jiang and the Guomindang, even though the spring of 1927 saw more bloodshed between communists and the right-wing Guomindang supporters. While other factors contributed to the current dispute between China and the Soviet Union, their early relations were not conducive to establishing trust and cooperation.

The struggle between the Guomindang and the Chinese communists was to last nearly 30 years. Among the events of this turbulent period, the Long March stands out as a political symbol and source of legitimacy and integration for the current communist regime. On October 16, 1934, some 100,000 Chinese communist men and women, led by Mao Zedong, burst out from Guomindang encirclement and began a march that ultimately took them some 6000 miles. This trek, which lasted an entire year and passed through 11 provinces, became a source of the party leadership's discipline and dedication, the spirit behind the contemporary sacrifices it has deemed necessary for China's modernization. In addition, it was instrumental in the survival and ultimate victory of the communist movement in China. By redistributing land and restructuring leadership and policies in territories under communist control, Mao communicated by deed the theories of a communist state. This was the key factor in gaining adherents to the successful communist drive for the control of China during the late 1940s.

The climax came in the years after World War II, when the communist forces succeeded in defeating the American-trained and -equipped forces of Jiang Kaishek. On October 1, 1949, Mao Zedong proclaimed the establishment of the People's Republic of China and raised the red flag in Beijing. The vision which Chairman Mao developed at this stage included the abolition of state power, the necessity of perpetual revolution, leadership by the working and peasant classes, the strengths of Chinese cultural traits, and the sanctity of labor. But even more important to that vision was a compulsive concern for social justice, equality, and economic modernization. Conscious of history, Mao recognized that ideas unaccompanied by action cannot in themselves be realized—that the construction of a new society is closely associated with the realistic need for economic development. There followed, between 1949 and 1952, a period of reconstruction and transition during which the government laid a basis for societal change through organization and education. Land reform was undertaken during this period, and China's planning commissions and party membership structures were organized. Most important, China stood up to a foreign power for the first time in its modern history in the Korean War (1950–1953).

Between 1953 and 1957, the First Five-Year Plan laid the foundation for industrialization, the modernization of agriculture, and the socialization of the economy. Progress was so encouraging that the leaders enthusiastically proposed the Great Leap Forward toward the first "communes" in 1958. The transition proved detrimental, however, to agricultural and industrial production. Morale problems and political reactions ensued, and the 1961–1965 period became one of consolidation, adjustment, and transition.

The Great Proletarian Cultural Revolution, which began in 1966, opened a new phase in socialist construction. While interpretations of the often violent Cultural Revolution vary, it undeniably represented Mao's last effort to instill the values of communism he held deepest: social justice and democratization of a bureaucratic state. One consequence was the removal of political leaders who had temporarily eclipsed Mao's control. Perhaps of greater moment was Mao's idealism and concern for maintaining the purity of the revolution. Mao believed that exploitation and privilege came from status differences and from the contradictions between mental and physical work and between urban and rural life-styles. Policies to rectify these conditions enacted during and after the Cultural Revolution included new measures to further equal status, education for peasants and factory workers, participation by workers' and peasants' councils in the management of factories and communes, and a requirement that students, economic managers, and party cadres experience physical labor on factories or farms. These acts were often eclipsed by unbridled extremism, particularly by the radical Red Guards.

Between 1975 and 1976 many of China's founding fathers died, including Premier Zhou Enlai (one of China's most influential and respected men) and the "Great Helmsman" himself, Mao Zedong. These deaths caused the most important leadership changes in China since the revolution. Following a year of struggle, two new factions emerged on top, one led by Hua Guofeng, the new party chairman and premier, and another led by Deng Xiaoping, deputy premier. Within five years, Deng had outmaneuvered the Hua faction, removing him and most of his followers from key positions. With the new leadership, China has opened up its doors to the outside world and increased trade and personal contacts. The ideological emphasis of the Cultural Revolution, a period during which China's economic growth was disrupted, has been replaced by

Fervent supporters brandish the Red flag and a portrait of Chairman Mao Zedong during a rally in favor of Mao's Cultural Revolution of the late 1960s. (Marc Riboud / Magnum)

a greater pragmatism in directing development. Under the slogan of the "Four Modernizations" (agriculture, industry, national defense, and science and technology), first put forward by Zhou, China is seeking to achieve substantial modernization by the year 2000.

Although China has undergone a profound transformation since 1949, it is important to appreciate the influence traditional Chinese culture exercises on China's political processes, including the way in which communism is interpreted and applied. Part of the success of communism in China is related to the similarity between its vision of a conflict-free society and the Confucian emphasis on social harmony. In addition, the conflicts that have taken place in China since 1949 have often pitted Mao's advocacy of social equality against the tendency of many party and government officials to abuse their power and privileges in ways reminiscent of the privileged class of Confucian-educated literati who ruled imperial China. The influence of Taoism, an early philosophical tradition which advocated responding to societal conflict by seeking internal peace and by adjusting to reality, is also evident. During periods of turmoil such as the Cultural Revolution, most people have adopted the strategy of simply going with the tide.

While the influence of tradition has been strong, China has not been immune to new influences. In the late nineteenth and early twentieth centuries, European inroads into China stimulated the development of nationalist and economic forces. The former encouraged a critical awareness of the existing social and political order; the latter created new classes other than peasants, landlords, and bureaucrats. Many of the new middle classes sought Western education for their children. Their foreign exposure threw them into a maelstrom of political debate, often revolving around Western liberal-democratic values and the suitability of those values to traditional Chinese culture, with its emphasis on authoritarianism and obedience. For many intellectuals, including Sun Yatsen, the preferred path was an eventual modified Western-style democracy; for others, such as the warlords, it was personalist authoritarian rule.

With the development of mass communications in the late twentieth century and further cross-cultural exposure, the two outlooks have again come into contention. The communists, while maintaining a hierarchical authoritarian party rule, have sought to remodel traditional patterns of government by introducing greater participation. Indeed, in neighborhoods, factories, and party subunits, citizen involvement, discussion, and (guided) decision-making have been widely encouraged. Competitive elections, albeit under Communist party control, and constitutional procedures for a variety of political needs have also been introduced.

When the British began to make inroads into China in the mid-nineteenth century, the Chinese, long accustomed to seeing themselves as the center of the universe, the possessors of all that is needed, suddenly became aware of major relative weakness. They were no match for the Western invaders militarily, nor was their economic system able to provide the base for a stronger government response. Furthermore, their system of government by means of a Confucian hierarchy seemed glaringly weak, yet there was no means of replacing it, even if alternatives could be agreed on. The result was often nationalist fanaticism, random reactions of frustration prompted by this new reality and the desire to acquire what was needed materially in order to defeat the West. In 1978, as in 1908, after attempts at withdrawal and self-reliance, China's lead-

Figure 1.4 SOME IMPORTANT EVENTS IN CHINESE HISTORY

1122 B.C.	Zhou dynasty—age of warring feudal states, Confucius, Taoist school.
206 B.C.	Han dynasty—centralized control of China.
A.D. 618	Tang dynasty—development of bureaucracy based on Confucian examination system.
1644	Qing (Manchu) dynasty—sustained contact with West begins in mid-nineteenth century
1911	Fall of Qing dynasty.
1912	Republic of China is formed—Sun Yatsen becomes the first president.
1912–1949	Years of chaos—Jiang Kaishek wins nominal control; Japanese war and communist revolt ensue.
1934	The "Long March" of Mao Zedong's communists.
1949	Communists win control of China's mainland—the Mao era begins.
1958	Great Leap Forward.
1966–1969	Great Proletarian Cultural Revolution.
1976	Zhou Enlai and Mao Zedong die. Hua Guofeng and Deng Xiaoping assume party and state leadership.
1980	Huo Guofeng replaced by Zhao Ziyang as premier and Hu Yaobang as party leader.
1987	Zhao Ziyang replaces Hu Yaobang as party leader following student demonstrations in several cities.

ers decided to seek ideas from the West. In the latter years of the monarchy it was religion, clothing, education, and political ideas, indeed anything that was Western; in the post-1978 era, Western-style discos, clothes, movies, plays, and music have been readily taken in along with Western ideas concerning private enterprise and competition.

Despite the humiliations of the past and the uncertainties over how much should be borrowed from the West, China has made important strides toward statehood since the revolution. In the post-Mao era, efforts to establish a state based on the rule of law are proceeding, and the arbitrary rule of revolutionary leaders has disappeared. Communications—roads, radio, television, films—have contributed to the formation of a single national identity, as have the unifying efforts of the Communist party. Today, it is a much more confident China that embraces the challenges of social, economic, and political development.

MEXICO AND NIGERIA: COLONIALISM AND ITS AFTERMATH

Mexico and Nigeria are both Third World countries, countries attempting to overcome economic and political underdevelopment. Although both have been colonies of Western powers, their experiences differ in key respects. Whereas Mexico had its Indian and European populations integrated under colonial rule, Nigeria has had its ethnic divisions reinforced. Whereas Mexico has had a long time since independence in which to overcome some of the problems of nationhood and state formation, Nigeria has had only a brief period—decades rather than centuries—to achieve these goals. For both, however, the experience with colonial rule—three centuries (1519–1821) of Spanish control for Mexico and one century (1861–1960) of British rule for Nigeria—left centralized political control, a modern bureaucracy, European religious influences, and European economic and political ideas.

Because of this inheritance, Mexico and Nigeria, like many colonially gestated countries, have been left with "split personalities," historically inherited contradictions. From European and American influences has come a widely held faith in constitutional government, democratic elections, and the arbitration of disputes by means of laws and courts. Nevertheless, the reality of each country's historical experiences has included authoritarian takeovers of elected governments and periods of arbitrary rule. Political leaders and parties often espouse social justice, but the predominant political pattern is still one characterized by privilege, favoritism, and the abuse of power.

Mexico: Toward a Modern State

Mexican society, much more than its North American counterparts, is an amalgamation of indigenous and European civilizations. Prior to the Spanish invasion of 1519, most of the territory now known as Mexico was incorporated into the highly advanced Aztec empire, which had been established through conquests of earlier Indian civilizations in the thirteenth and fourteenth centuries. When the Spanish arrived with their firearms and horses, they experienced little difficulty in conquering the Aztec empire; indeed, they were at first welcomed by the Aztecs, whose religion foretold that one day a white god would descend to rule over them. Although the Aztec and other indigenous civilizations vanished under Spanish rule, Indians themselves survived to a greater extent in Mexico than in English-speaking North America, mainly because they were used extensively as laborers on large estates or in the silver mines that provided much of the colony's income. The conditions under which Indians worked were often harsh and exploitative but—again in contrast to the United States and Canada—the intermarriage and interbreeding of Indians and Europeans occurred to such an extent that *mestizos* (those of mixed Spanish and Indian blood) eventually became the largest group in Mexican society. With the formation of a mestizo-dominated society, Mexico largely eliminated one common source of instability confronting Third World countries—the existence of large, hostile ethnic or racial communities.

Certain features of Aztec civilization facilitated the imposition and consolidation of Spanish rule. Spain at the time of the conquest was governed by an absolute monarch and dominated socially and economically by a rich landed aristocracy. Aztec civilization, too, was hierarchically organized—with warriors and priests on top, serfs and even slaves below—and rigidly authoritarian in its political structure. In addition, although Aztec religion was very different from Christianity, the native attachment to a series of gods associated with the planting cycle and with war proved to be readily transferable to the religion imposed by the Catholic missionaries from Spain. The Spanish church merely replaced local gods and temples with its own saints and churches and co-opted indigenous religious practices into its own festivals and celebrations. With cyclical patterns as the basis of the indigenous worldview, a passivity or acceptance of life's fate could also be expected to affect postconquest political orientations: one just accepts the bad turns of life as part of nature's cyclical offerings, so one accepts without protest the bad things that governments do. This outlook was well suited to the imposition of authoritarian rule.

After three centuries of Spanish rule, Mexico broke free of Spain in the Wars of Independence (1810–1821). Reacting against the control of the colony by a small Spanish-born elite, the founders of the new republic adopted a constitution which incorporated many features of the U.S. presidential system of government. The autocratic rule of Spain had poorly equipped Mexican society for representative government, however, and the balance of power between the Congress and the presidency prescribed in the constitution was soon subverted into out-and-out presidential domination. A long period of political violence and turmoil followed independence, as rival strongmen or *caudillos* took over power only to be challenged by other caudillos. In all, 30 different presidents served in the republic's first 50 years, almost all of them military officers, and governments averaged one per year. The most notorious of these caudillos was General Antonio López de Santa Anna, who fought on both sides of the Wars of Independence, lost Texas to the Americans in 1835, signed the treaty ceding all territories north of the Rio Grande to the United States in 1846—and still managed to return to power (for the eleventh time) in 1853.

Distaste with Santa Anna was one of the principal factors motivating the liberal takeover of power in 1854 and the launching of what became known as the Reform (1854–1872). To check the power of the Catholic Church, which had been closely associated first with Spanish rule and then with authoritarian dictatorship, legislation was passed ordering the selling off of all church estates. This was followed in 1857 by the promulgation of a new constitution providing for numerous democratic rights, restrictions on the church's powers, and expansion of public education. The church retaliated by excommunicating all officials who swore allegiance to the new constitution; conservative elements in the army followed suit by staging a coup d'état in 1858. Under the leadership of an Indian, Benito Juárez, the liberals managed to regain power in 1861—only to find the state's finances in such desperate straits that payments on foreign loans had to be suspended. With the United States preoccupied with its own civil war, Mexico's creditors, Britain, Spain, and France, seized the opportunity to strike back by sending in a military expedition; France went one step further by imposing a monarchy under Archduke Maximilian of Austria. Maximilian's rule was short-lived, however, for disappointment among conservatives with his reluctance to restore to the church its former estates and U.S. pressure on France to end its involvement in Mexico led to Maximilian's isolation and defeat by liberal forces. Juárez was restored to power once again, and he ruled democratically until his death in 1872.

The period of the Reform is one of the few bright spots in nineteenth-century Mexican history, but it was quickly followed by one of its darkest marks, the dictatorship of Porfirio Díaz (1876–1910). Although the *Porfiriato* was an era of economic growth, the development of factories, railroads, and large commercially oriented agricultural estates was achieved principally through foreign investments, and the benefit to Mexicans was mainly confined to a Spanish-descended elite. Moreover, free elections, free speech, and freedom of the press were all curtailed, and the regime resembled more a police state than a democratic republic.

The excesses of the *Porfiriato* led directly to the Revolution of 1910, the most significant event in Mexico's postcolonial history. The opening phase of the revolution was a violent one as revolutionary caudillos, including such romantic-heroic figures as Pancho Villa and Emiliano Zapata, struggled against counterrevolutionary forces for control of the state. By 1914 the revolutionaries under Venustriano Carranza were firmly in charge, and three years later they introduced Mexico's present constitution. In line with its American model, the constitution provided for a presidential system, separation of church and state, a federal structure, universal male suffrage, and extensive civil rights. Significantly, in reaction to Díaz's long rule, presidents were prohibited from seeking reelection. More radical were the constitution's social and economic provisions, which included state ownership of all land and natural resources, a promise of agrarian reform including land redistribution in favor of the peasantry, free primary education for all, and labor rights such as the eight-hour day and the legal recognition of unions.

The constitution went much further than Carranza would have preferred, and his reluctance to implement its more radical features, together with his efforts to circumvent the prohibition on reelection by imposing his own choice as successor, led to his downfall. Like his two immediate predecessors, Carranza was assassinated. The next president was the popular general Álvaro Obregon, who bolstered his public support by allying with a new national trade union organization, the Regional Confederation of Labor (CROM), as well as with various agrarian and civic organizations. Obregon was followed by his close associate, Plutarcho Calles, who helped to form the National Revolutionary Party (PNR), which converted the informal linkages with labor, peasant, and business groups into a single political organization that also included regional and military representation.

The presidency of Lázaro Cárdenas (1934–1940) furthered the consolidation of the new regime. In institutional terms, Cárdenas transformed the PNR into the Mexican Revolutionary Party (PRM). At the heart of this change was a restructuring of the party to consist of four sections: labor, peasants, a "popular" sector representing middle-class groups, and the military. The Cárdenas presidency also saw greater attention paid to the social and economic promises of the revolution, including land redistribution, the development of state (as opposed to church) primary education, and most significantly, the nationalization of foreign oil companies, which had resisted turning over ownership of their claims to the state.

Cárdenas' party, later renamed the Institutional Revolutionary Party (PRI), has ruled Mexico throughout the post-World War II period. Its development as an effective instrument of government has transformed Mexico into one of the most stable countries in the world. From the earliest days, Mexico has had constitutions which were only minimally followed, elections which were often controlled, Congresses which were virtually powerless, and courts which were neither objective nor law-abiding. Although these characteristics have not disappeared, Mexico under PRI rule has experienced several decades of relative peace and order.

The development of strong single-party rule in Mexico has also meant that the threat of military intervention has waned. The failure to include a distinct military sector in the new PRI symbolized the military's withdrawal from partisan politics; its influence now passes through the appropriate cabinet ministries rather than through the party. The interests that are represented in the PRI are handled primarily through patronage—the awarding of government jobs, contracts, and so forth—and through policy decisions which attempt to meet the major expectations and needs of each sector. In addition, since 1958 the practice has developed of alternating the presidency between liberal and conservative wings of the party. By these means, different points of view are represented within the PRI. Nevertheless, the authoritarian tradition perseveres in the domination of the political system by the president, in the virtual absence of competitive elections—opposition parties are allowed to win in some districts but are not expected to challenge the PRI's control—and in the government's willingness to use force to repress student demonstrations or other movements of protest.

Apart from the long tradition of authoritarianism counterposed by democratic and egalitarian thrusts, several other legacies from Mexico's past continue to influence the country's present political life. Despite government efforts to achieve centralized control from Mexico City, regionalism remains a powerful force in Mexico. One particularly important expression of regionalism is the tradition of *caciquismo*, a type of political rule administered through local political bosses *(caciques)*. Although the caciques are in effect agents of the central government, they remain free to do as they please within their fiefdoms as long as they maintain order and collect the assigned taxes. Caciquismo is a direct outgrowth of the Spanish type of colonial rule, under which the viceroy granted local leaders or chiefs extensive prerogatives in return for keeping the population quiet. The caciques used their powers to pursue their own interests and those of the wealthy landholders who supported them. This tradition became even more entrenched in the century after independence, due to the instability of the central government. Caciquismo has proved to be a lasting legacy from the colonial era, manifested in a modified form in the political and social power exercised by the governmental party's local leaders. Efforts by the PRI federal elite to counter the irresponsible rule of local party bosses, which have included transferring local leaders, appointing local leaderships, and attempting to control local elections, have met with only limited success.

Another legacy from Mexico's past is nationalism. Deep in Mexico's culture is the loss of face resulting from foreign aggression. The series of American interventions in the nineteenth and early twentieth centuries had a profound effect on Mexican national consciousness. While the rebellion against Spain produced some sense of Mexican identity, it was not until Santa Anna's defeat in the war of 1846—which entailed the humiliating loss of Texas, California, Arizona, and New Mexico—and France's control of Mexico in the 1860s that Mexico became noticeably more nationalistic. From these developments and the later manipulations of Mexican politics by the United States arose a strong sensitivity to Mexican national integration and independence.

Anti-Americanism has been particularly important in Mexico because the emphasis on regional goals and regional policies pursued by local political bosses has tended to undermine efforts to build a Mexican national community. Even national leaders have frequently been unconcerned with national political integration. Since their ascendancy has been based on personal appeal and military prowess rather than a well-established set of national political rules and loyalties, they have had little incentive to promote a sense of nationhood. For these reasons, leaders who have felt the need to arouse national loyalties have often done so by fomenting extreme nationalism directed at a foreign enemy, and the United States is the most obvious target. This tendency can be detected in a very powerful symbol of nationalism, the Revolution of 1910. In that struggle, the revolutionaries had to fight not only conservatives in Mexican society but also occasional American support for the conservative cause. Much of the radical content in the constitution of 1917 bespeaks a strong desire to be rid of foreign influences: the 1938 expropriation of foreign oil company holdings, which provoked outbursts of nationalistic jubilation at the time, was based on a constitutional provision granting ownership of the subsoil to the state.

A persistently difficult, if not worsening, legacy is the problem of class. The class structure that evolved during the colonial era was based primarily on race. At the top of the class pyramid were the whites: first Spaniards from Spain, then Spaniards born in Mexico *(creoles)* who had privileged political, social, and often economic positions. Next were the mestizos and below them the Indians. On an even lower level were people of other mixed racial backgrounds and blacks. While the overall position of mestizos has improved immensely, there still remains a large sector of the population—composed primarily of Indians and rural mestizos—who have remained largely excluded from the mainstream of Mexican society. This sector, estimated at about 25 percent of the population, does not partake in any meaningful way in national political life. Indeed, among these people, the concept of Mexican national identity itself is very poorly developed. Perhaps 5 or 10 percent of the total population are scarcely aware that the government exists. The others are apathetic about politics because of poverty, illiteracy, or despair. Much of this marginal population lives in remote villages, whose isolation gives rise to localism and separatism. For these people, the village or tribe is the primary object of the individual's loyalty and the only meaningful political unit. Outsiders, whether agents of the national government or members of neighboring tribes or villages, are regarded with suspicion and sometimes hostility.

Mexico's political culture in general may be described as transitional. Apart from the substantial, if diminishing, sector of the popula-

Figure 1.5 SOME IMPORTANT EVENTS IN MEXICAN HISTORY

1519	Arrival of Cortes and the Spanish conquistadores.
1810–1821	Wars of Independence.
1835	Texas revolts from Mexican authority and establishes a republic.
1846–1848	Mexican-American War, in which Mexico loses lands north of the Rio Grande River.
1857–1872	The Reform, led by Benito Juárez.
1876–1911	Rule of Porfirio Díaz.
1910–1917	The Revolution.
1917	New constitution provides for social reform.
1929	Founding of the National Revolutionary Party, forerunner of the Institutional Revolutionary Party (PRI).
1934–1940	Presidency of Lázaro Cárdenas—important social and economic reforms.
1977–1978	Revelation of major oil deposits.
1985	Major earthquake hits Mexico City.
1988	PRI confronted with first serious challenge to its presidential and congressional candidates; aftermath threatens viability of PRI as single dominant party.

tion that is uninvolved in and largely unaware of national politics, the sector of the population that is aware of the national government is mainly concerned with the government's output and its effects on them. On the one hand, they accept the government as legitimate—although their loyalties often focus on the person of the president—and feel considerable pride in the revolution, but on the other hand, their most frequent contacts with government involve the bureaucracy, which they regard as corrupt, arbitrary, and inefficient. These contacts give rise to political cynicism and frustration, which discourages active involvement in attempts to influence government. Furthermore, reverence for the revolution itself fuels cynicism, for its oft-repeated lofty goals are still far from fulfillment.

Nigeria: Trials of an Emerging State

Like Mexico, Nigeria is a layered polity. Its indigenous heritage, which is considerably more varied than Mexico's, has not been eliminated or assimilated. In fact, a multilinguistic and multireligious context strongly influences the unfolding of the new Nigerian state. Nigeria's colonial experience under the British is also part of the layering process, melding adopted parliamentary, legal, and administrative models into traditional political practices.

When the British first made political inroads into the area now known as Nigeria, they encountered a diverse set of cultures and political systems. Among these was the Bornu Kingdom, whose people had migrated centuries earlier from Sudan to the north of Nigeria. To the west of Bornu were the seven Hausa states, seats of Islamic culture straddling trade routes to the north and south. To the south lay the Yoruba Kingdom and its very rich and flourishing cultural offshoot, the Benin Kingdom. To the east were the Ibos and other minority groups living in small-scale political units.

The British did not act with foresight and intelligence in building their colony in Nigeria. It was not regarded as among the most important of Britain's African colonies, and it simply grew piecemeal from the annexation of Lagos in 1861 until 1914, when it acquired its present boundaries through the amalgamation of the predominantly Muslim north with the southern kingdoms to form the Colony and Protectorate of Nigeria. The consolidation of Nigeria under British rule obscured important cultural, political, social, and economic differences among the various communities that composed the colony. For example, the Ibo in the southeast were decentralized, each Ibo village remaining largely autonomous. Political power within the Ibo village was dispersed, and opportunities existed for democratic participation. Positions of leadership were the result of individual achievement rather than birth. The Yoruba community to the west had a complex centralized monarchy, the king claiming descent from the legendary Oduduwa, founder of the capital of Yorubaland. The status of other Yoruba towns was a function of the closeness of the hereditary link between their leader and the king. In the north, the Muslim Hausa-Fulani system was a highly centralized bureaucratic empire with strong theocratic overtones.

British and other European missionaries sought to introduce Christianity to the peoples of Nigeria, along with such other Western values as individualism, education, efficiency, and capitalism. However, differing communal group values meant that the impact of colonial rule varied from one region to the next and from one tribe to the next. For example, because the Ibo culture granted status on the basis of personal achievement (whereas the Hausa-Fulani determined status by an individual's birth and/or social ties), the Ibos were generally more willing to take advantage of educational opportunities. The southern animistic religions proved more vulnerable to Christianity than did the highly developed Islamic religion in the north, and the Christianized portion of the population was often readier to accept other Western cultural and economic values than were the Islamic peoples, who rejected Christianity.

British colonial governance was based on indirect rule through a colonial bureaucracy and indigenous leaders. A British governor-general, assisted by a variety of national and regional advisory groups, ruled the colony. While these councils sometimes included Nigerian representatives, their influence was limited; the governor-general relied more on the two British lieutenant-governors, one for northern Nigeria and one for southern Nigeria. The regional governments they headed provided basic services (health, education, police), but with little colony-wide coordination. This lack of coordination between regions, together with the British practice of relying heavily on tribal leaders to administer British policies, tended to perpetuate traditional social, economic, and political structures and to encourage regional disparities. For example, the British collaboration with the Muslim emirates in the north led to the exclusion of Christian missionaries from the north. While missionary-run schools educated southerners, the north lacked any significant mass education. In the long run this meant that national politics and the civil service would be dominated by the better-educated southerners and that northerners would be suspicious of political dominance by the less numerous southerners.

In 1922 the governor-general provided Nigeria with a constitution. It established a Legislative Council, which included the first popularly elected Africans to sit in a colonial council in all of British Africa. The Legislative Council had its limitations, however. For one thing the Nigerian population permitted to participate in the election of native members was severely limited. Even more significant for the course of later events was the exclusion of northern Nigeria from participation in the legislature. Thus, the first governing body with Nigerian membership was oriented toward the south, and the economic and political development of the north began to lag further behind that of the south.

While the electorate eligible to vote for the Nigerian Council was small, this did not prevent the emergence of nationalist political leaders and movements. Among the first Nigerian nationalist leaders was Herbert MacCauley, a civil engineer and journalist trained in Britain. In 1923 MacCauley formed the Nigerian National Democratic Party, one of Nigeria's first political parties. The activities of the party were centered in Lagos, and it increasingly found itself more involved in western regional politics than in nationalist causes. In reaction, dissatisfied educated youth formed more militant nationalist movements, which opposed colonial rule and attempted to rally support for national self-determination. In 1944 MacCauley and other nationalist leaders joined in forming the National Council of Nigeria and the Cameroons (NCNC). Nearly all the major nationalist movements, trade unions, and youth groups became associated with this common front for constitutional change and self-rule.

Perhaps the most significant feature of Nigerian politics to this point was the virtual exclusion of northerners from national Nigerian politics. Not until 1946, when the British governor-general imposed a new constitution, did northerners begin to become involved in national politics. The new constitution created a legislative council, with northern members, in Lagos. This reform came too late to assuage northern fears of discrimination by southerners, however; the economic and cultural disparities between north and south were by then well established. In addition, the constitution established regional assemblies in the three regions into which the colony had been divided in 1938: the Northern Region dominated by the Hausa-Fulani peoples, the Western Region by the Yorubas, and the Eastern Region by the Ibos. This had the effect of entrenching regional differences.

The growing strength and vigor of Nigerian nationalism quickly undermined the 1946 constitution. In 1951 a new governor-general issued yet another constitution, this one somewhat more sensitive to Nigerian nationalist aspirations. The regional governments were further strengthened and endowed with full governmental systems. Representatives to regional legislatures were thenceforth directly elected, and representatives to the federal legislature, formerly elected by popular vote, were selected indirectly by regional legislatures. Now that elections were taking place on the regional level, regional politics became all the more important. The Yorubas decided to form a political party separate from the increasingly Ibo-dominated NCNC. The new party, known as the Action Group, competed primarily within the Western Region. In the north the Northern People's Congress, which had been organized in 1948, won control of the Northern Region legislature. Cooperation between these ethnically and regionally based parties in the national legislature was often tenuous. One early sign of the growing political tensions between regions appeared in 1954, when the Action Group and the NCNC jointly supported a resolution in the Federal House of Representatives calling for full independence by 1956. The northerners were reluctant to support such a motion since they felt the need for more time under British rule to prepare for direct political competition with the more politically astute southerners. With their motion doomed to failure because of northern opposition, the members of the Action Group and the NCNC walked out of the legislature. When the northern delegates departed, they found an angry crowd of proindependence nationalists awaiting them. In retaliation, northerners rioted and revenged themselves on southerners living in the north.

Yet another constitution was adopted, this time with considerable involvement on the part of Nigerian political leaders. This constitution reduced centralized control and enhanced the power of the regions. The central government was assigned carefully and narrowly defined responsibilities, and all other government functions were left to the regional governments. In addition, the bureaucracy and court systems were shifted from the central government to the regional governments. It was this constitution that carried Nigeria toward independence.

Nigeria was one of 17 former African colonies to win independence in 1960. Although the pros and cons of the legacy of colonial rule can be debated, two signal failures characterized British rule in Nigeria. First, the basic British policy that no colony should place an economic burden on the motherland meant that it was not until after World War II that Britain began to take seriously the responsibility of providing education, health services, and public works and fulfilling other government obligations in Nigeria. And when these investments finally began to be made, Britain did not distribute them equally throughout Nigeria. The fact that the southern regions benefited more than the Northern Region tended to exacerbate regional and ethnic tensions. The second failure of British policy was the rigidification of ethnic differences as a result of indirect rule and loose federalism based on ethnically defined regions.

Despite the high expectations of Nigerian nationalists, the achievement of independence was not sufficient to create the authority necessary for governing a country anxious to modernize and plagued with numerous economic and social challenges. Within a few years ethnic tensions had developed into the core of a self-destructive political conflict. This situation led to manipulations of election results, to intensification of ethnic hostilities, and ultimately, in 1966, to two military coups. The first coup, in January, deposed the civilian regime; the second, in the summer, altered the military leadership. The ultimate victor in these coups was General Yakubu Gowon, who headed Nigeria's regime for the next nine years.

The military regime changed the political system by banning the existing political parties, prohibiting the creation of new ethnic parties, and instituting military rule in the 12 states which were set up to replace

Federal troops on patrol in Biafra, the Ibo homeland whose attempt to secede from Nigeria set off a bloody civil war in 1967. (© Bruno Barbey / Magnum)

the regions. The decision to abolish the regions, together with resentment over the slaughter in 1966 of 30,000 Ibos living in the north, provoked the Eastern Region, the home of the Ibos, to secede from the country and declare itself the Republic of Biafra in 1967. The Biafran Republic was put down in a bloody civil war which lasted until 1970. Clearly, what was needed was some means of coping with ethnic hostilities in the future. There were frequent calls for a return to democracy, but finding a political formula that would satisfy the distrustful ethnic communities and win general acceptance from Nigerians proved elusive.

What followed was a cascade of governments. In 1975, following discontent over corruption in government and Gowon's failure to restore democracy, he was ousted from power. His successor, General Murtala Mohammed, was assassinated a year later and succeeded by General Olusfgun Obasanjo. Under Obasanjo, a new democratic constitution was prepared, and in 1979 elections were held which brought Alhaji Shagari to the presidency. This regime, known as the Second Republic, lasted only until 1983, when another military leader, General Buhari, overthrew it and introduced "military discipline" to government. Many found that his government demonstrated too much discipline and too little performance, and in 1985 he, too, was overthrown, this time by General Babangida, one of his trusted colleagues.

From Nigeria's indigenous cultures have come several characteristics that affect the country's present politics. One of these is the presence of both authoritarian and democratic influences. Among Nigeria's many ethnic groups, there are some such as the northern Hausa-Fulani who have a heritage of authoritarian, neofeudalistic hierarchical structures and others, like the eastern Ibo, who practice consensual decision-making among all male members. These differing traditions influence perceptions of how government should be organized—in particular, whether it should be democratic or authoritarian in character—and thus contribute to Nigeria's present political instability.

Political instability has taken the form of a cycle of repeated military coups—six between 1966 and 1986—interspersed with voluntary reimpositions of civilian regimes. During each authoritarian interlude, demands for a return to constitutionalism have appeared. During each civilian regime, doubts about the performance of the existing constitutional framework have marked its tenure. This dualism has its roots both in the colonial stewardship, which created a substantial number of better-educated elites strongly socialized to expect democratic governance, and in certain indigenous cultures, which, as we have seen, contain strong traditions of authoritarianism.

Another significant aspect of Nigerian political culture concerns kinship and ethnic loyalties. Most Nigerians readily learn that their first identification is with their family and that they must obey elders. Akin to this is loyalty to the ethnic group—Ibo, Yoruba, Hausa-Fulani—above all other nonkin groupings. It is thus difficult to get people to look beyond these local interests to make political judgments conducive to molding a national interest. For example, bureaucrats and politicians tend to see their role as one of funneling benefits to themselves, their relatives, and their ethnic groups, rather than serving the public interest as a whole. Public supplies, equipment, and even decision-making authority often become available to the highest bidder, with the benefit going to the individual and his kin group. One of the principal reasons why governments have been overthrown so often in Nigeria is the prevalence of corruption in government.

Strong ethnic loyalties have also generated profound distrust between ethnic groups and therefore profound distrust of the central government. The tension between central control and regional autonomy led to civil war between 1967 and 1970; it has also encouraged the formation of new territorial units to accommodate regional interests. In 1962 an additional region was created; then in 1967 the regions were replaced by 12 states. The next major change occurred more than a decade later, when 19 states were carved out to replace the 12 states; in 1987 two new states were added. While these structural changes were aimed at pacifying the regionalists, the centralists have often had their way by establishing central control over state governments during the periods when the military rule. Thus, the democratic regimes have been federal—to appease ethnic sensibilities—while the periods of military control have been centralized—to check ethnic antagonism and maintain unity.

Ethnicity has also led to a politics of violence. The precolonial pe-

Figure 1.6 SOME IMPORTANT EVENTS IN NIGERIAN HISTORY.

1861	British annex Lagos and establish control over Nigeria.
1914	Nigeria formally becomes a colony of Great Britain.
1952–1954	Britain takes steps toward African participation in government to prepare for independence.
1960	Nigeria becomes an independent federal state within the Commonwealth.
1963	Nigeria becomes a republic.
1966	Two military coups end civilian government; General Gowon assumes control.
1967	The military government alters the regional governmental structure by forming 12 states; the Eastern Region secedes and forms the Independent Republic of Biafra; civil war ensues.
1970	Secessionists capitulate; General Gowon announces a general amnesty.
1975	Gowon overthrown by new military coup led by General Murtala Mohammed.
1976	Mohammed assassinated; General Obasanjo takes over.
1979	Second Republic established with Alhaji Shagari elected president.
1983	General Buhari overthrows civilian government.
1985	General Babangida deposes Buhari.
1988	Military regime begins phased return to civilian rule.

riod was often marked by violent conflict among ethnic groups. After independence, matters quickly degenerated into an extremely bloody civil war, but the violence did not end there, despite government efforts to promote reconciliation. In the 1980s a series of violent political activities associated with Islamic fundamentalist politics have occurred in the north, and the violence and corruption associated with the 1983 election campaign prompted a second overthrow of democratic government. A cohesive political community with an accepted, nonviolent means of settling political differences has yet to be consolidated in Nigeria.

CONCLUSIONS

In this chapter we have seen numerous examples of the ways in which both history and foreign influences have shaped political development. The process of political development had its roots in Western Europe and in particular among the two feudal kingdoms of England and France. Whereas England developed relatively spontaneously under the influence of market forces and within the protective umbrella of early political centralization, national integration, and relative security from foreign attack, France's greater vulnerability to attack and less complete national integration led it to adopt a more authoritarian solution. The inability of royal absolutism to keep pace with the emerging wealth and power of capitalist and parliamentary England was one of the factors that precipitated the French Revolution, which changed France's course of development and revealed to the world the power available when rulers and ruled unite under the rubric of the nation-state.

The other four countries all changed under the impact of the spreading power of the advanced states of Western Europe. In the case of Russia, her exposed position on the periphery of Europe stimulated the development of a highly centralized and autocratic state; China, in contrast, had already developed an imperial state structure before the influence of the West had made itself felt. In neither case, however, was the state structure strong enough to meet the challenge of the West; both ultimately underwent revolutionary transformations which retained authoritarian control but added the ingredient of highly united and mobilized masses, an idea implicit in the concept of the nation-state, in order to catch up.

Mexico and Nigeria differ from Russia and China in that there was no single, indigenous political structure before the arrival of Westerners; both in effect became states after having undergone a period of colonial rule. Mexico differs from Nigeria, however, in that its Spanish conquerors became absorbed into the population to a substantial degree and in the much longer period of independence it has enjoyed. Both factors have enabled Mexico to achieve a much greater degree of national integration and state-building than has been the case in Nigeria. Regionalism still plagues both countries, but Mexico has been able to control those forces by means of a single dominant party, the PRI. In Nigeria it has been the military that has suppressed regional tendencies and established central control. Moreover, Mexico, like China and the Soviet Union, has been able to use ideology to build legitimacy for the state. Nigeria, lacking a single unifying ideology, is beginning the task of developing its political structures under the severe strain of an aware, critical, and highly divided population. Its problems mirror those of many Third World countries today.

chapter 2

Political Frameworks

INTRODUCTION

One of the pleasantly surprising characteristics of the modern state is that its claim to sovereignty over territory and people usually does not extend to the point of tyranny. This political self-control often finds its ultimate embodiment in a constitution, a set of fundamental rules or principles to which governments are willing to subject not only their citizens but also themselves. The willingness of governments to keep their activities within constitutional bounds can be a powerful source of *legitimacy* for a regime. Legitimacy refers to the perception on the part of citizens that a given system of government is morally right; where it exists, it provides a surer basis for regime survival than force alone could ever do. Although legitimacy may be created in other ways, it is "rational," according to the German sociologist Max Weber, only if it is based on the regime's conformity to a generally accepted constitutional and legal order. Weber felt that a rationally based legitimacy represented the best and most modern foundation for a state.

Constitutions are written to establish the institutions that make and enforce public decisions, to indicate orderly procedures by which officials running them are chosen and replaced, and often to declare the basic values (rights, duties, and freedoms) that each citizen may expect to see honored by those officials and institutions. However, not all legitimate regimes operate in accordance with the prescriptions of written constitutions. In Britain, for example, there is no such document—yet the exercise of political power can hardly be described as arbitrary or tyrannous. In France, a written constitution does enjoy considerable legitimacy, but in practice its prescriptions are not followed in every significant area. Other states such as the Soviet Union have written constitutions that describe institutional forms but do not govern the most important power relationships. Generally speaking, the more discontinuous a country's political development, the more likely it is that its leaders decided at some point to rewrite the constitutional "rules of the game." But, by the same token, revolutionary leaders with goals of radical change often have been reluctant to tie themselves down to the niceties of constitutional procedure. Even without radical goals, a constitution may remain a lifeless appendage in societies where the idea of constitutionalism, that is, of formal limits on the exercise of political power, is itself an alien one.

The gap that often exists between political practice and constitutional principle does not mean that written constitutions are unimportant; rather, the point is that there is often a complex interplay between formality and reality in a political system. The existence of a constitution does not guarantee that there will be checks on the power of government, but where checks exist, it is often in the form of a written constitution that they find expression. We tend to think that the protection constitutions provide against the abuse of power flows from their declarations of basic human rights, but constitutions more often establish *structural* means by which political power can be kept within certain bounds. These structural devices include (1) a vertical division of powers in which subnational units, such as states or provinces, are given their own powers independent of the central or "federal" government and (2) a horizontal division in which power is dispersed among two or more separate institutions of the central government. The rules which establish how the personnel of government are to be chosen may also act as a check on the abuse of power, particularly if they provide for the right of citizens to make those choices. In this chapter we shall consider how alternative constitutional arrangements in each of these areas structure politics in our six countries.

The Vertical Division of Power

The vertical or territorial division of power refers to how political power is divided or shared between a country's central government and governments that exist for subunits of the country. All countries have local or regional governments, and in all cases these governments exercise real authority. The critical issue is whether that authority exists independently of the central government or whether it is subject to the scrutiny or control of the center.

There are three basic formats in which this dimension of political power is arranged: the confederal, the federal, and the unitary. Of the three, the confederal format is by far the least centralized. In a confederal state, authority ultimately rests with the member units, not with the state itself. The member states of a confederation, in other words, are themselves sovereign. A contemporary example of a confederal system is the European Community, more commonly known as the European Common Market. The European Community groups together 12 countries, including Britain and France, which have agreed to delegate a variety of powers in such areas as trade, tariffs, industrial development, and agriculture to a common set of institutions. There is also a European Parliament directly elected by the peoples of all 12 countries to give some popular input into the decision-making of the Community. Although the member states have agreed formally to abide by the decisions and rules of the Community, the tradition has developed that any country can veto any decision which it feels is contrary to its national interest. This tradition has recently been brought into question, but even if majority rule becomes more common, the European Community has no means of enforcing its decisions against a recalcitrant member state; it lacks, in other words, the crucial component of sovereignty.

Because of this weakness of the center, a confederation stands little chance of functioning well in a world of nation-states. The European Community has succeeded in many respects, but only because it has not tried to be a "country" in its own right. Where the participants of a confederation seek to form a single country, it will generally be necessary to transform the confederation into a federation. The United States, which began life as a confederation in 1777, adopted a new constitution in 1789 to effect such a change.

The characteristic that defines a federation is the formal division of powers between the central or federal government and the governments of the member units which together form the federation. Ideally, those powers which belong to the subunits are beyond the reach of the federal government and vice versa. Some effort is usually taken to allocate powers between the two levels of government according to where they are better exercised. Thus, foreign relations and defense are invariably given to the federal government; local government and education commonly fall within the purview of the subunits. These arrangements are spelled out in a constitutional document and protected by a supreme court, whose interpretations are considered binding on both levels of government. *ie/ U.S.A*

In practice, the lines of division between the powers of the center and those of the subunits are often blurred. This is due in part to the difficulties inherent in attempting to delimit for all time completely separate areas of competence, but it is also the result of a tendency for federal governments to involve themselves in areas formally under the jurisdiction of the subunits. Sometimes this intervention can be contestational, as when the United States government acted—where certain individual states would not—by putting suspected killers of civil rights activists on trial not for murder (since murder is a state crime) but for violating the victims' civil rights (a federal offence) by killing them! In other cases, the expansion of federal authority is a cooperative affair, for subunits often need the financial help of the federal government in order to discharge many of the costly responsibilities they bear, particularly in such areas as health and education. In return for such aid, federal governments often impose conditions or standards that amount to a considerable degree of de facto control of those areas.

The most centralized format is the unitary system of government. In a unitary state, all authority is vested in the central government. Local and regional governments still exist and they often exercise considerable powers, but their exercise of power rests on the pleasure of the central government. The laws under which they operate are national ones; the decision-making functions that they have are delegated from the center.

One way to visualize the distinction between subnational governments in federal and unitary states is to draw an analogy with municipal governments in North America. In both the United States and Canada there are local-level governments (towns, cities, counties, etc.), state or provincial governments, and central governments. Because both countries are federations, the states or provinces enjoy a certain independence from the central government—they have powers which the national government cannot touch.[1] One of these powers is the power to regulate local governments. Using this power, the states or provinces typically enact laws that specify which taxes local governments may raise, which services they must provide, and so forth. Those statutes, however, can be changed at any time by the state or provincial governments. In a unitary state, all levels of government below the central government exist in this same situation of dependence. They may exercise considerable powers and raise substantial revenues, but they do so only because, and for as long as, the central government authorizes it.

Most of the world's countries have opted for the unitary format. In part, this is because it corresponds most closely with the nation-state ideal, whose crucial property is the existence of undivided sovereignty. Where federal formats have been adopted, it is generally for one or more of the following reasons: (1) the country possesses substantial religious, linguistic, racial, or ethnic diversity that is geographically based; (2) the sheer size of the country makes centralized governance difficult; (3) there is a relatively low level of threat from other states. The rationale for the first reason is straightforward. Where differences among the peoples inhabiting different regions of a country are significant, federalism affords a means by which each such region can exercise a considerable degree of control over its own affairs. The likelihood that the people of those regions will feel that their rights or interests are being ignored or

---

[1]Only a constitutional amendment can do that, and in both countries such amendments require the consent of a large majority of the states or provinces themselves.

sacrificed to those of other groups or regions will therefore be much less. Similarly, large countries, even ones with relatively homogeneous populations, are especially likely to experience regional diversity and the consequent impetus to decentralize decision-making in order to make it more effective and responsive to regional needs. For these reasons, five of the six largest countries in the world are formally federal (China is the exception). In the Soviet Union, for example, ethnic and regional diversity is formally acknowledged in the existence of separate republics and other nominally autonomous territorial units. In the state structure, the unit representing the majority nationality (the Russians), called the Russian Soviet Federated Socialist Republic, contains more than half the country's population, but separate and much smaller republics have been created for ethnic minorities such as the Armenians, the Ukrainians, and the Latvians (hence the country's full title, the Union of Soviet Socialist Republics).

The third factor, the degree of exposure to foreign threat, is an especially powerful one, so powerful in fact that it often negates the other two factors. The United States and Canada can afford to be federal because of their relative isolation from other powerful states,[2] but many other countries have felt less free to introduce meaningful decentralization of authority, despite the advantages that decentralization can bring. In the Soviet Union, a state created in the midst of foreign invasion, the federal structure designed to respect non-Russian ethnic identities is largely symbolic; in reality the central government is in control of all republic-level governments.

There is a further aspect of this factor that should be borne in mind. The threat from foreign rivals may not only have encouraged a centralization of political power but also have stimulated a belief that only a profound societal transformation will allow the country to catch up or keep pace with its rivals. In Chapter 1 we saw that both France and Russia were caught in the bind of having centralized power effectively under absolute monarchs but of having stifled economic development in the process, thereby exposing the regimes to criticism and discontent. The revolutions that ensued did not lead to greater decentralization, despite popular anger at the arbitrary authority exercised by the old regimes, but they did entail a modernization of social, economic, and political structures.

The issue of societal transformation is particularly salient for new states created in the process of decolonialization, where centralized control has frequently been adopted in order to direct the daunting process

---

[2]Canada and the United States are not, of course, isolated from each other. Because Canada has always had a much smaller population than its neighbor, Canada's federal structure, established in 1867, was designed to give much more power to the center than was the case in the United States. With the disappearance in the twentieth century of fears of a possible U.S. invasion, Canada has actually become the more decentralized of the two countries, reflecting its greater regional and ethnic diversity.

of modernization more effectively. Ironically, it is not at all clear that centralization is the answer to the problems of economic development. The Soviet Union industrialized very rapidly between the two world wars under highly centralized governmental control, but other countries, such as South Korea and Taiwan, have done very well in recent years with more decentralized private enterprise systems. This ambiguity has created a great deal of division in the Third World over how much economic control governments should exercise, but there is much less uncertainty in the political sphere. Inspired by the nation-state ideal that equates strength with national unity, and disillusioned in many instances with the lack of progress in integrating distinct ethnic identities into a larger national identity, Third World states have more often than not chosen centralized, authoritarian political control. If minorities have demanded greater autonomy or control of their own affairs, the response has typically been greater repression rather than greater decentralization.

The Horizontal Division of Powers

The horizontal division of powers refers to the extent to which political power in a given level of government is concentrated in a single institution or dispersed among two or more institutions. In most communist regimes, power is concentrated in the Political Bureau or "Politburo" of the Central Committee of the Communist party. At the other extreme, the powers of the United States federal government are divided or "separated" among three formally coequal branches: the president, the Supreme Court, and the Congress. The Congress in turn is *bicameral,* that is, divided into two bodies, the Senate and the House of Representatives. The contrast between these two extremes has led many observers to conclude that authoritarianism is characterized by the concentration of powers and democracy by their separation. Certainly this was the guiding idea of the American founding fathers, who saw the separation of powers as a means of preventing governmental tyranny of the sort they perceived in the reign of George III of England, against whose authority the 13 colonies had rebelled. Nevertheless, the fact is that most democracies in the world today have a degree of concentration of power much closer to that of the Soviet Union than that of the United States.

Why is this the case? The answer to this question lies in the origins of democratic regimes. Most democracies in the world today are located in Western Europe, and they developed in countries that were once ruled by kings or emperors. As social forces emerged which opposed monarchical rule, they sought representation for themselves in popular assemblies or parliaments. Eventually, by revolution or evolution, parliaments in many European countries came to assume sovereign authority from their monarchs. The development of parliamentary sovereignty meant that cabinet members or "ministers," who formerly worked under a monarch's direction, were henceforth subject to the authority of the country's parliament. Increasingly, they were drawn from among the members of the parliament itself. In effect, the cabinet, including its leader, often known as the "prime minister," became a committee of the parliament, exercising authority at its pleasure and removable by it at any time. This is a very different situation, indeed, from that in the United States, where the president and his cabinet are responsible not to Congress, but only to the electorate at four-yearly intervals.

The concentration of ultimate political power in a parliament composed of hundreds of members may not seem to be very concentrated at all, but appearances can be misleading. Certainly there are cases where a parliament is divided into numerous factions or parties, each competing with the others for power and none able to emerge dominant. But it more often happens that a single cohesive party or *coalition* (alliance) of parties controls a majority of votes in the parliament and is able to govern unchecked by opposing forces. The leaders of such a party or coalition form the cabinet and from this position control both the executive and legislative branches of government. In principle, their followers in the parliament could rebel against them and remove them from power whenever they wished, but this is unlikely to happen for several reasons: (1) leaders and followers, as members of the same party or parties, probably share very similar political views; (2) it is often the leaders' popularity that ensured their followers' election to the parliament in the first place; and (3) the leaders are able to offer all sorts of benefits, including promotion to the cabinet, as rewards for their followers' loyalty and obedience. In this scenario, a prime minister and his senior cabinet colleagues possess a degree of political control which American presidents, faced with an independent and often hostile Congress, can seldom expect to experience.

Another striking feature of parliamentary systems is that their fusion of executive and legislative roles is usually unchecked by the third branch of government, the judiciary. In theory, the principle of parliamentary sovereignty means that a parliament can do as it likes or, more specifically, that there is no written bill of rights or other constitutional provision that limits its activities.[3] In practice, the principle of parliamentary sovereignty is often tempered by traditions of law that restrict what parliaments can do. Nevertheless, there is a great deal of difference between the role of the courts in a parliamentary system, which is confined by and large to applying the law as it exists to particular cases, and their role in a presidential system, which also includes the power to strike down laws deemed to be unconstitutional.

The concentration or fusion of powers in the hands of a single-party

---

[3]The main exception occurs when the system is also federal and therefore has a division of powers between the central government and the subunits enforceable by the courts.

leadership which forms the cabinet, dominates a majority in the parliament, and is largely unrestrained by the courts has both advantages and disadvantages. On the plus side, it means that a single party elected to implement a given political program or platform can do so without the checks an American president faces. Things that the cabinet feels need to be done can be done, and the electorate knows whom to hold responsible for the successes or failures of government in the next election. On the minus side, the system presupposes a great deal of trust in politicians, especially those of parties one doesn't support, for they may be given a degree of power not all that different from that of the Soviet or Chinese Politburos—they, too, are committees that control executive and legislative powers in their countries. Another potential weakness is that the efficiency of parliamentary government—its ability to get things done— is by no means certain, for it derives not from the rules or structure of the system but rather from the nature and number of parties in the parliament. Specifically, it presupposes that there are parties with coherent programs and obedient members (known as "disciplined" parties) which are capable of winning a majority of parliamentary seats, either singly or in stable alliance or coalition with other parties. If there is no majority party in the parliament and it proves difficult to find two or more parties that can put aside their differences and form a durable majority coalition, the result will usually be a great deal of governmental instability. Since coalition cabinets last only as long as they are agreed on what to do in government and can keep the support of a parliamentary majority, it is possible to see several different cabinets within the four- or five-year life span of a single parliament. Situations of this sort have at times made several parliamentary systems, including those of France, virtually unworkable.

Political Succession

One of the best indicators of the extent to which a regime considers itself accountable to the popular will is its mechanism for replacing leaders. In the absolute monarchies of the eighteenth century, the succession of leaders had nothing to do with the people; it was a matter of heredity alone. As liberal and democratic forces gained strength in the nineteenth century, they sought to replace hereditary succession by a more rational system: elections. In today's world, there also exists a variety of other means of succession, of which internal decisions by the leadership of a single ruling party or violent takeovers of power by rebels or the military are by far the most common. Each method tells us something about the nature of the system, its degree of legitimization, and its governing ideology.

The declaration that sovereignty resides with the people underlies the right of adult citizens in the United States to choose their president. Nevertheless, the American founding fathers had some lingering doubts about the wisdom of the people, and they introduced the device of an electoral college to mediate between the will of the voters and the selection of a president. This has not proved to be a serious impediment to democracy, however, since the college's choice almost always has reflected the will of the majority of voters. The direct election of a leader represents the clearest expression of the democratic ideal but, as the American example suggests, it is not very common. In parliamentary democracies, even the theory runs against it. The doctrine of parliamentary sovereignty means, in practical terms, that the vast majority of the voters do not vote for the prime minister. Instead, they elect their local parliamentary representatives; only the latter have the authority to create or remove prime ministers.

As in the American system, the indirect nature of this selection process can be circumvented in certain circumstances. Although voters in parliamentary systems cast their ballots only for a local representative, it is likely that they also have in mind the leaderships of the candidates' parties. If a single party wins a parliamentary majority, it is usually the case that it has also received more votes in the election than any other party. When this happens, the new prime minister and cabinet, chosen from the leadership of the winning party, can be thought of as having been elected by the people at large.

The structure of communist rule, as we have described it, appears remarkably similar to that of parliamentary systems: both are headed by small committees of top leaders in whose hands executive and legislative powers are concentrated. One of the areas where communist systems deviate from parliamentary democracies concerns the separation of powers: the autonomy allowed the judiciary in parliamentary systems to interpret the law without political interference or "guidance" is generally much greater than it is in communist systems. The area of succession provides another point of differentiation. In communist systems, succession is usually a matter that is kept strictly internal to the party and is more the product of personal and factional maneuvering than of orderly elections. In the Soviet Union, the absence of a well-established and open means of succession has meant that only once has the top leader, the general secretary of the party, left office before he died. Often there is a period of political paralysis at the highest levels of government as the leader's health deteriorates, and there is much uncertainty both at home and abroad as to whether he is still alive and in control and who will replace him when he dies.

Succession in communist states like the Soviet Union and China at least has the virtue of legitimacy: the people for the most part accept the party's right to govern and to choose leaders in any manner it wishes. In many of the world's newer states, no legitimate method of succession has yet developed. Where the regime itself lacks legitimacy—often because one ethnic group dominates it—or where the military feels free to take over the reins of power when things are no longer to its liking, succession often becomes a matter decided by force or the threat of force. In this sense, a good indication of the legitimacy of a country's governing institutions is given by the degree of orderliness in its transfers of power from one leader or set of leaders to the next.

BRITAIN AND FRANCE: DEMOCRATIC ALTERNATIVES

Britain and France both fall in the category of liberal democracies; in fact, much that is characteristic of modern liberalism and democracy, both theoretically and in practice, originated in one or the other of these two countries. Their experiences with liberal democracy have nonetheless been quite different. Britain's parliamentary democracy developed over a long period of time in a more or less consensual manner. Today, despite some questioning that has come in the wake of Britain's economic decline, it still enjoys a great deal of popular legitimacy. Part of the reason for this support is that parliamentary democracy in Britain has proved a stable and largely effective form of government.

France's experience with parliamentary government, on the other hand, has been far more negative. The trauma of the French Revolution left the country divided over the value of representative democracy, a division that was reflected in an oscillation of authoritarian and representative regimes that lasted over a century and a half. Although parliamentary democracy became the predominant form of government in France after 1875, its inherent instability and ineffectiveness kept it constantly under a cloud of criticism. In 1958 it was finally replaced by a mixed form of government that combines parliamentary and presidential features. Consequently, a comparison of the experiences that Britain and France have had with democratic government can reveal much about the strengths and weaknesses of its two principal variants, parliamentarism and presidentialism.

Britain: Classic Parliamentarism

The constitutional framework of the British government is one of the most unusual in the world because it is so largely unwritten. It does include certain written documents of great historical importance, such as the Magna Carta (1215) and the Bill of Rights (1689), which limited the king's authority over his subjects, but most of its rules and principles are not specified. Rather, they are the result of a long evolutionary process in which certain ways of doing things simply arose and gained acceptance. Tradition and precedent matter a great deal in the British political system, and the fact that they are not codified in a definitive written text does not prevent people from acting as if they had the force of law—nor the courts from giving them the force of law. The British revere their constitution, even if they cannot tell you precisely what it is.

Unitary Government   One of the most important historically derived principles of British government is that it is unitary. We have seen that the process of nation-building in the early modern era involved a substantial concentration of authority in the monarch or sovereign (hence the term "sovereignty"). When parliamentary forces wrested sovereignty away from the monarchy in the turbulent seventeenth century, they placed it not in the people (this was a predemocratic era) but in the Parliament itself. As local governments expanded and took on new functions such as education and public health in the nineteenth and twentieth centuries, they did so under the watchful eye of an all-powerful national government.

Today the local councils which run municipal and county governments are elected democratically but nevertheless remain closely regulated by the central government located in the London borough of Westminster. They may collect certain taxes on their own, but the bulk of their funding comes directly from Westminster. In recent years, the Conservative government of Prime Minister Margaret Thatcher, increasingly concerned about the growth in local government spending, has set limits on overall expenditures by local councils. Councils which have refused to comply with these limitations have been prosecuted in court or abolished altogether, as happened to the metropolitan councils of London and six other large cities in 1986.

In the 1960s and 1970s movements arose in both Scotland and Wales which sought greater autonomy or even outright independence from a central government seen by many as dominated by English interests. In response to this pressure, legislation was passed authorizing the establishment of regional parliaments in Scotland and Wales. But when the issue was put to referenda in both countries in 1979, it was soundly defeated in Wales and passed by so slim a margin in Scotland (51.6 percent) with so low a turnout (32.9 percent) that the plan was abandoned. It appears that even in the Celtic peripheries of Britain, the idea of centralized, unitary government is still very strongly entrenched.

Fusion of Powers   Extreme centralization also characterizes the structure of the national government, although a superficial glance at its institutional makeup might suggest a different conclusion. The state is formally headed by a monarch who appoints the prime minister and cabinet to run the government and who must sign all bills before they can become law. The task of writing the bills is vested in a Parliament which itself is bicameral: both the lower house, the House of Commons, and the upper house, the House of Lords, debate and vote on legislation. The arrangement, formally speaking, is thus similar to the division of powers in the United States among president, House of Representatives, and Senate. The reality is far different.

The monarch in Britain occupies an important role as an embodiment of the authority of the state, as a symbol of reverence and national pride, and as a living link to the country's past. The actual political power of the monarch, however, is virtually nonexistent. It is true that the present monarch, Elizabeth II, consults regularly with the prime minister and examines all important government documents. Nevertheless, the prime minister is completely free to ignore her opinions, while she is obliged to sign anything the prime minister submits to her. Moreover, she is expected to be above politics and may not express political opinions or preferences in public. Even her personal life is watched by Parliament, which annually grants her a living allowance. The continuing reverence that she receives from almost all sections of the British public is due in large measure to her distance from politics and political differences. As head of state, she performs most of the ceremonial duties attached to that role, leaving the prime minister free to get on with the more serious matter of running the government of the country.

A similar distance separates the appearance of bicameralism from the underlying reality. Like the monarchy, the House of Lords, composed traditionally of the highest ranks of the aristocracy, was once a very powerful institution. With the advance of democracy, its powers, too, have been severely curtailed. The sole power which it may exercise in the legislative process today is one of delay: it can hold up financial legislation it considers unwise for a period of no more than one month and other legislation for up to a year. Naturally, it may also suggest changes or improvements in the legislation it is considering and, away from the political limelight, it is often in a good position to arrive at sensible suggestions. But, again, the prime minister and cabinet are free to reject its ideas at will. Perhaps its most useful function for the prime minister is as a source of reward: professional achievement or political service is often acknowledged by naming the individual a "life peer,"

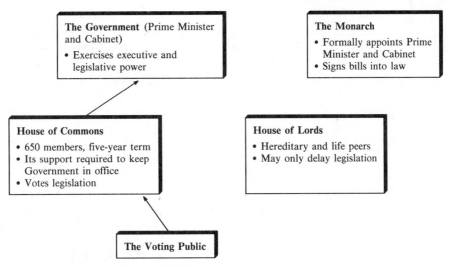

Figure 2.1 Basic institutions of British government.

that is, giving him or her a nonhereditary title of nobility and a seat in the House of Lords.

With the erosion of powers of the monarchy and the House of Lords, power has come to be concentrated in the House of Commons. The word "Parliament" and the title "Member of Parliament" or "MP" are now used almost exclusively to refer to the Commons and its membership. Yet even here, appearances can be deceptive. The parliamentary system of government which Britain pioneered is only truly parliamentary when MPs are free to speak and vote as they like. Where disciplined parties prevail, and especially where most of the membership of Parliament is organized into just two large parties, it is much more likely that the prime minister and cabinet will be the dominant force in the political life of the regime.

As we have seen, the source of this cabinet dominance resides, strangely enough, in the very dependence of cabinets on parliamentary support for their survival. According to the rules of the parliamentary system, if a party or coalition of parties is in control of a majority of votes in Parliament, it can place its own leaders in the cabinet and can keep them in that position of power. As long as their followers or "backbenchers" in Parliament maintain their support, their leaders in cabinet will enjoy virtually unchecked control over the executive and legislative functions of government. It is possible, of course, that backbenchers in the majority party rebel against their party leaders or that no party or coalition controls a majority in the first place, in which case one party, usually the largest, will form a "minority government" dependent on the support of one or more other parties in Parliament for its survival. But in Britain the tradition has been—at least since the late nineteenth century—one of single-party majority governments supported by disciplined parties in the Commons. The freedom of individual MPs to vote as they like in the British Parliament is, in effect, sacrificed on the altar of strong, stable cabinet government.

Let us look more closely at how cabinet government works in Britain. After each general election, the monarch asks the leader of the majority or largest party to form a government, as the prime minister and cabinet together are known. This government then seeks the approval of the House of Commons, which will be automatic when the party has won a majority of seats in the election. In theory, the prime minister is in a "first among equals" relationship with his or her cabinet colleagues. According to the (unwritten) doctrine of collective responsibility, the entire cabinet is accountable to Parliament for all decisions or actions taken by any cabinet minister, including the prime minister. This means that all decisions or actions of consequence should have been agreed on in advance by the cabinet as a whole.

Here, too, reality departs somewhat from theory. The prime minister is in fact much more than a first among equals. For one thing, the cabinet ministers are of her choosing, and she can dismiss them at will without seeking parliamentary approval. As noted above, her party does have the option of removing her from the leadership position, and hence from the prime ministership, but it is extremely unlikely that a party would remove an incumbent who had led it to victory in the preceding election. Such a display of internal disunity would almost certainly damage the party's image in the eyes of the electorate. Another resource which the prime minister has is control over the agenda of cabinet meetings. Since all significant actions or decisions contemplated by a minister must be approved by cabinet, the prime minister's control over cabinet business makes it unlikely that anything of significance will be decided without her approval. The reverse, however, is not necessarily true. Many decisions, especially in foreign affairs, have been taken by prime ministers without consultation with the full cabinet. Overall, the ability of the prime minister to dominate the cabinet and her backbench supporters in Parliament rests on the strength of the doctrine of party discipline, the ability of the prime minister to reward loyalty with high offices and honors, and the importance of her personal appeal in winning elections. Although only the voters of her own constituency have the opportunity to vote directly for a party leader, it is widely understood that an essential ingredient in a party's winning a majority of parliamentary seats in a general election is the personal appeal of its leader. This gives the leader, as prime minister, tremendous leeway in running the government.

The indirect manner in which prime ministers are chosen creates the possibility that the electorate's preferred party leader is not the one who becomes prime minister. This could happen either if the party that receives the most votes does not win the most parliamentary constituencies or if the majority party decides to change its leaders in midterm, thereby making a prime minister out of someone who had never sought the electorate's approval for that position. Winston Churchill, the nation's wartime leader, became prime minister in 1940 in this fashion. Chosen by Parliament to lead a coalition government composed of all parties, he did not submit his leadership to the electorate's approval until the war was over in 1945—at which time he was soundly defeated!

Both of these possibilities underscore the point that British government is based on the principle of parliamentary, not popular, sovereignty. All the electorate is expected to do is elect members of Parliament. The parties control the selection (and removal) of leaders. Since leaders are important in winning votes for a party, a popular leader will have tremendous authority within his party. A leader who leads his party to an election victory can therefore expect to dominate the government that he will be asked to form; but if he loses an election he may lose not only the prime ministership but the party leadership as well. While cabinet government may often resemble "prime ministerial government," the prime minister's authority depends very much on ability to gain and keep the electorate's consent. This ensures a strong element of popular control in the parliamentary system of government.

France: Parliamentarism Revised

Extreme centralization of authority has been the most salient characteristic of French government since the seventeenth century. According to legend, the French King Louis XIV once declared, *"L'état, c'est moi"* (the state, it is I); two centuries later, a French minister of education boasted that he could look at his watch and know which page of which textbook every French child was studying at that very moment. In French political culture, concentrated authority is generally viewed in a positive light, and even today most French citizens would regard the power of the French state—a relic of the absolute monarchy—to be an essential feature of national life.

A Hyperunitary State   The centralized system of administration created under the monarchy and refined by Napoleon in 1799–1815 treated France as if it were conquered territory. Under Napoleon, each of the 88 (now 96) "departments" into which the country had been divided in 1790 was governed by a high state official known as a prefect. The duty of the prefect was to uphold the authority of the state in his department, and the powers granted him to perform this function were vast. He controlled local police and coordinated the work of all government ministries in the department; even so trifling a matter as installing street lights had to go through him to the appropriate ministry in Paris for approval. After the establishment of the Third Republic in 1875, the units of local government, known as "communes," were each granted the right to elect mayors and municipal councils, but they could do little without the prefect's consent. He supervised their activities, approved their budgets, and took responsibility for implementing any decisions they reached with his approval. Almost as if it were headed by children, local government was considered to be under the "tutelage" of the state and its field representative, the prefect.

To some extent, this system of strong state control over local affairs was circumvented by a practice known as the "accumulation of mandates." Given the extreme dependence of commune mayors on the local prefect, mayors often found it useful to seek election to other bodies as well, such as the departmental and regional councils and especially the country's parliament. From the latter position, they could exercise some degree of influence over government policy and over the activities of the state, particularly as it affected their department or commune. This gave them a degree of leverage over the local prefect and encouraged a close cooperation between prefect and mayors that tempered the will of the state with sensitivity to local concerns.

In 1982 the Socialist government of President François Mitterrand decided to take matters several steps further in the direction of local control. The government formally ended the system of tutelage by making municipal, departmental, and regional councils responsible for taking and implementing decisions affecting the areas they represent; prefects might assist them, but their permission is no longer needed to get things done. In addition, it was decided that the power of councils to raise revenues, hitherto tightly restricted, would be expanded to correspond to their greater responsibilities. So major a reform may be expected to create difficulties at times, but it does represent the first serious attempt, after years of debate, to remove local government from the ubiquitous grasp of the state and place it squarely in the hands of locally elected representatives.

The Experiment in Quasi-Presidentialism   Historically, the tacit conflict between the representatives of the interests of the state and the representatives of local interests also took place in Paris. During France's parliamentary Third (1875–1940) and Fourth (1946–1958) Republics, however, the result was often much less satisfactory. Mayors or other local leaders elected to the National Assembly to defend their localities against the state and its representatives, the prefects, may well have created a rough balance in their localities, but they did so only at a considerable cost in terms of effective parliamentary government. As we saw in the British case, parliamentary government achieves stability and effectiveness when parliamentary representatives are willing to put aside much of their freedom of action and submit themselves to the discipline of a small number of tightly controlled parties. Only then can cabinets get on with the business of governing the country without having to fear being removed from office at any moment by an obstreperous parliament. To the extent that the individual parliamentary representative remains free of party discipline in order to better defend the interests of his particular locality, on the other hand, cabinet stability becomes more problematic. With numerous, poorly disciplined parties as its norm, France under the Third and Fourth Republics became notorious for its short-lived and ineffective cabinets.

The weakness of governments in the Third and Fourth Republics may seem surprising for a state as centralized as France, but there were good reasons for it. France's turbulent and occasionally revolutionary past had left the country profoundly divided over the kind of regime it should have, over the proper role of the Catholic Church in society, even over the desirability of modernization. These divisions fragmented the political party spectrum and made it very difficult to develop broadly based parties that could hope to win a parliamentary majority. The coalition governments that formed often could not agree on any course of action, and when compromises were made by leaders of the different parties in cabinet, the followers frequently refused to support them. In addition, the very strength of the state made it appear so potentially dangerous—especially if it fell into the wrong hands—that many parliamentary deputies felt that their prime task had to be to guard against attempts by the state or a cabinet to wield that power effectively. Often this meant that cabinets were defeated in the Parliament on the most minor of issues—it made the point more tellingly.

In normal times, the deputy's overriding concern to defend local interests against the power of the state and those who might attempt to abuse it undoubtedly had its value, but in times when government action was desperately needed, the system did not respond well. One such occasion was the challenge emanating from Nazi Germany in the latter 1930s, which French governments proved too weak to match. Another was the challenge created by the 1958 takeover of the French colony of Algeria by the army. This mutiny, supported by French settlers in Algeria, was motivated by the army's sense that Paris was not sufficiently keen on prosecuting the war against the native National Liberation Front, which was fighting for Algerian independence. Fearing a possible army takeover of France itself, the politicians in Paris turned to the war hero General Charles de Gaulle to save the situation. De Gaulle agreed to take over the reins of power, but his price was high: he demanded the right to have a new constitution drafted.

De Gaulle had been convinced for a long time that a pure parliamentary system was inappropriate for France. In his view, France needed stronger leadership than its weak and short-lived cabinets seemed capable of providing. His new constitution therefore proposed a system of government comprising two levels: at one level, the parliamentary system, complete with prime minister and cabinet, would continue to operate much as before, but at a higher level there would be a powerful president, not responsible to the legislative branch, who would ensure the overall functioning of the state and take ultimate responsibility for defense and foreign affairs. De Gaulle became the first president of this Fifth Republic and, with his forceful style of charismatic leadership, managed not only to maneuver the country through the traumatic experience of granting independence to Algeria but also to establish his regime as by far the most widely supported since the revolution of 1789.

The constitution of de Gaulle's republic attempts a merging of the principles of presidential and parliamentary government in order to benefit from the advantages of each. Accordingly, the constitution gives considerable powers both to the president and to the Parliament and cabinet. It is the president who selects the prime minister and cabinet, who presides over cabinet meetings, and who must sign all government bills or decrees for them to come into effect. If the Parliament passes bills that he dislikes, he can ask it to reconsider. He may also dissolve the National Assembly and call new elections (although only once per session). He may even bypass the Parliament altogether and submit a proposal to a national referendum. If he feels a crisis is at hand, he can declare a state of emergency and rule by decree for up to six months. The strong presidency is the chief innovation in this constitution and has been largely responsible for its popularity and success.

The French Parliament is composed of two houses, the National Assembly, which is elected for a term of five years, and the Senate, one-third of which is elected by local and regional councillors every three years. Although both houses vote on legislation, it is the National Assembly which is the more powerful body. Not only is it more directly representative of the electorate's will, but the prime minister and cabinet depend on its support alone. Moreover, if the National Assembly and the Senate disagree on a piece of legislation and no compromise can be worked out, the cabinet and the National Assembly together can override the Senate's objections.

The framers of the constitution of the Fifth Republic were concerned to limit the instability engendered by an all-powerful parliament. Part of their solution, as we have seen, was to create a powerful president untouchable by the deputies; another was to diminish the powers of the Parliament itself. According to the constitution, the Parliament meets for two sessions of about three months each year. There is a list of areas in which it can legislate, but all other areas are regulated by governmental decree. The government (i.e., the prime minister and cabinet) requires the support of the National Assembly but, for the government to be

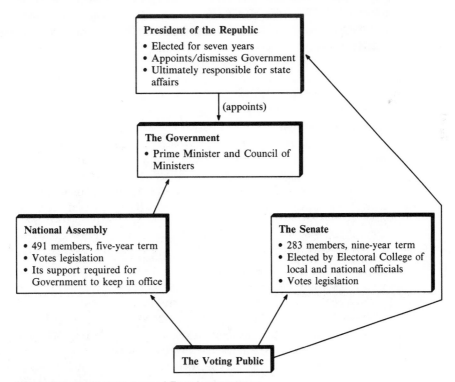

Figure 2.2   Basic institutions of French government.

removed from office, a censure motion must be passed by an absolute majority of deputies—not just a majority of those deputies who take part in the vote. Defeat of a government bill does not entail the resignation of the government unless the government declares that it is staking its survival on the passage of the bill; but if it does so, the bill also must be defeated by an absolute majority. Under this provision, even a bill that has been defeated by a relative majority in the National Assembly could become law. In addition, the National Assembly has 70 days to pass or defeat the budget; otherwise it becomes law as it is. The Parliament may not propose any amendments to the budget or any other bill that involves increases or decreases in public expenditures; the government, in other words, controls the purse. Finally, the government may reject all amendments and demand that its own version of a bill be put to a vote; if it also makes passage of the bill a matter of government survival, the government's version of the bill will become law unless an absolute majority is willing to oppose it and bring down the government as well. In short, the government gets its way unless there is a majority in the National Assembly determined to remove it from office.

Standing between the president and the Parliament is the government itself, that is, the prime minister and cabinet. The government's overall responsibility, according to the constitution, is "to determine and direct the policy of the nation." This suggests some degree of parity or balance between the authority of the head of government, the prime minister, and the head of state, the president, but things have not worked out that way. In 1962 de Gaulle had the constitution amended to provide for the direct election of the president by all adult citizens, rather than by an electoral college of local and national public officials. This direct, personal mandate from the electorate has given the president immense authority. Following the example of de Gaulle, who seemed to regard prime ministers as his executive assistants removable at will, French presidents have come to be the supreme figures in government. Like U.S. presidents, they are not subject to the possibility that a legislative majority, or their cabinet colleagues, could decide to remove them from office. Unlike their American counterparts, however, they escape the checks that a fully independent legislature could apply, for in order to defeat a president's legislative proposals, the National Assembly must be willing to remove his prime minister and cabinet as well. Since the establishment of the regime, this has never happened because presidents have almost always enjoyed the support of docile, disciplined majorities in the National Assembly. Indeed, so powerful is the presidential principle in France that when a Socialist, François Mitterrand, was elected to the presidency in 1981 after 23 years of conservative rule, the electorate promptly returned a Socialist majority to the National Assembly in the legislative elections held the following month.

The mixture of parliamentary and presidential principles in the constitution of the Fifth Republic does create the possibility that presidential predominance could evaporate quickly, however. French politics is divided between the Left (mainly the Socialists) and the more conservative parties of the Right. If a left-wing president faces a right-wing National Assembly or vice versa, then one may expect that the president's power would be substantially undermined. The constitution grants the president the right to choose a prime minister who will execute his will, but if that prime minister and his cabinet are opposed by a legislative majority, they will not be able to survive in office and perform that function. In such a situation, the president may be forced to submit to a government and a legislative program that is not to his liking or risk complete deadlock with the National Assembly.

It might be thought that a divided executive of this sort is unlikely to occur because the electorate will always tend to favor the same party or coalition in both the presidential and parliamentary elections, as it did in 1981. But even if the electorate does have this inclination, the rules may stand in its way. The Socialists won in both elections in 1981 because a Socialist won the presidency first and immediately used his power to dissolve the National Assembly and call new parliamentary elections. But the president is elected for seven years, the National Assembly for only five. Thus, the next National Assembly elections had to occur by 1986, two years before the next presidential elections. In those elections, a majority was won by the parties of the Right, but they could not "dissolve" the president and call new presidential elections. Of course, President Mitterrand could have resigned, thereby forcing new presidential elections (there is no vice-president to replace him), but he chose instead to allow the right-wing majority to form a government and implement its program. The result was a marked diminution in presidential authority and noticeable discord within an executive divided between leaders of antagonistic parties. This was a novel format, indeed, for a country that has become accustomed to strong presidential rule, but apparently one that was not displeasing to the electorate: when Mitterrand called parliamentary elections after being reelected in 1988, the voters chose not to give his Socialist party a majority.

THE SOVIET UNION AND CHINA: COMMUNIST ALTERNATIVES

Both the Soviet Union and China are governed by regimes which came to power by means of revolution with the intention of fundamentally transforming their societies according to the teachings of Marxism-Leninism. Among the most important principles they have adopted or adapted from this body of doctrine are the necessity of abolishing private property, the paramountcy of the welfare of society as a whole over the rights of the individuals who compose it, and the leading role that the Communist party must play throughout society and government. The first principle has meant that the state in each case has assumed the task of directing and coordinating the drive to establish a modern industrial economy; the second implies that in pursuing its goals the state has been unwilling to tolerate interference from individuals or groups that seek to delay or thwart its objectives. Most important, the third principle signifies that the formal institutions of government have operated more as tools by which the party can impose its will than as autonomous decision-making institutions in their own right. This gives the discussion of the governmental structures of communist regimes a somewhat unreal air; we must always bear in mind that there lurks a power behind the power of government—the ruling Communist party. Nowhere is this better illustrated than in the communist regimes of the Soviet Union and China.

Soviet Union: Single-Party Oligarchy

In 1977, amid considerable fanfare, the USSR adopted its fourth written constitution. The document contains a lengthy preamble and 174 articles spelling out an elaborate system of representative institutions, electoral procedures, and citizens' rights. Allowing for numerous clauses referring to certain doctrines of Marxist-Leninist ideology and sanctifying socialist ownership of property, it reads much like the constitutions of liberal democracies—and yet the country's experience has demonstrated that the realities of political power exist primarily outside the constitution. Those realities are hinted at in Article 6, which identifies the locus of that power: "The leading and guiding force of Soviet society and the nucleus of its political system . . . is the Communist Party of the Soviet Union."[4]

It is the "leading and guiding" role of the CPSU, the only party allowed to exist, that defines the nature of Soviet politics. The CPSU has an elaborate set of written rules; these do not describe the party's workings in every respect, but they do serve as general operating guidelines and can be perceived as a kind of party constitution.[5] The party's structure and functions will be discussed in Chapter 5, but it is important to note from the beginning that the substance of governance is shaped by the party and that all the governing institutions from the lowest village councils to the Supreme Soviet and the Council of Ministers are led and guided by party members. The division of tasks between government and party institutions is nowhere specifically written up; however, a system has evolved in which the overlapping functions of party and state on all levels have come to be understood. The political structures are large and

---

[4]This article further describes the party's role: "The Communist Party . . . determines the general perspectives of the development of society and the line of domestic and foreign policy of the USSR, directs the great constructive work of the Soviet people, and imparts a planned, systematic, and theoretically substantiated character to their struggle for the victory of communism." The Soviet constitution is reprinted in Donald D. Barry and Carol Barner-Barry, *Contemporary Soviet Politics: An Introduction,* 2nd ed. (Englewood Cliffs, N.J.: Prentice-Hall, 1982), pp. 361–389; cited from p. 363.

[5]The complete CPSU rules are reprinted in Barry and Barner-Barry, ibid., pp. 390–405.

complex, and they involve the active participation of thousands of people.

Perhaps it seems odd that a political system dominated by a single-party oligarchy has such an elaborate institutional structure, but the institutions serve important purposes. First, the top leaders cannot do everything; they need a network of subordinates to administer their decisions. In a country as vast as the USSR, whose government assumes a wider range of functions than that undertaken by Western governments, many individuals must be entrusted with the day-to-day tasks of running the affairs of state and party, as well as planning and managing the complicated state-run economy. In all these tasks, countless questions arise about the interpretation and application of policies drawn up by the central authorities; such questions require numerous decisions on the part of state and party bureaucracies at every level.

Second, the political institutions not only have functional purposes but also serve to validate the country's political mythology. Just as the monarchy before 1917 was buttressed by an official church with its belief system and its emblems of symbolic appeal, the Soviet state bases itself on an official ideology, Marxism-Leninism, and a system of myths centering on the Great October Revolution, the workers' soviets, and the memory of Lenin, who is venerated not just as a founding father but as a heroic figure of almost saintlike proportions. Today's political institutions embody the ideological proposition that the Soviet Union is a state of the working class and that its government, in theory, is open to the participation of a wide representative portion of this class. This wide participation is not equivalent to democratic rule as we know it in the West, however, for the functions and responsibilities of the Soviet government are defined and controlled by the Communist party, which claims the authority to speak on all matters on behalf of the workers' interests.

A Formal Federalism   Bearing in mind that the institutions of the state are in every instance subordinate to those of the party, we can nonetheless examine their structures as the constitution defines them. On the vertical plane, the Soviet Union is a federal state divided into territorial units coinciding roughly with many of the USSR's ethnic and national boundaries. There are 15 union republics, whose lands contain the largest and culturally most cohesive national populations (see Table 2.1). Some of these peoples, for example the Lithuanians, Latvians, and Estonians, have a history of independent statehood; others, such as the Ukrainians, have long aspired to independence or autonomy.

One step below the union republics are 20 so-called autonomous republics, all but four of which are located within the enormous land mass of the largest republic, the RSFSR. Also within some union republics are 18 autonomous *oblasts* (provinces) and national *okrugs* (districts), with less structural autonomy than the autonomous republics. Each of these subunits has its own set of governmental institutions, in

Table 2.1 THE UNION REPUBLICS OF THE USSR

Russian Soviet Federated Socialist Republic (RSFSR)
Ukraine
Moldavia
Belorussia
Lithuania
Latvia
Estonia
Georgia
Armenia
Azerbaidzhan
Kazakhstan
Uzbekistan
Turkmenia
Tadzhikistan
Kirghizia

one or another degree reflecting the structures of the central (federal) government. The subunits administer many details of state policy and official business, but their powers are clearly subordinate to those of the central authorities. In principle, the union republics have the right to secede from the USSR, but this right has never been exercised, and it is quite unthinkable, given current circumstances, that an act of secession will in fact ever occur.

On the intermediate levels of politics, there are signs that indigenous elites frequently make use of the federal structures to enhance their power, or to gain access on behalf of their republic to influence those within the central decision-making institutions. This trend is not acknowledged directly by Soviet authorities; it takes place in the realm of what some Western observers call "cryptopolitics," that is, an informal pattern of bargaining and jockeying for influence within the complex structures of both the state and the party. It hardly amounts to an institutionalized system of power-sharing, but, as we shall see in Chapter 5, cryptopolitics plays a significant role in the workings of the Soviet polity.

The Governmental Structure   The basic governmental unit at all levels is the *soviet* (council). The soviets symbolize the tradition of the Great October Revolution, when workers' soviets formed the backbone of Bolshevik power. Today, "soviets of people's deputies" exist in villages, towns, and cities, as well as on the district, regional, provincial, and republican levels, each subordinate in authority to the soviet at the next higher level. At the top is the Supreme Soviet, a bicameral body composed of the Soviet of the Union and the Soviet of Nationalities. Both chambers of the Supreme Soviet are elected by popular vote every five years.[6] Deputies to the Soviet of the Union are chosen from single-member districts of approximately 300,000 inhabitants; deputies to the Soviet of Nationalities are

[6]In 1988, a special party conference adopted a proposal to create a 2,250-member Congress of People's Deputies, which in turn would select a smaller Supreme Soviet headed by a powerful president.

elected roughly on the principle of ethnic, or ethnoregional, representation. The two chambers are equal in size (750 deputies each) and have the same legislative responsibilities.

The Supreme Soviet hardly bears comparison with the French or British legislatures. Composed of nonprofessional politicians, the Supreme Soviet usually convenes only once a year for one or two weeks; during this time, the deputies' purpose is to ratify legislation put before them by the professional politicians, and this they typically do by unanimous vote. Moreover, the process by which the deputies are chosen differs fundamentally from British and French elections, as only the Communist party may nominate candidates. In the past, only one candidate stood for election to a given position; this held true for local and regional councils as well as the Supreme Soviet. This practice changed in 1987, when multiple-candidate elections were introduced in a limited number of districts, with the intention of gradually expanding the practice more widely. In all cases, candidates are still nominated by the CPSU, and

Lenin's statue looks on as Soviet General Secretary Mikhail Gorbachev addresses the Supreme Soviet, November 1985. (TASS from Sovfoto)

therefore a multicandidate election means that communists (or, in some instances, non-party members who nonetheless have the party's approval) run against one another. Voters do not choose among candidates professing different ideologies, so the choice often boils down to issues of personal popularity and integrity.

According to the constitution, the Supreme Soviet is the highest body of state authority, but in actuality it is not. Above it are the Presidium of the Supreme Soviet and the Council of Ministers, both of which are formally elected by the Supreme Soviet. The Presidium acts as a kind of collective presidency, comprising nearly 40 members led by a chairman, who performs the ceremonial duties pertaining to his position as head of state. The Council of Ministers includes more than 100 heads of ministries, representing not just the usual cabinet departments characteristic of Western governments—finance, defense, foreign affairs, and so on—but also the specialized ministries that direct many branches of the state-owned economy (for example, the Ministry of the Aviation Industry). The chairman of the Council of Ministers, also referred to as the premier or prime minister, presides over yet another, and more powerful, body: the Presidium of the Council of Ministers, composed of approximately 10 to 15 first deputy chairmen and deputy chairmen. It is the Presidium of the Council of Ministers, together with the highest-ranking members of the Presidium of the Supreme Soviet, who are believed to be the most important governmental shapers of legislation.

Although the top governmental organs and their leaders play sig-

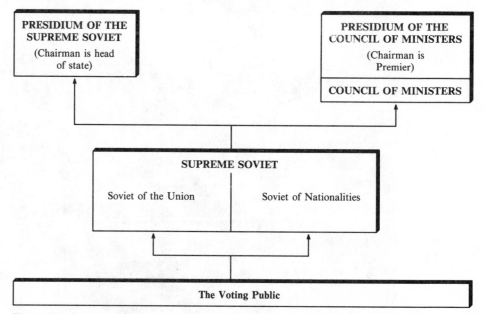

Figure 2.3 Soviet government structures, federal level.

nificant roles, the real seat of power lies with the Politburo and the Secretariat of the Communist party's Central Committee. This is true at every other political level, as well: the highest party organs do not just share power with the highest governmental bodies but in fact dominate the power structure—in the republics, the regions, cities, and on down to the lowest level. At the top, the Politburo makes the major policy decisions affecting the entire country; the Secretariat implements party policy, controls all organizational affairs, and oversees personnel appointments by means of what is called the *nomenklatura*.[7] Both the Politburo and the Secretariat are headed by the general secretary, currently Mikhail Gorbachev.

At least superficially, the Politburo bears comparison with the British cabinet in its ability to shape policy, both foreign and domestic, and in its leadership structure. In policy-making, it is clear that these two bodies play the most important role in their respective countries. The Politburo's power is somewhat greater, however, because it does not have to submit its policies to the scrutiny and criticism of a parliamentary opposition. The general secretary, like the British prime minister, is a bit more than first among equals. Although he does not personally appoint the other members of the Politburo, a strong general secretary can persuade his colleagues to change the Politburo's membership to his liking. The Soviet leader can also influence the composition of the party's Central Committee and maneuver his supporters into other political positions, but he wields such power over party personnel not by direct appointment but by persuading other ranking officials. Like the British prime minister, the general secretary holds his post at the behest of his party; in practice, however, the Soviet chief cannot be removed by a revolt within the lower party ranks, but only by his colleagues on the Politburo—and that has happened only once in the history of the USSR, to Nikita Khrushchev in 1964. Finally, and most significantly, the general secretary and his colleagues do not have to worry about being voted out of power by the public; they are answerable, in theory, only to the Communist party and, in reality, only to each other.

Just as the institutions of government are penetrated and dominated by the party, so too are the courts. Most judges and procurators (prosecuting attorneys) are party members, and all are chosen on the advice of the party authorities at the appropriate levels. The courts consider the interests of the party's will to be above all other principles of legality, including the rights of individuals spelled out in the Soviet constitution. Persons accused of political crimes are judged not on the basis of their constitutional rights, but on whether or not their actions have harmed the interests of the socialist community as determined by the norms of

---

[7]The *nomenklatura* is a list of positions for which the party's approval is required before a person can be appointed to, or removed from, any of them. It is not restricted to posts within the party but, rather, extends to many leadership positions throughout Soviet society.

the ruling party. The courts have been consistently severe in applying this criterion; those accused of political crimes have usually found it very difficult to disprove the charges brought against them. During the Gorbachev period, there has been some movement toward greater judicial independence in criminal cases; political cases, however, are still judged according to the standards set by the CPSU.

Political Succession   For years, Western observers debated and speculated about the Soviet succession problem. Neither the constitution nor the party's written rules spell out procedures for the selection of a party chief, and the ambiguous nature of collective leadership makes it unclear just how powerful the general secretary is. All these factors combine to paint a picture of mystery and intrigue around the issue of succession. And indeed, in the rise of Stalin and Khrushchev, there was intrigue aplenty. Stalin succeeded Lenin in the midst of a crisis that lasted more than a decade; Stalin's real and imaginary rivals were ousted from the party or even killed, and both the party and the larger society underwent a major upheaval. Stalin's death in 1953 precipitated another leadership crisis, at the end of which Khrushchev emerged as the victor; this crisis was confined mostly to the higher ranks of the party, however, and there was little turmoil among other political or social groups.

Beginning with the removal of Khrushchev, a pattern was established. Khrushchev was voted out of his position by a majority on the party's Presidium (Politburo), and the same majority named his successors: Leonid Brezhnev became first secretary (later, general secretary), and Aleksei Kosygin took the position of premier, which Khrushchev had also held.[8] After more than 18 years under Brezhnev's leadership, the party found itself facing the succession issue three times within 28 months. Each time, the general secretary died; each time, the Politburo calmly elected a new one: Yuri Andropov in 1982, Konstantin Chernenko in 1984, and Mikhail Gorbachev in 1985.

The succession process now appears to work smoothly, behind closed doors and among the members of a tight party oligarchy (on the death of Chernenko, the Politburo consisted of only 10 full members and 6 candidate members). The obvious weakness in the process is that party leaders are chosen for indefinite terms; a party chief can be removed, but this is difficult since it requires a kind of conspiracy among his opponents throughout the top ranks of the party—as in the removal of Khrushchev. In 1988, a special party conference proposed to address this problem by limiting party officials to two five-year terms.

The Politburo, therefore, remains supreme, a collective authority at the pinnacle of the Soviet regime. The constituency of the Politburo is a product of the ambiguities inherent in oligarchy. The members of this

[8]Khrushchev's party title at the time was first secretary, and the policy-making committee was known as the Presidium of the Central Committee. In 1966 these names were changed to general secretary and Politburo, as they had been called during the Stalin era.

all-powerful group rise to the top through a combination of distinguished party service, aggressive self-advancement, and loyalty to persons already in power. Underlying every appointment to the Politburo is an obscure and complicated process through which factional rivalries, policy debates, and interest articulation play themselves out. Soviet leaders like to give the impression that their actions are taken in complete harmony. The truth is more complex; the differences among the members of the party elite are by no means as serious as those that disrupted party unity after the death of Lenin, but they exist nonetheless. By now, however, the Soviet political system has evolved patterns of institutional behavior and decision-making that are quite stable. They are not defined by the written constitution, but they are well understood by members of the party oligarchy.

China: A "People's Republic"

China, like the Soviet Union, has promulgated a series of constitutions, the first in 1954, with subsequent versions in 1975, 1978, and 1982. The first constitution of the People's Republic of China reportedly was five years in the making; according to Chinese officials, more than 150 million people participated in various stages of the process. While the formal structures of government were laid out in that document, however, their prescribed functions were not always realized. For example, between 1949 and 1979, the National People's Congress—the top lawmaking body—met only infrequently, and congresses at all levels ratified legislation prepared elsewhere rather than creating new laws themselves. The Cultural Revolution of the latter 1960s further disrupted constitutional processes. The emergence of Deng Xiaoping as top leader since 1978 has led, however, to a strengthening of important state structures. While human rights have not consistently been respected, Deng has generally tried to encourage the creation and implementation of government procedures and to curb arbitrary party rule.

A Unitary State   China's formal governmental structure is that of a centralized unitary state. Unlike the Soviet Union, there is no pretense of federalism. Each of the successive constitutions has clearly articulated the unitary nature of the Chinese state. Thus the succeeding constitutions closely parallel the existing political reality, namely centralized political control.

Although central government is the key decision maker, several levels of government have been developed to administer this very large and diverse country. Immediately below the central government are the 11 military regions. They are often called on for administrative assistance in times of severe social or political tensions. During the Great Leap Forward and the first phase of the Cultural Revolution, this unit of government was activated to assist central government administration.

The most significant level below the central government is the provincial level. It includes 22 provinces, the five autonomous regions (several populated by minority peoples), and the three major cities—Beijing, Shanghai, and Tianjin. The provinces are historical units dating back to the earliest days of the Chinese state. The administrative unit below the province is the prefecture, of which there are around 150 throughout China. Originally they were to function as adjuncts to provinces, but they soon developed a life of their own. Below them are county-level units, including smaller cities and sections of larger cities. Their functions include administrative control over public works and economic enterprises such as mines and factories.

Between 1958 and 1980 the communes performed a major role in the administrative hierarchy, although one of declining significance. Their sizes tended to be either too small or too large to meet the ambitious expectations which the government or party had for them. They were to be the center for political administration, for industrial and agricultural economic activity, as well as for social functions such as education, care for the aged and infirm, health care, finance, and security. In a sense, they were to be the core of communist life in the new society.

Since 1979, the functions of the commune have been dispersed among other official units. One of these is the township, which took over the political role of the commune at the local level in 1982. Under the 92,000 townships are neighborhood and workplace units in urban areas and, in rural areas, some 820,000 villages. Earlier on, villages had formed production brigades, which were responsible for meeting production targets set by the communes. More recently, villages have been able to develop their own targets and make more decisions locally concerning such matters as the types of items to be produced. Generally, however, the quantity of goods and the specific products to be produced are still determined under pressure from higher levels of government. To gain more leverage, the village has had to develop its own economic base. It is allowed to tax the production team (the unit below it), and it has begun to innovate by expanding its own light industries. Indeed, it has become the core of the industrial revolution sweeping the Chinese countryside in the middle and late 1980s. The village uses its funds to provide educational services, primary as well as adult literacy courses, some welfare projects, community water, and fish ponds.

The lowest level of the rural hierarchy is the production team. It comprises a hamlet or sometimes a section in a larger village. For decades, it has served as the basic accounting unit for agricultural production. Increasingly, however, agricultural resources such as land, animals, and tools are being transferred to individual households. Under this "responsibility system," households are responsible for production decisions and may even earn profits on production that exceeds specified quotas.

The Governmental Structure   While China's constitution makes references to the real authority, the **Chinese Communist Party (CCP)**, it vests the formal authority and in many ways the day-to-day authority with the governmental structures of the state. The constitution provides for a body of legislative organs, the people's congresses, which are to be the source of "democratic" power. At the zenith of this set of legislatures is the National People's Congress (NPC). Comprising about 3000 delegates elected by provincial congresses, it now meets once a year to discuss and ratify legislation passed down from the authoritative party organs (to be discussed more fully in Chapter 5). The NPC also has the formal power to choose the Standing Committee, which represents it when the full Congress is not in session; to select the head of state, the president (an honorific post which was vacant between 1969 and 1983), and the head of government, the premier; and to approve the composition of the State Council. As was the case with legislation, these decisions are usually taken first within the party and then submitted to the NPC for automatic ratification.

Although the NPC exists primarily to ratify policies made by the party, with the growth of economic liberalization and the corresponding encouragement of individual responsibility, it has become the scene of growing independence. In 1987 the Standing Committee actually threw out a new enterprise law, claiming that it was not "ripe." In addition, there were reports of individuals complaining about the premier's report and calling for closer supervision of the government by people's congresses at all levels.[9]

The State Council is the executive organ of the highest state authority. Under the premier, it executes and administers the affairs of state. The Council is composed of the premier, several vice-premiers, and the ministers who head the ministries and commissions of the central government. Since the State Council can be quite large, it has a Standing Committee composed of the premier, vice-premiers, senior state councillors, and a general secretary. The State Council's functions include implementation of the national economic plans and the state budget; direction of cultural, educational, and public health services; management of affairs concerning national minorities and overseas Chinese; and, finally, national security. Under its control, numerous ministries run the business of the national government.

Beneath these structures are congresses at various local levels, including the provincial, county, and township levels, with associated government departments and officials. The core administrators and indeed the decision makers at all levels of government are centrally appointed officials. They form an extensive hierarchical network of cadres, perhaps 20 million strong,[10] that runs the affairs of government under the close scrutiny of the party. By the mid-1980s, lower-level government officials had been granted considerable latitude to make decisions pertaining to

---

[9]*Christian Science Monitor* (April 13, 1987), 10.
[10]Hong Yung Lee, "Deng Xiaoping's Reform of the Chinese Bureaucracy," *Journal of Northeast Asian Studies* (June 1982), 21–35.

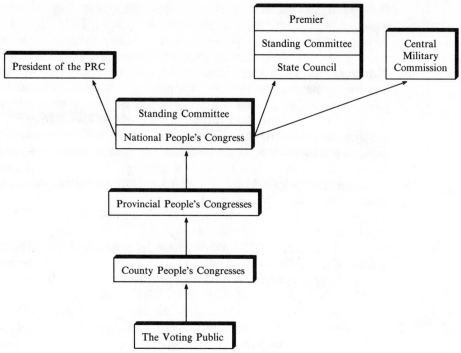

Figure 2.4 Basic institutions of Chinese government.

local needs; however, ultimate authority has remained in higher party and government bodies.

Leadership Selection The constitution provides for elections to the National People's Congress and to other congresses each five years. Election to the NPC is to be done by members of the congresses at the provincial level. Delegates to these congresses are, in turn, elected by county congresses. It is only at the latter level that the population at large participates directly in the electoral process. In 1979 a new electoral law was passed allowing for multiple candidates at all levels. How important this reform will become is unclear, however, because the party continues to maintain control over the nomination process.

Although the National People's Congress is formally responsible for selecting the top leadership of the government, these decisions, too, are generally worked out within the party. This largely hidden process involves a competition among top leaders to form coalitions with support groups in the key party areas and in the military in order to win backing for their own positions within the party. They are then able to influence—albeit slowly—the composition of key decision groups, such as the party's Politburo and its Standing Committee.

Attempts to realize the constitutional promise of freely elected government officials have mainly been confined to the lowest levels of the political system, and the results have been less than satisfying to those expecting reform. Those expectations grew in the wake of the 1978–1979 "Democracy Movement," which manifested itself in a plethora of public comments placed on billboards. Here ordinary citizens let out their feelings on particular issues and indeed on the system itself. Among the issues raised were serious questions about the fairness of the 1980 local elections and, in particular, the degree of party interference in those elections. In 1986–1987 the movement resurfaced and appeared to be making much more headway, but a series of student demonstrations in favor of democratic reforms encouraged the government to clamp down once again.

The dilemma China's leadership faces over how much autonomy to allow individuals and governmental institutions is also reflected in the legal system. Like its predecessors, the 1982 constitution describes a system of courts and procuratorates culminating in the Supreme People's Court, which supervises justice by the local people's courts and by the special people's courts. During the Cultural Revolution the legal system suffered severe setbacks. For example, in 1967 the chief procurator was publicly ridiculed, and in 1968 the president of the Supreme Court was driven to suicide. It was not until after the Cultural Revolution that the courts and procuratorates commenced functioning effectively again, albeit under the continuing inspiration and guidance of the ruling party.

In general, the Communist party's political priorities continue to supersede its constitutional proclamations. The governing elite's priority is for a managed political order rather than a competitive political system. It seeks control over the direction of public policy and therefore over the organs responsible for public decisions; and it allows nothing to come in the way of its maintenance of power. Nevertheless, in recent years the party has mandated orderly procedures and developed structures for public decision-making, leadership selection, and conflict management, and has sought to distinguish clearly its functions from those of the government.

MEXICO AND NIGERIA: THIRD WORLD POLITICAL STRUCTURES

Given the difficult task of creating political order in Third World countries, the processes of selecting and implementing constitutional processes are important. If constitutional processes fail to take hold, as is the case in many Third World countries, political development is greatly retarded. That is not to say that the process of political development does not proceed at all; debate and discussions on political formulas, the use of legal institutions such as courts of law, and even the occasional attempt at elections do occur. But none can replace the ultimate acceptance and habitual use of a constitutional process.

Both Mexico and Nigeria turned to foreign models in developing their constitutions. The Mexicans in their constitutions of 1824, 1857, and 1917 adopted the United States' presidential system as their model, while Nigeria under British guidance adopted the British parliamentary pattern after independence. During the formative years of both countries, federal structures were employed to cope with centrifugal regional forces. In both cases, the regional forces put too great a stress on the fragile structures, and military intervention resulted. However, Mexico's federalist presidential system has managed to survive to this day, although it has undergone lapses and considerable modifications; Nigeria's original parliamentary framework was cast aside in 1966 after just six years in operation. In 1979 a presidential system was attempted, but by 1983 a military government had once again taken over.

Mexico: Unrestrained Presidentialism

Mexico's current constitution, promulgated in 1917, is successor to and inheritor of a political tradition whose previous manifestations include two formal constitutions and various adaptations by a long line of military and civilian leaders. The current Mexican political framework is a federal presidential system with a bicameral legislature, an appointed judiciary, and a set of reserved powers for the states. In fact, the most powerful forces in the actual political formula are the presidency and the dominant political party, the Institutional Revolutionary Party (PRI). However, the party itself is not specifically dealt with in the constitution.

Mexico's constitutions have differed in the degree of power conferred on the federal government and in the limitations on privileges granted to the church. For many years, the church, the military, and the traditional landed elite were the major political forces in Mexico. The first constitution (1824) failed to create a political system that could withstand these forces, and the regime fell victim to a long series of military takeovers. The 1857 constitution, also modeled on that of the United States, was an attempt to remedy these weaknesses. It incorporated the right of judicial review and abolished some privileges of the army and clergy.

Many provisions of the 1857 constitution were incorporated in the 1917 constitution. These include the presidential system, a bicameral legislature, and a federal system with parallel executive-legislative structures for the 31 state governments. The 1917 constitution was the first modern constitution to posit that it is the government's duty to provide for the people's social welfare. It severely limits the role of the church, long a powerful force in the country's socioeconomic and political fabric, by prohibiting clerics from voting, engaging in political activities, or running primary schools. The constitution vests ownership of natural resources and land, including the subsoil, with the state and promises land redistribution to the poor. It provides for social rights as well as political liberties, guaranteeing the rights of workers to bargain collectively and to organize labor unions. Like its predecessor, this constitution was not a social contract to which the people had assented. Developed and promulgated by the elite, it reflects a compromise between two ideologies: the capitalist and libertarian values held by the wealthy landed classes, and the goals of social justice and secularization sought by peasant and labor groups.

Federalism?   Nominally, Mexico is a federation of 31 states and one federal district. Each state has the right to elect its own governor and legislature. The state governments have the legal power to raise revenues through taxes and to allocate expenditures within the constitutionally defined areas of their jurisdiction. In practice, the federal structure has been emasculated. The constitution grants the federal Senate the power to appoint a new state governor when the government of any state has broken down. In the past the federal government used this power on a number of occasions to depose state authorities who were unwilling to follow directions from Mexico City; it is now rarely used because the PRI controls not only the federal government but also the governorships and legislatures of all the states. Furthermore, while states have the constitutional power to raise their own funds, all are in fact heavily reliant and some virtually totally dependent on the federal government for necessary revenues.

The Ministry of the Interior directly supervises Mexico's state and local governments; indeed, the minister of the interior, through the president, has the power to remove local as well as state officials. State governments consist of a governor and a unicameral legislature. Below the state governor and state legislature are the municipal governments, each headed by an elected mayor and council. Local governments usually wait for the central government to develop programs to solve their problems, and this dependence is reinforced by the federal government's practice of preempting local initiatives. The central and state governments' control of education, construction, and public works further debilitates local government, as does its almost total reliance on higher levels of government for its funding.

Presidentialism   Perhaps the best explanation for the weakness of the Mexican federal system is the political preeminence of the president of the republic. Indeed, the constitutional and real powers of the president make him unrivaled as the dominant figure on the Mexican political scene. Although limited to one 6-year term, the president is an extremely powerful leader. Formally, his responsibilities are similar to those of the president of the United States, but his actual powers are much broader. The Mexican president has the power not only to initiate legislation and veto measures passed by Congress but also to delay implementing legislation and, in the absence of congressional action, to implement policy by decree. In practice, the president can count on the cooperation of the Congress to pass the legislation he desires—and little else.

In addition to the generous powers provided by the constitution, his control of the PRI and his popular appeal enhance the president's ascendancy. The PRI controls all aspects of politics at all levels, and the president, as the effective head of the party, uses this control to support his actions. While the party is pluralist in composition and lacks the discipline of a governing communist party, it is a powerful political force that the president can marshal for his ends. The president also benefits from the support of the population. Presidential elections are given considerable attention not because the contest is likely to be close (in fact, the PRI candidate has always won), but because it offers the PRI candidate the opportunity to build an almost personal rapport with the masses. During the campaign the candidate's name and picture are ubiquitous, and he makes an effort to expose himself to as much as the population as possible. For many Mexicans, the president personifies the PRI, the revolution, and Mexico itself; he is a paternal figure who has replaced the *patrón* of old as the object of total commitment and political loyalty. To these considerable powers of the president must be added control of the military and the capacity to use it for political ends. For example, when a protest movement developed in the Yucatan in 1969 over alleged electoral fraud involving the PRI, the president ordered troops to seize the ballot boxes and restore order.

The president is, in effect, an elected benevolent dictator for the duration of his six-year term. He can use his position to promote social change, as did Cárdenas (1934–1940) with agrarian reforms and López Mateos (1958–1964) with medical care, or to maintain the privileges of a few and inhibit social change that adversely affects them, as did Miguel Alemán (1946–1952). In spite of his powers, the president must interact with interest groups, party members, and the formal governmental structures (the judiciary, the Congress, the bureaucracy, and local and state governments). He is not free of political pressure from these and other sections of society, and his success in achieving his goals depends on his ability to win the support of at least some of these groups.

The second of the three supposedly equal branches of the Mexican government is the legislature, which has two chambers: the Senate and the Chamber of Deputies. The Senate has 60 members elected for nonrenewable six-year terms. In practice, all are members of the PRI selected by the president. The lower house, the Chamber of Deputies, has 500 members, each elected in a single-member district for a three-year term. As of 1988, 150 of these seats are allocated to opposition parties; the PRI controls the remaining 350 seats. The participation of minority parties sometimes leads to more enlightened debates, but does little to threaten the overall domination of the Chamber by the PRI majority.

In terms of actual power, the president clearly dominates the Congress. The overwhelming majority of the president's proposed legislation is passed by the Congress unanimously; the rest of his proposals are passed nearly unanimously. Occasionally the president uses the Congress as a means of testing public opinion on potentially controversial issues before taking a stand. On other occasions, highly controversial and divisive issues with little potential for partisan advantage (e.g., abolition of the death penalty) are left for the Congress to thrash out without presidential guidance. In spite of its lack of power and independence, the Mexican Congress serves to legitimize the regime. As one study of the Chamber of Deputies concludes, "The public understands that the Chamber is subservient to the executive; nonetheless, because of the formal authority of the Chamber as national decision-making it stands as a symbol to assure the public that the government will act in a responsible manner."[11]

The constitution of Mexico creates a system of courts, headed by a Supreme Court, to administer the law. Unlike the Mexican Congress, the Supreme Court actually does manifest a certain degree of independence. Nevertheless, political influence is still an important fact in decisions at all levels, including the state court system and local judicial structures. This problem of political intervention is accentuated by the fact that members of the judiciary are always appointed by government officials, usually reflecting the PRI executive's predilections.

Presidential Succession   In the past, the transfer of power from one leader to the next was a traumatic event in Mexico. During the nineteenth century military coups or revolts caused most changes of political leadership. Since the revolution, succession has gradually become regularized, and in the past half-century it has been accomplished without incident. The focus of the succession process is the nomination of the PRI candidate for the presidency. The nomination process involves much elaborate negotiation and maneuvering within the PRI. Needless to say, the incumbent president plays an important and often decisive part in the selection of the candidate. Once the PRI's candidate has been designated, there ensues a brief period of political uncertainty while the candidate builds new loyalties in the PRI and develops a personal bond with the Mexican people. As he does so, he inevitably weakens the incumbent president's authority, and most presidents attempt to delay the nomination of a successor as long as possible to minimize the length of the transition period. Despite the possibility of tension between the outgoing president and the nominee, the process of succession has functioned smoothly since 1940.

Nigeria: Experimenting with Political Frameworks

If a state required nothing more than people and territory to be said to exist, Nigeria has completed some two and a half decades of statehood. However, if it is the development of a constitutional-legal system that

[11]Rudolph O. de la Garza, *The Mexican Chamber of Deputies as a Legitimizing Agent of the Mexican Government and Political System,* Institute of Government Research Series, no. 12 (Tucson: University of Arizona, 1972), p. 24.

marks the state, including rules and procedures for managing political conflicts peacefully, Nigeria's experience with statehood has barely begun. None of the attempts at building a legal basis for the state has survived the test of time. Civilian government failures, frustrated constitutional thrusts, and a military that sees itself as a monitor of the political order have all retarded state-building in Nigeria.

A Succession of Frameworks   The seeds of Nigeria's failures to find an acceptable and workable political framework can be traced to its colonial experience. By uniting groups with differing political, social, and religious values and no prior history of political cooperation, Britain contributed to the creation of severe ethnic tensions. Moreover, the federal structure through which Britain ruled the colony, although clearly responsive to ethnic interests and points of view, strengthened regionalism and allowed differing regional political traditions and institutions to develop. In short, the political framework acknowledged and accentuated ethnic and regional differences, while doing little to promote national integration or weaken interethnic distrust. However, it is questionable whether any alternative political framework—short of creating separate countries—would have been more successful. The federal structure was a British concession to Nigerian demands for greater regional autonomy, and ethnic tensions were probably unavoidable whatever the political framework.

Nigeria's first postindependence constitution was modeled on the British parliamentary system with a governor-general, officially the British monarch's representative, undertaking the largely ceremonial duties of a head of state. In 1963, Nigeria became a republic and these duties were taken over by a president, elected by the Parliament. The Executive Council or cabinet, headed by the prime minister, was selected from the majority party in the House of Representatives, whose 312 members were elected from single-member districts. The country's regional tradition was expressed in a federal structure with strong regional governments and a federal Senate. Most of the 54 senators were chosen by their regional governments to represent the regions, but had little power. They could merely delay legislation and vote on constitutional amendments and alterations of constituencies.

The constitutional framework of the First Republic, as the regime came to be known, never really took root. Structures existed but did not achieve general acceptance because of the strong ethnic-regional divisions present in the country. Mistrust among ethnic groups was reinforced by abuses of the federal scheme, which was flexible enough to encourage those who would assert themselves at the center but too lacking in legitimacy and support to prevail against regional centrifugal forces. The first major abuse was the 1961 effort by the government of the Northern Region to eliminate its political opposition. In a parallel move, opposition at the federal level was reduced when the federal ruling coalition of the Northern People's Congress and the Ibo-dominated NCNC took advantage of a squabble in the Western legislature to suspend the Western Region's government and break up the west's leading party, the Action Group. In addition, the northern-dominated federal government had the 1962 census redone because it showed a significantly lower proportion of the population living in the north; to southerners, this appeared as a blatant attempt to preserve northern domination of the federal Parliament (parliamentary seats were allocated to regions according to population). With alienation and violence running high in the Western Region as a result of blatant manipulation of the 1964 federal election and a subsequent Western Region election by the NPC and its allies, the military intervened in January 1966 and put an end to civilian rule.

The need to eliminate regional cleavages as the major source of political conflict motivated the military's intervention. General Ironsi abolished the regions but did not replace them with any other form of subnational administrative unit. The resulting de facto unitary government, as well as Ironsi's moves to integrate the civil service, further increased mistrust and led to another coup in the summer of 1966 that brought General Gowon to power. Gowon, under military auspices, created 12 states, dismissed the Parliament, and established in 1967 a constitution that created a military government. In place of parliamentary rule, a Supreme Military Council appointed ministers to rule at the national level. The military elite also sought to expand its influence on local political decision-making; the military governors and the state commissioners chosen by them—often with federal and local elite input—exercised considerable power over the local districts and villages. Furthermore, civil servants representing federal ministries gained greater leverage in local political decision-making.

This military-dominated format persisted through most of the 1970s, even though the reinstatement of civilian-elected government had been promised for 1971. Finally, in 1979, a new constitution providing for a presidential system based on the American system came into effect. The executive branch of government was headed by a president elected by universal suffrage to a four-year term. In an effort to limit the ethnic problem in presidential elections, the constitution required presidential candidates to select vice-presidential running mates from outside their own ethnic or regional communities. The winning candidate not only had to gain a majority of the votes but also had to secure "not less than one quarter of the total votes cast in each of at least two-thirds of all the states in the federation." The legislative branch consisted of a National Assembly with two houses: a House of Representatives (450 members) and a Senate (5 members from each state). For a bill to become law, it had to pass both houses of the National Assembly and to be signed by the president. If the president vetoed a bill, it could have become law only if passed in each of the houses by a two-thirds majority. *Different from U.S.*

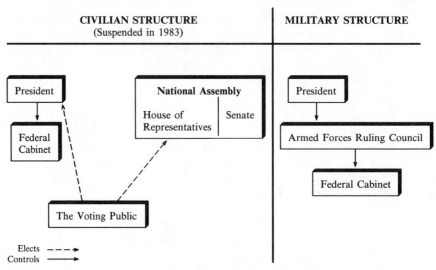

Figure 2.5 Civilian and military government structures in Nigeria, federal level.

Although the constitution of the Second Republic represented a concerted effort to arrive at a workable formula for democratic government, it became mired in widespread corruption and allegations of electoral fraud and was overthrown in the aftermath of the often-violent 1983 election campaign by Major-General Muhammadu Buhari. Since the Babangida coup of 1985, Nigeria has been ruled by a 28-member Armed Forces Ruling Council (AFRC) headed by a president. Under the AFRC is the Federal Cabinet, which exercises executive responsibility at the federal level. Military governors appointed by the president and assisted by Executive Councils are in charge of the state governments.

One area that has been allowed a certain measure of autonomy is the court system. The Nigerian judicial system is an amalgamation of British and traditional Nigerian influences. It consists not only of the Supreme Court of Nigeria and various Western-style courts beneath it but also of Sharia Courts to administer Islamic law in the north and various customary courts to dispense traditional law in other regions. Although the military has the power to appoint judges, British-inherited traditions of judicial independence continue to act as a constraint on political influence in the administration of the law.

Federal Versus Unitary Governance   As noted earlier, the British introduced a federal formula to mollify the various ethnic communities that came under the umbrella of the Nigerian state. This direction was repudiated in the military coup in 1966, when General Ironsi attempted to create a unitary state by abolishing the states and creating centrally controlled provinces in their place. This failed and General Gowon, who succeeded him, restored the federal concept, creating 12 states to replace the four regions. While the attempt to implement the federal idea was present, the practice of federalism in an inherently centralized military regime is somewhat contradictory. In 1976 Murtala Muhammed helped undercut state power by reducing their size (creating 19 states out of 12) and making them more dependent on the center.[12] Revenue collection, for example, was centralized. Under the Second Republic, the federal concept was given new life. State governors and legislatures were independently elected and considerable decision-making latitude was left to these governments and to local government. The Buhari coup ended this and restored the military conception of federal rule—direct central military control over the states.

Although Nigeria is presently ruled from the center by a military government, it is unclear just how long this situation will last. In 1986 indications were given by the Babangida regime that decision making might be opened up. In early 1986 President Babangida said he would allow "for debate on the future of Nigerian politics. A political bureau would be established to study a new political program to prepare for a handover of power."[13] He also suggested that the task would be to find a just system—above all a Nigerian solution, one that would allow participation and equitable distribution of wealth and opportunities. By 1987 plans had been drawn up which would lead to the full restoration of a presidential regime by 1992. It remains to be seen whether these plans will come into fruition, or whether leadership selection will continue to be determined in the barracks rather than through the ballot box.

CONCLUSIONS

We have seen that one of the most basic challenges any country must face is the provision of widely accepted mechanisms by which political leaders can be chosen and political decisions affecting society made and that one of the most common obstacles to meeting this challenge is the existence of ethnic, regional, or class cleavages that inhibit the emergence of a single national will on these matters. One solution to this dilemma lies in the recognition and accommodation of diversity through either vertical or horizontal divisions of powers (or both); the former allocates considerable authority to autonomous states or provinces in recognition of the fact that different problems may be faced and different solutions preferred in different regions of the country; the latter checks the potential for abuse of governmental powers by splitting authority among distinct institutions of central government. Another solution is to use the powers of government to impose the will of those who control it on a divided and potentially recalcitrant population.

[12] In 1987 the number of states was increased to 21.
[13] *West Africa* (January 13, 1986), p. 106.

Britain is a classic example of how the early achievement of national integration (particularly within England itself) and the early development of central state institutions permitted a relatively easy evolution toward democratic government. In Britain today, power is centralized both vertically and horizontally, not because rulers were led to impose unity on a divided population but because national integration is advanced enough and the legitimacy of state institutions strong enough that the need for checks on government authority is not strongly felt. France also developed the institutions of the modern state relatively early, but there the state did emerge in part out of the need to impose internal unity on a divided country. Although the need for a strong state has been felt by the French for centuries, the political disunity of the country tended to make a parliamentary form of government rather unstable and ineffective. For France, the solution has been to graft a powerful presidency onto the parliamentary framework.

In the Soviet Union and China, the circumstances were rather different. In those countries, the traditions of authoritarian rule combined with significant degrees of regionalism and a strongly felt need for state-led modernization to produce systems of government that, while resembling parliamentary democracies in their institutional frameworks, are actually single-party dictatorships. While it would be incorrect to assume that their governmental structures are irrelevant or that they lack legitimacy, we must always be aware that the formal dictates of constitutionality or legality can at any time be sacrificed to the political will of the ruling party leadership.

Third World countries, because they so often lack long histories as independent states, frequently face great problems in maintaining national unity and in establishing effective and legitimate governmental institutions. In these circumstances, the attempt to accommodate diversity horizontally through a checks-and-balances system of government or vertically through federalism is likely to give way to authoritarian solutions. Although both Nigeria and Mexico set out to be federal states, Mexico is in practice highly centralized and Nigeria has become so under military rule. Mexico, however, has achieved much more in the overall institutionalization of government, that is, in developing regularized processes for making and implementing public policy decisions and for transferring power from one set of leaders to the next. Regional and religious cleavages are now much less severe in Mexico than in the past, and the military—formerly a destabilizing factor—has been brought under control. However, one debilitating problem remains: Mexico's failure to deal with its serious class cleavages. Class division, as we shall see in the next chapter, is the factor most likely to destabilize Mexican politics.

With a far shorter history of independence, Nigeria has much farther to go in the pursuit of stable political institutions. The coups of 1966 and 1983 were setbacks in that regard, but Nigeria's military rulers have maintained a commitment to democratization. It remains to be seen whether the military's attempts to alter the conditions that destroyed earlier political frameworks, to regulate ethnic conflict, and to improve social and economic conditions will provide a firmer basis for liberal democracy in Nigeria.

chapter *3*

Society and Politics

INTRODUCTION

Politics is never a world unto itself. Since politics concerns the processes by which societies are governed, political systems or polities are necessarily in relationships of mutual interdependence with their societies. Most people are aware that governments create and enforce decisions that regulate human behavior; from the taxes we pay on consumer goods to the traffic rules that govern the way we drive to work or school, the impact of governmental decisions on our daily lives is unmistakable. Much less attention is given, however, to the opposite process, which involves the ways in which society influences political decision-making. Although less evident in our daily lives, the effect that demands and constraints emanating from within society has on the functioning of the political arena goes to the very essence of what we mean by politics. In this chapter we shall explore some of its dimensions.

The most obvious way in which the society at large affects politics is by presenting problems which the political system must attempt to solve. When high levels of unemployment, inflation, or poverty are generated with the economic system of a developed country, it is government that is usually expected to tackle the matter. Similarly, social problems such as crime, urban decay, or violent demonstrations regularly challenge governments to find appropriate remedies.

Often governments can do little more than ameliorate the impact of these problems. One major reason for this is that these problems frequently emanate from or touch upon profound societal divisions, known as *social cleavages,* that are strongly rooted and capable of generating intense conflict. Generally speaking, we may divide social cleavages into two basic categories: (1) those based on fundamental divisions of religion, language, ethnicity, or race and (2) those based on "function" or relative position in the economic order, including class cleavages. A third type, geographically based or regional cleavages, is also salient in many societies but generally reflects either economic differences or cultural/ethnic differences (or both) and therefore can be subsumed under the first two categories.

Since social cleavages lie at the heart of so much social, economic, and political conflict, it is not surprising that they have become a topic of great disagreement and debate within the social sciences. Two of the most important issues debated concern which type of cleavage is the more basic or central and whether there are effective and morally acceptable means by which cleavage conflict can be kept within reasonable bounds. These issues, which often pit Marxist against non-Marxist scholars, are examined in the following two sections.

The Primacy-of-Class Debate

Many of the founding fathers of social science, including Karl Marx, believed that the first category of cleavages was destined to die away in modern industrial societies. As industrialization proceeded, they felt that such "preindustrial" bases of division as religion and language would gradually lose their significance and be replaced by the class cleavage. Marx, in particular, argued that as industrial capitalism matured, societies would increasingly become divided into just two fundamental and antagonistic classes: those who owned property (the *bourgeoisie*) and those who did not (the *proletariat*). By property Marx did not mean personal possessions but rather what is often termed "the means of production, distribution, and exchange," that is, businesses that provide goods or services for profit. Under capitalism, Marx felt, the basic impulse of the bourgeoisie is to retain as much as possible of the earnings of its businesses for itself. As a result of the bourgeoisie's proclivity to maximize profits, the class of workers or proletarians—which actually performs most of the work in those businesses—will become ever more impoverished. Eventually, a realization or consciousness that the capitalist system is unjust and exploitative will come to prevail among the ranks of the proletariat. Since the bourgeoisie will want to preserve at all costs the system that profits it so well, Marx predicted that the proletariat will ultimately be driven to violent revolution in order to overthrow capitalism and establish a more just system based on the common ownership of property. In Marx's perspective, such a development corresponds to the direction of historical development; just as feudalism was replaced by capitalism, so capitalism will have to give way to the next (and final) stage in human history, the era of communism.

To what extent are these beliefs correct? Consider the belief that ethnic and cultural cleavages die away with modernization. Certainly, one can point to cases where modernization has caused, or at least has been accompanied by, this effect. In Britain, the antagonism between the Scots and the English, which often involved bloodshed in the past, has diminished a great deal over the centuries, and the Scots have been assimilated to the extent of having largely lost their native language. The same may be said of ethnic minorities such as the Bretons in France. In the United States, modernization has eroded the cultural and economic distinctiveness of the American south, and a civil war between regions of the country now seems quite inconceivable.

Two decades ago, it was common for observers to project these developments onto a world scale. Many felt that the spread of films, television—even rock music—would foster a homogenization of cultures around the world, a "global village" as Marshall McLuhan put it.[1] Surprisingly, it now appears that the enhanced communications and more rapid transportation that come with modernization have more often had the opposite effect, at least in the shorter term: They have made individuals more aware of just how much they and their people differ from other peoples. Indeed, it may be exposure to other cultures that crystallizes cultural identities. This appears to have been the case in many former colonies, where the process of mobilizing individuals from different ethnic or religious groups to fight for independence has hampered the subsequent task of forging a single national identity after victory has been achieved. An early example is the Indian fight for independence from Britain. Hindus and Moslems had lived together peacefully for some time in the Indian subcontinent, but the mobilization of both communities to fight British control abruptly ended that state of affairs. Once the British had conceded independence in 1947, violence of such intensity occurred between Hindus and Moslems that the leaders of the dominant Hindu community felt obliged to agree to the partitioning of India and the creation of a separate state, Pakistan, for the Moslem minority.

In the past, it was usually assumed that such problems were symptomatic only of the early stages of development, but it is now clear that even in the developed world, the existence of separate ethnic, linguistic, or religious identities often continues to pose problems or suddenly creates problems long after integration was thought to have been achieved. In the Soviet Union, authoritarian one-party rule since 1917, combined at times with heavy reliance on terror and police state tactics, has largely failed to dissolve the cultural distinctiveness and ethnic awareness of

[1]H. M. McLuhan, *Understanding Media: The Extensions of Man* (New York: McGraw-Hill, 1964).

many of the non-Russian peoples who constitute nearly half of the country's population. The early goal of forging a "new Soviet man" has had to be quietly set aside. In the 1960s and 1970s, American scholars came to the realization that the image of the United States as a great "melting pot" is overdrawn: ethnic (not to mention racial) identities have survived surprisingly well, even though most citizens are, or are descended from, immigrants who voluntarily left their own native lands. Nor have the much older nation-states of France and Britain escaped a resurgence of peripheral nationalism in recent years. In France, Breton and Occitan groups, fearful of the total extinction of their languages and cultures, have begun to demand greater recognition for their ancestral tongues, including the right for their children to study those languages at school. In Britain, Scottish and Welsh nationalist groups have gone beyond language rights to demand autonomy for their countries. While such demands have failed to elicit majority support within these groups, the fact that they have arisen and received considerable support after centuries-long processes of assimilation of the groups into larger nation-states is cause for considerable wonderment.

Western scholars generally approach the issue of social cleavages from a very different perspective than do Marxists. Instead of looking at them in terms of their supposed place in the flow of human history, they have focused instead on the means by which cleavage conflicts can be kept within tolerable bounds. Regimes basically have two options in managing social cleavages: they may use the power of the state to repress dissent, or they may provide mechanisms through which differences between sectors of their populations can be reconciled. The class cleavage provides an excellent illustration. Few in the West deny that it exists, but most feel it has been handled reasonably well in democratic societies by granting workers the right to form unions and negotiate (or strike) for better wages and working conditions, as well as by extending to them the right to vote for parties or leaders who promise to advance their interests in government. Thus, the legal recognition of economic and political rights for the working class, which largely occurred in Western countries in the period from the late nineteenth century to the early twentieth century, has provided workable mechanisms by which its claims for a larger share of society's wealth can be advanced. In contrast, communist regimes, which assert that they are ruled by their working classes, in reality keep their working classes subordinate to their overall employer, the state, through the state's control of unions and its willingness to use the criminal justice system to stifle dissent. Occasionally, rumors of a factory strike filter out of the Soviet Union, but these rumors are typically denied by the state, which continues to maintain that class actions such as strikes cannot and therefore do not occur in socialist societies. Where such activities cannot be denied, official government sources may blame them on outside agitators or spies working for the Western powers.

Apart from the effect engendered by granting workers economic and political rights, many Western social scientists have concluded that class conflict has remained of limited intensity in democratic countries because, contrary to the Marxist thesis, economic disputes are inherently *easier* to resolve than differences that touch on religious, linguistic, or ethnic/racial concerns. Most economic disputes are ultimately about money, and since money can be divided up in any number of ways, it is generally possible to find a middle position or compromise that gives something to each side. When religious belief or ethnic prejudice enters the picture, however, an acceptable compromise is often much more difficult to achieve. In the 1970s, the question of whether or not to legalize divorce proved to be highly divisive in Italy because it violated a central tenet of the teachings of the Roman Catholic Church and was felt by many Catholics to be a matter that could not be left to individual choice. Today, in the United States and elsewhere, a similar stance is taken by Catholics and fundamentalist Protestants with respect to abortion: it offends their religious and moral beliefs to such an extent that they will acknowledge no possibility of compromise (many "pro-choice" supporters are just as adamant).

If ethnic or racial prejudice is involved, it becomes especially difficult to reason out a solution to disputes. In Canada, much of the recent trouble between English and French speakers ultimately comes down to an unwillingness on the part of some English speakers to acknowledge the rights of French Canadians to have their language used in government, law courts, and educational institutions. Behind such beliefs may lie nothing more than a feeling of discomfort at hearing a foreign language spoken or at having to coexist with others who clearly do not share the same cultural values, norms, or practices. The presence of visible differences, as in race, seems to lend itself particularly well to the propagation of notions of superiority or inferiority that can hamper well-meaning attempts at equal treatment. Given the resilience of these kinds of divisions, it is not surprising that class often appears the least dangerous, rather than the most dangerous, of cleavages.

How do the Marxists respond to these points? First of all, they have recognized for a long time that workers can be "bought off" by capitalists through wage increases, recognition of the right to form unions, and other concessions. It is bound to be difficult to convince a worker to remain faithful to the cause of world revolution when his family is starving and he needs gainful employment. Even if he is not in desperate need, cash in hand naturally seems a lot more sensible to many than waiting for the distant goal of revolution.

This response does not fully address the issue, however, since workers could accept the money but still remain aware of the basic injustice of the system. Other considerations have therefore been brought into play. The first consideration is that workers in a market-oriented society become socialized into accepting its norms and values. One of those values is "possessive individualism,"[2] the idea that each individual's ultimate goal is to provide for his own (and his family's) material well-being. Marxists argue that it is especially difficult in a climate of possessive individualism to accept and cooperate fully in collective action such as strikes or revolutionary movements, which demand that the individual sacrifice his personal short-term advantage for the future good of his fellow workers or of the working class as a whole. In addition, it is often alleged that a much more active process of socialization is at work in capitalist societies. Those who control the levers of the economy, Marxists believe, also control the state and most of the other dominant institutions in society—the military, the mass media, the schools and universities, even the churches. Through these institutions, messages are put out that downplay the idea of class antagonism and emphasize instead values of patriotism, harmony, and the basic rightness of the society and the economy in its present form. In this respect, the state has a very important role to play. Marxists believe that the state is ultimately responsible for the survival of capitalism and the prevention of socialist revolution; it must therefore take an active role in nurturing values and orientations which support society and government as it is. In the pursuit of this goal, the state relies heavily on patriotic and nationalistic values and symbols, including the flag, the national anthem, and a substantial dose of ceremonial pageantry. It fosters a perspective on history that places great emphasis on the "glories" of the country's past and the virtues of its present. State-controlled educational systems are essential in this task: they propagate a vision of society that is basically benevolent, skirting over historical instances of class conflict or oppression and avoiding any mention of the possibility that society could be structurally flawed.

At this point, the issue tends to become more a matter of personal belief than of empirical evidence, for it begins to touch on fundamental conceptions of human nature. Clearly, governments do socialize people, particularly young people, into the ways of their economic and political systems. Just as clearly, they portray these systems as right, fair, just, and so forth. Is this manipulation? It is, if one believes the systems in question are inherently bad. Marxists often premise their rejection of Western societies on the argument that even if the material circumstances of workers have improved since Marx's time, what really matters is control over one's destiny, and the levers of power in capitalist societies are firmly in the hands of the bourgeoisie. One can be well-off in terms of wages, Marxists argue, but still be alienated or incomplete as a human being. The media, especially through advertising, attempt to teach people to focus their aspirations on the acquisition of material goods, but human nature is such that possessions alone cannot lead to human happiness. Thus, at the base of Western capitalist societies, despite their

[2]C. B. Macpherson, *The Theory of Possessive Individualism* (London: Oxford University Press, 1962).

wealth, Marxists believe they have found a fundamental flaw that must, and should, lead to their destruction.

Many non-Marxist Western scholars have accepted the thrust of this perspective without endorsing its conclusion of revolution. It has been pointed out, for example, that certain classic theorists of democracy, including Aristotle and Jean-Jacques Rousseau, emphasized the importance to the individual of having a say in shaping the environment in which he lives. Rousseau also argued that democracy could not function well if disparities between individuals in wealth were too great, for the possession of wealth brings with it disproportionate power and influence. Using these arguments, a sizable school of thought has emerged since the 1960s advocating the introduction of some measure of "industrial democracy" so that the workplace would be more democratic and employees less subject to authoritarian rules and therefore less alienated. A similar line of thought was pursued by the psychologist Abraham Maslow, who hypothesized that there exists a hierarchy of human needs, beginning with physical safety and sustenance and followed by the higher-level needs of belongingness, esteem, and finally "self-actualization," that is, aesthetic and intellectual satisfaction.[3] Once the lower-level needs have been taken care of, Maslow argued, people naturally seek to satisfy the higher-level ones. Since material existence has been largely assured in Western countries, Ronald Inglehart has interpreted this hypothesis to mean that nonmaterial demands including more participation by the individual in government, on the job, and in the community (which he views as part of "belongingness") should become more important as political issues.[4] Survey data analyzed by Inglehart have indeed revealed indications that a political value reorientation of this sort is under way in Western democratic countries, particularly among the younger generations.

What is common to most of these viewpoints is the belief that Western societies are basically sound and can evolve or reform themselves to overcome any pressing deficiencies related to their economic systems. Only time will tell for sure whether this or the Marxist prediction is the more accurate, but what of the apparently much more salient noneconomic cleavages? Where they are not regarded as idiosyncratic or due to die away, the most common response from the Marxist school is to attribute the strength of cleavages based on ethnicity, race, religion, or language to their connection to social class. Thus, ethnic or racial groups conflict in situations where one group exploits or represses the other economically; in a situation of equality, it is argued, such groups would not be antagonistic. Once again, there is an important kernel of truth in this position. Usually, antagonism based on eth-

---

[3]A. H. Maslow, *Motivation and Personality* (New York: Harper, 1954).

[4]R. Inglehart, *The Silent Revolution: Changing Values and Political Styles Among Western Publics* (Princeton, N.J.: Princeton University Press, 1977).

nicity or culture does involve groups that are unequal in power and wealth; the economic inequality between Catholics and Protestants in Northern Ireland or, to cite a more extreme example, between blacks and whites in white-dominated South Africa is a fundamental source of discontent in those societies. But the Marxist interpretation also contains the implication that since class is at the root of the matter, true class alliances and class conflict should emerge at some point. This means that, sooner or later, the white working class in South Africa should unite with its black counterparts to overthrow the rule of the white bourgeoisie. Similarly, Protestant and Catholic workers in Northern Ireland should unite against their Protestant and Catholic bourgeois employers. Neither prediction seems at all likely. It is quite clear that the ethnic/religious cleavage in Northern Ireland and the racial one in South Africa stand in their own right; they cannot be reduced to differences of class. Indeed, if class alone mattered, the Marxist interpretation would lead us to expect that the bourgeoisies of the two societies would have been able to contain these conflicts through their manipulative control of the mass media and the educational systems, which they have manifestly not been able to do.

The Management of Cleavage Conflict

The position of most Western social scientists, as we have seen, is that noneconomic cleavages are likely to be more difficult to contain within manageable bounds than economic or class cleavages. This raises an interesting question of its own: What limits the manifestations of noneconomic cleavage conflict in most divided societies, particularly those which are unwilling or unable to use force to repress dissent? One obvious means of quelling potential discontent is to grant equal political and economic rights to all citizens, but it must be recognized that this may not be enough. If a widespread prejudice exists against a particular group, a formal equality before the law will not necessarily end the discrimination it suffers from in society. If a clash of fundamental religious beliefs is at stake, neither side may be willing to let a majority of votes decide the issue. The more intensely held the beliefs, the more deep-seated the prejudice, the less likely it is that pragmatism and compromise can diffuse the point of contention.

The Crosscutting Cleavage Hypothesis   A major hypothesis that has been put forward to account for the phenomenon of conflict containment states that cleavages of both types become manageable to the extent that they *crosscut* or overlap one another. This hypothesis contains both psychological and sociological components, as the following example illustrates. Consider the case of a Catholic steelworker in the United States who is an active member of both his parish church and his trade union. As a church member, he interacts with other Catholics from a variety of walks of life, including presumably members of the middle class. With them he shares certain religious, moral, and ethical beliefs that form the basis of their association. As a union member, on the other hand, he unites with other workers, Catholic and non-Catholic, with the objective of exacting as much as possible in wages and benefits from management. The psychological component of the hypothesis holds that it will be very difficult for this Catholic steelworker to be intensely hostile toward either non-Catholics or members of the middle class because he has something in common with each group. He cannot hate non-Catholics so easily since he cooperates with them to fight their middle-class employers; but neither can he hate the middle class, for he interacts with and shares basic beliefs with middle-class Catholics that are contradicted or opposed by non-Catholics, including many of his working-class brethren. The result of these cross-pressures will be, according to the hypothesis, a moderation in the individual's opinions and attitudes. Issues that touch on religion or class will not be seen in black-and-white terms as "us" versus "them," since on each type of issue the "them" includes people who would be part of the "us" on the other issue type.

The sociological component of this hypothesis concerns whether the individual's society is structured so as to produce this result. Specifically, the salient cleavages in society must crosscut or overlap one another in order to generate the conflicting pressures that lead to moderation. If they coincide so that, to pursue the example, all Catholics are members of the working class and all non-Catholics belong to the middle class, the opposite effect should be produced. Whenever the steelworker is involved in a labor dispute, he would be pitted against not just members of a different class but members of a different religion as well; his antagonism should therefore be all the greater. An additional sociological facet of the hypothesis is that society must be highly organized; if the steelworker was involved, say, only in his union, the moderating effect of interacting with middle-class Catholics would not take effect, or at least not to the same extent.

The Consociational Alternative   The crosscutting cleavages hypothesis assumes that a society's social structure is the prime cause of cleavage conflict and implies that there is very little anyone can do about it if it so happens that the structure is not conducive to political moderation. Several European political scientists have pointed out, however, that there exists an important class of *segmented* societies in Europe which have managed to function in a stable and democratic fashion despite the presence of deep societal divisions that do not crosscut one another. This group includes, or has included, such countries as the Netherlands, Belgium, Switzerland, and Austria. The basic condition for the success of these *consociational democracies,* as Arend Lijphart has termed them, is a profound desire on the part of leaders of all segments to make their political systems work in spite of the cleavages that divide them.[5] Usually, this commitment involves a willingness to respect the fundamental interests of each segment, regardless of whether the segment is in power or not. Majority rule, in other words, is kept within strict limits. A second feature of this arrangement is that most of the benefits that governments control are allocated in proportion to the size of the segments. Thus, if a party representing one segment receives 40 percent of the vote, it should receive not only 40 percent of the seats in the country's parliament but also 40 percent of public sector jobs and public housing units for distribution to its supporters, and so forth. The proportionality in the allocation of government benefits implies a third feature of consociational democracies, the high level of organization of each segment. To the extent that each segment handles its own affairs, the likelihood of friction between the segments will be reduced. It is essential, therefore, that each segment have the organizational infrastructure to assume a wide array of public functions. In addition, if an individual's organizational life is bound up in segmental organizations that take care of most or all of his public needs, he will be more likely to follow obediently the decisions and policies of his segment's leadership. This is seen as necessary because the leaders of each segment must make compromises with the leaders of the other segments if the system is to survive, and their followers have to be willing to acquiesce in those compromises. In a sense, a high degree of segmental organization may be thought of as the sociological condition that compensates for the lack of crosscutting cleavages to moderate political divisions.

The desire to make the system work is central to the consociational solution; without it, no amount of segmental organization or proportionality will suffice. The Netherlands, the textbook case of consociational democracy, has had centuries in which to develop consociational practices to reconcile its Calvinist and Catholic citizens. Austria, another major example, developed its consociational system after the bitter experiences of civil war between its two segments, the Socialists and the Catholics, in the 1930s, war and military defeat in the 1940s, and finally occupation by foreign powers, which lasted until 1955. Such circumstances are, however, quite rare; in today's world few countries are as old as the Netherlands or as humiliated as Austria in 1945. It is perhaps for this reason that consociational democracies are not common, even though there is no scarcity of cleavage-ridden societies.

The Third World Dilemma   The newer states that emerged from the process of postwar decolonization are particularly likely to find themselves plagued with the problems of severe ethnic antagonism. In many cases,

[5]A. Lijphart, *The Politics of Accommodation: Pluralism and Democracy in the Netherlands,* 2nd ed. (Berkeley: University of California Press, 1975).

they emerged from colonial territories which lumped together distinct peoples who had had no previous tradition of living together in the same polity. Their struggles for liberation called for the creation of ideologies that emphasized unity and nationalism, not cultural and ethnic diversity. Consociational practices would have seemed ill-suited to their requirements because they are, in a certain sense, the very antithesis of the nation-state ideal: they demand the jettisoning of the goal of "one nation" in order to preserve the unity of the country. In its emphasis on decentralization, consociationalism is akin to federalism; but, like federalism, it finds little favor with leaders whose task involves fighting off external enemies or catching up with more advanced countries.

Leaders in these situations are far more likely to opt for authoritarian government, seeing in democracy, especially if it entails consociational arrangements, the seeds of disunity and dismemberment of the country. Often in such cases, the preferred model is the Soviet Union, which used one-party control to help keep a diverse country together and force through economic development. Where socialism is not adopted, the solution may simply be a military dictatorship, lacking the ideological justifications of the Soviet model and relying much more exclusively on the use of force to control dissidence. The use of force, however, often breeds forceful responses in the form of riots, guerrilla movements, and perhaps even full-fledged civil war, as Nigeria experienced in the late 1960s.

The Ideological Dimension of Conflict

A final noteworthy feature of social cleavages is that they are often associated with conflicting ideologies or belief systems. Where economic inequalities are particularly strongly felt, workers and their leaders usually turn to some version of Marxist ideology in order to account for their present situation, to suggest a better future, and to mobilize support for that goal (their employers are just as eager to espouse and propagate a free-market ideology). Ethnic or racial differences often generate ideologies which rest upon some version of genetic or cultural superiority: The "white man's burden" of the British imperialists; the "civilizing mission" of the French Empire; the Nazi doctrine of Aryan superiority are major twentieth-century examples. Religious differences are especially touchy because what might be permitted or even lauded in one faith may be anathema to another. Frequently, religious conviction spills over even more directly into politics. In Iran, the overthrow of the Shah in 1979 was orchestrated by religious leaders who sought to establish an "Islamic Republic," a state guided by fundamental Islamic beliefs and morality.

The importance of ideological differences does not rest solely with the fact that they are the verbal expressions of underlying social cleavages; their significance is also related to their tendency to survive the circumstances of their birth. In France, the outbreak of revolution in 1789 divided the country between those who supported the revolution's democratic goals and those who preferred a monarchy, a division of belief that largely reflected contemporary differences in social class and religious belief (since the Catholic Church favored monarchism). Yet that basic division persisted for over a century and a half. Even today, the best predictor of whether a French citizen will vote for the Left (Socialists or Communists) or the Right is how frequently he or she goes to church—in spite of the fact that the church assumes a stance of neutrality vis-à-vis elections.

Ideologies also acquire a life of their own because their appeal is often rooted in basic human propensities. Liberal ideologies often appeal to the propensity to bargain, to resolve differences, to achieve harmony through compromise. More authoritarian ideologies value unity, strength, and control as a means of achieving a better society. These propensities are not simply reactions to a given situation; often they reflect differences in political culture that may have existed for very long periods of time. Thus, when Nazi Germany collapsed in 1945, the Western allies sought not just to expunge the Nazi ideology of Aryan racial superiority but also to eliminate what they saw as its cultural mainstay, the German predisposition to authoritarianism. A massive program of reeducation of adult Germans and reform of the school system was undertaken in West Germany, with what appears now to have had quite remarkable results.[6] As with the consociational solution to social cleavages, however, the solution of resocialization to different values is one that most probably can be effected only in certain fairly unusual circumstances, such as the total discrediting of the previous belief system. We are therefore much more likely to see conflict emanating from profound social cleavages as a prominent feature of politics in many of the world's states for a long time to come.

BRITAIN AND FRANCE: CLEAVAGE MANAGEMENT IN LIBERAL DEMOCRACIES

Both Britain and France are pluralistic in their social and political structures; that is, they permit their citizens to organize themselves freely into groups for a wide variety of purposes. The pluralistic theory of democracy assumes that society contains a wide variety of different interests that must be allowed expression and that government should be at least somewhat responsive to those interests. It also assumes that social competition and conflict are inevitable and indeed may well be beneficial to society. Thus, the doctrine implicitly rejects the Marxist premises (a)

[6]For a good account of these changes, see D. Conradt, "Changing German Political Culture," in G. Almond and S. Verba, eds., *The Civic Culture Revisited* (Boston: Little, Brown, 1980).

that the existence of social cleavages, particularly between classes, necessarily indicates that the social system is defective in some respect and (b) that a different social system would eliminate such cleavages.

This is not to say that any degree of conflict is welcomed by believers in pluralistic democracy. Clearly, there must also be some forces of cohesion to counteract the divisive tendencies of untamed cleavage conflict if the system is to survive at all. Both Britain and France, two very old nation-states, have developed strong bonds of allegiance and loyalty that help to moderate tensions and keep them, for the most part, within manageable bounds. There have been occasions in recent times, however, when they have been severely pressed by social conflicts. In this section we consider the principal cleavages that affect British and French societies, the forces that act to contain them, and the likely evolution in the balance between the two.

Britain: Conflict on Several Fronts

A British political scientist once observed that "class is the basis of British politics; all else is embellishment and detail."[7] What he had in mind was the strong tendency for middle- and upper-class voters to support the Conservative party and for working-class voters to vote for the Labour party. Class structures British society much more profoundly, however, than is indicated solely by voting patterns. Class differences are noticeable not just in income, occupation (white collar or blue collar), and education but also in such matters as accent, speech patterns, dress, favorite sports, residence, and type of schooling to an extent that can scarcely be imagined by North Americans. A well-delineated system of class distinctions is one of the most prominent inheritances from Britain's feudal and aristocratic past, and its presence is felt, consciously or not, by all Britons.

In principle, class should largely be a matter of individual achievement: the higher-status jobs and larger incomes are supposed to go to those with better business skills, greater intellectual abilities, and so forth. Although this is true to a certain extent in Britain, much of what class differences represent in British society is *ascriptive,* that is, related to the station in life into which one was born. Using accent as an unspoken criterion in hiring is a good example; so is the establishment of different types of schools to educate the children of different classes. Since the 1960s, the Labour party has attempted to address the latter form of social differentiation by creating so-called comprehensive secondary schools. These schools have been established to replace the two-tier state system of "secondary modern" schools teaching vocational skills to working-class children and grammar schools catering to the

---

[7]P. Pulzer, *Political Representation and Elections: Parties and Voting in Great Britain* (New York: Praeger, 1967), p. 98.

academic aspirations of middle-class children. The object is to reduce the distance between social classes by educating all children in the same institutions[8] and to delay segregation into vocational and academic streams until the full potential of each child has had an adequate opportunity to demonstrate itself. To North Americans, who know such institutions simply as "high schools," nothing seems more normal, but in Britain, where schoolchildren had previously been selected for one stream or the other at the very early age of 11, it has been a highly controversial innovation. The Conservative party sees comprehensive schools as a threat to educational standards; its opponents would argue that what they represent is a challenge to the ability of the middle class to keep academic performance, and hence higher-status careers, as fully within the embrace of its offspring as it has been in the past.

The potential for class conflict in Britain has been apparent since the early nineteenth century. The industrial revolution, which began in the late eighteenth century, stimulated the growth of a large urban working class whose grievances—from poor housing and working conditions to low wages and high food prices—provoked considerable unrest in the first half of the 1800s. Karl Marx and Friedrich Engels, two of the fathers of the communist movement, studied the conditions of the English working class and concluded that England would lead the world in the revolutionary overthrow of capitalism and its replacement by communism. That this was not merely wishful thinking on the part of revolutionaries is indicated by the considerable extent to which the matter also attracted the attention of conservative, middle-class Britons. The notion that England was really constituted of two nations, the rich and the poor, was made famous by no less a figure than the Conservative prime minister Benjamin Disraeli, who pushed through the Second Reform Act in 1867, extending the vote to most urban workers. His hope was that the admission of the working class into the political arena would allay its radical potential and make workers loyal and law-abiding citizens—and perhaps even Conservative party supporters as well.

Disraeli's belief that the working class could be successfully incorporated into the political system turned out to be largely true, although whether it was gratitude, increasing prosperity, passive acquiescence, or indoctrination that ultimately dissipated working-class unrest is a subject of considerable debate, as we saw in Chapter 1. What is undeniable is that when trade unions turned their attention to politics, their efforts bore fruit in the form of a Labour party dedicated to a peaceful, parliamentary route to change. Nevertheless, the potential for a flare-up of class confrontation has remained a feature of British life. In 1926 a bitter, six-month general strike was staged by the union movement to fight

---

[8]For the same reason, the Labour party has also proclaimed the goal of abolishing private schools, known in Britain as "public schools," which have for centuries educated most of Britain's elites. The party has yet to act on this very controversial commitment.

wage rollbacks imposed by employers and supported by the government. In the depression years of the 1930s, hostility between classes became especially severe. It declined considerably in the affluent years of the 1950s and early 1960s, but as Britain's economic situation deteriorated in the 1970s and early 1980s, labor unrest and radicalism increased once again.

Today, the situation is almost schizophrenic. On the one hand, the union movement declined in numbers and support in the face of large increases in unemployment between 1979 and 1985 and of a Conservative government, led by Prime Minister Thatcher, which has taken on the task of whittling down its power and legal rights. On the other hand, many unions have come increasingly under the influence of radicals outrightly devoted to ending capitalism and introducing some form of socialist economy. For them, the economic decline in Britain is ample testimony to the fact that capitalism does not work (at least in Britain) and must be replaced.

The polarization reached a climax in the 1984–1985 coalminers' strike. The strike was launched at the instigation of the Marxist leader of the National Union of Coalminers (NUC), Arthur Scargill, who wished not only to protect mining jobs and improve wages but also to bring down the Thatcher government. Fearing that strike action would not be supported by the rank and file of the union if it were put to a vote (as required by the union constitution), Scargill persuaded the union executive to declare a strike anyway. The result was a bitter year-long work stoppage, supported by most miners but opposed by a sizable minority and marred by considerable violence against those who continued working. In the end the strike failed, but it left both a split union movement and a legacy of considerable bitterness against the government, which owned the coal mines and had so vigorously opposed the NUC. It was symptomatic both of the weakness and division in the union movement in recent years and of the increasing radicalization of a portion of workers who see their jobs and their unions threatened by a government bent on promoting free enterprise and economic efficiency at all costs.

The periodic manifestations of intense class-based hostility in Britain can be explained in part by the lack of crosscutting cleavages in Britain. When Disraeli spoke of two nations, he had in mind two classes which hardly interacted at all, except in relationships of master and servant or employer and employee. Even today, the differentiation noted earlier in accent, residence, and type of schooling bespeaks two subcultures that are isolated one from each other to a considerable extent. In contrast, the similarity between classes in the United States, particularly in accent, suggests the greater fluidity of its society. Another indication of the greater mobility of American society is the enormous shift in population from the northeast of the country to the prosperous south and west that has occurred since 1970. The northern part of Britain, once the prosperous cradle of the industrial revolution, has experienced economic decline and higher unemployment since the 1920s, but a population shift of American proportions to the much more prosperous south has not taken place. Instead, governments have been expected to institute policies designed to attract or keep industry and jobs in the north—something which would be unheard of in the United States. Many of the "bailouts" of declining British industries by the government, often criticized as being inefficient uses of public funds, have been motivated by concerns over high unemployment in northern areas. Increasingly, political commentators in Britain have been using the metaphor of "two nations" to refer to the unprosperous, largely working-class north, where the Labour party is predominant, and the prosperous, middle-class south, controlled by the Conservatives. This suggests a coincidence of region with economic condition that could create severe problems in the future if economic circumstances do not improve.

The Struggle in Northern Ireland   The crosscutting cleavage hypothesis can be used to even greater effect to explain the most severe cleavage conflict in the United Kingdom, the "troubles" in Northern Ireland. The rift between the two communities of that province is usually cast in terms of religion, but this is misleading; Protestants and Catholics, after all, coexist perfectly well throughout the Western world. What the labels "Protestant" and "Catholic" really represent in Northern Ireland is a cumulation of cleavages. One cleavage is that of ethnicity. Most Protestants are

Women supporters of the IRA demonstrate against a 1976 march for peace in Northern Ireland as London's "bobbies" (police) look on. (Chris Perkins / Magnum)

descendants of Scottish immigrants brought to Ireland in past centuries to colonize it; the Catholic community is composed of the native Irish. In addition, the two communities live geographically separated lives, with their own neighborhoods, pubs (bars), and community institutions; very little interaction between Protestants and Catholics takes place. Finally, the Catholic community is less well-off economically, a factor that is aggravated by the perception among Catholics that the Protestant-dominated regional governments of the past discriminated against them. Thus even the provision of equal rights to both communities has not been a factor acting to moderate the distrust and antagonism that riddle the province.

In the 1960s the hostility between the two communities in Northern Ireland degenerated into violent confrontation. When Catholics demonstrating in favor of reform came under attack from Protestants, the British government sent in the army to protect the Catholic minority and keep the peace. However, these clashes and the presence of the British army encouraged a resuscitation of the Irish Republican Army (IRA), a terrorist group which had fought for Irish independence early in the century and now seeks to annex Northern Ireland to the Irish Republic. IRA bombings and attacks against Protestants, the police, and the British army in turn stimulated the formation of Protestant paramilitary organizations, which have not refrained from using terrorist tactics themselves. The result has been a continuing spectacle of hatred and violence which the British government and army, caught in the middle, struggle to contain.

The situation in Northern Ireland seems ripe for a consociational solution, for it is clear that the Catholic community will never accept a return to the previous form of government, a regional parliament controlled by the Protestant majority, which the British government abolished in 1972. Westminster did take steps in the direction of consociationalism in 1973 by introducing a power-sharing arrangement between the Catholic and Protestant communities, but it was sabotaged by a Protestant general strike which crippled the province. It is not just the Protestants, however, who oppose a consociational arrangement. The IRA and other Catholic underground organizations are dedicated not to helping the Catholic community get a fair deal in Northern Ireland but to dislodging Northern Ireland from the United Kingdom entirely. Thus, the will to make the system work—the crucial ingredient in any consociational solution—is absent from key groups on both sides. Even the more modest British-Irish agreement in 1986 to set up a consultative committee on Northern Ireland provoked violent demonstrations, death threats against the police, and strikes on the part of Protestant groups which fear that any cooperative arrangement with the other side is but a prelude to the annexation of Northern Ireland by the Irish Republic.

The Level of Strife in Britain   The troubles in Northern Ireland and the bitterness provoked by the strikes of coalminers and other disaffected unions in recent years may evoke an impression of the United Kingdom as a strife-torn country. This impression would be misleading for several reasons. For one thing, the situation in Northern Ireland has had relatively little impact on Britain itself. British political parties are united on the need to keep peace in Northern Ireland and to resist demands from the "Loyalists" (Northern Irish Protestants) for a return to a Protestant-dominated regional government. There is relatively little public sympathy for the Loyalists in largely Protestant Britain, and although IRA bombing campaigns, which have struck England as well as Northern Ireland, are condemned by most Britons, few believe that repression against the Catholic minority in Northern Ireland is the answer. The policy of working with the Irish Republic to resolve differences is generally accepted at all levels of British society, and the most common public attitude is that the Irish situation is a separate, isolated problem that is perhaps unresolvable and probably not worth dwelling upon.

Despite the militancy of some labor union and political leaders, the class cleavage in Britain is also far from being explosive. Disraeli's hope of the 1860s that the working class could be won over to conservatism has been partly realized; about one-third of the working class votes for the Conservatives, providing the party with nearly one-half of its total vote. Most workers, even those who belong to unions, do not approve of the aims and activities of radical union leaders such as Arthur Scargill, and the coalminers' call for a general strike by all unions against the government was ignored by the other large unions in the country. Radicals attribute this acquiescence to "false consciousness" on the part of the working class, the result, they believe, of the manipulation of ideas by the dominant institutions of society. In so doing, they tend to forget that England (where most Britons live) has been a well-integrated country since the Middle Ages, with a strong sense of national identity since at least the sixteenth century, and that its economic, political, and military successes throughout most of the modern era have strongly reinforced these bonds of community and aided their extension to Wales and Scotland as well. The violence in Northern Ireland and the unrest in the labor movement over the past two decades should not obscure a background of strong patriotism and community-mindedness within Britain itself that have been forged over many centuries of national existence.

The Race Problem   There is a third cleavage, however, that falls outside traditional bonds: that between white Britons and a small but growing minority of nonwhites, made up mostly of emigrants from former British colonies in the West Indies and the Indian subcontinent. In a society not accustomed to thinking of itself as multiracial, it is perhaps not surprising that discrimination and prejudice against nonwhites have become widespread. Today, unemployment is exceptionally high among nonwhites, and it undoubtedly contributed to the outbreak of violent race riots in Bristol in 1980 and Brixton in 1981. The unemployment situation has even fostered resentment between immigrant groups. A racial disturbance in 1985 in Birmingham involved attacks by West Indians against businesses and shops owned by (East) Indians and Pakistanis, who were perceived as having prospered far better than West Indians. British governments have responded to the problem of race by tightening up immigration laws to control the entry of nonwhites into the country, but that has not prevented the emergence of an anti-immigrant National Front party advocating the repatriation of nonwhites to their native lands (despite the fact that many nonwhites were born in Britain). The poor state of race relations is a problem which most Britons, used to nothing more troubling than the occasional protests of Welsh or Scottish nationalists, have been slow to appreciate; they may have to take it much more seriously in the future.

France: The Decline of Cleavage Conflict

Traditional stereotyping opposes a united, law-abiding, and pragmatic Britain to a cleavage-riddled, violence-prone, and highly ideological France whose next revolution always seems just around the corner. These stereotypes, like all stereotypes, are exaggerated, but they do contain a germ of truth: There is no question that over the past two centuries France has been more unstable politically and more cleavage-ridden than Britain. Today, a contrast between the two countries still exists but it takes a very different form: While Britain has experienced increased social conflict in recent years, France has seen instead a relaxation of the social antagonisms that formerly plagued its national life.

The "Two Frances"   The fundamental rift that provoked so much political instability in France began, as we have seen, with the revolution of 1789. The democratic principles of the First Republic (1793–1795) were undermined first by Emperor Napoleon and then, on his defeat, by the reimposition of the monarchy in 1815, but they did not die away. Throughout the nineteenth century, France remained bifurcated between those who supported a monarchy or another Napoleonic Empire (the Right) and those who favored a republican form of government (the Left). This cleavage was strongly reinforced by religion, for the Catholic Church in France had closely aligned itself with the monarchical cause and even, at times, became implicated in plots to overthrow democracy. Class also coincided with this political-religious cleavage to a considerable extent because the working class, isolated from the larger society in working-class suburbs and subjected to low wages and harsh working conditions, sided strongly with the prorepublican, anticlerical Left. To the limited degree that cleavage lines crosscut, the expected moderating effect was undermined by the low level of voluntary group activity in France. For the same reason, a consociational solution to the country's divisiveness was not in the cards. The absence of a rich organizational life of either the crosscutting or segmental variety reflected the lack of strong bonds of social trust in France, a legacy of the absolute monarchy and of the divisions and instability which characterized the country after 1789. Even as recently as 1976, this lack of trust has been labeled "the French disease" and identified as French society's main problem by a leading politician in a book of the same name.[9]

The social and political conflict that seemed endemic in France up to World War II evaporated surprisingly quickly in the changed circumstances of its aftermath. What had changed most was France's economic situation. Whereas France had lagged behind Britain, Germany, and the United States in industrial development and economic prosperity before 1945, the 1950s and 1960s saw very rapid economic growth. The effect of this growth on France's social structure has been dramatic. For one thing, it stimulated a large migration from the countryside to the cities, reducing France's huge reservoir of impoverished peasants and thereby eroding the social isolation and "compartmentalization" that had characterized much of French society in the past. For another, rising levels of affluence undermined the resentment and alienation with the working class. In the 1950s the Communist party of France, devoted to the goal of socialist revolution and closely aligned with Moscow, could count on the votes of between 20 and 30 percent of French voters, mainly from the working class. Today its support has dwindled to the 10 percent range, and its claim to represent the revolutionary aspirations of the French working class no longer bears scrutiny.

The religious cleavage has also receded in the postwar decades. One reason for this is undoubtedly the general decline in organized religion that has occurred throughout most of the Western world in this period. A second and perhaps more important reason is the reorientation of the Catholic Church in certain key areas. The church now tends to regard religion as much more a private, personal matter and, correspondingly, involves itself far less in partisan politics. The distaste for liberal democracy that was characteristic of the Catholic Church in Europe before the war largely died after the experience of fascism and Nazism; today's Catholic Church now seems more likely to criticize right-wing dictatorships, such as those in Latin America, and to support the establishment of democratic regimes. In France, it has even become possible to be a devout Catholic and a member of the Socialist party, a combination of loyalties that would have been highly unlikely 25 years ago.

The decline in social divisiveness in France has undoubtedly been sustained in large measure by the establishment and consolidation of a political regime that all segments of society could support. In the 1950s France seemed out of step with itself. The economic miracle and the flight to the cities had already begun, yet the country was still burdened with an unstable parliamentary system operated by numerous weak,

[9]Alain Peyrefitte, *Le Mal Francais* (Paris: Librairie Plon, 1976). The English version of this book is *The Trouble with France,* trans. William R. Byron (New York: Knopf, 1981).

fractious, and increasingly irrelevant parties. The institution of the Fifth Republic changed all that. De Gaulle's regime combined the strong, stable executive authority admired by the Right with the democratic principles demanded by the Left. Although the Left was reluctant to endorse the regime when it was first established, perhaps fearing de Gaulle's own authoritarian tendencies, it soon had to reckon with the fact that the regime not only functioned stably and effectively but also was immensely popular with the electorate, including the Left's own voters. There were, to be sure, setbacks in the consolidation of the regime. In 1968 the future of the regime was brought into question by an outbreak of student demonstrations in Paris and elsewhere which eventually stimulated a general strike of several million workers. For well over a month, the entire country was paralyzed, and only de Gaulle's calling of legislative elections brought the country back to normal. Although many in France were sympathetic at first to the demonstrations against the government, which under de Gaulle often appeared aloof and high-handed, the more basic temper of the country was exhibited in the election returns, which gave the Gaullist party a landslide victory. De Gaulle himself left politics a year later, but the regime has continued to function well in his absence.

Race and Ethnicity in France   Although the French have moderated their long-standing differences and now seem more united than they have been for centuries, France is no longer as "French" as it used to be. Like Britain, France has attracted a sizable minority of immigrants from her former colonies, particularly Algeria and Tunisia. These immigrants were welcomed in the 1960s, when labor shortages existed in France's booming economy and immigrants proved willing to take on many of the low-paying and unpleasant jobs such as garbage collection and street cleaning that the French preferred to avoid. Today, with much higher levels of unemployment, antagonism and discrimination against these immigrants have become widespread. The government has attempted to alleviate the situation by offering financial incentives for immigrants to return to their lands of origin, and it has also tightened up the rules governing immigration and residency permits. Nevertheless, as in Britain, an overtly anti-immigrant party, the National Front, has emerged in recent years. In the 1986 and 1988 parliamentary elections, the National Front's surprisingly strong performance—just under 10 percent of the popular vote—has brought race to the center of political debate and made the possibility that the French are racist at heart an issue of much soul-searching in the media.

Race is not the only issue of this sort to trouble the French political scene. For some time, there have been small but active movements in Brittany and in the south of France which seek to preserve their non-French linguistic and cultural heritages. More significantly, in Corsica, originally an Italian-speaking island, the National Liberation Front of Corsica (FLNC) is conducting a campaign of bombings and assassinations to further its cause of independence from France. This movement does not enjoy the level of popular support of the IRA in Northern Ireland, but it is one more sign that the task of ensuring ethnic and racial peace in a country accustomed to thinking of itself as ethnically homogeneous will present a major challenge to the government and the major political parties in the years to come.

THE SOVIET UNION AND CHINA: PLURALIST SOCIETIES UNDER SINGLE-PARTY RULE

Marxist doctrine, as we have seen, maintains that class is the one fundamental basis for cleavage in modern capitalist societies and that all other bases for division, including ethnicity, religion, and language, are destined to decline in significance. Because of the primacy of class, the official ideologies of both the Soviet Union and China proclaim the need for just one political party, the Communist party, which will lead the victorious struggle of the proletarian class (including the peasants) over the former ruling class of bourgeoisie and landlords. As a result of this perspective and the repressive practices which have often followed from it, these regimes are often seen as totalitarian monoliths exercising complete control over their helpless citizens. In both countries, however, the efforts to mold a new type of citizen whose socialist consciousness and loyalty to the regime would supersede preexisting religious or ethnic ties have largely failed. This is especially true of the Soviet Union, where about half the population is ethnically non-Russian. Moreover, the attempts by both regimes to eliminate class differences have not prevented the emergence of large distinctions of wealth and privilege. Neither country is as homogeneous or as free from cleavage-based conflict and rivalry as their governments would have us believe.

Soviet Union: Contained Diversity

Lenin and the Bolsheviks inherited from the tsars one of the most culturally heterogeneous countries in the world. To this day, the Soviet Union is a land of abundant human diversity. The tidy villages and small towns of Latvia and Estonia resemble their counterparts in northern Germany or Scandinavia, while in Soviet Central Asia the scene is more reminiscent of Turkey or Iran: women in wide-legged trousers and turbaned old men on donkeys populate streets lined by houses of sun-baked clay. Moscow, a city of massive concrete apartment complexes, has one of the most comprehensive and efficient subway systems to be found anywhere, but there are towns and villages in Siberia where people live in rude wooden huts and the mud streets are often impassable.

Religion and Ethnicity in the Soviet Union   Officially, the USSR is an atheist country, but it is nevertheless home to several major religious traditions. The Russian Orthodox Church remains the largest denomination, as it was under the tsars. Other religions recognized by the state include

Roman Catholicism, the largest church in Lithuania; Lutheranism, predominant in Latvia and Estonia; and Islam, widespread in Central Asia. There are also large communities of Baptists in the RSFSR and the Ukraine. The Jewish community has been reduced by persecution and emigration; 1.81 million ethnic Jews live in the Soviet Union today (20 percent fewer than in 1959), and only an estimated 60,000 practice their religion.

Several smaller sects operate without the state's recognition and are treated as illegal organizations. These include the Pentecostalists, Jehovah's Witnesses, and Seventh-Day Adventists. In parts of the Ukraine there are still remnants of the Uniate Church, which practices the Eastern Orthodox rites but adheres to the authority of Rome; the Uniate Church was officially disbanded and made illegal during Stalin's time.

The party has always considered religion anathema to the long-range goals of communism; religious beliefs, according to Marxist-Leninist ideology, divert people's energies from the construction of a better material life and enslave them to reactionary authorities. The state has alternated between campaigns to eradicate religion (as in the 1930s and again in 1960–1961) and a grudging toleration of it. Since the 1970s, the authorities have allowed the registered sects to conduct worship services with little interference but have strictly prohibited church involvement in social or political matters. Atheistic instruction is required of schoolchildren, and churches are not allowed to counter by offering classes in religious education. Over the years, the number of churches and synagogues has greatly diminished and the proportion of worshipers has shrunk to a minority of the population overall.[10] But those who do practice tend to be firm in their beliefs, holding to them despite strong pressures from employers, educators, and local party authorities.

The churches have generally stayed out of politics, but some individuals and small groups—especially from among the officially unrecognized sects—have engaged in political dissent on religious grounds. In some cases, the crosscutting effect of religious and ethnic identity has intensified dissent among minorities, as, for example, among Catholic Lithuanians and Uniate Ukrainians.

For a country of such national diversity, the USSR has seen remarkably little ethnic conflict; national revolts have not occurred since the civil war of 1917–1922. The quiescence of the non-Russians cannot be taken for granted, however. Small-scale incidents of unrest are known to have occurred in Lithuania, Georgia, and the Ukraine during the 1970s, and it is possible that unreported incidents took place elsewhere. The Soviet security police deal with such matters quickly and firmly, as they have dealt with such well-known cases as the Jewish "refuseniks" who

[10]This by no means indicates that the number of believers is small. The Russian Orthodox Church has an estimated 30–50 million adherents, primarily living in the RSFSR, Belorussia, and the Ukraine. Among the native populations of Central Asia, totaling some 30 million, probably one-half or more practice Islam; of the Lithuanians (total 2.85 million), an estimated 80 percent or more are Catholics.

Table 3.1 **MAJOR ETHNIC AND NATIONAL GROUPS IN THE
SOVIET POPULATION, 1979**

Group	Number (millions)	Percent
Total population	262.08	100.00
Russians	137.40	52.42
Ukrainians	42.35	16.16
Uzbeks	12.46	4.75
Belorussians	9.46	3.61
Kazakhs	6.56	2.50
Tatars	6.32	2.41
Azeris	5.48	2.09
Armenians	4.15	1.58
Georgians	3.57	1.36
Moldavians	2.97	1.13
Tadzhiks	2.90	1.11
Lithuanians	2.85	1.09
Turkmenians	2.03	0.77
Germans	1.94	0.74
Kirgiz	1.91	0.73
Jews	1.81	0.69
Chuvash	1.75	0.67
Latvians	1.44	0.55
Bashkirs	1.37	0.52
Mordvinians	1.19	0.45
Poles	1.15	0.44
Estonians	1.02	0.39

Source: Soviet census data, reprinted in Ronald J. Hill, *The Soviet Union: Politics, Economics and Society* (London: Frances Pinter, 1985), p. 65.

have publicly complained about their treatment and demanded the right to emigrate. After years of demonstrations and police recrimination, news of which has provoked a public outcry in the West, substantial numbers of Jews were allowed to leave during the late 1970s and early 1980s. Jewish emigration subsequently slowed down, however, and many still await permission to emigrate, including some who have been incarcerated for their public protests.

The period of Gorbachev's reforms—the so-called *perestroika,* or "restructuring"—has seen an increase in nationalistic unrest. Renewed demonstrations have taken place in Lithuania, Latvia, and Estonia; incidents were reported in 1986 and 1987 among the Kazakhs and the Crimean Tatars, and in 1988 violent clashes broke out in Azerbaidzhan between Azeris and the Armenian minority. Police dealt mildly with the Baltic demonstrations and that of the Tatars, allowing them to take place without violence; the Azeri–Armenian conflict, in contrast, required the official use of force.

On the subject of ethnicity and nationalism, official Soviet attitudes have had to undergo a change. Lenin, like Marx, underestimated the strength of nationalism, believing that economic development and material abundance would make people shed their nationalistic sentiments.

Modern Soviet leaders, however, have seen that nationalism dies hard, and they find themselves having to be alert to problems caused by the resulting social cleavages.

The state's policies allow for the expression of cultural traditions but do not accord ethnic groups the right to organize for community action; the structures of federalism are not set up for this, nor may ethnic groups petition for community rights outside the federal structures. In language policy, the state pursues a type of bilingualism in most non-Russian areas, allowing for education, commerce, and media communication in the local language. Russian, however, is the lingua franca and, therefore, mandatory for all who wish to hold positions of authority.

Marxist-Leninist ideology envisions the assimilation of all citizens into a unified "Soviet" identity, valuing "proletarian internationalism" rather than the officially disparaged "bourgeois nationalism." This is a vague and distant goal at most, and in practice it seems to spell Russianization. The state pursues its assimilationist objective through incentives: members of ethnic minorities who learn Russian and display "internationalist" sentiments have opportunities for higher education, social mobility, and power that are generally not accessible to those who hold tight to their ethnic identities. But such opportunities are in any case not available to everyone and are apparently not attractive to some. Many choose to retain their ethnic customs and are allowed to do so as long as they pose no challenge to the political system.

Within the vast reaches of the Soviet Union, one finds many exotic ethnic and regional traditions. Here a professional couple in Uzbekistan choose to be married in a traditional ceremony. (TASS from Sovfoto)

Russianization is apparent in the ranks of the CPSU, where ethnic Russians dominate the highest levels of the party hierarchy and occupy positions of authority even within many of the non-Russian localities. This does not mean that non-Russians are excluded from power; Stalin, born Joseph Djugashvili, was a Georgian, and a number of powerful contemporary leaders are non-Russians, including Eduard Shevardnadze, a Georgian who became foreign minister in 1985, and Geidar Aliyev, an Azeri (Azerbaidzhani), who was considered one of the most powerful members of the Politburo between 1984 and his dismissal (perhaps because he was a rival to Gorbachev) in 1987. Like Stalin, however, these men lost much of their ethnic identity along the road to power; Aliyev even changed his Muslim name to give it a secular Russian form.

Thus, quite in contrast to the consociational idea, in which the political system is designed to harmonize a culturally pluralistic populace, Soviet policies have attempted to diminish the diversities. However, the long-term goal of assimilating the entire body politic into a common "Soviet" identity remains elusive. For the time being, unrest among minorities is not an acute problem, but in the longer run, some Soviet authorities are concerned, especially given the fact that certain minority populations are growing much more rapidly than the Russians. This is particularly true of the largest Central Asian nationalities—the Uzbeks, Kazakhs, Tadzhiks, and Turkmenians—among whom a population explosion is occurring that threatens to alter dramatically the USSR's ethnic balance. To date, there is little evidence of political nationalism among these peoples, but the rise of militant Islamic fundamentalism across the borders in Iran and elsewhere in the Middle East gives the Russians cause for alarm.[11]

Class and Privilege   Closely related to the ethnic and regional diversity in the Soviet Union are social and economic inequalities. The Russian Empire under the tsars was a land of stark inequalities, with little or no industrial development taking place in most regions of Siberia, Central Asia, and the Caucasus and education in these areas at a very low level; among the native populations in Central Asia, for example, the literacy rate before the Bolshevik revolution was only 2 to 3 percent.[12] Since the 1930s, industry has grown tremendously in all regions, educational standards have risen dramatically, and the material quality of life has greatly improved. Still, there remain disparities among the republics; in those with the highest economic level, Estonia and Latvia, per capita

---

[11]One reason for the Soviet military intervention in Afghanistan, beginning in 1979, may have been official fears that a victory by the Islamic rebels over the Soviet-backed Afghan regime might stir the religious and ethnic sentiments of Muslims in Soviet Central Asia.

[12]F. Wheeler, *The Modern History of Soviet Central Asia* (London: Weidenfeld and Nicholson, 1964), p. 97.

income may be as much as twice that in Uzbekistan and Tadzhikistan. Educational standards also vary substantially; Jews, Georgians, Armenians, and Russians have the greatest access to secondary and higher education, while Moldavians, Lithuanians, Tadzhiks, and Kazakhs have the least.[13]

Soviet sociologists divide their society into two classes, the working class (85.1 percent of the total population, according to the census of 1979) and the collective-farm peasantry (14.9 percent). This division confuses somewhat the conventional Western distinction between the industrial and agricultural work forces, as the working-class category includes workers on state farms (large farms, roughly on the scale of American agribusiness concerns, owned and managed by the state, as opposed to farms owned collectively by those who work them); if these are added to the peasantry, approximately 21.5 percent of the total population is employed in agriculture—a high proportion by modern standards. The working class is subdivided into the categories of manual and non-manual workers; the latter category encompasses all "white-collar" personnel—persons in management, administration, and the technical professions—and includes the subcategory known as the intelligentsia (defined as those with higher education or specialized secondary education).[14]

Officially, the Soviets tend to downplay the inequalities in their society. Differences in the relative levels of wealth and social status do exist, however, and not just between regions and ethnic groups: there are noticeable differences between urbanites and rural dwellers, among the many occupational groups, and among people of differing educational levels. Moreover, particularly noticeable differences exist between the life-styles and prestige of the intelligentsia and those of the rest of society. The intelligentsia occupy positions of great respect in the eyes of their fellow citizens, and they have access to better housing, greater travel opportunities, and generally higher salaries than other workers or peasants.

There is yet another gap that cuts across occupational lines, that between party members and nonmembers. Besides the obvious discrepancies of power, there are more subtle differences in material life-style; party members have access to special stores offering certain goods not available to the general public, and they often find it easier to buy such "luxury" items as automobiles and video players. Party membership makes it easier for an individual to travel abroad, and within the Soviet Union numerous holiday resorts are reserved exclusively for party members. It would be unthinkable for any official to admit it publicly, but by

---

[13]D. Lane, *The End of Social Inequality? Class, Status and Power Under State Socialism* (London: Allen & Unwin, 1982), p. 87.
[14]Ibid., pp. 34–53.

many objective standards, the party—and especially the party elite—has taken on the characteristics of a privileged class.[15]

Who can achieve membership in this privileged club? Soviet statistics on the social backgrounds of party members show some ambiguities, but in general it appears that nonmanual workers, particularly the intelligentsia, are represented in disproportionately greater numbers than their share in the total population, peasants in slightly lesser relative proportion, and manual workers significantly lesser.[16] Leaders tend to be better educated than the rank and file, and this tendency increases toward the very top of the CPSU.

In an oligarchical system such as that of the USSR, the power elite makes the rules of politics and defines the legitimate issues. This does not mean that the Soviet system is completely unresponsive to the needs of social groups. In one way or another, the elite must pay attention to its subjects; in the most negative way, the security police infiltrates many corners of society in order to keep tabs on citizens and forestall challenges to the elite's authority. But the state has shown itself to be responsive in more positive ways, too, by bringing economic progress to the backward regions, by raising educational standards, by providing health care and inexpensive public transportation and state-funded cultural programs, and in many other respects. This beneficence has its limits, but it is indicative of the fact that the Soviet elite rules not only for the sake of power itself but also from a vision of societal welfare.

The precise nature of this vision, of course, is defined by the party oligarchy. To a degree, the oligarchy's rule is conditioned by diverse and competing demands on the system of resource allocation, fought out in limited ways through the cryptopolitics of the party's internal workings, but it is within the oligarchy that the critical decisions are made. The myth of working-class rule notwithstanding, the Communist party elite still believes it necessary, more than 70 years after the Great October Revolution, to govern on behalf of, rather than with the consent of, Soviet workers.

China: Equality or Performance?

Communist regimes, for ideological reasons, are particularly concerned with class differences, and nowhere has this concern been more manifest than in the People's Republic of China, where class cleavages inherited from the old order were especially severe. Edgar Snow's account of China in the mid-1930s gives some idea of the extent of the problem:

[15]In the 1950s Milovan Djilas, once the second-ranked leader of communist Yugoslavia, identified the class nature of party members' privileges in his book, published in the West under the title *The New Class* (New York: Praeger, 1957).

[16]Ronald J. Hill, *The Soviet Union: Politics, Economics and Society* (London: Frances Pinter, 1985), p.77.

Have you ever seen a man—a good honest man who has worked hard, a "law-abiding citizen," doing no serious harm to anyone—when he has had no food for more than a month? It is a most agonizing sight. His dying flesh hangs from him in wrinkled folds; you can clearly see every bone in his body; his eyes stare out unseeing, and even if he is a youth of twenty he moves like an ancient crone. . . . Children are even more pitiable, with their little skeletons bent over and misshapen, their crooked bones, their little arms like twigs, and their purpling bellies, filled with bark and sawdust, protruding like tumors. . . . The shocking thing was that in many of these towns there were still rich men, rice hoarders, wheat hoarders, money-lenders and landlords, with armed guards to defend them, while they profiteered enormously. The shocking thing was that in the cities—where officials danced or played with sing-song girls—there was grain and food, and had been for months.[17]

Before 1949, China's major industries were largely in the hands of foreign investors; they and the Chinese merchants, the military, and the landed elite dominated a highly unequal society. The pronounced class cleavages of prerevolutionary China provided fertile ground for the spread of Chairman Mao's analysis of the status quo and prescriptions for change. One of his followers recalls the intensity of prerevolutionary class antagonisms:

My fellow students were nearly all the sons of landlords or merchants, as few poor boys ever got to school. I studied at the same desks with them, but many hated me because I seldom had any shoes and my clothes were poor and ragged. I could not avoid fighting with them, when they cursed me. If I ran to the teacher to get help, I was invariably beaten by him. But if the landlords' sons got the worst of it, and went to the teacher, I was also beaten.[18]

With the establishment of the revolutionary regime, extraordinary efforts were devoted to eliminating class differences. The aggregation of agricultural land into collective farms and, later, into agricultural communes resulted from land reforms undertaken to abolish the system of landlords and tenant farmers. The government expropriated foreign-owned industries and commercial enterprises and gradually converted all other industry and commerce to state ownership. The regime also made a special effort to provide political and educational opportunities to the classes that had previously been deprived of such benefits.

Interestingly, one of the first steps the Chinese took toward the elimination of class conflict was the identification of individuals with clear-cut social classes. The regime classified the rural population into former landlords, rich peasants, middle peasants, or poor peasants. Students were subdivided into three broad classes: (1) revolutionary classes, consisting of the children of workers, poor peasants, lower-middle peasants, revolutionary martyrs, revolutionary cadres, and revolutionary soldiers; (2) backward classes, made up of the children of landlords, rich peasants,

[17]Edgar Snow, *Red Star Over China* (New York: Grove Press, 1944), pp. 226–227.
[18]Ibid., pp. 328–29.

capitalists, "rightists," and "bad elements" (criminals, thieves, loafers, and former Guomindang officials); and (3) the middle range or free professions, including the children of doctors, teachers, technicians, middle peasants, and shop clerks. Once such class ties were identified, the new communist regime could give preference to those who had been disadvantaged under the old regime and limit the influence of those who had exploited others. The middle-range group was regarded as having particular potential, because many of its members had accepted the party's leadership.

Student sensitivity to class origins was encouraged in party and educational activities. One student noted:

> We spent a great deal of time studying the origins and distinguishing characteristics of different social classes. As a result, the concept of class was very much in our minds. Everybody was evaluated in terms of his social class background. This did not mean that we had outright conflict within the school; actually, everybody continued to get along well enough. It was just that we began to grow more aware of an individual's class background and there was a tendency to explain his conduct in terms of this factor.[19]

A major obstacle to the elimination of class differences is the tendency for new classes to emerge as the old are destroyed. As Soviet experience indicates, the elimination of classes rooted in capitalism may well be followed by the emergence of classes characteristic of a communist society. In a large state undergoing economic and social change, it is inevitable that social class differences develop between urban and rural residents, government administrators and those they govern, professionals and nonprofessionals, and educated and uneducated people.

In attempting to lessen the consequences of the new social classifications, Mao utilized several devices. One such device was the mass migrations undertaken to minimize the differences between urban and rural life. Doctors, teachers, entertainers, and other skilled or talented individuals were moved from the city to the countryside with the aim of providing the rural population (still about 80 percent of the total population) with the cultural attractions, medical care, and educational opportunities available only in the cities. The regime also sought to promote equality by requiring those of higher social status to exchange jobs with workers and peasants. Thus, industrial managers worked on assembly lines or in the fields at harvest time; students and professors spent part of each year performing manual labor on farms or in factories; farmers and workers joined the revolutionary committees that made decisions about the operation of their communes or factories.

The most dramatic and far-reaching of the Chinese attempts to

[19]Ronald Montaperto, "Revolutionary Successors to Revolutionaries," in *Elites in the People's Republic of China,* ed. Robert Scalapino (Seattle: University of Washington Press, 1972), p. 596.

disrupt the natural trends toward bureaucratization and class differentiation have been the mass revolutionary movements. Periodically, Mao used these movements to destroy the privileged bureaucracies he saw developing in order to prevent the emergence of new privileged classes and to perpetuate the social and economic equality that existed within the communist movement during its long struggle for power. Mao was willing to do so even at the cost of disrupting society and slowing economic development because, in his perspective, the revolutionary spirit of equality took precedence over stability and economic progress.

The struggle against class differentiation divided the party and ultimately culminated in the Cultural Revolution. Liu Shaoqi, premier from 1959 to 1969, led a faction seeking a more pragmatic approach to national development. This faction opposed Mao in several key areas. For example, Liu went against the *xia fang* movement which sent leaders back to the countryside, arguing that leaders were scarce and were needed in their managerial positions. He also introduced personal incentives and private farm holdings. To promote industrial efficiency, Liu argued in favor of applying cost-benefit criteria designed to produce profits. Mao opposed these deviations from his view of socialism, arguing that they would lead to exploitation by powerful and privileged individuals. A related issue in this conflict was the "red versus expert" debate. Mao sought in the early 1960s to launch a campaign promoting the importance of commitment to socialist principles and the need to resist the "sin" of status. Again, the entrenched urban elites and experts, including many in high party positions, opposed the campaign. The political conflict over the dangers of class and status was resolved for a while by the Cultural Revolution, which was a triumph for Mao's egalitarianism. Liu and his followers were expelled from their positions in the party and in the government, and throughout the country individuals more closely associated with intellectual than proletarian pursuits were sought out for ridicule and punishment.

Mao's victory did not prove to be lasting, however. Many of those who shared orientations similar to Liu's were restored to office following Mao's death; their rise to ascendancy has meant that the choice between equality and modernization now favors modernization. With this choice has come a renewed emphasis on merit for educational advancement, work evaluation, and earnings. Indeed, in recent years media stories about the emergence of a small number of wealthy industrialists and farmers abound, and black markets in money and consumer goods like televisions, videocassette recorders, stereos, and automobiles are notorious. It remains to be seen whether heightening differences in wealth will become a major problem for a regime which, until recently, was strongly egalitarian in its social and economic orientations.

Ethnic and Regional Pluralism in China   In terms of absolute numbers, Chinese ethnic minorities account for only about 5 percent of China's population. Though 95 percent of the population is ethnically Han (the dominant Chinese ethnic group), the Han Chinese speak a number of mutually unintelligible dialects. The majority speaks one of the northern dialects commonly called Mandarin, and in recent years Mandarin has been promoted as the basis of a new national language. Other important dialects used by Hans, principally in the south, include Wu, Cantonese, and Hakka. In addition, several provinces have their own distinctive dialects. The linguistic diversity of the Hans is rendered somewhat less complex by the existence of a universal script that can be read by all Han Chinese. Nevertheless, language differences often affect interregional social attitudes and relations. For example, note the pleasure some southern students derived from their linguistic advantage over a group of northern (Beijing) students during the Cultural Revolution:

> We were repulsed by the conceit the Beijing Red Guards displayed and thoroughly enjoyed putting them on. Beijing dialect was commonly used all over the country, so we knew what they said; however, when we spoke in Cantonese, the Beijing Red Guards could not understand us. We cursed them and they simply smiled.[20]

Among the small minority that is non-Chinese are numerous ethnic minorities, many with their own religious persuasions. For example, some 6 million Tibetans are Lamaist Buddhist, with their own religious-secular leader, the Dalai Lama. The various minorities (mostly Turkic) on China's northern border are an essential part of its 14 million Muslim population, larger than that of many Muslim countries. There are also an estimated 5 million Christians in China.

The Chinese communist regime has strongly discouraged ethnic cleavages in the interest of pursuing the construction of socialism and modernization. Its goal is to eradicate the minorities' national aspirations without destroying their cultures. Ideally, for example, Tibetans will come to view themselves not as Tibetans, but as Chinese citizens of Tibetan descent. Integration is seen as requiring the establishment of a uniform political culture and the development of a new Chinese citizen who will be supportive of a communist society.

While China has generally succeeded in achieving this goal, it still faces problems in integrating the border-based ethnic groups psychologically with the rest of the country. Ethnic groups that straddle the country's frontiers are difficult to integrate into the national community and also pose a potential for international conflict if both states claim the ethnic group and its homeland. This is particularly true of the Sino-Soviet border, which is poorly defined and disputed by both China and the Soviet Union. Several ethnic groups—notably the Uighurs, Monguls, Kazakhs, Tadzhiks, and Kirghiz—overlap this border. Each side has

---

[20]Gordon A. Bennett and Ronald N. Montaperto, *Red Guard: The Political Biography of Dai Hsiao-ai* (New York: Doubleday, 1971), p. 134.

made claims on territories now held by the other and manipulated ethnic groups to support these claims. The result has been a prolonged border dispute that periodically flares into open military confrontation and battle. So far, military clashes have remained limited, but the potential for a more serious political and military showdown clearly exists.

A particularly difficult problem for China is Tibet. China has claimed sovereignty over Tibet since conquering it in the eighteenth century. In 1914 Tibet achieved relative independence under British sponsorship in order to serve as a buffer state between British India and tsarist Russia. In 1950 the Chinese reoccupied Tibet and announced its integration into China as an autonomous republic. China curtailed the powers of the Dalai Lama, Tibet's religious and secular leader, installed Chinese communist leaders, and encouraged the immigration of Han Chinese (a strategy that has also been used in Inner Mongolia). In 1959 the Tibetans revolted against Chinese rule and the curtailment of the powers of their religious orders. China crushed the revolt and the Dalai Lama fled to India. The Chinese replaced him with the Panchen Lama, who was expected to be more cooperative. He, too, proved insufficiently compliant, however, and in 1964 the Chinese removed him from office. Further evidence of Tibetan unrest came to light during the Cultural Revolution, when Red Guard activities, including the destruction of monasteries, aroused great resentment in Tibet.

Since 1979, Mao's successors have attempted to accommodate Tibetan sensitivities. This has included paying more respect to traditional Tibetan culture and religion, opening Tibet to tourism, and permitting Tibetans a market economy with freedom of production, pricing, and marketing. The Chinese government appears to be interested in winning back the Dalai Lama from exile, which would allow them to be free of the colonial image they have held since their 1950 occupation of Tibet. However, these concessions have not been sufficient to overcome alienation and anger among Tibetans. In 1987 the Chinese government experienced a major setback when demonstrations demanding autonomy from China broke out. The repression of these demonstrations, which occurred at a time when Western tourists were present, was highly embarrassing to Chinese authorities still trying to overcome the stigma of colonialism.

A Changing China   China in the post-Mao era has undertaken major social, economic, and political changes, and with these changes have come new social forces and pressures. Urbanization is occurring at a brisk pace; between 1978 and 1985, some 60 million peasants switched from agricultural production to other trades.[21] In urban areas, students and professionals such as engineers, journalists, and technocrats have become

[21]*Christian Science Monitor* (March 10, 1986), 11.

more outspoken and politically active. In the rural areas, an expanding sector of well-to-do peasants and entrepreneurs is vying with party cadres for power and influence; indeed, the Communist League's most popular attraction in recent years has been a rural speaking tour by rich peasants on the topic "How to get rich on contract lands."

China's attempt to deal with class differences has taken many turns. Initially, it involved homogenization, a direction which reached its apogee in the Cultural Revolution, but in the post-Mao period the class issue has taken a back seat to economic growth. This has meant that those seeking to move ahead are free to do so, even if it results in the emergence of major income inequalities. So far, the political concern has been with excessive corruption, not with inequality as such, but this could change if reality becomes too inconsistent with official ideology, which espouses a classless society.

The attempt to deal with ethnic problems has also varied. The early oppression of minorities and attempts to "sinoize" them gave way in the post-Mao era to acceptance of ethnic differences. But the differences between Han and various minorities within China's borders have not dissolved. Indeed, the Islamic rebirth following Khomeini's "Islamic revolution" in Iran has become a powerful force among Muslim peoples in China as in the Soviet Union and could lead to considerable unrest. In addition, prejudices combined with strong differences in perceptions of the social order, in particular differences between traditional and modernizing viewpoints, aggravate the problem of ill-will between the Han Chinese and the minorities. A critique of party cadres in Tibet, published the year before the outbreak of demonstrations and violence, reported that cadres "arbitrarily interfere in the masses' freedom of religious belief and even remove Buddhist scriptures on the grounds that they are spiritual pollution"—acts, which, a regional cultural bureau official told the party central committee, "have seriously hurt people's feelings." The state religious affairs bureau even admitted that the bulk of China's some 1,000 lamaseries were desecrated or destroyed during the Cultural Revolution.[22]

MEXICO AND NIGERIA: DIMENSIONS AND CHALLENGES OF NATION-BUILDING

At first glance, Nigeria and Mexico appear to represent two distinct configurations of social cleavages: Nigeria with strong ethnoregional divisions, and Mexico with clear socioeconomic class divisions. However the picture is substantially more complex owing to the coincidence in both countries of multiple cleavage lines. In Mexico, class distinctions coincide to a large extent with a rigid stratification pattern based on race,

[22]*Far Eastern Economic Review* (January 30, 1986), 22.

with Indians at the very bottom of the ladder. Nigeria's social structure is even more complex. The three main ethnic groups in Nigeria are differentiated not only by region but also by religion and by life-style. In both countries, processes of modernization are adding new lines of cleavage and new tensions to their already divided societies. As in much of the Third World, major social cleavages such as these present formidable problems for governments attempting to maintain or establish social harmony and foster economic development.

Mexico: The Challenges of Class and Race

The evolution of Mexico's class structure is typical of a country undergoing economic development. Since the turn of the century, Mexico's upper and middle classes have grown substantially, but the lower classes, including both urban proletariat and rural peasantry, still constitute a large majority of the total population. Moreover, the gap between the very poor and the very rich is both large and increasing. In 1950 the average income of the wealthiest sector of society was 12 times that of the poorest sector, by 1964 it was 18 times, and by the mid-1980s the ratio had become 20 to 1.[23] These statistics reflect the stubborn persistence of class differences despite the doubling of the country's annual gross national product (the total output of goods and services per year) in the past quarter-century. Mexico's urban slums contain increasing numbers of persons who exist only at the subsistence level; an even larger percentage of the population ekes out a marginal existence in the rural areas.

Urban poverty and rural poverty are two distinct phenomena. Despite subsistence-level incomes or unemployment, city dwellers have greater access to opportunities and amenities than do the rural poor. Cities offer more and better schools, more cultural diversity, and higher-paying jobs. Sanitation, though poor in urban slums, may be considerably better than what is available to those lowest on the rural social scale. Urban slum housing, bad as it is, often surpasses the mud adobe huts and dirt floors of the rural masses. Running water, health clinics, schools, and movie theaters are all available in the neighborhood of the urbanite; for the rural resident, they may be miles away at best. While there are some relative advantages in urban as opposed to rural poverty, however, neither is tolerable. In fact, the alienation and psychological isolation that compound the material sufferings of the urban poor suggest that it is the possibilities rather than the realities of urban life that make cities so attractive to rural immigrants.

Mexico's class disparities have had profound political consequences. During the 1910–1920 decade, class tensions led to an anarchic

---

[23]V. Alba, *The Mexicans* (New York: Pegasus, 1970), pp. 242–243; World Basics, *World Development Report 1984* (Oxford: Oxford University Press), pp. 272–273.

Table 3.2 OCCUPATIONAL STRUCTURE IN MEXICO
(PERCENT OF TOTAL EMPLOYMENT)

Year	Agriculture	Industry	Services
1940	65.4	12.7	21.9
1950	58.3	15.9	25.7
1960	54.1	19.0	26.9
1964	52.3	20.1	27.6
1976	40.0	30.0	30.0
1980	33.0	33.0	34.0

Source: Banco de Mexico S.A.

civil war in which peasant armies fought government forces and each other. Eventually, the lower classes were organized into labor and agrarian interest groups. Labor was actively recruited and ultimately instrumental in Carranza's successful 1915 drive for the presidency. Since that time, the peasant and labor sectors have become an integral part of Mexico's politics through Mexico's dominant party, the PRI.

The ability of labor and the peasantry to identify with their occupational groups and along class lines has stabilized Mexico's political system and provided long-term payoffs to both groups. While these payoffs have been minimal, especially for the peasants, the elite realizes that its position is dependent on the support of these groups and does take steps to maintain their support. As we shall see in Chapter 4, a pattern of dependence centering on patron-client links is an important integrating structure in this regard, reflecting and, in fact, institutionalizing class relationships. It is characterized by hierarchical and unequal reciprocal relations in which patrons clearly dominate exchanges of material goods (money, clothes, and food) and status (jobs, offices) for votes from their "clients."

There is a wide gulf—indeed a chasm—between the massive numbers of very poor and the handful of very wealthy people in Mexico and, as we have seen, no evidence that it is narrowing. Furthermore, tensions are likely to increase as more Mexicans move from rural settings, which are relatively isolated from politics, to urban ones, where they become aware of politics and are accessible to political organizers. This phenomenon might pose a serious threat to the regime should the poor become convinced that the government is failing to meet their needs. Recently, discontent has been widespread over the government's slow handling of the reconstruction of homes in Mexico City after the 1985 earthquake and over government austerity measures, including the reduction of subsidies on food staples such as beans, flour, and tortillas, which have come in the wake of falling oil revenues and the cost of servicing a huge foreign debt. While the family structure helps to buffer class realities and frustrations in Mexico, these developments could produce an underlying resentment which might someday target the government, the party, or the privileged elite.

For the most part, the leadership has successfully deflected the blame for economic discontent onto others: the church, greedy, corrupt bureaucrats, and foreigners. Until the 1988 elections, the PRI, the republic's presidents, and the revolution had thus avoided blame for continued inequities. Furthermore, the regime has proved capable at times of responding to serious threats by enacting reforms that undercut resentment toward the regime itself. Nevertheless, resentment came to the forefront in the 1988 elections as support for PRI candidates, including its presidential candidate, declined sharply. The future stability of the regime hinges on the leadership's continued ability to direct blame away from itself and to respond to imperative needs for reform.

Racial Divisions in Mexico   A century and a half after independence, Mexico is still troubled by the racial cleavages it inherited from its Spanish colonial past. While approximately two-thirds of the population are mestizos, there are more than 3 million Indians, of whom about one-third speak only their native languages.

A noted Mexican scholar, Gonzales Casanova, has argued that a form of internal colonialism exploits the Indians. Municipal centers controlled by Ladinos (mestizos) "exercise a monopoly over Indian commerce and credit, with relationships of exchange unfavorable to the Indian communities."[24] These commercial monopolies, he argues, isolate the Indians from other centers or markets and thus result in their dependency. Furthermore, Indians are exploited as laborers and sharecroppers, living in virtual peonage in exchange for minimal wages. Indians are also distinguished from similarly impoverished mestizos by the unique characteristics of their existence:

> Indian communities have . . . a predominantly subsistence economy, with minimal money and capitalization; lands unsuitable for crops or of low quality, unfit for agriculture because of hilly terrain, or of good quality, but in isolated locations; deficient crop-growing and cattle-breeding because of low quality seeds and inferior animals smaller than the average of their kind and pre-Hispanic or colonial techniques of land exploitation; a low level of productivity; standards of living lower than those of the peasants in non-Indian areas, exemplified by poor health, high rates of mortality, including infant mortality, illiteracy and the presence of rickets; lack of facilities and resources, such as schools, hospitals, water and electricity; promotion of alcoholism and promotion of prostitution by hookers and Ladinos; aggressiveness among communities, which may be overt, or expressed through games or dreams; magic-religious culture; economic manipulation through the imposition of taxes and a status-bound economy; and . . . political manipulation.[25]

Perhaps more important than geographic isolation is psychological isolation, the source of the Indian's reluctance to make demands on gov-

---

[24]Gonzales Casanova, *Democracy in Mexico* (New York: Oxford University Press, 1970), pp. 85–86.
[25]Ibid., p. 87.

ernment. The Indian tends to regard himself as uninvolved in the politics and economy of the national state. He is usually uninterested in the government's activities and does not desire to know more about them. This apathy derives in part from cynicism about what government can or will do for him and in part from the sense that the Indian way of life is superior to that of the rest of society. The Indian outlook prompts him not to confront and master his environment, but to accept and live in harmony with it. These attitudes explain why the unassimilated Indian population is not a source of instability in contemporary Mexican politics. As one scholar noted of the Indian: "If it is outside his nature to conquer his environment, he will scarcely demand that the government do it for him."[26]

The assimilation process is not easy for those Indians who undertake it. Other Indians ostracize those who begin to accept modern culture, and it is often difficult for them to find a place in society once they leave their native villages. There is no governmental obstacle to the integration of the Indians, but the regime has shown little interest in actively promoting assimilation. Periodic efforts have been made to teach Spanish to Indians and to improve communication with remote tribes by constructing roads and installing telegraph or telephone lines. But these efforts have lacked adequate financing and sufficient government commitment to be successful. Similarly, land reforms aimed at fulfilling the revolution's promise to give land to Indians and poor mestizos have done little to improve the position of the Indian: only one-fifth of all Indians possess land of their own.

The Mexican government's attitude toward the Indian is paradoxical. On the one hand, it idealizes the Indian as the oppressed victim of colonialization and the tyrannies of the nineteenth century and as a revolutionary hero and chief beneficiary of the revolution of 1910. Ancient civilizations are praised and studied by one of the world's finest archeological museums, and the cultural richness of contemporary Indian life is highly valued. On the other hand, the government largely ignores the Indian. Few efforts are made to improve the quality of the Indians' lives or even to fulfill their basic health and nutritional requirements. Divisions within the government over whether Indians should be encouraged to assimilate into Mexican life or should preserve their own way of life partly explain this inactivity. As frequently happens, such a split results in a minimal policy—in this case, literacy drives and the introduction of the Spanish language—which is unlikely to change the Indians' lot dramatically.

Religion as a Source of Cleavage   Since Mexico's independence, religion has been a perpetual subject of political debate. While nearly all Mexicans

[26]Robert E. Scott, *Mexican Government in Transition,* revised ed. (Urbana: University of Illinois Press, 1964), p. 65.

are Catholics, Mexico has shared with other Catholic countries sharp divisions over the proper extent of the church's influence on society and politics. Conflict between clerical and anticlerical elements among the creoles and middle-class mestizos played an important part in the turmoil of the nineteenth century, and the struggle to separate church and state was long and bitter. The 1857 constitution formally separated church and state, but the church continued to wield enormous political, social, and economic power. Enforcement of the anticlerical provisions of the 1917 constitution by Calles in the 1920s led to an armed uprising, and further revolts occurred in the 1930s when certain state governors used the powers granted them in the constitution to limit the number of priests permitted to officiate in their states. By the late 1930s, the relationship between the federal government and the church had become one of peaceful coexistence, although in the early 1940s many Catholics were attracted to the *Sinarquista* movement, which advocated restoration of a hierarchical religious-led state. This movement succeeded in electing a governor in Guanajuato before the rise of the National Action Party, a more moderate conservative Catholic party, undermined its political aspirations.

New Challenges The predominant sources of social change in Mexico are rural and urban modernization. These forces are spawning new groups and challenges for the Mexican government. In the countryside, government support for irrigation, fertilizers, and pesticides, as well as access to markets, has produced a new class of well-to-do peasants. In addition, there are opportunities for the lowest of the dispossessed to migrate to the United States or, in some cases, to find work in the large commercial agricultural enterprises in the northern Mexican states. Once there, many are able to take advantage of greater educational opportunities to learn to read and write and, equally important, to learn how to organize politically. When they return, these "changed" Mexicans are often more aware, more involved politically, and more likely to be a source of dissent if government policy is insensitive to local needs or if it is abusive.

In the urban areas, professionals and small-business people have also become more cynical of the government and occasionally have sought to express themselves publicly. Nevertheless, it is students and the urban poor who have been the most visible of the rising urban political forces. How they express this discontent will be discussed in the next two chapters.

Since the revolution, the Mexican government has adopted a consistent tack with regard to cultural pluralism. It has learned by trial and error that the best way to deal with these groups is to co-opt them, that is, to integrate them into the controlling political party. The initial coalition brought together labor, peasants, the military, professionals, and business groups. This process of adaptation to new social forces has continued. The problem for the government is that it has not always been able to control the dissenters within each of the groups. In the past, oppression was used to achieve conformity, but it is by no means assured that such means will always be effective in preventing the creation or spread of alternative political forces.

Nigeria: The Quest for National Unity

Political division on the basis of socioeconomic class generally becomes more pronounced in the early and middle phases of a country's social and economic development. With Nigeria's attempts to develop commerce, industry, and manufacturing, and with the growth of government, class increasingly has become a factor in Nigerian society. While class distinctions are in evidence, however, they have not become determinants of psychological identification, nor have they given rise to partisan activities, as in Mexico. This is attributable to the dominance of fundamental ethnic and regional identifications that cut across class lines.

Ethnoregional Cleavages in Nigeria   There are 18 different ethnic groups and nearly 400 linguistic subgroups among the approximately 92 million people of Nigeria. The three main groups are the Hausa and Fulani of northern Nigeria, the Ibos of southeastern Nigeria, and the Yoruba of southwestern Nigeria. Table 3.3 indicates the relative sizes of the several ethnic groups that make up the country's population. Each of the three main groups is centered in a single region, although some members of each reside in other regions; there are also several minority groups in every region. Figure 3.1 shows the locations of the principal groups. The Hausa-Fulani, the Ibos, and the Yorubas are clearly differentiated from each other by language (each has its own distinctive language and several dialects), by religion (the Hausa-Fulani are mainly Moslem; the Ibos and Yorubas are mostly Christian), and by life-style (the Hausa-Fulani are nomadic tribes; the Ibos and Yorubas are more sedentary, urbanized, and educated). The generally coincident nature of linguistic, religious, and life-style cleavages along tribal lines renders the gulf separating the various cultural groups in Nigeria both wide and deep.

While the presence of three major ethnic groups, each with its own political network and region, would challenge any new country, large-scale migrations have enhanced Nigeria's problems. Under colonial rule considerable numbers of Ibos and Yorubas moved to the north, and Hausa traders moved to all parts of the nation from the north. Each relocated ethnic group founded a union to maintain its customs, cultural attributes, and ties to its home region. As is frequently true of those impelled by ambition to relocate, many of the immigrants were more successful than the average inhabitants of the localities to which they had moved, which tended to heighten resentment among the dominant ethnic group.

The system of indirect colonial rule employed by the British helped

Table 3.3 MAJOR ETHNIC GROUPS IN NIGERIA

Ethnic Group	Estimated Population (millions)	Percent
Hausa-Fulani	26.7	29
Yoruba	18.4	20
Ibo	15.6	17
Tiv and Plateau cluster	8.3	9.0
Kanuri	4.6	5.0
Ibibio	5.5	6.0
Idoma	2.4	2.6
Edo types	3.0	3.3
Ijaw	1.8	2.0
Bororo (pastoral Fulani)	1.4	1.5
Nupe	1.1	1.2

Sources: Derived from official *Nigerian Census,* vol. 3 (1963), and *New York Times Encyclopaedic Almanac* (1972). These selected groups do not represent the total population.

to institutionalize Nigeria's linguistic, ethnic, and regional differences. The British recruited the most respected native leaders, who were often granted considerable political authority, and employed the ethnic unions to administer politics at the local level. The result was that the authority of tribal rulers was enhanced, regional outlooks were perpetuated, and interaction among Nigeria's numerous ethnic groups was discouraged.

Socioeconomic disparities engendered by regionalism also contributed to the problem. The gravity of early social disparities between regions is evident in the following figures: in 1963 there were some 2.5 million primary students in southern Nigeria and fewer than 0.5 million students in the north, even though the north contained more than half the country's population. Similarly, power consumption, a good indicator of economic development and prosperity, was much greater in the south (270 million kilowatt-hours in 1964) than in the north (40 million kilowatt-hours).[27] Resources have been distributed inequitably in Nigeria, and the more developed regions have tended to be reluctant to share their resources with other regions. This problem became acute when the Northern Region, because of its larger population, succeeded in gaining political control in the 1960s. Resentment aroused by the use of this power precipitated the military coups of 1966 and ultimately the Biafran secession and civil war of 1967.

Civil War in Nigeria   When the dust had settled after the first military coup of 1966, General Johnson Aguyi-Ironsi was at the head of the new military order. General Ironsi, although an Ibo, was committed to the national unity of Nigeria. Like many others in the military, he put professional and national interests above ethnic loyalties. However, rumors circulated that Ironsi was under the influence of Ibos. Ironsi's efforts to

[27]R. L. Sklar, "Contradictions in the Nigerian Political System," *Journal of Modern African Studies* 3 (1964), 204–205.

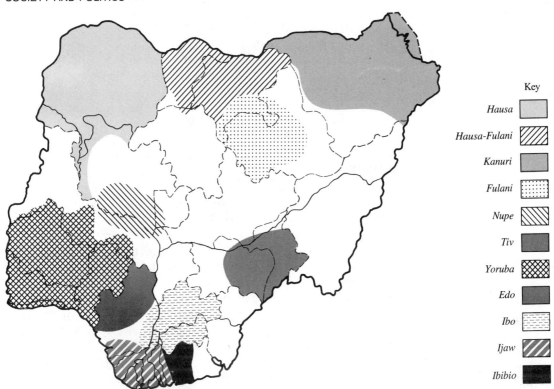

Figure 3.1 Nigeria's principal ethnic groups. (*Source:* John M. Ostheimer, *Nigerian Politics,* p. 10. Copyright © 1973 by John Ostheimer. By permission of Harper & Row, Publishers.)

merge the civil services of the various regions fed these rumors because it was a reform that undermined regional-ethnic control of the bureaucracy and of civil service jobs. In addition, competition among ethnic groups over markets, land, political positions, employment, educational opportunities, and even language was growing. The tendency was widespread to blame competition from other ethnic groups for an individual's inability to find a job, secure the desired education, or find adequate housing. This high level of ethnic tension made it difficult for the Hausa to accept rule by an Ibo. The northern Hausa feared an Ibo plot to gain national political control and acted to prevent this from happening. Their first target was the large Ibo population that had settled in the north. In May 1966 there occurred attacks on the Ibo immigrant population in the north. In July, a second military coup resulted in the murder of Ironsi and the ascension of General Gowon, a Tiv who had the full backing of the Hausas.

Attacks on Ibo immigrants continued in the north, especially in the city of Kano. By the autumn, violence in the north had reached a peak, and the Ibos began to flee to the south. In October, Hausas with automatic weapons attacked Ibos arriving at Kano's airport. The result was a bloodbath in which several thousand Ibos were massacred; more than 1 million were forced to flee the north.

The Ibos now demanded more autonomy through a confederal formula ensuring greater powers for their regional government. Negotiations toward this goal failed, and in May 1967 the Eastern Region seceded, declaring itself the Republic of Biafra. The Nigerian military immediately launched a two-pronged attack on the east; the civil war was under way. After an initial Biafran advance, the Nigerian army was successful in reducing the territory of Biafra. However, decisive victory eluded both sides and there ensued a war of attrition, in which the Nigerian forces cut off the flow of urgently needed food, medicine, and military supplies to the Biafrans. After 2½ years and an estimated 1 million casualties, Biafra surrendered in January 1970.

The Present State of Tensions   Although the war did not eliminate ethnic tensions, there is now greater ethnic harmony in Nigeria than at any time since independence. Under the leadership of General Gowon and his successors, development has proceeded in all parts of Nigeria. However, industrialization and economic progress should not be seen as automatic solutions to the problems of cultural pluralism. In the past, economic development in Nigeria has contributed to ethnic antagonisms by accentuating interregional economic differences and encouraging the migration of ethnic groups from their home regions to the cities, which led to concentrations of ethnic minorities in urban areas and heightened tensions. If, as in the past, development is unevenly distributed, regional disparities will increase and the resulting tensions may once again pose a serious threat to political stability.

The diffusion of Islamic consciousness from all parts of the Islamic world is helping to add a religious dimension to the ethnic issue. By the 1980s the emergence of this dimension had become very pronounced. There were incidences of Islamic groups in the north protesting or seeking to seize power locally, only to be put down by federal military interventions. In 1986 even the issue of whether Nigeria should be a member or an observer in the Islamic Conference Organization based in Saudi Arabia turned into an emotional national debate.

Nigeria's military governments have attempted to remedy weaknesses inherent in the previous governmental structures that made ethnic conflict almost inevitable. They have encouraged ethnic peace through institutional changes, including the substitution of 21 new states for the former regions (albeit with a great deal of central government control), multiethnic recruitment for public institutions, the creation of multistate-run firms, the promotion of English as the national language, and more evenhanded social and economic development programs. The government has even gone to the extent of shifting the federal capital from Lagos to Abuja, away from the influence of Yoruba economic pressures and bureaucratic access.

Nevertheless, the road to ethnic harmony in Nigeria seems likely to be a long one. Where cultural cleavages coincide with geography and where political institutions are fragile, as during a country's first few decades of independence, political stability is bound to be difficult to achieve. Military control has provided a short-term solution to the problem, but the pressures to restore democracy have not abated. Indeed, stimulated by the oil boom of the late 1970s, a large group of professionals, businesspeople, and students has come to the fore and will likely play an increased role in politics in the future. Prominent members of the bar, the medical profession, the military, and the government bureaucracy have made it a point to speak out on public issues, and the restoration of democracy—when it comes—is not likely to be greeted with passivity. Whether it will be the occasion of further ethnic hostilities remains to be seen.

CONCLUSIONS

The histories of Mexico and Nigeria illustrate the impact that social cleavages can have on three major problems of developing countries: national integration, political development, and economic modernization. The problem of overcoming ethnic cleavages, in particular, does not lend itself to easy answers. The consociational solution seems to work best for religious and class cleavages, but there is little or no evidence that it can cope with the intense hostility generated with ethnic differences. Probably the best strategy is to accept the existence of separate ethnic groups and to minimize their likelihood of engaging in conflict among themselves or with the state by practicing evenhanded nondiscriminatory policies. In the long run, social and geographic mobility and the development of crosscutting affiliations characteristic of complex industrialized societies may weaken such ethnic affiliations. Effective use of the mass media can further respect and tolerance, particularly by exposing all citizens to the nation's cultural diversity.

If none of these options seems particularly promising, it is because the problems posed by social cleavages, especially nonclass cleavages, are extremely difficult to resolve. We have seen in the cases of Britain, France, and China that even in countries which have had centuries of independent existence, serious cleavages can still occupy the political arena. States such as the Soviet Union, Mexico, and Nigeria, which have been assembled much more recently out of ethnically distinct peoples, face far more serious problems. In the Soviet Union, seven decades of single-party rule, often with high degrees of violent repression, have failed to eradicate ethnic and religious diversity. In Mexico, a degree of political stability is due to the unifying symbol of the 1910 revolution and the backwardness of the Indian minority, but it is not clear how long it can last in the face of rapid population growth and hard economic times brought on by the slump in export earnings from oil. Nigeria, the newest state, is also the one most pressed by severe ethnoregional cleavages, and only military force maintained its territorial integrity in the 1960s. It, too, is suffering today from a sharp decline in revenues from its most important export, oil, and increasing population pressures.

Despite their successes in maintaining order, the single-party and military government solutions are not necessarily final. As increasing levels of education and better communications make people more eager for some voice in determining the texture of their lives, demands for greater autonomy and more participation are likely to increase. In all four countries ruled by one or the other of these formulas, calls for greater personal freedom and greater respect for ethnic and religious diversity can be heard. Not all of these demands threaten the unity of these states, but they do challenge the ability of political leaders to find acceptable compromises between the reality of diversity and the ideal of a unified nation-state to which most of them subscribe.

two

POLITICAL ACTORS

chapter 4

The Citizen in Politics

Democracy, as the Greeks understood it, was a form of government which the modern world does not and cannot know.

H. D. F. KITTO[1]

INTRODUCTION

In the city-states of classical Greece, the ideal of citizen participation in the life of the polity achieved one of its highest expressions. The Greeks of the fifth century B.C. believed that the citizen's complete fulfillment could be realized only if he had a say in the governing of his community. The good life required not only good laws and good government—those could be provided by a benevolent dictator—but also the experience of having participated in their creation. This experience was important not because it allowed the citizen to advance his own interests, but because it forced him to put aside his own views and consider the welfare of the community, to weigh carefully arguments made by other citizens, and to strive to arrive at decisions and laws that embodied wisdom and justice. The pursuit of justice marked the virtuous life, and for the Greeks virtue was the highest goal of human existence.

Political arrangements which strike us as quite bizarre were adopted in order to realize these values. In the city-state of Athens, for

[1]H. D. F. Kitto, *The Greeks* (Harmondsworth, England: Penguin, 1957), p. 9.

example, governmental and military leaders were selected each year by lot from among the male citizenry, and the ultimate decision-making body for the city-state was the assembly of all male citizens. The idea that the political viewpoints of ordinary citizens should be conveyed to government by elected representatives, which is known as "representative democracy," was alien to the Greek conception of the ideal system of government. If the citizens as a whole were to rule, the Greeks felt that it had to be in a direct fashion. The Greeks introduced the concept of democracy into Western civilization, but what they had in mind was very different from what we find in liberal democracies today.[2]

The democratic experience of classical Greece has fascinated people for well over 2000 years partly because popular rule of any sort goes against the grain of much of premodern and early modern history. Rome, which ultimately absorbed the Greek city-states, changed from a republic governed by an elected senate to an empire ruled by an emperor. After the fall of the Roman Empire, the Germanic peoples occupying much of Europe were governed by kings elected from among the leading nobles of their realms; over the centuries, however, these kingships gradually became hereditary. In the sixteenth century, the hereditary basis of royal rule was elaborated into the theory of the "divine right of kings," which argued that the king and his family had been chosen by God as his instrument of temporal (worldly) rule and thus that any challenge to the power or will of monarchs was not only illegal but sacrilegious as well. This theory was used to provide intellectual support for the establishment of absolute monarchies in many European states.

The intellectual edifice justifying autocratic rule, imposing though it was, did not forestall all opposition to its claims. In England, the aspirations of the Stuart monarchs for untrammeled authority provoked a successful resistance movement on the part of those who argued that the constitutional traditions of the country stipulated a division of power between monarch and Parliament. After the removal by Parliament of James II in 1688–1689, all future English monarchs had to acknowledge that, ultimately, sovereignty rested not with them but with their nation's representatives. In France, where absolutism had triumphed in the seventeenth century under the Sun King, Louis XIV, the challenge came not so much on the basis of tradition as from the new ideology of "reason." The eighteenth century was the age of the "Enlightenment," when any social institution which could not stand up to the standards of rationality came under intense criticism and ridicule; the absolute monarchy, with its quasi-religious justification, was a favorite butt of attack. In the place of divine sanction, the philosophers of the Enlightenment advanced the idea that there existed a "natural law" above the will of kings.

---

[2]Ancient Greek democracy differed from our own in another way as well: it excluded women and slaves. It was thus a highly participatory democracy, but only for those recognized as citizens.

Under natural law, subjects were entitled to such rights as equal treatment before the law and freedom from arbitrary arrest, imprisonment, or seizure of their property. Eventually, the idea took hold that government should rest on the consent of the governed, to reflect, as it was often phrased, the "general will" of the community.

With the development of the idea of the general will, we begin to see not only the reemergence of democratic political philosophy but also a crucial splitting or bifurcation of that philosophy into two streams which are still very much present today. The first stream, which became entrenched most strongly in the Anglo-American democracies, holds that democracy consists of a competition between different interests or segments of society, with the prize of governmental power going to whichever side wins a majority or plurality of votes. There is no suggestion that one point of view or philosophy is more correct than any other; as long as basic democratic rights and freedoms are respected by all sides, power belongs to the side with the greatest voter appeal. The political arena in this perspective is seen as similar to a marketplace where each competitor tries to sell his product (his political program) to as many customers (voters) as he can. If the product proves to work poorly, customers will switch to another product the next time around. The general will in this interpretation means nothing more than the will of the majority.

Another interpretation of the general will was developed by one of the greatest of the Enlightenment thinkers, Jean-Jacques Rousseau. In Rousseau's conception, the general will represented the interests of society as a whole; it was a higher moral standard, beyond that of the mere "appetites" or desires of individuals, to which government and law should conform. Rousseau believed that people would obey governments and laws which embodied the general will because in so doing they would be, in effect, obeying their own higher moral selves. Thus, for Rousseau, it was not enough that a system of government allows the will of the majority to prevail; as he put it, only "obedience to a law which we prescribe to ourselves is liberty."[3]

Some have suggested that Rousseau's conception of the general will is a progenitor of twentieth-century communism. Whether Rousseau's thought actually influenced Marx or Lenin is questionable, but there is no doubt that the theory and practice of Marxism-Leninism follow a very similar orientation. Communist societies operate under the premise that there is only one political program, Marxism-Leninism, that embodies the highest aspirations of society as a whole. Unlike other ideologies, Marxism-Leninism is "correct" both scientifically, since it corresponds with and explains the direction of history (from feudalism to capitalism to socialism and, eventually, communism), and morally, since only under it can people be truly free. It follows, therefore, that competitive elections

[3]Jean-Jacques Rousseau, *The Social Contract and Discourses* (New York: Dutton, 1954), book 1, chapter 8, p. 19.

are inappropriate; instead people have to be led to understand that only one party, the communist party, represents their true or ultimate interests.

Few in the West accept this line of thought. Instead, Western democratic systems operate on the premise that voters can decide for themselves which party or program best represents their interests, provided that all parties have a roughly equal opportunity of presenting their messages. The purpose of politics, according to the dominant Western view, is not to create the conditions for the evolution to a superior form of society; rather, political parties appeal to voters on the basis of meeting legitimate needs and overcoming problems within the context of the existing society.

The fact that this conception of democracy rejects the idea that there is a single political ideology superior to all others is usually seen by its supporters as an advantage, but it does raise a difficult question: If each party competing in the political arena represents the will or point of view of one particular sector of society, who represents the general will, that is, the interests of the country as a whole? In Britain, for example, the Labour party receives most of its votes from the working class, while the middle class votes predominantly for the Conservative party. Both parties claim to embody the national interest, but might they not simply advance in government the interests of the classes which support them? It would be nice to think that politicians will place the national interest above that of their own party or its supporters, but as we shall see, most people in Britain do not believe that they do. The role of special interests or, as Rousseau would call them, "particular wills" raises concerns among many about the fairness and representativeness of Western democracies today.

Another potential problem often seen in liberal democracies relates to the limited role played by ordinary citizens. For the ancient Greeks, the essence of democracy was participation by the individual. Only by involving himself in the process of governing society, they believed, could the individual realize his full intellectual and moral capabilities. In a similar vein, Rousseau argued that participation in the political process would teach men to put aside their selfish private desires and advance policies that would be acceptable to all, that is, policies that reflect the general will of the community. Political participation, in other words, would not only make people freer, but would make them better, more responsible individuals as well.

In order to achieve these ideals, both the Greeks and Rousseau believed that the small city-state was the ideal political unit. Nowadays, however, most people live in much larger political units, units too large to permit every citizen to participate directly in public decision-making. In today's representative democracies, a small number of individuals exercise a full-time political and governmental role, while the majority of citizens do not involve themselves in politics beyond the simple act of voting at periodic elections (and many do not even do that). Some have argued that this is not only necessary but also desirable: Since the average citizen knows very little about politics, they believe that it is best that he limit his input to registering his satisfaction or dissatisfaction with those in office once every few years. Limited popular participation also makes it easier, they believe, for government officials to get on with the business of actually running the government; it is therefore a more efficient arrangement.

Others, however, find these arguments excessively "elitist." They feel that there is a far too limited role for the citizen in the society which claims to be democratic and that it leads to alienation of the individual from his government and opens the door to distrust, anger, and even violent protest against the authorities. Only by opening up government to genuine, widespread popular participation, they argue, can democratic societies be truly integrated and individuals come to feel in control of their social and political environment. Whether large states such as those considered in this text could be opened up to significantly higher levels of participation without impairing governmental efficiency has been one of the most intensely debated questions among political scientists in recent years.

Who Participates?

Many of the advocates of a more participatory society place a great deal of emphasis on the educative or self-fulfilling role of participation. Just as the reading of literary classics is supposed to enrich a person's intellect and emotions, so the active involvement in politics is held to add a dimension of satisfaction essential to the complete enjoyment of life. As with the reading of great literature, however, active involvement in politics is undertaken by only a relatively small proportion of the population in most countries.

In considering who participates, it is important to make a distinction between voting and other forms of participation. In countries which permit elections, it is almost always the case that a majority of citizens cast ballots in national elections. In Western countries, this majority generally comprises between 55 and 85 percent of the eligible population; in communist countries, where great pressure is put on the citizens to vote, the turnout is often above 99 percent. When we say that participation is low in most societies, therefore, we do not mean voting but rather other forms of political activity such as joining a political party or organization, getting involved in political campaigns, or running for office. The true activists, those who devote substantial time to the latter types of political activities, generally number less than 1 or 2 percent of the adult population.

Part of the reason for this is the low salience of politics in the lives of most people. The day-to-day concerns of earning a living and raising a family occupy the attention of most people most of the time, and what leisure time is available is generally devoted to the pursuit of private interests such as hobbies, friendships, and popular forms of entertainment. In comparison with these familiar facets of life, politics is bound to seem rather remote and unimportant. For the most part, only a particularly gripping political event, such as the assassination of a leader or the outbreak of war, can rivet the attention of an entire country. In many Third World countries, the natural tendency to be concerned with the immediate circumstances of one's existence is intensified by the sheer difficulty of making a living and accentuated by low levels of literacy and poor communications, which dampen political awareness. Long experience with authoritarian rule, whether by native leaders or by colonial rulers, can also reinforce the tendency to regard politics as a realm inappropriate for personal involvement.

There is a price to be paid for low involvement in politics, however. It stands to reason that a political system will be more likely to respond to the needs and wants of those who are active in it than to the needs and wants of those who are not. Participation is important, therefore, not just because of the educative or psychological benefits it may engender but also for the greater opportunities it affords to gain some of the benefits that governments control. In systems which allow citizen participation, then, why aren't more people politically active?

We have seen that the lack of political involvement can be explained in part by low interest in or awareness of politics, but this is far from being the whole story. Certain fundamental sociological factors influence who participates and who does not. One major factor is class or socioeconomic status. It is a common finding of research into participation that individuals who are higher on the socioeconomic scale tend to participate more. It appears to be the case that education in particular engenders in the individual certain traits that are associated with higher levels of political activity. Obviously, education can provide certain factual information on how the political system of one's country works and, perhaps, some information on the major political issues facing the country as well. More important, however, education can convey a sense of *political efficacy,* a personal feeling that one can comprehend the abstract concepts of the political world such as "left" and "right" or "socialist" and "conservative," that one can use these concepts to reason through a political position, and that one can effectively communicate that position to others, including government officials. Efficacy, in short, involves the sense of confidence that one can be an effective actor in the political arena, and it seems to be an important ingredient in actual political involvement. Ironically, the effect of education in stimulating political involvement tends to mean that the people who participate the most, the better educated, are generally the ones who need government benefits the least. In politics, it is often the case that "he who has, gets."

Another example of how attitudes affect political involvement can be found in differences between participation levels of men and women. It seems to be universally true that women are, or at least were, less interested and active in politics. Traditionally, women in most societies were socialized into believing that politics and government were male preserves, and they were often legally excluded from the political process as well. In Britain, for example, women did not become fully enfranchised until 1928; in France, they had to wait until 1945. Today, attitudes have changed considerably and there is little difference between turnout rates of men and women in national elections. Nevertheless, despite the emphasis put on equality between the sexes in communist societies and the strength of women's movements in most liberal democracies in recent years, women are still enormously underrepresented at the level of elected officials. In 1983, only 24 women were elected to the 650-seat British House of Commons; in the Soviet Union just 12 women could be counted in the 370-seat Central Committee of the Communist party in 1986. In many countries, awareness of just how out of date this sex imbalance is has been increasing, but it is also evident that traditional stereotypes and attitudes of this sort are very difficult to change.

Citizen Roles in the Third World

In much of the Third World, political participation is hampered by low levels of economic development. Where life is a daily struggle for mere subsistence, people have little time, energy, or interest in the world of national political affairs. Illiteracy and poor communications are bound to place limits on the extent to which people are even aware of the national political scene. The world of the traditional peasant is largely confined to the immediate village in which he lives and works.

Authoritarian rule, common in traditional societies, often reinforces this outlook. Before 1911 China was ruled for millennia by emperors supported by an elite class of mandarins who administered the country in the emperor's name. Russia emerged in the early modern period under the supreme and eventually absolute authority of its tsars. Many smaller political units were governed by kings, tribal chiefs, or military conquerors. It is not surprising in these circumstances that obedience has been the natural response of many peoples to the exercise of political authority.

The independence movements that swept Latin America in the nineteenth century and Africa and Asia after World War II attempted to counteract many of these tendencies and orientations. The struggle for independence involved considerable efforts to make colonial populations more politically aware, to encourage their involvement in efforts to found an independent regime, and, very often, to proselytize ideologies that emphasized democratic or populist norms. After independence, these movements usually went on to establish political regimes that allowed for or even encouraged popular participation.

Unfortunately, many of these regimes have had difficulty meeting the expectations of their newly aroused populations. The promise of economic development which inspired so many in these movements has more often than not been followed by disappointment and frustration. Frequently, social mobilization in multiethnic states did not create a new national identity so much as it stimulated tribal or ethnic consciousness, and politics in many of these states has tended to reflect less the restrained norms of government and opposition that one finds in developed countries than an intense, sometimes violent, antagonism between rival ethnic and racial communities. The frustration with economic failure, the hostility between ethnic groups, and the long tradition of authoritarian rule are all factors that have encouraged authoritarian takeovers of political power in Third World countries, particularly by the military. Where this happens, the opportunities for democratic participation by the citizenry are inevitably curtailed.

One of the major obstacles to the stable functioning of democratic governments in the new states of the world is the lack of legitimate channels for popular participation. In the absence of a well-developed party system or representative institutions that command widespread loyalty, frustrations and demands are likely to spill over into confrontation and violence. Such occasions often serve as pretexts for the introduction of military dictatorships. The repression which follows usually solves the immediate problem of establishing order, but unpopular repressive regimes are seldom able to stimulate the enthusiastic cooperation of the population in the pursuit of goals such as economic development and nation-building.

A more effective way in which citizens are linked up to government in many countries is through *patron-client* networks. Such networks are composed of hierarchical relationships between individuals who control some measure of political power (patrons) and individuals who seek the benefits which they control (clients). Often patrons are prominent local-level figures such as major landowners who are willing to provide jobs, government assistance, and other benefits in return for political support and loyalty. There is generally an air of corruption about patron-client relationships because of the favoritism involved in allocating government resources to particular clients, and well-organized networks are often referred to as political "machines." The activities of patron-client networks may also hamper economic development, since government jobs and contracts tend to go to those with the best contacts rather than to those who are best qualified or make the lowest bid. Nevertheless, many social scientists have argued that they perform an essential function in providing assistance and opportunities to the poor and needy at times when governments are unwilling or unable to do so directly.

Human Rights

A less desirable feature of many developing countries is scant regard for basic human rights. Where the norms and practices of democracy are poorly developed, recognition of the right to oppose governments freely is also likely to be withheld. Where ethnic hostilities, economic setbacks, or political unrest provokes takeovers of power by civilian or military dictators, repressive practices such as imprisonment without trial, torture, or even execution can be expected to follow. None of this is unique to the developing world, however. Regimes guided by a single, dominant ideology such as Marxism-Leninism have generally been unwilling to tolerate opposition to their goals. Frequently, what would be considered legitimate acts of opposition in liberal democracies—such as criticizing the government—are regarded as criminal, even treasonous, by these regimes.[4]

There is, however, a strong trend in recent years in the direction of greater recognition of human rights. An important step in this direction was taken in 1975 when the United States, the Soviet Union, Canada, and the states of East and West Europe signed the Helsinki Accords. From the Soviet point of view, the benefit of the accords was that they guaranteed the present borders of European countries, but the accords also included, at the West's insistence, a section committing all signatories to respect basic human rights. Since that time, human rights movements have arisen in the Soviet Union, Czechoslovakia, and elsewhere demanding the strict adhesion of their governments to those provisions. The repression of these movements has evoked criticism from Western countries and served to keep human rights issues in the forefront of world attention.

In the Third World, the pressure for human rights has been less systematic and intense but, increasingly, organizations such as Amnesty International have been successful in focusing worldwide concern on the plight of political prisoners in countries such as Chile and South Africa. It seems that as technology increases our ability to communicate across the world, awareness of violations of human rights is also likely to increase. While human rights are not the same as democratic rights (e.g., the right of citizens to choose the country's rulers), one of the most basic aspects of the citizen's role in politics is his right to voice political opinions and receive fair treatment from the judicial system of his country. The pressure for governments around the world to recognize these rights is clearly on the increase.

BRITAIN AND FRANCE: CITIZEN ROLES IN LIBERAL DEMOCRACIES

We live in an age in which political participation in some form is a normal adjunct of social existence; the forces of social mobilization,

[4]Liberal democratic governments may also violate human rights, but because they permit the existence of a political opposition and a free press which can detect these violations and an independent court system capable of punishing or rectifying them, human rights abuses tend to be less common.

aided immeasurably by mass communications technology, have seen to that. In countries which consider themselves to be liberal democracies, such as Britain and France, political participation has generally been made into a positive virtue, even a duty that all citizens should fulfill. But do they fulfill it, and what effect does their participation have? These are questions that have aroused lively debate among political scientists.

The questions that surround the nature of political participation in liberal democracies have generally had to do with two seemingly contradictory goals: the desire to make the political system responsive to citizen participation, and the desire to control citizen participation so that it doesn't interfere with the proper functioning of the system. The first goal embodies the ideal of democracy; the second, the goal of effectiveness. Opinions differ primarily over how much democracy is compatible with effective government.

Keeping participation within manageable bounds in democratic regimes generally entails the provision of legal and nonviolent channels by which citizen input can be delivered to government. In liberal democracies, these channels include the right to vote for one's preferred candidates, the right to express one's opinions freely, and the right to support, join, or even form organizations, including political parties, that attempt to carry one's political beliefs into the governmental arena. All of these rights exist, and are exercised, in Britain and France. However, there also exist in both countries powerful traditions of governmental authority and autonomy. The essence of these traditions is that governments, and those who control them, know better what the art of governing is all about and therefore should be allowed considerable freedom in exercising that function. These traditions, which owe their credibility to the fact that both Britain and France were successful states long before they were democracies, tend to work against the idea of citizen control over government, even when that control takes legitimate, peaceful forms. The exact degree of citizen involvement that can, and should, be allowed thus remains an open question in both countries.

Britain: An Awakening Citizenry?

Until recently, the British political system has been regarded as predominantly deferential; that is, the balance between citizen input and governmental efficiency was tilted noticeably in favor of the latter. As noted in Chapter 1, evidence for the tendency of the British to defer to governmental authority has been seen in the slowness with which voting rights were extended to the adult population and in the acquiescence of the population in that gradual course of reform. More direct evidence has come from public opinion surveys. A 1964 survey by Butler and Stokes produced the findings reported in Table 4.1, which show that most citizens do not involve themselves in politics or political campaigns beyond the act of voting in national elections. Although the vast majority of citizens

Table 4.1   FREQUENCY OF FORMS OF MASS PARTISAN ACTIVITY IN BRITAIN

Activity	Percent
Held some local party office	0.3
Took part in active campaigning at general election	3
Went to political meeting during general election campaign	8
Subscribed to local party	14
Were at least nominal party members (including membership through trade unions)	25
Voted in local elections	43
Voted in general election	77
Followed general election campaign via mass media or personal conversation	92

Source: D. Butler and D. Stokes, *Political Change in Britain* (New York: St. Martin's, 1969), p. 25.

followed the campaign through the media, only 8 percent reported going to a political meeting or rally, and only 3 percent took an active part in campaigning for their preferred candidate or party in the 1964 election.

Voting in a national election is the one basic political act that all citizens in a liberal democracy are expected to do, but we must not lose sight of how limited an act it is. For electoral purposes, Britain is divided into 650 constituencies or "ridings" of roughly equal size, and each citizen has the right to vote for his preferred candidate in the riding in which he resides. It is a single-member plurality system, which means that the one candidate who receives more votes than any other wins the riding, regardless of whether he has won a majority of votes or not. Voters who supported losing candidates are not directly represented in Parliament; their votes, in a sense, are "wasted."[5] Moreover, unlike the American system, ordinary voters in Britain do not have any voice in choosing the candidates who will run in each constituency; that is left to party members alone. Table 4.1 shows that only 14 percent of respondents in 1964 subscribed to a local party organization,[6] which is the basic party unit that selects most parliamentary candidates; no more than 8 percent attended candidate selection meetings. Most important, because Britain operates under a parliamentary system of government, casting a ballot for one's preferred candidate for constituency MP is the only voting act permitted citizens at the national level. They do not have the right to vote for a prime minister or any other national political figure.

The act of participation in national elections in Britain is facilitated by an automatic registration system in which a permanent list of voters is kept by the government and updated annually. Since fewer potential voters are left off the registration rolls than in the United States, where

[5]It is often argued, however, that they gain indirect or "virtual" representation through other candidates of the same party who won in their constituencies.

[6]The difference between the 14 percent who subscribed to a local party and the 25 percent who were at least nominal members can be explained by the fact that for many workers, union membership automatically confers membership in the Labour party.

Table 4.2   VOTER TURNOUT IN BRITAIN AND THE UNITED
             STATES (PERCENTAGE OF ELIGIBLE
             ELECTORATE VOTING)

British general elections		U.S. presidential elections	
Year	Percent	Year	Percent
1964	77.1	1964	63.3
1966	75.8	1968	62.3
1970	72.0	1972	57.1
1974 (Feb.)	78.8	1976	55.8
1974 (Oct.)	72.8		
1979	76.0	1980	55.1
1983	72.7	1984	52.9
1987	75.4		

Sources: D. Leonard and R. Natkiel, *The Economist World Atlas of Elections* (London: Hodder and Stoughton, 1987), p. 131, 140; *The Manchester Guardian Weekly* (June 21, 1987), p. 3.

registration depends on the individual's initiative, voting rates in British general elections are much higher than in American elections. As Table 4.2 shows, about 75 percent of the electorate usually turns out at the polls in British general elections, compared with an average of less than 60 percent in presidential elections. In addition, because there is only one choice to make in a British general election—the choice of a local constituency MP—voting is much less complex than in the U.S. system, which provides the voter with the right to vote for a wide range of positions, from president to county court judge. There are separate local-level elections in Britain as well, but there the voters' role is limited to electing unpaid local councillors; usually only about 40 percent of the electorate bothers to participate. Voting in Britain is thus both relatively easy and relatively uncomplicated, but is such a limited degree of participation in political affairs enough?

Those who believe that it is enough generally base their position on one or both of the following observations. First, there is considerable evidence to show that the vast majority of voters have only a weak understanding of the nature of the political system and of the issues and ideological differences that are involved in partisan competition. In a sample taken in 1963, Butler and Stokes found that only 13 percent of the British electorate fully understood the idea that the public exercises its control over government by choosing among competing parties in elections and believed that Britain conformed to that ideal. In contrast, 40 percent had not caught on to the idea, although it is, according to the authors, the central principle of liberal democracy as it is practiced in Britain.[7] Butler and Stokes also found that few respondents ordered their responses on

[7]D. Butler and D. Stokes, *Political Change in Britain* (New York: St. Martin's, 1969), p. 34.

issues in an ideologically consistent manner or were able to interpret the concepts of "left" and "right" and apply them to the major political parties. For every explanation such as the following, given by a London transport supervisor:

> To the left means increased social welfare benefits, the elimination of private wealth, and nationalization. To the right means the preservation of private wealth and the reduction of expenditure on social benefits,

they received four such as this, from a Sheffield lubricating engineer:

> Well, when I was in the army you had to put your right foot forward, but in fighting you had to lead with your left. So I always think of the Tories [Conservatives] as the right party for me and that the Labour party are fighters.[8]

The second point in favor of limited citizen participation in politics follows from the first. The reason that politics is so poorly understood by the general public, it is argued, is that politics does not seem especially salient or relevant to most people. They are content to leave such matters to the professional politicians, trusting that they will do what is best for the country. This, of course, is the basic idea of deference. Admittedly, if deference were total, there would not be any democracy at all, for democracy implies that the people exercise ultimate authority. But given the public's limited interest in or understanding of politics, perhaps it is best, they argue, that the public involves itself only to the extent of exercising an overall judgment of the government's performance once every four or five years.

Unfortunately for the defenders of limited popular involvement in government, it seems that the British public may no longer be willing to accept this role. In a public opinion survey conducted in 1974, Marsh found that a substantial proportion of the public did not express the high level of trust in government that has usually been assumed of Britons. His data, presented in Table 4.3, indicated that most Britons do not believe that government and politicians can be trusted to do what is right, to tell the truth, or to place the country's interest above that of their party most or all of the time. This distrust of leaders, moreover, seems to be associated with discontent over the limited role that individual citizens play in the political process. An official government commission investigating popular attitudes toward the system of government in Britain in the early 1970s found considerable dissatisfaction with the accessibility of government and a widespread desire for more participation.[9]

When access through official channels is blocked or limited, one

[8]Ibid., pp. 208–209.
[9]Commission on the Constitution (Kilbranden Commission), Research Paper no. 7, *Devolution and Other Aspects of Government: An Attitude Survey* (London, 1973).

Table 4.3   TRUST IN BRITISH GOVERNMENT

	Just about always (%)	Most of the time (%)	Only some of the time (%)	Almost never (%)	Don't know/refused (%)
How much do you trust the government in Westminster to do what is right?	7	32	47	10	3
When people in politics speak on television, or to the newspaper, or in Parliament, how much, in your opinion, do they tell the truth?	3	22	60	10	4
How much do you trust a British Government of either party to place the needs of this country or the people above the interests of their own political party?	7	28	45	15	5

Source: Alan Marsh, *Protest and Political Consciousness* (London: Sage, 1978), p. 118.

may expect that nonofficial channels will be used. Despite the impression of a largely docile British public, Marsh's 1974 survey turned up surprisingly high levels of support for the idea of protest. Nearly four-fifths of his respondents reported that they were willing to engage in legal forms of protest such as signing petitions and participating in demonstrations; a significant one-fifth also declared that they were willing to engage in illegal forms of protest, including rent strikes or blocking traffic. Fully 56 percent agreed with the idea that there are occasions when it is justified to break the law in order to protest against something the individual feels is harmful or unjustified.[10]

Just how commonly are such beliefs translated into actions? This is very difficult to determine in any precise way, but the trend seems to be in the direction of higher levels of protest and confrontation. The decision by the government-owned National Coal Board to close down a number of pits provoked a year-long coalminers' strike in 1984–1985, which involved numerous violent confrontations of a very serious nature between strikers, police, and nonstriking miners. Britain's agreement in 1980 to allow the United States to stock cruise missiles at its base at Greenham Common provoked illegal squatting at the entrance to the base by thousands of women, whose plight at the hands of the police garnered considerable support for the nuclear disarmament movement. The 1986 decision by a newspaper owner to fire his print workers because

[10]A. Marsh, *Protest and Political Consciousness* (Beverly Hills, Calif.: Sage, 1977), p. 155.

their union had resisted the introduction of automated printing equipment led to a virtual siege of the new plant by his discharged employees, supported by radicals and members of other unions. These examples alone should not be taken to mean that Britain is turning into a violent society or that its political system is seriously under threat, but, together with the survey evidence, they do suggest a greater willingness to question or challenge authority than has hitherto been the case.

Like the British system of government itself, the right of Britons to engage in protests or other forms of political expression is not set down in any constitutional document. Nevertheless, many basic civil rights, such as equality before the law, have long traditions in Britain, and all rights normally protected in liberal democracies receive vigilant enforcement from an independent judiciary. The principle of parliamentary sovereignty does mean that British governments can override human rights if they wish; the most famous recent example was the policy of imprisoning suspected IRA terrorists without trial in the early 1970s. The policy was not especially effective in curtailing terrorism, however, and proved to be an embarrassment to the government when several of those arrested appealed to the European Human Rights Commission on the basis that they had been tortured, contrary to the European Human Rights Convention which Britain had signed. The government's embarrassment suggests the key check on parliamentary sovereignty: the fact that Parliament is ultimately responsible to what appears to be an increasingly less deferential public.

France: A Citizenry on Guard

The political system of the Fifth Republic offers French citizens considerably more opportunities for participation than exist in Britain. Because the Fifth Republic incorporates elements of both the presidential and parliamentary systems of government, French men and women have the opportunity to vote both for their local National Assembly deputy and for the president of the Republic.[11] National Assembly and presidential elections are, in fact, separate events which normally do not occur at the same time: The presidential term of office is seven years, while the National Assembly stays in power for five years at most.

In addition, the unusual two-ballot majority electoral system employed in most National Assembly elections frequently offers the voter an extra opportunity to vote for each office. For legislative elections, the country is divided into 577 districts of roughly equal size, each of which elects one deputy to the National Assembly. However, unlike the system in Britain or the United States, it is not a simple plurality system. To win a district, a candidate must receive a majority of the votes cast in the

[11]The upper chamber of the French legislature, the Senate, is elected by local and regional representatives rather than by the public at large.

French Socialist leader François Mitterrand campaigning vigorously in a successful bid to be reelected president in 1988. (Lionel Cironneau / AP)

district. If no candidate wins a majority of votes—which is usually the case—a second election is held a week later. For this second round, all candidates who did not receive at least 12.5 percent of the votes are dropped from the ballot; others may simply choose to withdraw themselves and endorse alternative candidates. As a result of these two processes, second-round ballots generally have fewer candidates and hence a greater likelihood that one of them will win a majority. At this stage, however, the plurality rule takes over: The candidate with the most votes wins, whether or not he has received a majority of the votes cast.[12]

Presidential elections in France are run on very much the same lines. In the first round, a candidate must receive a majority of the votes cast in order to be declared the winner; otherwise, a second round is held two weeks later. In the second round, only two candidates may remain in the race. These will be the two top candidates in the first round, unless one of them voluntarily decides to withdraw (in which case the third candidate in the first round will take his place on the ballot). Since there are only two names on the second ballot, one of them will inevitably win a majority.

For both National Assembly and presidential elections, the extra

[12]In 1984 the ruling Socialists introduced a proportional representation system which allocated parliamentary seats according to the percentage of the popular vote each party won regionally. The Right, returned to power in the 1986 elections, promptly restored the two-ballot system.

round offers the voter an opportunity to reflect on his choice in light of how each of the candidates fared the first time around. He may, for example, cast his ballot for a relatively unpopular candidate in the first round in order to demonstrate his true feelings, then switch on the second round to another choice with a better chance of winning the election. In legislative elections, the political parties typically collaborate to facilitate this process. For example, the two main parties of the Left, the Socialists and the Communists, compete intensely for votes on the first round but usually also agree that in each district that has not already been decided, whichever of their candidates gets fewer votes in the first round will step down and urge his supporters to vote for the other candidate of the Left in the second round. In this way, the chances of one of their candidates winning the constituency is maximized. The parties of the Right also engage in this form of electoral collaboration among themselves. Thus, because of the two-ballot system, voters in effect have the opportunity to vote for their preferred party in a multiparty race in the first round and then, having seen the results, vote for their preferred side (Left or Right) in the second round.

A third way in which French citizens are afforded greater opportunities for participation is through the system of local government. The 96 departments into which France is organized contain more than 36,000 communes, each of which has its own elected mayor and municipal council. Since municipal councils have at least nine members, the number of elected officials in France at any one time is staggering: nearly half a million, or 1.8 percent of the total electorate.[13] Until recently, participation in local government was more impressive for its scale than its content, for in the highly centralized French system of government, municipal councils had relatively few powers to exercise on their own. The Socialist government elected in 1981 changed this picture drastically, however, by introducing sweeping reforms giving local governments far greater powers to manage their own affairs. The full ramifications of these reforms have yet to be demonstrated, but it is clear that the exercise of political authority, even if it is only over local issues, is something that will be experienced at one time or another by a substantial proportion of the entire French population.

The high level of involvement in local-level government is matched in France by high levels of voter participation in elections at both levels. As Table 4.4 shows, about 80 percent of registered voters in France typically turn out for national elections; for local elections the figure of about 75 percent is equally impressive. As in Britain, part of the reason for the high turnout levels in national elections is the voter registration system, which is automatic and comprehensive. It is possible that the sharp divisions that are still perceived between the Left and the Right in France also stimulate turnout, particularly at the local level.

[13]H. Ehrmann, *Politics in France,* 4th ed. (Boston: Little, Brown, 1983), p. 102.

Table 4.4   VOTER TURNOUT IN FRANCE (FIRST BALLOT)

Presidential elections[a]		National Assembly elections[b]		Local elections[c]	
Year	Percent	Year	Percent	Year	Percent
1965	84.8	1958	77.1	1959	74.7
1969	80.5	1962	68.7	1965	78.2
1974	83.5	1967	80.9	1971	75.2
1981	81.5	1968	80.1	1977	78.8
1988	81.5	1973	81.3	1983	67.8
		1978	83.4		
		1981	70.9		
		1986	78.3		
		1988	65.8		

[a]*Source: Facts on File,* volumes 1965, 1969, 1974, and 1981; *Manchester Guardian Weekly,* (May 1, 1988), p. 1.
[b]*Source:* H. Ehrmann, *Politics in France,* 4th ed. (Boston: Little, Brown, 1983), p. 220; *Le Monde* (June 7, 1988), p. 1.
[c]*Source:* V. Wright, *The Government and Politics of France,* 2nd ed., (London: Hutchinson, 1983), p. 291.

Despite the opportunities for citizen participation and the extent to which they are used, there remains in France a strong tradition of extralegal protest. France, as we have seen, possesses a powerful state tradition, the product of a centuries-long process of national unification under the monarchy. However, the absolutist direction that state-building took in France left almost no room for popular participation. The revolution of 1789 represented to some extent an explosion of frustration and anger against the closedness and inefficiencies of the monarchy, and it ushered in a strong egalitarian and participatory stream in French political culture. In the two centuries since the revolution, the French have demonstrated on numerous occasions their willingness to enter dramatically and even violently upon the political stage when the moment seems right. The last of these "moments of madness,"[14] as they have been called, occurred in 1968 when a student-worker strike involving several million people virtually shut down the country for weeks. Like earlier such moments, the "events" of 1968 involved no concrete demands or objectives; it almost seemed a case of protest for its own sake.

The outburst in 1968 caught most observers by surprise, not just because there was no obvious reason for it but also because it was thought that the establishment and consolidation of the Fifth Republic had ended France's problems in finding a generally accepted and workable political system. Whatever 1968 stood for, it was not a protest that was channeled through the legitimate outlets for participation provided by the regime. Even the French Communist party, which advocates the creation of a communist system in France, was unable to control or direct the strike activities of its own unions. The protest bypassed all authority and seemed all the more threatening because of that fact.

[14]A. Zolberg, "Moments of Madness," *Politics and Society* 2 (1972), pp. 183–208.

Table 4.5 POLITICAL TRUST IN FRANCE, BRITAIN, AND THE UNITED STATES

	Just about always (%)	Most of the time (%)	Only some times (%)	Almost never (%)	Don't know/ refused (%)
France					
How much do you think we can trust the people who govern to do what is right?	12	35	38	10	6
Britain					
How much do you trust the government in Westminster to do what is right?	7	32	47	10	3
United States					
How much do you think we can trust the government in Washington to do what is right?	5	48	44	1	2

Sources: (Britain) A. Marsh, *Protest and Political Consciousness* (Beverly Hills, Calif.: Sage, 1977), p. 155; (France and U.S.) J. Ambler, "Trust in Political and Non-political Authorities in France," *Comparative Politics 8* (October, 1975), 43.

The importance of a protest such as that which occurred in 1968 can be truly appreciated only when it is placed in the context of the very long French tradition of suspiciousness of governmental authority, a tradition which has affected both democratic and authoritarian regimes. In the unstable and ineffective Fourth Republic, it was normal for only 20 to 30 percent of the population to indicate satisfaction with the government's performance and for half or more to indicate dissatisfaction with the administration of justice in the country.[15] The Fifth Republic has brought with it much higher levels of satisfaction with governmental performance and, as Table 4.5 shows, a level of trust in government that is above that of Britain and just slightly below the American level, but the picture changes considerably when attention is turned to the state itself. Survey evidence has indicated that only 50 percent of French respondents feel that administrative decisions were usually or almost always just, and two-thirds of respondents feel that the administration would always win in a conflict between it and a citizen. Only 15 percent feel that their explanation of a problem would be taken into account by governmental officials in reaching their decision.[16] These findings contrast with earlier survey evidence showing that over 80 percent of British and American citizens expect equal treatment from government and that about one-half expect their points of view to be given serious considera-

[15]J. Ambler, "Trust in Political and Non-Political Authorities in France," *Comparative Politics* 8 (1975), 39.
[16]Ibid., pp. 33–34.

tion by governmental officials.[17] Thus, despite the greater satisfaction with the Fifth Republic, there seems to be an underlying distrust of the state that could still provide the basis for large-scale protest and demonstration in the future. The uniqueness of French politics is that these moments of national protest are often unpredictable and may catch a perhaps overly complacent political leadership totally by surprise.

The suspicion of authority that has characterized French political attitudes and behavior also finds expression in a strong concern for human rights. Indeed, since the revolution of 1789 and its famous Declaration of the Rights of Man and the Citizen, France has been at the forefront of concern for human rights. Yet, paradoxically, the countervailing emphasis on the authority of the state has led to limits on civil and democratic rights. Until the latter 1970s, for example, governments blatantly controlled and manipulated the reporting of news and denied opposition parties equal access to the publicly owned airwaves. Since then, the government monopoly on broadcasting has ended and reporting is now much more balanced, but the state still has the authority to dissolve political organizations and newspapers, powers which are used against extremist causes such as those which advocate or employ violence to promote their aims. Despite such state prerogatives, however, it remains the case that French citizens by and large enjoy the full panoply of human rights that their ancestors did so much to define and propagate in past centuries.

THE SOVIET UNION AND CHINA: CITIZEN ROLES IN SOCIALIST COUNTRIES

In liberal democracies, political participation is usually a matter that is left to individual citizens; most governments do little more than encourage their citizens to exercise their franchise at election time. In communist states, participation is typically neither as spontaneous nor as voluntary. The dominant communist parties act as the major stimulants of citizen activity, creating a strong obligation to become involved in the achievement of such party-defined goals as the demonstration of support for communist rule, the attainment of production goals, and the rooting out of dissent.

The centrally directed nature of mass participation in communist states is readily understandable. For one thing, communist governments are dedicated to the quickest possible transformation of traditional societies into modern industrialized societies. This task requires discipline and central direction to harness and channel human resources. Secondly, many of the prerequisites to spontaneous political participation—notably a literate and affluent population—are missing in communist states, or were so in the critical period after the assumption of power.

[17]G. Almond and S. Verba, *The Civic Culture: Political Attitudes and Democracy in Five Nations* (Boston: Little, Brown, 1965), pp. 70, 72.

Finally, and perhaps most importantly, the Leninist concept of the party's leading role has underlain the party elites' efforts to direct all political action.

The efforts of the Communist parties of China and the Soviet Union to stimulate mass participation have been successful in many respects. Relative to Western democratic systems, a very large share of the populations of both countries is involved in political or community activities and organizations. In China, for example, workers can be found after factory hours in discussion groups, reflecting on the relationship between culture and politics or the roles they can play in national development; students spend their vacations working alongside peasants in the fields; women volunteers control traffic in towns and cities. However, the nature and extent of participation are determined by the party leadership; at times the limits of permissible activity have been expanded, at other times constricted. Thus, the repressive conditions of Stalin's rule inhibited participation in the Soviet Union in the 1930s and 1940s, but with the "thaw" of 1956 freer expression and greater citizen involvement were encouraged. In China the Hundred Flowers Campaign of 1956–1957 was a period of expanded participation; it was followed by a period of tightened control that lasted until 1966. Then, under the aegis of the Great Proletarian Cultural Revolution, China went through a highly participatory—although far from democratic—phase. At present, the trend in both the Soviet Union and China seems to be toward government decentralization and greater citizen participation, but the extent to which either ruling party will allow this participation to escape its guidance and control is likely to remain limited.

Soviet Union: A Symbolically Participatory Regime

The long centuries of Russian autocracy bred a populace mostly inclined to view political authority with a mixture of deference and apathy, but containing a tradition of sporadic revolt and a subculture of restless intellectuals. Today, Russians overwhelmingly display the deferential side of that legacy, but a small contingent of dissidents keeps the tradition of intellectual rebellion alive. Most of the national minorities have also inherited a deference to authority; for some of them, however, their dislike of the dominant Russians continues to color their attitudes toward the Soviet state. The political elite, like the tsars and boyars of the past, views the general public with distrust and keeps a watchful eye on both Russians and minorities for signs of any unrest.

These traditions have naturally favored the perpetuation of a strong state whose power is not seriously challenged by popular will. And yet, the regime that has developed rests its claim to legitimacy on a revolutionary mythology based on the Marxist-Leninist vision of a state ruled democratically by the working class. According to that theory, the party seized power in the name of the workers' soviets and set up a dictatorship of the proletariat. This workers' dictatorship was necessary, the communists maintained, because the supporters of the old regime were eager to regain power and had to be kept in check by force. Once the supporters of the old regime (the aristocracy and the bourgeoisie) were liquidated or neutralized, only the working class and the peasantry would be left. In time, the dictatorship of the proletariat would give way to a *socialist* system; the peasantry would eventually merge with the working class, and the world's first true democracy could be established, based on the absence of an exploiter and an exploited class. In 1936 the Soviet Union was officially proclaimed a socialist state.[18] This did not yet mean a totally classless society, for there still remained a large peasantry. In theory, that poses no problem for working-class rule today, for the peasants, whose economic and cultural life is fully organized within the collectivized agricultural system, are presumed to have no conflict with the working class.

Guided by the official mythology, the communist elite has created institutions and processes that are designed to include workers in the system that is nominally theirs, but the elite nonetheless reserves to itself the right to determine the "general will." Thus, the "ruling class," that is, the working class, does not actually rule in the sense that we in the West understand the concept, but it does participate in political life to a greater degree than the populace of Western liberal democracies—even if that participation is often only symbolic.

Political participation in the Soviet Union can entail joining the Communist party and becoming active in its work, as either a volunteer or a salaried official; serving as a member of an elected soviet, from the local level to the Supreme Soviet; taking part in the activities of the trade unions; joining the KOMSOMOL (youth league); or becoming involved in community self-help organizations. Literally millions of people participate in these capacities. In 1982, for example, more than 2 million citizens were serving as deputies of local soviets, and as of 1984 membership in the CPSU totaled 18.4 million.[19] Even larger numbers are members of the KOMSOMOL and the trade unions.

Community self-help organizations exist in every town and village, though their activities may vary from place to place. In general, they divide into three functional groups. The first includes those set up to control and prevent minor deviant or criminal behavior: local citizens' courts (called comrades' courts) and voluntary militia groups. The second are neighborhood, block, or (in large residential units) house com-

---

[18]According to Marx and Lenin there is, of course, yet another stage of development to come, that of *communism,* a form of society in which all share equally in the material wealth of the community. The Soviets accept this idea but explain that communism will be a long time in the building; in the meantime, Soviet society has entered a stage that the party now describes as *developed socialism.*

[19]R. Hill, *The Soviet Union: Politics, Economics and Society* (London: Frances Pinter, 1985), pp. 100, 75.

mittees, whose task it is to mobilize citizens for various projects being undertaken by the local soviets; the committees' tasks also include reporting on people whose behavior or attitudes may displease the local authorities. The third are voluntary organizations whose functions include a number of community services not always adequately provided by the agencies of the local soviet; these can range from firefighting and sanitation brigades to senior citizens' councils. Up-to-date statistics on participation in community self-help organizations are hard to come by, but Theodore Friedgut reported that in 1963 those in the Sakhalin oblast (province) alone had a total of 87,710 members; the significance of this figure becomes apparent when we consider that there are 130 oblasts in the USSR.[20]

There are, in addition, a number of less active ways in which nearly all citizens participate in political life. They include discussions, led by party members, of public issues and policies; attending political education classes; turning out to march and demonstrate on patriotic holidays; and, of course, voting in elections for the Supreme Soviet and local and regional governments. In contrast to comparable activities in the West, which tend to be voluntary and therefore limited to those who choose to be politically active, these forms of participation in the USSR are expected of citizens, and virtually everybody engages in them. Some do so with enthusiasm and a sense of purpose; others consider their participation a waste of time or a necessary burden.

All citizens aged 18 and over have the right to vote. The Communist party decides who will stand for election in every instance, and no opposition party is permitted. Despite the fact that some elections are now contests between two or more candidates, the lack of an opposition ensures that the ruling party will go unchallenged. Still, the elections are taken seriously as a demonstration of citizens' loyalty and a ceremony substantiating the mythology of the workers' state. Voters are made to feel that their participation is important; election day is a festive occasion, and party activists and members of the mobilization committees work hard to get out the vote. Among voters there is a vague sense that they may get in trouble if they do not vote, although Friedgut's authoritative study found no evidence that those who intentionally decline to vote are punished.[21] Soviet officials generally report voter turnout at about 99.8 percent of the electorate. There is reason to believe that this statistic is inflated, but not by much; Friedgut estimates, as an example, that the accurate figure for the 1970 elections to the Supreme Soviet was around 97.5 percent.[22]

Nonvoting can be a way of showing disapproval of the electoral system or of the candidates selected by the party. Another way of showing

[20]T. H. Friedgut, *Political Participation in the USSR* (Princeton, N.J.: Princeton University Press, 1979), p. 245.

[21]T.H. Friedgut, op. cit., p. 115.

[22]Ibid., p. 117.

disapproval is by voting against the candidates put up for office by crossing their names off the ballot. Voters are not allowed to write in an alternative selection, so a vote against the party's candidate(s) is not a vote *for* someone else. As a majority of votes is required to elect a deputy, it has occasionally happened that the voters have turned down a candidate by casting a majority of negative votes. The incidence of candidate defeat is statistically minuscule (in 1975, about 1 in 70,000); it has happened mostly at the village level, rarely at the district level or in the voting for a city soviet, and never for a republic soviet or higher.[23]

It is a common misconception in the West that Soviet officials are distanced from, or even inaccessible to, their citizens. This may be true of high party and state figures, but local leaders in fact appear to be more accessible than are most of their Western counterparts. Citizens commonly turn to their local soviet deputies with complaints about public services such as housing or pensions—so commonly, in fact, that the soviets' staffs are often overburdened by requests for help. They are not always able to help, or to do so promptly, but they nearly always acknowledge the complaints or requests and make an effort to deal with them within their capabilities. Frequently, citizens who do not receive satisfactory results from local authorities appeal to higher authorities, even to their deputy to the (federal) Supreme Soviet. Thus the right to petition public authorities is taken quite seriously in the Soviet Union.[24]

The most important forms of political participation take place in the Communist party. Before the revolution, Lenin had conceived the ideal party as a compact and highly disciplined group capable of operating clandestinely within the hostile environment of the tsarist police state. Even in Lenin's lifetime, however, the party increased in size from fewer than 24,000 members in January 1917 to over 300,000 by the time of the October Revolution. Today, 1 in every 10 adults is a party member.

Men make up approximately three-fourths of the CPSU membership, and, generally speaking, the proportion of women becomes increasingly smaller in the higher leadership ranks. In recent years, there has been no woman on the Politburo and only one (of 11) on the Secretariat of the Central Committee. As to nationality representation, the statistics are more equitable, though there is still a tendency to overrepresentation of the Russians, especially at higher levels. Table 4.6 gives a recent breakdown of total CPSU membership by nationality.

As in Lenin's day, party members are disciplined and loyal, but it should be remembered that they are also human beings who are not set apart from other citizens but live and work within their community; they are fathers and mothers, wage earners, consumers. They differ from

[23]Ibid., p. 130.
[24]In contrast, S. Verba and N. Nie, in *Participation in America* (New York: Harper & Row, 1972), found that only about one in five Americans had ever turned directly to a local leader or official with a problem.

Table 4.6   CPSU, COMPOSITION BY NATIONALITY, 1977

Nationality	Number	Percent
Total	15,994,476	100.00
Russians	9,679,129	60.5
Ukrainians	2,561,129	16.0
Belorussians	580,833	3.6
Uzbeks	333,907	2.1
Kazakhs	292,936	1.8
Georgians	265,625	1.7
Azeris	241,677	1.5
Armenians	239,460	1.5
Lithuanians	110,934	0.7
Moldavians	72,331	0.5
Latvians	66,402	0.4
Tadzhiks	65,477	0.4
Kirghiz	51,112	0.3
Estonians	50,984	0.3
Turkmenians	50,269	0.3
Others	1,331,584	8.4

Source: Official CPSU data, reprinted by R. Hill and P. Frank, *The Soviet Communist Party* (London: Allen & Unwin, 1981), p. 39.

other members of society in that they have chosen to serve the ends of the party and the party has chosen to bring them into its membership. As a rule, they are more politically conscious than other citizens, and although some may join the party primarily for the resulting benefits to their career or material life-style, most do so from a sense of commitment and responsibility. "Joining the CPSU," as two observers have written, "is the most significant act that an individual can perform, as momentous in its way as the decision by those of different persuasions to become 'dissidents'."[25]

And what of the dissidents, those to whom the Western media devote so much attention? They, too, are political participants, though their participation takes place on the fringe of the Soviet polity. Opposition to the party or its leadership is considered antisocial behavior, and those who engage in it risk prosecution, imprisonment, exile, or in some cases punitive confinement in mental institutions. Protests and strikes are not allowed; demonstrations, parades, and other forms of public gathering normally require permits from the authorities, and permits are not granted for the purpose of unofficial political expression. This does not mean that all forms of criticism are forbidden; within limits, it is permitted to criticize individual party and government leaders of the lower and middle levels, and the Soviet press frequently prints letters from citizens complaining about inefficiency or arrogance on the part of officials. How-

[25]R. J. Hill and P. Frank, *The Soviet Communist Party* (London: Allen & Unwin, 1981), p. 20.

ever, the socialist system, the party as such, and the top leadership are not acceptable targets of public criticism.

Despite the impression given by the Western media, open political protest by groups or individuals is rare and has no mass support in the Soviet Union. The dissidents, nearly all of them drawn from the intelligentsia, are nevertheless courageous and deserving of admiration. Because of official harassment and surveillance by the KGB (secret police), they are unable to band together in organizations and cannot easily communicate with each other. The dissidents represent several differing political and philosophical tendencies, from Marxist-Leninists who are disturbed by the party's compromises of its humanitarian principles, to religious dissenters who reject communism as an atheistic doctrine. The dissident ranks encompass members of national minorities who protest ethnic discrimination, as well as a small movement of Russian nationalists who value their cultural roots and resent the ideology of "internationalism."

The broad issue most acutely raised by the dissidents best known in the West is that of human rights and civil liberties. A handful of persons once prominent have taken the dangerous step of speaking out; the best known have been historian Roy Medvedev, who has been careful to stay mostly within the bounds of law and has thereby avoided punishment; nuclear physicist Andrei Sakharov, one of the men involved in the development of the Soviet hydrogen bomb in the 1950s, who spent long years under house arrest in the provincial town of Gorky before finally being released in late 1986; Nobel Prize-winning writer Aleksandr Solzhenitsyn, who in 1974 was exiled to the United States after nearly a decade of harassment; and world-renowned cellist Mstislav Rostropovich, who was deprived of his Soviet citizenship during a lengthy period of residence in the West. In 1976–1977, Helsinki Watch Committees were formed by dissidents in numerous localities to monitor noncompliance with the human rights clauses of the 1975 Helsinki Accords, signed by the Soviet government. In their efforts to publicize the plight of persecuted dissidents, the Watch Committees managed to bring together a wider base of activists than had ever before cooperated; Christians, Jews, ethnic minorities, opponents of psychiatric treatment for political prisoners, and others joined forces to the extent possible. Within two years, however, some of the group's leaders found themselves beginning long terms in prison, and by 1982 the activities of the Watch Committees were greatly curtailed by the government's pressures.[26]

With respect to human rights, the Soviet constitution presents two faces. On the one hand, it acknowledges all the civil rights incorporated

---

[26]In 1986 the founder and head of the Moscow Helsinki Watch Committee, Yuri Orlov, was released from a prison camp in Siberia after more than eight years and allowed to emigrate to the United States as part of an apparent swap involving a Soviet citizen convicted in the United States of spying and an American journalist, Nicholas Daniloff, arrested in Moscow on charges of espionage.

into the constitutions of Western democracies: freedom of the press, freedom of religion, free speech, and so forth. On the other hand, the Soviet constitution clearly restricts these rights, specifically by asserting (Article 39) that individuals may not exercise them in a way that interferes with the interests of the community. Further clauses explain that individual rights are granted not for their own sake, but for the purpose of strengthening and developing socialism (Article 50); that agitation or propaganda aimed at subverting Soviet authority is not allowed (Article 70); and that citizens have the right to practice their religion, but, while they are free to conduct atheistic propaganda, they are not free to make religious propaganda (Article 52).[27] These constitutional restrictions serve to justify a variety of repressive activities undertaken by the state in the professed interests of the socialist community.

Western regimes and private human rights organizations have often criticized the USSR's human rights behavior in strong terms and reminded the Soviet leadership of its commitment to the Helsinki Accords, as well as the Soviet government's acceptance of the Universal Declaration of Human Rights. The Soviets have countered in several ways. They argue, in the first place, that their government has the right to punish those who openly challenge the basis of their political system, and they point to certain fringe elements in Western societies who, they say, have been persecuted for their political activities, such as Russell Banks, the leader of the radical American Indian Movement. In addition, the Soviets accuse the West of ignoring what they consider to be a basic human right, the right to employment; noting the especially high unemployment rates in North America and Western Europe during the early 1980s, Soviet spokesmen point out that their system provides a job for every able-bodied worker, thereby protecting the citizen from the hardship and indignity of joblessness.

The Gorbachev regime has taken modest steps toward liberalization. In 1986–1987 more than 100 dissenters were released from prison, and the rate of politically motivated arrests reached its lowest level since the Khrushchev period. Aware that social and economic progress depends on new ideas and innovative problem-solving approaches, Gorbachev and his associates appear to agree that it is worth whatever political "risk" is involved to free some of the creative minds that have been locked away. The liberalization is thus far only a partial change, however, and its ultimate dimensions are not yet clear.

How do we evaluate political participation in the USSR? Certainly, the average Soviet citizen has scant effect on policy-making and negligible input into the selection of governmental representatives. On the other hand, the political system involves the citizen in frequent activities that carry an important symbolic meaning. These activities are not, strictly

[27]Darrell P. Hammer, *The USSR: The Politics of Oligarchy,* 2nd ed. (Boulder, Colo.: Westview, 1986), pp. 177–180.

speaking, voluntary, and many people no doubt feel some resentment about the fact that they are expected to participate. And yet very few are driven to rebel or speak out against the system or its practices. The circulation of dissent via the *samizdat* ("self-published") underground press is limited to perhaps a few thousand readers at most, and there is every reason to believe that the vast majority of Soviet citizens are unsympathetic to, or unfamiliar with, the cause of the dissidents.

For the individual, then, there is a curious and fundamental difference between politics in the Soviet Union and politics in the West. In the West, the individual citizen decides whether or not to support a party or a cause, to canvass or participate in fund-raising, and even to vote, and he may freely choose (as many people do) not to become involved in politics at all. In the Soviet Union, everyone is expected to vote and to participate in other political activities; those who choose not to be so involved distinguish themselves from their peers and invite the criticism of their local Communist party committee. Politics, as Westerners are inclined to understand the term, involving policy debates and authoritative decision-making, remains the prerogative in the Soviet Union of a tight oligarchy; but politics in the broader sense, involving a range of activities that engage the citizen on a regular basis in one or another aspect of public life, is far more widely participatory in the USSR than in the West.

China: The Ebb and Flow of Participation

Before the collapse of the monarchy in 1910, politics in China was the preserve of the nobility (including the monarchy), the landed elite, the bureaucratic elite, and to a limited extent the bourgeoisie or emerging merchant class. The peasants, who composed the great bulk of the population, challenged the status quo only when their situation became intolerable. During the 1930s, when China was entering the early stages of industrialization, the urban working class began to become more outspoken; nevertheless, politics still largely excluded it. Although China is not yet fully industrialized, the communist regime has altered this rather limited participation in several significant ways. Nevertheless, there is an inevitable tension between the desire to involve the people in the political process and the desire to control that involvement so that it does not pass beyond the bounds of the Communist party's control and direction.

Although China proclaims itself a "people's republic," elections have played a very circumscribed role in Chinese politics until recently. Direct elections are limited to a relatively low level of political office, the County People's Congresses. The delegates so chosen elect the next level of public officials, the delegates to the Provincial People's Congresses, who in turn elect the National People's Congress delegates. Thus, while the British prime minister is chosen indirectly by MPs, the Chinese have gone a step further by inserting two more levels between directly elected delegates and the highest government leadership. There are also elections in various other local organizations, including direct elections of team leaders at the production team level. In most cases, however, the party must approve the candidate or slate of candidates for the position in question.

Elections in urban areas are held primarily by secret ballot, whereas those in rural areas have tended to be by show of hands. The 1953 electoral law allowed this procedure in order to overcome the barrier of illiteracy. Although approximately 85 percent of the eligible voters turn out, elections have not generated a great deal of popular enthusiasm. Citizen enthusiasm for elections appears to have been undermined by disillusionment with some of the candidates, who in earlier elections were chosen without sensitivity to public opinion, and by the failure of the local congresses to fulfill their functions. People realize that citizen involvement in elections is encouraged with the objective not so much of eliciting choices but of legitimizing choices already made. Thus, the Chinese government's role in political participation is simultaneously a stimulating and an inhibiting one, and the net effect may often be one of discouragement.

While "hot and cold" shifts in government policy toward popular input have continued into the post-Mao era, important changes toward democratization have occurred. Among the most significant are the present leadership's encouragement of greater public expression, its increased attention to public opinion, and its desire to open up the process of selecting public officials. In recent years, public opinion has increasingly been sought to determine potential support for new policy initiatives. In 1986 the *Economic Daily* sampled people in 17 cities to determine their attitudes toward economic and governmental reforms. They found that a significant proportion of respondents believed the reforms would succeed and that many felt they were proceeding too slowly.[28] In a survey released in 1987, some 56 percent of young people (under 25 years of age) believed that "China has a certain degree of democracy but still needs improving."[29] Greater democratization was in fact the intention of an electoral law passed in 1979, which allowed for the possibility of multicandidate elections for a variety of local offices. Corresponding legislation affecting internal party elections has also been passed. These reforms have met with problems and resistance, however. At times there were too many candidates, and officials have had to intervene to reduce their numbers. For example, in 1987 some 17,000 candidates came forward in elections to the 240-seat Beijing People's Congress. In addition, although party members tend to do better in the selection process, some officials have feared the new system will mean the end to their authority.

[28]Cited in the *Beijing Review* 26, no. 1 (January 1987), 8.
[29]*Christian Science Monitor* (October 3, 1987), p. 1.

Nevertheless, democratization appears to have the continued support of top party officials such as Deng Xiaoping.

A form of political participation unique to China is the mass movement or mass campaign, an attempt to mobilize the emotional and physical strength of the people to achieve specific goals established by the leadership. The party has aimed the most important mass movements at transforming the society from its prerevolutionary state to socialism. Among the most noteworthy are the Hundred Flowers movement of the late 1950s, which allowed open criticism of party practices, and the Great Leap Forward of the early 1960s, which attempted a rapid spurt toward socialism and industrialization. Perhaps the largest of all the mass movements was the Great Proletarian Cultural Revolution in the late 1960s.

The Chinese leadership resorts to the mass movement to counter apathy and stimulate citizen participation in politics. The mass movement represents a temporary intensification of the pressure to participate and a channeling of citizens' efforts toward chosen objectives. The leadership hopes that the experience of participation will change the masses' ideas and behavior patterns permanently. There is considerable evidence that behavior is more likely to change through actual participation than in response to persuasion but little evidence that the changes will be lasting. In a sense, mass participation in the transformation of social institutions is a huge "psychodrama" aimed at modifying individual and collective traditional behavior. Given traditional patterns of socialization which emphasize dependence on authority, it probably requires a strong push from above to break ingrained habits of dependence. But the process is slow and there are many setbacks, as is sensitively conveyed by a Red Guard's description of the early stages of the Cultural Revolution:

> In all of the excitement, it seemed as though the Red Guards were to sprout like bamboo. However, we soon came face to face with the reality that we didn't know how to organize. In the past, we would simply have used the leadership structure that already existed, but that was not possible. We had to decide who was to be eligible to join the Red Guards, what the specific goals should be and what its relationship with the Preparatory Committee established by the work team should be. We pored over the newspapers hoping to find the answers. All that we found, however, were reports in praise of the Red Guards. These kept our enthusiasm at a peak but were of no help in solving the main problem.[30]

Since the Cultural Revolution there have been other mass movements or campaigns (see Table 4.7). One of the more minor ones, the campaign around Lei Feng, illustrates both the cyclical nature of the process and the degree to which these campaigns are used to advance

[30]Gordon A. Bennett and R. N. Montaperto, *Red Guard: The Political Biography of Dai Hsiao-ai* (Garden City, N.Y.: Doubleday, 1971), pp. 72–73.

Table 4.7 MOVEMENTS AND CAMPAIGNS SINCE 1969

	Time Period	Goals or Targets
Anti-Lin Biao	1971–1972	Against Lin Biao and his supporters
Anti-Confucius	1974–1975	Against Zhou Enlai and moderates
Water Margin	1975–1976	Against Zhou Enlai, Deng Xiaoping, Hua Guofeng
Study the Dictatorship of the Proletariat	1975	Against Zhou Enlai, Deng Xiaoping, and the fourth NPC policy programs
Campaign against Capitalist Roaders	1976	Against Deng Xiaoping
Campaign against the Gang of Four	1976–1978	Against Jiang Qing and the radicals in the CCP, army, and bureaucracy
Emulation Campaign in Railroads	1977	Railroad efficiency and security
Sanitation Campaign	1978	To improve sanitation and public health
Four Modernizations Campaign	1978	For industrialization, technological development, economic change
Democracy Movement	1978–1979	Against opponents of Deng Xiaoping
Four Great Freedoms Campaign	1978–1979	For the "four freedoms": speaking out freely, airing views fully, holding great debates, and writing big character posters
Anti-Crime Drive	1983	Against corruption by government and party officials
Anti-Spiritual Pollution	1984–1985	Against "corrupt" foreign thought and liberal movies and music

distinct policy directions taken within the party. In the 1960s Lei Feng was brought to the attention of the Chinese as a model communist. He was selfless and did countless anonymous good deeds for others. After the introduction of economic reforms in the 1980s, the ideal communist youth came to be seen much more as a seeker of individual advantage. But conservatives in the party, long concerned by these "Western" influences among the young, got their chance to counterattack in the wake of the suppression of the 1986–1987 demonstrations for democracy. Lei Feng was brought back in a second national campaign and eulogized as a pliant, unquestioning party follower. As Lei put it:

A man's usefulness to the revolutionary cause is like a screw in a machine. It is only by the many, many interconnected and fixed screws that the machine can move freely, increasing its enormous work power. Though a screw is small, its use is beyond estimation.[31]

Voluntary civic action is another form of mass participation at the local level. Volunteer labor performs many basic services, including sanitation, firefighting, and traffic control. Committees of volunteers often set or administer policy for such small social units as apartment buildings, collective farms, and factories. The use of volunteer police and even judges serves as an effective deterrent to nonconformity. While the penalties they can mete out are limited, they tend to be more severe than those given by trained police and jurists. Often community service is used as a punishment for minor offences.

Since the economic reforms of the late 1970s, considerable citizen involvement has taken place in a myriad of local groups, where individuals seek to influence teachers, business organizations, local government, or party officials. The main issues are those associated with the allocation of scarce resources affecting economic units. Other issues subject to local group consideration include health, education, food distribution, and family size (official policy is that couples should have only one child).

Political involvement for many individuals also takes the more informal but highly significant form of patron-client relationships known as *guanxi,* in which individuals seek advancement and influence by attaching themselves to those of higher status. For example, a few local influentials may back a particular individual's candidacy to the County Congress. That individual in turn will be approached by groups seeking to promote a leader for the provincial level, who in turn will be called on to support a group seeking national offices. If the local people line up with a winning coalition, their status will also rise. Their requests for jobs, funding, educational opportunities, or other favors granted by government or party will more likely be honored.

Women have generally had far fewer opportunities for participation than men. One study of urban bureaucratic elites found that 94 percent were male.[32] Within the party itself, only about 10 percent of party members are women, and they are rarely found in leadership positions. In the military, in the party, in factories, and in government bodies at all levels, however, the numbers of women have been increasing; in 1983, for example, 21 percent of the delegates at the Sixth National People's Congress were women.

Efforts continue to improve women's social and political position. The regime has been particularly conscientious in its efforts to overcome

[31]*Christian Science Monitor* (March 6, 1987), p. 11.
[32]Kao Yingmao, "The Urban Bureaucratic Elite in Communist China," in *Communist China: A Functional Reader,* ed. Yung Wei (Columbus, Ohio: Merrill, 1972), p. 191.

the traditional oppression of women. In addition to enactment of laws guaranteeing equal treatment, the equality of women is emphasized in socialization efforts. For example, a study of Chinese films found that many had feminist themes and that women had leading roles more frequently than men.[33] Films play a prominent role in adult socialization in China and, through the depiction of heroines, the leadership has sought to overcome traditional attitudes toward women.

In general, opposition to the Communist party or its leadership is considered antisocial behavior subject to prosecution. The government regards protest demonstrations, parades, and strikes as unacceptable appeals to the masses over the heads of the party and its leadership. Criticism of individual party and government leaders at the lower and middle levels is, however, acceptable and encouraged within limits. The Chinese press frequently prints letters criticizing party and government leaders for inefficiency or arrogance. Such criticism helps keep the party responsive to the people and combats bureaucratic lethargy.

There are signs that China may be undergoing an evolution in citizens' roles, one which could affect both political orientations and, ultimately, the political system itself. This process is occurring primarily in response to party encouragement. In 1979 individuals and groups began to bring their grievances to the attention of other citizens (through wall posters) and to the government. In one of the bolder manifestations, several hundred demonstrators from northern provinces came to Beijing to seek jobs, housing, and food. They took their demands to the very center of power, the Zhung-nanhai in the "forbidden city," where the Communist Party Central Committee and the party chief, Hua Guofeng, resided.

The "Democracy Movement," as it was called, was in fact a political manipulation by Deng Xiaoping against Hua Guofeng. When he had successfully turned the tables on his political opponents, the movement was promptly terminated, at least in its overt form. However, in 1986 Deng again perceived a political opportunity. Frustrated students in many cities in China were allowed to protest. In Shanghai more than 20,000 students attracted crowds of over 70,000 in their marches to the municipal hall. They were seeking legalized student demonstrations, more democracy, economic reforms, and an end to police abuses. The press was initially silent on the matter, while local officials responded that students have a right to express their grievances. As before, it was a combination of spontaneous citizen concern and political leadership objectives that allowed the demonstration to take place. Eventually, when matters seemed to be getting out of hand, the demonstrations were crushed and the leaders responsible removed.

Nevertheless, open dissent is becoming much more common in

---

[33]John H. Weakland, "Chinese Film Images of Invasion and Resistance," *China Quarterly* 47 (July/September 1971), 439–470.

China. For years artists and intellectuals were labeled dissenters because their work did not fit into prescribed lines or directions. Today, debate is raging within the party over whether art and literature should be totally subordinate to politics, and reported incidents of open dissent abound. In one incident, a deputy editor of the *People's Daily* reportedly lost his job because of his ideological dispute with a senior party leader over the issue of humanism.[34] In another incident, one of the successful candidates for local election was a cook who had criticized the minister of commerce for failing to pay his bill for meals.[35]

Political dissent inevitably raises the question of individual or human rights and, in particular, the issue of how well protected individuals are when they protest against the state. In revolutionary periods, human rights are often not respected, even by groups who claim to be struggling to achieve them. The leaders of the Chinese Revolution stressed the need to destroy the institutions and individuals that in the past had brought misery and repression to millions of Chinese, but in their struggle against privilege and social oppression, the rights and freedoms of many, particularly those seen as former exploiters, were abused.

After Mao's death, his successors seemed somewhat less interested in pushing for equality and social justice; their priority has been to promote rapid industrialization. This has prompted a tension between the need for more individual initiative in the economic sphere and the desire to maintain tight state control in the political sphere. China's post-Mao constitutions have guaranteed civil rights and, as noted earlier, democratic movements have appeared. Nevertheless, on both occasions they were suppressed. In addition, Amnesty International has reported numerous cases of persons in China being punished because of their political beliefs or membership in a faction that is out of power. In one well-publicized case, Wei Jingsheng, a leader of the Democracy Movement in 1978–1979 and editor of a journal advocating democracy as "the fifth modernization," was arrested and put on trial as a counterrevolutionary. He argued, in his defense, that Article 45 of the 1978 constitution granted him the freedom to speak, to write, and to debate. He was sentenced to 15 years in prison.

To understand this situation, one must take note of the way in which democracy is perceived by the Chinese. Chinese political thought has traditionally assumed an identity of interests between the state and the people. Harmony is a prime Confucian objective. To achieve this harmony, the norm is that rights can be revoked whenever it is deemed necessary in order to protect the national interest. In contrast, Western democratic norms hold that laws which are inconsistent with basic individual rights should be invalidated. In a sense, China's view supports a

[34]*Christian Science Monitor* (July 2, 1986), 9.
[35]Brantly Womack, "The 1980 County-Level Elections in China: Experiment in Democratic Modernization," in *Asian Survey, 22* no. 3 (March 1982), 269.

state-centered system of rights, whereas Western thought gives preference to individual rights.

MEXICO AND NIGERIA: NATIONAL CONSCIOUSNESS, ALIENATION, AND MOBILIZATION

In former colonies such as Mexico and Nigeria, it is frequently during
the period immediately preceding independence that individuals with
limited knowledge of the world outside their village or kinship group
become aware of their membership in a larger political body. They may
even be mobilized to fight for nationhood. If political instability and
turmoil follow in the wake of independence, however, the result may be
apathy, alienation, and withdrawal from the uncomfortable new reality.
Nigeria and Mexico have both followed this pattern. Nigerian enthusiasm was very high during the late 1950s—the eve of independence—and
the early 1960s. Mexico experienced the same phenomenon in the first
two decades of the nineteenth century. Both country's citizens later confronted the bitter realities of postindependence conflict and instability.

With time, the process of modernization can be expected to undermine traditional orientations toward the world. Education, the mass
media, and urban employment expose individuals to new experiences
that broaden their horizons and lead to a wider range of social and
political involvements. As a result, individual predispositions to participate in politics may well increase. In Mexico, these processes have already begun to affect large sections of the population; in Nigeria, they are
just beginning to make themselves felt. For both countries, their net
effect is likely to be one that challenges the prevailing authoritarianism
of their current regimes.

Mexico: Limited Participation, Limited Protest

Until recently, citizen participation in Mexico was quite limited. This is
due in part to the control of the ruling PRI and the widespread faith in
its commitment to fulfill the promises of the revolution (for example,
better living conditions, jobs, and land reform) and in part to the relatively low level of development of the country. As in much of the Third
World, the social conditions that encourage participation—literacy, mass
media exposure, urbanization—are absent or poorly developed in Mexico. Of Mexico's 48 million citizens aged six or over in 1979, more than
10 million were illiterate; in fact, the rural population was almost evenly
divided between literates (48 percent) and illiterates (52 percent).[36]

Certain attitudes unlikely to support political participation are especially prevalent in Mexico's less developed areas. Oscar Lewis described a typical peasant, Pedro Martinez, as follows:

[36]*C.B.S. News Almanac, 1978* (Maplewood, N.J.: Hammond Almanac, 1979).

He shares many peasant values—a love of the land, a reverence for nature, a strong belief in the intrinsic good of agricultural labor, and a restraint on individual self-seeking in favor of family and community. Like most peasants, he is also authoritarian, fatalistic, suspicious, concrete-minded and ambivalent in his attitudes toward city people.[37]

Studies have confirmed the prevalence of authoritarianism, lack of trust in others, and passivity, especially among peasant and lower-class communities. One study of a Mexican village found that sociopolitical relations were characterized predominantly by submissiveness and fatalism (49 percent), and by authoritarianism (36 percent). In only 7 percent of cases were democratic tendencies in evidence.[38] A study of schoolchildren also found a prevalence of authoritarianism involving a general lack of trust, decisions not to participate, patterns of personal dependence, and a lack of confidence in political parties. These attitudes were most common among lower-class children.[39] In addition, numerous studies have shown that fewer than one-fifth of adults expect to receive serious attention to their viewpoints from the police of the bureaucracy, even in urban areas. Attitudes such as these are hardly likely to stimulate active participation in politics.

The low level of political involvement in Mexico is illustrated by the difficulty of arousing interest in elections. In one early study, 45 percent of the Mexicans interviewed said they paid no attention to election campaigning.[40] Voting in presidential elections, nevertheless, is often quite high: 72 percent voted in the 1976 election and 70 percent in 1982. Moreover, studies of voting patterns in Mexico have shown that voter turnout is often highest in those areas where competition from the opposition party is least and in less developed areas.[41] This finding is at odds with the experience of the United States and other competitive systems, in which turnout is higher in areas that are more competitive or more developed economically. Mexico's variance from this general rule is explained, at least in part, by the fact that the people perceive voting for the PRI as a means of expressing loyalty to the regime and of encouraging the government to dispense more favors in their region. The same influences do not operate to encourage involvement in political organizations, however. Thus the PRI leadership has a difficult time eliciting participation in campaign and party activities, and success is often attributable to the skill of an aggressive and appealing leader in motivating others to join in undertaking political action.

[37]Oscar Lewis, *Pedro Martinez* (New York: Random House, 1964), p. xxxii.

[38]E. From and M. Maccoby, *Social Character in a Mexican Village* (Englewood Cliffs, N.J.: Prentice-Hall, 1970), pp. 262–263.

[39]R. Segovia, *La Politization del nino Mexicano* (Mexico, DF: El Colegio de Mexico, 1975), pp. 52–54, 121–130.

[40]G. Almond and S. Verba, *The Civic Culture* (Boston: Little, Brown, 1965), p. 109.

[41]Barry Ames, "Bases of Support for Mexico's Dominant Party," *American Political Science Review* 64 (March 1970), 153–167; R. Segovia, op. cit., p. 81.

Although interest in partisan and electoral matters is low on average, Mexicans tend to be willing to engage in civic projects for the benefit of the community. Motivated by leaders with visions of social change, Mexicans frequently involve themselves in civic action. In Oscar Lewis's study *Pedro Martinez,* we glimpse this willingness to become involved in voluntary civic service:

> I was always serving my village, as president of the committee on national fiestas, as inspector of the parks, as inspector of charcoal production, as president of the commission to get drinking water for the village and, of course, I always volunteered for the *cuatequitl,* the collective working party.[42]

In addition, the lack of involvement in the democratic political process is compensated for in part by the ability to use patron-client networks to influence government. It is not uncommon for an ordinary individual to seek assistance from the mayor or local PRI leader, the key patrons at the local level. In exchange for his service, the local patron is likely to call on the client for his and his family's votes in the following election. The disadvantage in this procedure is that demands coming from the lower classes can be dealt with by the authorities in a piecemeal and dilatory fashion, while the need for more general reforms is ignored.

Political participation in Mexico often takes such violent forms as demonstrations, riots, political assassinations, and occasionally guerilla warfare. The inadequacy of nonviolent means of seeking redress for grievances largely explains the prevalence of violence in politics and in society in general; in the view of one observer, the Mexican "is compelled to resort to drastic expedients, that is, to express in shouting and shooting what he is unable to express through legal means."[43] Furthermore, the tradition of violence in Mexican history has created a political culture that validates violence as a means of political expression. Mexican men's *machismo,* or assertive masculinity, is often expressed in violent behavior.

The potential for protest and violence is amply illustrated in Mexico's recent past. Large-scale student strikes in 1968 resulted in a government massacre of hundreds of students. By the mid-1970s, at least a half-dozen terrorist groups operated in various parts of Mexico; bank robbery, kidnapping, and assassination were among their favored tactics. Peasants have become active in protests as well. During President Echeverría's term (1970–1976), the government's decision to grant some land to peasants in the northern state of Sonora led peasants to grab other lands and to engage in violent protests. Peasant land seizures spread to nearby states until government forces removed the peasants from "illegally" seized land pursuant to a court ruling against Echeverría's land

[42]Oscar Lewis, op. cit., pp. 260–261.
[43]Victor Alba, *The Latin Americans* (New York: Praeger, 1969), p. 44.

grants. In the winter of 1980–1981, Indian peasants of Santa Fe protested a government decision to build a nuclear power station in their region. With the help of U.S. Indians and local tourist leaders, they were able to defeat the proposed nuclear installation. In July 1986, some 10,000 National Action Party (PAN) supporters in Ciudad Juárez occupied the bridge between that city and El Paso, Texas, to protest alleged fraud in an election in which the PRI defeated the PAN.

A Spanish culture legitimizing machismo heavily influences women's roles as well. Machismo requires that men treat "good" women with outward dignity and ceremony but restrict them to the socially prescribed roles of subservient housewife and mother. Until recently, society has tacitly discouraged women from pursuing education or occupations outside the home. Mexican women did not receive equal citizenship or the right to vote until 1953, and they voted in a presidential election for the first time in 1958. Although enfranchised, women continue to have much lower rates of political participation than men.

The trend in Mexico is generally toward greater citizen participation in organizations and associations and toward transference of participatory attitudes fostered by these experiences in the political arena. The growth of the middle class and the spread of mass communications have accelerated this process. Mexico's particular labor migration pattern is also having a major impact. Millions of Mexican laborers have gone to the United States for jobs, and there they have become aware of their own relative deprivation and oppression and how they might alter that condition. However, there is an important mitigating factor: the government's frequent use of strong repressive measures to discourage or eliminate potential opposition to the PRI.

Mexico's record on human rights is less than commendable. While the large numbers detained, arrested, or shot during and after the 1968 student demonstrations are the most conspicuous example, the government's treatment of labor and peasant revolts is equally noteworthy. In the 1973–1977 period, more than 257 people disappeared during antiguerrilla campaigns in the state of Guerrero. When violent clashes occurred in 1977 between peasants and the military, more than 30 peasants died. Civil rights organizations in Mexico have claimed that some 376 persons disappeared during the late 1970s. In 1986, an Amnesty International report stated that "torture... remains in common use by the police forces, particularly as a method to obtain confessions as a basis for criminal prosecutions." As a Mexican human rights leader, Rosario Ibarra de Piedra, put it, "We have denounced torture for ten years. We have no indication it has diminished." She further charged that there are 475 political prisoners being held illegally and clandestinely by the government.[44]

Some progress has been recorded in the field of human rights. Presi-

---

[44]*Christian Science Monitor* (October 11, 1986), 19.

dent José López Portillo's administration (1976–1982) released some 500 political prisoners, many held since the 1968 student riots, and legalized both the Mexican Communist party and a far-right party. Nevertheless, in 1984 there were still reports of opposition figures being kidnapped and of dissidents disappearing, and human rights activists staged a hunger strike at the legislative palace, demanding information on political prisoners and on those who had disappeared. In 1986 the Mexican legislature considered a bill which included a prison term for police officers found guilty of torture, and President de la Madrid appointed a new attorney general with instructions to end torture by the ministry's agents. It remains to be seen whether these steps will bear any positive fruit, but the pressure for reform is likely to continue from Mexico's increasingly less placid and deferential population.

Nigeria: Participation Within Limits

Participation in Nigeria faces many obstacles, quite apart from the suspension of democracy by the military in 1983. Foremost among them are the existing social conditions of the country and its traditional patterns of political socialization. Concerning social conditions, the adult literacy rate in 1980 was only 34 percent,[45] the per capita annual income about $1200.[46] Moreover, communications are poorly developed in much of the country: there are only 1.9 telephones for each 1000 people and only 9 newspapers for each 1000 inhabitants.[47] Such low levels of education and exposure to politics clearly act to limit the potential for political involvement on the part of large sectors of the Nigerian population.

Prior to independence, Nigerian political participation was limited to local kinship or tribal elites. The elites were selected by age, by skills such as bravery, or by religious prestige. Among some ethnic groups, males over a certain age were also involved in community decisions. Since independence, conflicting socializing forces have been operative, and the overall effect is often unconducive to political participation. It is common for family-kinship groups to inculcate in their members trust of those within the familial context and distrust of those outside, orientations which are not likely to foster the development of national political loyalty or a sense of civic duty. Furthermore, the varying socialization patterns of different tribal units aggravate ethnic tensions by inculcating dissimilar and sometimes conflicting political and social values. For example, northern children are likely to learn to respect theocratic authority and to manifest unquestioning obedience. They are also likely to

[45]The World Bank, *World Bank World Tables,* 3rd ed., vol. II, *Social Data* (Washington, D.C.: World Bank, 1983), p. 69.

[46]S. Sinclair, *Third World Economic Handbook* (London: Euromonitor Publications, 1982), p. 38.

[47]Charles Taylor and M. Hudson, eds., *World Handbook of Political and Social Indicators,* 3rd ed. (New Haven, Conn.: Yale University Press, 1983.)

observe and internalize an authoritarian style in relationships and to apply its norms to potentially participatory situations. In contrast, Ibos and Ibibios tend to be socialized into individualism, competition, and high parental expectations of excellence and achievement, especially in the marketplace, orientations which have noticeable democratic as well as capitalist components.

The impact of ethnicity is evident in patterns of political participation. Not only do different patterns of socialization produce differing propensities to participation and differing assumptions about the kinds of involvement that are appropriate, but also the strength of ethnic identities has caused participation to be strongly oriented around ethnic concerns. Even before the highly divisive civil war of 1967–1970, the focus of political participation was regional and ethnic rather than national. It remained so during the brief Second Republic (1979–1983). National elections might have been expected to enhance citizens' commitment to national political activities, but ethnic and regional considerations nevertheless prevailed. For the Nigerian voter, choosing between national parties and taking stands on national issues were less significant than selecting the candidates most likely to protect his parochial interests.

One reason for the strength of ethnicity is that the strong kinship and village ties of traditional Nigerian society generally give rise to patron-client relationships. These relationships are hierarchical in nature, with those who possess valuable property, status, or high office developing followings among those of lesser means and status. For example, a propertied Ibo may well be a member, or the head, of his village council. If he also has a relative who is influential in the armed forces or a federal ministry, he will be able to assist villagers of less status with, for instance, recommendations for federal jobs. In exchange for such favors, he receives their future support and recognition of his leadership status.

Regional differences in Nigeria make generalizations about the role of women in politics difficult. Historically, women have played important political roles in parts of Nigeria; Ibo women, for example, have enjoyed considerable economic and social rights and status and have exercised political influence. As early as the 1920s, Ibo women organized and fought against a rumored special tax on women. No peaceful battle, the "women's war" of 1929 resulted in the deaths of some 50 women before order was restored. In other parts of Nigeria, however, women's social, economic, and political roles have been severely circumscribed. This is particularly true in the areas of the Muslim north, where women are not encouraged to attend public schools or to involve themselves in politics.

Women have had the right to vote in Nigerian national elections since 1954. While levels of interest and participation vary from one region to the next, it is not unusual to find women's unions and associations defending their political and social rights. Such groups even existed in

Table 4.8   ELECTORAL TURNOUT IN
              NIGERIA'S FEDERAL
              ELECTIONS, 1964–1983

Year	Turnout (%)
1964	28
1979	34
1983	39[a]

[a]This election was marred by charges of fraud and violence and nullified by military coups four months later.

Source: Charles Taylor and D. Jodice, *World Handbook of Political and Social Indicators,* vol. 1, *Cross National Attributes and Votes* (New Haven, Conn.: Yale University Press, 1984), table 2.5, p. 77.

the upper echelons of some political parties. One sign of their improving position is the fact that women had representation at the 1978 Constitutional Assembly.

There is evidence of a contrast between Mexico and Nigeria that is noteworthy. A 1966 study found that 70 percent of the Nigerians surveyed talked about politics often or sometimes, while only 30 percent claimed never to talk about politics.[48] This finding indicates an unusually high interest in political discussion, more typical of highly developed countries such as Britain than of developing states. In comparison, 66 percent of Mexicans surveyed claimed never to talk about politics, and only 32 percent talked about politics often or sometimes.[49] This evidence undoubtedly reflects the ethnic and political turmoil that preceded the military coups of 1966, but it also indicates that there are conditions conducive to political participation in Nigeria.

Although political interest has been high in Nigeria, voter turnout (Table 4.8) has been very low. One prominent reason for this is the cynicism of most Nigerians, led by their media. This is expressed in doubts about government's capacity to govern and in concern over the widespread presence of corruption in public organizations. In the Nigerian press, one often finds comments such as the following:

Often, however, what do we find? Mediocres. Men who have no idea what to do, or where to start. Men overcome by the sheer terror of Government House. Men who imagine that their turn has arrived—not to demonstrate their vision and the muscles—but to collect their "share". Government House would then be turned into the rendezvous of strange men and even stranger women; of curious parties and scandalous deals. Outside, the waiting crowd would be treated to stunning silences and empty rhetoric. Each time the governor opens his mouth the only remarkable thing would be his bad breath.[50]

[48]J. MacIntosh, *Nigerian Government and Politics.* Evanston, IL.: Northwestern University Press, 1966, p. 302.

[49]G. Almond and S. Verba, *The Civic Culture,* p. 79.

[50]Sanala Olumhease, "Government House," *This Week* (September 8, 1986), 8.

Press criticism may abound, but there are limits, and these demonstrate the potential for abuses of individual rights. In late 1986 Dele Giwa, a prominent Nigerian journalist and editor of *Newswatch*—a publication often critical of the government—received a package from the Office of the Commander in Chief with a marking that only the addressee should open it. He did, and the bomb inside blew him and much of his house up. Previously he had been "invited in" by the inspector general of police for 14 days because of an article he had written criticizing the government and later called back to police headquarters to make a statement with regard to his criticisms of current state policy.[51]

Despite incidents of this sort, Nigeria's record on human rights is less controversial than that of many other Third World countries, including most of Africa. This is primarily because of the widespread support for the creation of a "workable" constitutional framework and for a limited role of the military. Each coup has brought with it numerous detentions, many of which were justified by military officials as being in response to corrupt practices. Others—such as the case of a government critic freed by the High Court after his arrest by the military in March 1977 or the arrest of a famous entertainer who frequently criticized the government and its policies in his music—are less ambiguous. Nevertheless, a strong and relatively free press and an independent judicial tradition—legacies of British colonial rule—do act to limit the extent of human rights abuses.

Nigerians now are in a transitional period. Many still retain traditional values, but education, the media, travel, and work represent a new set of socializing experiences that are beginning to have an effect. Schools orient students beyond the family and village to the country and the world and to norms of economic development and social change. They expose children to citizenship roles, social awareness, and national loyalty. The media also play a major role in providing information and shaping orientations. Newspapers and the Nigerian Broadcasting Corporation are increasingly important sources of attitudes toward the government and thus toward participation. Although the ethnic basis of parties and interest groups and the numerous military coups clearly have been obstacles, the difficult but necessary process of transcending parochial conceptions of civic roles does appear to have begun.

CONCLUSIONS

Citizen participation is an accepted principle in all six countries examined here, as indeed it is in most other countries. Two factors greatly color the extent and nature of participation, however. The first is the assumption that widespread participation can take place without challenging the ability of the state to maintain order, to govern effectively,

[51]*Newswatch* (Nigeria) (November 3, 1986), 13–17.

and to avoid threats to its territorial integrity. The most obvious case where this assumption could not be met is Nigeria, where the military has stepped in twice to overthrow civilian democratic regimes plagued with antagonistic ethnically based political parties, massive governmental corruption, and repeated instances of electoral fraud. Even well-established democratic states can be led to suspend democratic procedures where public order is threatened. Britain, for example, has had to suspend the regional parliament in Northern Ireland because its perpetual domination by Protestants had led to unequal treatment of Catholics and helped to rekindle Catholic terrorist activities and demands for unification with the Republic of Ireland. A basic, if unwritten, assumption of democracy is that it must proceed in an orderly and stable fashion; where that condition cannot be met, democracy is unlikely to be allowed to survive.

The second factor governing citizen participation is related to the goals of the regime. Where participation in itself is the prime goal, a relatively free reign is likely to be allowed to citizen involvement in the political process. Where the regime's leaders have in mind the radical transformation of society, however, it is unlikely that participation can be allowed to find its own expressions. Instead, participation is channeled into the forms that sustain the task of social reconstruction. In communist regimes, as we have seen, there is a constant tension between the desire for widespread and enthusiastic involvement of the masses and the determination to keep that involvement within bounds that do not challenge the party's control of society or its goal of building a communist future.

The tension between public input into the political process and the desire of leaders to be unhindered in the exercise of the tasks of governing is not unique to communist regimes. In democratic regimes, the principles of democracy are often considered to be served if most citizens vote just once every few years. When large numbers of people decide to involve themselves more directly in politics, as they did in France and the United States in the late 1960s, their leaders often feel threatened. The state of citizen involvement in politics is always one of balance and tension, and in comparing regimes, one should consider both the pervasiveness of participation and its degree of autonomy from governmental control—realizing that both have their limits.

chapter 5

Interest Groups and Political Parties

INTRODUCTION

In modern representative regimes, elections constitute the principal formal means for involving citizens in the political process. This involvement is usually quite limited. Elections in communist countries are held primarily to show continued public support for the current leadership and policies of the ruling party; serious opposition is not allowed expression. Liberal democratic states permit the citizenry to exercise choice among competing candidates and parties, but once that choice is made, citizens are usually not called on to demonstrate their political views for several years. Modern polities are simply too large to be governed through the direct, highly participatory democratic procedures that flourished in the city-states of ancient Greece.

The public's role in political life is not, however, limited to the occasional episodes of voting. In the long periods between elections, individuals as individuals can do relatively little to affect politics, but individuals organized into *groups* can do a great deal. Much of the dynamics of day-to-day political life revolves around the relationships between government officials and groups representing major ethnic, religious, or social groups, powerful economic or institutional interests, or popular causes. Groups may be thought of as linchpins between the needs and desires of individuals, on the one hand, and the power and resources of governments, on the other. In democratic societies especially, they are necessary, if imperfect, substitutes for the continuous involvement of all citizens in the life of the polity that was the hallmark of the direct democracy of the ancient Greeks.

The importance of groups for democratic politics resides in their ability to *aggregate* or gather together the opinions and beliefs of large numbers of ordinary citizens and *articulate* them in the form of coherent sets of beliefs and demands that are conveyed to government. Since there may be a great many different political opinions current in any society, groups perform a valuable role in simplifying the spectrum of beliefs and demands into a smaller, more manageable number. This need not guarantee that resolutions will be found to all problems—the groups involved in any one issue may be diametrically opposed to each other— but it does establish a basis on which the political system can begin to cope with the complexity of modern society's needs and aspirations. Nondemocratic regimes face similar exigencies. Although they are not so keen to recognize the right of groups to make demands on government, even the most repressive dictatorships usually require the support of at least some interests, such as big business, large landowners, or the military, and therefore must respond at times to their points of view. Group politics, in one fashion or another, is a significant feature of virtually every regime in the world today.

There are two basic types of groups in political life: interest or pressure groups and political parties. In principle, both are concerned with having government enact policies favorable to the people or causes they represent, but they differ in one crucial aspect: interest groups advance their interests by attempting to influence those in government to adopt policies favorable to their cause, while political parties advance their interests by seeking government office itself. In this chapter we first examine the role of interest groups in political life and then turn to the role of parties in the politics of liberal democratic, communist, and Third World regimes.

Interest Groups and the Political Process

The formation of interest groups is an inevitable by-product of societal development. In very primitive societies where every individual is a farmer or a hunter, there is seldom much incentive to form organized groups. As societies become more differentiated economically and socially, interests characteristically diverge. In early modern Europe, the interests of merchants who wanted stronger government to break down restrictions on trade often collided with the interests of landowners who wished to preserve their autonomy and isolation from central government. During and after industrialization, the desire of industrialists to keep wages, taxes, and operating costs as low as possible clashed with working-class demands that governments grant the right to form unions and strike, establish safe working conditions in factories and mines, and provide for the needs of those unable to work or to find work. As processes of social mobilization have made ethnic, religious, or linguistic groups in plural societies more self-aware, organizations demanding equal or even preferential treatment for those groups have also tended to appear.

Interest Groups in Pluralist Settings   A variety of types of interest groups can be identified, but perhaps the most important distinction is between groups which act mainly to convey demands or opinions from the sectors of society they represent to government and groups whose primary function is to assist the government in maintaining control over society. As we have seen, societies which allow interest groups to form freely and spontaneously in order to advance distinct points of view are known as pluralist societies. The concept of pluralism forms the basis for one common interpretation of liberal democracy, that is, as consisting primarily of the competition of organized interests in the political arena. The role of government in this interpretation is to evaluate the demands of each of these competing interest groups and arrive at decisions that reflect, to some degree, a fair compromise that respects the legitimate expectations of each group. It is often assumed that governmental leaders are neutral in this competition, that is, that they have no particular interest of their own except that of pleasing as many voters as possible in order to increase their chances of being reelected.

The success of rival interests in liberal democracies depends on a variety of factors. One set of factors concerns the assets or resources of the various groups, including the strength of their organizations, the cohesiveness of their memberships, and the size of their financial resources. At one extreme there are many potential interests, sometimes called "informal interest groups," that are not organized at all or are organized so poorly that their influence in government is minimal. A good example is the elderly in many Western countries, who are more likely to live in poverty and require assistance than the rest of the population but who have been largely unable to organize themselves into cohesive interest groups. At the other extreme, relatively small groups with good financial resources and strong membership support can get benefits far out of proportion to their electoral weight. In the United States the most famous example is the National Rifle Association, which has been highly effective in preventing handgun control legislation by mobilizing its members to support politicians who favor its cause and to punish those who do not—even though surveys show that a large majority of Americans favor such controls. Generally speaking, it is easier to organize "producer groups," groups representing those who provide the goods or services that society needs, such as doctors or farmers, than it is to organize larger, more heterogeneous consumer groups, such as patients or supermarket customers. Consumer groups by and large must hope that political leaders will remember that informal interests, although lacking cohesive organizations or persuasive lobbyists, often comprise very large numbers of voters who may become alienated if narrow special interests have their way too often.

A second type of factor affecting interest group success in liberal democracies is the openness of the political system to lobbying by pressure groups. The freer an elected representative is to make up his own mind and vote as he likes in the legislature, the more likely he is to become a target of lobbying. If the system is such that he depends on voluntary contributions from interest groups and their supporters for campaign funds, he is likely to be especially receptive to the appeals of interest groups that are important in his constituency. This does not mean that his political opinions and his legislative votes are "bought," for his concern to defend his constituency's interests and to be reelected may well have led him to be responsive to those interest groups in any case. But it does mean that successful interest groups are usually those that aim their appeals at politicians who are susceptible, because of the nature of their constituencies, to the groups' particular needs.

In systems which impose a high degree of party discipline, such appeals to individual legislators are far less likely to be productive. In most parliamentary systems, there is enough party discipline to ensure that the most an individual legislator can do is attempt to persuade his party leaders of the validity of a particular interest group's appeal; in most circumstances, he is not free to vote as the interest group would wish him to unless the party leaders also decide to do so. In such situations, it obviously behooves the interest group to concentrate its lobbying on the party leadership. One consequence is that interest groups representing broader interests are more likely to be successful than those representing narrowly focused interests. In many European democracies, business interests are advanced by a single national organization which attempts to represent business as a whole rather than by particular companies, while a single union organization defends the interests of organized labor, the disadvantaged, and the unemployed. In the former case, the lobby can gain access by arguing that economic prosperity depends on following its advice; in the latter case, by pointing out that it represents a huge mass of voters. Since campaign financing in disciplined parties is usually centralized as well, such large and powerful interests are more likely to be able to contribute the huge sums of money such parties require and to command attention for that reason.

Lobbying by interest groups often extends beyond elected officials to encompass bureaucrats as well. One reason for this is that many bureaucrats are in positions that allow them to decide just how government policies and legal statutes are to be applied. In addition, elected officials frequently turn to professional bureaucrats for advice on which areas of government activity need to be reformed and on what form the changes should take. Even for commitments made during an election campaign or decisions taken in office by a leader or party, the expert advice of senior bureaucrats on how best to implement them is usually essential.

The increase in government responsibilities that accompanies economic development has often facilitated access by interest groups. In the West, the activity of governments has expanded since World War II to touch on just about every area of their complex economies and societies, and with this expansion has come the necessity of enlisting the cooperation of organized interests in most sectors of social and economic life. Often this cooperation takes formal, institutional form as governments set up permanent consultative committees composed of senior government officials and representatives of the affected interests (usually business and labor). These committees become important sources of information for governments and sounding boards for new ideas before they are presented to the public; in exchange, they afford those interests represented on them the opportunity to press their views and raise objections to new legislative proposals before the government becomes publicly committed to them. Some observers have argued that this development means the replacement of pluralism by "corporatism," a system of government in which various organized interests are in effective control of their sectors of activity. The extent to which corporatist arrangements have been established varies greatly among democratic countries, but their growth in recent decades highlights the importance governments attribute to interest group cooperation. Indeed, in some democracies the need to enlist the aid and cooperation of outside interests in governing has been so strongly felt that, where no relevant interest groups existed, governments have encouraged their formation so that they can participate in consultative committees.

Interest Groups in Authoritarian Settings   The fact that governments can encourage the creation of groups suggests that groups may not always be autonomous entities articulating genuine public concerns. In liberal democracies, even interest groups created under government encouragement have generally become autonomous spokesmen for their memberships, but in more authoritarian systems, groups are often set up by governments to exercise a *control* function within society. This is particularly true of communist governments, which create and maintain networks of mass organizations to encompass virtually every aspect of political, economic, and social life. Outwardly, these organizations may have the look of large interest groups, but they are not called by that term and, except in rare instances, do not play the role of interest groups in political decision-making; that role is played, if at all, by informal groupings within the political elite, who influence the top party leaders by expressing the needs or desires of the institutions they represent.

The extent to which an authoritarian regime will place importance on such subservient organizations depends largely on its overall aims. A simple dictatorship, particularly a military one, may be content with the passive acquiescence of the population, preferring to reserve to itself all involvement with political affairs. A regime of this type would be concerned only to prevent the emergence of groups that could turn into centers of opposition. Regimes with more sweeping goals of societal transformation, however, are unlikely to be content with an acquiescent population. In the Soviet Union and China, the ultimate aim is to create a new society whose citizens are morally and ideologically equipped to rule themselves. Before that goal can be achieved, the entire working class must enthusiastically share the vision, and its members must be conditioned to think of themselves as equal participants in political life. Mass organizations such as trade unions, youth leagues, and women's associations are expected to play a leading role in this process. As with elections, these organizations enlist a wide spectrum of the populace, and the authorities point to them as evidence of democratic participation in the affairs of their societies. A limited degree of public concern and criticism can be expressed through the channels of these organizations, but their most important functions are the means they provide for the ruling party to monitor the political behavior and (to the extent possible) attitudes of the populace, to propagate and justify its ideology, policies, and actions, and to mobilize its members for party-directed political activities—hence the term "transmission belts" frequently used to refer to these organizations.

How well mass organizations of this type fulfill these functions is another matter. Because they serve as means through which social life is penetrated and controlled by the regime, these organizations often generate among their members not enthusiasm but apathy. In the USSR, for example, workers have not failed to notice that the unions created to represent their interests are led by party functionaries whose primary loyalties attach to the state. As a result, the unions have functioned more often as tools to achieve management goals such as maximizing production than as a means for achieving better wages and working conditions; wages, working conditions, and other such issues are not neglected by union leaders, but it is evident that their first priorities lie within their organizations' control, propaganda, and mobilization functions. By and large, people join the unions and other mass organizations because they believe it is expected of them, not because they find in the organizations' activities a meaningful political experience—and certainly not in the expectation of influencing the policy decisions of the top party leaders.

The overall conclusion one reaches in the study of interest groups is that they are necessary to the governance of modern societies. Because government activities touch on so many sectors of societal life, these sectors must organize and appeal to government if they are to achieve many of their goals. Conversely, leaders attempting to govern large, complex societies need information on what society's needs and wants are, and they also need the cooperation of organized sectors of society in effecting policies to address those concerns. This suggests that the relations between groups and governments are inherently reciprocal or two-way in nature. A major differentiating criterion between pluralistic and authoritarian systems, however, concerns the direction of influence that predominates. In pluralist systems, the predominant direction is from groups to government; for authoritarian regimes, it is generally the reverse. Excessive imbalance in either direction, however, can create problems: just as too much influence by interest groups in liberal democratic systems can emasculate the ultimate authority of elected governments, so too much governmental control of groups in authoritarian regimes can leave them hollow, lifeless shells. For these reasons, the exact nature of the balance of governments and interest groups is a highly salient dimension of political analysis.

Political Parties in the Political Process

Political parties form a second major linchpin between citizen and government in most states. Whereas interest groups may attempt to influence governments in favor of the particular needs of their members, parties seek to realize the objectives of the people they represent through the attainment of government office itself. Because of this representational character of parties, they are found in virtually all contemporary states. Even dictatorships usually feel the need to buttress their power through the creation of a political party that can generate popular support for the leader. For the most part, only states that do not recognize any active role for the citizen in politics prohibit the existence of parties.

While almost all states have at least one party, it is certainly not the case that all parties are alike. Although parties may be distinguished on a number of grounds, observers most commonly concentrate on two criteria. The first criterion is internal to parties and concerns the particular ideologies or sets of fundamental beliefs that define their goals. The number of distinct ideologies that could inspire political parties is potentially vast, but most parties seem to fall within a limited set of general ideological types, of which conservative, liberal, Christian democratic, socialist or social democratic, and communist are the most common. It is often the case that the party name states the ideological orientation quite explicitly, as in the case of the British Liberal party or the Chinese Communist party. In other instances, an ideological category can be fitted to the party quite readily. For example, the Gaullist party in France (officially known as the Rally for the Republic) is usually identified as conservative and the British Labour party as social democratic in ideological orientation. Nevertheless, there are parties and even whole party systems which escape these ideological categories. This is particularly likely to be true of a new state like Nigeria, where ethnic and regional divisions have formed the basis for parties after independence.

The second distinguishing criterion is external in the sense that it is related not to the nature of the parties themselves so much as to the number of parties that exist in the political system. The most basic distinction in this category lies between one-party states and states that permit a plurality of parties to operate freely. As we shall see, there is a great deal of difference between parties that monopolize political power in a state and parties that must operate in a competitive context. In addition, competitive party systems differ according to the number of parties they contain; 2-party systems do not function in the same way as 10- or 12-party systems. Thus, it is important to consider not only what a party stands for and who leads it but also how many parties it must compete (or cooperate) with.

Parties in Liberal Democratic Systems   The major defining characteristic of liberal democracies is their recognition, in both law and practice, of the right to form political parties and compete for governmental office freely and fairly. This is not the same thing as saying that all systems with more than one party are liberal democracies. Certain communist states such as Poland and East Germany also permit the existence of other parties besides the Communist party. Although these smaller parties are allowed to win a few legislative seats, they are not free to challenge seriously or even to criticize the control of the ruling Communist party. A somewhat similar situation exists in Mexico, where the ruling Institutional Revolutionary Party or PRI exercises a dominance over the political system undisturbed by the smaller parties, which in general support its rule. These "hegemonic" party systems, as they have been called, permit the appearance of multiparty competition while denying its substance: the right of any party to compete on equal terms with the ruling party.[1]

Parties which accept and operate under a liberal democratic framework generally conform to the pluralistic assumptions underlying it. These assumptions hold that politics is primarily a matter of competition between different interests or points of view, with the right to govern going to the party which manages to convince the electorate that what it has to offer, whether it be its leadership or its program or "platform," is the best available. In this sense, there is no right or wrong in liberal democratic politics, just more or less popular.

The pluralistic world of competing interest groups requires a competitive party system in order to work effectively. In most democratic countries, there are hundreds or even thousands of organized interests that want to influence the direction of government policy. Not only do parties offer candidates for public office who reflect different points of view in society (interest groups could do that themselves) but also, and more important, they aggregate the vast array of demands and expectations into a much simpler range of alternatives. Given that the interests of organized groups may differ among themselves in any number of ways, parties in liberal democracies tend to identify and reflect the most

[1]G. Sartori, *Parties and Party Systems* (Cambridge, UK: Cambridge University Press, 1976), pp. 230–238.

basic societal divisions, be they ethnic, linguistic, or based on class. In this way, parties organize the range of political alternatives into a limited set which voters can more readily comprehend and act on.

Basic social cleavages do not automatically translate into political parties in a one-to-one fashion, however. Other factors, such as the nature of the system's institutions, can exercise a powerful influence on the party system. In the U.S. system, for example, the winner-take-all presidency acts as a powerful constraining factor on the number of parties. Since victory generally goes to the presidential candidate who wins the majority of votes, if either the Democrats or the Republicans were to split into two smaller parties or factions each offering a different candidate, it is likely that the other main party's candidate would win handily. The presidential system therefore provides a strong incentive for both parties to remain united. A similar effect has been demonstrated in France, where the introduction of the directly elected presidency in 1962 contributed significantly to the reduction in the number of political parties.

Another institutional factor that has often been touted in this role is the nature of the electoral system. It has been argued that the electoral system used most often in the Anglo-American democracies, the single-member plurality system, encourages the survival of just two political parties. The single-member plurality system requires that a party win a plurality of votes (more votes than any other party) in a constituency in order to elect a representative to the legislature. Thus, a smaller party that receives, say, 20 percent of the vote in each constituency in the country will probably not win any constituencies at all; it will, in other words, be severely underrepresented and perhaps even forced out of existence. By the same token, larger parties can expect to be overrepresented in the legislature. The result of this process is therefore a tendency toward the survival of just two parties, the minimum number needed for competitive politics. Proportional representation or PR systems, in contrast, are held to encourage multiple parties because, through various often complex formulas, they attempt to give each party the same proportion of legislative seats as it received in votes. A party receiving only 5 or 10 percent of the popular vote, for example, would expect through PR to win 5 or 10 percent of the legislature's seats, thus proliferating the number of parties represented in the legislature.

Although there is some truth to this proposition, important qualifications need to be made as well. First of all, there is no doubt that single-member plurality systems do penalize smaller, third parties if their support is fairly equally spread throughout the country, but if their support is concentrated geographically in a smaller number of constituencies, they could still win their fair share (or more) of legislative seats. More important, proportional representation cannot artificially stimulate the creation of new parties where there is no demand for them. Proportional representation is simply a system that allows the divisions in the country to be accurately reflected in the legislature. In fact, historically, it has been the countries with serious societal cleavages that have opted for PR as an electoral system precisely in order to establish fair representation for all significant viewpoints. In other words, it has not been PR that divided the political spectrum, but a divided political spectrum that created the need for PR.

What consequences follow from a highly divided political spectrum? Basically, a divided political spectrum poses a very serious challenge to liberal democracies if it inhibits or prevents the formation of stable majority governments. This is most likely to occur if the legislature contains sizable "antisystem" parties, that is, parties that do not accept the legitimacy of the democratic system itself.[2] The most common examples of antisystem parties are the communist parties of Italy and France, although the fascist or Nazi parties of pre-World War II Europe also qualify. Because of their extreme views, antisystem parties are usually considered ineligible for membership in governing coalitions; this means that majorities have to be constructed from the prosystem parties nearer the center of the spectrum. If the antisystem parties control 30 to 40 percent of the legislative seats, as is usually the case in Italy for example, a majority coalition must get its 50 percent support from the remaining 60 to 70 percent of the representatives. This can be difficult to do, especially if the prosystem parties are themselves sharply divided, which often happens in societies with serious social cleavages.

In many Western democracies, the intense divisions of the past have subsided in recent years as growing affluence has moderated class differences, as increasing secularization of society has diminished religious hostilities, and as new issues such as environmental protection have emerged and cut across old divisions. Politics in the Western world is increasingly becoming less "programmatic" and more media oriented, that is, less bound up in ideological and policy differences and more concerned with the images and leadership styles of political leaders. For some, the concentration on personal style as opposed to policy content is a worrisome development; nevertheless, most would agree that the lessening of ideological hostilities has made liberal democracy a more workable system of government today in many countries than it was in the past.

The Party in Communist Systems   Communist parties approach the political world with a perspective very different from those of liberal democratic parties. This perspective does not envisage the public good as flowing from the free competition of political parties and ideas; rather, the public good is associated with the total triumph of one particular philosophy, Marxism-Leninism.

Once the party is in power, its role is to lead the way in the creation

[2]G. Sartori, *Parties and Party Systems* (Cambridge, UK: Cambridge University Press, 1976), pp. 131–200.

of a truly communist society. Most citizens, strongly influenced by capitalist values, cannot be expected to know what this course of social reconstruction entails and may lose sight at times of the ultimate advantages that the sacrifices required of them will win. A ruling communist party must therefore establish and maintain extremely close contact with all sectors of society, educating people in the values and ideals of Marxism-Leninism, stimulating their enthusiasm and their energies for the task of constructing the new society, monitoring them to ensure that there is no "backsliding" or lapse in communist rigor, and identifying those whose abilities and allegiances make them suitable candidates for leadership positions in society and the party.

To achieve these functions of control, guidance, and recruitment, communist parties are organized differently from most parties in liberal democracies. Rather than forming local units based on electoral districts, communist parties typically form small groups of party members, sometimes known as "primary party organizations" or "cells," based primarily in the workplace. Because work brings people together on a daily basis, this mode of organization is especially effective at maintaining enthusiasm and solidarity on the part of party members. Moreover, the location of party cells in factories, military units, schools, and offices facilitates the tasks of monitoring the activities of non-party members and encouraging their support for the party's cause. All other organizations, from the smallest community associations or clubs to the state bureaucracy itself, are permeated by party members for the same reason.

In communist societies, the higher-ranking personnel in any field of endeavor, from collective farming to scientific research, are likely to be party members. This is seen as an important factor in maintaining control over society, but it has the side effect that ambitious individuals may join the party simply to improve their chances of occupational mobility. Communists therefore take care to invite into their ranks only those who exhibit loyalty and dedication to the party's cause. In this, they are different from Western political parties, whose memberships are made up of all who can be persuaded to join. Communist party leaders take a dim view of "careerists" or other less dedicated members, and every once in a while a campaign is undertaken to remove any members deemed to be lacking the proper attitude. Even so, within such mass-scale organizations as the Soviet and Chinese Communist parties are many who have joined less from political enthusiasm than from the knowledge that their chosen careers stand to benefit.

Communist parties are structured according to the precepts of *democratic centralism.* The democratic element in this formula comprises the right to elect party officers at each level of the hierarchy and the right to discuss freely all issues under consideration by the party; once a decision is taken, the centralist principle that all must obey comes into force. In fact, the candidates for party positions at any given level are usually nominated at higher levels of the party and run uncontested. Moreover, decisions are generally taken at higher levels of the party and then reported downward through the structure; members at lower levels of the hierarchy seldom have the opportunity to suggest policy alternatives and, because of the centralist principle, do not have the right to criticize these decisions. The idea of centralism, in other words, triumphs over the idea of internal party democracy. This does not mean that party members are passive, however. Members are expected to take an enthusiastic and active role, spreading the party's message, encouraging popular support and cooperation, and reporting any signs of deviation or dissent. Those not prepared to make the required sacrifice in time and energy stand to lose the prestige and advantages associated with party membership.

The theory and practice of communism emphasize the dominant role the party must play in society. This principle of party domination extends to government itself, which is thoroughly permeated at all levels by party members. At the higher levels of government, it is entirely likely that all officeholders are also party members. The party itself has a structure parallel to that of government, and it is within the party structure that all significant policy decisions are taken. The task of the governmental structure is to execute those decisions; there is never any ambiguity as to which organization, party or government, is the ultimate authority. The top leader in communist countries is almost always the general secretary or chairman of the party, regardless of whether he fills the top governmental post.

In the West, ruling communist parties often conjure up an image of secret police, political repression, thought control, and enormous cruelty perpetrated against unwilling but helpless populations. Stalin's bloody rule over the Soviet Union in the 1930s and 1940s, the violence unleashed by Mao's Cultural Revolution in China in the 1960s, and the repression of the Solidarity trade union movement in Poland in the 1980s have added fuel to this image, but it would be wrong to see all communist rule in this light. In the Soviet Union and China today, the dominance of the party over government and all other areas of social life is based not on force but on a widespread acceptance of the party's leading role in society. Communist party rule in both countries enjoys genuine legitimacy, and their goal of constructing communist societies commands much respect and admiration throughout their populations.

Parties in Third World Systems The position that parties occupy in the political life of Third World countries varies enormously. In some states, there is a single, all-encompassing party that monopolizes or dominates political life; in others, there is a multiplicity of often weak and fractious parties; still others are ruled by military dictatorships that have abolished all parties and imprisoned their leaders. Relatively few are the states in which a stable, competitive party system has been established and consolidated as the means by which the public will can be reflected in government.

One reason for the scarcity of stable democracies in the Third World is that parties face particularly difficult problems in those states. Very often they must operate in political systems, copied from Western models, that have only recently been established and command little popular loyalty or allegiance. The process of achieving independence from colonial powers may have involved a strong element of social mobilization, and where this has occurred, expectations often run high as to what the new regime can achieve in a relatively short time. These expectations are bound to be disappointed when, as usually happens, economic development turns out to be much less smooth than was anticipated. In the absence of high levels of literacy or mass communications, parties may have difficulty in establishing strong roots in the electorate. Frequently, party systems form around ethnic or racial divisions, further exacerbating the low levels of national integration and raising the specter of succession struggles or civil wars.

A common solution of these problems involves the emergence of a single party which claims sole legitimacy for itself. This solution has been most successful where the party is led by a charismatic leader, particularly one who played a pivotal role in the country's struggle for independence or in a popular revolution. The writings of the leader may form the basis for a new doctrine which is used to mobilize the population behind the goals of economic development and nation-building, often to great effect. Where the dominant party comes to be associated with a particular ethnic group, however, its vision of a new national identity transcending the older ethnic identities may be viewed with suspicion by the other ethnic groups. They, in turn, may be perceived by the dominant party as threats to national survival. In such instances, single-party rule may be employed and justified as a means of repressing these groups and imposing order on society by force.

Another appeal of single-party rule is that it is often seen as a more satisfactory means for achieving economic development. Since the world economy is predominantly capitalist, it is natural to blame the country's underdevelopment on international capitalism and to find an alternative model of economic development in some form of socialism. Even when socialism is not adopted, the preferred development strategy generally entails a high degree of government involvement in, and control of, the economy to ward off excessive dependence on the powerful economies of the capitalist world. Either way, a one-party hegemony is bound to seem more efficient and effective than a divisive multiparty system.

Successful Third World parties are often structured on the basis of patron-client relationships. In developing societies, where the disparities between rich and poor are often very great, patronage is a highly effective way in which those with access to resources such as jobs, money, and government or private contracts can bind supporters or clients to them.

But there is a price to be paid. In Mexico, rampant corruption, patronage, and favoritism have certainly sustained the rule of the PRI, but they have also encouraged a great deal of inefficiency in government and in the economy, slowing economic growth and creating an enormous drain on resources. In the mid-1980s the alarming extent to which earnings generated by state-owned enterprises such as the national oil monopoly, Pemex, found their way into private bank accounts shocked Mexican society and even its PRI-controlled government. The widespread presence of corruption in one-party states in the Third World is one sign that the single-party solution, however attractive it may appear, is no sure answer to the problems of economic development.

Our case studies present a particularly good mix of party types and situations discussed in this section. Among the liberal democracies, Britain is a classic example of a stable two-party system, while the French case is instructive on the adverse effects of a highly fragmented and polarized party system and the ability of institutional modifications to transform it into a stable multiparty system. The Soviet Union and China are both good examples of the dominant-party mode of organization typical of communist regimes and its capacity to cope with heterogeneous populations and the daunting challenges of economic development. Among the Third World cases, Mexico illustrates well the domination of a hegemonic noncommunist party, whereas Nigeria has experienced a pattern of unstable multiparty politics that has occurred in numerous Third World countries.

BRITAIN AND FRANCE: GROUP POLITICS IN LIBERAL DEMOCRACIES

Britain and France are typical of liberal democracies in that they each have a huge array of interest groups attempting to influence public policy and a competitive party system seeking to convey a popular will into government action. In both countries, a certain tension may be detected between the need for government to respond to the demands of powerful interests and the need to enact policies that will prove successful with the electorate at large. However, the extent to which this inherent conflict is appreciated differs markedly between the two countries. British politics has been characterized for the most part by a remarkable lack of concern that the public interest might get shortchanged in the process of accommodating the expectations of large organized interests. In France, the notion, deriving from Rousseau, that the particular wills of groups within society are incompatible with the realization of the general will of the nation is much more solidly anchored in the political culture.

This attitudinal difference is related to major differences in the interest groups and political party systems of the two countries. In Britain, interest groups tend to be large, cohesive, and pragmatic in their policy orientations and to have good links with major political parties. France, in contrast, possesses a much more fragmented and ideologically oriented interest group structure, with weak or nonexistent links to major political parties. Until recently, the parties themselves have mostly been small, poorly organized, and lacking in firm roots in the general population; today they remain sharply divided along ideological lines. As we shall see, differences in the structure and orientations of group life account in large measure for the substantial contrasts that exist between the politics of the two states.

Britain: Collectivism in Decline

One of the more enduring characteristics of Britain's political culture has been the easy associability of its citizens. In the seventeenth and eighteenth centuries, the relative openness of British society allowed aristocrats to join with merchants and bankers in commercial and industrial enterprises and contributed substantially to Britain's rise to economic preeminence. Although industrialization brought with it a greater sense of class differences and consequently a greater isolation of the classes from one another, so strongly ingrained was the norm of associability that the right of workers to form unions to advance their interests, a right often staunchly resisted in other European countries, was fairly readily acknowledged by Britain's rulers.

As governments became ever more involved in regulating social and economic life in the twentieth century, trade unions and other organized interests were gradually drawn into the policy-making process. The challenges and sacrifices of the two world wars provided a major impetus for this development. Even during the darkest days of World War II, the British government began planning for a postwar future in which the hardships experienced during the depression years of the 1930s would be prevented or alleviated by government action. Out of this planning process came a commitment to a strong governmental role in managing the economy so as to prevent unemployment and encourage economic growth and an enormous expansion in social services for the less well-off. In the early postwar years, the essential structure of a welfare state was established, replete with "womb to tomb" coverage for virtually every social complaint, and governments sought the cooperation of organized interests to discharge these increased responsibilities more effectively. A vast structure of consultative committees grew up in response to this need, and political decision-making became so dominated by relations between organized interests and government that British politics came to be regarded as essentially "collectivist" or group oriented in nature.[3]

The process of involving organized interests more closely in governmental decision-making was greatly facilitated by the links that exist

---

[3]This term was first used by S. Beer, *British Politics in the Collectivist Age,* 2nd ed. (New York: Knopf, 1969).

between major producer groups and political parties. The closest connection in this regard is between the trade union movement and the Labour party. The Labour party is in fact a creation of the Trades Union Congress (TUC), an umbrella or *peak* association of trade unions representing most of Britain's highly unionized workers. It is possible to become a party member by joining a constituency-level party organization or by adhering to one of many cooperative societies affiliated with the party, but over 90 percent of the total party membership comprises workers whose union membership automatically makes them Labour party members as well. The unions' dominance of the membership rolls gives them the determining influence when policy issues are put to a vote at the annual party conferences; in addition, the unions choose 12 of the 29 members of the party's governing body, the National Executive Committee, contribute most of the party's financial support, and sponsor a majority of the party's MPs. Britain's other major party, the Conservative party, is not linked in any formal way with business interests, which are represented primarily by the Confederation of British Industries, but there is nevertheless a basic harmony of perspectives that is sustained by friendships, common memberships, and the dependence of the party on business contributions for most of its financial support.

Since the two major parties, Labour and Conservative, are associated with the interests of the union movement and big business respectively, it might be thought that the actions of each party when in office would be highly biased in favor of the interest that supports it. Although Labour governments are certainly more in tune with the TUC positions and Conservative governments respond more to business points of view, both parties have nevertheless been able to maintain a substantial degree of autonomy from their interest group connections. Electoral considerations have a great deal to do with this. The Labour party cannot hope to win an election with the votes of trade unionists alone, nor can the Conservative party win on the strength of middle-class votes; each must therefore appeal to a much wider spectrum of opinion if it is to have any hope of governing. This very practical consideration is reinforced by a strong norm in British politics that governments should put aside their narrow allegiances and govern in the interests of the nation as a whole. Indeed, both parties go to great lengths to portray themselves as the true representatives of the national interest; nevertheless, as we saw in Chapter 4, there is still a feeling among much of the public that the parties too often put their own advantage first.

Another factor fostering party autonomy is the desirability of enlisting the active cooperation of both business and labor in managing the economy. The vast network of government-sponsored consultative committees, composed primarily of government officials and representatives of both business and labor, emerged in the postwar era to facilitate cooperation. In many instances, the noncooperation of either business or labor would render the committee useless from the government's point of view. This has generally meant that Labour governments, although officially committed to socialism, have been concerned to assist the private economy, and Conservative governments, although committed to free enterprise, have accepted responsibility for managing the large number of industries nationalized by Labour governments.

Unfortunately, the fact that a widespread consensus was achieved in postwar Britain on a "mixed" (partly nationalized, partly private) economy managed by government with the cooperation of business and labor did not mean that economic prosperity was assured. As Britain's relative economic decline became increasingly apparent after 1960, the collectivist consensus began to unravel. The 1970s in particular were years of increasing economic difficulties, labor unrest, and disenchantment on all sides. For many union leaders and their members, the government's management of the economy came to mean that it was the unions who were expected to make sacrifices in wage demands in order to foster a national economic recovery that never seemed to come. Even under Labour governments, it appeared to many that the objectives of maintaining investor confidence in the economy and protecting the exchange value of the pound sterling were taking precedence over the goal of improving the living standards of the majority of the working population. Amid increasing rebelliousness among the rank and file of many unions, the rise of new, more radical union leaders, and the emergence of a substantial contingent of committed socialists in the constituency associations of the party, pressure to reform the Labour party increased enormously. In 1981 the party constitution was changed in several important ways. First, under the new rules the party leader is no longer chosen by the Labour MPs (known collectively as the Parliamentary Labour Party or PLP) but by an electoral college in which the MPs have 40 percent of the vote, the constituency party organizations 30 percent, and the unions 30 percent. The electoral manifesto or platform of the party, which formerly was drafted by the PLP alone, is now the joint responsibility of the PLP and the National Executive Committee; this means that the PLP can no longer decide by itself which of the policy positions adopted at the annual party conferences are to be acted on in government. Finally, the constituency party organizations were granted the right to "reselect" their local MPs between elections, which gives them the power to remove incumbent MPs if they are not satisfied with their parliamentary performance.

All three changes were meant to democratize the party by making its MPs more responsive to the party membership, but the effects have been quite controversial. Since constituency party organizations often have fewer than 500 members, small left-wing groups have been able to take them over in several cases and use their new powers to remove moderate MPs and replace them with more radical candidates. This development raises in an acute fashion the larger issue of whether democracy should mean a parliamentary party responsive to the party membership or a party responsive to Labour voters as a whole. It also raises the issue of whether the Labour party, open to radical penetration at the constituency level and more closely controlled by the unions than before, can ever hope to win an election in Britain.

In 1981 a small group of Labour MPs defected from the party to form the Social Democratic Party (SDP). They were moved to take this action by the fear that the changes introduced into the Labour party would open the way for greater radical influence and result in the adoption of extreme policy positions such as unilateral nuclear disarmament and a stronger commitment to socialism. The founders of the SDP had a strong preference for the moderate policies of the Labour party in past years, in particular its acceptance of a mixed economy, and they perceived an important advantage in having a left-of-center party without formal ties to organized labor and therefore better able to adopt policies acceptable to a broader range of opinion. Because small parties with scattered support tend to be underrepresented by the single-member plurality electoral system, the SDP entered into an alliance with another small moderate party, the Liberals, in order to increase its chances of winning parliamentary seats. By the mid-1980s, the Social Democratic-Liberal Alliance had become a significant third force on the British political scene.

The breakdown of the consensus politics of the 1950s and 1960s also received impetus from developments in the Conservative party. While Labour supporters were often alienated by the sacrifices they felt the workers were forced to accept for the sake of the economy, many Conservatives came to see the power of the unions and the costs of the welfare state as major constraints on economic growth. Margaret Thatcher, who became party leader in 1976, committed the party to the idea that economic decline could be reversed only if people became more self-reliant and less dependent on the state and if tax rates were reduced so that there are greater incentives to work harder. Prime Minister Thatcher and her supporters in the party believe that efficiency and economic growth will come primarily from the free operation of a market economy, and they no longer accept the idea that nationalized industries serve any public good. Although the Conservative party boasts of a powerful mass organization of over a million individual members organized through constituency party associations, it has traditionally allowed a great deal of authority to its leader. Thatcher has used this authority to fashion her cabinet out of loyal supporters of her positions and to impose most of her programs on the party backbenchers. Many within the party feel that her desire to unravel the welfare state and her willingness to tolerate high levels of unemployment violate the traditional Conservative concern for the plight of the poor, but there has been as yet no movement to democratize the party by making the leader more responsive to the party rank and file or even to its elected MPs.

While the two major parties became more polarized in the 1980s, it

British Prime Minister Margaret Thatcher campaigning during the general election of 1987. With the victory of her Conservative party, Mrs. Thatcher became the first prime minister in this century to win three consecutive elections. (Dave Caulkin / AP)

does not appear that the electorate followed suit. In a 1983 survey, 50 percent of British respondents regarded the Labour party as "far left" or "substantially left" in its political position, but only 4 percent applied those labels to their own political beliefs; correspondingly, 48 percent of respondents felt that the Conservative party was "far right" or "substantially right" in its ideological position, but just 11 percent placed themselves in the same categories.[4] This distancing of voters from the two major parties was reflected in the decline of their share of the total vote from 87.5 percent in 1964 to 70 percent in 1983 and in a related decline in the proportion of voters who consider themselves to be supporters of either party from 81 percent in 1964 to 70 percent over the same period.[5] It was also reflected in the popularity of the SDP-Liberal Alliance, which received nearly as many votes as did the Labour party in the 1983 election.

For a time, it appeared that the rapid rise of the Alliance would transform the party system, but the 1987 election brought a severe set-

[4]Gallup poll, June 22–27, 1983, as reported in R. Rose, *Politics in England,* 4th ed. (Boston: Little, Brown, 1986), p. 294.

[5]I. Crewe, "The Electorate: Party Dealignment Ten Years On," *West European Politics,* 6, no. 4 (1983), table 3.

Table 5.1   **VOTES AND PARLIAMENTARY SEATS WON IN BRITISH ELECTIONS, 1979–1987**

	1979		1983		1987	
	Votes (%)	Seats (%)	Votes (%)	Seats (%)	Votes (%)	Seats (%)
Conservatives	43.9	53.4	42.4	61.1	42.3	57.7
Labour	43.9	42.4	27.6	32.2	30.8	35.2
Liberal	13.8	1.7	—	—	—	—
Liberal-SDP Alliance	—	—	25.4	3.5	22.6	3.4
Others	5.5	2.7	4.6	3.2	4.3	3.7

Sources: A. Birch, *The British System of Government,* 7th ed. (London: Allen & Unwin, 1986); *The Manchester Guardian Weekly,* May 1987.

back to the Alliance's prospects. This setback came not so much from a decline in popular support for the Alliance as from the workings of the single-member plurality electoral system. As Table 5.1 illustrates, the effect of the electoral system in the 1983 election was to underrepresent the Alliance severely: with 25.4 percent of the popular vote, it won just 23 seats, or 3.5 percent of the total House of Commons. A similar result occurred in 1987: 22.6 percent of the popular vote gave the Alliance just 3.4 percent of House of Commons seats. Although the Labour party was somewhat more popular in 1987 under its new leader, Neil Kinnock, it is likely that the Alliance's failure to increase its popular support is due principally to discouragement over its extreme underrepresentation in the Commons. Discouragement showed in party ranks as well: following the election, the SDP voted to disband itself and seek a union with the Liberals. While the Social Democratic challenge is gone for the time being, the lesson has not been lost on Labourites. Many within the party, including the leader himself, are seeking a reconsideration of some of the more extreme party policies—such as widespread renationalization of industry and the abandonment of nuclear weapons—that fueled the SDP's rise and contributed to three successive electoral losses for Labour.

France: Fragmentation and Polarization

The associational life of France has long been noted for its relative weakness. This weakness is manifested not so much in a shortage of organizations as in their relatively low levels of membership and active involvement and in the highly fragmented character of the overall interest group infrastructure. The low level of involvement in interest groups has often been interpreted as a consequence of the strong cultural norms of egalitarianism and individualism that limit the willingness of the French to associate with others to advance common interests; as for the interest group fragmentation, it reflects in large part the strong ideological conflicts that have divided the political arena in France. As noted earlier, the overall weakness of associational life in France receives philosophical justification in Rousseau's argument that the general will of society should always prevail over the particular wills of its different sectors or subunits.

The consequences of this weakness of associational life can be seen most clearly in the domain of industrial relations. Rather than having one large association of unions, as in Britain, the French labor movement is divided into three organizations, each with a distinct ideological position. The largest of the three is the General Confederation of Labor (CGT), which is linked informally to the French Communist party. Second in size and importance is the Democratic French Confederation of Labor (CFDT), which began as a Catholic trade union movement and is now close in its sympathies to the Socialist party. Finally, there is the Worker's Force (FO), which espouses to a mildly reformist stance. Because these movements are opposed ideologically and compete among themselves for members, they usually do not cooperate in actions against employers. This lack of cooperation makes it much more difficult for strikes and other forms of collective action to succeed, and their lack of success further discourages membership. It has been estimated that, at most, only 24 percent of French workers are unionized, a figure that compares poorly with the 55 percent level of unionization in Britain.[6]

The ineffectiveness of French unions encourages their tendency to emphasize ideological conviction over pragmatic gain. When success at the bargaining table or on the picket line seems so difficult to achieve, it is natural to blame the capitalist system itself and to develop political programs based on its fundamental reform or even its demise. Ideological opposition may be a way of attracting the support of alienated or angry workers when their concrete demands cannot be achieved, but a major cost is involved. The unions' emphasis on left-wing ideology has greatly lessened their influence with the mostly conservative governments of the Fifth Republic, and it has also encouraged employers to ignore or bypass them as much as possible. Neither of these developments has helped the unions to advance the material interests of their members.

Because collective bargaining works less smoothly in France than in most other Western countries, there are occasions when anger and frustration spill over into outright protest or violence. The last major outburst occurred in 1968, when a student strike against university authorities mushroomed into a general strike involving between 6 million and 7 million workers. These strikes were not organized, led, or even encouraged by the unions, which were caught quite by surprise. Nor were they motivated by particular, concrete demands. At the height of the crisis, the government met with unions and business leaders and arranged a substantial across-the-board wage increase as well as im-

---

[6]Sources for these data are H. Ehrmann, *Politics in France,* 4th ed. (Boston: Little, Brown, 1983), pp. 193–194; S. Jackson and D. Miller, *The Closed Shop* (Aldershot, UK: Gower, 1982), p. 20. In recent years, levels of unionization in most Western countries have been falling.

provements in social security provisions, but even these concessions did not immediately quell the protest. Only after several weeks of national paralysis and the government's announcement of new elections did the country begin to return to normal.

The fragmented character of the interest group structure and the ineffectiveness of interest group bargaining processes are in evidence in other domains as well. France has a very large agricultural sector, and successive governments have always been willing to fight hard for higher farm price support levels within the European Community, which sets these levels for its 12 member-states. Throughout most of the postwar period, governments have also been willing to collaborate closely with the agricultural peak association, the National Federation of Farmer's Unions (FNSEA), in efforts to modernize the agricultural sector and establish better living standards for workers. Nevertheless, the privileged, almost corporatist relationship that the FNSEA has enjoyed with successive governments has not prevented the fragmentation of the agricultural lobby into hundreds of different national organizations attempting to defend the interests of agriculture, nor has it precluded the frequent resort by farmers to demonstrations, traffic blockages, and mass dumpings of produce on highways to vent their anger and pressure government officials directly.

The weakness, fragmentation, and ideologism of the interest group infrastructure in France are long-standing characteristics that seem to be firmly rooted in political culture and history; 30 years ago, the same could be said of France's party system. The parliamentary Fourth Republic (1946–1958) was a classic example of a highly polarized and fragmented party system, with numerous weakly organized and ideologically divided parties, large antisystem parties on the left and right, and unstable coalition governments. Since that time, however, the party system has gradually consolidated into four major units, which compete for popular support across the country. This development, stimulated by the disrepute into which the Fourth Republic had fallen and by the introduction of a directly elected presidency in the Fifth Republic, has allowed stable and effective governments to become the norm in contemporary France.

The evolution toward larger, better organized parties began with one of the antisystem movements of the Fourth Republic, the Gaullists. Throughout the brief history of the Fourth Republic, Charles de Gaulle and his supporters had been committed to the establishment of a new system of government characterized above all by strong executive leadership. When de Gaulle introduced his new quasi-presidential constitution in 1958 and became the Fifth Republic's first president, his popularity helped the party, then known as the Union for a New Republic (UNR), to become the dominant party in the country. The apogee of the party's success was reached in the elections held just after the massive student-worker demonstrations of 1968, when it became the first party ever to win a parliamentary majority in France. Following de Gaulle's resignation in

1969, however, the party's grip on the reins of power began to slip. After 1974 it no longer controlled the presidency; by 1976 it had lost the prime ministership as well. Worse still, in the 1978 legislative elections it lost its place of preeminence in the party system, sinking to a position of approximate equality with the other three party groupings.

In 1977 the party reorganized itself under the leadership of Jacques Chirac and adopted a new name, the Rally for the Republic (RPR). As the name suggests, the party has retained its strong support for the institutions of the Fifth Republic, but in certain areas its program has changed significantly. In the 1960s, de Gaulle attracted the support of a broad cross section of the population by stressing such themes as national independence, economic modernization, and greater participation by all citizens in decisions affecting their lives. As the party's popularity declined, its support became increasingly confined to more conservative sectors of the population, particularly the middle classes, practicing Catholics, and women. The new policy orientation reflects this shift by downplaying the role of the state in economic modernization and abandoning the theme of participation. The party now stresses such standard conservative themes as reliance on the free market to generate economic growth, "privatization" (i.e., selling off) of nationalized industries, and opposition to big government. A strong commitment to an independent defense policy, including France's nuclear arsenal, remains a major legacy of the policies of de Gaulle.

It is unlikely that the RPR will simply wither away, since its conservatism does appeal to a substantial proportion of the population, but the party can no longer count on automatically dominating the political Right. In recent years a second large political force has emerged on the Right, led by Valéry Giscard d'Estaing. Giscard, the leader of the small Republican party, served as finance minister under both de Gaulle and his successor, George Pompidou, before running successfully for president in 1974. His commitment as president was to a more "centrist" policy, one that avoided the extremes of conservatism or socialism. The theme of progress toward a more just and humane society without running the risks of socialism appeals to many French voters, and in 1978 Giscard was able to consolidate his popularity by forming an alliance of small centrist parties under the banner of the Union for French Democracy (UDF). In each of the 1978, 1981, and 1986 legislative elections, the UDF has won nearly as many votes as the RPR; in 1988, it actually won more. Its future is clouded, however, by the fact that it consists of a loose alliance of small parties, none of which has a strong grass roots organization. To a considerable extent, the UDF remains the creation of one man, and, in the absence of a strong organizational base such as the Gaullists have been able to create, its future must be deemed uncertain.

The creation of the Fifth Republic presented a challenge to all of the old political parties, but no political force met that challenge more successfully than did the Socialists. The original Socialist party, known as the French Section of the Workers' International (SFIO), had been a large and successful party during the 1920s and 1930s, but had declined substantially during the Fourth Republic and even further in the first decade of the Fifth Republic. A largely spent force, the party dissolved itself in 1969 and regrouped under a new label, the Socialist Party (PS). With the assumption of the party leadership by Francois Mitterrand in 1971, the PS began a dramatic, decade-long rise to political supremacy. In policy terms, the PS is committed to the demise of capitalism and the inauguration of a socialist society by democratic means; under Mitterrand's leadership, it also committed itself to allying with the Communists as the best means of achieving political power. In 1972 the two parties negotiated and signed the Common Program of the Left, which called for sweeping reforms of government including the nationalization of numerous private firms and the end of the French nuclear deterrent. Under the banner of the Union of the Left, Mitterrand came within 1 percent of winning the presidency in 1974, but the alliance did not prove able to withstand the growing popularity of the Socialists, whom the Communists rightly perceived as being its principal beneficiaries. In 1978 the Union of the Left broke up and the Right managed once again to win the legislative elections. The Socialist momentum was not to be denied, however. In 1981, Mitterrand won the presidential election, promptly used his authority to call new legislative elections, and led his party to a massive electoral victory. The PS became only the second party in French history to win a parliamentary majority.

The electoral victory of the Socialists in 1981 opened the way for the French Communist Party (PCF) to have a share in government for the first time since 1948. But the appointment of four Communists as ministers in the new Socialist government could not disguise the serious decline that the Communists had suffered at the polls. In the immediate postwar period, the PCF, buoyed by its major role in the underground resistance to the German occupation, was the most popular political party in the country, commanding about 30 percent of the vote nationwide. It soon declined to between 20 and 25 percent of popular support, but this figure was still sufficient to allow it to dominate the left-wing opposition to de Gaulle. The rise of the Socialists in the 1970s denied the PCF its predominance on the left, however, and by the mid 1980s its support had fallen to about 10 percent.

At present, the PCF finds itself in a doctrinal dilemma. Long considered the most "Stalinist" of West European communist parties because of its unwavering support for the Soviet Union, it began a process of liberalization in the late 1960s and early 1970s in order to broaden its appeal. The Soviet invasion of Czechoslovakia in 1968 elicited PCF criticism of the Soviet Union for the first time, and by the mid-1970s the party had renounced the doctrine of the "dictatorship of the proletariat" as a necessary and intermediary stage before communism and declared its commitment to the achievement of communism through democratic means. These reforms facilitated the establishment of the Union of the Left but did not win over much new support for the party. The lack of democratization within the party itself, its long history of support for the Soviet system, and a general perception among voters that it was "safer" to support the Socialists undermined the Communists' ability to keep pace with the PS. The 1978 decision to abandon the Union of the Left only made matters worse: within the party there was considerable resistance to the sudden decision to revert to the old ways, while electorally the party's decline only accelerated. It is unlikely that any changes in strategy or doctrine can reverse the party's descent; the pervasive working-class alienation that nourished the party's appeal in the past has been eroded by economic growth and modernization, and for moderate left-wing voters the Socialists represent a much more acceptable choice than the "party of Moscow."

The Fifth Republic has seen the intensity of its party politics decline, but the process is far from complete. Within both the left and right blocs, the member parties do cooperate electorally to the extent of agreeing to support a single candidate per constituency in the second round of legislative elections; each bloc, moreover, has demonstrated the ability to form a stable governing coalition of its two main member parties. But the bipolar or two-sided nature of politics in the Fifth Republic encourages fierce struggles between Gaullists and Giscardians and between Socialists and Communists for supremacy within their respective blocs. The combination of within-bloc competition and the normal between-bloc competition serves to keep hostilities among parties intense at a time when the French public has become much less polarized ideologically than it was in the past. Furthermore, although one extreme party, the PCF, is in serious decline, the 1980s have seen the sudden rise of an extreme party on the right, the National Front. The strongly anti-immigrant position of the Front has kept the Giscardians and the Gaullists wary of it, but its surprisingly strong showing in recent elections suggests that it could become a significant factor in French politics in the future. Indeed, one reason why the right-wing government of Prime Minister Chirac restored the single-member plurality electoral system in 1987 (the Socialists introduced proportional representation in 1985) was to deny the Front the number of parliamentary seats that its popular vote warrants under PR.[7] Neither the intrabloc rivalries nor the rise of the National Front presages a return to the ideological fragmentation and governmental instability of the Fourth Republic, but they do help to keep the political temperature much higher in France than in most other Western democracies.

THE SOVIET UNION AND CHINA: LIMITED PLURALISM UNDER SINGLE-PARTY CONTROL

Interest group activities in the Soviet Union and China differ from those in liberal democracies in that the groups which affect policy most are not

---

[7]It worked: in 1988, the National Front managed to win just one seat in the National Assembly, even though its popularity had not decreased.

formally organized and not officially acknowledged. Groups that are formally organized and officially acknowledged, on the other hand, are party-controlled; they are mass organizations, and the party utilizes them to mobilize their members for political action. Under certain circumstances the party permits these groups some autonomous action and tolerates, or even encourages, their contributions to policy-making, but the groups usually exercise discretion in bringing their points of view to the attention of party leaders and decision-makers. It would be wrong to dismiss the influence of groups in contemporary Soviet and Chinese politics, but it would be equally wrong to assume that because groups participate in policy-making they do so with an openness and persuasiveness equal to that of interest groups in Britain and France. The difference between the activities of groups in communist states and those in liberal democracies is attributable to the Communist party's dominance of the political scene.

While the Soviet Union and China have these basic characteristics in common, they do differ in the extent to which unified party control has been consistently exercised. The Soviet Union has always maintained an unquestioned domination over the infrastructure of Soviet mass organizations and has managed to preserve a front of party unity, despite the occasional power struggles that have occurred between powerful leaders and their followers. In China, groups such as trade unions have at times been much more vocal in demanding freedom from official control, and the party itself has experienced moments when factional struggles have flared into the open. But, while the Chinese appear to be more willing to tolerate developments that escape official control, it remains as much a basic tenet of the Chinese Communist Party (CCP) as of the Communist Party of the Soviet Union (CPSU) that ultimate control must remain exclusively in the party's hands.

The Soviet Union: The Party and the General Will?

As compared with parties in liberal democracies, the Communist Party of the Soviet Union stands in a very different relationship to society. The CPSU's monopoly on power exempts it from having to win voters' support or court interest groups. Soviet ideology holds that the party itself embodies the interests of the working class, and since political interests are seen as *class* interests, conflicting interests were eliminated along with the elimination of conflicting social classes. Therefore, in theory, there is no need for autonomous organizations to aggregate and articulate the interests of society's groups; whatever disputes may arise can be reconciled by the party, acting as the arbiter of the general will. This means that the party is connected to the mass organizations—the trade unions, the KOMSOMOL youth league, and others—in much the opposite way from that in which Western interest groups are connected to political parties. Rather than groups defining their own interests and supporting the party in return for representation of those interests, as happens in the West, the party determines the nature of the mass organizations and, in the main, defines their interests for them.

This is not to say that the mass organizations are powerless. Their leaders do carry some authority within the party; the head of the All-Union Central Council of Trade Unions, for example, is invariably a member of the CPSU Central Committee and, from that position, can help the party leadership shape labor policies. Similarly, the leaders of the KOMSOMOL have some input into the shaping of policies related to the problems of young people. The mass organizations' influence on decision-making is limited, however, by the complexity of their structures, the party's centralized hold on the prerogative of policy-making, and the difficulty of access to the highest ranks of the party hierarchy. Only the very top officials of the mass organizations have any chance to influence decisions made by the party's Politburo, and because the Politburo members hold their positions at the behest of each other (rather than because of their support from any interest group constituencies), they are not obliged to "deliver" policies that benefit this or that group.

It is, nevertheless, possible to describe a process of interest group politics within the Soviet elite, as long as we allow for the way in which the Soviet political system functions, that is, as long as we do not assume that Soviet interest groups operate as do interest groups in Western democracies. T. H. Rigby has described the working of what he calls "cryptopolitics," a process by which ministry officials, department heads, mass organization leaders, and other members of the elite influence party decisions about the distribution of resources among the many state organizations. Although this process is unacknowledged publicly, it occurs within the Soviet system much as it does within the managerial structures of, say, General Motors or Exxon Corporation. Cryptopolitics, in Rigby's words, is

> not overt and channeled through specialized "political" institutions, but covert, masquerading as the faithful performance of assigned organizational roles. It involves competition between constituent organizations and their formal subdivisions, biased reporting of information relevant to the formation or vetting of policy, informal networks or cliques, the use of personal powers to reward friends and punish enemies, and bias in the execution of policy so as to facilitate or prejudice its success or to favor certain affected interests rather than others.[8]

Whether we should consider this process as comparable to Western interest group politics is open to debate, but it is important to understand

[8]T. H. Rigby, "Stalinism and the Mono-Organizational Society," in R. C. Tucker, *Stalinism: Essays in Historical Interpretation* (New York: Norton, 1977), pp. 58–59. Rigby argues that such informal competition within the system took place as early as the 1930s, though the process of cryptopolitics obviously operates with much greater pervasiveness in the post-Stalin era.

its implications. Politics, according to a classic definition, entails the authoritative allocation of social resources. All complex societies contain groups, whether formally organized or not, each with its own claim on the allocation of resources. The Soviet Union, despite the mono-organizational form of its political system, is not different in this fundamental respect. It is distinguished from liberal democracies in that the competition for the benefits of political decisions takes place informally and out of the public's view. As in the West, the most important aspects of this competition occur among an elite, but it is an elite that is more restrictively defined than that among whom Western interest group politics takes place; primarily, the process occurs within the upper ranks of the Communist party.

The CPSU is structured in a pyramid of authority. Members of the cells or Primary Party Organizations (PPOs) elect delegates to either the rural district party conference (if they live or work in a village), the town conference (if in a town), or the borough conference (if in a city); each of these conferences elects its own executive committee and also selects delegates to the next higher conference, and so on up the line. (See Figure 5.1.) At the top of the pyramid is the Party Congress, nominally the highest party unit. Party Congresses are convened only about once every five years, however, and, much like the Supreme Soviet, serve mainly to ratify decisions already made by the Central Committee or, more accurately, the Politburo of the Central Committee. Though the election procedures within the party operate from the bottom up, candidates are chosen by higher party units, and thus the electoral process turns out to be a series of ratifications, too.

Power flows downward from the Politburo and its Secretariat to the republic, provincial, and local party organs. It is the duty of every party unit and every party member to carry out the policy decisions made by higher-ranking committees. Because this entails many tasks involving virtually all aspects of politics, economic affairs, and social life, a large number of people, called *apparatchiki,* are employed full-time to staff the party apparatus.

It is no exaggeration to say that the party has an army of dedicated persons at its command; indeed, party membership is 10 times the size of the Soviet army and more than 3½ times that of the USSR's total military personnel. Allowing for those who may be less than fully committed to the party's purpose, one must nonetheless stand in awe of the manpower recruited for political service. Thanks to this mass organization directed largely from above, the party's policies are put into effect and monitored across the Soviet Union's vast expanse.

This implies an enormous array of tasks in the direction and supervision of social and economic activities. Indeed, supervision and control are the central functions of the party on all levels, and several intricate methods are employed to carry out these functions. First and foremost is the party's role in choosing people for leadership positions, not only in

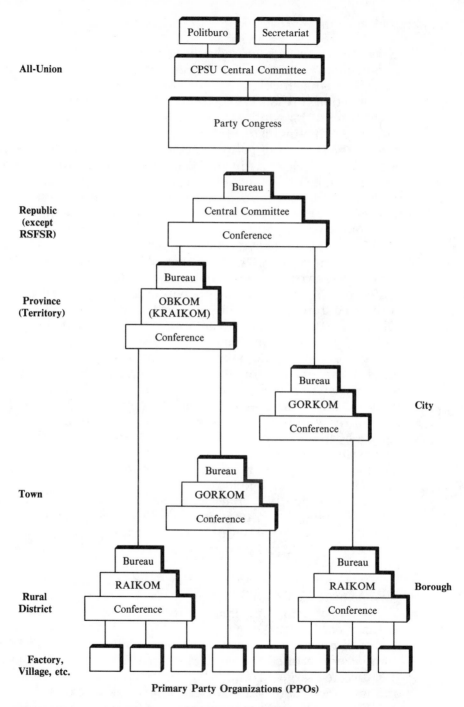

All-Union

Politburo

Secretariat

CPSU Central Committee

Party Congress

Republic (except RSFSR)

Bureau

Central Committee

Conference

Province (Territory)

Bureau

OBKOM (KRAIKOM)

Conference

City

Bureau

GORKOM

Conference

Town

Bureau

GORKOM

Conference

Rural District

Bureau

RAIKOM

Conference

Borough

Bureau

RAIKOM

Conference

Factory, Village, etc.

Primary Party Organizations (PPOs)

Glossary—OBKOM: Oblast committee; KRAIKOM: Krai (Territory) Committee; GORKOM: Gorod (City/Town) Committee; RAIKOM: Raion (District) Committee.

Figure 5.1 Major organs of the Communist party of the Soviet Union. OBKOM, Oblast committee; KRAIKOM, Krai (Territory) Committee; GORKOM, Gorod (City/Town) Committee; RAIKOM, Raion (District) Committee. (Adapted from R. Hill and P. Frank, *The Soviet Communist Party*. London: Allen & Unwin, 1981, p. 47.)

political organizations but in economic and social institutions as well. The *nomenklatura* system which governs personnel choices within the party extends also to positions of responsibility outside the party. By means of this system, the party committee charged with the authority of appointment or approval—for example, the RAIKOM of a city borough—will keep two lists: one specifying positions that need to be filled, the other containing the names of individuals judged by the RAIKOM secretariat to be qualified for the posts. Extensive records are kept, detailing the candidates' backgrounds and indicating any positive or negative qualities. In the case of particularly important posts, the party committee may have the prerogative of naming the person for the job; for less sensitive positions, it may confirm the suitability of a candidate or exercise veto power over a decision taken by authorities outside the party. In any case, the system virtually ensures that individuals who oppose the party's general policy lines will not assume positions of responsibility.

Very frequently, though not always, it will be party members or even party officials who head factories, educational institutions, collective farms, and other organizations. This pattern of overlapping leadership further guarantees that party policies are carried out everywhere, and just to make doubly sure that they are, the party maintains Control Committees which monitor activities throughout society. Meanwhile, the public is kept informed of current policies and reminded of their obligations as citizens by the party's propaganda functionaries, who fill the newspapers and the air waves with political messages and deliver countless lectures on political and ideological subjects to audiences of all ages.[9]

Is the public persuaded? That is hard to say, for public opinion surveys bearing directly on political attitudes are not routinely taken. Behavioral evidence, however, certainly indicates that the party's authority is not questioned, save by a portion of the small dissident community; thus it would appear that the general public accepts the party's rule as legitimate. As to whether or not the CPSU would ever submit its legitimacy to a genuine electoral test, that question would strike party officials—and, quite probably, most of the voting public—as irrelevant. In any event, there is no alternative political force immediately visible on the Soviet scene.

Why, then, must the party maintain such an extensive system of controls over society? That, too, is a difficult question, and the answer may involve elements of custom, habit, and unquestioned assumptions about the nature of politics as much as it involves practical necessity. Certainly the history of Russia has conditioned the populace to accept centralized authority as normal and, the ideals of the 1917 revolution notwithstanding, it is apparent that authoritarian elements in the political culture are stronger by far than democratic impulses.

---

[9]In the Soviet context, the word "propaganda" does not carry the negative connotations it takes on in the West, but nevertheless there is widespread acknowledgement, even by many CPSU spokesmen, that party propaganda tends to be unimaginative, ineffectual, or even irritating to the public.

In addition, there is the scale of political transformation implied in the communist ideal: to create a society of equal men and women striving collectively in self-government. Although the goal can be stated simply, the task is enormous for a multicultural—indeed, multiracial—society of some 270 million people, especially when nothing in their past has prepared them for self-government. Such an ambitious goal might be elusive anywhere, but the degree to which the Soviets have missed the target after 70 years of Communist rule is remarkable. Still unable to deliver on its visionary promises, the party feels compelled to continue reassuring the public about the communist future while making sure there is no backsliding toward the capitalist past. For now, and for as far into the future as one can imagine, party control continues to overwhelm the ideal of workers' self-rule. The party remains distrustful of the public—a fact ultimately demonstrated by the extensive role of the KGB (security police) in surveillance throughout society.

It should be understood that the role of the security police has been modified over the years. The reign of terror that prevailed during the Stalin era, characterized by a widespread net of arrests, torture, and executions, often arbitrary, has given way to a system of surveillance and enforcement that utilizes methods which are generally less extreme. To be sure, a "Gulag" of prisons and internment camps still exists, particularly in Siberia, much as the well-known writer Aleksandr Solzhenitsyn has described it, to punish not only criminals but political offenders as well.[10] Compared with the Stalin era, however, the full repressive power of the KGB affects relatively few people today. In the main, the regime today relies more on social pressure to induce political conformity than on arrest and incarceration.

The control over society exercised by the party and the KGB is far from total. Even under Stalin's rule, pockets of resistance, in spirit if not in public behavior, are known to have existed. Today, many people choose to distance themselves from the party by attending church, participating in unapproved forms of entertainment, or living consciously nonpolitical lives (to the extent that is possible in a community where people are expected to be politically involved). It may seem as if the party is omnipresent, but there are areas of privacy—among the family or with close friends—where its penetration is minimized.

China: Evolving Roles for the Party and Interest Groups

As in other communist systems, formal interest groups in the People's Republic of China have exercised primarily a control function. While some have prerevolutionary origins, all are sanctioned and monitored by the party by means of the interlocking leadership structure characteris-

[10]A. Solzhenitsyn, *The Gulag Archipelago,* 3 vol. (New York: Harper & Row, 1974–1978).

tic of all large Chinese organizations. Such groups do, however, also serve to transmit individuals' reactions to policy to the party and bureaucracy. They are encouraged to provide this feedback, within circumscribed limits, but it is clear that their primary role is to help carry out party policy and educate the masses about communism.

Since 1949, interest or secondary groups in China have taken two forms: those based on membership in a common occupational or class category and those based on membership in a residential unit or movement. The first type includes organizations such as the All-China Federation of Trade Unions, the Women's Federation, the Youth League, and various organizations of small businessmen and landlords that have emerged with the recent economic reforms encouraging small-scale private enterprise. Residential committees—the second type—serve to organize groups that might otherwise be isolated, such as housewives. They are involved in transmitting party policies to the lowest levels of the society, but they are also very active with local problems, such as sanitation, fire and safety services, and potable water supplies. By dealing with these civic problems, they provide opportunities for citizen participation at the lowest levels. In addition, temporary groups have formed from time to time around a single cause. Some of these, such as those involved in the Great Leap Forward and the Cultural Revolution (especially the Red Guards), developed extensive memberships and organizational structures.

A major dilemma for interest groups in communist states is the difficulty of serving both the party and their own clienteles. This problem is well illustrated by the Chinese trade union movement. The All-China Federation of Trade Unions is one of China's largest and best known interest groups. Although the federation's leaders come from and belong to the party, the immediate pressure of the workers often prevails over the external, if more powerful, political party pressure—that is, until the party intervenes to reassert control. For example, workers succeeded in having the right to strike included in the 1975 and 1978 constitutions; but the party soon decided to oppose it, and it was removed from the 1982 constitution. The dilemma of union officials, caught between party and worker pressures, is well expressed in the following comment by one of their number:

> We are Party members and according to Party discipline, must subordinate ourselves to resolutions of Party organizations: otherwise we might be labeled "syndicalists", "agitators for independence from the Party", or "tailists", etc., and might even be expelled from the Party. On the other hand, we are elected by the workers to speak for their interests and should subordinate ourselves to the will of the majority of the workers, otherwise we would be accused by the workers of being the "tail of the administration" and would be discarded by the workers.[11]

[11]Quoted in Paul Harper, "The Party and the Unions of Communist China," *China Quarterly* 37 (January–March 1969), 109.

Under the leadership of Deng Xiaoping, the party has gradually removed itself from interference in labor relations. To prevent discontent, workers' participation in management of both state-owned and cooperative-run enterprises has been enhanced. Indeed, workers' congresses have evolved to the point where they provide an effective voice influencing party policy in areas of workers' interests. Nevertheless, workers remain at a disadvantage in a scheme of priorities which places modernization above most other social and economic objectives.

Chinese interest groups utilize resources similar to those of groups in Western political systems. They often have their own press and films, mass meetings, and monetary resources from membership contributions or from the party. Their success is dependent on their leadership and its persuasive skills. When these function poorly, as is true of interest groups in more open political systems, their cause may well be hindered. Because China shares or has shared certain characteristics associated with low political involvement—low rates of literacy, low media exposure, and nearly nonexistent political competition—interest group activity has often been ineffectual. Only the most skilled and confident of individuals and group leaders have succeeded in making their concerns heard.

One particularly vocal group is the intellectuals. While not as well known as their Soviet counterparts, intellectuals have been actively involved in open criticism of government policies as well as in writing unapproved literary and dramatic pieces; the 1958 Hundred Flowers Movement and the later Cultural Revolution brought their activities and perspectives to the fore. It is clear, however, that criticism of the authorities and free artistic expression usually surface during periods of official government encouragement. On these occasions, the party leadership or portions of it encourage interest groups to speak out against a given policy or leader in order to use this "public" protest as a pretext to change policy. An outstanding post-Mao example is Deng Xiaoping's manipulation of the Democracy Movement of 1978–1979 against his opponent, Hua Guofeng. Once he had achieved his objectives, Deng immediately suppressed the movement.

In China the center of political power is the Chinese Communist party. Its current structure is depicted in Figure 5.2. The ultimate source of authority within the party is the National Party Congress (NPC). It is chosen indirectly through a hierarchy of lower-level congresses, each of which chooses delegates to the next highest level. The penultimate level consists of the Provincial Party Congresses, which select the National Congress delegates. Party rules now call for the National Party Congress to be held every five years; so far 13 have been held since 1921.

The National Party Congress formally elects (or ratifies) a Central Committee, which meets when the whole body is not in session. While congresses have been infrequent, there have been numerous plenary

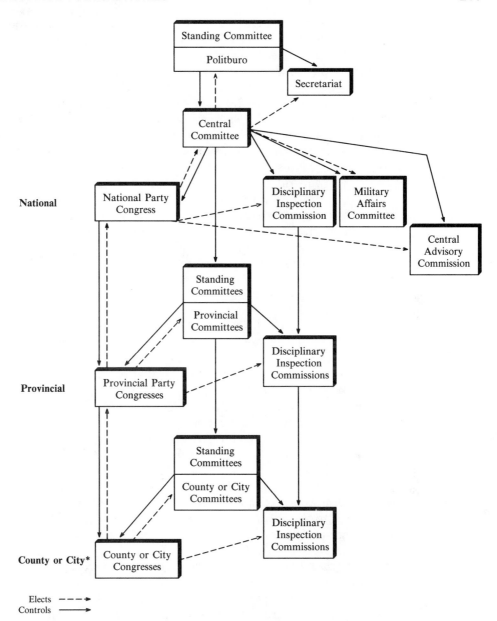

Figure 5.2 Major organs of the Chinese Communist party.

Elects --→
Controls ──→

*Lower levels, which include Basic Party Committees, General Branches, and Branches (the lowest level) all mirror this basic structure.

sessions of the Central Committee. The Central Committee includes most of the party's leaders and meets primarily to ratify or modify decisions made by the Politburo or the Politburo's Standing Committee. Both the Central Committee and the National Party Congress are deemed too unwieldy to conduct day-to-day decision-making.

In theory, the Central Committee elects the Politburo and its Standing Committee; the reality is that the latter two bodies are self-appointed and in control of the composition of the Central Committee. The Politburo and, in particular, the Standing Committee make most of the important policy decisions. Since 1980 the Secretariat of the Central Committee, which had been abandoned by Mao during the Cultural Revolution, has been revitalized. The Secretariat is where the day-to-day business of the party is administered under the head of the party, the secretary general. It has seven departments, covering organization, liaison with the fraternal parties abroad, propaganda, united front work, publication of the *Red Flag* and *Peoples' Daily,* policy research, and party schools.

Among the other important organs formally subordinated to the Central Committee are the Military Affairs Committee, which oversees the military, the Central Advisory Commission, made up of party members with at least 40 years' service to the party, and the Disciplinary Inspection Commission, charged with seeing that party policy is implemented and handling internal disciplinary matters. In addition, *party fractions* or ad hoc working groups exist in all state interest group organizations. Their often delicate job is to monitor and rectify deviations from the party line. As in the Soviet Union, the party also has organs that coincide and overlap with lower-level state institutions. For example, there are six regional party bureaus responsible for political activities in the provinces, autonomous regions, and special cities.

The numerous top-level party institutions and their shifting tasks have provided the leadership of the CCP with a flexible hierarchical structure for party decision-making. For example, when the Central Committee ratified Mao's 1958 decision to launch the Great Leap Forward, it bypassed the Politburo entirely. What lies behind this flexibility, however, is often an intense power struggle. Thus, the Cultural Revolution's attack on ideological deviation among some party officials reflected a severe conflict between Chairman Mao's faction and that of Liu Shaoqi dating back to the failure of Mao's Great Leap Forward. Chairman Mao did manage to purge Liu's faction and regain face, but Premier Zhou's ability to protect individuals such as Deng Xiaoping meant the survival of factions capable of shifting the balance toward rapid modernization after Mao's death in 1976.

The intraparty struggle that followed Mao's death ended at the Twelfth Party Congress in 1982 with the consolidation of Deng Xiaoping's position as dominant leader in the party. The congress was marked by his reforms: secret ballots reportedly were used in provincial party elections; more than one candidate was permitted for each position; and the proceedings were televised throughout the country. The culmination of Deng's efforts to reform the party occurred at the Thirteenth Party Congress in 1987, when Deng effectively transferred power to Zhao Ziyang and replaced 10 senior members of the Politburo with 7 younger and less conservative people. By resigning his own position in the Central

Committee, installing Zhao as general secretary of the party, and replacing so many Politburo members with his own followers, Deng has sought to transfer power to a new generation of leaders who will continue the basic lines of reform which he introduced.

The intense, if periodic, conflicts over control of the party suggest something about the role of the party in China. Its main tasks are leadership recruitment, ideological guidance, and social control, which it seeks to achieve by administering the government, directing the modernization and socialization of society, and managing social conflicts. In a system in which the state makes most decisions about resource allocation and runs most firms and agricultural organizations, the party's responsibility for managing society is indeed massive. Although they are not accountable in elections, leaders are sensitive to the success or failure of their efforts. This means that accountability often takes the form of intraparty competition, a phenomenon also characteristic of noncommunist single-party systems.

The party is at once ideological, personalist, and pragmatic. It is ideological in that it advocates a coherent set of ideas and ideals: the development of the country along socialist lines. It is personalist in that during crises and conflict of leadership, appeals are often made to support the prestige of individuals such as Chairman Mao. It is pragmatic in that when such socialist objectives as equality of salaries or socialization of agriculture conflict with practical necessities, it is often the ideals that are set aside. Thus, shortly after the ideological frenzy of the Cultural Revolution, China made an accommodation with its ideological enemy, the United States, to achieve greater security vis-à-vis the Soviet Union and to acquire the technological inputs necessary for more rapid modernization. More striking have been the changes under Deng Xiaoping, which have made economic development and social modernization the dominant goals even at the cost of compromising socialist principles. For example, a limited amount of private enterprise has been permitted, as have the large income differentials that tend to result from it. Deng has also sought to institutionalize the government's role and to increase its autonomy from the party, particularly in the area of economic policymaking. The effect has been to increase the prominence of public offices and to weaken the role of personalities dramatically since the days of Mao. How long the direction and role that Deng has cast for the party will continue is a major undecided issue in the often turbulent world of Chinese politics.

MEXICO AND NIGERIA: INTEREST GROUPS AND PARTIES IN DEVELOPING COUNTRIES

The status of interest groups and political parties in Mexico and Nigeria clearly reflects their respective levels of development. Mexico, whose industrialization dates back to the late nineteenth century, has developed occupationally based groups representing labor, peasants, businessmen, professionals, students, and even, to a limited extent, consumers. Nigeria, with a much shorter history of political and socioeconomic development, has experienced the emergence and consolidation of groups with strong ethnic and regional bases. Although the principal interest groups are (or were) linked up with political parties in both countries, the patterns are quite different. In Mexico, the main groups are incorporated in the ruling PRI and help to sustain its control of political power; in Nigeria, the main ethnic associations became linked to hostile and antagonistic ethnically based parties. The result is that Mexico has lived for several decades under stable, single-party rule, while Nigeria has seen the overthrow of two democratic regimes in its short history.

Mexico: Interest "Sectors" and the Dominant Party

Mexico's interest groups vary in type and degree of autonomy. Although many groups are totally independent, the largest and most important ones enjoy a close, interdependent relationship with the ruling PRI. Indeed, three major associations are formal "sectors" of the PRI, representing portions of the "revolutionary family": workers, peasants, and "popular" or middle-class interests. Their major activities include organizing individuals with common interests to initiate or modify government policy and serving as channels for communication from government to the society. Dissent and intergroup competition are allowed, provided that no group challenges the PRI's overall control.

The peasant sector is organized as the National Peasant Confederation (CNC). Based on a myriad of rural labor leagues, the CNC draws most of its support from the *ejiditarios,* small farmers working communally owned lands *(ejidos)* that in many cases were provided in government-sponsored land reform programs. For these farmers, membership in the CNC is mandatory. Because they received their land from the government, the ejiditarios tend to be loyal to the regime. They are also highly dependent on the government. Their plots are small and often only marginally arable, and they depend on the government-run Ejido Bank for credit to purchase seed and fertilizer to maintain their farms and families. Political disloyalty to the PRI may result in withdrawal of credit and therefore the destruction of their livelihoods. The dependence of the peasants naturally limits the autonomy of their interest group vis-à-vis the party leadership and the government. In practice, the leadership of the CNC and the peasants themselves can be counted on to give loyal support to the PRI and its leaders.

The labor movement also has limited autonomy with respect to the PRI and the government. It is divided into two major blocs: the United Workers' Bloc (BUO), which is closely tied to the regime, and an anti-BUO coalition composed of unions favorable to the regime but hostile to the BUO. The Confederation of Mexican Workers (CTM), which represents almost two-thirds of all union members in Mexico, dominates the BUO, by far the larger of the two blocs. The CTM alone has a membership of over 2 million. Within the official labor section coalition but opposed to the BUO is a bloc of leftist unions, the strongest of which is the Revolutionary Confederation of Workers and Peasants (CROC), with some 120,000 members. Conflict within and between the blocs weakens the labor movement and facilitates its control by skillful political leaders.

The popular sector, represented by the National Federation of Popular Organizations (CNOP), is the most heterogeneous of the three official sectors. It is primarily middle class in composition, representing such groups as civil servants, members of cooperatives, small-farm proprietors, small merchants and industrialists, professionals, artisans, women's organizations, youth groups, and even moral movements. Unlike the ejiditarios, who must join the CNC, and most workers, who must belong to a PRI-affiliated labor union, the members of most of the groups associated with the CNOP joined voluntarily. This fact gives the popular sector greater autonomy than those groups with respect to the PRI and the government and causes the CNOP to be more responsive to the interests of its clientele in order to retain their membership. These factors, coupled with the growing tendency of the party and the government to draw on the CNOP for its top leadership, make the CNOP a very powerful branch of the revolutionary coalition. Of the three sectors, the CNOP has the greatest access to top-level decisionmakers.

Although not officially members of the PRI family of interest group sectors, most business and employer groups are assured of a political voice. Defined in statutes as "organs of consultation of the State for the satisfaction of the needs of national commerce and industry," the most powerful of these groups are the National Confederation of Industrial Chambers and the National Confederation of National Chambers of Commerce. Membership is compulsory for businesses with more than a handful of employees. These groups are often able to influence legislation by commenting on and even modifying legislative proposals that affect their interests. Although these groups represent only 0.5 percent of the total population, they can effectively utilize their support in the media and among the highest public officeholders, party members, and administrators—often including the president—to achieve their goals.

Because various official interest groups affiliated with the PRI have not always met the expectations of their clients, competing groups have emerged. These groups, which do not belong to the PRI alliance, attempt to pressure the government from without and often play important parts in Mexican politics. For example, since the 1960s some business groups unaffiliated with the popular sector of the PRI have acted through the media, government contacts, and the opposition National Action Party (PAN) to protest government moves toward the nationalization of industry. In addition, there have been attempts to organize independent peasant groups. Here, the government tends to be less tolerant, however; when a major militant group, Civic Action, emerged in the 1970s, the government sought out and killed both of its leaders.

The PRI has been and, despite the dramatic increase in citizen protests since 1970, still is adept at co-opting emerging groups as they gain significant stature or preempting them by granting desired concessions. While this skill has been a primary factor in its maintaining power over so many years, it has both costs and benefits for the groups. They are assured a hearing and participation in the major political game: competition for resources within the officially sanctioned party. However, if their leaders become too interested in status and official favor, they may sell out their groups' interests. Labor leaders, for example, have been known to set a price primarily beneficial to themselves for the termination of a strike. At one point in the late 1930s it was reported that the Mexican Chamber of Commerce distributed to trusted businessmen a list of top labor officials and the prices they charged to settle labor disputes.[12] Employers and labor leaders benefit in such situations, but the workers' movement is weakened. The ensuing resentment has prompted many defections, but rebel groups have a difficult time combating adversaries that can retaliate with governmental pressure, the law, and other sanctions.

The origins of this system of one-party domination reside in the presidency of Calles. He was made aware of the need for a means of perpetuating the ideals of the Mexican revolution by a threatened military revolt in 1923 just after he became president. The threat was countered successfully by armed peasants and workers, and Calles decided to move beyond personalist leadership cliques by forming a party, the National Revolutionary Party (PNR), that would institutionalize the de facto peasant, labor, and military base on which the revolution had been built. His concept of an institutionalized party composed of these groups did not foreclose the possibility that those opposed to the revolution would form their own party, but it did involve the consolidation of the "revolutionary family" into a single ruling political coalition. President Cárdenas (1934–1940) took the process one step further by transforming the PNR into the Mexican Revolutionary Party. The new party, founded in 1938, included four sectors: the peasants, labor, the military, and the popular sector. The military sector of the party was merged with the popular sector in 1940. President Alemán in 1946 changed the party's name to Institutional Revolutionary Party (PRI), but its style and character had been well established during the regimes of Calles and Cárdenas.

The PRI is characterized by factional differences between its left and right wings. The left favors realization of the revolution's promise; the right opts for control and gradual social and economic change con-

[12]Martin Needler, *Politics and Society in Mexico* (Albuquerque: University of New Mexico Press, 1971), p. 11.

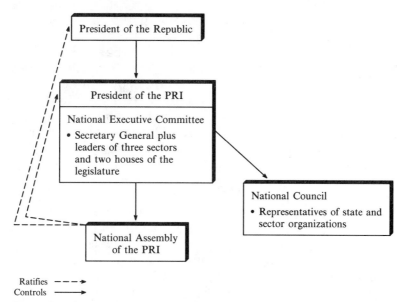

Ratifies $----\rightarrow$
Controls $\longrightarrow$

Figure 5.3 Organizational structure of the PRI.

sistent with maintenance of existing structures. But the influence of competition and interaction among the party's three sectors and associated interest groups prevails over left/right polarities. For example, there is a tradition that the PRI nominates to the Chamber of Deputies a representative of the sector that is strongest in each legislative district.[13]

The PRI's structure is personalist and hierarchical. During the regime of each president of the republic, the PRI becomes his personal party. His closest potential rival is the National Executive Committee (CEN) which has seven members: the president of the party, a general secretary, secretaries for each of the three interest sectors (labor, popular, and peasants), and representatives of the Chamber of Deputies and the Senate. To a large extent, all are dependent for their offices on the president.

Formally, the most authoritative party organ is the party's National Assembly, which is supposed to select its candidate for president of the republic. In practice the National Assembly is subordinate to the CEN and the president. It ratifies policy decisions made by the CEN and others at high levels; the CEN controls its membership and convenes its meetings. The PRI also has a National Council, which represents the party organizations of the 31 states and the three constituent interest sectors. It is through the National Council that the CEN regulates state-level party activities. The CEN, with its power to control state and municipal party membership and policy directions, clearly dominates the party

[13]Martin Needler, op. cit., p. 12.

structure, although, as noted above, its powers are subject to the intervention of the president.

The Mexican political structure is characterized by an advanced version of patron-client relationships. Within the PRI there are numerous cliques. An individual member advances by joining and working for the clique most likely to achieve dominance. If his clique is successful, the aspirant may acquire sufficient financial resources and position to enable him to develop his own following. This patron-client structure is somewhat exceptional, however, in that clients may also be members of occupational interest groups, such as the peasants or laborers, and may seek collective rewards for the groups they represent rather than for themselves.

The PRI dominates Mexican politics. Since its founding it has never lost a presidential or gubernatorial election. Nevertheless, with the growth of Mexico's middle class, which now constitutes approximately 30 percent of the population, numerous opposition groups have emerged. Apart from dissident interest groups, opposition is provided by "official parties" affiliated with the PRI network and other parties that are genuinely independent. Among the parties on the right of the political spectrum are the Authentic Party of the Mexican Revolution (PARM), the National Action Party (PAN), and the Democratic Party of Mexico (PDM). PARM, the "official right" party, supports PRI presidential candidates and manages to win a few seats in the Chamber of Deputies. PAN is the only effective opposition party on the right. Founded in 1939 to preserve the political influence of the Church and the private enterprise system, PAN has loose connections with the international Christian democratic movement. The PDM, legalized in 1979, is the successor party to neofascist groups active in the 1930s and 1940s. The PDM's program is now closer to Christian democratic positions than to fascism. The left of the opposition spectrum consists of two parties, the Popular Socialist Party (PPS) and the small Mexican Communist Party (PCM). The PPS, formerly the "official left" party, joined other leftist and nationalist parties in 1988 to form the National Democratic Front (FDN). Its presidential candidate, Cuauhtemoc Cardenas Solorzano, won an impressive 31 percent in an election marred by accusations of government fraud. The Front also won several Senate seats—the first time the PRI has lost senatorial contests—and became the leading opposition group in the Chamber of Deputies.

The extent of the PRI's domination can be seen in the presidential election results presented in Table 5.2. As noted earlier, the domination of Mexico's party system by the PRI is largely due to the PRI leadership's skill at co-opting potentially threatening opposition groups. Nevertheless, the tide of dissent has been rising in the past two decades, particularly in the north. This has occurred partly as a result of a series of electoral frustrations for the PAN, which is popular in that region. In several elections, the PAN and its numerous followers in the states of

Sonora, Nuevo Leon, and Chihuahua have taken to the streets to protest what many felt were fraudulent elections. These protests became even more vociferous in the 1980s.

In response to the growing frustration, and in particular in the wake of increased protests in the north following the 1985 and 1986 elections (where massive fraud was alleged by the opposition parties), reforms were offered by the PRI. These included the provisions passed by the Chamber of Deputies in 1986 to enlarge the Chamber from 400 to 500 members and allocate 150 seats for the opposition, to have half of the Senate elected each three years instead of all members each six years, to create an 80-member elected Assembly for the capital, Mexico City, and to use transparent ballot boxes. But the most controversial aspect of this legislation left little doubt about the reform's intent: it stipulated that the PRI and its allies would not lose power even if they received less than 51 percent of the vote.

Nigeria: Communal Interests and Suspended Parties

At present, Nigeria's political parties are dormant and must await military consent to renew their activities and confront the tests of time and popular support. Interest groups still function, however, straddling the line between traditional (precolonial) and modern pursuits. Though neither interest groups nor parties are free to function as they did under civilian rule, the histories and styles of the political parties during the two republics contain clues to the roles they will probably play if and when the military permits the reestablishment of stable civilian constitutional rule.

Table 5.2 PRI'S MAJORITY IN RECENT PRESIDENTIAL ELECTIONS (PERCENTAGES)

Year	PRI	PAN	FDN	Others	Total Votes Cast
1934	98.19	—	—	1.81	2,265,971
1940	93.89	—	—	6.11	2,637,582
1946	77.90	—	—	21.80	2,293,547
1952	74.31	7.82	—	17.85	3,651,201
1958	90.43	9.42	—	0.13	7,483,403
1964	88.81	10.97	—	0.20	9,422,185
1970	85.82	14.00	—	0.17	13,892,624
1976	98.69	—[a]	—	1.31	16,925,880
1982	71.63	16.41	—	11.96[b]	22,539,272
1988	50.40	17.10	31.10[c]	1.40	19,100,000

Source: Daniel Levy and Gabriel Szekely, *Mexico. Paradoxes of Stability and Change* (Boulder, Colo.: Westview, 1983); *The New York Times* (July 15, 1988), 3.

[a]PAN did not officially run candidates in 1976. There were, however, three write-in candidates who polled 1 million votes among them.

[b]In 1982 most of the opposition vote after PAN went to leftist parties. In addition, 1 million votes for the fourth largest bloc were anulled.

[c]In 1988 Cuauhtémoc Cárdenas led a coalition of leftist parties under the National Democratic Front (FDN) label. The election generated claims of massive fraud, including widespread destruction of ballots.

Nigeria's earliest interest groups were ethnic based, and British colonialism was the main impetus to the development and proliferation of such groups in both northern and southern Nigeria. Among the earliest ethnic-based interest groups was the Egba society, formed in 1918 to represent the Egba sect of the Yorubas. In the 1930s Ibo émigrés formed unions to maintain their culture and customs in Lagos and other areas outside Iboland. They collected funds, engaged in politics, and worked to preserve the Ibo language, tribal songs, history, and moral beliefs among émigrés. They also provided contact with the home village and such social benefits as mutual aid, financial assistance in case of illness, funerals, and the return of the deceased to his or her ancestral lands. In the north, the emirs formed their own organization, the Northern People's Congress, in response to the growing political involvement of the Ibo and Yoruba ethnic associations. Most of the ethnic associations were multifunctional, serving as a base for social, cultural, religious, and financial as well as political undertakings.

The political functions of these groups are highly germane to the development of cleavages that have contributed to the destruction of the postindependence republics. Some of these ethnic unions served as tax collectors for the colonial government before independence. As pressure groups they prevailed on local authorities for hospitals, dispensaries, better roads, and other public services. They also had a direct political role, sometimes acting as equivalents of formal governmental bodies in their regions.

The effect of this political involvement was to facilitate the emergence of ethnically oriented political parties. In some cases, the ethnic unions were the source of the key political factions in regional political parties and their dissident offspring. In other cases, the ethnic unions provided a core of electoral support for the political parties affiliated with them. Such was the case with the Ibo State Union and its affiliates in eastern Nigeria, which preceded the Ibo-dominated National Council of Nigeria and the Cameroons (NCNC). These ethnic-based associations continue to be active politically, though their party affiliates no longer function.

Urbanization and economic development have caused functional interest groups based on common occupations, tasks, or professions to emerge in Nigeria. There are, for example, labor, medical, student, and farmer groups. Although less than 5 percent of Nigeria's working population are wage-earners and only 2.4 percent are union members, labor is among the more active and important of these functional interest groups.[14] Nevertheless, the political and economic influence of the labor movement has been minimal, in large part because of efforts by the military governments to curtail it. In 1985 the government imposed a

---

[14]G. Kurian, *Encyclopedia of the Third World,* 3rd ed. (New York: Facts on File, 1987), vol. 2, pp. 1483–1484.

wage freeze and ordered unions affiliated with the labor movement's peak organization, the National Labor Congress, to suspend collective bargaining for a year. Although unions may now bargain with their employers and even go on strike, strikes are forbidden while disputes are being considered by the Industrial Arbitration Panel or the National Industrial Court, government-created bodies set up to resolve labor disputes.

With a few notable exceptions, most of the functional interest groups did not associate themselves with the ethnically based political parties during the First and Second Republics. When the functional groups tried to form political parties that would cut across ethnic lines, they were unsuccessful. Instead, the relationship between ethnic interest groups and the ethnic-based political parties predominated, perpetuating communalism, frustrating national integration, and prolonging political instability.

As we have seen, the roots of the linkage between ethnic groups and parties lie well in the past. Unlike many other colonies which fought for independence after World War II, Nigeria did not develop a single nationalistic and revolutionary independence movement. The NCNC, formed in 1944, at first opposed ethnic and regional divisions and fought for more self-determination, and ultimately total independence, for Nigeria. But it was not lost on distrustful western Yorubas that the leader of the NCNC was an eastern Ibo. They feared Ibo control of the Western Region via the NCNC. Not long thereafter, the Society for the Descendants of Oduduwa was formed to protect Yoruba political rights. By 1948 this group had formed the core of what was to become the main party of the Yorubas, the Action Group (AG). Its original goal was to gain control of the Western Region's government. Later, as was the case with other regional and ethnic-based parties, the Action Group became involved in national politics with the objective of defending its ethnic group's political and economic rights. As noted earlier, emirs in the north responded to these developments by forming the Northern People's Congress (NPC).

The political parties claimed to have coherent ideologies, but theory was seldom stressed. The NCNC spoke of "pragmatic African socialism" and the AG of "democratic socialism," but the most socialist in content and intent was the small Socialist Workers and Farmers Party (SWAFP). This party appealed in particular to labor union members and landless peasants but was relatively insignificant and attracted only a small membership.

The three regional and ethnic-based parties—the NCNC, NPC, and AG—became the key factors in Nigeria's electoral and parliamentary system after independence. Given this structure, political conflict was inevitably ethnic. The parties' primary concerns were success at the ballot box, maintaining political control within their regions, and representing their group's interests in the distribution of government funds and political positions. Unfortunately, the frustration and mistrust engendered during these elections fueled communal violence and increased political haggling, and the growing turmoil prompted the military coups in 1966 that abolished the party system in Nigeria. Political parties were formally proscribed by the military dictatorship from 1966 until 1978.

Why did the party system give way to military rule? Perhaps the outstanding causal factor in the party system's decay was the contradiction between its regional and ethnic basis and the overriding need to achieve national integration. The lack of established political norms defining the role of oppositions and the lack of respect for the will of the electorate also contributed; the cheating in the October 1965 Western Region elections was undoubtedly the nadir of the First Republic's party system. Nevertheless, it is to the background factors, especially the weakness of crosscutting functional interest groups and the tenacity of ethnic identities, that one must look for the sources of these problems.

Political parties were permitted to operate again in 1978 in anticipation of the return to civilian rule, and elections to choose a president, a federal Senate and House of Representatives, and state governors and legislatures were held in 1979. Five parties contested these elections. They each had some link to the past parties, although there was some attempt to bridge over ethnic and regional differences. As the new constitution prescribed, the presidential election was conducted among balanced tickets; for example, a presidential candidate from one region would run with a vice-presidential candidate from another.

Among the parties and candidates in the 1979 election was the National Party of Nigeria (NPN). Many of the leaders of this party, including its presidential candidate Shehu Shagari, can be traced to the NPC. Another major party to enter the competition was the United Party of Nigeria (UPN). Its leader, Chief Obafemi Awolowo, was actively involved with the independence movement as well as founder of the Action Group. Dr. Nnamdi Azikiwe, an independence leader, founder of the Ibo-dominated NCNC and former president of Nigeria, led the Nigerian People's Party (NPP). A group within the NPP rejected Azikiwe's leadership and formed another party to compete in the elections, the Great Nigerian People's Party (GNPP). It nominated Alhaji Waziri Ibrahim, a Moslem, as its presidential candidate. This was not the only party to suffer a split over leaders. Some of the members of the NPN who rejected its conservative policies split off to form another party, the People's Redemption Party (PRP). Alhaji Aminu Kano, who had long opposed Hausa-Fulani rule in the north, became its presidential candidate.

In the elections, the NPN emerged as the strongest party and its leader, Shagari, was elected president. In spite of the attempts to create integrated parties, the election results strongly reflected both historical enmities and ethnic voting patterns. For example, the Yoruba candidate, Awolowo, won 80 to 90 percent of the western Yoruba vote, and Azikiwe and his Ibo-led NPP won a large majority of the eastern (Ibo) vote. The parties differed little on ideology or platform; in essence, the same ethnic biases that marked the previous attempt at democracy emerged anew.

The new civilian government found itself in both good and bad times. The oil-based economic prosperity led to a heady confidence and, with it, massive corruption. There were political fights, called "bash-ups," as the NPN moved aggressively to establish itself in the east and west and win over factions from the other parties. This heightened the tensions and conflict associated with the 1983 elections, which saw the NPN significantly increase its vote and its control of the National Assembly and the state governorships (see Tables 5.3 and 5.4). At this juncture, amid mounting frustration over the widespread election fraud and corruption, the military intervened in 1983 to end this second episode of civilian government. The leader of the coups, Major-General Buhari, suppressed all political activities, shut down the political parties, and imposed a strict military regime.

Clearly, the fundamental problem thwarting democracy in Nigeria is the persistence of strong ethnic and regional cleavages. Given that some of the touchiest issues, such as revenue allocations and economic development, have regional and ethnic underpinnings, the prospect for the development of class-based parties seems slender. While the party names changed in the Second Republic, the politics did not. There was widespread fraud in the 1979 and 1983 elections and considerable misuse

Table 5.3 NIGERIAN PRESIDENTIAL ELECTIONS OF 1979 AND 1983

Party	Percent of Votes Cast	
	1979	1983
National Party of Nigeria (NPN)	33.8	46.0
Unity Party of Nigeria (UPN)	29.2	30.1
Nigerian People's Party (NPP)	16.8	13.6
People's Redemption Party (PRP)	10.3	6.8
Great Nigerian People's Party (GNPP)	10.0	2.5
National Alliance for Progress (NAP)	—	1.1

Table 5.4 NIGERIAN SENATE, HOUSE, AND GUBERNATORIAL ELECTIONS, 1979 AND 1983

Party	Percent of seats in federal Senate		Percent of seats in federal House of Representatives		Percent of governorships won	
	1979	1983	1979	1983	1979	1983
NPN	37.9	64.7	37.4	59.1	36.7	68.4
UPN	29.5	14.1	24.4	8.1	26.3	15.8
NPP	16.8	14.1	17.4	10.6	15.8	10.5
PRP	7.4	5.9	10.9	9.0	10.5	5.3
GNPP	8.4	1.2	9.6	—	10.5	—

by politicians of funds allocated to development purposes. Ultimately, divisiveness, corruption, and an attitude of "what is public is mine" brought on the same political fate for the Second Republic's democratic experiment as the First's, namely military intervention. The military's determination to act as a monitor and to intervene if it feels conditions warrant is clearly a factor that limits the survival chances of any future party system.

CONCLUSIONS

Interest groups and political parties are frequently the most prominent actors in a political system. Where they operate effectively, they serve as bridges between citizens and the state, conveying the needs and concerns of the public to government in a coherent and meaningful way. This task of representation is of paramount importance in liberal democratic states such as Britain and France, where several parties compete for the public's allegiance and for political power. However, even in nondemocratic systems such as China and the Soviet Union, interest groups and parties seek to determine and meet needs of the public.

Parties and interest groups can assume a variety of forms and tasks. One difference between party systems that has attracted much attention is the number of parties. Many in the West consider the only acceptable pattern to be the competition of two or more parties, but it must be remembered that competitive party systems haven't always functioned well. The Nigerian case suggests that party competition during the early stages of development may be divisive and even explosive, and the French experience during the Third and Fourth Republics indicates that it can lead to weakness and instability even in states with long histories of independent existence. The single dominant parties of Mexico, China, and the Soviet Union may not be democratic as we understand the term, but they at least have proved successful at providing stable government and orchestrating social and economic change.

Whatever their nature or number, interest groups and political parties must be present and operative in a modern state. Interest groups provide alternative means of political representation that compensate for the low levels of direct citizen participation in most political systems and serve as informal but essential partners of government in drafting and implementing policy. They are thus important in ensuring effective and responsive government. Even more important is the overall impact of political parties on the political system. The presence of powerful parties is vital to the development of stable political institutions. Where effective dominant parties have prevailed, the course of political development has been made easier. The success of the PRI and the CPSU in providing Mexico and the Soviet Union with political institutions and procedures illustrates the role parties can play in the political development and promotion of political stability in developing countries. In contrast, the failure of the Nigerian parties and their part in exacerbating ethnic conflict paved the way for civil war and military rule. In China, the CCP has had difficulty making the transition from guerrilla activity to running a government, but it is now well on the way to establishing institutions and procedures that can provide a stable political framework.

Although the stability of party structures is a good indication of the overall stability of the political system, it would be inaccurate to designate the party system as the only causal factor in the establishment and maintenance of political stability; other factors such as leadership skills and political norms and attitudes must also be considered. Nevertheless, the contribution of the party system to overall stability is highly important. Where political parties falter or disappear, the political system may no longer be able to channel or meet the needs of a politically mobilized populace. The failure of parties is thus often a prelude to military rule, bureaucratic stagnation, or both.

chapter 6

Political Leadership, Civilian and Military

I was going to make myself formidable intellectually, morally invulnerable, and make all the money that it is possible for a man with my brains and brawn to make in Nigeria.

OBAFEMI AWOLOWO
Former Regional Premier

INTRODUCTION

A central aspect of the politics of any country is the quest for public office. Although the personal rewards to be gained by undertaking this quest can be great, political leadership involves more than the use of power to enrich oneself and one's friends or to satisfy personal whims. The quality of leadership matters greatly to the overall functioning of any political system, and the recruitment of leaders is one of the most important tasks a political system performs. In many countries, the top leader or leaders play such a vital part in the political process that their individual abilities and characteristics determine the political fate of millions.

What is a political leader? We may define political leaders as individuals who hold public office—whether elected, appointed, or by force—and/or who make authoritative decisions affecting the public. This definition includes both formal occupants of positions of power and those who wield actual power, whether or not they hold government positions. This chapter examines political leadership by looking at the general environment in which leaders operate and at the types, contexts, and characteristics of political leadership. Since the military hold or have held political power in a great many countries, attention will also be paid to the military as political leaders and, in particular, to the conditions which encourage the military to enter the political arena.

Political Leadership in Civilian Regimes

Civilian regimes, other than monarchies or closed aristocracies, generally hold open the possibility that any citizen can rise to a position of political leadership. Nevertheless, certain background characteristics and personality traits are associated with the attainment of political power and its effective exercise. In this section we consider some of the attributes of successful political leaders as well as the contraints imposed by the contexts within which leaders operate.

Routes to Political Leadership   In most of the world's civilian-led regimes, positions of political leadership may be sought by anyone who wishes to do so. Few avail themselves of this opportunity, however. We saw in Chapter 4 that political participation in general tends to be dominated by the better educated, and this is especially true of the quest for political office. The world of politics is a complex one, remote from the everyday lives of most people, and aspiring politicians are usually found among those whose education or family background has stimulated an interest in or an understanding of larger community or national issues.

Certain careers facilitate involvement in politics. Journalists who report on political affairs, bureaucrats who administer government policies, and lawyers who deal with the application of laws are naturally led to take an interest in politics and to feel that they have some understanding of it. The ease with which one can leave a career temporarily is also a factor that influences the decision to enter politics. Lawyers, in particular, are often able to go into politics for a period of time without jeopardizing their legal careers; indeed, in many cases even an undistinguished or unsuccessful political career can improve a legal practice by making the lawyer's name better known in the community.

In both competitive and single-party regimes, the groundwork for launching a political career is usually laid with voluntary service to a political party. Part of the task of party officials is to select suitable candidates for political office, and those who, often by virtue of their professional backgrounds, are able to demonstrate to party officials that they possess superior knowledge and abilities—such as the ability to communicate effectively to audiences—are more likely to be invited to seek political office. In some countries, experience in local government is expected before seeking national political office; in others, new recruits go into national politics directly. In either situation, however, many years of apprenticeship in government as well as substantial support within a party are required before an individual can expect to attain high political office.

Leadership Characteristics and Skills   Politics involves conflict and cooperation for public office and favored policy outcomes. Seeking and holding office are the objectives of political leaders, and success depends to a large degree on the leader's personal traits and skills. Among the characteristics that influence leadership performance are socioeconomic background, political style, and such personality traits as the ability to command respect and the knack of finding innovative solutions to problems.

The socioeconomic backgrounds of a country's leaders—their occupations, class affiliations, education, and wealth—are important to understanding their leadership. For one thing, the leaders' socioeconomic traits may be important indicators of the country's level of integration and therefore of the workability of its political system. A society in which individuals from diverse backgrounds are drawn into politics may be less divided than one in which leaders from the lower classes or from minority ethnic groups are noticeably absent. Also, the socioeconomic characteristics of the leadership may reveal informal linkages between leaders in various parts of the political system. For example, similar levels of education and socioeconomic status may facilitate cooperation and mutual understanding among leaders of different parties or between labor leaders and business leaders. Both of these forms of integration may bear on the political stability and legitimacy of the system.

Another aspect of leadership is the leader's political style. Political style reflects such features as the leader's ideological commitment and disposition to be active or passive in decision-making. Those at the zenith of a political system always have more power than those at lower echelons; however, the extent to which that power is used varies with the leader's conscious or unconscious assumptions about the duties of office. A leader who is strongly committed to an ideology, particularly an ideology that proposes a vision of a radically different society, may be much more highly motivated to participate actively in political decision-making than one whose orientation is toward maintaining things more or less as they are. Alternatively, the dispositions, needs, or achievement-oriented socialization of some leaders may impel them to active roles, regardless of their ideological commitments.

Closely related to political style is the leader's personality. There is much evidence to show that leaders' attitudes on positions are often less influential than are their personalities in affecting voting decisions in competitive systems. Television brings the candidates into the living rooms of voters, and a candidate's ability to project the image of a confident and amiable leader may be more important than his or her position on specific issues. "Print is for ideas," as the saying goes, but on television it is personality and image that are exposed and communicated.

A particularly important aspect of personality is the ability to command respect. The successful leader is able both to elicit the respect of the people and to use this respect as a means of gaining support and of extracting services and sacrifices from lieutenants and followers. In democratic countries, where continued tenure in positions of political leadership requires electoral victory, leaders must expend a great deal of time and energy maintaining the respect of voters. In communist countries, leaders may also receive popular respect for making beneficial social changes or leading a popular revolution, as did Fidel Castro and Mao Zedong. More important than popular respect, however, is the respect of other party leaders, whose willingness to support the projects of top leaders is essential to their success. Gaining their respect requires different skills than does mastery of public opinion, notably organizational skill, ideological acuity, and the ability to forge alliances with key individuals and powerful groups such as the military, the bureaucracy, or the secret police.

Other significant personality resources for a leader include an innovative mind. The leader who can generate new ideas and approaches to a country's problems—alone or through advisers—is invaluable. The ability to discern the needs and demands of the populace is also important. Leaders need to establish and maintain links with citizens, interest groups, and lower-level officials in order to avoid being cut off from the needs, concerns, and expectations of the public. Where the citizenry is passive, the leadership may have to determine its needs without waiting for demands to be made. The leader who desires change must discern needs even in the absence of demands and must stimulate public interest and support for his or her plans.

The Context of Leadership   There is no such thing as a truly all-powerful or absolute political leader. No matter how powerful a leader may seem, there are always at least some constraints at work. Even Stalin and Hitler were constrained by the limitations of their countries' resources, by technological obstacles, and by the need to depend on others to carry out their orders. Most leaders are also subject to existing political norms and patterns, which they must either accept or try to alter. The prevailing political culture not only provides norms of popular participation but also defines norms and expectations concerning leadership styles. For example, a political culture that emphasizes deference toward authority may foster the emergence of strong and aloof political leaders. Among patterns, none is more common than the patron-client pattern typical of Third World countries. In systems where this pattern is prevalent, successful leadership may depend less on a leader's public image or other personality attributes than on the ability to maintain patron-client networks by providing a steady flow of rewards in the form of jobs, loans, letters of recommendation, advice, and prestige.

Political culture also determines the types of political power that will be accepted as legitimate. Generally speaking, political leaders must operate within the context of legitimate power or authority. For example, a leader wishing to exercise dictatorial power over society might expect serious obstacles in a political culture whose norms emphasize democracy and limited government. The German sociologist Max Weber delineated three types of legitimate authority on which leadership may draw: traditional, charismatic, and rational-legal.[1] *Traditional* authority rests on beliefs in the sanctity of traditional institutions and the individuals who occupy traditional positions of authority. Examples are monarchies, aristocracies, and tribal chieftaincies. *Charismatic* authority is characterized by public acceptance of a ruler's right to rule because of a belief that he is endowed with exceptional powers or qualities. A crisis environment often gives rise to the emergence of this type of leadership; Hitler, Stalin, de Gaulle, Mao, and many other leaders have legitimized their exercise of power by promoting belief in their extraordinary or unique characteristics. *Rational-legal* authority is based on acceptance of the legality of established rules and of the right to govern of those who come to power in observance of these rules. Examples include many of the developed states, both democratic and nondemocratic, in which rules prescribing certain procedures for acquiring positions are observed.

As this categorization implies, the type of political authority depends largely on the level of development of the country in question. Before the impact of modernization, deference to traditional institutions with rich symbols of authority and respect, such as monarchies, was common. The struggle for national independence is often accompanied by the emergence of charismatic leaders, whose appeal is based on their own personal characteristics and on the vision of a new society which they uphold. Leaders, even charismatic ones, are not immortal, however, and some more permanent basis for authority must be established. In communist countries, authority is generally vested in the party, and constitutional and legal rules generally respect the party's preeminence; at the bottom, however, the party's claim to legitimacy rests not on these rational-legal elements but on a charismatic premise, that is, the belief that the party has a unique collective insight into the processes of history and the needs of the community. In many Third World countries, no basis for legitimate authority exists; instead, there is a struggle between democratic forces, often representing an emerging middle class of students, professionals, and businesspeople, and more traditional or authoritarian sectors. Countries such as Mexico and Nigeria have seen democratic regimes overthrown by the military or *caudillos* in the name of restoring order or traditional values. Imposed and maintained by force, these regimes, too, may prove to be short-lived. In contrast, all highly developed noncommunist countries have well-established democratic political systems in which authority is rational-legal in nature.

[1]Max Weber, *The Theory of Social and Economic Organization* (New York: Free Press, 1947), pp. 324–429.

In addition to the limits imposed by the political culture and by accepted sources of legitimacy, the leaders are usually obliged to act within an established political framework. Where the regime has formalized effective constitutional procedures to check possible abuses of power, or where it allows others to question the actions of government leaders, leaders may be less free to do what they like than they are in more authoritarian contexts. The nature of the political party system, the degree of centralization of power, and the activities of outside interest groups are among the other factors that may constrain a leader. These kinds of constraints are considered more fully in Chapter 7, which deals with the processes of decision-making.

The course of political events also affects leadership. During an emergency or threatening situation, leaders may be able to exercise more authoritarian rule and to allot less time for consultation and consensus formation. Thus, in the United States, presidential powers expanded dramatically during the Civil War, the two World Wars, and the Vietnam War. Conversely, periods of relative peace may inhibit even highly ambitious leaders from reaching their full potential power. Foreign intervention, natural disasters, and economic depressions also affect the functioning and success of leaders.

While the constraints on leaders are many, it is important to realize that leaders may use the resources of public office to bolster their authority and achieve their goals. The most obvious resources available to them are rewards such as money, goods, services, jobs, and honors, which may be employed to gain the cooperation of others. Leaders may also attempt to use symbols to manipulate public opinion. Symbols that trigger emotions of patriotism and devotion, such as the national flag, the national anthem, past heroes, historical events, the military, and national projects, can be highly effective in mobilizing public opinion and action to serve a leader's ends. The importance of the manipulation of these symbols is apparent in the control over the media exercised by governments of all types throughout the world.

More ambitious tactics may also be used in the attempt to consolidate power. One tactic involves the use of co-optation, such as is employed by Mexico's ruling Institutional Revolutionary Party (PRI). If an opposition party becomes too powerful, it is given the choice of joining with the PRI or being eliminated. Another possibility, which also occurs in Mexico, is institutionalizing the sharing of power among different intraparty factions. This is more easily achieved, however, with class or functional than with communal cleavages. Ethnic and religious communalism tend to be highly explosive, as the cases of Northern Ireland and Nigeria demonstrate, and governments cannot overcome such fundamental cleavages as easily as they can co-opt labor unions. Given this fact, the most common remedy in communally divided societies is the elimination of political competition altogether. It is often under such circumstances that the military intervenes.

Political Leadership by the Military

Among the more common phenomena in the world today are military takeovers of political power. Military takeovers are usually staged by members of the officer corps, although on rare occasions leaders have emerged from the noncommissioned ranks. In cases involving higher-ranking officers (colonel or above), the leaders are typically oriented toward organizational efficiency and economic development. While espousing professionalism, the attitudes and behavior of military leaders reflect those of their society as well. The desire for a better life for themselves, their friends, and even their ethnic group is as much in evidence among them as among civilian politicians.

The resources of military leaders are also akin to those of civilian leaders, with one important exception—their greater access to coercive force. Yet, organizational skills and personality characteristics are important to their performance and their credibility; coercion is not a ready guarantee of either success or survival. Often, military leaders have lost power at the hands of their fellow officers or of a disgruntled civilian population because of their failures in office. In Argentina and Brazil, for example, the masses have gone to the streets to demand—and get—the end of military government.

Why the Military Intervenes   The military can play many roles in politics, ranging from subtle pressure on civil servants and political leaders to control of a country's political and economic processes. Among the most common military tasks is the maintenance of national security against external threats, which usually involves only minimal domestic political action by the military. However, in times of all-out war, the priority accorded the war effort may enhance the military's influence in domestic politics. Furthermore, the military may become politically involved because civilian leaders have manipulated public fears about national security.

The military's role in countering domestic security threats leads more readily to interference in domestic politics. Where police forces are unable to maintain internal security, the military is used to preserve domestic peace. In Third World countries, rebellion by ethnic, linguistic, or regional minorities or segments may be of a magnitude that the police cannot control. This phenomenon is not limited to developing countries; several industrialized countries have employed military force to maintain domestic order. Repeatedly during the civil rights and antiwar protests of the 1960s, the United States called on the National Guard to control public dissent; Poland imposed martial law in 1981–1983 under the leadership of General Jaruzelski to thwart the powerful independent trade union known as Solidarity; and Britain today maintains a substantial military presence in violence-prone Northern Ireland.

There is always a latent danger that military leaders might refuse to protect the regime or might be more eager to protect it against some threats than others. Military leaders in noncommunist countries are usually readier to defend the regime against alleged communist threats than against threats emanating from the far right; just such an alleged left-wing danger was used to justify the military dictatorship in Greece from 1967 to 1974. In addition, persistent use of the military to control domestic political disorders may politicize military leaders even if the military has a past record of political neutrality. For example, the Chilean armed forces had traditionally tended to abstain from politics prior to the early 1970s, when President Salvador Allende grew to rely on them to quell civil disturbances; in 1973 Allende's civilian government fell victim to a military coup.

Whether military leaders decide to step over the line separating influence from control is largely dependent on the domestic political context. Where the public regards civilian political leaders and institutions as legitimate, the military is unlikely to try to overthrow the regime. An attempted military coup in such a situation would probably either fail, with disastrous effects on the military, or precipitate a civil war, an outcome most military leaderships are anxious to avoid. On the other hand, where legitimacy is tenuous or lacking, the threat of military coups is likely to be much greater.

Military intervention is also a function of a country's state of political and economic development. Countries in the first years of independence face many challenges. Demands for urban development, housing, sanitation, schools, and jobs often severely strain the limited capacities and resources of governments. Conflict between ethnic, linguistic, and regional groups over the allocation of scarce resources or participation in national policy-making puts immense stress on any government, new or old. If political institutions able to regulate and channel political activities are missing, or if they have failed to win general acceptance, *praetorianism*—the propensity of the military to intervene—is likely to prevail.[2] In such societies, as one writer points out, "each group employs means which reflect its peculiar nature and capabilities. The wealthy bribe; students riot; workers strike; mobs demonstrate; and the military coups."[3] Indeed, the absence of effective and legitimate political institutions may leave the military as the only organized force capable of governing. In such a political vacuum, it is almost inevitable that the military will play an important and determining part. For these reasons, military coups are frequent in developing states that lack accepted political institutions and very rare in developed states with institutionalized and legitimized political frameworks.

[2]The term "praetorianism" derives from the Praetorian Guard in imperial Rome, whose influence became so great that it could control the selection of new emperors by threatening to deny its protection of, or to act against, the Senate.

[3]Samuel P. Huntington, *Political Order in Changing Societies* (New Haven, Conn.: Yale University Press, 1968), p. 196.

The attitudes of military leaders toward their role in society also affect the military's propensity to intervene. Chief among the attitudes likely to induce military intervention is the notion that the military is the guardian of the country's most fundamental values and interests, as opposed to the partisan and sectional views of politicians, parties, and interest groups. If civilian leaders act in ways military leaders feel do violence to the country's "true" values, military leaders may step in to defend the country from the politicians. As one Bolivian president (and military officer) put it, the army should be the country's "tutelary institution . . . watching over the fulfilling of laws and the virtue of governments."[4] The values defended by the military may be the country's constitutional principles or, more commonly, narrower values such as defense of the status quo and of privileged groups.

Military officers often view themselves as efficient organizers of people and material. The hierarchical command structure of the military may seem to them preferable to the slow-moving and inefficient state bureaucracy. Military leaders may be distressed by the corruption of politicians who pursue self-serving goals. In such circumstances, they may seize power in order to cleanse the state by removing corrupt politicians or incompetent officials and replacing them with presumably efficient and honest military leaders.

Finally, military officers are often particularly concerned with economic modernization and expansion. Advanced technology means greater military capacity; economic prosperity means more funds for military appropriations. In states where trained technicians are in short supply, military officers may want to set their technical personnel to the tasks of economic development. Believing themselves to be in command of the best modernizing force in the country, they may stage a coup to promote economic and social reform.

The Military as Modernizers   Since military intervention occurs most frequently in developing countries, and since coups are often justified on the grounds of social change and reform, one might ask how effective military leadership is in promoting economic development. There is no clear-cut answer to the question; it is a matter of debate among experts on military politics.[5] Those who argue on behalf of a modernizing role of the military point to the backgrounds of the military themselves. Military officers tend to spring from the newer middle-class sectors, as opposed to the older landed elite, and are better able to identify with the middle-class elites in industry, government, and the professions. The military's technical orientation and its experience with the latest technology can be important in societies where the overall level of technological devel-

[4]Ibid., pp. 225–226.

[5]For a summary of some major arguments on both sides, see H. Bienen, ed., *The Military and Modernization* (Chicago: Aldine-Atherton, 1971).

opment is relatively low. Moreover, military leaders have a strong interest in promoting the technological development of the country because such improved technical capacity will increase the military's capabilities. Finally, the military is sometimes idealized as an effective modernizer because of its allegedly efficient hierarchical organization, which in many developing countries may be more highly developed and less prone to corruption than governmental and private bureaucracies.

Other evidence casts doubt on the effectiveness of military regimes in pursuing economic modernization. Military regimes, although publicly committed to economic development, have sometimes expended most of the state's resources on military undertakings and equipment. Moreover, the much-vaunted organizational skills of the military are not easily redirected from military planning and organization to the tasks of economic planning and modernization. The Spartan qualities that are often cited as desirable attributes of the military may not always manifest themselves; in many developing countries, military rule has also brought a large dose of wastage and corruption.

Numerous studies of countries—with both military and civilian regimes—suggest that as economic modernizers, militaries are not particularly effective in stimulating increased agricultural productivity, industrialization, and educational expansion. According to one cross-national study, only in tropical Africa is there a strong positive correlation between military regimes and positive changes in agricultural productivity, industrialization, and economic expansion; in other parts of the world military rule has produced economic decline rather than growth.[6] The pattern seems to be that military governments achieve higher rates of economic growth in the least developed countries but that civilian governments do better in relatively more developed non-Western countries.

Essential to political modernization is the development and gradual increase in effectiveness of political institutions, especially of political parties. When military regimes inhibit the development of political parties, prohibit elections, or prevent other political bodies from operating— as many have done—political institutionalization is retarded. In countries with severe regional, linguistic, or ethnic divisions, the military may be able to prevent opposing forces from pursuing their interests through their own parties and thus contain the possible adverse effects of such cleavages for the time being. However, regional or ethnic interests in such countries as Nigeria and Ethiopia have aroused such high levels of conflict that violence has erupted and threatened or destroyed national unity despite the presence of military regimes.

[6]Eric A. Nordlinger, *Soldiers in Politics: Military Coups and Governments* (Englewood Cliffs, N.J.: Prentice-Hall, 1976), p. 170. See also R. D. McKinlay and A. S. Colhan, "A Comparative Analysis of the Political and Economic Performance of Military and Civilian Regimes: A Cross-National Aggregate Study," *Comparative Politics* 8, no. 1 (October 1975), 1–30.

Civilian Attempts to Control the Military In most liberal democracies, the norm of civilian mastery is usually well established and accepted by military leaders without question. Typically, democratic forms of government rely on a strict hierarchy of authority in which civilians head the military; for example, the president of the United States serves as commander-in-chief and appoints civilian secretaries of the navy, the air force, and defense. Communist governments, too, generally maintain strict civilian control over the military (Poland is the main exception). Nevertheless, praetorianism is widespread, particularly among the newer states of the Third World. As Table 6.1 reveals, overt military dictatorships rule in about one-fourth of the Third World countries; in sub-Saharan Africa the proportion rises to 40 percent.

In newer states, where the norm of civilian mastery is often poorly established, asserting and maintaining civilian control are clearly difficult. One approach that has been successful in several countries with past histories of military intervention is to develop political counterforces to offset the natural advantage the military derives from its control of the instruments of force. Political parties, for example, can be powerful counterweights to military power. Parties can be used to organize public support for the regime and thus raise the specter of civil war in

Table 6.1   REGIME TYPES OF THIRD WORLD COUNTRIES, GROUPED BY REGION, 1986

	Military dictatorships (%)	Civilian dictatorships (%)	Monarchies (%)	One-party modified or partial democracies (%)	Democracies (%)
Middle East and North Africa ($n = 19$)	21.1	26.3	36.8	5.3	10.5
Africa South of the Sahara ($n = 45$)	40.0	20.0	6.7	26.7	6.7
East and South Asia ($n = 23$)	21.7	17.4	8.7	13.0	39.1
Latin America ($n = 32$)	12.5	0	0	68.8	18.8
All countries ($n = 119$)	26.1	15.1	10.1	18.5	30.2

Source: Derived from G. T. Kurian, *Encyclopaedia of the Third World,* 3rd ed. (New York: Facts on File, 1987).

the event of an attempted military coup. A similar strategy is to create rival quasi-military organizations ostensibly to defend domestic security, such as the national police force in the Philippines. In some Third World countries, peasants may develop their own armed guerrilla units to counter the military forces. As noted earlier, the Mexican case suggests another means of civil control: co-optation. Co-opted military leaders are appointed to civilian policy-making positions in governmental bureaucracies, enterprises, and the ruling political party and thus merge with the bureaucracy and the leading party.

According to one authority, praetorianism is most likely in societies in which

> The dominant social forces are the great landowners, the leading clergy, and the wielders of the sword. Social institutions are still relatively undifferentiated, and the members of the ruling class easily and frequently combine political, military, religious, social, and economic leadership roles. The most active groups in politics are still basically rural in nature. Families, cliques, and tribes struggle unremittingly with each other for power, wealth, and status.[7]

The actual decision to intervene may be provoked by a variety of factors, including economic stagnation, political instability, and immobilism. Perceived threats to the military's professional interests, defense budget cuts, and ascendancy over the military by a rival policy group may also constitute grounds for military intervention. The desire for upward mobility has been noted in studies of direct military political involvement; the military is clearly an important social route upward in societies where traditional elites dominate status roles. For these reasons, to the extent that civilian leaders are able to effect significant degrees of modernization of their societies, the prospects of mastering the military will be enhanced.

BRITAIN AND FRANCE: LEADERSHIP IN LIBERAL DEMOCRACIES

The political regimes of Britain and France, like those of most other Western democracies, enjoy high levels of legitimacy and unchallenged civilian control of government. While these features have been part of the fabric of British politics for centuries, however, they have been consolidated in France only in the past 25 years. The case of France shows that economic development does not automatically translate into legitimate civilian-led government, although it is clearly conducive to it.

Another feature that Britain and France share is the domination of leadership positions by individuals of elite educational and occupational backgrounds. To some, the elite backgrounds of political leaders contradict the spirit of democracy, if not its letter; others point to the need for

[7]Samuel P. Huntington, op. cit., p. 199.

democratic governments to have highly trained and able people at their helm. While certain backgrounds do favor successful political careers, it is important to note that leadership is not a closed-shop affair in either Britain or France and that talented men and women of diverse backgrounds can and do break through the barriers to achieve positions of political leadership.

Britain: Collegial Leadership by a Civilian Elite

A distinguished student of British politics once noted that British democracy is "government of the people, for the people, with, but not by, the people."[8] Although no country is actually ruled by its people, literally speaking, politics in Britain has seemed to many observers to be the preserve of an especially narrow elite. In the nineteenth century, MPs were not paid salaries, and their ranks were dominated by those wealthy enough to support themselves. Even in the twentieth century, positions of social and economic prominence have tended to open the doors to political careers, and a very substantial proportion of MPs have been educated at prestigious "public" (i.e., private) schools such as Eton or Harrow, often followed by attendance at the elite universities of Oxford and Cambridge. In the House of Commons elected in 1983, for example, fully one-half of MPs had been educated in private institutions.

The high proportion of MPs with elite educational backgrounds is somewhat deceptive, however, for it masks an important difference in the recruitment of the two major political parties. Although Conservatives have almost exclusively come from well-off middle-class or upper-middle-class families, the Labour party has been highly successful at bringing individuals from more modest backgrounds into politics. Before World War II, the vast majority of Labour MPs began their working lives as manual workers or union officials, and even today about one-half of Labour MPs have not received a university education. According to the rules of the party, a prospective candidate for Parliament must be nominated by a group affiliated with the party, and the affiliated groups consist mostly of trade unions. In the 1983 elections 55 percent of the victorious Labour candidates were "sponsored" by a union, which means that most of their election expenses were paid by the sponsoring union, in return for which they were expected to represent the union's interests in Parliament.

The contrast between the class origins, educational attainment, and occupations of Labour and Conservative MPs has been a profound one for most of the twentieth century and has tended to make British politics appear as much a clash of cultures as a struggle for political power. In recent decades, however, the differences have become less noticeable.

[8]L. S. Amory, *Thoughts on the Constitution* (London: Oxford University Press, 1947), p. 31.

Labour MPs, even those sponsored by unions, tend increasingly to come from the ranks of the university educated; correspondingly, the ranks of the Conservatives now contain more university-educated members and fewer members who attended only an elite public school. Nevertheless, differences in backgrounds still remain. Conservatives are far more likely to have come from business or the older established professions such as law and medicine; a majority of Labour MPs, in contrast, are recruited from the working class or so-called communicating professions such as teaching, journalism, and group and party organization. Conservative MPs are much more likely to combine their political duties with business or professional careers; Labour MPs are more likely to treat politics as a full-time job.

In all political parties, the selection of candidates for the House of Commons is the prerogative of local constituency organizations. The Conservative party maintains a list of approved candidates, selected by national party headquarters, from which constituency party executives draw up a short list of names to put before their constituency associations as vacancies occur. Labour party headquarters also maintains an approved list, and candidates nominated by groups affiliated with local party organizations are interviewed by the local parties' General Management Committees (GMCs), which make the final choices. In 1980 the Labour party rules were changed to make it mandatory for MPs to be "reselected" before each election. The main impact of this rule has been to allow some left-wing-dominated GMCs to replace MPs whom they judged to be too moderate. Although the National Executive Committee has not been pleased with some candidate selections, it has generally endorsed them except where party rules had been violated in the selection process.

Prospective parliamentary candidates are not expected to have had experience in local politics. Although political parties compete in local

Table 6.2 OCCUPATIONAL BACKGROUNDS OF BRITISH MPS, 1983

	Conservatives (%)	Labour (%)
Established professions (law, medicine, accounting)	25.9	10.5
"Communicating" professions (teaching, political organization, journalism)	16.9	32.5
Other professions	4.0	1.4
Business	35.8	9.1
Armed forces	4.5	—
Civil service	4.0	4.8
Farming	4.8	0.5
Manual labor	1.0	33.5
Other	3.0	7.7

Source: Derived from D. Butler and D. Kavanaugh, *The British General Election of 1983* (London: Macmillan, 1984), pp. 236–237.

council elections, positions on local councils are unpaid and are usually pursued by individuals who regard politics as an interesting or valuable part-time hobby rather than by those who wish to make a career of it. Nor is it necessary to reside in the constituency in which one wishes to be a candidate for Parliament. In fact, the vast majority of MPs do not have roots in the constituency they represent, and there is no expectation that they will establish any. A candidate who is defeated in one constituency is perfectly free to seek nomination in another. The goal for a candidate is to be nominated in a "safe seat," that is, one that is usually won by his or her party, and it may take more than one attempt to achieve that goal. Because the focus of national politics in Britain is almost exclusively on national or international affairs, this practice is accepted readily by voters; they realize that their MP, governed by party discipline, is not free to vote according to the interests of the constituency in any case.

While political experience is not a prerequisite for becoming an MP, accession to the cabinet—where political power is concentrated—is another matter. Unlike the situation in the United States, where cabinet officers may be drafted from any walk of life, cabinet portfolios in Britain are filled only by those who are members of the House of Commons or, less often, the House of Lords. In fact, 10 to 20 years of apprenticeship in Parliament is usual before a first appointment to the cabinet. During this period, ambitious MPs or peers will probably try to impress their party leader with their loyalty and skill in parliamentary debates. In addition, an MP whose party is in power may win an appointment as a junior minister, assisting a cabinet minister with the management of a government department. Longevity in Parliament, loyalty to the party, and skill in debating and administration are the tests that determine who will ultimately rise to cabinet status.

What is not expected of a would-be cabinet minister is experience of a nonpolitical sort. Apart from cabinet posts concerned with the law, such as the solicitor general, which are usually filled by ministers with some legal training, a minister need know nothing of the business of a department before assuming its control. There is no tradition of departments concerned with the economy being headed by ministers with business or economics backgrounds, for example. Similarly, the political neutrality of the civil service has meant that senior civil servants are not recruited into politics by the parties and, for the most part, do not enter politics of their own accord. Politics is considered a career in its own right, even if it is combined—as it often is among Conservatives—with outside careers in business or law.

A good example of a successful rise to political power is that of Britain's present prime minister, Margaret Thatcher. Mrs. Thatcher first became actively involved in politics as a student at Oxford University in the late 1940s. She attended a Conservative party conference as a delegate from Oxford and soon received the nomination to run for the party in the constituency of Dartford. Unfortunately for her, Dartford was not a safe Conservative seat, and she lost in both the 1950 and 1951 elections. Realizing that her entry into national politics depended on being nominated for a safe seat, Thatcher worked tirelessly for the party. She participated actively as a supporting speaker in various constituencies in the 1955 election and subsequently tried on three occasions to secure a nomination in a seat which had become vacant, but without success. Finally, she was nominated in the constituency of Finchley, which she carried for the victorious Conservatives in the general election of 1959.

It had taken Thatcher 12 years to become an MP but, once in Parliament, she was able to impress her superiors and move up quickly. Within a year of her election, she won parliamentary approval to introduce a private bill, but party leaders persuaded her to introduce another bill which they favored instead. Her effective leadership in piloting that bill through Parliament led to the offer of a junior ministerial post as parliamentary secretary to the minister of pensions. In 1964 the Conservatives lost power, and the party leader, Alec Douglas-Home, resigned and was replaced in 1965 by Edward Heath. Thatcher supported Heath for the leadership and was rewarded by a position in the "shadow cabinet," the group of party leaders each assigned to speak for the party in Parliament on a given subject area. At first assigned to the shadow treasury team, Thatcher was later appointed by Heath as Conservative spokesperson for power, then transport, and finally education. When the Conservatives were returned to power in 1970, the latter responsibility was carried over into a cabinet appointment as secretary of state for education. Despite her relatively rapid rise from backbench MP to cabinet minister, 20 years had passed since Thatcher first stood as a Conservative candidate for the House of Commons. During that time she had acquired very considerable political skills in debating and electioneering, but it is noteworthy that none of her cabinet or shadow cabinet responsibilities bore any direct relationship to her professional training as a barrister (trial lawyer).

The concentration of political power in the hands of the cabinet is reinforced by the doctrine of collective responsibility, which holds that the cabinet as a whole is responsible to Parliament for the conduct of government. Cabinet decisions are therefore collective ones, and ministers must support them publicly—regardless of whether they personally agree with them—or resign. These customs produce a highly collegial style of leadership in Britain, in which compromise and pragmatism generally characterize governmental decision-making.

The prime minister's role largely supports these tendencies. Although British prime ministers, like American presidents, have the right to choose their cabinets, there are important limitations on their ability to impose their own views that American presidents do not share. As noted earlier, prime ministers must appoint their cabinets from among the ranks of their party's parliamentary representatives. These individuals are usually political leaders in their own right, and they often command considerable respect from the party rank and file. In addition, although the prime minister is head of government, he or she is not head of state. Popular expressions of patriotism tend to be directed to the Queen, who performs the lion's share of the symbolic ceremonial duties associated with a head of state. The prime minister therefore appears less like an august figure symbolizing national pride and more like a partisan politician, as open to criticism as any other.

In recent years, there has been a noticeable tendency for the personalities and public images of party leaders to assume much greater prominence, especially during election campaigns. Television is largely responsible for focusing attention on party leaders at the expense of the other candidates or of the parties themselves. Although most Britons do not have the opportunity of voting for their prime minister directly, many regard a vote cast for the local candidate for Parliament as really a vote cast for the candidate's party leader. In addition, political news between the elections tends to concentrate to a very large extent on the actions and words of party leaders. Some observers argue that this has made British politics more "presidential" in style, but it remains the case that party leaders must make decisions in conjunction with senior party figures. For the ruling party, these individuals are usually members of the cabinet; for opposition parties they form the shadow cabinet. The influence of the cabinet or shadow cabinet on party leaders is largely hidden from public view, but it exists nonetheless.

The military plays a relatively small role in British politics, much smaller than in many other democratic countries. Historical experience accounts for the military's nonpolitical orientation. Parliamentary supremacy was established in the seventeenth century as a result of two clashes between parliamentary forces and the monarch. The first of these episodes, the English revolution of 1640, eventually led to the dissolution of Parliament and the creation of a military dictatorship under the Puritan general Oliver Cromwell. This event created a mistrust of the army among parliamentarians, and once Parliament was finally in control it adopted the strategy of permitting only a small army, which had to receive authorization as often as every six months.

Britain was able to curtail its army so severely because it had little need for land-based forces: it shared no borders with major adversaries. As an island power, Britain placed the main emphasis of its military policy on the "senior service," the navy. A powerful navy can enable a country to extend its influence overseas, and the British navy became the instrument by which a vast empire was created. Navies, however, are not suited to seizing political power. Military takeovers require land-based forces, as British parliamentary leaders were well aware.

The legitimacy of parliamentary government in Britain and the long parliamentary experience expected of cabinet ministers have meant that, like civil servants, career military figures seldom attempt political careers. Nor is there a military lobby such as exists in the United States. Since political power lies with the cabinet, the lobbying of Parliament would be of little use, and it would probably be considered improper if it were attempted. Military officers are expected to maintain a position of political neutrality and refrain from making political statements of any sort—and they generally do. The military's contact with government takes place through the Ministry of Defense, headed by a cabinet minister, the secretary of state for defense. As in other policy areas, policy related to defense is the responsibility of the cabinet as a whole.

The Royal Navy is now a much smaller force than it was when Britain "ruled the waves," and the military's size (333,000 personnel in 1983) now corresponds more to that of a middle power than a great one. These changes have been accepted by military leaders apparently without protest. One reason is that Britain still plays an important military role, particularly through its independently controlled nuclear forces. In fact, the Thatcher government plans to increase Britain's nuclear forces enormously through the acquisition in the 1990s of a fleet of U.S.-made Trident nuclear submarines. But by far the more important reason for the military's quiescence is the well-ingrained tradition of military subservience to parliamentary governments. In Britain the military does not "monitor" politics, nor does it embody the country's highest ideals; it is simply a tool of Parliament and Parliament's civilian leaders.

France: The Consolidation of Presidentialism

Political leadership is regarded in France with much more ambivalence than it is in most other democratic countries. On the one hand, there is widespread admiration for such strong leadership figures as the Sun King, Louis XIV, and the military heroes Napoleon Bonaparte and Charles de Gaulle. On the other hand, ambitious leaders are often distrusted; after all, the reigns of both Louis and Napoleon were marred by incessant warfare and entailed considerable suffering for those who had to bear the costs and sacrifices of their leaders' ambitions. During the Third and Fourth Republics, parliamentary life was characterized by a strong sense of egalitarianism among the deputies, and attempts by prime ministers or other party leaders to exercise authoritative leadership or to build up popular followings were widely resented and often punished by defeat in parliamentary votes.

It was precisely the absence of strong leadership in the parliamentary republics that sustained General de Gaulle's conviction that a new type of political regime had to be installed following World War II. After heading the liberation government of 1944 to 1946, de Gaulle retired from political life when it became clear to him that the principal political parties were set on creating another parliamentary regime. The opportunity to establish a presidential republic came 12 years later, in 1958, when a revolt by army officers fighting the independence movement in Algeria led fearful deputies to ask de Gaulle to assume power. It had been an established practice for the French Parliament to turn to outside leaders in moments of crisis, and in earlier episodes these "temporary dictators" had been deposed as soon as the crisis was over. De Gaulle prevented this result by demanding as his price the right to have a new constitution drawn up, and it was this constitution, ratified by a national referendum in 1958, which established the Fifth Republic.

The influence of de Gaulle's leadership style as the Fifth Republic's first president was an extremely important one. Although the constitution specified a division of authority between prime minister and president, de Gaulle exercised supreme power in a highly autocratic fashion, appointing and dismissing prime ministers at will and treating his cabinet as if it were little more than administrative machinery to execute his wishes. On one famous occasion, he even violated his own constitution by staging a referendum without parliamentary approval on an amendment to make the presidency a directly elected office. The Constitutional Council ruled the referendum unconstitutional, but it was held anyway, and with overwhelming popular support de Gaulle's initiative prevailed. Subsequent presidents have lacked de Gaulle's heroic stature, but they have generally followed his precedent of dominating government. Only with the election in 1986 of a right-wing parliamentary majority to oppose the Socialist president, François Mitterrand, was presidential power curtailed, but most authorities regard this situation as exceptional and expect strong presidential rule to remain the norm of French government.

What made de Gaulle's style of leadership popular was his success in providing stable and effective government, in presiding over the fruition of France's postwar economic recovery, and in staking out an independent role for France in world affairs. In the popular mind, national weakness—as illustrated by the crushing defeat at the hands of the Germans in 1940—became associated with weak and unstable parliamentary government, and de Gaulle was able to regenerate national pride through his decisions to remove French forces from NATO (the military arm of the Atlantic Alliance), to build an independent nuclear deterrent, and to establish better relations with the Soviet Union and China. The circumstances which led to his departure from politics—a referendum defeat in 1969—probably reflected a degree of disenchantment with his aloof and autocratic style, but de Gaulle's 11-year exercise of power nevertheless helped to legitimate the idea of presidential leadership, a conception that is universally accepted in France today.

Although the innovation of a strong presidency has changed the character of French politics dramatically, other political leadership roles bear much continuity with previous regimes. The absence of party discipline or stable governments in the parliamentary republics meant that the deputy's primary role was to defend his constituency's interests in Paris. Often, deputies and senators were elected from among the ranks of local officials such as mayors or departmental councillors, and they retained these positions while they served in the Parliament. Party discipline now leaves the individual deputy much less free to vote according to his constituency's interests, but the practice of combining local and national offices has persisted in the Fifth Republic. Because of the weakness of grass-roots party organization, individuals must make names for themselves in local politics if they wish to maximize their chances of launching parliamentary careers.

The ranks of those elected to national political office tend to overrepresent lawyers, doctors, and business executives, much as they do in other democratic countries. There are, however, certain peculiarities to the mix of occupational backgrounds in the French Parliament. The National Assembly, unlike the British Parliament, contains a very low percentage of manual workers, despite the strong representation of the Socialist and Communist parties. In 1981, when the Socialists won an absolute majority in the National Assembly, only 3.1 percent of deputies originated as blue-collar workers.[9] On the other hand, teachers, professors, and other intellectuals make up a surprisingly high proportion of deputies (over a third in 1981). In the past, the substantial presence of academics has been used to explain the noticeably ideological style of French politics, but it is equally possible that it is the ideological style that attracts so many intellectuals to politics.

Another occupation that is highly overrepresented is the civil service. About 23 percent of the deputies elected in 1981 were former civil servants, the vast majority from the upper ranks. Although civil servants are expected to administer the policies of any elected government impartially, it is permissible for them to be associated with a particular political party or to leave the civil service temporarily to pursue other careers without losing rank or seniority. In the National Assembly, they often assume leadership roles on committees because of their administrative and technical expertise, and their representation is even stronger on the executives of most political parties and in the cabinet. In fact, they may already have had a taste of politics before entering the National Assembly. Ministers in France typically appoint personal "cabinets" of advisors to assist them in running their departments, and many of the appointees are civil servants from other departments.

Unlike parliamentary regimes, there is no expectation in France that cabinet ministers will be chosen from among those elected to the National Assembly or the Senate. Indeed, the constitution makes the two positions incompatible; any member of Parliament who is appointed to the cabinet must resign the parliamentary seat. This provision was put in to achieve a certain degree of separation of powers between the executive and legislative branches, and it has allowed presidents to appoint civil servants directly to head departments of government. The practise

[9]Le Monde, *Dossiers and Documents, Les Élections Législatives de Juin 1981* (June 1981), p. 84.

Table 6.3   OCCUPATIONAL BACKGROUNDS OF FRENCH DEPUTIES, 1978

	Gaullists (RPR) (%)	Centrists (UDF) (%)	Socialists (%)	Communists (%)
Teaching	13.0	8.0	42.2	24.4
Liberal professions	27.2	31.2	16.6	6.6
Upper business	29.2	28.6	10.8	1.2
Upper civil service	24.0	23.2	18.6	1.2
Middle-range business and civil service	1.3	—	8.8	10.5
Farming	2.6	7.1	—	7.0
Shopkeepers, artisans	1.9	1.8	—	1.2
White-collar labor	—	—	1.0	11.6
Manual labor	—	—	2.0	31.4
Other	0.5	—	—	2.5

Source: Derived from D. Gaxie, *Revue française de Science politique* 30, no. 1 (February 1980).

of appointing civil servants as cabinet ministers enables presidents to enhance their own authority and control over the cabinet, since civil servants lack political followings of their own and are totally dependent on their president's favor. It has also added an element of administrative expertise to the direction of government affairs. However, many observers have questioned the democratic responsiveness of a system of government that permits nonelected leaders to run government departments, yet lacks the checks and balances of the American system to keep them in control.

Although the civil service is heavily represented in positions of political leadership, the military by and large is not. In large part, this reflects the fact that the Fifth Republic was created as a result of a serious incidence of mutiny. In May 1958, French settlers in Algeria, fearful that the government of the day was contemplating negotiations with the Algerian National Liberation Front (FLN), staged an insurrection in Algiers. The army leadership in Algeria came out in support of the settlers and made preparations to invade metropolitan France. De Gaulle's assumption of power quelled the revolt, but as he moved cautiously toward the inevitable granting of independence to Algeria—which finally occurred in 1962—army officers in Algeria once again became restive. In 1961, just after a national referendum had approved independence for Algeria, a military insurrection was staged by army officers in Algeria, and it was followed by the formation of the so-called Secret Army Organization, which committed numerous acts of terrorism in both Algeria and France. In order to combat these activities, President de Gaulle assumed emergency powers, as provided for by Article 16 of the constitution, and used them to set up two new military courts to try officers involved in activities against the state and to purge the army of disloyal officers. Faced with a determined and popular leader, the army's attempts at resisting political authority were easily suppressed.

Oddly enough, it was the example of de Gaulle that the army officers in Algeria used to justify their mutiny. In 1940 General de Gaulle himself disobeyed orders by refusing to surrender to the Germans and fleeing instead to England, where he set up a provisional government. De Gaulle justified his actions by claiming that he represented France's true interests, which had been betrayed, he believed, by the French government when it signed the armistice with Germany. The generals in Algeria made a similar claim, but in reality the circumstances were very different. The French army, which had suffered a humiliating defeat in 1940 followed by another in Vietnam in 1954, was determined to win in Algeria at any cost in order to restore its lost honor. Its professional officers, after years of fighting colonial wars, did not fully realize that opinion in France was less concerned with colonial victories than with rebuilding France's economy and society and achieving some degree of political stability. As de Gaulle consolidated his new regime, the French public was easily persuaded to abandon Algeria, and die-hard opinion to the contrary proved to be the dream of but a small and isolated minority.

De Gaulle's forceful action to bring the military to order was successful largely because of his enormous stature as a military hero. His efforts to enhance France's international standing also contributed; by removing France's military forces from the control of the NATO High Command and embarking on a nuclear armaments program capable of defending France from any enemy, he created a new role for the military to replace the old one of resisting the rising tide of decolonization. This new role, moreover, has proved to be a source of consensus in French society. Since the 1960s, the military has never found itself at odds with substantial sections of the population; the policy of military self-reliance, including its corollary, the possession of nuclear arms, has met with no significant opposition within France. Ultimately, however, the return of the military to its traditional role of quiet obedience can be attributed to the consolidation of a legitimate civilian regime. As in other Western democracies, it is the support that the constitutional regime enjoys among the public that ensures that military officers obey the decisions of their civilian superiors.

COMMUNIST STATES: FROM HEROIC TO INSTITUTIONALIZED LEADERSHIP

First-generation political leaders in a communist country are generally those who led their party's successful takeover of power. The second leader generation, more often than not, emerges from a succession battle among the top party factions following the leader's death. Subsequent generations evolve regular patterns by which new leaders are chosen; these patterns may be more or less explicitly formalized, but there does appear to be a tendency toward the institutionalization of leadership recruitment and succession. In the course of this evolution, charisma tends to give way to coalition management as the dominant trait of the party chief, and among his highest associates, plain political "savvy" or technical skill becomes the criterion of advancement.

Leadership patterns in the Soviet Union and China mirror the two countries' differing stages of revolutionary and economic development. The revolutionary generation long ago passed from the Soviet scene, replaced by an elite characterized by growing diversity and technical specialization. The Soviet military, never a serious threat to civilian rule, participates in policy-making but shows no sign of seeking greater political power. In China, on the other hand, the last members of the revolutionary guard are only now making their exit, and the postrevolutionary generation is struggling to find its way to a systematic process of elite recruitment and development. In this, they must strike a balance between the revolutionary zeal that built their new society and the practical needs of a modernizing economy, while at the same time they attempt to maintain civilian dominance over an army with a long tradition of political activism.

Soviet Union: The Oligarchs

With the exception of the Stalinist dictatorship, the Soviet Union has always been ruled by a civilian oligarchy.[10] This is not to deny the fact that individual leaders have stamped the political system with their own style and personality; Lenin and Khrushchev were strong-willed leaders whose personalities dominated the oligarchies of their day, and Brezhnev's conservative style colored the working of government for 18 years. Only Stalin, however, ruled the USSR with unchecked power.[11] Even Lenin, a highly charismatic person who might have become a dictator had he wished to, preferred to govern through three committees, the Politburo, the Secretariat, and the Orgburo (organizational bureau). Mikhail Gorbachev, like his predecessors Khrushchev, Brezhnev, Yuri Andropov, and Konstantin Chernenko, leads the high party elite but makes no major policy decisions on his own.

How many persons make up the Soviet oligarchy? This question poses one of the mysteries of the Soviet political system; some of the clues to it are publicly known and some are not. Certainly, the Politburo

[10]It is hard to say exactly when Stalin assumed absolute power, but if we date his dictatorship from sometime in the early 1930s, as does T. H. Rigby, that means the Soviet government was effectively ruled by one man for about 20 of its now more than 70 years. See Rigby, "Stalinism and the Mono-Organizational Society," in R. C. Tucker, ed., *Stalinism: Essays in Historical Interpretation* (New York: Norton, 1977), pp. 53–76.

[11]Of course, even Stalin could not make every governing decision himself. The difference between one-man rule and collective leadership, as Rigby has aptly explained it, is that a dictator makes every decision he chooses to make—and no one challenges his right to do so.

occupies the center of the power elite. However, the Secretariat of the CPSU Central Committee also makes many crucial decisions, and the Presidium of the Council of Ministers appears to make some. Certain key members of the larger Central Committee often figure in policy decisions, particularly the chiefs of the Central Committee's specialized departments concerned with areas such as agriculture, the various branches of industry, party organizational affairs, propaganda, and other matters. In addition, the first secretaries of the party on the level of the republics are frequently consulted on important issues, especially when their local constituencies are specifically affected. Thus it is difficult to put a number on the size of the power elite. We can, however, assume that it is no smaller at any given time than the voting membership of the Politburo (that is, between about 10 and 15 persons) and may include many more.

The top military officials also make up part of the oligarchy, but at no time since the Bolshevik Revolution have the armed forces posed a serious threat to civilian control. That may seem odd, given the fact that the Soviet military occupies a position of high visibility and public esteem and commands an enormous share of the state's resources. Civilian leaders agree that a powerful military organization is necessary to defend the country and pursue its interests abroad, but they are also aware that the army they have created could become a rival to the ruling Communist party. Therefore, the regime has devised elaborate means of political control over the military.

The party, in the first place, permeates the armed forces. Nearly all military officers are party members, and most of the recruits belong to the party or the KOMSOMOL. Within each armed forces company (about 150 people) is a political unit headed by a party appointee called a ZAMPOLIT, whose responsibilities include the continuing political education of the troops and the maintenance of party discipline among them. In addition, agents of the KGB are assigned to each division to deal with the political behavior of the troops and to keep a watch on the ZAMPOLITs as well.

The party, finally, sees to it that the interests of the military are represented in the top decision-making bodies. The minister of defense is on the presidium of the Council of Ministers, and in recent years it has become standard practice for him to be at least a candidate member of the party Politburo. Three of the last four defense ministers, including the current one, Dmitri Yazov, have been army generals. Together with certain sympathetic civilian members of the power elite, they have traditionally wielded a strong influence within the oligarchy, yet without ever having challenged the rule of the Communist party.

Several qualities characterize the persons who make up the high party elite. In the first place, they are all committed Marxist-Leninists. This does not mean that they are a like-minded group of dogmatists wedded to an unthinking philosophical approach; indeed, they are capable of disagreeing with each other on a wide range of issues involving the interpretation of their common ideology. But they all accept the basic premises of Marxism-Leninism: they value the socialist form of economic ownership, they believe that their society is moving toward a historically determined ideal, and they are convinced that their political structures and processes represent the highest form of human organization.

Although some members of the high party elite are co-opted into the oligarchy from careers outside politics, most work their way up through lengthy political apprenticeships beginning in a local or regional party organization. Formal education is not an absolute prerequisite for party leadership, but over the years the proportion of CPSU leaders with higher education degrees has increased enormously (see Table 6.4). All the full members of the Politburo as of 1987 held university or technical degrees, and several had earned more than one.

Traditionally, there have been few women in the party's top ranks. General Secretary Gorbachev has vowed to increase their representation

Table 6.4   HIGHEST EDUCATION LEVEL OF LOCAL AND REGIONAL CPSU SECRETARIES

Year	Higher education[a] (%)	Secondary education (%)
Secretaries of counties, cities, *okrugs*		
1947	12.7	33.4
1957	28.1	15.3
1967	91.1	2.6
1977	99.3	0.1
Secretaries of provinces, *krais,* republics		
1947	41.3	29.4
1957	86.8	5.6
1967	97.6	1.0
1977	99.5	0.4

[a]It is important to note that the Soviet source classifies as "higher education" the courses of study, more accurately characterized as programs of political and ideological training, offered by the Higher Party School and the Academy of Social Sciences. Given a more conventional definition, Professor Bialer estimates that higher-education degrees would have been earned by approximately 75 percent of the party secretaries on the county and city levels and 85 percent of those on the provincial and republic levels as of 1977. Despite this problem, however, the Soviet data are useful for showing the strong trend to more education over the years.

Source: Official Soviet data, as reported in Seweryn Bialer, *Stalin's Successors: Leadership, Stability, and Change in the Soviet Union* (Cambridge, UK: Cambridge University Press, 1980), p. 174.

in high positions, but for the time being, power remains mainly in the hands of men. Other imbalances, of a smaller degree, exist in the makeup of the elite. City dwellers are slightly more apt to attain power than rural folk, the technical intelligentsia more than other social strata, and Slavs, especially Russians, more than other nationalities.

Soviet leaders do come from all social backgrounds, however. The Politburo itself contains men of blue-collar and peasant origins, as well as sons of schoolteachers, white-collar workers, and high government officials. General Secretary Gorbachev, as the son of a peasant, shares common social origins with Khrushchev and Stalin, but Brezhnev's father was a metalworker and Lenin's a civil servant. For advancement to the party's highest ranks, therefore, social origin appears not to be a determining factor.

What does matter is one's ability to command respect and authority among other party members. As a leader rises through the lower ranks, it is especially important that he develop the informal support of specific individuals higher up, for it is through just such connections that new leaders climb to power. Toward the very top of the party hierarchy, political advancement depends crucially on one's connections. Some Western observers have guessed, for example, that Gorbachev rose to the top because he was a favorite of the late General Secretary Andropov and (perhaps) the longtime powerful Politburo member and party ideologist Mikhail Suslov. Gorbachev, in turn, may have "sponsored" several new members elevated into the Politburo since 1985.[12]

It is not simply blind loyalty that distinguishes potential party leaders from others. Throughout their careers, party leaders must demonstrate ability to administer the offices they attain: they must thoroughly understand official procedures, both formal and informal; they must show that they are capable of maintaining discipline among the party rank and file; they must manifest some degree of sensitivity to the needs of the general public; and they must develop either a wide-ranging familiarity with public issues or a specialist's understanding of one or more policy areas, for example, agriculture or industrial organization.

As in any political system, communist or capitalist, politicians in the Soviet Union must also be skilled at promoting their own careers and defending the positions they have achieved. As the Soviet system has developed, much of the uncivil quality in political life has diminished; defeated rivals are not executed or imprisoned, as they were in Stalin's time, and deadly conspiracies do not characterize the inner workings of the Kremlin. Nevertheless, a politician's life is worrisome. The failure of a major policy initiative can cost a leader his authority or even his career. A shift of power in the party's top ranks can redound throughout the

---

[12]Such connections between "sponsors" and protégés are never explicit and generally cannot be verified. Accordingly, some Western observers dispute the connection between Gorbachev and Andropov or Suslov. See, e.g., Darrell P. Hammer, *The USSR: The Politics of Oligarchy,* 2nd ed. (Boulder, Colo.: Westview, 1986), p. 151.

lower levels of the hierarchy, and those who were connected to an ousted leader may quickly find themselves removed from office, too. Once a high-ranking leader is removed from power, he has scant hope of making a comeback and generally suffers the humiliation of being officially forgotten—as in the case of Khrushchev. Because matters of power and personnel are decided behind closed doors, there is always an element of uncertainty surrounding one's position; even the general secretary cannot be secure, for if he should lose the confidence of his colleagues on the Politburo, they are empowered to remove him.

Soviet leaders are conscious that their authority is constantly being tested, even if the test never takes the form of democratic elections or policy referenda. The high party elite do not hold their positions unconditionally; politics in the post-Stalin era is no longer a game played for life and death, but leaders do answer to each other and can be removed by the consensus of their peers. Khrushchev rose to power by mobilizing coalitions against several formidable rivals, and he himself was removed by another such high-level conspiracy. Under Brezhnev's leadership the Politburo stabilized, and no conspiracies against the general secretary emerged. That this was so is a tribute to Brezhnev's attention to personnel policy, something about which Gorbachev apparently learned much. As a new general secretary settles into the job, he seeks to build coalitions that will fortify his position and bolster his authority. Usually, this entails a reshuffling of leading personnel up and down the hierarchy. During the first year of Gorbachev's leadership, a majority of the Politburo members were changed; two who lost their seats were potential rivals for Gorbachev's position: Viktor Grishin, the powerful head of the Moscow party organization, and Grigory Romanov, former first secretary of the Leningrad party committee. The same year saw more than one-third of the government ministers replaced, as well as 14 of the 23 Central Committee departmental chiefs and dozens of party leaders on the levels of the republic, province, county, and the largest cities.[13]

A strong general secretary, therefore, can do much to shape the contours of his party. Since Stalin, there have been three strong general secretaries, and each has attempted to remold Soviet politics according to his preferences. Khrushchev, whose personal style was straightforward and impetuous, pushed the party to enact bold policies that were often ill-chosen or poorly designed. Partly because his programs sometimes did not work, and partly because he failed to pay sufficient attention to party cadres, Khrushchev eventually lost his authority and was forced from office. Brezhnev, far more conservative in temperament, was meticulous about overseeing personnel matters and worked hard to build a broad intraparty consensus for his policy lines. As a result, policy tended to be cautious and even unimaginative, but Brezhnev succeeded

---

[13]Thane Gustafson and Dawn Mann, "Gorbachev's First Year: Building Power and Authority," *Problems of Communism* 35, no. 3 (May–June 1986), 2.

in maintaining his position at the head of the CPSU even as he was overtaken by illness and old age, and he died in office.

Brezhnev's experience suggests that, despite the hazards of power, a general secretary who successfully establishes his authority can count on the cooperation of his colleagues. Politics at the top, then, is a mix of opportunity and danger. There exists the opportunity to lead, to build effective governing coalitions, and to shape all areas of policy—and there exists the danger of making too many mistakes, losing authority, and falling from power totally.

Mikhail Gorbachev followed two elderly general secretaries, Andropov and Chernenko, who both died after short terms in office. Under Brezhnev the political system had stabilized, but policy had bogged down amid competing elite groups and governmental action was hampered by a sluggish bureaucracy. Gorbachev brought to his job a dynamism that had been missing since the days of Khrushchev and a polished intelligence that contrasted with the stodgy image projected by his immediate predecessor Chernenko. Quickly, the personalities who served as spokesmen for the regime, both at home and abroad, changed; gone were the dry bureaucrats in rumpled suits, replaced now by a younger generation of press secretaries who dressed well and spoke Western languages fluently. The change was not only one of image, and Gorbachev soon made it clear why he put so much effort into reshuffling the top ranks of government and party: he planned to embark on a program of controversial reforms aimed at revitalizing the economy and encouraging the freer flow of ideas.

In the process, Gorbachev encountered opposition among the party elite and the bureaucracy. In 1987 he persuaded the Politburo to approve his plans for economic reform; sweeping changes were foreseen, referenced by the watchword *perestroika,* or "restructuring." The plans were adopted by the CPSU Central Committee and ratified by the Supreme Soviet. In 1988, reforms that would significantly liberalize the political system were proposed. Under the surface, however, conservatives within the power elite continued the intraparty debate over the scope of the reforms as well as the speed with which they would be implemented. Thus the nature of the "Gorbachev era," at least in its early phases, appeared to be that of an ongoing struggle among the members of the oligarchy over the dynamics of change.

China: The Passing of Revolutionary Leadership

China's leaders, civilian and military, operate in a political system dominated by a centralized Communist party but sometimes significantly affected by pressures from other sectors of society, including the army. The party determines public policy and controls the placement of personnel in important public offices, and the party's top leadership is responsible for maintaining the strength and quality of cadres. However, the party has often been far from unified in its approach to such matters, and the serious disruptions that have broken out—in the wake of the Great Leap Forward, during the Cultural Revolution, and during the Democracy Movement of the late 1970s—have reflected divisions within the party and the military, in particular between coalitions supporting ideological purity and those favoring pragmatism or reform. Military officers take part in this factional fighting and often influence the selection of leadership and the maintenance of power.

Constituting the top levels of the party leadership is a group of persons with generally similar backgrounds as well as shared experiences in party service and political education programs. Until recently, the very highest ranks have been dominated by the elderly; at the Twelfth Party Congress in September 1982, the average age of Politburo members was 80.[14] Few high party officials are women; as of the late 1970s, for example, only 14 full members of the Central Committee, and 24 alternate members, were women. Chinese leaders tend to be of middle-class rather than working- or lower-class origin, and they are considerably better educated than the overall population. These qualities are less pronounced among leaders on the lower levels, but the trend throughout the party's official ranks increasingly favors those who are well educated and professionally trained.

Like their Soviet counterparts, Chinese leaders are firmly committed to communism and, until the 1980s, treated Marxist-Leninist ideology as a guide to action. In the course of time, their party has gone through fluctuations in doctrinal rigidity. Often a period of ideological relaxation has been followed by an abrupt reversion to orthodoxy and a forceful reassertion of traditional doctrines. For example, the relatively liberal Hundred Flowers Campaign during the mid-1950s was followed by the rigorous imposition of ideological orthodoxy during the Great Leap Forward. Domestic policy in this area does not necessarily correlate to foreign policy; policies of international detente, in which ideological goals are deemphasized in favor of doing business with capitalist countries, may be accompanied by intensification of ideology at home and repression of dissenters. On balance, the political style of the 1980s has been one of tactical flexibility rather than doctrinaire rigidity. The current Chinese leaders believe, as Lenin did, that they must apply revolutionary principles to real situations and not simply repeat abstract Marxist slogans.

Leadership recruitment and mobility can be determined by either patronage or merit. Under the first pattern, prevalent during most of the postrevolutionary era, leaders are recruited and promoted because of their loyalty to some more prominent party or government leader. In many cases, particularly during times of radical policy lines, the key criterion is "redness," or ideological rigor. The second pattern, stressing

---

[14]This changed substantially at the Thirteenth Party Congress (1987) as a result of Deng's leadership changes.

technical skills or expertise, has become more important during periods of decentralization and consciously pragmatic modernization programs, in particular from 1957 to 1960 and again after 1978. Given China's ongoing economic development policies, expertise is increasingly likely to be the basis for the recruitment and promotion of leaders.

As in the Soviet Union, the uncertainties of power force leaders to defend their positions carefully. Although they do not face the threat of being thrown out of office at the next election, Chinese leaders do devote considerable time and energy to preserving their positions in the party hierarchy. Those who neglect this task may find themselves abruptly disposed of. Thus, a leader not only must perform his assigned job according to the expectations of his peers and superiors but also must understand the shifting configuration of power within the complex Chinese oligarchy—and must always be wary of his opponents.

At the top of the party high command, the Chinese experience with leadership succession has been a turbulent one. During the long tenure of Mao Zedong, second-level leaders came and went, and the answer to the question of who would succeed Chairman Mao changed with the times. On two occasions Mao named his own successor, but neither ever came to power; the first, Liu Shaoqi, lost favor with Mao in the mid-1960s, and the second, Lin Biao, was implicated in an abortive military coup in 1971 and fell into disgrace.

After Mao's death in 1976, a fierce succession struggle took place between Hua Guofeng and the so-called Gang of Four. In this, Hua prevailed; not only did he secure the party leadership, he also had the key members of the Gang arrested and jailed. Hua became party chairman, premier, and head of the Military Affairs Committee, but his victory was short-lived; his erstwhile allies, those who had helped him defeat the Gang of Four, forced Hua to resign from all these positions one by one. The reformist group, led by Deng Xiaoping, came to the fore.

Another example of the uncertainties of power is illustrated by the case of Hu Yaobang, a close associate of Deng. In the fall of 1986, the CCP's plenum was debating the impact of economic and political reform on social and political values. By December, the debate had spilled over to the streets. There were mass demonstrations at which intellectuals and students appealed for political democracy. The protests were put down firmly, and Hu Yaobang, who sympathized with the intellectuals, paid the immediate price of these demonstrations. He was removed from the party chairmanship and replaced by Zhao Ziyang.

It is worthwhile to examine the personal style of China's two major post-1949 leaders, Mao Zedong, for so long the driving force of Chinese communism, and Deng Xiaoping, the reformer of the 1980s. Chairman Mao was a revolutionary of vision and enthusiasm, a man of action and skill. His life was dedicated to remolding an ancient society toward a single end—the creation of communism. He was, in a sense, a romantic; in contrast to the dull prose through which most politicians speak, Mao sometimes expressed himself in poetry, as in the following verse, which reveals his impatience:

How many urgent tasks
Have risen one after another!
Heaven and earth revolve
Time presses
Ten thousand years is too long.
We must seize the day
The four seas rise high
The clouds and the water rage
The five continents tremble, wind and thunder are unleashed,
Until not a single one remains[15]

The changes Mao sought reflected the social ideals he believed in: participation, egalitarianism, and freedom through human development and industrialization. Among Mao's firmest beliefs was the conviction that human potential, once freed and focused, can achieve any degree of social change. Realizing that information is one of the most powerful resources of leadership, he kept abreast of ongoing programs and outcomes. He acted flexibly to maintain political power and promote his policy objectives; when he deemed a certain decision necessary to keep up the momentum of socialist construction, he submitted it to the decision-making body most likely to provide the needed support. If he felt he would be outvoted by the Politburo, he would convene a small group such as the Politburo's Standing Committee. If he lacked support there, he might convene an expanded meeting of the Politburo with invited nonmembers; alternatively, he would turn to the Central Committee or even to ad hoc state conferences. Ultimately despairing of these groups, he launched the Cultural Revolution as a means of achieving his goals, relying on the energy of the masses.

In contrast to Mao's revolutionary romanticism, Deng Xiaoping's style is one of pragmatism. Born in 1904, Deng rose through the ranks of the CCP as a protégé of Premier Zhou Enlai, whom Deng met as a student in France in 1920, and it was from Zhou that, more than 50 years later, Deng inherited the program of the "Four Modernizations." Deng's career has had its ups and downs; a member of the CCP Politburo as early as 1945, he became minister of finance, secretary general of the party Central Committee, and vice-chairman of the National Defense Council, but in 1956 Deng was removed from his posts. The party reinstated him in 1973, and he became deputy premier. Subsequently, he rejoined the Central Committee and, a few months later, the Politburo. As undisputed leader since the late 1970s, Deng has emphasized economic reform consistent with the Four Modernizations and encouraged the rise of technocrats in the party. Although Deng stepped down from the Central Com-

[15]*New York Times,* February 22, 1972, p. 3.

Chinese leader Deng Xiaoping (left) and Premier Zhao Ziyang voting at the Thirteenth Party Congress in 1987. Note that Deng still wears a traditional jacket, while his heir apparent is dressed in Western clothes. (Reuters / Bettmann Newsphotos)

mittee in 1987, he was able to install Zhao Ziyang, who as premier had spearheaded China's rapid economic modernization since 1980, in the party chairmanship. In addition, Deng managed to have Li Peng (the adopted son of Zhou Enlai), an engineer educated in the Soviet Union and experienced in major development projects, chosen as premier. Li is also a member of the Politburo's Standing Committee. With these and other appointments, Deng's legacy appears safe for the foreseeable future.

In the post-Mao period China has begun to institutionalize political leadership change and move toward a meritocracy. This has coincided with a change from the dominance of revolutionary values to those of socioeconomic modernization. Without meaning to emulate the Soviets, the Chinese have developed a bureaucratic system akin to that of the USSR, and perhaps in time they will evolve a regularized process of leadership transition such as that which now exists in the CPSU. Chinese leadership roles, however, are not clearly delineated; the key decisions on policy and the transfer of authority will probably continue for a while to shift among powerful individuals in the Central Committee and the Politburo. Still, the old style of personal leadership—the revolutionary-charismatic style of Mao Zedong—appears to be giving way to the rule of an executive committee, and that, in a communist system, is a sign of progress in the institutionalization of political processes.

What about the Chinese military? From the beginnings of the CCP, Mao had always accepted the Leninist doctrine of party primacy, but he realized that the success of the revolution in China depended on the formation of an army. The revolutionary struggle in China lasted from the early 1920s until the communist victory in 1949. Throughout this "pre-liberation" era, the Chinese Communist party and its military arm, the People's Liberation Army (PLA), were united in pursuit of revolutionary victory through military action. Well organized and efficient, the PLA played a vital political role after 1949, as it was responsible for consolidating power in many parts of China where party cadres were scarce. Indeed, not until four years later was the party itself able to gain effective control in certain provinces to the point where its rule, rather than that of the army, prevailed. Thus, the Chinese communists have a legacy of party-military collaboration that complicates the problem of civilian dominance.

Several times since 1949, external threats have led to preparation for actual or potential military conflicts: the Korean War (1950–1953), the Vietnam War (1965–1973), and border disputes with India (1962–1987), the Soviet Union (1964 to the present), and Vietnam (1977 to the present). These events, as well as the tensions aroused by the Cultural Revolution, contributed to the involvement of the military in politics. Moreover, Chairman Mao used the army on occasion as a weapon to combat his opposition within the party. Though frequently drawn into politics, however, the military has rarely taken political initiatives on its own—the most prominent exception being Marshal Lin Biao's attempted coup in 1971. Unlike many other developing countries, China has so far been successful in managing the military.

The civilian elites have developed several means of controlling the armed forces. First, there are a number of party and state institutions, starting at the top with the party's Military Affairs Committee; both Mao and Deng Xiaoping have headed this committee, which oversees the military's actions and advises the party on military policy. The parallel state institution is the Central Military Commission, which is headed by the chairman of the Military Affairs Committee. Party committees operate throughout the military hierarchy, and Soviet-style political officers are assigned to all levels. In contrast to the Soviet practice, however, the military commander of a given unit has at times also been the political officer, limiting somewhat the party's independent control.

Periodic shifts in military structures and personnel have enhanced civilian authority by weakening the political ties that might otherwise grow up in a given province or between given sets of leaders. In addition, high-level military officers such as Lin Biao, who overstepped the political bounds as determined by the party, have been purged. Finally, the armed forces have been employed in such civilian enterprises as farming, industry, education, health programs, and heavy construction. These activities help to relieve boredom among the troops during peacetime; they also serve to keep them integrated into society by participating in the country's development process.

Civilian supremacy has not gone unchallenged, however. The peak of military influence was reached during the Cultural Revolution, as Mao used the army to bolster his authority and radicalize the populace. Initially the army trained and directed some of the Red Guards, but later it was used to round up dissident students and send them to the countryside for reeducation, as well as to close the universities that had been their base of support. Eventually the military took on important civil and economic functions, including operation of the communication and transportation systems, from which its power spread to factories, schools, cities, villages, provinces, and even the highest ruling political bodies. By the Ninth Party Congress in 1969, the military controlled voting majorities on the Politburo and the Politburo's Standing Committee and occupied many additional positions of power on the national and provincial levels. Of 2350 counties, 2000 were under military rule.

The party began to reassert its control following the attempted military coup in 1971. Mao engineered a purge of the officers involved by expanding the membership of the Military Affairs Committee and reorganizing the command of the Beijing military region. By 1973, the decline in the military's influence was evident. Civilian leaders have ever since been shy about calling the army into politics. When Hua Guofeng moved against the Gang of Four, for example, he employed a security guard rather than regular military units to make the arrests. Further attempts to control the military have come under Deng's leadership. At the Thirteenth Party Congress in 1987, the changes in the Politburo's membership involved the removal of conservative military leaders and their replacement by moderates. Moreover, only 16.5 percent of the new Central Committee chosen at that Congress are professional military officers.

Still, the politicians know the armed forces are important to them. During the 1986 outbursts among students and intellectuals, Deng Xiaoping had to turn to the Military Affairs Committee. The conservative majority on the committee apparently insisted that the military's support would be contingent on Deng's taking a firm stand with the students and sacking some reformist leaders, Hu Yaobang becoming the principal scapegoat.[16] As this example illustrates, the relationship between the party and the military continues to be one of a delicate balance between civilian control and the army's potential clout.

MEXICO AND NIGERIA: TOWARD THE INSTITUTIONALIZATION OF LEADERSHIP

Leadership patterns in Mexico and Nigeria clearly reflect the two states' different stages of political development. With a much longer history of independence, Mexico has developed and institutionalized a pattern of leadership roles that serves to bind the country together. The public has

---

[16]*Far Eastern Economic Review* (March 19, 1987), 59–61.

certain expectations about how leaders will be recruited and how they will act in public office. The transformation from traditional leadership, however, is by no means complete; patron-client bonds continue to be of vital importance to leadership recruitment and interaction, and there are still elements of *caciquismo.*

In Nigeria, the institutionalization of new leadership roles has not been accomplished. Traditional leadership patterns, which differ from one region to the next, continue to characterize much of the political elite. Some have claimed that the military coups and civil war destroyed emergent national political roles, but it is equally probable that the army stepped in because there were no civilian political leaders capable of unifying the fragmented society. As is true of virtually all aspects of Nigerian life, ethnic and regional differences significantly affect the leadership system. Consequently, national leaders—as opposed to regional and ethnic leaders—have not yet been able to assume authority throughout the community as a whole. Apparently, one of the aims of the military rulers has been to provide a set of national leaders—even if they must be "civilianized" military figures.

Mexico: Controlling Praetorianism

Central to the context of political leadership in Mexico are the PRI and the role of the president. As long as PRI dominance of government continues, aspiring leaders must pursue their political careers under its auspices or almost certainly be excluded from top-level office. The PRI shares many aspects of its decision-making power with other organizations such as the church, business and financial corporations, foreign investors, and in some cases local landowners and social notables, but it is only through the party that political leadership is recruited and developed.

The president is the key political actor, but he sits atop a system that is more complex than it appears at first glance. Each president develops his own autonomy in the shadow of his predecessor, and he presides over a country in which governors and municipal leaders are skilled at developing their own autonomous powers. Despite the ultimate authority of the president to intervene in local matters, many lower-level officials exercise important political prerogatives and privileges.

Mexican political leaders come from a wide variety of socioeconomic backgrounds, and it is possible for individuals of humble peasant origin to reach the highest levels of political leadership, including the presidency. As to regional origins, there are indications that the national leadership is disproportionately drawn from the four most populous states of Mexico: Veracruz, the Federal District, Puebla, and the state of Mexico. Most have had university educations, primarily in law and generally at the National University of Mexico. In the past, disproportionate numbers of leaders were drawn from the armed forces, but since 1940 there has been a decline in military participation at the top levels of government.

A notable feature of Mexican leaders is their relative lack of ideological commitment. The revolution was socialist in orientation and goals, but from the beginning its leaders were pragmatists rather than ideologues. Socialist goals and sentiments remain an important part of the Mexican revolutionary tradition, but mainstream PRI leaders rarely invoke the ideology or symbolism of socialism. Even leaders who have implemented major economic reforms have been guided less by ideology than by their assessment of the reforms' political consequences.

A second aspect of the Mexican leadership style is authoritarianism. The president's powers are great, and those who have held the office have proved willing to use them, whether ruthlessly to suppress dissent or courageously to launch major social reforms. The president controls 80 percent of the total public budget, makes appointments to the courts and most public offices throughout the country, and has the authority to dismiss state and municipal governments.

Closely related to authoritarianism is a third feature of the Mexican political style, personalism. Because of the president's charismatic and symbolic appeal, his personality dominates the political scene during his six years in office, but authoritarianism and personalism permeate all of Mexican politics. The patron-client system and *caciquismo,* both long-established practices, are founded on personal loyalties and traits rather than on loyalties to, or the formal powers of, institutionalized public offices. The *caciques* are the traditional embodiment of local authoritarianism, as one student of *caciquismo* writes:

> As long as the *cacique* does not clash with the government in power, his authority sometimes borders on sovereignty. . . . When a *cacique* actually dominates the local administration, the agents of the central government must obey him if they want to keep their jobs.[17]

As influential as the *caciques* have been historically, they are now gradually losing their local authority to public officials. The mystique of power and status that has been a keystone of the *caciques'* position is being eroded by increased education, greater exposure to the media, and the growing public involvement in politics. The passing of the *caciques* by no means signals the end of local fiefdoms, however, for the new public officials, in the tradition of the *caciques,* tend to be no less authoritarian in their conduct.

In a system where individuals wield so much personal authority, one of the most important leadership skills is the ability to balance contending interests to enhance one's flexibility and power. Sometimes this

[17]Jacques Lambert, *Latin American Structures and Political Institutions,* trans. Helen Katel (Berkeley: University of California Press, 1967), p. 312.

requires a politician to develop counterforces and play off one interest against another. In all cases it is necessary for a leader to make appointments shrewdly, building a support base through the strategic placement of loyal appointees.

Although most political leaders rise to the top through the PRI, there does exist another route, namely through direct co-optation. Promising leaders of dissident groups or marginal political parties are sometimes lured into the system by offers of high-ranking positions. While this path is far less trodden than that leading through the ranks of the PRI, it is important as a way of diffusing opposition and preventing excessive inbreeding in the leadership.

In rising through the PRI, an aspiring young "politico" will generally become involved in a patron-client relationship. Typically, his career will begin when he joins the clique of an established politician. After successfully performing tasks for his patron, he may be promoted to higher positions if his patron is in turn successful in serving those above him. Eventually the young politician may develop his own circle of followers, who will perform tasks to solidify and promote his status. His route may take him through the service of several patrons before he reaches his peak.

It is in this way that recent Mexican presidents have risen to the top. Miguel de la Madrid, president from 1982 to 1988, got his start during the 1950s as a law student of José López Portillo, who preceded him in the presidency and named him to two cabinet positions. Similarly, de la Madrid's successor, Carlos Salinas de Gortari, who has served in the bureaucracy and in the cabinet, is a former student of de la Madrid at the National University. The careers of both men, which entailed long and complicated political apprenticeships, would undoubtedly have found-

Carlos Salinas de Gortari was designated in 1987 to become the ruling PRI's candidate for the presidency in the 1988 elections. (Sergio Dorantes / Sygma)

ered somewhere along the way had they not been connected to powerful patrons.

The PRI and its complicated patron-client networks are a phenomenon of the current era, but for many years of Mexico's history the typical route to political power led through military service. In fact, twentieth-century Mexico is a good example of a developing country that has succeeded in establishing civilian control over an army with a long-standing tradition of intervening in politics. Throughout the first hundred years of Mexican independence, attempts were made to establish constitutional governments, but each one aroused opposition; more often than not, who would hold power was determined by the gun rather than the ballot box. The vast majority of Mexico's rulers between 1821 and 1917 were military figures. During the same period the army controlled the nation's budget and sometimes spent more for military purposes than the total revenues collected by the government.

The 1917 constitution provided for civilian control of the armed forces and prohibited active military officers from holding elected public office, but the army continued to play a major part in politics for another 20 years. Over time, however, the political power of the military ebbed. All of Mexico's presidents in recent decades have been civilians, and there have been few military officers in other high federal or state posts. The army's claim on the national budget declined from 44 percent of all federal governmental expenditures in 1924 to only 1.4 percent in 1983.[18] Once the kingmaker and mainstay of politics, the Mexican army today is a model of subservience to civilian members.

Several factors combined to bring the Mexican military under civilian control. The development of effective political institutions created the kind of political environment conducive to the downfall of praetorianism; chief among them were the presidency and the PRI, which proved capable of responding to the interests of a variety of social forces and thus minimized the social discontent that often fosters military intervention. Formalized rules for governing and succession have eliminated the political uncertainty that had in the past given the army a reason for assuming power. Over time, the party co-opted and absorbed the military by allowing it to develop its own sector alongside the peasant, worker, and popular sectors; by 1940 the military's political strength had declined to such a degree that President Avila Camacho abolished the military sector of the PRI and incorporated it in the popular sector.

As in China, army units have been assigned to economic and social projects, diverting their attention from politics and eliciting their commitment to the social aims of the state. Civilian tasks performed by the

[18]P. G. Casanova, *Democracy in Mexico,* 2nd ed. (New York: Oxford University Press, 1970), p. 207; U.S. Arms Control and Disarmament Agency, *World Military Expenditures and Arms Transfers 1985* (Washington, D.C., 1985).

military have ranged from the management of armaments plants to the promotion of adult literacy in rural areas. On retirement, military officers are frequently offered comfortable positions in private business—an attractive and lucrative alternative to political activism.

Conspiracies have been prevented through close surveillance of the military and its officers, directed by the president. In the past, Mexican generals would develop regional power bases that defied central control and sometimes provided a base from which to undertake a coup. To prevent this, recent civilian leaders have periodically rotated commands and officers, reducing the generals' ability to develop regional political fiefdoms.

Over the years, Mexican leaders have shown much ingenuity in creating counterforces to the military. Today it is the party that stands as the primary organization counterbalancing the army's power, but earlier politicians developed other means. Porfirio Díaz, who ruled from 1876 to 1911, formed a rural police force which he controlled. President Carranza (1917–1920) recruited labor brigades to combat the peasant armies of Villa and Zapata. President Cárdenas (1934–1940) won popular backing through land and social reforms and, when challenged by the military, created peasant and labor militia forces. His successful resistance to the army in 1938 ended the last major military threat to civilian rule in Mexico.

Lacking a serious external threat, the military's main task today is internal security, which frequently involves it in politically relevant activities such as antiguerrilla action, riot control, suppression of student demonstrations, and control of electoral problems. The military's role in such affairs raises the possibility that the government may become dangerously dependent on the armed forces, particularly if the level of social unrest should rise precipitously. After half a century of unchallenged civilian supremacy in Mexico, most observers expect the pattern to continue, but in two recent Latin American cases—in Chile and Uruguay—similar traditions of military noninvolvement in politics were destroyed by prolonged periods of instability and civil disorder. It is possible that such instability and conflict in Mexico might prompt the military to intervene in politics and act independently to restore order. Recent public opinion evidence suggests that the army might be welcomed in such a case. With the government on the defensive over a series of electoral frauds and policy failures, including high unemployment, inflation, and deflated expectations regarding the oil bonanza, a 1985 poll asked Mexicans to state which elements in society "lie" most to the public; 59 percent mentioned politicians and 26 percent said public officials, but only 2 percent considered the military to be more untruthful than other elements.[19]

[19]Jorge G. Castaneda, "Mexico at the Brink," *Foreign Affairs* 64, no. 2 (Winter 1985–1986), 292.

Nigeria: The Military in Power

In contrast to the regularized pattern of Mexico's leadership, the leadership system of Nigeria has been shaped by rapid and fundamental changes. These shifts mirror the tumultuous changes in the political system during the twentieth century, from colony to independence to civil war and alternating periods of civilian and military rule. Traditional Nigeria was characterized by hereditary elites in the emirates of the north, kingdoms in the west and midwest, and decentralized lineage systems in the eastern regions. British colonial rule brought to the forefront educated professionals and civil servants, who competed with traditional leaders in forming political organizations and helping the British administer their colony. Upon independence, power gravitated to those who could provide goods and services and who gained recognition through hierarchical patron-client linkages. Efforts to establish a constitutionally defined leadership system were short-circuited, moreover, by the 1966 coup and the long civil war. After the coup, a military elite supported by bureaucrats ruled; in subsequent years, this elite has continued to dominate Nigerian national politics despite periodic changes of personnel and a four-year attempt at civilian rule (1979–1983).

Part of the problem is that Nigeria, unlike many emerging states, has had no national charismatic leader to rally the people behind the cause of nationalism.[20] Each region and communal group had its own heroes and leaders. Some regional leaders who came into federal public office sought to win acceptance as leaders of the whole country, but supporters and opponents alike continued to perceive them as regional or communal leaders. Since the civil war, some success in gaining acceptance as national figures has been achieved by the military leaders, but they continue to confront deeply rooted regional and ethnic sentiments as well as differing local leadership systems.

Each Nigerian region has a unique pattern of leadership and a correspondingly separate style of recruiting its leaders. Those of the north, where most current Nigerian leaders come from, are the most traditional. Historically, the main subunits of the north, for example, the Hausa political system, were almost independent kingdoms within the Sokoto empire. Rule was autocratic and hierarchical, from the sultan on down. Key elite positions came to be dominated by the Fulani. Public office meant social status and could lead to great personal wealth.[21] This traditional pattern, characteristic of the Hausa-Fulani, persists to a considerable extent today, although in the upper leadership ranks expertise and competition have come to replace heredity as the principal means of advancement to leadership.

[20]However, Nnamdi Azikiwe came very close to being a national leader in the "preregional" phase (1940–1950).
[21]M. G. Smith, "The Hausa of Northern Nigeria," in J. L. Gibbs, ed., *Peoples of Africa* (New York: Holt, Rinehart & Winston, 1965), p. 81.

In contrast to Hausa authoritarianism, the Ibos of the east developed leadership councils composed of elders who govern by consensus and with the acquiescence of the community. As in other parts of Nigeria, two leadership systems exist, that of formal political offices and that of the traditional councils. Traditional village leadership is dominated by well-to-do men—those who produce the most food, own the most property, or can afford to court their neighbors' support by granting favors and holding large social gatherings. Economic achievement is the basis of political recruitment, and the group most important in the process is the clan hierarchy.

The traditional Yoruba systems had kings whose prestige derived from divine sources. In practice, however, the king shared power with councils whose members included hereditary chiefs and representatives of major territorial and associational groups.[22] Since the Yoruba kings could be removed by their councils, they were not as active or as politically secure as Hausa kings. Nor did the Yoruba kings accumulate property or fiefs as did the Hausa kings. Entrepreneurial activity among the Yoruba created a class of individuals whose wealth sometimes equaled that of the kings.

Given the strength of these differing regional traditions, it is not surprising that modern-day Nigerians have difficulty agreeing on a national leadership, and the intensity of civil conflict from the late 1960s to the early 1970s tragically illustrated the scope of the problem. The lack of national civilian leadership has created a political vacuum which only the armed forces have been able to fill consistently since the early years of the First Republic.

The military chiefs who have succeeded each other in ruling for most of the time since 1966 show both similarities and differences in their backgrounds. All have been northerners, but not all have been Hausas; General Yakubu Gowon, who ruled for the longest period (1966–1975), was a member of a minority ethnic group. A Methodist by religion, Gowon was educated in colonial schools and later at the Sandhurst Royal Military Academy in England. In contrast, the man who overthrew Gowon, Brigadier Muritala Rufai Muhammad, was a Hausa and a Muslim, and so, too, are the men who have seized power in the 1980s, Major-General Muhammed Buhari (1983–1985) and Major-General Ibrahim Babangida (1985–present). The sole civilian president during the past two decades, Shehu Shagari (1979–1983), was also a Hausa and a Muslim, but his vice-president, Dr. Alex Ekuwueme, was an Ibo. Thus it appears that northerners, specifically Muslim Hausas, have an edge on the top power position, although they do tend to bolster their position by making alliances with representatives of other important social groups.

The socioeconomic backgrounds of the larger military-political elite run the gamut from the humble origins of most to the millionaire

[22]P. C. Lloyd, "The Yoruba of Nigeria," in J. L. Gibbs, ed., op. cit., pp. 547–582.

family and Oxford education of Lieutenant Colonel Ojukwu of eastern Nigeria. As in civilian society, patron-client ties among the military-political elite are an important factor in advancement. And while members of different ethnic groups have become prominent, there is evidence that ethnicity is a salient factor in the formation of patron-client relations within the officer corps and between military and civilian elites; close ties between civilian leaders and officers of the same ethnic groups help to bridge some of the inherent political gaps in Nigerian society.

President Shagari's political life illustrates the blending of traditional and modern influences. Shagari was born the son of a village chieftain. His early education was in an Islamic school, but later he studied education in England. He served in the regime of General Gowon in several ministerial positions. He helped to promote education in his native Sokoto, starting nearly a hundred elementary schools. His last position prior to being elected president in 1979 was in private industry as the head of the Peugeot automobile firm in Nigeria.

Although ideology is less important among Nigerian elites than ethnoregional identity and personal connections, those who rule do take seriously the need to develop policies and programs commensurate with some set of political or social goals. Since 1966, the military leadership has emphasized national economic development, ethnic reconciliation, and political reform. Basing its authority on a variety of support systems, the elite tolerates and even encourages input from tribal chiefs and other traditional regional leaders, as well as from newer technically trained elites. However, as Figure 6.1 suggests, the military has not been reluctant to take care of its own needs.

In examining the reasons for the dominance of military rule, it is worthwhile to consider the differences between Nigeria and Mexico. In the first place, Mexico has a much longer history; its nationhood rests on more than a century and a half of unified political independence, and in the course of that time strong attachments have grown between the people and their central government. The Mexican state thus has a basis of support that has allowed it to develop civilian institutions strong enough to govern without requiring the particular kind of discipline that, in Nigeria, only the military seems able to impose on society. In a real sense, comparing Nigeria and Mexico as they both are today overlooks the fact that when Mexico was as young a country as Nigeria is today, it too was persistently vulnerable to military rule.

Like the Mexican army of the mid-nineteenth century, today's Nigerian army itself is a relatively young organization. It was created by the British during the colonial era. As a product of British colonial rule, it inherited some of the values and norms of British civil-military relations, and in its early years officers and troops alike were socialized to accept civilian control over the armed forces. Prior to independence, however, the military was under the control of the British, and it has not subsequently learned to submit to *Nigerian* political institutions. More-

over, more than 80 percent of the officer corps had been foreigners (Brit-
ishers and others) before independence, and the many new officers who
had to be rapidly trained and upgraded had little time to absorb the
British tradition of loyalty to civilian control.

This newly nationalized army, led by a mostly inexperienced officer
corps, immediately confronted tasks that had a politicizing effect on it.
Its main task was to maintain internal security during the increasingly
frequent lapses in political and social order, entailing the suppression,
early on, of politically motivated riots. Called in to impose order where
the civilian government could not, many military officers quickly came
to understand that the force under their command was more viable than
the authority of the civilian state, particularly given the fundamental
cleavages in the society over which the civilian government was helpless
to assert its control. Thus the first attempt at civilian rule, from 1960 to
1965, gave way to the power of the military.

The second attempt at civilian rule, from 1979 to 1983, also failed.
Although the government of President Shagari served through one complete term, its authority was badly damaged by a severe economic recession as well as allegations of fraud and corruption leveled by both the
military and the opposition. But the Buhari regime proved itself no better
than its civilian predecessor, and after 20 months the military, led this
time by Ibrahim Babangida, intervened again.

The Babangida regime revealed that the Buhari government had

Figure 6.1 Military expenditures as a percentage of GNP in Nigeria. The GNP
(gross national product) is a measure of the total value of goods and services
produced in a country in one year. Note the generally lower level of military
expenditures during the period of civilian rule from 1979 to 1983. (*Source:* U.S.
Arms Control and Disarmament Agency, *World Military Expenditures and Arms
Transfers,* Washington, 1985, p. 75.)

arrested and harassed journalists and others who criticized the government. Moreover, the economic crisis had continued unabated, and there was some evidence of corruption by top military officials in the regime.[23] The Buhari government had based its rule on Hausa-Fulani control, and the Babangida regime has sought to restore regional harmony by diversifying the ruling group. Babangida himself enjoys a greater personal popularity than his predecessor.

Even so, his government faces problems which would be difficult for any group of leaders, civilian or military. Reliant on revenues from oil exports, Nigeria has been jolted by the drop in world petroleum prices during the 1980s, and, as the recession persists at home, Nigeria's leaders know they have to make fundamental reforms in their country's economic structure. The underlying social conflicts, too, are not about to disappear. While addressing the economic and political problems in a more open fashion, the Babangida government appears reluctant to undo all the misdeeds of the Buhari group, continuing, for example, to exert political pressure on the press.

Thus the reasons for persisting military rule in Nigeria remain strong and the bases for civilian rule weak. If Nigeria is to return to real civilian rule, as is planned, effective civilian political institutions and political parties must be created. Any civilian government must be capable of preventing or quickly overcoming social disorder, or new military action would be extremely likely. In light of recent experience, the prospects for the consolidation of a permanent civilian regime do not appear bright.

CONCLUSIONS

In all six countries political leaders are differentiated from the public by better educations, better economic positions, and, in all but the Soviet Union, higher social class origins. They are more frequently drawn from dominant cultural groups than from minorities. These findings are not surprising, since these socioeconomic characteristics tend to be associated with greater interest in politics and greater propensities to participate. That leaders are, in these terms, unrepresentative does not necessarily mean that public policy will slight underrepresented classes and groups. It frequently happens that individuals of upper-class origins initiate social and economic reforms that fly in the face of their presumed class interests. By the same token, it is not uncommon for leaders from lower-class backgrounds, once elevated to the political elite, to become insensitive to the concerns of the underprivileged. The point is that socioeconomic backgrounds do not inevitably determine elite attitudes and values.

Leadership styles and skills differ from one state to the next in

---

[23]Larry Diamond, "Nigeria Update," *Foreign Affairs* 64, no. 2 (Winter 1985–1986), 330.

accordance with political institutions, traditions, and values. However, two traits were found to characterize the leadership of all six countries: pragmatism and personalism. Even the allegedly ideologically committed communist leaders demonstrate flexibility in applying their doctrine to concrete situations. Flexibility is not always a virtue, however. There is a danger in many countries—especially the Western democracies—of sacrificing principles for the sake of political expediency. If political leaders give in to the demands of powerful interests whose aims are self-serving, they may betray the long-range interests of the community as a whole. What is expedient is not always what is best.

In one matter, it makes little difference whether a state is old or new, communist or democratic, developed or underdeveloped: when civilian political institutions prove unable to perform the tasks expected of them by the people, the armed forces may abandon their normal role as guards against external attack and become the country's political "gods," ousting and installing political leaders. Thus, when civilian authorities were unable to cope with grave social and political crises in France during the Algerian war, in China during the Cultural Revolution, and in Nigeria when ethnic tensions reached the point of explosion, the armies intervened politically to install new leaders, fill the political vacuum, or completely replace the civilian government. The transformation of the military from guards to gods is likeliest to occur during periods of prolonged political turmoil, because at such times the military may be the only organized group capable of preventing further decay or civil war.

In many Third World countries, especially those in Latin America and Africa, tendencies toward both democratic and military modes of governance exist. Yet, once a tradition of military intervention is established, it is difficult to nullify the political pretensions of the armed forces and reassert the norm of civilian control. Having successfully intervened in the past, the military is readier to do so in the future. Furthermore, a military regime often lacks the knowledge and incentive to develop effective civilian government structures, which may in turn lead to further military takeovers when things appear to be getting out of control. The job of imposing civilian authority on a politicized military is arduous. That it can be accomplished, however, is demonstrated by the reestablishment of civilian authority in France and, more dramatically, by the abolition of a century-old tradition of praetorianism in Mexico.

three

POLITICAL PERFORMANCE

chapter 7

Making Public Policy: Structures and Styles

INTRODUCTION

People often associate policy-making with smoke-filled rooms where politicians wheel and deal in the exchange of goods and values, including the public offices they covet. But the bombing of a village, the construction of a school, and the promise of "a chicken in every pot" are also aspects of the policy-making process. In this process, governmental actors such as cabinet ministers, legislators, and administrators interact with each other, with individuals and groups outside government, and with other governments to formulate policy that will affect the public. In this chapter we examine how political issues are born and why some issues are never submitted to the policy-making process. We then explore how political decisions and policies are made: the participants, the settings, and the styles of decision-making are all considered. Finally, we discuss the very important role played by public bureaucracies in the policy-making process. In the subsequent chapters of Part Three, the nature and outcomes of policy decisions relative to three important areas of political performance—economic development, political stability, and change—are examined.

The Origins of Political Issues

Governments exist to address problems and provide services that cannot be tackled effectively by private individuals or groups. In many cases, the services provided are so obviously "governmental" that they are scarcely, if ever, questioned: law enforcement agencies, courts of law, and armed services for national defense fall in this category. For many other areas of public need, the extent to which government is involved varies greatly from one country to another. In Britain and France, for example, it is taken for granted that the national government should provide universal health care services at very low or no direct cost to the citizen; in the United States, however, this assumption is apparently not accepted by the majority of the public or their political leaders. It is normal in most communist countries to expect the government to provide employment for every well-bodied citizen; governments in the West are normally expected to assist in promoting an economic climate conducive to job creation and may even establish public works projects or offer subsidies to employers to take on extra workers, but a promise of jobs for all would be considered highly extravagant, if not morally wrong.

As these examples illustrate, the climate of prevailing political beliefs and orientations in a society affects which public needs are addressed by governments and which are not. The beliefs and opinions of the actors involved in policy-making matter a great deal as well. Clearly, political leaders who believe that the private sector (the market economy) should take care of as many needs as possible will be less eager to offer public solutions than political leaders who believe that the state has an obligation to provide a wide range of social services for its citizens, regardless of the citizens' ability to pay. Often, however, leaders are not left free to pick and choose which issues they will address. A great deal of the political process involves the interaction of government authorities and leaders of organized interests who seek government cooperation or assistance with problems they face. The weapons these interest group leaders bring to bear on decisionmakers may include the ability to withhold cooperation with government or to refuse to perform services needed by the economy or the society, the attraction of media attention to their needs, and, in the extreme, the threat to mobilize public opposition to the government.

The effectiveness of each of these weapons depends on the nature of the organizations and issues involved and on the type of political system within which they function. We noted in Chapter 4 that, in democratic societies, interest groups that are well organized are better able to attract government attention to their concerns because their access to the media and their ability to get their followers to withhold support, cooperation, or services are likely to be greater. Doctors, who control a vital service and are usually well organized, tend to get much more favorable attention from government than do groups such as the handicapped, who are on average less affluent, less well organized, and not in command of a vital service. Although almost everyone would prefer to have less pollution, environmental protection has generally received low priority on governmental agendas, in large part because politicians believe that voters are not effectively mobilized or organized around this issue.

In communist systems, interest groups and institutions are highly penetrated by the ruling party, but they can still advance demands and create pressure on political leaders to respond to their concerns. Here, too, some interests are more effective than others. Although the military does not constitute a serious threat to civilian rule in the Soviet Union, it represents an influential institutional force whose demands on government resources are generally accorded a great deal of respect. The high priority the Soviet regime gives to its military competition with the West also allows industries that are essential to defense production to make strong claims on government resources. The same is true, for obvious reasons, of the KGB. This competition, which lacks official recognition and therefore exists within the realm of cryptopolitics, is nonetheless a central feature of policy-making in the Soviet Union.

In the boom years of the 1950s and 1960s it was commonly thought that governments in Western countries would always have the resources necessary to address recognized social problems. The more difficult economic climate of the past 20 years has forced governments to reconsider this position. While problems such as natural disasters or nuclear accidents continue to receive immediate political attention, politicians often choose to ignore or minimize other problem areas, such as urban homelessness, that are less likely to attract the attention or touch the lives of the majority of the voters. In nondemocratic systems, political leaders need not even be concerned with the effect on voters of ignoring political issues, since they can't be voted out of office. Public opinion does matter to them, however. A discontented public may be unwilling to contribute its full energies to achieving societal goals, or it may participate in strikes, demonstrations, or personal acts of protest that attract unfavorable world attention. Although the degree of governmental control of society may be great enough to prevent a mass uprising, popular discontent could prompt a coup d'état by others within the government, party, or military elites, especially if the regime is poorly institutionalized and lacking in legitimacy. For these reasons, leaders in nondemocratic countries usually attempt to control the emergence of issues by controlling the media and its coverage of events. Disasters such as airplane crashes may go totally unreported; other events or situations may be reported in such a fashion as to favor the activities and policies of the leadership. In underdeveloped countries, political awareness, literacy, and mass communications may be so poorly developed that the ability of large numbers of the public to react to events or mobilize around them is very weak; political leaders in these circumstances may exercise power with little concern for assuaging public opinion or addressing public needs.

The emergence of political issues out of the needs and goals of society and its various subdivisions thus depends on a number of factors.

The prevailing ideological and cultural values and objectives, the structure of organized interests in society, the level of development of the country, and the type of regime it has—particularly whether it is democratic or not—all shape the complex processes giving birth to political issues. Finally, we must also bear in mind that there is a certain element of unpredictability in the process. A leader may emerge with a particular personal concern for a problem or objective that cannot be explained by its appeal to other citizens; alternatively, a problem may suddenly begin to attract attention even though no leader or party is championing it. Perhaps most significant of all is the fact that many issues result from developments that occur outside a country's borders. The need perceived by France's postwar leaders to promote economic development was occasioned by the country's humiliating defeat by Nazi Germany in 1940; had the Nazis not taken over power in Germany, this need might never have been felt. Today, the state of most noncommunist economies is strongly influenced by the state of the world economy, and leaders often find that they must cope with economic problems originating in distant parts of the globe. The birth of political issues is neither totally predictable nor totally controllable, and much of the excitement of politics resides in this element of spontaneity that infuses the changing agenda of political concerns.

The Who, Where, and How of Policy-Making

Patterns of policy-making vary considerably from one country to the next, but certain regularities may be observed. First of all, in nearly all political systems, three major participants are involved: political officeholders (presidents, prime ministers, and sometimes legislators), bureaucrats, and affected interest groups. Political officeholders are usually responsible for the most important policy decisions because they possess the greatest political power and because their political futures may depend on the overall performance of government. Bureaucrats often must interpret policy as they administer it, and they can also influence overall policy decisions by manipulating the kind of information they pass on to the political decisionmakers. Bureaucrats may also participate directly in deliberations about policy. Interest groups serve as sources of information and sometimes directly influence the policy-making process, particularly in liberal democratic systems. Other frequent participants include political parties, the military, and individual citizens.

The locales of policy-making are subject to great variation. Most political systems formally vest lawmaking authority with representative legislatures but, more often than not, these institutions do little more than legitimize decisions made elsewhere. For example, the lengthy debates and formal votes of the British House of Commons usually serve only to legitimize policies decided on in cabinet meetings, party caucuses, or negotiating sessions among government officials and interest group representatives. This does not mean that the parliamentary debates are meaningless: they offer the opposition an opportunity to propose alternative policies; they help to inform the public on the pros and cons of the government's proposals; and they may lead to refinements of those proposals. Similarly, in France and Mexico, although policies are debated at length in their legislatures, real decision-making power on major policies is not to be found in those institutions. At an extreme is the Soviet Union, where the legislature meets only a few days a year to ratify unanimously the government's decisions. Even there, however, traditions of legalism and obedience to constitutional procedures entail the formal adoption of major policies by the Supreme Soviet.

Legalism and constitutionalism are norms absent in many other parts of the world. In certain periods in some countries, such as Nigeria and China, the near absence of institutionalized procedures has meant that ad hoc arrangements are or have been the predominant characteristic of policy-making. Practical and political needs determine whether a decision is made in a party meeting, a military staff session, or a conference between local notables and government administrators. The procedures, setting, and participants may be entirely different for the next policy decision. Shifting patterns of policy-making need not be considered inferior to regularized patterns; indeed, the improvisational nature of this kind of decision-making may be an asset in countries undergoing rapid change, where the locus of political power is shifting and transitory alliances are necessary to build support for policies.

The style of policy-making may take any of three general forms: elite dominant, in which a very narrow circle of leaders at the top of the political hierarchy determines policy; closed bargaining, in which policy is made through bargaining among a larger although still limited number of participants; and open bargaining, in which policy is the product of negotiation among most of those interested in the policy at hand. One might expect the open-bargaining style to characterize the policy process in liberal democracies, but this is not always the case. Issues affecting national security may be addressed by a very small closed group of decisionmakers. A restricted number of participants often sets other policies, especially those that do not become controversial or visible to the public. Only a few of the most controversial subjects give rise to open bargaining by large numbers of participants. In communist countries, decision-making tends to be concentrated at the top levels of the party hierarchy; nevertheless, as noted earlier, numerous organizations with distinct and often competing policy goals—including the military and the myriad functional ministries and local administrative and economic organizations—play significant roles in the process. Although military or single-party rule in many Third World countries often places limits on the nature and extent of interest group participation in policy-making, the existence of competing patron-client networks and of interests which are not as fully penetrated or controlled as they are in communist systems may make the policy-making process more open and more inclusive than it is in most communist systems.

Another aspect of the style of policy-making concerns whether it is "incremental" or "rational." Generally speaking, most policy-making is incremental; that is, it takes place piecemeal in response to immediate needs and demands rather than as part of a carefully thought out overall plan. Policies often emerge from the accumulation of decisions on current issues and consequently lack clear identification of overall goals, thorough consideration of all alternatives, or full evaluation of possible outcomes. This is especially true in liberal democracies and Third World countries, where a variety of interests and influences emanating from within government and outside it can affect policy outcomes, but it is also true in communist countries, despite the greater degree of centralized control over decision-making that their leaderships exercise.

While incrementalism characterizes most policy-making, attempts are often made to achieve greater efficiency through a rational style of policy-making. Rational decision-making has a powerful appeal. We would like to envision our political leaders setting public policy through a well-defined rational process that provides for full examination of all possible alternatives, an assessment of the probable costs and consequences of each, consultation with impartial experts and representatives of affected groups, and an attempt to coordinate each policy with others and with the overall goals of the government. We would also like to see them put aside such political considerations as the effect of a decision on their ability to remain in office, basing their decisions instead on the good of the country or a broad sector of the public. Ideally, leaders should be able to make decisions free of the influence of narrow interest groups, such as a medical group wishing to limit the number of new doctors in order to maintain its members' high earnings. In brief, we want policy-making to be rational.

The rational approach to policy-making is most commonly applied to areas such as economic planning and government budgeting, where decisions are primarily allocative—how much should be allocated where or to whom and when. Generally speaking, the greater the degree of control a government seeks over the country's social and economic development, the more it will rely on high degrees of planning. In communist systems, for example, comprehensive plans have been adopted in the effort to bring about major changes in existing social and economic structures and relationships and to accelerate economic development. Where governmental controls are less extensive, the rational approach may be limited to altering spending patterns in the government's administrative units in order to control budgeting overruns or to enlisting the voluntary cooperation of the private sector in achieving agreed-on goals.

A major difficulty with rational policy-making, particularly in its

Figure 7.1 SOME KEY CHARACTERISTICS OF RATIONAL AND INCREMENTAL POLICY-MAKING STYLES

Rational policy-making	Incremental policy-making
Takes a longer-range view	Takes a shorter-range view
Aims at transforming society	Aims at satisfying voters/supporters
Attempts to consider all public needs	Considers politically salient needs only
Defines a single set of goals	Allows multiple, conflicting goals
Establishes specific targets to be met	Does not specify targets
Allocates resources according to a comprehensive plan	Allocates resources as needs/demands arise
Looks for optimal solutions	Looks for improvements
Downplays the role of special interests	Recognizes legitimate place for special-interest concerns

more comprehensive forms, is that it assumes an underlying simplicity: that a country has a single set of goals, that all needs have been considered in arriving at those goals, that the actions chosen can realize the goals, and that nothing unforeseen will emerge to disrupt the process. But the governing of complex societies and economies is seldom so straightforward, and leaders are often unable to anticipate events. For example, no Western leaders foresaw in September 1973 that within a month a Middle East war would provoke an Arab oil boycott leading to severe energy shortages and bringing an end to the long postwar economic boom in the West. Apart from unforeseen events, what most often confounds attempts to introduce greater rationality is precisely that these schemes are rational: they assume the rational use of resources to reach objectives, when in actuality ideological and political criteria often outweigh both economic rationality and the overall goals sought by leaders. Thus, the ideologically based belief in the superiority of collective farms prevents the leaders of the Soviet Union from advocating their abolition, despite decades of evidence that they are not as productive as private landholdings. Political criteria that interfere with rational decision-making involve the very important need to satisfy political supporters, including voters in democratic systems, clients in systems with extensive patron-client networking, and organized interests in systems of all kinds; even the most altruistic leaders must concern themselves with retaining their hold on public office and power.

In practice, no political system even approximates the ideal of rational policy-making. Often precedent or tradition determines a policy without anyone's subjecting that policy to critical examination; indeed, in many instances it may be neither practical nor politically wise to disturb traditional ways of doing things even in the name of greater rationality. Moreover, other obstacles can interfere even when the desire to achieve rationality is present. Decisionmakers rarely have the time or resources to consider all possible policy alternatives and often lack information on the costs and consequences of those that are considered. Impartial experts are not always available, and when they are, they frequently give conflicting advice. In most political systems, the pressures exerted by interest groups tend to reflect more the special needs of their clienteles than the public interest as a whole, and civil servants may be more intent on protecting their own bureaucratic empires than on achieving the government's policy objectives. Related policy decisions may have to be made separately, as events demand, rather than in coordination with one another or with overall objectives. Objectives may conflict with one another, and it may be impossible either to realize or to abandon them without offending important political actors or influential interest groups. The necessity of responding to immediate problems or dealing with powerful cross-pressures often leads to a "satisficing" style of policy-making, in which outcomes are satisfactory to those involved rather than optimal in themselves. In Britain this kind of policy-making is often referred to as "muddling through," an apt description of policy-making in most parts of the world.

Bureaucracies: The Challenge of Political Control

No consideration of the processes of policy-making would be complete without examining the central role played by state or public bureaucracies. A public bureaucracy is a complex system, usually hierarchical in structure, with specialized tasks, a body of rules, and a system of records and precedents. It is usually subdivided by function; thus departments or ministries of agriculture, defense, finance, health, and communications are typical government departments. At the apex of each department are the department's ministers and assistants, usually all political appointees, and frequently one or more senior civil servants. Typically, the political leaders who fill the top positions have the responsibility of ensuring the organization's conformity to the decisions of the government. Subordinate to the top level of leaders and officials are the subagencies and staffs that perform specific portions of the department's mission.

Bureaucrats or civil servants may be selected in several ways: through the "spoils" or patronage system, in which they are chosen on the basis of service to political leaders or the party; through the merit system, in which they are selected on the basis of administrative or technical abilities; or through some combination of the two. The spoils system usually gives way to the merit system as a state modernizes; one partial exception, however, is the United States, where it can still be found at state and local levels of government.

Ideally, bureaucrats simply execute policy decisions made by the political leadership; whatever their own partisan or ideological convictions, they obediently follow the directions of political leaders. In practice, bureaucracies virtually never limit themselves to this role. In modern governments with extensive social and economic responsibilities, bureaucracies acquire a political influence far greater than organizational charts suggest. Rather than existing to serve the leadership, they themselves make policy on a daily basis. To a degree, this is desirable and inevitable, since the execution of laws requires bureaucrats to apply abstract statutes to real-life situations. However, bureaucracies often act like interest groups, pressing government for policies they want. Bureaucracies can also ignore decisions made by the political leadership: lethargy and outright resistance can delay or sabotage virtually any program.

Studies of bureaucracies tend to cast them as heroes or villains. Those who see bureaucracies as villains argue that they cannot be controlled by their political masters and pose a threat to democratic values because expertise and bureaucratic self-interest tend to replace the will of the people. Among the chief obstacles to political control of the bureaucracy is the "numbers game": in Britain, for example, some 100 politicians are charged with controlling more than a half-million civil servants. Compounding ministerial ineffectiveness is the frequent turnover of ministers; many political leaders have only a short time in which to become familiar with and gain ascendancy over the bureaucracy. An associated problem is the lack of technically qualified politicians available for ministerial roles. Democratic governments are elected to represent the will of the electorate, and they are responsible for the conduct of government affairs during their tenure in office. If they fail to control the actions of the bureaucrats, the notion of democratic responsibility is rendered null and void. But the problem of controlling the bureaucracy is not unique to democracies. Authoritarian and dictatorial regimes must also guard against bureaucratic lethargy and sabotage of policies sought by the political leadership.

Those who see bureaucracies as heroes emphasize the rational and efficient administration achieved by the technicians who efficiently implement policy. In contrast to the supposedly inexperienced and untrained political hack, the bureaucrat has special training and/or long experience in public administration. Furthermore, the bureaucracy is seen as imparting stability and continuity to government. During periods of political turmoil, the uninterrupted activities of the bureaucracy may cushion the system from chaos and prevent total collapse. Finally, bureaucracies may be sources of innovation and political initiative, which is particularly valuable in developing countries where interest groups are poorly established and expert advice is not otherwise available to political leaders.

Despite its imperfect realization, the norm of political dominance over the bureaucracy is widespread. Nearly every political system has procedures and mechanisms to promote the loyalty of the civil service to the political leadership. Most political leaders want to see their decisions implemented in the way they were intended and consequently devote considerable time to surveillance of their bureaucracy's performance.

BRITAIN AND FRANCE: PUBLIC POLICY-MAKING IN LIBERAL DEMOCRACIES

Policy-making in liberal democracies is conditioned by the pluralistic context within which it operates. In liberal democracies there is a clear delineation between public and private spheres of activity, and it is generally only in the public sphere that the government exercises direct control. A great deal of what occurs in society—including decisions by large organizations and corporations that have widespread social repercussions—lies outside its reach. To the extent that government does involve itself in social and economic concerns, there is likely to be a plethora of organized interests which attempt to influence the nature and direction of this involvement.

Britain and France illustrate well the pluralistic quality of democratic policy-making. Governments are chosen by means of national elections in which competing parties and leaders present alternative proposals for popular approval. They possess rich infrastructures of freely organized interests which attempt to influence government policy-making. To a large extent, the existence and activities of these groups reflect the relatively high degree of involvement of the governments in the social and economic life of their respective countries. Governments in Britain and France not only have assumed responsibility for the overall functioning of their economies but also have taken on the task of ensuring a wide variety of social services, including extensive public housing and state-financed medical and hospital care. The scope of state activities finds another reflection in the large size of their state bureaucracies, whose experience and expertise in administering so sweeping a range of state activities make them necessary partners in the development of new policy initiatives. Thus, policy-making generally involves a diversity of actors and inputs—party, interest group, and bureaucratic—each of which is capable of having a major effect on policy outcomes.

Britain: The Politics of "Muddling Through"

Britain presents a classic example of the incrementalist approach to policy-making. Interestingly, the growth in the size and responsibilities of British government was due in large measure to a deliberate effort at rational planning. As a result of wartime planning designed to prevent a recurrence of the hardships of the 1930s, commitments were made that government in the future would provide a comprehensive set of social welfare programs and manage the economy so as to ensure full employment. After the war, however, the idea of continuing economic planning was resisted by both unions and business, while socially, the basic framework of the "welfare state" was established very quickly and required little additional planning. Moreover, both Labour and Conservative parties accepted these policy innovations and competed largely on the basis of which one could manage them better; as a result, a "politics of outbidding" emerged as each promised a little more in the way of social expenditures in order to garner extra votes. Incrementalism thus became the major characteristic of postwar British policy-making, and economic growth—essential to fulfilling the commitments of full employment and an expanding welfare state—became its most central concern.

Apart from the broad consensus on social and economic policy, the victory of incrementalism reflected the multiple influences on policy-making that are typical of liberal democracies. The ability of major groups such as doctors or unionized workers to resist or disrupt policies that they oppose can be considerable, and British governments have generally preferred to legislate policies that have first been cleared with the major affected interests. The perceived necessity of involving organized interests in the execution of the growing responsibilities of government became institutionalized into a tripartite consultative process involving, in many instances, representatives of industry, labor, and government. Often, the desire of governments to appease these interests led to the abandoning of carefully developed plans for significant change or their weakening to make them more acceptable to all concerned.

A good example of the pressures toward incrementalism emanating from interest groups can be found in the field of industrial relations. In 1969 the Labour party proposed to improve Britain's lagging economic performance by instituting penalties for unions which went on strike in violation of their contracts. However, strong union opposition to making labor contracts legally binding obliged the party, which depends on union support, to abandon the proposal. When the Conservatives passed an Industrial Relations Act in 1971, which included a very similar provision, not only did the Labour party oppose it, but most of the unions refused to register under the act or to recognize the National Industrial Relations Court which it created. When Labour was returned to power in 1974, one of its first steps was to repeal the Industrial Relations Act. The goal of the act had been to improve industrial relations, but its effect was the very opposite: the numbers of working days lost in strikes reached levels not seen since the General Strike of 1926.[1] Chastened by this experience, the Conservative governments of the 1980s have adopted a much more cautious and incremental approach to reforming industrial relations.

Incrementalism is also fostered by the several stages of review and refinement involved in the policy-making process. Major policy decisions in the British system of government are the responsibility of the cabinet,

[1] D. Kavanaugh, *British Politics: Continuities and Change* (Oxford: Oxford University Press, 1985), p. 313.

headed by the prime minister. Although cabinet positions are filled by members of the same party, cabinet ministers may not always agree with one another on policy questions. One reason for this is that each cabinet minister has the duty to advance the interests and perspectives of his or her department, and this can often lead to conflict with other ministers. Ministers of defense typically fight for more money for the armed services, for example; ministers in charge of education usually want to see more funds directed to schools and universities. Governments seldom have enough resources to finance every minister's proposals, and often a great deal of give and take must occur before a policy initiative can gain full cabinet approval.

There are three major ways in which this interministerial competition is regulated. First of all, any policy proposals coming from a department must have Treasury approval before they can be presented before cabinet. The Treasury's role is to scrutinize policy proposals with the government's policy priorities and the overall state of its finances in mind, and it has to be convinced both of the proposal's relative merits in comparison with proposals from other departments and of its affordability. In fact, the Treasury reviews the programs and budgets of every department each year and may demand cuts in departmental spending where it judges them necessary or justifiable.

Interdepartmental consultation represents a second method of controlling rivalry within the government. This consultation occurs through an elaborate committee structure which includes cabinet committees composed of ministers of different departments, as well as interdepartmental committees of civil servants and mixed committees of ministers and civil servants. Cabinet committees are particularly important in coordinating policy and working out disagreements within major areas of government activity such as the economy, defense, and foreign affairs. Because of the high work load of the cabinet, a great many decisions that in theory are taken in the cabinet are actually taken in these committees. A cabinet minister who has lost a decision in committee may not take the issue to the full cabinet without the approval of the committee chairman; for the most important committees, the committee chairman is usually also the prime minister.

The prime minister constitutes the third and, in some ways, the most important coordinating force in the cabinet. In principle, the prime minister is no more than a first among equals in the cabinet; in reality, the prime minister's role is much greater. Some political scientists have argued that the prime minister's power over cabinet is so great that the system of cabinet government has been replaced by "prime ministerial government." Although this claim is somewhat exaggerated, the power of the prime minister, especially a popular and determined one, should not be underestimated. The prime minister determines the composition of the cabinet, sets the agenda, and chairs its weekly meetings. This leadership role allows the prime minister to guide discussions and give form to the consensus on any issue. If the cabinet is seriously divided on an issue, the prime minister may not be able to force through the decision that she or he prefers. Nevertheless, the overall conduct of the government is the responsibility of the prime minister and, in the conflict between different ministers and departments, it is largely the prime minister's task to set the priorities for governmental action.

The Treasury's responsibility for vetting new policy proposals, the importance of ministerial and interdepartmental committees in coordinating policy, and the prime minister's leadership role in guiding the overall course of government policy-making represent major checks in the policy-making process. Although their purpose is to improve coordination and planning—and thus to render policy-making more rational—the net effect of these consultative and review processes is often to force policy proposals to conform to political considerations such as the overall balance of political power among ministers and ministries within the government and the probable effects that the policies would have on public opinion. Frequently, it seems that the greater the number of people within government who examine a new proposal, the greater the number of objections that arise against it and the more it must be "watered down" if it is to survive at all.

There are three other potential sources of influence in the policy-making process in most political systems: the political parties, the legislature, and the state bureaucracy. Generally speaking, parties in liberal democracies range between two extremes: parties in which the leadership has a free hand to determine policy and parties where a deliberate effort has been made to keep the leadership accountable to the party rank and file for major policy decisions. In Britain, the Conservative party clearly falls in the first category: policy is left to the party leader and her or his senior colleagues in the parliamentary party. In contrast, the Labour party is structured to give ultimate policy-making power to the Annual Party Conference and to the National Executive Committee (NEC) which is elected by it. The Parliamentary Labour Party (PLP) and the NEC have the prerogative of deciding which of the conference's policy resolutions are put into the party's election manifesto or platform, and past Labour governments have been allowed considerable latitude to ignore or go against official party policies. Nevertheless, both the Annual Party Conference and the NEC are dominated by the big trade unions and the PLP has to be careful not to offend them—as it found out in the case of industrial relations.

The British House of Commons has very little real authority to modify policy proposals, since party discipline generally ensures that the ruling party's policies are supported by its parliamentary majority. However, effective criticism by opposition parties, particularly the kind that exposes unforeseen deficiencies or loopholes in proposed legislation, can prompt the government to amend its own legislation. Similarly, widespread discontent within the rank and file of the majority party can lead the party leadership to backtrack. Government policy proposals are usually discussed with party backbenchers before they are introduced into Parliament in order to minimize the possibility of exposing divisions within the party to the public eye.

Finally, there is the role of the civil service. The civil service in Britain is recruited on the basis of merit, right up to the highest levels. Unlike the situation in the United States, where incoming presidents attempt to ensure political control of the bureaucracy by appointing most of its top leaders themselves, it is assumed in Britain that senior civil servants can serve any government impartially and fairly. Despite occasional complaints by former Labour ministers, the system of civil service neutrality has generally held up well and continues to be supported by all parties.

Nevertheless, the civil service's influence on policy-making can be very great. Civil servants generally have much greater expertise in the management of government business than do politicians, who come and go with the changing fortunes of electoral politics. In fact, although elections occur every four years or so, ministers may expect to head their departments for only about two years before being moved elsewhere. In any case, their rise to political power is usually due more to their political skills, as demonstrated in election campaigns and House of Commons debates, than to their management skills. In office, much of their time must be devoted to party, parliamentary, and constituency duties, and they are often hard-pressed to master the workings of their department on a part-time basis. As noted earlier, the task of political control is daunting: a relatively small number of politicians must manage the activities of several hundred thousand civil servants. It is not surprising, in such circumstances, if ministers find themselves merely reacting to proposals developed and presented by their senior civil servants rather than taking the initiative in policy-making themselves.

This unbalanced state of affairs has led many British political scientists to wonder whether the cabinet really controls the civil service. Although opportunities exist for senior civil servants to "guide" their ministers, obstruct the ministers' wishes, or simply wait until the ministers are replaced, there are considerations which limit these strategies. In the first place, parties usually compete in elections on the basis of policy alternatives which they publicly commit themselves to adopt in office. Not all election promises are acted on, but the major ones—those which have the attention of the prime minister and other senior ministers—cannot easily be resisted or subverted by manipulating the inexperience or ineffectiveness of a single minister. Second, the civil service exists in its present form precisely because it is perceived by all parties as essentially neutral. Were it to attempt serious obstruction of cabinet decisions, steps would undoubtedly be taken to ensure greater political control. In fact, so great has been the civil service's desire to demonstrate neutrality that civil servants often take it on themselves to translate election commitments by the major parties into draft legislation even before the outcome of the election is known.

The myriad influences on policy-making in Britain—from both inside and outside the ranks of the governing party—suggest the extraordinary complexities of the overall process. It is not surprising that political leaders find themselves largely locked into the existing structure of policy or that the net effect of their efforts while in office usually amounts to incremental or moderate change at most. It is at times when the normal course of life has been severely disrupted—such as during and immediately after World War II—that the most sweeping changes have been instituted. At other times, fundamental reform is difficult even for a system of government such as Britain's that is not hindered by a formal system of checks and balances.

France: Centralized Policy-Making

The influences and obstacles affecting the policy-making process that come from organized interests, from intraparty and interparty rivalries, and from the bureaucracy are common to all liberal democracies and constitute a great deal of the ebb and flow of their day-to-day politics. France is no exception to this generalization. However, in France three factors have helped to prevent the policy-making process from becoming derailed by too many cross-pressures. The most innovative of these factors is undoubtedly the creation of a Planning Commission to handle longer-term social and economic development. The high degree of concentration of decision-making power in the executive in the Fifth Republic also limits inputs from outside interests. Finally, the existence of ministerial cabinets of appointed officials to help ministers run their departments provides a means by which political control over the state administration can be enhanced.

France has had a long tradition of state involvement in industrial development, and the necessity of rebuilding after the devastation of World War II, together with the desire to modernize economically to prevent future military defeats, encouraged French leaders to institute a system of national five-year plans for social and economic development. In the early postwar years, the principal value of the planning process was that it was able to bypass the weak and divided parliamentary governments of the day. Instead of working with politicians, the civil servants of the Planning Commission worked directly with representatives of industry and labor in the definition and realization of national goals. These goals included not only industrial reconstruction but also such matters as expanding the university system and controlling inflation. Although the national plans were voluntary, the government was able to use a variety of means (discussed more fully in Chapter 8) to enlist the cooperation of industry in achieving their objectives.

During the Fourth Republic, each plan was submitted to the National Assembly for approval, but the elected politicians, aware of their own internal divisions, usually found it best to avoid interfering too much. The advent of the Fifth Republic changed this situation substantially, however. With the executive headed by a powerful president supported by a stable parliamentary majority, there was no longer any compelling reason to preserve the plans' independence. Presidents and prime ministers, responsible to the electorate for the overall state of the economy, have felt it desirable to involve themselves more in the process of social and economic policy-making, and the importance of the plans has diminished accordingly.

According to the constitution of the Fifth Republic, executive power is divided between the president of the republic and the prime minister. Until 1986, however, each president has had a majority in the National Assembly willing to follow his lead. This has permitted presidents to appoint (and dismiss) prime ministers and other ministers at will and to exercise general surveillance over government policy, while allowing the Council of Ministers to manage the day-to-day operations of government. Between 1986 and 1988, a new situation emerged with the division of executive power between the Socialist president, François Mitterrand, and the Gaullist prime minister, Jacques Chirac. Although both still attended the weekly meetings of the Council, for most matters the National Assembly's right-wing majority allowed Chirac to be the dominant force in policy-making. Thus, even in the absence of a presidential majority, the tradition of strong executive leadership prevailed.

Part of the task of strengthening the executive in the Fifth Republic's constitution involved weakening the Parliament's authority. The ability of the Parliament to stop the government's policy proposals was limited through a number of innovations, including the blocked vote, the requirement of an absolute majority to sustain a vote of nonconfidence, and the ending of the right to alter the amount of public expenditures (see Chapter 2). Equally important has been the development of disciplined majorities within the Parliament who have been willing to support the government's actions almost without question. These characteristics of Fifth Republic Parliaments remove much of the important role the Parliament used to play in policy-making and have tended to discourage lobbying of deputies by organized interests; interest groups must now use other channels if they are to have an impact on policy in the highly centralized Fifth Republic.

One means by which interest groups can attempt to get their voices heard is through the maze of consultative organs—some 500 councils, 1200 committees, and 3000 commissions—that bring together interest group representatives and state bureaucrats.[2] There is, in addition, the Economic and Social Council, composed of representatives appointed by

[2]Henry Ehrmann, *Politics in France,* 4th ed. (Boston: Little, Brown, 1983), p. 204.

major interest groups and the government, which considers proposed legislation in the social and economic spheres and gives both the government and the Parliament its considered advice. Nevertheless, many interest groups have found that their ability to communicate their needs and influence policy remains very limited. One reason for this is the tradition in France of seeing interest groups as representatives of particular (and therefore selfish) wills of subsections of society and the state as embodying the higher general will; another is the centralization of authority around the president and, between 1986 and 1988, the prime minister—individuals who are not easily accessible to interest groups. One consequence has been the frequent resort to protests and demonstrations to attract the government's attention and action. It often seems as if the best way to get results in the absence of meaningful consultation with the government is to take to the streets. The 1986 student demonstrations against proposed university reforms was one of the more notable of these events, and it achieved its desired result: an embarrassed government withdrew the legislation.

The dominance of the presidency in the Fifth Republic has also had a dampening effect on the ability of political parties to influence policy. As in Britain, the control of policy by party memberships is less highly developed among the parties of the Right than it is in the principal party of the Left, the Socialists. The RPR originated as a movement dedicated to supporting the leadership of Charles de Gaulle rather than as a distinct ideological force in itself. Its coalition partner, the UDR, consists of a number of small, elite-led centrist parties brought into alliance by Giscard d'Estaing in 1978 to support his own presidency. Long years in office have habituated both groups to the principle of leadership control. The Socialist party, in comparison, is organized into recognized factions which compete actively with one another to influence policies decided on at party conferences; ideology is taken very seriously within the party. Nevertheless, during the period of Socialist majority government (1981–1986), the PS found itself obliged to follow President Mitterrand's increasingly conservative shifts in policy. Although there was noticeable discontent among more left-leaning elements within the party, the custom that the president determines policy without party constraints prevailed.

Unlike the Parliament, the political parties, and the organs for interest group consultation, the state bureaucracy is well placed to exercise a continual and powerful influence on policy-making. There is a tradition in France that the state—which essentially means the bureaucracy—is the guardian of the national interest. This sentiment was reinforced during the long periods when France was victim to frequently changing cabinets and regimes. During these periods of political instability, it was natural for state officials to see themselves as the true rulers and protectors of the country.

Civil servants are well trained to exercise this role. In contrast to Britain or the United States, where higher administrators are recruited from universities or business and trained on the job, the higher echelons of the French bureaucracy are staffed by individuals who have been trained in specially designed state institutions. These institutions, known as *grandes écoles* ("great schools"), are more prestigious and more difficult to get into than any of France's universities. They tend to breed a narrow, self-conscious elite that is convinced of its own unique abilities to manage the affairs of the state. This sense of superiority is often reinforced by privileged social backgrounds, for a large proportion of this elite are recruited from Parisian upper-class and upper-middle-class families, many with traditions of senior state service.

Self-confidence as well as the exceptionally rigorous and demanding training of the state elite make it a powerful independent influence on policy-making. This influence takes place most noticeably through the Council of State. The Council of State is the highest administrative tribunal of France, and much of its duties involves adjudicating cases where the state is alleged to have violated the rights of citizens. But the Council also has the right to examine all government bills and decrees before they come into effect. Although its advice is not binding, governments almost always submit to its opinions.

Bureaucratic influence on policy-making also occurs through the more subtle molding or resisting of the actions and opinions of ministers by their more experienced (and more permanent) civil servants. This tendency is well recognized in France, however, and a unique institution has been developed to cope with it. France is similar to Britain (and dissimilar from the United States) in that an incoming government does not have the right to replace senior bureaucrats with its own appointees. What ministers can do to facilitate control of their departments is to appoint their own ministerial cabinets—groups of 10 to 30 people who act as the minister's eyes and ears in the department and who counter the advice and experience of senior bureaucrats with their own. Many appointees are party officials or other political figures who can advise on the political and partisan implications of given decisions (something bureaucrats may not want to or be able to do), but these cabinets also include bureaucrats seconded from other departments who are capable of exercising oversight on the technical and administrative aspects of making and administering policy. By setting one group of senior bureaucrats against another, ministers may be able to understand and control policy in their departments more effectively than would otherwise be the case.

Although the French political system has developed three significant means—national planning, centralization of power around the executive, and ministerial cabinets—to help ensure that policy-making does not escape political control or become too fragmented or piecemeal, the results are not always what one would expect. Planning worked well in the early years because of its detachment from the normal political processes, but rivalry with the Ministry of Finance, which had formerly handled economic affairs, and concern by presidents to exercise more direct control over economic policy have undermined its influence. The centralization of power around the executive has allowed coordination of policy in priority areas, but it has also left many groups and institutions—including Parliament and interest groups—cut off from the policy-making process and has led to numerous confrontations and protests. The use of ministerial cabinets certainly assists ministers with the difficult task of controlling the policy-making and implementation of their departments, but it does not prevent administrative sabotage or inertia. As a Gaullist deputy advocating a reform was once told by his prime minister (Pompidou):

> When (the Ministry of) Finance is against a reform, it has little chance of happening. When Finance and the ministry involved are both against it, it has absolutely none. Except if the matter is of such political importance that the Prime Minister or the President of the republic imposes a decision. Unfortunately, this isn't the case with this matter. Alas, I can do nothing.[3]

France does not differ in this regard from other societies; the dynamics of policy-making in France represent simply another variant of the multifaceted and conflict-prone business of making public policy in democratic societies.

THE SOVIET UNION AND CHINA: POLICY-MAKING IN COMMUNIST STATES

One might expect that policy-making by communist governments would approximate the rational model. Communists, after all, have well-defined goals derived from their ideology; they are self-conscious about making policy decisions that will pursue these goals; they are committed to some degree of centralized planning and decision-making; and they have the political ability to resist the shifting winds of public opinion. In fact, however, policy in communist states is never quite as rationally made as it seems on the surface, and although the state persists in drawing up elaborate long-term plans, policy-making often becomes reactive and incremental, suggesting that "muddling through" is not unique to Western democracies.

Communist states differ from other political systems in the extensive scope of their administrative tasks. In Western countries the operations of government are limited, even in countries with a lengthy tradition of welfare statism, because most industrial and commercial enterprises are privately owned and state planning and regulation take second place to private management. In communist states the government owns and controls most enterprises, the party ultimately controls all social organizations, and state-controlled bureaucracies provide all

[3]A. Peyrefitte, *Le Mal Francais* (Paris: Plon, 1976), p. 238.

social services. The scope of government activity thus reaches into all areas of society and includes many tasks that Western systems leave to nongovernmental bodies.

The Soviet Union: Conservatism and Reformism

Even before the Bolshevik Revolution, both leaders and citizens of the Russian Empire had grown to understand that the realm of public policy was wide, encompassing areas of economic development and planning, cultural affairs, and other matters that Western governments concerned themselves with marginally or not at all. After 1917 the Soviet state expanded its responsibilities further. Marxist-Leninist ideology, its guiding purpose being the creation of an ideal new society, has given impetus to a scope of public policy touching on every significant aspect of the community's life. The communist leadership assumes that all, or nearly all, human activity falls within the purview of public policy. The community appears to accept this assumption, by and large, though dissidents and fringe elements would dispute it. This is not to say that citizens welcome the state's interference in private affairs without grumbling, but the right of public officials to make policy across the vast field of issues addressed by the party and state does not appear to be widely questioned.

The underlying goal of Soviet policy is, and has always been, the radical transformation of society. This is taken to be a long-term, ongoing purpose which will continue to motivate the formation of specific policies until the ultimate goal of a communist society has been attained. In the earlier decades of Soviet rule, the pursuit of this radical goal entailed equally radical policy measures, exemplified by the programs of War Communism and the "Third Revolution" of Stalin. Although policies derived from a program that might be termed rational-visionary, they were implemented in a fashion characterized more by fanaticism than by rationality. Yet from these backgrounds emerged a pattern of policy creation, institutionalized in the five-year (economic) plans, that has continued to this day to provide a rational framework for the entire scope of public policy.

Since the Stalin era, however, the style of policy-making has become more complex. Its basis remains the formulation of five-year plans (FYPs) elaborated in painstaking detail, but the day-to-day realities of governing require the Soviet polity to respond incrementally to the needs of the moment, to make adjustments when one or another aspect of the plan goes awry, or even to reconsider major portions of the current FYP. Under Gorbachev's leadership, the system appears to be moving toward a partial decentralization of decision-making in some aspects of economic policy, but, on the whole, public policy remains highly centralized.

If Soviet policy-making after Stalin changed from rational-visionary to a blend of rational and incremental styles, it has also lost most of its radical quality. Policymakers still profess to be pursuing the ideal of a communist society, characterized by the disappearance of the coercive state and the freely willed sharing of the community's wealth, but their behavior indicates that the ideal is a long way off. In the meantime, existing "contradictions" in society must be resolved by policies that either preserve the status quo (conservative policies) or attempt to improve on the way things are currently being done (reforms). The successive post-Stalin regimes have exhibited differing mixtures of conservatism and reformism. None has been willing to alter radically the basic features of the system—one-party rule, state ownership of industry, and so on—but all have attempted to modify aspects of the system in major or minor ways.

Under Khrushchev's leadership, the party undertook a number of far-reaching initiatives only to see many of them aborted and criticized as "harebrained schemes" during the more conservative Brezhnev years. The abandoned approaches included not only such poorly conceived ventures as the Virgin Lands program, an attempt to develop agriculture in regions of Siberia ill suited to cultivation, but also more promising efforts such as Khrushchev's modest relaxation of controls over cultural and artistic life.

During the Brezhnev years (1964–1982), the Politburo worked mostly by consensus, seeking to maintain a balance amid the cryptopolitics of interest groups competing for the resources of the state. The period was not devoid of reformist policies, specifically in the area of economic organization and management. However, the Brezhnev approach to reform was cautious and ambivalent, favoring piecemeal changes which disturbed the status quo as little as possible. As a result, the "reforms"—outside observers fell into the habit of referring to them in quotation marks because of their compromise nature—usually failed to improve significantly on past policies, and, unable to win over the opponents of more substantial reforms, the leadership often retreated to previous ways of doing business. Thus, muddling through became the party's characteristic modus operandi.[4]

The Brezhnev years left a mixed legacy. On the one hand, the political system stabilized and policy lines became more predictable than they had been under Khrushchev's leadership. The economy prospered modestly, and the government pursued a military buildup that lifted the USSR to genuine parity with the United States. Dissent was controlled, by repression when other means failed, but this was a positive achievement from the leadership's point of view—and a factor in the government's stability that stood in marked contrast to the internal strife of several other communist-ruled countries, most notably China and Po-

---

[4]Seweryn Bialer, *Stalin's Successors: Leadership, Stability, and Change in the Soviet Union* (Cambridge, UK: Cambridge University Press, 1980), pp. 298–305.

land.[5] On the other hand, the Brezhnev Politburo slipped into a predominantly reactive and incremental style of policy-making that failed to respond adequately to long-term problems of growth and development. The leaders' "satisficing" approach to decision-making succeeded in preventing the rise of any intraparty opposition, but at the cost of imaginative programs. By the early 1980s the Politburo had grown old, the economy showed signs of stagnation, and the state and party bureaucracies had settled into patterns of inertia.

The accession of Gorbachev immediately brought a new look to the political style, though it took some time for policies to begin changing. Gorbachev made it clear that he wanted the government to enact reforms, particularly in the structure and management of the economy. Early on, he moved to build support for his policy initiatives by promoting the advancement of like-minded party officers into top-level positions. Under Gorbachev's leadership the party fostered an atmosphere of *glasnost'*—literally, "speaking out," or, as it has been more often translated by the English-language media, "openness." The Soviet media were encouraged to discuss problems in economic management, consumer goods supplies, and the responsiveness (or unresponsiveness) of government and bureaucracy. *Glasnost'* spread to the intellectual community, where literature and the arts flowered modestly in the mid-1980s, and even, cautiously, to the ranks of dissidents as Andrei Sakharov and other critics of the government were allowed into the community once again. The policy of *glasnost'* clearly served Gorbachev's other policy aims, for the more open public discussion of managerial and bureaucratic problems made it difficult for those who opposed reform to stand their ground and tilted the balance toward the power of the reformers.

The experience of the early Gorbachev years sheds some light on the nature of the Soviet policy process. In the first place, it confirmed that policy-making has remained the province of the party's top ranks, first and foremost the Politburo. At the same time, it demonstrated that policy is not determined by one person only, no matter how prominent the current leader may appear to be; Mikhail Gorbachev established himself publicly as a dynamic spokesman for reform, but behind the scenes he found it necessary to exercise all his powers of persuasion and manipulate the party personnel procedures to bring his supporters into positions from which they could bolster his program of economic *perestroika*—even though there remained many in the power elite who either opposed the reforms or wished to see their implementation restricted.

Policy-making neither begins nor ends with Politburo decisions. The Politburo relies on the input of party and state commissions, agencies, and bureaus and often shares its ultimate decision-making responsibilities with the CPSU Secretariat and the Presidium of the Council of

[5]Seweryn Bialer, "Soviet Policies in the 1980s," in E. P. Hoffmann and R. F. Laird, *The Soviet Polity in the Modern Era* (New York: Aldine, 1984), pp. 841–842.

Ministers. In all cases, major policy initiatives must be approved by the CPSU Central Committee and ratified by the Supreme Soviet. For new departures, such as the Gorbachev economic reforms, the support of regional party organizations is crucial, and often the general secretary himself will travel around the republics to gain the necessary approval. It is never entirely clear what takes place when central party leaders thus solicit support in the provinces, but one can assume that bargaining about budget allocations and regional leaders' prerogatives plays a significant role.[6]

In the process of policy-making, many discussions take place, and over the years an increasing effort has been made to bring the public into them. Outside the official ranks, however, the word "discussion" does not accurately describe the process; rather, party leaders serve to inform groups of citizens about the nature of policy and explain the meaning and operation of new programs. In this way, the party seeks to keep the public informed of its policies as they develop.

Although the general lines of policy are decided by the highest CPSU organs, not all significant issues are resolved at that level. As in other governments, policy questions must be researched, facts about the current situation must be studied and projections into the future drawn up, and an almost infinite range of circumstances and problems and tasks and personnel needs must be defined in terms of finite alternatives. All ministries and their divisions, as well as the specialized bureaus of the party, draw up programs within their areas of responsibility—steel production, banking, cinematography, magazine publishing, and so on. As this myriad of factors is explored and studied by the bureaucracy, decisions are constantly being made about what is important, which facts are pertinent, which problems need to be solved, and what range of alternatives should be considered.

The Politburo and other decision-making bodies must sort out many organizational claims to the country's resources, and in that sorting-out process the complicated and largely secret game of cryptopolitics is played out. The military services claim their share of resources; the republics each claim theirs; agriculture, heavy industry, construction, consumer industries, culture, science, and education—all these interests are represented in the policy-making process. In meetings of the highest party and state councils, the competing claims must be reconciled within the limited capabilities of Soviet society.[7]

Generally speaking, the more delicate the issue, the fewer the persons involved in deciding it. As in Western countries, the most sensitive decisions having to do with foreign policy and especially national security are taken by a handful of top officials in secret. Unlike the situation

---

[6]It is known, for example, that Brezhnev had secured a fair amount of independence for *oblast* (province) party chiefs in return for their loyal support.

[7]Darrell P. Hammer, *The USSR: The Politics of Oligarchy,* 2nd ed. (Boulder, Colo.: Westview, 1986), pp. 225–238.

in the West, however, the major decisions about domestic policy lines are also taken behind closed doors, even though there may have been considerable public discussion beforehand. For issues like the framing of the yearly economic plan or the FYP, in contrast, the number of individuals involved will be very high as layer upon layer of the state planning bureaucracy makes its input.[8]

Alfred G. Meyer, a longtime American observer of the Soviet Union, once wrote that the political system appeared to be moving toward an ideal of "participatory bureaucracy."[9] And indeed, the role of the vast Soviet bureaucracy looms so significantly over policy that it must be taken into account by every general secretary. Politburo decisions are nearly always couched in overall terms and then handed down to bureaucracy departments, where they must be translated into practical details. For a policy to be effectively implemented, it must have at least the grudging acceptance of all those responsible for carrying it out. Bureaucratic recalcitrance, caused by a fear that one's responsibilities may be taken away (or the converse, that one might suddenly shoulder responsibilities one does not want), can obstruct the application of a policy and even bring about its failure. And in the course of implementing a policy, the bureaucracy defines its final shape.

Just as Soviet leaders are aware of the potential power residing in the armed forces, so too they are wary of the bureaucracy, and they have built into the system numerous checks. In the first place, positions in the bureaucracy are staffed through the mechanism of the *nomenklatura,* which is controlled by the party Secretariat. Most key officials of the bureaucracy are party members, and they are under constant pressure to carry out the party's program faithfully. All offices of the bureaucracy are watched over by members of the People's Control Commission and the KGB. In addition to these control factors, the bureaucracy is motivated, to an extent, by the knowledge that those who serve the party's goals in an exemplary manner are candidates for promotion. All in all, the control factors are probably more effective than the reward system in checking tendencies to bureaucratic obstructionism, but both serve to reinforce the party's centralized command.

To illustrate the Soviet policy-making process, let's look more closely at the case of the economic reforms which were formally adopted in 1987. (The nature of these reforms and their effect on economic structures are discussed in Chapter 8.) It had long been officially acknowledged that economic performance was unsatisfactory, and many leaders concluded that some degree of reform would be desirable. Action was held up, however, by the conservatism of an aging Politburo and, espe-

[8]Ned Temko, "Soviet Insiders: How Power Flows in Moscow," part 2, in *The Christian Science Monitor,* February 23, 1982.

[9]Alfred G. Meyer, "The Soviet Political System," in Hoffmann and Laird, op. cit., p. 767. Meyer's tongue-in-cheek term recalled the phrase "participatory democracy" popular among American left-wing movements.

cially, by the rapid turnover of the Politburo's leadership between 1982 and 1985. With the accession of Mikhail Gorbachev to the general secretaryship, the first element of a major policy shift was put in place.

Studies of the economy and its results in recent years were undertaken; in some cases, studies had already been completed but shelved because of their disquieting conclusions—these were reviewed by the new leadership. In an oligarchy like that of the CPSU, changes in policy require the support of many powerful persons. Gorbachev realized, therefore, that the next step was to ensure that enough reform-minded individuals were in authoritative positions, hence the replacement of numerous party leaders by Gorbachev supporters throughout the system and, in particular, a turnover of 11 Politburo members and the entire CPSU Secretariat between March 1985 and January 1987. Most of the Central Committee's department heads, who oversee the party's top-level policy study processes, were replaced. Thus, while the studies were taking place, they were coming more under the supervision and influence of reform-minded leaders. Simultaneously, problems in the economy were aired publicly in the press and media as *glasnost'* developed, thereby increasing the pressure for major policy changes.[10]

The studies having been carried out and the policy alternatives considered, Gorbachev and his advisors spent long hours persuading both central and provincial leaders to support their plans. The Politburo and other high-level authorities began working out the details, and in June 1987 the CPSU's official backing was sealed at a plenary meeting of the Central Committee. All that remained was implementation of the reforms—a task that promised months and years of refining the plan, testing it, putting it into effect piece by piece, overseeing and enforcing its many complicated provisions, evaluating, reevaluating, and adjusting. Along the way, it was anticipated that there would be many possible pitfalls—and even that conservative forces in the party or bureaucracy might capitalize on problems or frustrations caused by the reforms and delay or even reverse the momentum.

Soviet policy-making, then, is centralized and elite dominated, but with elements of closed bargaining within the oligarchy. To the extent that the public is involved, its role is passive; citizens are informed of the general policy lines, but they are not asked for their advice. To say this, however, is not to call the Soviet system a dictatorship. Because the realm of public policy covers such an enormous scope, the number of people involved in its making belies images of the Soviet polity based on concepts such as "dictatorship" or "totalitarianism." Perhaps Professor Meyer's half-serious term "participatory bureaucracy" is not far from the mark, bearing in mind that the party oligarchy reserves to itself the

[10]Although *glasnost'* meant a degree of openness unusual in the Soviet media, something similar had generally characterized this stage of policy-making even before the Gorbachev era, as the official press would be used to inform its readers of current policy directions and the need for any changes.

most important policy decisions and strives to maintain control over the bureaucratic structures through which any wide-scale participation takes place.

China: Ideology and Policy-Making

Underlying the development of China's policy processes has been a revolution driven by a powerful ideology which, until very recently, shaped the overall aims of social, economic, and political policy. The revolutionary ideology has impelled the party to seek dramatic changes, often through major policy innovations and grandiose projects. Especially during Mao's lifetime, policies were intended to mold minds, alter social structures, and reshape the economy. The Great Leap Forward (1958) was designed to alter radically agricultural production and rural lifestyles; the Great Proletarian Cultural Revolution aimed at reinculcating socialist thought and purging "reformist" opponents of Mao. These massively scaled projects were implemented by cadres of party and government bureaucrats, who shifted with each turn of the policy wind. The new programs themselves frequently were implemented and then abandoned, often rapidly. The post-Liberation drive to provide China with a modern economy by promoting the development of large-scale heavy industry was followed, for example, by a program that called for backyard steel furnaces, the extreme in small-scale industry. Similar instability in the political scene is illustrated by the shift from the liberalism of the Hundred Flowers Campaign of 1956–1957 to the mobilization of the Great Leap Forward, beginning in 1958.

Two aspects of this style of policy-making proved costly to the country and left a bad taste with those who lived through the Mao years. The first aspect was its extremism. Under Mao, radical changes in policy would typically be introduced on a countrywide basis with mass campaigns to build support, rather than on an experimental basis in a few regions. Second, the apparent impulsiveness with which major policy innovations were introduced and then changed meant that party and government officials often resisted new policies for fear that if they became too closely associated with them, future policy reversals could leave them on the wrong side of an issue and might jeopardize their careers. This plus the traditional conservatism of the peasantry undermined even carefully thought-out policy initiatives.

Since Mao's death and the changeover from the revolutionary to the modernization phase, policy changes have been less dramatic and more incremental and pragmatic. This is not to deny the extent of the changes resulting from Deng Xiaoping's economic reforms, which include the full-scale implementation of the Four Modernizations as well as limited economic privatization. However, such radical, society-wide campaigns as the Great Leap Forward and the Cultural Revolution appear to be things of the past. The party and government still lead the way in deter-

Figure 7.2   POLICY SHIFTS WITHIN THE CHINESE COMMUNIST PARTY, 1956–1987

1956	Eighth National Party Congress (NPC). Liu Shaoqi announces transition to socialism realized and class conflict ended.
1957	Hundred Flowers campaign unleashes criticism of party; "antirightist" campaign attacks these critics.
1958	Great Leap Forward launched; Eighth NPC line rejected.
1959	Eighth Plenum of Central Committee (CC) rejects Defense Minister Peng's criticisms of the Great Leap Forward, launches campaign against "right opportunism."
1961	Ninth Plenum of CC retrenches after admitting errors of Great Leap Forward.
1962	Tenth Plenum ends retrenchment; beginning of new offensive by Mao.
1963–1966	Maoism advanced in People's Liberation Army by Defense Minister Lin Biao.
1965	Mao calls for assault on revisionist policies.
1966	Eleventh Plenum adopts Cultural Revolution; Lin becomes party vice-chairman.
1968	Liu Shaoqi purged.
1969	Ninth NPC. Lin named Mao's successor; party formally committed to Mao's line.
1971	Lin dies in coup attempt.
1973	Tenth NPC. Leftist line reaffirmed; radical "Gang of Four" confirmed in Politburo.
1976	Radicals purge Deng Xiaoping from premiership; Hua Guofeng becomes premier, arrests Gang of Four.
1977	Eleventh NPC. Hua's policy of the Four Modernizations announced, still within framework of Mao's continuing revolution; Deng reinstated.
1978	"Practice faction," including Deng, attacks Hua's moderate Maoism; Democracy Movement criticizes Mao and Cultural Revolution; Third Plenum of Eleventh NPC breaks with Hua's policies; Deng's protégé, Zhao Ziyang, becomes premier.
1982	Twelfth NPC. New constitution introduced; goal of quadrupling output by 2000 announced.
1987	Thirteenth NPC. Zhao becomes party chairman; many conservatives on Politburo resign; individual initiative and private enterprise are encouraged.

mining the key issues, but many other groups have made a determined effort to place their own interests on the agenda. They include workers concerned with such issues as bonuses and salaries, peasants demanding the right to determine their crop selection, and students wishing to select their own representatives. As Chinese society modernizes further, it is likely that more issues from sources outside the ruling elite will be brought to the attention of the decision-making groups.

Mao dominated the policy process during the first two decades of communist rule. Mao consistently pursued China's ideologically defined overall goal—the use of human potential and technology to establish a participatory, egalitarian, industrialized socialist society—with skillful leadership tactics. In developing policy, he sought the participation of individuals, usually party officials, who were involved at various levels. Once he had heard the range of opinions and alternatives, he posited his own summary view, which he then expected to be translated into action. Before action could take place, however, the process had to go through several further steps. Mao's decisions were usually framed in terms of objectives rather than means of implementation; the details had to be worked out by the political bodies responsible for policy-making. These might include the State Council, the Politburo, the Military Affairs Committee (MAC), and at times special Central Committee plenums—varying as Mao saw fit. Policy objectives were publicized by means of articles and editorials in the media, various types of national congresses, and local cadre groups, and implementation was dependent on the response from government ministries and provincial or commune-governing bodies.[11]

The crucial factor in the process was Chairman Mao's leadership style and skills. Mao absorbed massive amounts of information; he kept abreast of proceedings at party meetings, performance problems, and other matters of concern to him, utilizing this information to maintain his influence over the policy-making processes. By alternating his use of decision-making bodies, he prevented any single group from consolidating power and inhibited the institutionalization of decision-making mechanisms, thereby keeping the crucial decision-making power in his own hands.

Even so, there were times when the process threatened to get out of control. The party elite and mass groups sometimes opposed Mao's policies. During the Cultural Revolution conflicts over policy-making were frequent among groups and individuals at the party center, between the center and the local units, and between military and Red Guard organizations. Evidence of widespread factionalism and autonomous local decision-making became abundant. Local party and Red Guard units often disobeyed commands from the center during and after the Cultural Revolution. Because policies were heavily weighted with ideological objectives, many resulted in extensive short-term costs. For example, the dramatic structural changes of the Great Leap Forward led to a decline in food production, and the Cultural Revolution caused the disruption of established institutions, including the entire school and university systems, which were closed for up to four years. When Mao went into semiretirement during the late 1960s, Zhou Enlai assumed the day-to-

[11]The best commentary on China's policy process is Michael Oksenberg, "Policy Making Under Mao, 1949–1968: An Overview," in John M. Lindbeck, ed., *China: Management of a Revolutionary Society,* (Seattle: University of Washington Press, 1971). See also Paris H. Chang, "Research Notes on the Changing Loci of Decision in the Chinese Communist Party," *China Quarterly* (October–December 1970), 169–193.

day decisions, although Mao maintained a keen interest in their direction. But the realities of decision-making had begun to change. The 1970s saw shifting patterns of personal authority, especially as high-level individuals jockeyed for power following Mao's death. Under Mao's successors, Hua Guofeng and Deng Xiaoping, ideological rigidity has lessened. The new leaders have taken a no-nonsense approach to economic development, severely criticizing those who had previously brought chaos to China's productive system. Their approach signaled a major turn in both the style and substance of policy.

Today, major decisions are usually accompanied by considerable politicking and persuasion. Position papers circulated by individuals and party branches often give rise to lengthy and lively debates. As in many Third World countries where there are close interpersonal relations among those who are politically active, policy-making in China takes place on two levels. On one, the government attempts to make policy rationally, developing programs and allocating resources to meet needs. On the other level, there is evidence that those with close personal relations to the policymakers receive priority in both the fashioning and implementation of policy. In China, such "pull" is called *guanxi.*

Commonly, the public is informed of new policy directions by wall posters. For example, wall posters widely proclaimed the shift from "red" to "expert" in the post-Mao era. Changes in policy have frequently been accompanied by an attack on opponents and frequently by changes in the top elite. This happened in the years following Mao's death, as Hua Guofeng and Deng Xiaoping fought their battle over the intensity of policy change and, ultimately, power.

One of the most important changes in the post-Mao era has been the increased importance of institutions in making policy. This is not to deny the personal power of individual leaders such as Deng Xiaoping, but institutional groups have settled into a more stable pattern of hierarchy and functionality. China's supreme policy-making groups today are, in descending order of importance, the Politburo's Standing Committee, the Military Affairs Committee, the Politburo, and the Party Central Committee. Their policy decisions tend to be couched broadly and are translated into operational terms by the government's State Council. Most of the high officials who head ministries and commissions also hold positions in the party hierarchy, which serves to facilitate communication and party control.

Long-term planning, usually in the form of five-year plans, is done under the State Council's authority by the State Planning Commission. The plans focus on selected areas, such as the sectors of development (agriculture and industry), and on setting priorities for heavy and light industry, agriculture, consumption, and investment allocations. In the 1980s considerable effort has gone into implementing the economic reforms. This has meant integrating market considerations into planning and deciding which areas of production and services will be allocated to nongovernmental enterprises. While central planning has remained the mainstay of economic policy, the reforms have had a profound impact on this process, as private activities have been encouraged to compete increasingly with the planned sector.

Party control over policy persists beyond the planning stage. It is exercised not only through the appointment of party members to top ministerial positions but also through the party branches, which ensure that the party policy is carried out in all governmental and economic organizations. Party committees permeate the governmental hierarchy and economic organizations at all levels. The party-directed mass organizations—unions, peasant associations, women's associations, the Young Communist League—also aid in party control.

Still, controlling China's policy-making machinery—which includes the military, the Communist party, the government administrative structures, and the massive network of state-run economic enterprises—is a big task. The party and governmental hierarchies alone comprise some 20 million officials. Moreover, the system is hierarchical, privileged, and at times riddled with corruption. It is also personalistic, in that personal relationships can often determine success or failure in rising through the system.

As one might expect of a system so large and ridden through with the privileges of power, there are problems. Certainly, for a revolutionary party claiming service to the people as its official raison d'être, chief among its concerns are corruption and the decline of idealism. Self-interest and cynicism abound, and according to some observers, those who are attracted into the civil service as young people see it primarily as a way to personal advancement or access to privileges such as faster promotions, better housing, educational opportunities, use of a car, and chances for travel.[12]

Mao was consistently wary of the bureaucracy, and he used mass movements such as the Great Leap Forward and the Cultural Revolution to shake up the bureaucracy, to emphasize revolutionary ideals, to combat bureaucratic resistance to central direction, and to ensure his personal political preeminence. The reestablishment of the bureaucracies during periods of consolidation, however, demonstrated Mao's realistic acceptance of their importance in governing and changing society. Other means of keeping bureaucracies "responsive" in China include mass participation in enterprise management, mandatory manual labor by officials and technical personnel, periodic public criticism and self-criticism, and return-to-the-countryside campaigns. The uses of mass movements and other forms of participation serve a similar function to the procedures for public accountability in liberal democracies. Questioning, then, becomes the citizen's right and a way to control or influence public policy directions.

[12]Orville Schell, *To Get Rich Is Glorious: China in the 80's* (New York: Mentor, 1986), p. 93.

In 1983 an official campaign was begun to curb abuses within the bureaucracy. In addition to moral reforms, there were attempts to eliminate inefficiency—for example, by reducing the numerous layers of structures between state industrial enterprises and various ministries. The party's reforms reduced the bloated bureaucracy and attempted to improve its sense of dedication; they also sought to change modes of communication between the bureaucracy and the masses in order to keep civil servants better informed of actual conditions among the public and lessen the hostility many people felt toward the bureaucracy.[13] Additional campaigns in 1986 and 1987 brought corrupt cadres to trial for serious offenses and, in many cases, resulted in death sentences.

MEXICO AND NIGERIA: PROBLEMS OF POLICY-MAKING IN DEVELOPING COUNTRIES

In most parts of the Third World there is a tendency toward greater demands on governmental decisionmakers. Governments are expected to provide social welfare, promote economic development, control the influence of foreign powers, and solve a host of other social, economic, and political problems. The policy-making capabilities of many Third World countries, however, are weak. In most cases, the policy-making process is tightly controlled by a small elite and offers little opportunity to mobilize mass participation in social change. In some cases, change is blocked by powerful forces committed to the status quo, such as military hierarchies, bureaucracies, churches, business interests, and foreign investors. In other cases, the political leadership has the power to bring about change but is prevented from doing so by its own ideological blinders.

Policy-making patterns vary too much within the less developed world for any one or two countries to be typical, but Mexico and Nigeria offer useful contrasting examples. Mexico's institutions are older and hence more developed than those of Nigeria. Nigeria offers an example of policy-making under military rulers clearly committed to free enterprise. The Mexican government runs a number of state enterprises in what is a mixed economy but, as is the case in many Third World countries with socialist leanings, the private sector remains large and its values, including the primacy of private enterprise and market mechanisms for distribution of goods and services, dominate.

Mexico: Policy-Making Under PRI Control

In Mexico, as in many Third World countries, the government plays the role of referee, deciding which issues are to be addressed through policy

[13]Liang Heng and Judith Shapiro, *After the Nightmare: Inside China Today* (New York: Macmillan, 1986), p. 90.

and which not. Citizens may approach their congressman, senator, governor, or mayor to make a claim, but unless they belong to a government-organized group the response is likely to be no more than a polite hearing of their case. This is particularly so if the claim requires a major policy adjustment, such as land redistribution, the creation of jobs, sanitation, or educational opportunities. If the demands are taken up by an official government-sponsored interest group, they may be translated into public policy, but often the policy is only a symbolic response to the group's requests. That is, legislation may be enacted which mentions the need for policy change to address the problem, but it falls short in implementation; funds are not allocated, for example, or the bureaucracy is not pushed to apply the law.

Since the 1917 revolution, Mexico's policy-making network has developed a great measure of stability. The major participants in the policy process at the top level are the president and his cabinet of ministers. Beneath them are the PRI's three active sectors: the peasant, labor, and popular sectors. In addition, the military, the church, economic elites, representatives of state and local government, and an expanding number of socioeconomic associations all participate.

While a two-way flow characterizes the policy-making process in general, the usual direction is from top to bottom. It is an elite-dominated system with both formal and informal channels. The formal process involves presidential initiative, congressional approval, and ultimately a ministerial or ad hoc commission with members from the affected groups that hammers out the details of implementation. The informal channels, highly individualistic and based on patron-client relationships, deal mostly with minor issues and policy requests that flow from bottom to top. All in all, the system demonstrates a curious mix of authoritarian and pluralistic patterns aiming at a wide consensus.

The formal process usually begins with a proposal by the president, although in some policy areas the inspiration for a given policy may come from a federal cabinet minister or department head. Competing elite groups use their leverage with the president to gain concessions. If the president has decided on a given policy, he may consult relevant ministers or bureaucrats about the proposal. Thereafter, the original proposal may be modified, and a law will be proposed to the Congress. It is then passed by the Chamber of Deputies and the Senate, the PRI deputies voting unanimously in support of the measure.

Implementation of the law requires the support of the interest groups involved and may also require that the definition of the law be sharpened. For this, the president may appoint an ad hoc commission, which serves until its mission of defining the law and gaining the acceptance of the involved groups is complete. In this process the policy is further modified. The president's guidelines and intent must prevail, but the commission—and the involved groups represented on it—may well define the real content of the policy. An example is President López

Mateos' decision in 1961 to amend the Mexican constitution (Article 123) to allow profit sharing for employees of corporate enterprises.[14] He appointed a special commission whose responsibility was to determine the details of profit sharing. This necessitated a choice between two alternatives, one supported by the business sector and another favored by the unions. The presidential commission decided on a solution that was more favorable to the unions than to the employers, but both finally agreed. A consensual policy was thereby formulated, and it became law.

Among the most powerful groups influencing the policy processes are the landed elite, including both the large ranchers and the more successful *ejiditarios* (beneficiaries of the land reform programs), and wealthy businessmen, whose success, in many cases, has been enhanced by the government's role in aiding their enterprises. Industrial policies are often made in consultation with the National Confederation of Chambers of Commerce. Although not part of the PRI, the Chambers of Commerce are at least as powerful as the labor and farm sectors of the ruling party. Their influence is clearly evident in the government's investment priorities, which have strongly favored economic infrastructure and industrial investment over education, credit for the *ejidos,* housing, and agricultural extension. Thus, while many interest groups influence policies, they are by no means equal in power.

Business interests, though strong, do not always prevail, as we have seen in the case of the profit-sharing legislation. It is part of the president's task to create policies that unite, rather than divide, his party's diverse support groups. Indeed, the president's ability to manipulate interests to maximize support for his (and his party's) preferred policies can significantly limit or increase the power of the privileged sections of Mexican society.

As is true of leadership recruitment, patron-client hierarchies are the basis of the informal policy structures. Policy output frequently reflects the government's desire to create "obligations" or loyalties to the PRI. Individuals and groups requesting government assistance realize, or are made to realize, that such assistance comes at the price of present or future political support. This is true of all levels, from major interests at the federal level to villagers using the occasion of a government minister's visit to appeal for a new clinic for their village. In the latter case, such requests are sometimes granted, but the response typically takes the form of a symbolic payoff: a verbal assurance that the minister understands the villagers' problem and that action will be forthcoming. Limited, particularistic payoffs are often granted at the local level—loans and part-time jobs, for example—but these hardly constitute a solution to the complex poverty-rooted problems that plague the average villager's life.

[14]Susan Kaufman Purcell, "Decision Making in an Authoritarian Regime: Theoretical Implications from a Mexican Case Study," *World Politics* (October 1973), 28–57.

A great deal of policy is made on the subpresidential level, in part because the state is extensively involved in public enterprises. The federal government controls subsoil natural resources and irrigation systems, for example, and invests heavily in transportation and communication: railroads, commercial aviation, maritime transportation, telegraph, newsprint, motion picture distribution, and even the nominally private telephone company. The government also controls or has interests in such other industries and services as electric power, petroleum exploration and production, iron and steel production, petrochemicals, textile mills, truck and auto assembly, the country's largest meatpacking plants, banking, and consumer distribution. The state and its ministries are constantly involved in policy-making for these industries, which employ large numbers of workers and affect businesspeople and consumers throughout Mexico.

Policy-making processes extend hierarchically down to the state and local levels. The president has considerable influence through the state PRI organizations; he and the federal executive branch also control most of the finances of local governments. The president can influence the allocation of many other important rewards to individuals, groups, and politicians, including pet projects, credit for business and industry, government jobs, and political appointments and promotions.

Although beholden to the president, governors are also powerful. They are intermediaries for the president and the dominant force in local politics. Most municipal governments are limited to such routine matters as tax collection, road building, and public services; the more important projects are the responsibility of the governor and his assistants.

Local officials are appointed to three-year terms, which gives them little time to gain the administrative experience needed to manage their communities' affairs. Because there are often no state or local plans to guide expenditures, the door is open to myriad particularistic demands, and funds are often allocated on the basis of status and influence. Given this state of affairs, the federal deputy and his relatives are much more likely to have government projects in their neighborhoods than is the resident of a poor *barrio* (neighborhood).

With influence dispersed among so many political actors, there is little logic or cohesion to policy outputs. The business elite gets protectionist policies even while concessions are simultaneously made to foreign investors; programs for redistributing land to the landless exist side by side with increasing credit opportunities for wealthy landowners. Efforts to rationalize policy-making have taken place, however. There is, for example, growing momentum toward urban and regional planning, which if carried through could result in attempts to rationally allocate labor and resources. Another step in this direction is the attempt, begun by President Luis Echeverría during the 1970s, to bring technocrats—experts in engineering, industrial management, and economic planning—into the cabinet, rather than political loyalists. Nevertheless, Mexico has thus far resisted the implementation on a national scale of sophisticated socioeconomic plans or grand projects analogous to the Soviet Union's industrialization drive or China's Great Leap Forward.

Because Mexico gives priority to the market system in allocating resources and values individual liberty over social justice, policies tend to develop incrementally. That is, they are limited in scope and generally emerge in response to immediate needs. Villagers may ask local officials that a road be repaired or that running water be piped to their area. If they have enough influence or if the officials are so disposed, their requests may be fulfilled. If the pressures are sufficiently great, state or federal officials may respond to the demands. In fact, most projects tend to be allocated in this way. Once an objective becomes a matter of national policy, particularistic political pressures determine allocations. Such policies thus bring about partial changes, not comprehensive ones.

While Mexico's PRI and the president's cabinet are responsible for developing most of the country's public policies, civil servants contribute to the actual shape of policy through their role in its implementation. Implementation can be as significant an arena for policy-making as the initial stage of goal formation. Just as interest groups can influence the making of policy through pressures on cabinet ministers and committees, they can affect the implementation of policy by putting pressure on bureaucrats. It is during the stages of implementation that opportunities for corruption are most prevalent. Officials generally receive modest salaries and can be easily swayed by bribes. The possibility of bribery increases the political efficacy of the wealthy at the expense of those unable to pay bribes, and it also interferes with the accurate evaluation of policies.

As is true of many Third World bureaucracies, there are widespread allegations of corruption in the Mexican civil service. It is hard to determine the actual extent; it may well be true, as one observer concluded some years ago, that the vast majority of Mexican bureaucrats are honest.[15] However, there is clear evidence, especially among the upper levels of the bureaucracy, that the opportunities and rewards for graft are often hard to resist. Many ministers, agency heads, and directors of state-owned industries have taken their so-called *mordida,* or "bite", while in office. The administration of President de la Madrid made an attempt during the 1980s to weed out corruption by example, indicting the head of Pemex, the government petroleum giant, and Mexico City's chief of police. Although these cases were prosecuted, corruption persists in all ministries and in all state and local governments.

Contributing to the problem is the overlapping of politics and the bureaucracy. Young people who are interested in politics often begin

---

[15]Frank Brandenberg, *The Making of Modern Mexico* (Englewood Cliffs, N.J.: Prentice-Hall, 1964), p. 160.

their careers in the civil service, and former elected officials frequently move into civil service jobs when their terms of office expire. Despite reforms over the years aimed at a merit-based bureaucracy, political loyalty and service to the PRI still influence entry and advancement.

Nigeria: Policy-Making by a Military–Bureaucratic Elite

In Nigeria, as in Mexico, policy issues flow in two directions: through governmental commands from above and particularistic interests expressed from below. Where they conflict, as in the question of priorities for industrial sites or governmental credits, the government usually prevails over interest groups. If the regime is bent on a certain objective and believes that public demands exceed its will to compromise, it will hold the line against the pressures of any interest group. Thus, while both authoritarian and pluralistic tendencies exist, the Nigerian system under military rule clearly tilts toward authoritarianism.

Although since modified by the practices of military rule, Nigeria's policy-making processes have their roots in the constitution of the First Republic (1960–1966). In that system policy-making was dominated by cabinet ministers, the Parliament, regional leaders (both politicians and chiefs), and interest groups. Planning bodies existed, but they were concerned primarily with infrastructural development. Their plans were merely advisory and subject to acceptance by the politicians.

Between 1966 and 1979 and again after 1983, policy-making has been under the tutelage of the military rulers. However, because of disparities in qualifications—age, education, experience—between the military elite and top civil servants, the military still must rely heavily on the latter. Thus, although the Armed Forces Ruling Council (AFRC) is the most powerful policy-making body, members of the civil service have also been active in creating and implementing policies. Military rule has also brought a trend toward centralization of policy-making inasmuch as the central regime has co-opted issue areas traditionally left to the regions and states, such as education, health, and planning. Much tension between the federal military regime and the states has resulted from these centralizing efforts.

With the introduction of a presidential system in 1979, power was again decentralized and, at the federal level, subjected to checks and balances. The new constitution created competing sources of policy—the executive branch, the bicameral legislature, and the judiciary. At the local level, much authority was given to the district councils to develop policy in the areas of public health, sewage and sanitation, road maintenance, cemeteries, and such other services as street lights and public safety. Much of this pattern has survived the 1983 military takeover, although district and village governmental decisions concern mostly routine matters. In all cases, local leaders must work closely with governors, and it is primarily at this point, as in Mexico, that interest groups exert their pressures. Many governors are heavily involved in infrastructure and developmental efforts, working closely on a day-to-day basis with local civil servants and, in particular, with the permanent secretaries of state ministries, their counterparts at the federal level, Nigerian and foreign businesspeople, and local leaders.

The origin of issues has varied with the type of government. Under the Second Republic, policy initiatives could come from either legislative chamber, the president, or the various bureaucracies. In the civilian setting, the proliferation of interest groups and a relatively free press made it possible for many issues to be articulated from below. In the military framework, on the contrary, the government attempts to control the agenda of national issues.

In both the military and civilian frameworks, policy on the state level has been the carefully guarded domain of the governors, at least until recently. The military government of Ibrahim Babangida has attempted to open its processes to citizen petitioners, and this has been copied in some state capitals. According to at least one report, the result has been a rise in public involvement unmatched even in the Second Republic, as citizens have confronted their governors to demand improved health care delivery, better schools, road repairs, and relief from high taxes.[16]

As already noted, the civil service continues to play an important role under military rule, as it did in the civilian governments. Although strongly influenced by the British system, the bureaucracy has adopted its own set of practices within the realities of the Nigerian context. Civil servants enjoy high status. At all levels, they run what amount to mini-fiefdoms and often treat the public with disdain. In many cases, they have virtually unchecked power to grant or deny citizens' requests.

The strength of the Nigerian bureaucracy derives from its colonial background. Under British indirect rule the bureaucracy was subject to control by the British Colonial Office but was not politically responsible to the Nigerian legislature, nor in fact to the British Parliament. The scope of its activities was broad, encompassing the formulation and application of policy and even judicial tasks. As a result, the bureaucracy was more highly developed than such other political bodies as legislatures, parties, and interest groups. But it was "foreign," in that it was tainted with involvement in colonial rule and manned at the upper levels by Britons. Asserting political control over the bureaucracy upon independence was doubly difficult because of its foreignness and its institutional strength compared to other Nigerian political structures.

The first step was the "Nigerianization" of the bureaucracy—the replacement of British colonial civil servants with native Nigerians. This process was hampered by ethnoregional rivalries, and even when it was accomplished the results were mixed. On the one hand, psycholog-

[16]"State Governors Meet the People," *New African* (October 1986), 7.

ical and political dependence on the former colonial power was eliminated, but on the other, the civil service was weakened by overloading it with young and inexperienced officials. Even more important, the competition for positions in the civil service heightened ethnic tensions, especially between northern and southern Nigeria. Indeed, when General Ironsi in 1966 proposed to merge the civil services of the various regions, the fear that Ibo dominance would result exacerbated ethnic tensions in the crucial weeks leading up to the July coup, the secession of Biafra, and the civil war.

Through all the turmoil of the 1960s and 1970s, the Nigerian civil service survived more or less intact. Having adopted the British system of recruitment and promotion, which stresses the political neutrality of the civil servant and seeks to attract the best possible individuals by offering generous benefits, the civil service has retained much of its independent status. Indeed, under military rule, the influence of the bureaucracy has increased. Civil servants have headed most ministries and served in other positions of leadership as well. The disappearance of political parties and the weakness of interest groups have augmented the bureaucrats' freedom of action, for the pressures for concessions to special interests or the cronies of political leaders are no longer as great.[17] Moreover, since the 1970s the civil service has been further expanded, as state governments have joined with the federal government in developing their ministries' bureaucracies. In short, the bureaucracy, always strong, has seen its power increase under military rule to the point that it is the chief partner of the military in governing contemporary Nigeria.

These developments do not mean that it is immune to some of the illnesses afflicting other Third World bureaucracies. Nigerian news magazines frequently cite abuses of power by bureaucrats and claim that corruption costs the country millions of dollars annually; in 1984 numerous senior civil servants were jailed for corruption along with members of the Second Republic's government. Nepotism is another problem. The strength of familial bonds obliges many Nigerian bureaucrats to find civil service jobs for their relatives. The higher an official's position, the bigger the problem is, as both close and distant relatives will approach him seeking jobs.

The Nigerian civil service thus finds itself torn between the British traditions of political neutrality and meritocracy and the practices of corruption, nepotism, and clientelism characteristic of many developing countries. In addition, its ability to perform an enhanced leadership role effectively has been undermined by developments outside its control. Foremost among these is the decline in the price of oil in the 1980s, which has reduced the funds available for economic and social development. The uncertainty over the future of the present military regime also

---

[17]John M. Ostheimer, *Nigerian Politics* (New York: Harper & Row, 1973), pp. 121–123.

undermines bureaucratic performance; bureaucrats realize that their greater independence of special interests and local elites may be short-lived and that they ought not to alienate these groups and individuals too much.

CONCLUSIONS

The evidence from our six countries illustrates the basic fact that policy-making in all systems is a complex process involving many different forces and interests. This observation goes against much conventional thinking, which concentrates on the distinction between the incrementalism of noncommunist systems and the "rational" or centrally planned style preferred by communist regimes. Clearly, there are bound to be differences between policy-making by a ruling party which claims to have a unique and unchallengeable vision of a future to be constructed under its guidance and that by a ruling party which is simply trying to adopt policies that will help it win the next election. Nevertheless, the similarities are equally as striking. In communist systems, the manner in which the unique vision is to be achieved is open to considerable disagreement and dispute, and major institutional interests—the military, heavy industry, and the like—are usually able to show that responding to their particular demands furthers the overall objective of building communism. This means that conflicting policy proposals can be expected to emerge on any issue and that it is usually necessary to build coalitions of key leaders and groups in order to advance policies successfully; as in democratic systems, the result is often a great deal of tugging and jostling within the highest ranks—and policies that are either inconsistent or timid—until there are changes in leading personnel that allow new policy initiatives to be adopted and implemented. It also means that policies are subject to processes of evaluation and review to determine whether they are achieving their desired effects, particularly in light of competing claims. Nor are policies adopted without regard to public opinion. In fact, Soviet and Chinese leaders are generally reluctant to introduce policies that will antagonize the general public. The Communist party's claim that it always knows what the people want and acts in accord with the popular will is, at best, exaggerated, but the party leaders do attempt to keep informed about the attitudes of the people and usually act to minimize negative popular reaction to their policies.

There are two principal areas where the processes of policy-making in communist and noncommunist societies diverge. Although policy-making involves competition among interests and points of view in both systems, the competition is generally more hidden from public view in communist systems; interest groups do not publicize their causes and elections do not resolve the policy debates, which often lie hidden beneath the surface of an ostensibly unified oligarchy. The need to maintain the facade of a united elite inspired by a single vision also limits the range of admissible choices; options that seem too capitalistic, for example, may be bypassed or rejected for essentially ideological reasons. The second difference is that the "reach" of government policy is much greater in communist systems. Noncommunist countries like France and Nigeria have adopted national plans to promote social and economic development and at times have used very powerful incentives to gain the cooperation of economic interests, but neither has attempted to supplant the private economy with the command economy model characteristic of communist countries. The competition of interests is present in both communist and noncommunist systems, but the stakes of the contest, in this sense, are greater in communist systems.

The centralized policy-making that is a distinctive feature of communist states has both advantages and disadvantages. On the positive side, from the standpoint of the elite, it facilitates the maintenance of control over policy and society. It permits the marshaling of all human and material resources to move society in the desired direction. On the other hand, the scope of centralized planning poses enormous problems. All major decisions are governmental rather than private and must be consciously made by central bodies. This can overburden policymakers and fosters such bureaucratic vices as red tape, delay, "buck-passing," and reluctance to take responsibility.

Bureaucratic resistance and inertia are not unique to communist systems, however. In all political systems, there is a natural tendency for bureaucrats to concern themselves more with the needs of the organization that employs them than with the goals it is intended to advance and to place their own expertise on issues affecting their jurisdictions above the opinions of their political leaders. Communist regimes have developed the most extensive system of monitoring governmental responsiveness to party decisions, but every system of government must adopt some means of ensuring that bureaucrats follow the lead of their political superiors. Perhaps the reason that the idea of political control of public bureaucracies is so strongly emphasized in most political systems is that it is inherently so difficult to achieve.

chapter *8*

The Challenges of Growth
and Stagnation

INTRODUCTION

In premodern times, governments had relatively little to do with managing economic affairs. Apart from providing a system of justice to regulate disputes and protect private property (where the institution of private property existed), political leaders largely stood aside from the tasks of providing for the material conditions of existence. Most adult members of society were directly involved in providing for their own food, clothing, and shelter, and when crops failed, local communities were left to their own devices to weather the hardships as best they could.

In the twentieth century especially, governments have become much more involved in economic management. This change in the role of government has come about primarily because of industrialization and its effects on society. The most basic effect of industrialization is to provoke a massive transfer of working people from the countryside to urban areas and from direct involvement in food production to dependence on earned income to purchase the necessities of life. In the West, the industrial era has been characterized since its beginnings by cycles of economic expansion and recession, and when recessions hit, the result was often declining wages, widespread layoffs of workers, and enormous suffering. Many economists of the early nineteenth century, whose discipline came to be known as the "dismal science," responded to this problem with a traditional remedy: just as starvation and disease had always taken care of the problems of overpopulation in the countryside, so the same grim forces should be allowed to work their effects in the cities. After all, they reasoned, if excess labor is kept alive through the actions of the state, it will only produce more excess labor, thereby compounding the problem for future generations.

This hands-off approach was never totally accepted, even in the nineteenth century. In the countryside one could usually grow or gather enough food to survive a bad harvest; there was often occasional employment on the lands of the better off; and, if worse came to worst, work might be found in the towns and cities. Urban dwellers, however, have far fewer opportunities to produce their own food or to return to the countryside. A temporary downturn in the business cycle or even the bankruptcy of a single firm could leave thousands of families destitute almost overnight, and the desperation shared by such large numbers could easily generate riots, attacks on the rich, or even rebellion against the state; at the very least, crime rates could be expected to increase. Compassion for the needy thus combined with concern for social peace to provoke the governments of industrializing countries into action.

At first, that action mainly took the form of social legislation designed to alleviate the distresses caused by industrialization. Unemployment insurance and labor exchanges to assist individuals in finding work were among the first steps. The need for some form of relief for those disabled in industrial accidents and for those too old or sick to work was also appreciated. Governments began to concern themselves with the relationship between wages and food prices, realizing that if they became unbalanced, enormous lower-class unrest and radicalization could ensue. Tariff policy was often used to maintain an acceptable balance between the need to protect jobs at home and the opportunity to import cheaper goods from abroad. Still, the assumption was maintained that, apart from these necessary palliatives, the market economy should be allowed to function as freely as possible.

This confidence in the ability of markets to achieve satisfactory levels of production and employment was challenged most profoundly in the severe depression which began in 1929 and lasted until World War II. With tens of millions unemployed throughout the Western world, the idea that the market economy would correct itself without outside interference became less credible. The sufferings of the depression, combined with the enormous sacrifices demanded by governments of industrialized countries during the world war itself, stimulated a widespread belief in the West that governments must ensure the proper functioning of their economies in the future. The "dirty thirties," it was felt, must never be allowed to happen again.

This belief that governments must play a major role in economic management received added stimulus from the example of the Soviet Union, which departed on a fundamentally different course in the 1930s by ending private ownership of the means of production (including farms) and engaging in an enormous project of state-controlled industrialization. By the late 1930s the Soviet Union had substantially industrialized, and by 1945 it emerged as one of the world's two greatest military powers. The Soviet approach to economic management therefore seemed to be a remarkably successful one.

The example of the rapid industrialization of the Soviet Union had a particularly powerful influence on many new states, and it was directly applied in countries under Soviet influence, including China and most of East Europe. Even in underdeveloped countries that did not adopt the Soviet model, doubts often cropped up over whether rapid economic development was possible without substantial guidance from the state. With the populations of their countries growing rapidly—thanks largely to the introduction of Western medicine and sanitation standards—many Third World leaders concluded that they could not afford to wait until modernization came of its own accord. Thus, whether the socioeconomic system was capitalist or socialist, developed or underdeveloped, the central role of government in the management of economic affairs was accepted almost without question in the postwar era. Only in the past decade has it come into doubt.

The "Managed" Capitalism of the West

In the developed countries of the West, the theories of the English economist John Maynard Keynes were widely seen after 1945 as the solution to the problem of how governments could maintain the prosperity of their economies. Keynes argued that governments could regulate the overall level of economic activity by using their spending and taxing powers in a more imaginative fashion than they had previously done. Up to that time, economic orthodoxy taught that governments, like households, should maintain a balanced budget and avoid going into debt. Keynes pointed out that government indebtedness is not like the indebtedness of private individuals or organizations because governments have the power to tax those to whom they owe money, i.e., their citizens. Therefore, governments need not be excessively concerned with balancing their budgets; rather, Keynes maintained, governments should deliberately spend more than they receive in tax income during periods of recession in order to stimulate economic activity and help their economies pull out of the recession. Conversely, when too much spending threatens to drive up prices, governments should cut their own expenditures and raise taxes to reduce spending by others. In sum, Keynes advanced the idea that governments should use their spending and taxing powers to maintain an overall level of demand for goods and services that would be high enough to allow full employment but not so high that it generates excessive inflation. "Demand management" became the key to smoothing out the business cycle and maintaining economic prosperity.

Keynesianism seemed to work well for a quarter-century after

World War II, during which time the industrialized economies of the West experienced their most sustained period of economic expansion since the industrial revolution. The Keynesian approach was not consistently applied, however. Although governments were quite prepared to run deficits to stimulate economic growth, they were much less keen to risk displeasing voters by reducing expenditures and raising taxes when inflation threatened. The potential for inflationary problems was activated by the enormous increase in U.S. government expenditures to pay for the Vietnam War and President Johnson's antipoverty campaign in the 1960s; it was given an added push when the Organization of Oil Exporting Countries (OPEC) suddenly quadrupled oil prices in 1973. During the 1970s inflation became a severe problem in most Western countries, and it persevered even in times of economic stagnation. This unanticipated combination of inflation and stagnation, labeled "stagflation" by some, suggested to many the need for a new economic orthodoxy. The orthodoxy which came into vogue is known as *monetarism.*

Monetarist economists argued that inflation would be checked if the government controlled the rate of growth of the money supply more closely. The money supply involves not just coins and bills in circulation but also the creation of new money by such means as loans to individuals, corporations, and governments. The key task of government, therefore, is to set or influence interest rates and the level of government borrowing so that the money supply does not expand too rapidly. Monetarists also suggested that there was no need to offend trade unions by adopting wage freezes, as had been common during the 1970s as a means of controlling inflation. If the expansion of the money supply was kept within reasonable bounds, monetarists argued, unions would not be able to drive wages up too high because there would not be enough money available to pay them. Therefore what governments should do is step away from too close an involvement in the economy and concentrate instead on maintaining a monetary climate conducive to acceptable levels of economic growth and inflation.

In the 1980s most Western governments came to rely much more heavily on monetarist policies. In order to control monetary growth, interest rates shot up to unprecedented levels in the early 1980s. That action did check inflation—returning it to low levels not seen since the mid-1960s in most countries—but it did so at a considerable price. A severe recession set in as many businesses simply could not survive the skyrocketing interest rates on their loans, and unemployment rose substantially in Europe and North America. Since that recession, moderate economic growth and levels of inflation have returned to the industrialized West, but high levels of unemployment remain a problem, especially in West Europe.

The economies of the West are now in an uncertain state. In the 1960s Europe was so labor-hungry that it imported millions of Arab and

Table 8.1 INFLATION RATES IN WESTERN ECONOMIES

	Average annual increase in consumer price index (%)			
	1960–1967	1968–1973	1973–1979	1979–1983
Britain	3.6	7.5	15.6	10.7
France	3.6	6.1	10.7	12.1
Group of seven major capitalist economies[a]	2.7	5.5	9.4	8.4

[a]The group of seven includes the United States, Britain, France, West Germany, Japan, Canada, and Italy.

Source: Organization of Economic Cooperation and Development, *Historical Statistics 1960–1983* (Paris, 1985).

Table 8.2 UNEMPLOYMENT IN BRITAIN, FRANCE, AND THE UNITED STATES

	Unemployment rate (% unemployed)				
	1960	1970	1975	1980	1985
Britain	2.2	3.1	4.1	6.5	12.9
France	1.8	2.6	4.3	6.2	10.0
United States	5.5	4.9	8.5	7.1	7.1

Source: U.S. Central Intelligence Agency, *Handbook of Economic Statistics, 1986* (Washington, D.C.: Government Printing Office, 1986).

Turkish "guest workers"; by the late 1980s more than 15 million of its own citizens were unemployed. It is not just the recession of the early 1980s that hurt; much more significant in the long term are the inroads made by goods produced by East Asian countries, particularly Japan. Although certain countries such as West Germany are doing well in this regard, Europe as a whole is facing a serious technological challenge from abroad. Ironically, companies that do modernize in order to meet that challenge frequently do so by laying off excess labor and adopting labor-saving technologies instead, thereby adding to the unemployment problem, at least in the short run.

The economic realities of the 1980s and 1990s have created other serious problems as well. With a higher proportion of the population unemployed, the costs of unemployment and welfare payments have increased enormously. Those costs must be borne by the smaller proportion of the population that is working. Similarly, the elaborate social programs established in the 1950s and 1960s—which in Europe provide coverage for virtually every social need—are now much harder to finance than they were when nearly full employment and higher levels of economic growth kept government tax receipts at healthy levels. Moreover, the public does not seem disposed to accept cuts in these social services. How well the countries of the West will meet the technological, financial, and economic challenges that face them remains to be seen; what is clear is that the management of developed capitalist economies is no longer as straightforward or as successful as it was just 20 years ago.

To many in the West, the era of automatic growth, full employment, and robust tax revenues seems like a dream from the past.

Bureaucratic Stagnation in Socialist Economies

The type of state-owned and state-directed economy pioneered by the Soviet Union was intended as a deliberate alternative to capitalism. The Soviet Union achieved impressive rates of growth and industrialization during the 1930s, when most Western economies were mired in depression. From the Soviet perspective, the depression in the West signaled the approaching demise of capitalism, as foretold in the doctrines of Marxism-Leninism. Although capitalism survived those years and went on to prosper in the postwar era, the economic problems since 1973 have once again suggested to Soviet observers the "contradictions" of the capitalist system and its inevitable—although not immediate—destruction. It is their belief that capitalism will be superseded by the type of economic system they are in the process of developing.

The central feature of Soviet-style socialist economies is that the state rather than the market determines the allocation of goods and their prices. The appeal of this system is its rationality: instead of letting millions of consumer choices determine the allocation of resources, state decisionmakers can do so in light of the goals which the state wishes to realize. In theory, this means that unnecessary or frivolous demands will not take resources away from more important ones; the whims of the rich will not be catered to while the poor go hungry. For a country with limited resources and ambitious plans for rapid economic development—such as China and many other Third World states—the socialist model is bound to seem attractive. Moreover, the success of the Soviet Union's industrialization during the first three decades of centralized planning (1928–1958) gave credence to the model's effectiveness as a means of shortening the modernization process.

Central allocation of societal resources is not an easy task, however. Market economies largely let consumer demand determine the type and quantity of goods produced; in a centrally controlled or "command" economy, these decisions must be made by bureaucrats. It may be necessary to set millions of prices and production levels annually, and without the corrective that markets provide, the scope for miscalculation can be very large. Consider, for example, the production of a single consumer good such as cooking pots. In the Soviet Union, the decision on how many resources should be allocated to the production of cooking pots must be made by state planners. If they overestimate the demand for pots, enormous wastage can occur, but even if their predictions do prove to reflect demand accurately, there may still be inefficiencies. The easiest way to set production quotas in a large complex economy is to do so quantitatively, that is, by specifying how many tons of cooking pots each pot-making firm must produce. It is much more difficult to specify quality or stylistic standards. In market economies, firms which produce goods of inferior quality or unwanted sizes of styles risk bankruptcy; state-owned economies do not normally incorporate that risk. There is therefore little incentive for factory managers to change their product selection or improve their product quality to achieve greater consumer satisfaction; as long as they produce the quantities of goods the plan expects of them, they have done their job. Unwanted goods may be produced in enormous quantities because it is cheaper or easier than producing the types of goods for which there is genuine need.

Command economies have proved to be far more effective in achieving large increases in the production of basic goods, such as coal and steel, than they have with the more complex products that characterize a developed economy. Innovation may be seriously handicapped in an economy where there is no danger of going bankrupt or losing a job and perhaps little individual reward for new ideas. Soviet growth rates have slowed dramatically since the 1960s, and the production targets of the five-year plans (FYPs) are frequently unfulfilled. In both the Soviet Union and China, political leaders have come to realize that material incentives must be offered to encourage greater efficiency, harder work, and more innovation, however much this goes against the image of self-sacrifice that they are trying to mold.

In China to a very considerable extent, and in the Soviet Union more modestly, privately owned enterprise has been allowed to develop in recent years. The hope of their governments is that the incentive of profit will make these firms efficient and that the competition they provide will force state-owned firms to follow suit. Chinese and Soviet leaders can draw on the experiences of Yugoslavia and Hungary, both of which have had some success with programs permitting limited privatization—Yugoslavia since the mid-1950s and Hungary since 1968. The danger, however, is that free enterprise will prove too popular or too successful to be kept within the bounds of a socialist economy. It is likely that the largely covert struggle between factions within the ruling elites who favor these experiments in order to achieve more efficiency and factions who worry about their ideological consequences will continue for some time to come in both countries.

The Challenges of Economic Development in the Third World

During the optimistic years of the great wave of colonial liberations, it seemed to observers in both the developed world and the former colonies themselves that rapid economic development was just around the corner. With foreign aid from developed countries, loans from international agencies such as the World Bank, importation of Western technology, education of large numbers of young people in the universities of the developed world, and expansion of world trade, it was confidently expected that the advantages of industrialization would be experienced by a substantial and increasing proportion of the world's growing community of sovereign states. So great were the stakes in this worldwide process that the Soviet Union, the United States, and to some extent even China entered into a vigorous competition over which form—socialist or capitalist—this process would ultimately take.

The Soviet Union and the United States still compete overtly and covertly for influence in the countries of the underdeveloped world, but it has become increasingly clear that neither the aid and influence of the superpowers nor that of lesser powers involved in the Third World ensures that economic development will happen at all. The underdeveloped countries face enormous obstacles in their path, not least of which is the rapid growth in their populations. In many Third World countries, respectable levels of economic growth have occurred since the 1950s, but increases in agricultural and industrial production have been offset by increasing numbers of people, causing average personal incomes to remain steady or even decline. In the developed world, economic development was accompanied by a net migration of population from rural to urban areas as increasing agricultural efficiency meant that fewer people were needed to work the land and jobs opened up in the new factories and offices. In much of the underdeveloped world, population growth in rural areas has caused a migration to the cities to take place without a level of industrialization sufficient to absorb the influx of labor. Many governments find it necessary to expend large sums in subsidizing food prices for their urban populations in order to prevent massive suffering and violence—money which might have been used for economic development.

This problem may be addressed either in the countryside or in the cities, but each strategy has its obstacles. Consider first the countryside. In some countries, including Mexico and many other Latin American states, large agricultural holdings *(latifundia)* are concentrated in the hands of a few elite landowners. These landowners often pay their workers extremely low wages and use repressive measures to keep them in line; politically, their wealth and influence make governments especially responsive to their interests, which include the prevention of significant land reform. At the other extreme are the *multifundia:* countries such as France and Nigeria with profusions of small landowners. Their more equitable distribution of land helps to satisfy a basic peasant drive for land ownership, but the small size of the holdings, especially where inheritance systems result in subdivision of plots among the deceased's children, can condemn their owners to poverty. Smallholdings are especially vulnerable to indebtedness and loss of ownership by farmers unable to survive hard times. If farm subsidies or high tariffs on food imports are used to help this sector, however, the result can often be a drain on scarce government resources and maintenance of inefficient forms of agriculture that ultimately retard overall economic development.

Some countries have responded to this dilemma by creating agricultural cooperatives, in which private ownership of land is replaced by some form of collective possession. The Soviet Union was the first country to attempt a state-run collectivized agricultural system, but the results have been mixed at best. The elimination of the aristocracy ended the exploitation of the peasantry by a rich and largely idle class of landowners, but the fact that the peasants work land that is not theirs means that their efforts are less than wholeheartedly enthusiastic. The Soviet Union is richly endowed with arable land, but agricultural production has repeatedly fallen behind projected levels and the government has frequently had to import food from Western countries.

Agricultural production in the Third World has been aided by the scientific breakthroughs of the "green revolution," notably the development of high-yielding seeds that have increased the output of wheat, rice, and other crops enormously. Today, more than enough food is produced overall to feed the entire world's population. However, such yields require additional inputs including fertilizers, pesticides, and irrigation, and because the richer farmers are best able to avail themselves of these inputs, the disparity between rich and poor farmers often increases. Other modernizing developments have also had negative consequences. Many developing countries were encouraged to move away from subsistence agriculture and develop cash crops that could be sold on the international market; the profits could then be devoted to industrial development. Unfortunately for these countries, world prices for primary products such as agricultural goods tend to fluctuate wildly, and when prices are low a country can easily be caught in a closing vise as its revenues from foreign sales are dramatically reduced and its overspecialization in one or two cash crops denies it the ability to feed itself. Often, the only available remedy in these circumstances is borrowing from abroad to pay for food and other imports, a step which increases a government's foreign debt without contributing to its economic development or its ability to pay off that debt.

The alternative of encouraging industrial development has been equally plagued with paradoxes. One means of attempting to advance industrialization is through foreign investment. Companies from the developed world often find it advantageous to build factories in Third World countries because of their low wage rates, weak labor movements, and favorable tax structures, but the net effect of these investments on standards of living is usually quite marginal. Even investment projects involving hundreds of millions of dollars may offer permanent employment to only a few hundred or at most a few thousand individuals. Those employed in these enterprises earn good wages by local standards and often have fairly Westernized life-styles, but the gap between them and the rest of the population can be very wide. With a low standard of living overall, there often is little domestic market for manufactured goods; the factories created by foreign investment remain as isolated reminders of what has not been achieved, rather than sparks to stimulate the industrialization of the country. In such circumstances, the purchasing power of this new elite may be oriented toward imported products from the developed world rather than indigenous products, reducing the possibility of beneficial "spin-off" effects on the rest of the economy. Foreign investment thus may contribute more to developing a small Westernized elite eager to hang on to its privileges than to developing the country as a whole. Often, bribery and corruption become the methods by which this elite maintains its wealth, privileges, and power, and what resources are available are diverted into these channels rather than being used for their intended purpose.

The narrow impact of foreign investment on the economy, as well as the degree of foreign influence that it brings, has encouraged many Third World countries to attempt to insulate themselves from the world market. Frequently this involves the creation of state-owned industries and the erection of tariff barriers to minimize foreign competition. In communist countries, these methods were extended to include nationalization of most or all firms and strict control of imports, with the potential for problems noted in the previous section. Other countries attempt to combine nationalization with private enterprise and use high tariffs to limit but not cut off the entry of foreign goods. The problem with this strategy is that insulation from market forces can often spare domestic firms the need to make themselves as efficient as possible; nationalized firms, especially if they hold monopoly positions in their countries, may become prone not only to inefficiency but also to patronage and corruption. The result may be much slower growth than would occur if firms had to compete on more equal terms with each other or with foreign products. At worst, scarce government resources may be channeled into maintaining money-losing nationalized industries because they represent symbols of national independence, because they have become powerful corporate interests that the government dare not offend, or because they are valuable sources of patronage jobs for government supporters.

The challenge of economic development is thus a severe one. Industrialized countries of the capitalist West enjoy the highest standards of living in the world (apart from certain small oil kingdoms), but to many Third World leaders the benefits of economic development seem reserved for a select few countries. The argument of Western leaders that unfettered market forces can bring about economic prosperity seems suspect to many of them—especially in light of economic problems the developed countries are facing—and the experience of foreign investment has not been encouraging. On the other hand, the Soviet pattern of development, although impressive in its early stages, has clearly failed to match the performance of the capitalist model. Even if its success were not in doubt, it entails a degree of government control that exceeds the capabilities of many Third World countries. Various hybrid combinations of the two models have too often been marred by favoritism, excessive protectionism, patronage, and corruption to be effective instruments of development.

The challenges facing the developed countries are also daunting, although the level of economic prosperity is much higher. Within the capitalist world, divisions of opinion over economic theory and policy are perhaps more intense and more politicized than they have ever been, and an era of full employment and dependable economic growth has given way to one of rapid technological change, severe economic dislocations, and much harsher international competition. The intensification of technological competition in the West has made much clearer the relative backwardness of the socialist bloc economies, and the early response of importing Western technology—although still very much in evidence—has yielded to a realization that significant changes must be wrought in the structure of socialist economies if they are to keep up in the future. Steps toward stimulating private enterprise and initiative have begun, but the question of how far they should or must go still remains unresolved.

BRITAIN AND FRANCE: MANAGING ADVANCED CAPITALISM

Britain and France represent a significant contrast in the management of capitalist economies. Although the extent to which British governments have been prepared to intervene in the economy has at times been considerable—such as during the massive nationalizations of private firms in the 1940s or the price and wage controls of the 1970s—the basic approach of both Conservative and Labour governments has been a laissez-faire or noninterventionist one. In France, governments have been much more willing to guide or direct the economy, enlisting the cooperation of private industry in the achievement of goals which are essentially state-defined. The French approach seems to have met with greater success, but both countries today face serious economic challenges that have brought their different styles of economic management into question.

Britain: A Managed Economy

Britain entered the post-World War II era with a strong national consensus that economic conditions must never be allowed to return to their prewar depressed state. During the war, the British government—which was a coalition of all three parties—committed itself to the goals of full employment and the provision of social services "from the cradle to the grave." In the 1945 general election, the electorate rejected their wartime leader, Winston Churchill, and his Conservatives in favor of the Labour party, which was more closely associated with these goals. In power, Labour embarked on an ambitious program of nationalizing key industrial sectors (including coal, steel, railroads, road transportation, gas, electricity, and the Bank of England) and extending social services, most notably by creating the National Health Service to provide medical care to all without charge. For the most part, the (mainly Conservative) governments that followed in the next three decades accepted this thrust. By 1981 nearly one-third of the work force was employed by the state; the nationalized industries alone employed 8 percent of the work force and accounted for 11 percent of the total output of goods and services in the country.

Since the Labour party had been created to defend the interests of the trade unions, it resisted any suggestion that government involvement in the economy should be extended to free collective bargaining. Business leaders, too, preferred to remain free of government interference, and the result was that little attempt was made to develop an elaborate role for the government in economic planning after the war. Instead, governments of both parties settled for the Keynesian strategy of manipulating tax rates, credit, and government spending in order to achieve full employment. Wartime controls on industry, for example, were dismantled as soon as it was feasible to do so.

The goal of full employment was largely realized in the 1950s and 1960s but, unfortunately, Britain was not able to achieve the high rates of growth that continental European countries enjoyed. Instead, the British economy fell into a disastrous "stop-go" cycle as government efforts to employ the Keynesian strategy of increasing economic growth by stimulating consumer demand led to massive influxes of imports, balance-of-payment problems, and attacks on the pound sterling and had to be abruptly cut short on several occasions. In the 1960s attempts were made to introduce longer-term economic planning, but these initiatives got no further than the establishment of committees in which labor, industry, and government representatives could consult with one another. As inflation accelerated in the 1970s, exceeding levels experienced by Britain's competitors, both compulsory pay freezes and voluntary pay limits were attempted, but many unions either ignored them or undermined their results by seeking (and often getting) catch-up wage increases after the controls had been removed.

Table 8.3   BRITAIN'S SLOW GROWTH COMPARED TO FRANCE AND THE EUROPEAN
COMMUNITY

	Average annual increase in gross national product per capita[a] (%)				
	1961–1965	1965–1970	1971–1975	1976–1980	1981–1985
Britain	2.5	2.0	2.0	1.7	1.3
France	4.5	4.5	3.2	2.8	0.7
European Community	3.7	3.8	2.2	2.8	0.9

[a]Gross national product (GNP) is the total value of goods and services produced in a year. The table shows increases in GNP after the effects of inflation have been removed.
Source: U.S. Central Intelligence Agency, Handbook of Economic Statistics, 1986.

The increasing economic difficulties facing Britain forced governments to attempt various other strategies for improving the country's economic performance. In 1971 the Conservative government of Edward Heath passed the Industrial Relations Act, which made labor contracts legally enforceable and introduced a set of industrial tribunals to regulate labor relations. This legislation was actively resisted by the union movement, however, and a worsening climate of labor relations culminated in a long and bitter coalminers' strike during a period of severe oil shortages in 1973–1974.[1] With the energy-starved British economy half shut down, the Conservative government called an election on the issue of "Who rules, the government or the unions?"—and lost. The new Labour government promptly repealed the Industrial Relations Act and entered into a "social contract" with the unions. Under the social contract, the government agreed to increase welfare benefits in return for a commitment from the Trades Union Congress (TUC) to limit wage demands in order to curtail skyrocketing inflation rates. The agreement held for a few years, but by 1978 rank-and-file pressure to end wage restraint led several unions to strike for wage increases above the government's guidelines, and the unpopularity of these often bitter strikes during what was termed "the winter of discontent" contributed significantly to the electoral victory of Margaret Thatcher's Conservatives in 1979.

Another initiative of the Heath government aimed at stopping economic decline was the commitment to resist pressures to come to the assistance of troubled or declining industries. But when Rolls Royce—one of the world's largest manufacturers of aircraft engines—went bankrupt in 1973, the government felt obliged to rescue it. Throughout the 1970s, enormous government funds were poured into such failing industrial sectors as shipbuilding and automobiles. The loss of jobs that would have followed the bankruptcy of such large enterprises seemed too great a price to pay for strict adherence to the rule of the market. Critics charged, however, that the money would have been better spent on newer industries such as computing and biotechnology than on industries whose prospects for expansion and profitability were poor.

Another foray in the attempt to restore Britain's sagging economic fortunes involved membership in the European Community (EC), more commonly known as the Common Market. The six countries which formed the EC in 1957 sought to promote the economic integration of West Europe by adopting common economic and social policies and by removing barriers to trade among themselves. Among their most noteworthy achievements was the creation of the Common Agricultural Policy (CAP), which established common price support levels for farm produce across the EC. At first, Britain was reluctant to join the EC, but as the economic success of the Common Market countries became evident,

---

[1]The oil shortages were caused by the Organization of Petroleum Exporting Countries (OPEC), an Arab-dominated cartel, which cut off oil exports in response to what it saw as Western support for Israel in the 1973 Arab-Israeli war.

both Labour and Conservative parties grew more favorable to the idea. In the 1960s Britain's applications to join were rejected on two occasions, however, mainly because President de Gaulle of France believed that Britain was too closely associated with her overseas Commonwealth and with American interests to be a suitable partner in the construction of a more integrated Europe. Under President Pompidou, France became more favorably disposed to admitting Britain into the Common Market, and Britain formally joined in 1973.

Unfortunately, the year of Britain's accession to the Community was also the year that saw the OPEC oil embargo and the end of the long postwar economic expansion. Since 1973, economic growth within the EC has declined to a much lower level than was experienced in the 1960s, and it is not clear whether accession to the Community has been a net benefit to Britain's overall economic performance. In addition, the EC is structured in a way that is fundamentally at odds with Britain's economic needs. Because of the CAP, the Community allocates the lion's share of its total expenditures to agricultural subsidies, and only a relatively small proportion is available for industrial aid. Britain has a highly efficient agricultural sector, which is not in great need of subsidies, but a troubled industrial sector which could well benefit from greater Community assistance. Moreover, because Britain's agricultural sector is very small, employing only about 1.6 percent of the work force, Britain ends up paying far more to the EC through taxes and tariffs than it receives in payments to farmers. The irony of one of the poorer members of the EC (in terms of income per capita) paying greater net contributions than any other member state has not been lost on British governments, and they have been able to negotiate rebates from the Community on part of their excess contributions. But the basic problem remains: only a fundamental reform of the CAP would allow a significant reallocation of Community spending, but countries such as France and West Germany, with highly influential (and less efficient) farming sectors, are opposed to revamping the system which benefits them so well.

The Conservative government of Margaret Thatcher came to power in 1979 with a commitment to reduce government intervention and subsidization of the British economy and to tame the power of the unions. The immediate task of controlling inflation was handled by allowing interest rates to rise to unprecedented levels (as in other countries), and in the recession of the early 1980s the government held firm in its resolve not to rescue failing companies. Rising unemployment undermined the power of the unions, and the government succeeded in introducing some modest measures to limit union rights. In addition, government spending on many social services was cut, even though opinion polls continued to show that Britons would prefer paying higher taxes to reducing social expenditures. Prime Minister Thatcher saw the task of her government as one of creating the conditions under which the market economy could operate as freely as possible, and expenditure cuts were matched wherever feasible by tax cuts, which mainly benefited the better-off.

The government was aided in its task of reducing its borrowing and taxation by the huge revenues generated by the new oil fields of the North Sea and by the profits earned by selling off a variety of nationalized companies. The sale of British Telecom, the government-owned telephone and telecommunications company, was the largest stock offering in world history, and other major publicly owned companies, including British Air and British Gas, also brought in huge revenues to the Treasury. These sales represent the first major challenge to the postwar consensus on a mixed (partly public, partly private) economy, and it is the Conservatives' hope that by giving millions of Britons the opportunity to own stock in formerly nationalized companies, a taste for the private market economy will be inculcated throughout the population.

The overall record of the Thatcher government's experiment in monetarism and free-market economics is hotly debated in Britain. In its favor are the facts that inflation has been tamed, British economic growth has kept pace with the rest of Europe since 1980, and the productivity of industry has been rising faster in Britain than in most other countries. Mrs. Thatcher believes that if her policies are continued for a number of years, these trends will persist and the British economy will have become highly competitive and prosperous once again. The negative side of the record is worrisome, however. Unemployment rose from about 1 million to over 3 million by the mid-1980s, and Labour critics argue that the figure would have been over 4 million if the government had not changed the way it counts the unemployed. The output from

Many regions in Britain, particularly in the Celtic peripheries, have suffered enormously from the declines in traditional industries. Here, a desolate village in the once-prosperous coal-mining region of South Wales. (© David Hum/Magnum)

industry reached only 1979 levels in 1987, which may mean that the rise in productivity in the intervening years was due simply to the shedding of excess labor by hard-pressed firms rather than to any profound structural changes in British industry. More ominously, Britain became a net importer of manufactured goods for the first time since the early nineteenth century. Since Britain must also import about half of her foodstuffs, a trading surplus in manufactured goods or services is essential if Britain is to balance its books with the rest of the world. For the time being, the shortfall is made up largely by the export of North Sea oil, but the North Sea wells are rapidly becoming depleted and production is expected to decline sharply in the 1990s.

Recoiling from the high levels of unemployment, the Labour opposition has become less sympathetic to the free-market economy. The party is not yet prepared to adopt a program of socialization of the economy (although it does promise some renationalization of companies the Thatcher government has sold off), but there are strong forces within the party calling for an "alternative economic strategy." This strategy would involve erecting tariff barriers to reverse the job loss created by foreign imports and developing a strong government role in economic planning, including the ability of government to influence the direction and level of investment by private firms. Because this policy goes so strongly against the grain of British experience and would invite retaliation from the United States and the European Community in the form of tariffs against British products, it has not met with great popularity outside some party and academic circles. However, it does serve to illustrate the extent of the divergence in economic thinking in present-day Britain, and it underscores the seriousness of the economic problems facing a country which was once "the workshop of the world" and is now riddled with unemployment and threatened by foreign competition.

France: A Concerted Economy

France's economic performance since World War II has been little short of remarkable. Traditionally regarded as relatively backward in economic terms, with lower standards of living, less industrialization, and a larger peasant population than most developed countries, France embarked on a postwar "economic miracle" that catapulted the country to the forefront of economic development and prosperity. At first apprehensive about foreign competition, French industry found it could compete successfully in the larger markets of the EC. As industry flourished, an enormous migration to the cities eliminated many of the small, unprofitable peasant farms and opened the way for more efficient agricultural production. In the boom era from the late 1950s to the early 1970s, France experienced the highest growth rates in West Europe.

This turnaround was not the result of the unleashing of market forces. France has long had a tradition of state involvement in industry, and the experience of defeat and occupation by the Germans convinced many French leaders that the state must be used to build France's industrial strength to a level that would preclude further humiliations of that sort. Two tools were chosen for this task. One was the development, in cooperation with business and labor groups, of national plans to shape the directions of economic development; the other was the utilization of institutions under state control, including the Bank of France and other lending institutions nationalized after the 1944 liberation, to ensure that the priorities of the plans were respected.

The first plan (1946–1953) concentrated on rebuilding basic industries such as steel, cement, transportation, electricity, and agricultural machinery and fertilizers. These priorities were developed through a series of Modernization Commissions in the Planning Office, which brought together representatives of industry, labor, and state planners, and were subsequently ratified by the National Assembly. With the objective of the first plan achieved, subsequent plans have focused on such concerns as controlling inflation (especially in the 1970s), reducing unemployment, and enhancing international competitiveness (the 1980s).

The French refer to this process as one of "concertation," and this is usually interpreted to mean that, unlike planning in socialist states, French planning involves an essentially *voluntary* collaboration between government and the private sector. Although this is true, strictly speaking, the French state has powerful weapons to induce reluctant firms to cooperate with the plans' objectives. The state has influenced the private sector (a) through its massive buying power and its control, via the nationalized firms, of energy and transportation, (b) through its price controls and ability to grant exemptions if firms cooperate, (c) through its control of lending rates and limits, and (d) through large investment funds that it makes available to firms which invest according to the plan.

Although France has rarely been ruled by left-wing governments, the nationalized or public sector of the economy is one of the largest in the Western world. The French state controlled a number of monopolies (such as tobacco, telegraphs, and telephones) before the war, but it was during the liberation period that a truly massive expansion in state ownership was undertaken. The railroad, mining, electricity, gas, and nuclear energy industries, most of air and sea transportation, aircraft production, and banking, as well as sizable proportions of the insurance, automobile, and housing industries, became state-owned. With the aid of Marshall Plan funds from the United States, French planners were able to direct large sums of money into rebuilding the largely nationalized transportation and energy infrastructures of the country in the early postwar years, and since that time French governments have used their own resources to stimulate the development of industries where they perceive the national interest to be at stake. One prominent example is nuclear energy. Lacking significant coal, oil, or hydroelectric energy,

France has developed one of the largest nuclear energy programs in the world—some would argue the most successful as well. Where other Western countries have curtailed or halted their development of nuclear power in response to concerns over safety and the storage of nuclear waste, French governments have forged ahead to the point where nuclear power now provides most of the country's energy needs.

This enormous increase in government involvement in the economy was matched in social matters. France, like other West European countries, was able to channel much of its growing prosperity into social programs ranging from a national medical care plan to a huge expansion in the size and number of universities. One of the most unusual of these measures provides generous benefits to large families. Convinced that the defeat at the hands of the Germans in 1940 was due partly to France's smaller and declining population, French governments have maintained that the country is substantially underpopulated and that the state must intervene to stimulate population growth. The effect of this program is, however, uncertain; although the average number of children per family did increase in the 1950s and 1960s, it has declined in the economically more uncertain 1970s and 1980s.

The planning approach to economic and social development has diminished in importance as France has reached industrial maturity and as the more difficult post-1973 economic climate has tempted political leaders to control economic decision-making more closely. France's ability to go its own way economically is more limited now because its economy is much more integrated into the Common Market and the world economy. Problems originating from abroad, such as the oil embargo of 1973 and the rapid oil price rises of the 1970s, can easily disrupt the best of plans. Nevertheless, the planning process is still used to direct state investments in areas such as nuclear energy that have been identified as national priorities, and the state's role in directing the economy is still recognized as fundamental to France's future economic success.

The victory of the Socialists under François Mitterrand in 1981 led to a large increase in state involvement in the economy. The Socialists embarked on a massive program of nationalizing private firms, including the rest of the banking sector, and attempted to provide relief from the recession of the early 1980s by creating 200,000 new public sector jobs, shortening the work week, and increasing social benefits. This essentially Keynesian solution to the recession depended on the assumption that the world economy, and therefore France's, was about to enter a period of expansion which would increase government revenues to pay for these reforms. Unfortunately, the expected economic expansion never occurred, and as the franc slumped on international money markets, the government was forced to cut back spending, increase taxes, and even control wages and prices for a while. One commitment remained, however: the commitment to state investment. Not only did Mitterrand's government increase the funding available for research and development, it also launched the Eureka project, which now involves most West European governments in a program of stimulating research in areas of high technology to enable Europe to keep pace technologically with the United States and Japan.

In 1986 the Socialists lost control of the National Assembly to a right-wing coalition of Gaullists and Giscardians led by Jacques Chirac. Although the widespread nationalizations of the liberation period and the heavy use of state power to influence economic development are part of de Gaulle's legacy, the Gaullists under Chirac have become more influenced by the monetarist and laissez-faire ideas dominant in the United States and Britain. One of Chirac's first steps was to begin to denationalize the firms nationalized under the Socialists, and he also wanted to denationalize firms taken over under de Gaulle during the liberation period. Chirac's goal is to create a freer market economy, without price controls or the state's predominant role in shaping future economic trends. His ability to convince voters of the viability of this strategy is hindered, however, because the French have come to associate economic prosperity with state planning and state guidance of the economy. In 1988, Chirac lost the presidential election to Mitterrand and lost his majority in the National Assembly as well; for the time being, the nationalized industries are secure in Socialist hands.

The guidance that has helped French industry expand and modernize since the war was also employed to restructure agriculture. France's slow and incomplete industrialization had left the country with millions of peasants barely subsisting on small plots of land. Increases in agricultural productivity and profitability clearly depended on creating larger farms that could employ tractors and other machinery to increase output. When the EC's Common Agricultural Policy was established, its objective was to set price supports at levels which would gradually force smaller farmers off the land. Stimulated by the availability of jobs in France's expanding industries, huge migrations from the countryside did occur, and the proportion of the labor force employed in agriculture has declined from nearly 40 percent before the war to about 9 percent today. This trend has been slowed, however, by efforts of farmers' organizations since the 1960s to defend their way of life. The objective of these groups is to keep price supports at levels high enough to preserve the livelihoods of all their members, and they have proved quite willing to protest and demonstrate to draw attention to their views. As the Gaullists and the Giscardians came to rely more on the votes of the farmers and other more traditional sectors such as small shopkeepers, they became more susceptible to these appeals. Defending the income of farmers in the councils of the EC is much more popular than collaborating in a process of forcing them off the land—especially as high levels of unemployment mean that there are few jobs in the cities for farmers to go to. Similarly, defending small shopkeepers against the intrusions of supermarkets and the even larger "hypermarkets" earns votes for right-wing parties. Although both policies mean higher prices for consumers, even the Socialists—who pride themselves on defending the little man—find it difficult not to follow suit.

Agriculture is likely to become a major source of challenge in the future. The CAP has been very successful in stimulating agricultural output, but it finds itself in the position of having to buy up enormous quantities of produce for which there is no demand within the Community. The costs involved have greatly angered the British, but the CAP's policy of selling the surplus abroad at subsidized rates has equally angered the Americans and other large agricultural producers, who fear the loss of their export markets. The CAP, and with it the fate of millions of French farmers, has now become an international issue.

France at the present time finds itself at a crossroads. It has followed a unique and successful strategy of planned industrial development and, through the CAP, planned agricultural development as well, but both are now threatened by international forces. The Socialist government of 1981–1986 found that it is extremely difficult to follow a policy of economic expansion when the rest of the Western world is moving in the opposite direction. Even when French economic policy is not at odds with economic policy elsewhere, factors outside France's control, such as the price of oil, can easily disrupt it. The agricultural policies of the EC, which have benefited France's farmers greatly, are now challenged from inside the Community (Britain) and outside it (the United States) and no longer serve the goals of agricultural modernization. The present French government is attempting to remove the heavy hand of state influence from the economy, a policy more in line with policies in other Western countries, but it is not certain that economic performance will improve as a result. The successes of planning in the past and the seriousness of the economic challenge from abroad in the present suggest that the French state will continue to play a large economic role in the future.

THE SOVIET UNION AND CHINA: EXPERIMENTING WITH "MARKET SOCIALISM"

For most of their postrevolutionary histories, the Soviet Union and China have followed economic policies inspired by the pressing impetus to industrialize as rapidly as possible and structured by the Stalinist model of the command economy, an economic system owned by the state and directed by state planners. The intent in developing the command economy was to produce a system based on principles totally different from capitalist ones and capable of achieving results far better than capitalism could. These better results were to include not just faster growth and greater prosperity but also a more equal distribution of wealth than was normal in Western economies. Although the successes of the command economies in these two countries should not be underestimated, both countries are now involved in fascinating attempts to overcome the shortcomings that are increasingly evident in their economies by introducing greater reliance on market incentives and private enterprise. How far these experiments will be allowed to go and what effects they will have economically, socially, and politically are major unanswered questions in the study of communist regimes.

Soviet Union: The Ups and Downs of a Command Economy

No country in the world has undergone greater socioeconomic change in the past hundred years than Russia. A profoundly traditional society, Russia was jolted by the industrialization program of Tsar Nicholas II, but by the time of the first World War Russia still remained far behind Western and Central Europe. The ravages of the war plus three years of civil conflict reduced industrial production by 1920 to less than one-fourth the level of 1913. In the course of Lenin's NEP program (1921–1928), the economy managed to recover the ground lost, and the Stalinist policies of the following decade propelled the Soviet Union into the ranks of the world's industrial powers. Another world war set the country back again, and it was not until 1952 that the economy recovered to 1939 levels. Yet, five years later the Soviets shocked the world by launching the first artificial satellite, *Sputnik* ("fellow traveler"), into outer space, and by the end of the 1970s it was clear that the soviet military-industrial complex had achieved a warmaking capacity second to none. However, this was achieved at the expense of Soviet consumers, whose standard of living to this day is far below that of their Western counterparts and even below that of some other communist countries such as East Germany and Czechoslovakia.

Soviet leaders have never questioned the assumption that the state is responsible for planning and managing the economy, as well as providing a wide range of social benefits for its citizens. Thus, in addition to directly taking charge of economic production, the Soviet state administers a free, universal, and comprehensive health care program and provides tuition-free education at all levels (and even subsidizes living expenses for students in institutions of higher education). The state provides day care and summer camps for children, paid maternity leave, and old-age pensions; it subsidizes housing and invests generously in sports, culture, and other public activities. The quality of social goods and services can vary from region to region, and there is evidence that in many aspects—especially housing and medical care—it is everywhere lower than what middle-class Westerners would find acceptable, but in contrast to the United States with its large permanent "underclass," no Soviet citizen is excluded from standard services such as medical care.

Since the Bolshevik Revolution, the government's long-term social goal has been consistent even if its methods of pursuing it have varied. That goal has been the development of the Soviet Union into an economically advanced society capable of defending itself against its enemies while providing the material basis for a prosperity that can be shared by all. It was Lenin's belief that while the Soviet Union was progressing toward its goal of prosperity, workers' revolutions would topple the imperialist governments of other industrialized countries, and they would no longer threaten the existence of the Soviet state. Subsequent events have proved Lenin wrong on this count, and successive Soviet governments have believed it necessary to make military preparedness their first economic priority. In the current era, the government has maintained parity in the arms race with the United States while simultaneously policing its East European empire and striving to play the role of a global superpower elsewhere. With a gross national product only about one-half that of the United States, the Soviet Union has skimped on butter and invested heavily in guns.

The system of state planning and management which makes such a choice possible took on its basic structure during the 1920s and 1930s. Under the NEP the state was already centrally involved as the owner of heavy industry, transport, communications, and banking, but it restricted its planning activity to an essentially regulatory role. The Stalinist "Third Revolution" greatly increased the state's powers, eliminating all private ownership of land and capital and putting the central planners totally in command of economic resources. The first five-year plan was inaugurated in 1928; the plan in effect from 1986 to 1990 is the twelfth FYP.

At the apex of the economic policy-making structure today are the CPSU Politburo and the Council of Ministers (especially its Presidium). The Politburo makes broad decisions, such as those determining the share of resources to be devoted to military production, consumer goods, or agriculture. The Council of Ministers supervises a number of important specialized committees and agencies, including, first and foremost, the State Planning Agency (GOSPLAN) and the central bank (GOSBANK). The separate ministries are responsible for the sectors into which economic activity is divided—more than 100 in all—and GOSPLAN undertakes to coordinate the sectors, balancing the material requirements and fitting together the overall plan in all its details.

In industry, the system produced remarkable results during the first three decades of central command planning. (See Table 8.4.) Excluding the years of World War II, annual growth rates were higher than those of any other industrial country during a comparable period of its development. As a result, the Soviet Union achieved its basic industrialization with a speed unprecedented in history. Moving beyond that level, however, has proved to be difficult. Since the late 1960s the economy has slowed down; productivity has declined, and technology—outside the military sector—has lagged. The bureaucracy has become overwhelmed by the complexity of planning, and because of the centralized structure of command, individual plants and sectors are unable to innovate significantly. Growth rates have declined to levels that are consistently low, and FYP targets have not been met. (See Table 8.5.)

Soviet agriculture has never done well since it was collectivized. In

Table 8.4 SOVIET INDUSTRIAL GROWTH, 1928–1958

| Years | Average annual rate of growth in industrial production[a] (%) | |
	Soviet figure	Nutter estimate
1928–1937	16.3	12.1
1950–1955	13.1	9.6
1955–1958	10.3	7.1

[a]Official Soviet figures, given in the middle column, are presumed to be inaccurate. Independent data are not available except in the form of various estimates by Western economists. Those of W. G. Nutter, published in his book *Growth of Industrial Production in the Soviet Union* (Princeton, N.J.: Princeton University Press, 1962), represent the low limiting case, and one might justly guess that the truth lies somewhere between the two figures given for each time period. All the above data are cited from David A. Dyker, *The Soviet Economy* (New York: St. Martin's, 1976), p. 18.

Table 8.5 SOVIET GROWTH RATES, PLANNED AND ACTUAL

| Years | Average annual rate of growth: actual and (planned) (%) | | |
	GNP	Industry	Agriculture
1966–1970	5.0 (6.5)	6.2 (8.2)	3.7 (5.5)
1971–1975	3.0 (5.8)	5.4 (8.0)	−0.4 (3.7)
1976–1980	2.3 (5.0)	2.6 (6.5)	1.0 (5.0)
1981–1985	2.0 (4.0)	2.0 (4.9)	2.0 (5.0)

Source: U.S. Central Intelligence Agency, *Handbook of Economic Statistics, 1986*, p. 64.

the early years of the collectivization drive, many peasants resisted by slaughtering their animals and sometimes taking violent action against the authorities. The authorities' retaliation cost millions of human lives in what Stalin once described to Winston Churchill, in the middle of World War II, as his most difficult battle. In time, the government made a small concession to the peasants, allowing each household to farm a small "kitchen plot" privately as long as every individual contributed his or her share of work to the collective. The kitchen plots today make up no more than 3 percent of tilled farmland, but they produce as much as one-fourth of the USSR's food and, because their products are usually sold for higher prices than those of the collective, they account for as much as one-half or more of a given collective farm's income.[2]

Shortcomings in agricultural production have continued to plague

[2]D. Gale Johnson, "Agricultural Organization and Management," in Abram Bergson and Herbert S. Levine, eds., *The Soviet Economy: Toward the Year 2000* (London: Allen & Unwin, 1983), p. 124.

Large collective farms or *kolkhozy* dominate the rural landscapes of the Soviet Union. Here the wheat crop is being harvested at the V. I. Lenin *kolkhoz,* Moscow Region. (TASS from Sovfoto)

the Soviet economy and, together with lagging industrial output, signal a slow but definite crisis. In the consumer sectors, goods of inferior quality are produced, and to make matters worse, shoppers find chronic shortages of many items ranging from meat to toilet paper. As a result, workers lack incentive and morale is poor. Piecemeal changes introduced during the Brezhnev years failed to address the underlying structural problems, to which there are no easy solutions. Central accounting has become chaotic, as data processing technology has not kept up with the scope of the task. The arbitrary pricing system conceals inflationary pressures and makes it difficult for planners to calculate real costs. The very size and cumbersomeness of the command system ensure that waste, mismanagement, and corruption abound. In short, the economic structures have long been in need of major reform.

Ideas about structural changes in the economy have been discussed in the Soviet Union since the mid-1950s. During the 1960s controversy centered on proposals developed by the economist Yevsei Liberman, who adhered to the central planning model but advocated a change in the way success was measured; instead of aiming at gross output targets, Liberman argued, the plan should point industry toward greater efficiency by focusing on enterprise profits. To Western economists, this idea seemed commonsensical and indeed modest, but it implied a decentralization of control that many Soviet leaders found disturbing. "Libermanism" actually represented the middle ground between economists who advocated a still greater degree of decentralization and those who opposed any lessening of the central planners' authority. Prime Minister Aleksei Kosygin, seeking to create a consensus, persuaded the party and government to enact a partial reform that left the basic structures and practices intact, leading one Western observer to dub the program "The Reform That Never Was."[3]

In the meantime, Communist governments in Czechoslovakia and Hungary debated programs of decentralization and market pricing that went beyond the discussions in the Soviet Union. The Czech program was cut short when the reformist government fell following a Soviet military intervention, but the Hungarians enacted a sweeping reform which went into effect in 1968. Taken further during the 1980s, Hungary's policies have transformed that small country's economy into a mixture of state, cooperative, and private enterprise. Soviet leaders have watched the Hungarian developments with interest and periodically expressed their cautious support.

It was apparent that Soviet General Secretary Andropov, who succeeded Brezhnev, had economic reform in mind, but Andropov fell ill after only nine months in office, leaving policy matters in limbo. His successor, Chernenko, showed no great enthusiasm for major reform initiatives, and it was left to Gorbachev to make the official push for change. By the middle of 1987 the outlines of the Gorbachev program had fallen into shape, and the general secretary had secured for them the approval of the Politburo, the Central Committee, and the Supreme Soviet. Consciously recalling Lenin's NEP, the reforms envision a major decentralization of economic authority. The central ministries and such agencies as GOSPLAN will remain, but their responsibility will be reduced to that of drawing up guidelines, leaving to factories and enterprises the task of making detailed plans and setting wages. Gorbachev's advisers anticipate that, rather than being propped up by state subsidies (as has been the case), inefficient plants will be allowed

---

[3]Alec Nove, "The USSR: The Reform That Never Was," in L. Dellin and H. Gross, eds., *Reforms in the Soviet and East European Economies* (Lexington, Mass.: Heath, 1972).

to go under. Instead of progressing toward the goal of equality, the reformers accept the likelihood that wage inequalities will increase as the more efficient workers are rewarded. Even before the adoption of the reforms a limited number of small private services, such as restaurants, began to spring up, and the party leadership appeared to be taking seriously the idea that some collective farms might be broken up and rented to private farmers.

The Soviet Union thus moves toward the final decade of the twentieth century by appearing to retreat from some of its long-standing policy lines. The party high command took this new path in a spirit of realism that was colored by the awareness that the risks were high. The new policies would never be put to the vote of the Soviet electorate, but the leaders knew that the workers could "vote" by refusing to cooperate, not responding to the wage incentives aimed at increasing productivity. Moreover, the Gorbachev reforms were enacted against the opposition of many influential forces in the party and the government; if the program fails, the current party leadership knows its authority is in jeopardy.

The Gorbachev economic reforms fit into the party's larger vision of Soviet purposes. The USSR's role as an international power has heavily taxed the domestic economy. Supporting revolutionary movements abroad and aiding friendly Third World governments are risky and economically unremunerative ventures. Even maintaining a system of client states just across the border in Eastern Europe now appears, in economic terms, to involve more cost than benefit.[4] Participating in the world economy, as the USSR has done through increasing levels of trade and international borrowing, has served to emphasize the difficulty of competing in a world that insists on high-quality goods. Soviet leaders have no intention of withdrawing into an isolationist stance, but they fear that in the absence of substantial change their creaking domestic structures cannot for long sustain the high cost of active global diplomacy, let alone deliver on the long-postponed promise of material abundance for Soviet workers.

Approaching the twenty-first century, Soviet leaders evince a more sober attitude about their country and its prospects than Lenin and Stalin expressed in their times. The goal of material abundance shared equitably by all is still distant, and the ruling party is less certain of how to attain it than ever before. When one considers the immensity of the USSR and begins to weigh the natural and human potential that is still largely untapped, one must stand in awe of the ultimate prospects. After two decades of stagnation, Soviet leaders hope they have discovered the key to unlocking that potential.

[4]Morris Bernstein, "Soviet Economic Growth and Foreign Policy," in S. Bialer, ed., *The Domestic Context of Soviet Foreign Policy* (Boulder, Colo.: Westview, 1981), p. 247.

China: From Mass Mobilization to Material Incentives

The revolutionary social and economic changes promised by China's communist government presupposed state control of the economy. In the beginning, the Chinese also confronted the task of reconstruction after the devastation of the long civil war and World War II. State planning was adopted on the scope of that in the Soviet Union; the government took it on itself to set production quotas and prices, as well as determine distribution, for virtually the whole economy. As in the USSR, agriculture was collectivized and industry brought under state ownership. The first five-year plan was inaugurated in 1953, giving priority to heavy industry—a preference that would be reflected through the fifth FYP (1976–1980). Party and government cadres implemented policy at all levels. Since Mao Zedong's death, however, much of this sytem has been dismantled. This dismantling has created problems, but it also continued and, in some respects, intensified progress achieved by Mao's policies.

Although industrialization initially had the highest priority, rural development was most in need of attention after 1949. With more than 80 percent of the population, rural areas were potential markets for heavy industry and, more important, a source of savings for industrial development. Even more than in the Soviet Union, communist policies in China have brought dramatic change to the countryside. The Chinese regime has tried several fundamentally different approaches to rural development. The first method involved reforms in land distribution, the pooling of machinery, and cooperative farming, but failed to solve agricultural problems or meet industrial needs. Next, in one of the boldest and most massive social experiments in history, the government fostered the formation of communes, which were to combine the functions of agricultural and industrial production, trade, education, and defense. According to this reform, enacted in 1957–1958, each commune was to be a complete and self-sustaining unit that would bring the benefits of urban life to the village: schools, hospitals, tailor shops, public laundries, and even banking. Almost immediately, however, the commune system ran into problems of worker incentive, and the party retrenched. Large communes were broken up into production brigades and teams. In 1960 private plots and free markets were again allowed, if not encouraged, and by the mid-1960s more farm implements were owned by individuals than by collectives, and more time was devoted to private plots than to communal plots.[5] However, the Great Proletarian Cultural Revolution reversed this trend; the government reestablished the communes and instituted programs aimed at creating greater equality.

After the death of Mao, the policy line turned once again. Targets for the production of grain and other crops were dramatically increased.

[5]Chao King, *Agricultural Production in Communist China, 1949–1965* (Madison: University of Wisconsin Press, 1970), p. 67.

To reach these targets, the new party leadership in the late 1970s commenced an intense effort at mechanization. To increase incentives, the state raised the prices of food grains and other staples. By 1985 all state purchasing quotas were abolished except for grain and cotton. Free-market prices increasingly guide the decisions of farmers, a major change after some 35 years of centralized pricing. The small but important free market, which has always existed in China, was officially recognized as a means of exchanging surplus products, and farmers were again allowed the open use of their private plots.

Sizeable gains in agricultural production have resulted. Between 1979 and 1982, the government reported that the value of China's agricultural output had increased by 7.5 percent annually. During the same period the average peasant's annual income had doubled to 270 yuan; by 1985 the figure had risen to 355 yuan, an annual growth rate of 15 percent.[6] The effect of these gains has been partially offset by inflation, but the increase in items of personal comfort—better houses, more motor-bikes—demonstrates that rural China has progressed. Many other developing countries can boast similar gross statistical increases in food production and commercial crops, but their regional disparities and quality of life often cannot compare favorably.

A spin-off from China's agricultural development is the growth in small rural businesses—livestock raising, construction, transportation, and small factories and tourist services, along with more traditional occupations such as handicrafts. More and more laborers not engaged in agriculture are staying in the villages to participate in the booming rural industries. These have substantially increased the income and savings of peasants, as well as provincial tax revenues, and have even contributed to the growth of exports.[7]

China's policymakers have constantly had to weigh the balance between agriculture and industry and within the industrial sectors between heavy and light industry. Before the reforms of the late 1970s, the state determined what was to be produced, where industrial plants were to be located, how much would be invested, how enterprises would be managed, how high wages were to be, and what prices would be charged for products. Heavy industry was favored over light industry, with consumer goods having a particularly low priority. Most of the government revenues came from turnover taxes of the profits from state enterprises, urban and rural, yet as late as 1980 many of these—at least 25 percent—were being operated at a loss.

Like agriculture, China's industry has passed through periodic changes of official policy. The first FYP, its emphasis powerfully weighted toward capital goods production, benefited from large doses of

    [6]Orville Schell, *To Get Rich Is Glorious: China in the 1980's* (New York: Mentor, 1986), pp. 62–63.
    [7]See *Far Eastern Economic Review* (June 4, 1987), 78–80.

Soviet assistance, particularly in the machine industry, iron and steel production, and oil refineries. At the end of the first FYP, the party proudly announced that many targets had been overfulfilled, but the overly ambitious goals of the second FYP (1958–1962) fell victim to drought, poor planning and implementation of the commune program, and withdrawal of Soviet assistance as the two largest communist states entered into a bitter conflict over ideology, policy, and other issues. Delays and political repercussions of the Great Leap Forward resulted in the postponement of the third five-year plan until 1966. Production was hampered by the struggles of the Cultural Revolution, but some progress took place as the government placed emphasis on labor-intensive, small-scale industry and sought to promote greater regional diversification in industrial investment.

The 1970s brought policies aimed at the attainment of national self-sufficiency in both industry and agriculture, as well as a cautious opening to the West in trading patterns, but it was not until the post-Mao era that the government took major steps to accelerate the modernization of China. The "Four Modernizations"—industry, agriculture, science and technology, and national defense—were to be based on something new for China: market socialism.[8] The state continued to set targets, but once an enterprise met its target, it could thereafter produce according to market demand—if demand existed. The firm could look to the market for its raw materials rather than to state sources, and prices would be set by the market where possible. To survive, firms were expected to be profitable rather than to depend on state subsidies.

Implementing these reforms presented major challenges, in particular financing the modernizations and adjusting from state to market controls. Massive foreign purchases of technology were necessary, including such big-ticket items as entire steel plants, offshore oil rigs, and computers. To finance the imports, the government sought to accelerate oil and coal production and sell more exports. In late 1978, for the first time, China agreed to accept government-to-government credits and allow direct foreign investment. Increased labor productivity has been encouraged through wage incentives and promises of shop-floor democracy.

The impact of these policies has been considerable: by 1987 it was estimated that 65 percent of all agricultural products and 40 percent of industrial raw materials were no longer subject to strict state-administered prices.[9] In other words, this commerce has found its way to the growing system of free markets. Nevertheless, problems abound. In 1986 the targets set by the state were so far above demand that massive inventories were accumulated and factories had to figure out how to dispose

[8]Market socialism had been tested and implemented in Yugoslavia beginning in the 1950s, but its adaptation to the far larger Chinese economy could never be an exact copy of the Yugoslav model.

[9]*Far Eastern Economic Review* (June 18, 1987), 75–76.

of them. Moreover, concealed unemployment exists in the form of fea-
therbedding and the overstaffing of many plants with cadres; a recent
estimate is that surplus personnel have accounted for about 15 to 20
percent of the total work force in state enterprises.[10] Pricing has been
complicated by the state's efforts to counter the impact of inflation; workers earning bonuses for their productivity, together with farmers profit-
ing from the private market for their goods, have strengthened the demand for many consumer products, but the government has tried to keep
retail prices stable to please the urban population even as the cost of
making the products goes up.

One of the reforms' impacts has been the demise of the "iron rice
bowl." Before the reforms, one could be assured of a secure job for life,
for full employment was one of the state's highest priorities. By the terms
of the reforms, however, industries do not have to keep surplus labor and
can lay off those who do not perform.[11] High unemployment has resulted
in rural and especially urban areas, and given the extent of featherbed-
ding and overstaffing, it could go much higher. One remedy for unemployment—though by no means a complete one—is the growth of private
enterprises, which in 1986 employed 11.6 million persons.[12]

The policies of market socialism and privatization are by no means
unanimously accepted by the party's leaders, and the politial debate
continues. In the 1980s party and economic leaders began asking
whether the state should continue to be the main actor in producing and
distributing the society's wealth or whether individual initiative should
take over more of these tasks—with all the social inequities that implies.
The debate on these fundamental issues provides one of the main sources
of political cleavage within the party.

China's leaders have attempted to eradicate the tangible sources of
poverty—economic underdevelopment and class barriers—but they have
also tried to change peoples' attitudes, particularly their motivation and
expectations. Socialist development, as it is understood by communists,
is based on human development. This implies more than the elimination
of poverty; it means opportunity, freedom from exploitation, and the
assurance of basic needs such as food, housing, health, and old-age care.
Full employment remains an important goal, although its realization has
been thrown into doubt by the post-1979 reforms, necessitating greater
reliance on the extensive welfare program built up since its legislative
beginnings in 1951. Workers are protected from income loss resulting
from injury, and some medical costs are paid as well. The same legisla-

---

[10]*Far Eastern Economic Review* (March 19, 1987), 77.
[11]In October 1986 the National Peoples' Congress passed a new law permitting the
hiring of workers on contract for a fixed duration, not permanently. Unemployment and
pension schemes are to be developed, with the contract workers contributing to these in
each pay period.
[12]Stanley Rosen, "China in 1986: A Year of Consolidation," *Asian Survey* (January 1,
1987), 45.

Table 8.6 COMPARISON OF OUTPUT OF MAJOR INDUSTRIAL AND
AGRICULTURAL PRODUCTS IN CHINA, 1978 AND 1986

Product	1978	1987
Grain (millions of tons)	305	391
Crude oil (millions of tons)	105	131
Cotton (millions of tons)	2.17	3.54
Pork, beef, mutton (millions of tons)	8.6	19.2
Coal (millions of tons)	618	870
Electricity (billions of kilowatt-hours)	257	446
Steel (millions of tons)	32	52
TV sets (millions)	0.5	14.5
Refrigerators (millions)	0.03	2.24
Washing machines (millions)	0.00	8.99
Cameras (millions)	0.18	2.15

Source: China Reconstructs (October 1987), 19.

tion provides for such collective welfare institutions as orphanages, sanitariums, and old-age homes.

In education, the party's policies have led to great changes since 1949. At that time, some 80 percent of the population was illiterate; within 25 years this figure had declined to less than 20 percent. Education through the primary level is now the norm, and the school system includes an extensive kindergarten program for students 3 to 6 years old. In an effort to avoid the usual dominance of higher education by the more privileged portions of society, the Chinese have made a special effort to extend the benefits of higher education to workers and peasants.

The push to modernize has required an intensified effort to train experts, technologists, and management personnel. Higher education in China had suffered from the anti-intellectual activities of the Cultural Revolution; universities shut down from 1966 to 1971, and research institutes closed their enrollments for 10 years. In 1978 China entered into agreements with several European countries, the United States, Canada, and Japan to take several thousand students from a broad range of studies, as there were at the time only 370 Chinese institutions of higher education. In subsequent years these numbers have increased, and China is simultaneously taking steps to improve its own universities and technical schools.

While education and the elimination of poverty are important to a modernizing society, both would be severely undermined by inadequate health. On the eve of liberation, there were in China fewer than 30,000 Western-trained doctors and one hospital bed for every 3200 persons; venereal disease was widespread, starvation was not uncommon, and the average life span was short. By the end of 1950 all brothels had been closed, and within a few years venereal disease had been nearly eradicated. By 1953 some 307 million people had been vaccinated against smallpox, essentially eliminating the disease; over 200,000 midwives had been retrained and 10,000 new maternal and child health workers

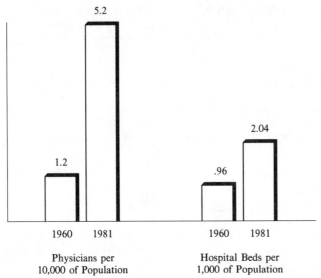

Figure 8.1 Health care services in China, 1960 and 1981. (*Source:*
World Bank, *World Tables,* 3rd ed., vol 2 (Baltimore: Johns Hopkins
University Press, 1983), p. 21.

trained.[13] Major campaigns were undertaken to eliminate parasitic diseases, rural health clinics were constructed, and a systematic effort was
devoted to the development of traditional forms of medicine such as
herbalism and acupuncture.

Over the two decades following the beginning of the first five-year
plan, China's health delivery system improved phenomenally (see Figure 8.1). The backbone of the program was the "barefoot doctor," the
name given to the many paramedics stationed throughout the country
and trained to treat less serious problems, promote preventive medicine
through public health programs, and serve as a communication link
with other health centers. These paramedics are still working, especially
in rural areas, and the public health programs are exemplary for developing countries, for they are based on clearly stated goals and a strong
governmental commitment, and they have been put into effect through
coordinated administrative efforts and widespread public support.

Overall, China finds itself with a mixed record in social and economic development. Many aspects of social policy, such as health care,
have proved highly successful and earned the regime a great deal of
support. In other areas, however, the record has been more uneven. In
education, laudable efforts to extend educational opportunities were interrupted for years by the Cultural Revolution, and China is still struggling to make up its losses in personnel trained in science and technol-

[13]Robert M. Worth, "Strategy of Change in the People's Republic of China," in Daniel
Lerner and Wilbur Schramm, eds., *Communications and Change in the Developing Countries* (Honolulu: University of Hawaii Press, 1967), p. 223.

ogy. Economic policy has experienced even greater disruptions and reversals, as ideological considerations have repeatedly taken policy in unsuccessful directions. The current emphasis on private enterprise and market mechanisms has produced impressive indications of economic growth, but it is opposed by many within the party and government hierarchies. Western countries find China's limited opening to capitalism heartening, but it is an ideologically charged decision and a sudden reversal in policy, such as has occurred several times in the past, cannot be ruled out.

MEXICO AND NIGERIA: ENDURING THE SETBACKS IN DEVELOPMENT

Mexico and Nigeria exhibit numerous qualities typical of Third World countries. The paramount challenge is rural development, for industrial development requires adequate and increasing supplies of food for a growing work force. In both countries, government action in this area has been inadequate. As the population has increased, the failures of rural development have become more evident in poverty and mass-scale migration to the cities. The governments have devoted much of their budgets to military and administrative expenses, leaving little for investment in public services, welfare, or research and technology. In the push to industrialize, both countries became dependent on foreign capital.

Mexico and Nigeria are different from most Third World countries, however, in possessing abundant oil reserves. Oil shortages and the resulting rising oil prices in the 1970s stimulated rapid economic growth in the two countries, and leaders confidently anticipated that, with such large revenues from oil, the attainment of full-scale economic development lay in the foreseeable future. With the bursting of the oil "bubble" in the 1980s, both must now face a much more difficult economic future.

Mexico: Economic Development and Nationalism

Mexico's economic policies show the same contradiction that colors its political life: claims of faith in the religion of the revolution versus realities that reflect the opposite. Popular rhetoric filled with promises of social justice, harking back to the times of Zapata and Cárdenas, coexists with the individualistic ethic of capitalism as expounded by presidents Miguel Aleman, Gustavo Diaz Ordaz, and Miguel de la Madrid. State involvement in the economy, though to some extent reversed since 1982, has generally grown over the past few decades and now includes direct ownership of major industries (such as oil and banking) and extensive regulation of private industry, imports and exports, and foreign investment; nevertheless the gap between the rich and the poor continues to grow. Mexico has been an oil-producing country since the

1930s and today has one of the largest oil reserves in the world, yet Mexico's economic development has been plagued by inflation, lack of confidence by foreign investors, levels of unemployment or underemployment exceeding 30 percent of the work force, and a lack of clear policy directions.

During the 1980s the world became familiar with Mexico's economic woes, which are serious and obdurate. Mexican cynics, long familiar with these problems, are inclined to see in their system a cycle that begins with a president entering office and assuming the "mess" of his predecessor. He spends the first three of his six years in a defensive position, trying to bring fiscal sanity to the operations of government, and the second half of his term pursuing a grandiose new development scheme to ensure that his name stands out in the history books. The scheme inevitably fails, of course, and the next administration starts the cycle again.

Mexico's economic problems begin in the countryside, for more than half the population is rural and employed in farming. Agricultural conditions are not universally good. Climate and soil conditions vary greatly; dry areas lack irrigation, whereas many of the more fertile areas frequently suffer from damaging storms. The distribution of land among peasants is very unequal, and many peasants, especially in the dry areas, barely eke out a living.

While the Mexican government recognizes the importance of rural problems, it has always had difficulty finding the means and the will to bring about the needed reforms. The government's rural development policy has had five major thrusts. First, it has experimented with land redistribution and expanded the availability of cultivatable land to the landless. Second, it has brought credit, technical services, marketing, and infrastructure (irrigation, roads, and electricity) to rural areas. Third, it has sought to increase the dispersion of industries to the countryside. In some areas, a fourth focus has been integrated regional development. And finally, the state has tried to improve rural residents' health and educational opportunities.

One of the main methods of land redistribution has been through the *ejido* movement, which came out of the Mexican Agrarian Reform Law of 1921. Under this reform, the village or community owns the land and divides it among its members. The federal government gives the individual title to the land, which can be handed down through inheritance but not otherwise transferred or mortgaged. Payment for the land takes the form of a tax of about 5 percent of the crop per annum. Since the mid-1970s, however, the government has backed away from land reform, stressing the commercialization of agriculture in the hope that security for the peasants will come, not with land, but with their "proletarianization" (i.e., conversion to factory workers).

In the meantime, state planners have focused on regional development, which has involved the attempt to consider each region's total needs and unique characteristics in economic planning. The concept of regionalism recognizes the inherent interrelationship of different aspects of the economy—for example, rural unemployment and the need for industrial jobs—within given geographic regions. To realize this approach, the government has established interministerial commissions to coordinate its development policies at the regional level.

Despite these efforts, rural development has remained disappointing. Production of wheat and corn reached the point of self-sufficiency but then tapered off in the 1970s, necessitating imports again. Peasants' living standards remain low, and farm income is growing more slowly than that of other sectors of the economy. Rural education opportunities and health services have improved, but nowhere are they adequate to meet needs. Moreover, high birth rates mean that the number of landless peasants tends to increase from one generation to the next; many seek work in the teeming cities, and millions have flowed across and through the northern border, legally and illegally, into the United States.

The de la Madrid government continued the trend of neglecting small farmers in favor of commercial agriculture. Public investments in agriculture have decreased, and prices for basic foods such as corn and beans have not kept up with inflation. Indeed, the peasants have been hit especially hard by inflation, while urban residents—seen by the government as a greater potential source of political instability—have been treated to food subsidies. Even these, however, were reduced during the mid-1980s when the Mexican government found itself unable to afford the scale of the subsidies any longer, thus dealing a sharp blow to the urban poor.

While the rural problems remain intractable, the government has concentrated increasingly on industrialization as the answer to Mexico's economic quandary. Ever since the inauguration of President Echeverría in 1970, the *tecnicos,* or university-educated specialists, have occupied the forefront of economic planning. Impatient with the old ways—reliance on persuasion, consultation, and popularity—the *tecnicos* have built their system around sophisticated development plans and efforts to make the most of Mexico's international relations.

Mexico's dealings in the world economy have undergone important shifts in recent decades. Traditionally reliant on exports of coffee, cotton, and sugar, Mexico began trading oil in 1974, and this has become by far the most important item in the country's foreign trade. Before the 1970s, most of the productive and extractive industries were foreign-owned. The Echeverría government moved to protect the country's resources by "Mexicanization"—restriction of foreign ownership in such key economic sectors as public communications, mines, and other natural resources. The government itself played a central role in this process, assuming control of public utilities, basic heavy industries (including petroleum and petrochemicals), and some mining enterprises. Foreign capital remained important, but it was carefully regulated by the terms of the 1973 foreign investment law.

The de la Madrid administration, however, saw a conflict between this policy and the desire for industrialization and economic prosperity. If Mexican industry is to compete internationally or survive in an unprotected domestic market, de la Madrid reasoned, it must utilize the latest in technology, and acquiring this technology means allowing foreign investors to bring it in. His administration overturned some of the rules of the 1973 law. It is, for example, once again possible for foreigners to own majority shares in companies operating in Mexico. To counter the dangers of too much foreign activity, the government tries to maintain control of capital, in particular by limiting capital flows out of Mexico.

Amid the increased foreign investment activity Mexico has found itself grappling with a burdensome international debt, which by the end of 1987 had surpassed $105 billion. The origins of that large debt lay in the world energy crisis of 1973–1974, when Mexico was still a net importer of oil, and by the end of the Echeverría administration Mexico's foreign indebtedness had reached $18.3 billion. During the term of López Portillo (1976–1982), however, revenues from oil exports climbed dramatically, encouraging the government to enter a program of massive economic development, to be financed by Mexico's own petroleum wealth. It was López Portillo's idea that, as long as the oil supplies lasted, the income from them could be used to build a diversified modern industrial base. The program ran into problems just as large doses of foreign investment began to pour in; inadequate road and railroad systems made the movement of raw materials and food supplies difficult, ports were congested, and urban centers were flooded with migrants at a rate faster than they could cope with them, aggravating the already obstinate shortages of housing, power, water, sanitation facilities, transportation, and schools. The newly gained dollar imports accelerated inflation in the urban areas: 17 percent in 1978, 28 percent in 1981, and 59 percent in the following year.

On the heels of the grand plans came two more shocks. First, inflationary pressures in the international currency markets drove interest rates up to historic highs. Then came the 1982 oil glut, causing the price of crude to fall from over $30 per barrel to below $12 by 1986. In the interim, Mexican banks and industrialists panicked. Millions of dollars were sent out of the country to "safety" in the United States and Europe. López Portillo nationalized the banks in late 1982 to decrease the decline of monetary reserves, but the damage could not be halted. Inflation continued its upward spiral, hitting 105 percent in 1986 and moving even higher in 1987; the value of the peso plummeted to a low of around 2500 to the U.S. dollar before the de la Madrid government revalued it to 2000 in late 1987. (See Figure 8.2.)

It is against the backdrop of mounting foreign debt and the disillusioned hopes of the López Portillo plan that Mexico's economic crisis

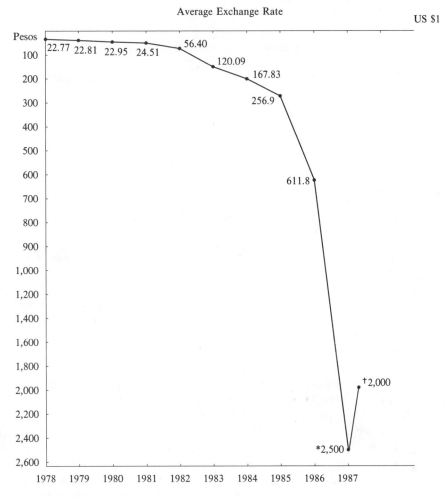

Figure 8.2 Fall of the peso, 1978–1987. (*Source:* The Economist Intelligence Unit, *Country Report: Mexico*, 1985, 1987).

must be viewed. De la Madrid, López Portillo's successor, pursued a more equitable distribution of industrial investment throughout the country and enhanced export competitiveness through research and technological innovation. One of the major decentralization moves focused on the northern border region, where some 300 plants owned by U.S. firms and employing more than 40,000 Mexican workers produce some $500 million worth of electronic products, textiles, and other goods annually.

To encourage industrial growth, the state has created a development bank, Nacional Financiera, S.A., that administers funds for the development of industries, infrastructure, and workers' housing. One of

Table 8.7   MEXICAN ECONOMIC GROWTH,
1979–1986

Year	Growth in real gross domestic product (%)
1979	9.2
1980	8.3
1981	8.0
1982	−0.6
1983	−4.6
1984	3.7
1985	2.7
1986	−3.7

Source: The Economist Intelligence Unit,
Country Report: Mexico, 1985 and 1987.

the leading sources of revenues in recent years has been the tourist industry, revamped to take advantage of the fact that foreigners find Mexican prices extremely favorable, given the low exchange rates of the peso. Together with the new foreign-financed industries in the border regions, the so-called *maquiladoras,* tourism and oil—benefiting from an upturn in international prices, finally, in 1987—are helping Mexico combat its economic crisis. Even so, the foreign debt continues to tax Mexico's resources. In 1985 interest payments alone came to $14 billion and took more than 55 percent of the country's export earnings. The balance was inadequate to finance domestic growth.

Thus it is that the Mexican economy, which showed impressive gains during the 1960s and 1970s, fell in the mid-1980s to negative growth rates. (See Table 8.7.) Development efforts have been damaged by erratic fluctuations in the international environment, nature's whims, and the weaknesses of the Mexican system—in particular poor organization and self-discipline. In addition, greed and corruption have caused many development programs to go awry, for leakages of funds to corrupt officials have mitigated much potential progress. In one of the largest scandals, officials of Pemex, the government's giant petroleum company, misallocated millions of dollars during the time its earnings went from $4 billion to over $20 billion a year.[14]

The economic problems of the 1980s have exacerbated long-running sore spots in social services and human welfare. Since the 1930s, peasants without land have been moving to the urban areas in ever-increasing numbers. This migration puts a strain on public services and creates a permanent underclass living at the bottom level of urban society. Mexico's municipal governments devote most of their resources to public works and make smaller allocations to education and welfare (often less

[14]James Street, "Can Mexico Break the Vicious Circle of 'Stop-Go' Policy? An Institutional Overview," *Journal of Economic Issues* XX, no. 2 (June 1986), 609.

Table 8.8   INFANT MORTALITY IN THE
SIX COUNTRIES

	Mortality per 1000 births
United Kingdom	10.2
France	9.0
Soviet Union	27.7
China	33.0
Mexico	53.0
Nigeria	114.0

Source: United Nations Statistical Yearbook, 1983–1984.

than 5 percent of their budgets). The extent and performance of services vary widely throughout the country. For those employed in factories, unions work effectively for higher wages and other benefits, but these advantages obviously do not help the unemployed. And for both the employed and the unemployed, urban housing is in perennial short supply. In particular, the population of the capital, Mexico City, now about 15 million, stretches the limits of the city's environmental and public capabilities.

Poverty in Mexico is widespread in both urban and rural areas. Wages are higher in urban areas, but the mass migration into the largest cities has made it increasingly hard for newcomers to find jobs. The government's approach to poverty focuses on industrialization, expanded education, and (as we have seen) a rather indifferent policy of land redistribution; these policies are piecemeal and inadequate in a country where "real" wages (i.e., wages after the effects of inflation have been removed) declined some 50 percent between 1978 and 1987.

Not surprisingly, the high level of poverty is reflected in the relatively low state of public health. Deaths from dysentery, pneumonia, and malaria are frequent; infant mortality is high compared with the rates of developed countries. (See Table 8.8.) Nutrition, too, is comparatively poor, as much of the typical Mexican's diet is starch. For a large part of the population, home consists of a shack with no sanitary facilities of any kind, and more than half the population does not have access to safe drinking water. Doctors are being trained and hospitals are being constructed, but neither is keeping up with population growth; in 1983 there was only one physician for every 2136 persons (compared to one for every 1850 at the beginning of the 1980s) and one hospital bed for every 863 persons (compared to one for every 530).[15] Relatively few of either are to be found in rural areas; in any event, few of the poor are covered by medical insurance and thus medical care, which is mostly private, is unaffordable for them.

Like health services, education is most available in urban areas and

[15]*United Nations Statistical Yearbook,* 1983–1984.

accessible primarily to the middle and upper classes. Peasants rarely complete more than three years of school, and typically they start late because of agricultural obligations to their families. Urban students are likely to complete six years of primary school and, if they are members of the middle and upper classes, even continue on to secondary school. For the masses, however, education brings simple literacy skills but few other results conducive to occupational preparation.

Perhaps the most serious social problem in Mexico is the persisting gulf between the very rich few and the impoverished many. So far, the governing PRI has been able to maintain the support of the poor despite its weak performance in reducing economic disparities. It has done so by manipulating revolutionary symbols and by uttering periodic reassurances of its commitment to greater equality.[16] Whether this approach will work in the future as the urban population grows and becomes better informed is open to question.

Nigeria: Ups and Downs of a Petroeconomy

Nigeria's three decades of independence have been accompanied by economic changes often seen in Third World countries, centering on the evolution from agriculture as the mainstay of the economy to increasing reliance on a growing industrial and service area. Unlike most underdeveloped countries, however, Nigeria has been blessed by large deposits of oil, and its economy, like Mexico's, has been greatly affected by oil.

The Nigerian government has attempted to give direction to the country's economic development through a series of plans. The first National Development Plan was in effect from 1962 to 1968. This was followed by a second (four-year) plan launched in 1970 and a third (five-year) plan in 1975–1980; it was in the first years of the third plan, nourished by the dreams of petrodollars, that the most rapid growth occurred, 8.5 percent per annum between 1974 and 1979. The dream then was to modernize Nigeria by the year 2000, when, it was estimated, the country's oil reserves would be diminished.

In the meantime, however, Nigeria's grand design has been set back by the decline in world oil prices and domestic political instability. Even before the decline in oil prices, it became apparent that the targets for Nigeria's third development plan would not be reached, and before the end of the 1970s the economy's growth rate had fallen into negative figures. The civilian government optimistically announced a new five-year plan in 1980, but in the midst of it, oil prices collapsed and it became clear that the targets of the plan would not even be approached. Subsequently, the policies of the military government have

[16]Charles L. Davis, "The Mobilization of Support for an Authoritarian Regime: The Case of the Lower Class in Mexico City," *American Journal of Political Science,* 20 (November 1976), 653–670.

Table 8.9   NIGERIAN ECONOMIC GROWTH AND FOREIGN DEBT, 1979–1986

	1979	1980	1981	1982	1983	1984	1985	1986
Real GDP growth (%)	−5.7	6.0	0.4	−5.3	−8.5	−5.5	1.3	−3.3
Total foreign debt, disbursed (U.S. $ billion)	3.3	4.3	5.9	12.5	18.0	18.2	18.4	20.0

Source: Economist Intelligence Unit, *Country Report/Nigeria,* no. 2/1987, and *Quarterly Economic Report/Nigeria: Annual Supplement, 1985.*

struggled to keep pace with what had become a serious foreign debt burden. (See Table 8.9.)

Although oil and other new industries have attracted a large portion of the work force, a majority of Nigeria's population still lives and works in rural areas, primarily in agricultural occupations.[17] During the 1960s Nigerian farmers produced enough to feed the whole population; before the oil boom agricultural goods provided 50 percent of the national income and, with forest products, 80 percent of the country's export earnings. In more recent years, however, production has not kept up with population growth, and food has been imported to make up the shortfall.

Much of the total agricultural output is subsistence production consumed by the farmers themselves. Cultivable lands represent a much greater proportion of all land—an estimated 37 percent—than in Mexico and indeed most other developing countries. Ownership for the most part takes the form of small, individually owned family plots, but there is in addition a large commercial plantation sector, much of which is foreign-owned. Key exports are groundnuts, palm oil (used in soaps and cooking oils), rubber, cocoa, and cotton.

The growing demand for food to feed the urban population has impelled the federal government to play an active role in agricultural development. Land tenure and distribution have been left mostly up to the states because of the regional variation in traditional land ownership customs, but the federal government has intervened to regulate commodity prices and taken other steps to aid production. In the 1960s experiments with various forms of agricultural cooperatives and even state-run farms were undertaken, particularly in the north, for the raising of livestock. Later, the state established its own national fertilizer company to augment the supply of fertilizers and reduce dependence on imports.

Nigeria's government has long favored the commercial sector of agriculture and tended to neglect the small farmers. Officials talk optimistically about feeding 120 million people by the early part of the next century, but their actions have been inconsistent and severe problems in other sectors of the economy have commanded their attention. In line

[17]As of 1983 an estimated 15.9 million people, or about 51 percent of the work force, were employed in agriculture (Economist Intelligence Unit, *Quarterly Economic Report/ Nigeria: Annual Supplement, 1985,* pp. 7, 10).

with a general austerity program, the federal budget for 1987 showed a major cutback in funds allocated to agriculture. (See Table 8.10.)

The industrial and commercial sectors of the economy have grown rapidly and, as of the late 1980s, account for more than 50 percent of gross domestic production. Most significant in this sector is the Nigerian oil industry, which boomed during the 1970s when Nigeria established itself as the world's seventh largest petroleum producer and the number one exporter of light, low-sulfur crude. By 1979 production exceeded 2 million barrels a day—the same as that of many Middle Eastern oil-producing states. In 1971 a National Oil Corporation was set up to provide for government participation in the industry, and in 1974 it was empowered to assume a 55 percent controlling share in all foreign oil companies operating in Nigeria. Several large refineries were built, and they produce most of the oil consumed domestically; because their capacities are not quite enough to satisfy demand, it is necessary to import some quantities of refined petroleum, although the amount is small compared with the amount of crude oil exported.

Revenues from oil exports became the backbone of industrialization; as a result of the petrodollars, the third National Development Plan foresaw a more than 30-fold increase over the second plan in capital investments—in new refineries, liquefied natural gas projects, and cement factories. With the drop-off in oil revenues during the 1980s, however, such projects were inevitably cut back, and other industries have not met the optimistic expectations of the 1970s.

The manufacturing industry, despite significant growth, still accounts for only a small proportion of national output (11.8 percent in 1985) and was badly damaged by the slump of the mid-1980s. There is a large potential market for manufactured goods in Nigeria, but indigenous industries have found it difficult to compete with the prices and quality of imported goods. The government has preferred to keep its distance from industrial management, leaving it in private hands, but the state has stepped in with regulations restricting foreign ownership and control. In doing so, it has discovered that well-trained management personnel are not as readily available as had been hoped.

Table 8.10 NIGERIAN STATE ALLOCATIONS TO AGRICULTURE, 1986–1987

Ministry/Department	Allocations (millions of naira)		Change (%)
	1986	1987	
Rural development	491.5	70.5	−85.7
Agriculture (crops)	215.4	170.1	−21.0
Livestock	31.1	12.7	−59.2
Fisheries	5.5	4.4	−20.0
Water resources	141.1	99.9	−29.2
Agricultural cooperatives	1.8	2.6	+30.8

Source: West Africa (January 12, 1987), 87.

Nigeria's international economic position has become a delicate one. During the 1970s and 1980s the balance of payments swung back and forth between surplus and deficit, and while the size of the foreign debt was not large compared with Mexico's, it was burden enough; in January 1987 the Central Bank missed payment on an international promissory note, causing concern through the world banking community. Moreover, Nigeria's nationalization policies have tended to discourage foreign investors. In 1978 a big client was lost when International Business Machines (IBM) left Nigeria rather than concede to foreign investment laws requiring certain industries, including computers, to be 40 percent Nigerian-owned.

To deal with the country's worsening economic problems, the military government adopted a two-year Structural Adjustment Program in 1986. The main objective of this program is to restructure and diversify the economy to reduce dependence on oil exports. The strategy employed to achieve this objective is market-based; the government seeks to reduce its own involvement in the economy by cutting its spending, particularly in the areas of price supports and subsidies, and by privatizing many state-owned or -controlled enterprises. The early results of the program,

Nigerian workers on an American-owned oil rig. Since the 1970s, the development of vast offshore oil reserves has made Nigeria a leading oil exporter—and highly vulnerable to fluctuations in the world price of oil. (Campbell / Sygma)

however, have not been encouraging: after its first year, exports had become even more dominated by oil, the manufacturing sector had contracted, inflation had risen as a result of the devaluation of the national currency, the naira, and many businesses had closed.[18]

With Nigeria's efforts at economic development and their setbacks have come other problems. As in Mexico, urban centers are growing beyond the capacity of governments to provide public services. Between 1960 and 1980 Lagos, the former capital, quadrupled its population, which has now surpassed 4 million. The problems are familiar throughout the Third World: too much automobile traffic, inadequate water supply systems and electrical power, slum housing, unemployment, and—even more serious—governmental mismanagement and corruption. The shortage of highly educated professionals means that local governments must often call on foreigners to study and propose solutions to their problems. Governments at all levels have found themselves overwhelmed, and though they have tried to help through such programs as the establishment of regional housing corporations, more often than not their programs have failed.

Nigeria's industrialization has paralleled agriculture in the sense that performance has fallen far short of aspirations. Major projects, such as a massive gas liquefaction plant to utilize the tremendous natural gas resources, have been long delayed. The optimists of the 1970s believed that oil revenues would enable Nigeria to meet its objectives of self-sufficiency in food and well-rounded industrialization, but overall performance has not been impressive. It is difficult to predict the future fluctuations in oil prices, so vital to Nigeria's continued development.

The economy has grown, but so has the population, and with this growth has come increased social needs. Government assistance to the aged and unemployed is limited to former government workers, so the major sources of economic security are still the extended family, the clan, and village associations. Even more than in Mexico, health problems in Nigeria are serious. Very high infant mortality rates testify to the weakness of the health delivery system. (See Table 8.8.) As in Mexico, modern medicine is available only to a limited degree to urban residents and infinitesimally to rural citizens. Many diseases are passed through water polluted by human and animal wastes. Nutrition levels vary regionally; for example, in the north, where the average life span is considerably shorter than in the south, vitamins A and C are chronically deficient in the diet. Yet vitamin C, necessary for resistance to disease, is present in palm oils available and heavily consumed in the southern part of the country.

With regard to education, too, Nigeria faces a severe challenge to

[18]*West Africa* (September 28, 1987), 1901–1904.

distribute opportunities justly and provide a meaningful educational experience. In the past, education was under regional, and later state, control because each region sought to preserve its own culture and values by controlling education through its separate systems: Muslim schools in the north and Christian missionary schools in the south. This arrangement produced disparities: the southern states spent more on education than did the north, and as a result there were more schools and students at all levels in the southern states than in the northern states. The central government found itself obliged to step in and develop a national schools policy that included direct control of the educational system. To date, performance has been less than spectacular—a discouraging fact given that, in a developing country, education is vital to the creation of a skilled work force.

CONCLUSIONS

Over the past four decades, the penetration of society by the state has increased in all political systems, whatever their ideologies. Even in liberal democracies with a tradition of clear distinctions between public and private issues, the tendency has been to grant a larger role to government. In part, the increased socioeconomic activity of government can be explained by rising public expectations. People no longer expect their governments to be passive and allow society and the economy to function on their own. Rightly or wrongly, government is expected to resolve or manage social conflicts and economic difficulties and to take action to prevent their recurrence. Failure to meet these expectations results in loss of support from the public, the military, or other key political forces.

Underlying the growth of governmental socioeconomic action is the complexity of modern societies and economies. Many current social problems, such as low-cost housing, mass transport, education, and public health services, are of little interest to private entrepreneurs. Nor can free markets alone provide solutions to critical socioeconomic problems: the allocation of increasingly scarce natural resources, energy development and utilization, environmental protection, and population control. Until the 1980s, the most common assumption was that governments would inevitably expand to take on these and other problems.

The desirability of governmental intervention is more in doubt today than it was just a few years ago. Can massive bureaucratic machines solve major social and economic problems? Will their solutions be better or worse than the original problems? Will they permit flexibility and responsiveness to local conditions and interests? Can they be controlled by the populace in countries where democracy is valued? In both capitalist and socialist countries, political leaders are increasingly confronting these questions and, in light of the economic difficulties of the 1970s and 1980s, coming to the conclusion that there are limits to what governments can do and should do in these areas. Today, the issue of how far government should step back from managing economic growth and development centers the political debate in countries on both sides of the East-West and North-South (developed–undeveloped) divides.

chapter 9

The Challenge of Political Stability

Since 1945, violent attempts to overthrow governments have been more common than national elections.

TED GURR[1]

INTRODUCTION

The world in which we live is rife with examples of political instability. The Middle East is a veritable powder keg as Israeli confronts Arab and Sunni Muslim confronts Shi'ite Muslim. In Africa, coups and civil wars are endemic, while in Central America, rebel movements struggle against both left-wing and right-wing governments, catching thousands of innocent victims in their cross fire. In Southeast Asia, Vietnam fights guerrilla movements opposing its occupation of Cambodia in a conflict that could involve both Thailand and China. Discontent and protest on the part of East Europeans against their Soviet-style regimes are standard fodder for the newspapers of the Western world, while in the West itself acts of terrorism and violence are by no means absent, as the case of Northern Ireland attests.

Despite, or perhaps because of, the prevalence of instability throughout the world, political stability is a highly desired value. Most people would prefer to live under a political system that can ensure a

[1]*Why Men Rebel* (Princeton, N.J.: Princeton University Press, 1970), p. 3.

stable environment in which order and the rule of law prevail. The problem is that the value of political stability frequently conflicts with other basic values, including nationalistic aspirations, religious fundamentalism, and the desire for economic advancement. In this chapter we examine the nature of political instability and some of its causes, before turning to a consideration of the ways in which it is addressed in our six case studies.

The Nature of Political Stability and Instability

Political stability is a concept that has been given numerous interpretations, but one point is indisputable: it does not refer to a state of changelessness or immobilism. Governments and, indeed, political systems themselves change over time, and in most cases these changes do not threaten political stability. Generally speaking, this situation is most likely to hold true when politics follows a set of well-accepted rules, often taking the form of a constitution, which prescribes methods for selecting political leaders, making public policy, and mediating political differences. Stable change thus involves a basic acceptance of the nature of a regime, without necessarily precluding peaceful efforts to reform it.

The meaning of political instability is less clear. Following from the above description of stable change, political instability is most often equated with the use of extraconstitutional means—such as force or the threat of force—to effect a change in regime. Examples include the military takeovers in Nigeria in 1966 and 1983 and the large-scale revolutions that inaugurated the communist regimes in the Soviet Union and China. There is, however, another common usage of the term, one that relates it to the frequency with which cabinet governments fall within a given regime. The rapid succession of cabinets in the Third and Fourth Republics in France and in the present Italian regime are well-known instances of this type of instability. What distinguishes it from the first type is that no breach of the constitutional rules takes place; it happens even when all political forces scrupulously respect the rule of law. Finally, political instability is often identified with incidents of political violence, including riots, acts of terrorism, and demonstrations directed against public authorities, whether or not they result in a change of government or regime. The terrorist attacks of Tamil rebels in Sri Lanka in the latter 1980s, the hostilities involving both Catholic and Protestant groups in Northern Ireland since the late 1960s, and the mass demonstrations against the military dictatorship in South Korea in 1987 fall into this category.

Although none of these definitions of political instability is wrong, each has its limitations. The most appropriate definition is undoubtedly the first one, which relates instability to extraconstitutional changes in regime. This definition ignores, however, serious challenges to a regime that fail to produce their intended effect.[2] The second meaning of political instability, which concerns the instability of cabinets, is quite limited in its applicability because it affects only parliamentary regimes; presidential regimes, for example, are immune because leaders are elected for fixed terms of office. As for political violence, although a large-scale challenge to the political order by rebel groups clearly brings the stability of a regime into question, terrorist attacks by small isolated groups—such as the bombings by Islamic terrorists in France in 1986—usually do not constitute threats to a regime's stability. Moreover, it is possible that demonstrations or riots may be repressed so effectively that no serious challenge to the regime's survival can be said to have taken place.

Much of the confusion over the term "political instability" may be avoided if we define two distinct types: (1) that which involves a serious attempt—whether successful or not—to alter fundamentally the nature of a regime or its policies by means which lie outside the accepted rules of the political game, such as force, and (2) that which follows from the inability of political parties to form stable coalition governments in complex multiparty parliamentary systems. In this chapter we are concerned primarily with the first type, which is by far the more important.[3] Political violence or protest will be discussed and evaluated in the context of its regime-threatening potential.

Factors Leading to Political Instability

There are a number of factors that can produce challenges to the stability of regimes, of which the antagonisms surrounding social cleavages, the disruptive effects of socioeconomic development, and the adverse impact of the world economy are among the most basic. In addition, two major intermediate factors—political institutions and political culture—must be taken into account. In this section we look briefly at each of these factors.

There is little doubt that serious social cleavages constitute one of the most common, if not the most common, sources of political instability. No social cleavages are more potent as sources of political instability than ethnic or racial differences. Among our case studies, Nigeria, with one civil war and six military coups in its brief history, represents a classic example of major ethnic divisions undermining the attempt to construct a unified and cohesive political community. Religion and ideology may also be divisive forces, for the conviction held by true believers that theirs is "the one true way" can lead to unwillingness to allow other groups to have access to political power. The 1979 revolution in Iran, for

---

[2]It also obscures the fact that there might be traditions, not strictly constitutional but accepted nonetheless, that allow the military to take over power in difficult times.
[3]The second type was dealt with to some extent in Chapter 5.

example, was motivated by the desire of Ayatollah Khomeini and his followers to construct an "Islamic republic," that is, a political regime led by religious leaders and guided by religious thought; in the process, non-supporters have been ruthlessly repressed. Ideological differences with other Chinese leaders lay behind the unleashing by Mao of the Cultural Revolution in the latter 1960s, which involved a great deal of instability and considerable violence against those perceived as resisting the ideological direction that Mao favored.

In Third World countries, cleavage-driven political instability often finds its stimulus in the problems and challenges of development. Traditional agrarian societies are usually headed by highly stable authoritarian systems of government, such as monarchies or tribal chieftaincies. As economic development begins to occur, however, traditional social and economic structures are altered. New groups including businessmen and Western-educated students emerge, often demanding a voice in public affairs; traditional groups such as peasants and artisans may feel they are being left behind. As a result, societies may become sharply divided between those who favor change and those who do not. The Iranian Revolution, for example, was in large measure a reaction to the intense program of industrialization and secularization conducted by the former Shah, who viewed the country's huge oil revenues as a tool which could be used to bring about the rapid modernization and Westernization of the country. The revival of Islamic thought and the impetus to scourge the country of Western influences receive support from sectors of Iranian society that were fearful of the destruction of their traditional way of life and its replacement with one guided by alien beliefs and values. In addition, there may be conflicts among those committed to development over how it should be pursued. Struggles which underlay the Soviet purges of the 1930s and the Cultural Revolution in China largely concerned differences of opinion within ruling circles over which direction the development of their countries should take. In these countries, the ideologies of communism and socialism have been interpreted less as forms of societal organization that will succeed mature or developed capitalism than as forms of organization designed to achieve development.

Economic conditions can affect the political stability of developing countries in other ways as well. Since World War II, there has been a global trend toward increasing economic interdependence and a lessening of self-sufficiency among both developed and underdeveloped countries.[4] While the growth of international trade, foreign investment, and loans has helped developing economies in many instances, it has also created severe and potentially destabilizing economic problems. For example, during the inflation-prone 1970s many developing countries borrowed huge amounts from both Western banks and international organizations in order to develop their economies. But when interest rates shot

---

[4]Global interdependence is explored more thoroughly in Chapter 10.

up to unprecedented levels in the early 1980s and produced a severe recession in the developed world, countries such as Brazil, Argentina, Mexico, and Nigeria found themselves in desperate financial straits. Not only had the interest payments on their loans increased enormously but also Western demand for their products, mainly commodities such as coffee and oil, fell sharply, cutting their export earnings and hence their ability to make their interest payments. Typically, international lending organizations such as the International Monetary Fund insist on cutbacks in government expenditures as their price for further financial aid; this, however, can lead to increased unemployment and a reduction or ending of subsidies on basic foodstuffs such as wheat or rice. In Brazil, riots among the country's poor followed the government's decision to raise food prices, and in 1987 the government decided to resist demands for more cutbacks and suspend its payments on foreign loans. Other countries are similarly poised between the need to adapt government policy to the expectations of foreign lending institutions and the possibility of provoking widespread unrest if hardships among their poor and needy are increased.

Even where the foreign debt load is not serious, dependence on world markets can cause severe problems that could lead to instability. While a handful of Third World countries such as South Korea and Taiwan have industrialized rapidly, most of the Third World has found it difficult to catch up industrially with the increasingly competitive developed world and must depend on the export of raw materials in order to import needed industrial and agricultural goods from abroad. Unfortunately, prices for raw materials fluctuate much more than do the prices of manufactured goods, and a recession in the developed world can produce much greater economic hardships in developing countries as prices for their commodities plummet. In countries where the livelihood of many depend on the export markets of just one or two commodities, the probability that serious unrest will follow a decline in world prices is all the greater.

Third World countries are particularly likely to suffer the strains of development and the vicissitudes of the world economy; since many were formed of different peoples and have had little time to mold new national identities, they tend to be especially vulnerable to cleavage conflict as well. But this is far from being the whole story. In seeking the sources of political instability, it is important to consider not just the root causes—social cleavages, developmental strains, and the like—but also the factors that aggravate or moderate them. One such mediating factor is political institutions. Because development can have such a disrupting effect on traditional societies, heightening political awareness and expectations of political participation for some and threatening traditional values and ways of life for others, Samuel Huntington has argued that the creation of political institutions capable of absorbing and channeling popular demands and expectations is essential if political violence and instability are to be avoided.[5] Such institutions take time to develop, however, and are therefore most likely to be found in the older countries of the developed world. It is for this reason, Huntington believes, that traditional societies as yet untouched by the forces of development as well as developed societies are generally more stable than countries at intermediate levels of development, producing a curvilinear or U-shaped relationship between level of development and political stability, as depicted in Figure 9.1.

One institution that is often employed to channel expectations of political participation and to direct economic development is the monopolistic political party. Where the problem of underdevelopment is compounded with the obstacles to national unity posed by severe social cleavages, single-party regimes may be seen as the most appropriate means by which the country can be kept together and its citizens mobilized to confront the daunting challenges of economic, social, and political development. Certain caveats must be made concerning this solution, however. As we shall see, Communist party rule in the Soviet Union and China has been accompanied at times by instability, or the threat of instability, stemming from internal party disputes over the direction policy should take and from the enormity of the social transformations the party has launched. In addition, it has involved on occasion a degree of coercion that few single-party regimes in the Third World have been able—and willing—to apply. In countries where single-party regimes have been less effective in controlling social divisiveness and generating economic growth, pressures to allow more pluralistic economic and political structures may be much greater and a struggle with democratic forces may become endemic to political life. Since ruling monopolistic parties, wedded to the belief in their unique suitability to guide the affairs of state, are unlikely to recognize the legitimacy of this struggle and institutionalize it through competitive elections, repression and instability often result.

Where effective political institutions have not emerged to deal with political instability, the military may feel tempted to intervene. As we saw in Chapter 6, military leaderships often see themselves as "monitors" or guardians of public order and cherished national values. They may also believe that they would be better governors than the civilian politicians and parties and that their technical and organizational expertise will enable them to lead the country along the path of economic development more effectively and more rapidly. In many cases, the expectation that economic conditions will improve under military guidance is not borne out, and the military government faces growing popular dissatisfaction and increasing demands for a return to civilian rule.

[5]S. Huntington, *Political Order in Changing Societies* (New Haven, Conn.: Yale University Press, 1968), p. 41.

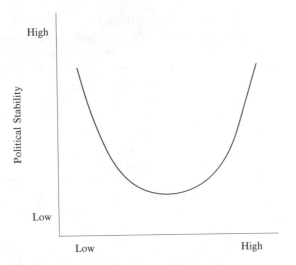

Figure 9.1 The U-shaped relationship between levels of economic development and political stability.

Too often, the response of military governments has been to use force to repress opposition to their rule. Even when military governments yield to these pressures and turn power over to civilians, it may be with the tacit understanding that they will intervene again if they so choose. Cycles of alternating civilian and military regimes have been characteristic of certain developing countries such as Argentina and Peru; Nigeria, which is now considering a third attempt at democratic government, may well be headed in the same direction.

Just as the Third World has been the prime focus for developing explanations of political instability, the experience of Western countries has provided fodder for explanations of stability. The most important thrust that has emerged from the study of Western regimes relates political stability to aspects of political culture. One very well known approach associates the stability of democratic regimes with the widespread acceptance of a set of "civic" norms and attitudes, including pride in the political system, trust in one's fellow citizens, and bonds of solidarity that cut across and moderate partisan divisions.[6] We noted in Chapter 1 that pluralistic political cultures—those in which pragmatic bargaining and reasonable degrees of social trust characterize the political arena—have been more conducive to the establishment and maintenance of democratic stability than have political cultures exhibiting low levels of social trust and strong ideological divisiveness. Nevertheless, it must be remembered that political attitudes of the latter type are more likely to

[6]G. Almond and S. Verba, *The Civic Culture* (Boston: Little, Brown, 1965) is the best example of this approach.

be present where sharp social cleavages divide the citizenry of a country and prevent the development of norms of social trust and cooperation, as in France after the revolution of 1789. Thus, attitudes identified as detrimental to stable democracy, although important, are more likely to be reflections of serious cleavage problems than independent causes of instability in their own right.

Another political cultural approach, developed by Harry Eckstein, has suggested that stability, whether democratic or not, follows from the degree of "congruence" or similarity between the authority patterns prevalent in the political system and authority patterns characteristic of other areas of social and political life.[7] For example, a society in which interest groups, political parties, schools, and even families are run along highly authoritarian lines is not likely to be fertile ground for the implantation of democratic government; conversely, a society whose institutions incorporate significant elements of democratic participation will not easily accept an authoritarian form of government. The basis for this relationship is socialization: people, according to Eckstein, are bound to prefer a form of government that exercises authority according to the way they are accustomed to seeing authority exercised in other spheres of their lives.

One advantage of Eckstein's theory is that it fits well with the situation in countries undergoing socioeconomic change, where instability often results from the conflict between more modernized and Westernized social sectors that wish to democratize government and traditional sectors that may prefer a more authoritarian regime. This would explain why highly traditional societies and highly developed societies are both more stable on average than societies that fall between the two extremes. But it also means that Eckstein's approach, like the previous one, describes an intermediate rather than an ultimate cause of instability. The important message in both approaches is that circumstances such as the existence of serious social cleavages or socioeconomic change do not themselves produce instability; people rebel against their government because of their attitudes or beliefs, not because the social structure impels them, unthinking, into action.

The Use of Force in Managing Discontent

The keystone to cultural interpretations of stability is the concept of legitimacy, the belief that the system of government is morally right. For a regime to be stable, it is often argued, most citizens must believe that it is legitimate. Clearly, a refusal to accept the legitimacy of government can prompt efforts by individual citizens to undermine its

[7]Harry Eckstein, *Division and Cohesion in Democracy* (Princeton, N.J.: Princeton University Press, 1966), appendix B.

functioning or to engage in mass demonstrations, as seen in Chile through much of General Pinochet's dictatorship or in Haiti under Duvalier and his military successors.[8] Often overlooked, however, are the long periods of time during which unpopular regimes have managed to govern undisturbed by public unrest. For example, the recent troubles in South Africa tend to make people forget that blacks remained basically passive for decades despite the existence of laws that deny them basic civil and democratic rights and assure them a much lower standard of living than whites; similarly, our attention to the activities of small groups of resisters in Nazi-occupied Europe camouflages the obedience, motivated by fear, of the vast majority of citizens in these countries to their foreign rulers during World War II. These examples indicate that public discontent is usually not enough in itself to cause political instability; the role of governments in managing discontent must also be considered.

There are several methods by which governments in potentially unstable circumstances can manage discontent so as to preserve their rule. In intensely divided societies, the consociational practices discussed in Chapter 3, which generally involve a division of government expenditures and jobs proportionally among the country's hostile groups, may be employed. While these have worked in some cases, interethnic distrust and suspicion have often proved too powerful to be assuaged by these forms of sharing power and resources. A second technique, practiced with success in Mexico and bearing some relevance to the Soviet Union, is to co-opt relevant sectors of society and their leaders within the embrace of a single ruling party. This approach depends on the development of a party that is capable of attracting the support and meeting the demands of large sectors of the population; in societies with deep cleavages, the more likely outcome is the formation of a number of hostile parties or rebel groups that convey these divisions into the political arena and accentuate them. For these reasons, the most widely used method for controlling discontent in countries where legitimacy is lacking remains the use of force, particularly by military or civilian dictatorial regimes. It is an unfortunate, but undeniable, fact that a dictatorial leadership in control of its military forces can usually defeat most opposition uprisings and prevent their recurrence. It is usually only when extreme unpopularity combines with a lack of will among leaders to fight back or an inability to ensure that the military will remain obedient that the fall of a dictatorial regime becomes possible. Legitimacy is a better guarantee of a regime's survival, but in today's world, force is at least as common a mainstay of governments.

[8]James C. Scott, *The Moral Economy of the Peasant* (New Haven, Conn.: Yale University Press, 1976), discusses several forms of citizen protest in a very insightful contribution on the processes of rebellion.

BRITAIN AND FRANCE: POLITICAL STABILITY IN LIBERAL DEMOCRACIES

The stability of democratic regimes rests on a number of interrelated assumptions. One assumption is that the institutions of democratic government will not be seriously challenged provided they remain essentially "neutral," that is, provided that they allow free and fair competition among politicians and parties for political office. Since voters have opportunities to change governments and governors, they are not expected to seek to change the system itself. It is also assumed that the occupants of government positions will respect the principle of popular control and will not try to hold on to power by force if the electorate should turn against them at the polls. Political ideologies which argue that one political party or movement should be accorded a permanent monopoly on political power are not expected to receive much popular support. It is taken for granted that the right to choose among several aspirants for power is sufficiently attractive to dissuade most citizens from subscribing to a political ideology that would deny the right of choice in the future.

In Britain and France, the political attitudes and behavior of politicians and citizens largely conform to these expectations. The vast majority of the citizens of both countries accept the political regimes which govern them and confine their expressions of discontent with government to such officially sanctioned channels as peaceful demonstrations, competitions, and, most important, the exercise of their right to vote incumbents out of office during national elections. Political parties in both countries understand and obey the rules of democratic politics; even the French Communist party has acknowledged officially that if it ever were to win a national election, it would respect the electorate's right to vote it out of office in a subsequent election. Where the two countries differ is primarily in the longevity of political stability; Britain is usually taken as a prime example of a centuries-old tradition of stability, whereas France up till the 1960s was a classic case of political instability.

Britain: The Long Road to Stability

If any one feature embodies Britain's long history of political stability, it is the longevity of the country's political institutions. Virtually all of the principal institutions of British government were in existence in the Middle Ages. First and foremost is the monarchy; since the Norman conquest of 1066, there has been only one brief period, in the seventeenth century, when a monarch did not reign over England. A national system of law courts was in place by the twelfth century to interpret and enforce the laws of the realm. Parliament began in the thirteenth century as a consultative organ between monarch and subjects, and by the fourteenth century the House of Commons had emerged as a separate body with distinct and important powers over government finance. The origins of the cabinet can be traced to the fifteenth century, and it had assumed its present role as the center of executive power by the eighteenth century. Only the huge and diversified civil service is of comparatively recent origin, but even here, key departments such as the Treasury have been around for centuries.

Concentrating solely on institutions can leave an exaggerated impression of changelessness, however; for while the institutions have survived in name, the role each plays in the political system has changed enormously over the centuries. The British monarch is still the head of state, but his or her effective power is virtually nonexistent. The designation of the country as a "constitutional monarchy" and of the government as "Her Majesty's Government" are polite fictions that cannot obscure the reality of Britain as a parliamentary democracy in which the monarch plays a very minor role. Similarly, the respect afforded the House of Lords as the "upper chamber" of Parliament masks the reality that it is almost as powerless as the monarch to affect government policy significantly. Power in Britain lies with the House of Commons and, more particularly, with the cabinet, although the latter institution is not mentioned in any formal constitutional document.

The continued existence of institutions long after their functions have been removed certainly suggests a degree of continuity with the past, but the process by which these institutions lost their powers involved considerable struggle and even violence. The contest for supreme power between monarchy and Parliament was ultimately resolved in the seventeenth century through recourse to force: two kings had to be removed from the throne (one by execution) and a civil war fought before the question was laid to rest. The determination of the hereditary House of Lords to preserve its coequal powers with the elected House of Commons provoked a major constitutional battle early in this century, which was ultimately resolved in favor of the Commons only when the king threatened to create enough new peers to swamp the membership of the upper chamber. Confrontations between the rival political forces of monarchy, aristocracy, and commoners never attained the cataclysmic proportions of the French and Russian revolutions, but there were occasions when the nature of the regime itself was under serious challenge and the stability of the entire political order imperiled.

Economic and social problems have also threatened at times to destabilize the political regime. The hardships and suffering that followed in the wake of the industrial revolution led to widespread unrest among the lower class in the first half of the nineteenth century. Demonstrations and riots, coupled with demands for political democracy, caused alarm throughout the propertied classes, and the issue of how to keep the lower classes "in their place" was seen as a major social and political dilemma. Most commonly, the response by the authorities to these challenges was repression, particularly during the period of the wars against revolutionary France (1793–1815) and during the hard years of the 1840s—a response that was hardly calculated to soothe feelings of alienation and bitterness.

What provided relief from these pressures and gave Britain the reputation for orderly, peaceful government that it enjoys to this day was not political reform but rather economic prosperity. By the second half of the nineteenth century, Britain's position as the dominant economic power of the day had been consolidated and the economic growth that accompanied industrialization had begun to have an effect on working-class standards of living. Legislation limiting the length of the working day and setting industrial safety standards provided important protections against the most flagrant abuses of factory life. In addition, the relative quiescence of the working class was rewarded by the gradual extension of voting rights to working-class males. Britain's position as the world's strongest and most prosperous country made it difficult to contemplate challenging the system in any case, and the parliamentary system of government was widely credited with being one of the keys to the country's industrial and imperial successes.

Although Britain's fortunes as an economic and political power are much reduced today, its political system continues to enjoy the support of the vast majority of Britons. Surveys done by the European Community have shown that while a majority of respondents believe society needs to be reformed gradually, only a small minority support revolutionary action to effect radical change. (See Table 9.1.) Another survey, conducted in 1978, indicated that only 11 percent felt that the present system of government "needed a great deal of improvement" (versus 82 percent who felt it worked "pretty well").[9] Survey evidence from 1982 revealed that Britons have roughly the same amount of confidence in institutions such as the legal system, the police, the civil service, and the legislature as do the citizens of the United States and other highly stable countries[10] and that only about 8 percent of the public believes that MPs are doing "a bad job."[11] Clearly, Britain's very considerable economic difficulties have not been translated by the public into discontent with the system of government; instead, Britons seem to make a clear distinction between the economy, which is seen as not functioning as well as it should, and the political system, which by and large is seen as an effective and appropriate means of governing the country.

The strong sense of national unity that exists among Britons undoubtedly acts to sustain loyalty to the political system even in the face of severe challenges. British democracy, like its American counterpart,

---

[9]L. Moss, Attitudes Toward Government, SSRC Research Report, HR5427, 1980, appendix p. 28.

[10]G. Heald, "A Comparison Between American, European and Japanese Values," Hunt Valley, Maryland Annual W APOR Conference, May 1982, table 4. Cited in R. Rose, *Politics in England,* 4th ed. (Boston: Little, Brown, 1986), p. 135.

[11]P. Kellner, "Who Rules Britain?" *The Sunday Telegraph,* October 24, 1982, cited in P. Norton, *The British Polity* (New York: Longman, 1984), pp. 360–361.

Table 9.1   ATTITUDES TOWARD SOCIETAL CHANGE IN BRITAIN

	Percent of respondents supporting the statement		
	1976	1981	1985
"The entire way our society is organized must be radically changed by revolutionary action"	8	10	5
"Our society must be gradually improved by reforms"	65	63	65
"Our present society must be valiantly defended against all subversive forces"	27	27	30

Source: Commission of the European Communities, *Eurobarometre,* no. 24 (December 1985), table 14.

survived the difficulties of depression in the 1930s and world war in the 1940s relatively unscathed, and it is not surprising that Britain's present economic difficulties have failed to discredit or destabilize the regime. This does not mean, however, that there are no potential threats to political stability in Britain. These threats do not come from the majority of citizens who are English and white, but rather from groups who are somewhat peripheral, racially or ethnically, to the mainstream of British life.

These peripheral groups fall into two categories: Britain's small but growing nonwhite minority and the ethnic minorities of the "Celtic fringe," in particular the Scots and the Irish. The race problem in Britain is of relatively recent origin. In the postwar era, immigrants from the nonwhite territories once ruled by Britain began to enter the country in considerable numbers. This flow of immigrants consisted largely of Indians and Pakistanis from Asia and blacks from the West Indies. While many of these immigrants have done well in Britain, the group as a whole has suffered from considerable discrimination and has been especially hard-hit by the high unemployment levels of the 1980s. British governments have acted to curtail the influx of immigrants in response to public opinion, but the size of the nonwhite minority—about 4.5 percent of the population—is already great enough to pose significant challenges to law and order. In 1985 serious urban riots in Liverpool and south London alerted the government to the dangers that can result if the problems of disadvantaged racial minorities are ignored.

There are considerably fewer Northern Irish than there are nonwhites in the United Kingdom, but the problems they pose to stability and the rule of law are much greater. The main reason for this is geography: Northern Ireland is geographically separated from the rest of the United Kingdom but contiguous with the Republic of Ireland (Eire). Many among the Catholic minority in Northern Ireland (which numbers about half a million) support the ultimate goal of the Irish Republican Army (IRA) of bringing Northern Ireland into the Irish Republic and tolerate its campaigns of bombings and assassinations designed to achieve that end. In addition, a proportion of the Protestant community stands behind the sometimes violent activities of Protestant paramilitary groups determined to resist such aims. Although IRA attacks have occasionally been staged in Britain itself, the violence is largely concentrated in Northern Ireland, and most Britons see it as a Northern Irish rather than a British problem. The fact remains, however, that in part of the United Kingdom law and order is maintained with the active assistance of the British army—and only precariously at that.

Sentiments of separatism have also become important in Scotland. In the late 1960s and early 1970s support for the idea of Scottish independence was bolstered by the discovery of oil deposits in the North Sea off the Scottish coast, which promised to assure Scotland's economic future. In the 1980s separatism increasingly is being fed by the opposite conditions: hard economic times and high unemployment. The recession of the early 1980s hit the northern parts of Britain, including Scotland, especially hard, and the recovery that has since taken place has been largely confined to southern England. Not surprisingly, it was the prosperous constituencies of southern England that gave Conservative Prime Minister Thatcher her electoral victories in 1983 and 1987; in Scotland, the Conservative party finds itself in deep decline, winning just 9 of 72 Scottish seats in the latter election. A feeling of alienation at being left out of the economic recovery and being ruled by a government that commands so little support in Scotland may lead in the future to greater support for the goal of Scottish independence.

The importance of these challenges from somewhat peripheral groups should not be exaggerated. The widespread sentiments of alienation in Scotland did not translate into votes for Scottish nationalist candidates, who won only three seats in 1987, one more than they had won in 1983. In Northern Ireland, Britain's fight against terrorism is even receiving the active cooperation of the government of the Republic of Ireland, which rejects the idea of forcibly removing that province from the United Kingdom. As for Britain's nonwhite minority, its geographic dispersal throughout Britain and its small size relative to the total population limit its potential for seriously threatening the political order. For the majority of United Kingdom citizens who are white and English, the regime enjoys, and likely will continue to enjoy, overwhelming support. What the British example does illustrate is that the achievement of political stability is never total and that challenges to the political order can arise whenever distinct groups feel disadvantaged relative to the rest of society.

France: Stability in the Making

For most of the two centuries since the French Revolution, France's main political problem has been instability. The cavalcade of authoritarian and democratic regimes noted in Chapter 1—which came and went at a rate of one every 15 to 20 years—suggested a society seriously at odds with itself over how political authority should be organized. Even within the longest-lasting regime, the Third Republic (1875–1940), instability abounded: over 100 different governments held office during its 65-year history and several attempts were made to overthrow it by force. The current regime, the Fifth Republic, appeared to be under serious threat during the student-worker demonstrations and strikes of May–June 1968, just 10 years after the regime had been founded. When student demonstrations broke out in 1986 over proposed university reforms, many observers wondered whether they represented a new manifestation of the tendency of the French to attack (and topple) their political regimes at frequent intervals.

France's political instability originated in the Old Regime. Instead of moving over time toward a system of parliamentary and eventually democratic government, as did England, French political development, up to the late eighteenth century, tended toward ever greater concentration of power around the monarch. Increasingly unpopular and ineffective, the monarchy fell during the revolution and was replaced by a republic, but excesses by its leaders and invasion by foreign powers ultimately paved the way for the dictatorship of the Emperor Napoleon. Napoleon's military defeat in 1815 allowed France's enemies to restore the monarchy but left the country divided among those who supported the monarchy's return, those who were committed to the revolutionary values of "liberty, equality, fraternity," and those who longed for the glory of the Napoleonic Empire. The variety of regimes after 1815—which included republics, monarchies, and another empire—reflected in large part the changing political fortunes of these rival groups.

France's turbulent and divisive political history has also had its effect on popular attitudes. We saw in Chapter 1 that the French have ambivalent attitudes toward authority: on the one hand, they believe that the country requires a strong state to govern it; on the other hand, they seem highly prone to reject authority and rebel against it. It may be that a willingness among the French to accept the need for some kind of authority at a rational level is, in a sense, balanced by a reluctance to invest any duly constituted regime with emotional commitment. Given the frequent regime changes, this withholding of emotional commitment is understandable; it must be difficult to accept any one regime as "normal" and "right" when its likelihood of being replaced by a very different one has been so high. In general, cynicism and skepticism about politics and government have been much more in evidence in France than trust and confidence, with the right to reject authority if it goes too far held in reserve.

Suspicion of government in general, together with the lack of consensus on the appropriate form of government for the country, has manifested itself at times in a tendency to distinguish between what is "legal" and what is "real" in France. This distinction was most vigorously and openly advanced during the 1930s by Charles Maurras, the leader of an extreme right-wing antiparliamentary movement. Maurras believed that the real France was monarchist, Catholic, and rural and that the parliamentary regime of the Third Republic—the legal government— was an alien political form foisted on this real France. This distinction justified Maurras' opposition to the regime and, ultimately, his support of the Nazi occupation. A less extreme form of this contrast has been (and to some extent still is) current among top civil servants. With governments lasting six to eight months on average in the Third and Fourth Republics, it was natural for higher administrators to see themselves as the true governors of the country, protectors of the interests of the state, while politicians came and went. This attitude was nourished not just by the short durations of governments but also by the tendency, discussed in Chapter 5, for elected politicians to represent more the interests of their localities (and pressure groups associated with their localities) than national perspectives. It was also stimulated by the periodic political scandals, which, to many, added an aura of corruption to democratic politics.

A similar line of thought was present for a very long time within the officer corps of the armed forces. Hostility to the fledgling Third Republic was common among the army's officer corps during the latter nineteenth century, and a failed military coup in 1889 ultimately provoked the government to a purge of antirepublican officers. The army remained basically quiescent until the 1950s, but the tendency to associate parliamentary government with weakness and betrayal of the country's "true" interests was rekindled when Fourth Republic political leaders began to contemplate seriously the granting of independence to Algeria. Algeria was not considered a colony in the normal sense; rather, it was a department of France, with representation in the National Assembly. To army officers fighting the rebel FLN in Algeria, giving up Algeria would have been tantamount to ceding a part of France itself, an act of betrayal even if it were done in a perfectly legal fashion. The mutiny of army officers in support of French colonists who seized control of the government in Algeria brought on France's last change of regime, the dissolution of the Fourth Republic and its replacement by the Fifth Republic in 1959.

Political instability has been a highly salient fact of French life for much of the last two centuries, but there were important elements of continuity and stability in French government that limited its impact. This is particularly true in the areas of law and administration. Laws passed under one regime, for example, typically remained in effect during subsequent regimes, even when the nature of the regime changed drastically. While new regimes certainly brought in new legislation or decrees that accorded with their political or policy orientations, in a great many areas where the state touches on the lives of its citizens, the basic framework of laws survived regime changes essentially intact. Similarly, the structure, methods of operation, and even personnel of the state bureaucracy generally continued not just from one government to the next but from one regime to the next. This continuity of personnel carried over to politicians as well. During the parliamentary republics, the frequent turnover of governments masked a surprisingly high degree of stability among cabinet ministers. When a government resigned or was defeated in the Parliament, more often than not it was followed by a government composed largely, if not entirely, of the same parties. As a result, individual party leaders often continued on in cabinet over two or more successive governments, providing stability of leadership despite the instability of cabinets.

This hidden continuity in the personnel, procedures, and laws of government furnished a basis on which a more general political stability could be achieved, if only an acceptable and workable form of government could be found. By the 1950s, the issue was no longer whether the regime should be democratic or not; what mattered was finding a system that would function more effectively and win greater public support. The answer de Gaulle arrived at was to check the possibilities for instability inherent in the parliamentary system by introducing a strong element of presidentialism. Although de Gaulle's Fifth Republic has been in existence for just three decades, it has demonstrated both stability and effectiveness and has garnered overwhelming support from the French public. The institution of the presidency has contributed to the popularity of the regime because it usually has meant that a single, powerful leader, accountable to the electorate at election time, is clearly in charge of the overall management of the state's affairs. The rudderless drift of government in the hands of unstable coalitions of parties unable to agree on major policy issues—a prime characteristic of the parliamentary republics—is no longer in evidence.

The presidency has augmented the stability and effectiveness of government in part because its existence encouraged the consolidation of the party system and the formation of stable majorities in the National Assembly. The process began very quickly under de Gaulle's presidency. So great was de Gaulle's popularity that the Gaullist party very quickly became the largest party in the National Assembly and, together with other, much smaller right-wing parties, was able to provide the president with an assured majority for his policies throughout his 11 years in office. The parties of the Left, in consequence, soon realized that if they were ever to win the presidency, they would have to present a credible alternative capable of winning at least 50 percent of the national vote. The result has been a degree of unity on both the Left and the Right that, although fragile at times, has made French elections an essentially two-sided affair and provided stable, disciplined majorities for all the governments of the Fifth Republic.

The massive demonstrations and strikes in 1968 seemed at the time to challenge the survival of the new regime, but the regime weathered the crisis well. The "events" of May–June 1968 clearly indicated some disenchantment with de Gaulle's aloof and autocratic leadership style as well as government actions or inactions in certain areas, but it is unlikely that the regime was ever really under threat. The legislative elections held shortly thereafter confirmed the strength of support for the government and the regime: the Gaullists won an absolute majority in the National Assembly and the opposition parties sustained considerable setbacks. De Gaulle, perhaps feeling that his personal leadership had been repudiated, resigned the following year, and the first transfer of power took place smoothly with the election of Georges Pompidou, de Gaulle's former prime minister, to the presidency.

There were other indications that the regime's support was not undermined by the protests of 1968 or the resignation of de Gaulle shortly thereafter. For example, a 1978 survey indicated that 56 percent of respondents thought the regime's institutions worked well (versus 21 percent who did not) and that two-thirds thought they assured stability.[12] At that time, however, two crucial challenges had still to be met: Could the regime survive a transfer of power to the Left, and could it survive a division of authority between a president of one side and a parliamentary majority of another?

In the 1980s both questions have been answered in the affirmative. In 1981 the Socialists won both the presidency and a majority in the National Assembly and proceeded for the subsequent five years to govern much as their predecessors had. For a time, four Communist leaders were even included in the cabinet; the only sign of protest came from the United States (and it was very much resented in France). In 1986 the final challenge was encountered when the Socialists lost control of the National Assembly. The constitution provides no clear guidelines for how authority is to be divided between president and prime minister in such a situation, but the dilemma was easily resolved. President Mitterrand, who still had two years left in his mandate, decided to accept the more recent verdict of the electorate and allow the new right-wing majority to proceed with the implementation of its program.

The Fifth Republic today appears to have addressed all the obstacles to stable government in France and to have won the support of the French public. It provides for strong leadership at the top, while improving the accountability of government to the public through the direct election of the president. In a 1985 survey only 5 percent of respondents believed that society should be changed through revolutionary action, a considerable improvement over 1976 (see Table 9.2). Such is the nature of French political culture that demonstrations and protests may be expected to occur from time to time, but they most likely will continue to be largely nonviolent and oriented toward challenging specific government policies rather than challenging the regime itself. The vital quality

[12]*L'Express,* September 25, 1978.

Table 9.2   ATTITUDES TOWARD SOCIETAL CHANGE IN FRANCE

	Percent of respondents supporting the statement		
	1976	1981	1985
"The entire way our society is organized must be radically changed by revolutionary action"	14	5	5
"Our society must be gradually improved by reforms"	67	68	70
"Our present society must be valiantly defended against all subversive forces"	19	27	25

Source: Commission of the European Communities, *Eurobarometre,* no. 24 (December 1985), table 14.

of political stability—so elusive for so long in France—has now become an undisputed feature of French political life.

STABILITY AND INSTABILITY IN THE USSR AND CHINA

Communist governments come into being amid great political instability, and while it cannot be doubted that one of their first priorities is establishing the stability of their ruling position, an equally compelling objective is the revolutionary transformation of existing social and political realities—a purpose that requires continued destabilizing actions. In the process of carrying the revolution forward, the ruling party often develops serious cleavages within its leadership ranks which can produce an unstable condition that persists for a long time. In the Soviet Union, the party's ruling position was firmly established within half a decade after the Bolshevik Revolution, but instability within the party elite persisted until some years after Stalin's death. In China, similarly, the party has managed to secure its position at the helm of the political order while serious conflicts among leaders have continued to occur. During the life of Mao Zedong, moreover, it was clear that the party engaged in policies meant to shake society periodically from whatever tendencies to complacency might have been forming, and usually these policies resulted in prolonged political instability. The contemporary regime in the USSR enjoys a position of high stability, both in its hold on the instruments of power and in its processes of elite recruitment and succession; in China, to the contrary, the stability of the party's ruling position overlies a continuing shakiness in the patterns of elite competition.

Soviet Union: A Stable Oligarchy?

There is in the West a popular notion, supported by certain political leaders, that the Soviet political system is inherently unstable. This notion stems from the traditional liberal belief that no government can endure unless its authority is based on the explicit will of the governed, as expressed in periodic free elections. The Soviet leaders, of course, scoff at the idea that their system is unstable, pointing out that their government has now lasted for more than seven decades—a time that has seen the disappearance of centuries-old European monarchies, the rise and fall of fascism, radical constitutional changes in countries as old as France and Japan, and the birth of new states in place of the colonial systems once ruled by the British, French, Dutch, and Portuguese. In terms of overall criteria—legitimacy, durability, and the management of internal conflict—the Soviet government approaching 1990 certainly appears stable, but are the appearances accurate?

If it is difficult in any case to measure a government's legitimacy, it is especially so in regard to the Soviet Union. Elections, as we know, are not a useful indication, and public opinion surveys, though not unknown in the USSR, do not give direct data on citizens' attitudes toward their government or its leaders.[13] However, in several respects that are clearly observable, a prominent Soviet affairs specialist concluded toward the end of the Brezhnev era, one should not doubt the legitimacy of the Soviet government:

> The legitimacy of the Soviet system is conditioned by its longevity, by its withstanding the tests of major crises and shocks, by its identification with great-power nationalism which unifies the masses and the elites, by the successful symbiosis of the messianic doctrinal elements of Marxism-Leninism with this nationalism, by the increase in the number and weight of the strata in Soviet society which have a stake in the system and particularly in its activities, by the basic unity of its elites, and by the complex way in which the system is integrated.[14]

The durability of the Soviet regime is the most obvious of these points. The governing system, based on a single-party oligarchy, has remained essentially the same since the Bolshevik Revolution. True, the style of decision-making changed (as did the flavor of the decisions taken) when Stalin gathered effective power unto himself, but even in usurping the decision-making authority of the Communist party, Stalin did not abolish it, and the post-Stalin leaders found the party's institutional base sufficiently intact to allow the rebuilding of its authority. Since the end of the civil war in 1920, there has been no serious challenge to the party's rule, and as of the late 1980s the emergence of any force capable of mounting such a challenge is almost unthinkable.

As far as its ability to manage internal conflict is concerned, the Soviet government has demonstrated itself to be among the most effective

[13]For a study of Soviet and East European public opinion on a range of issue areas, see Walter D. Connor, "Opinion, Reality, and the Communist Political Process," in W.D. Connor et al., *Public Opinion in European Socialist Systems* (New York: Praeger, 1977).

[14]Seweryn Bialer, *Stalin's Successors: Leadership, Stability, and Change in the Soviet Union* (Cambridge: Cambridge University Press, 1980), p. 205.

in the world. It is no small feat for a government to rule for seven decades over more than a hundred different ethnic communities. Occasional outbursts of unrest have been contained to local areas, and no widespread nationalist movement has developed—not even among the Armenians angered by their relations with the Azeris. Political and religious dissent has been kept to the margins of society. In recent decades the Soviet Union has seen no civil disturbances of a scope comparable to those in Poland during the 1970s and early 1980s and nothing like the mass manifestations of China's Cultural Revolution; there has been no regional violence like that which has persistently thrown the legitimacy of British rule in Northern Ireland into question; nor have there been urban riots like those that broke out in the black ghettos of the United States during the mid- and late 1960s. In comparison to these and indeed many other societies, the Soviet Union projects a picture of domestic tranquility.

Of course, this was not always the case. The revolutionary period, stretching through the purges of the late 1930s, was a time of great socioeconomic stress, the uprooting and even destruction of many families, extreme levels of violence, and tremendous human suffering. The civil war, the collectivization drive, the breakneck pace of industrialization, and the political terror all took countless lives, and even if the party's unparalleled use of coercion succeeded in securing its rule, its position atop a vast society that was at first rebellious and then beaten into submission could hardly be called stable.

As for today's stability, one could justifiably take issue with its basis. It comes at the cost of a persisting police state environment which deprives citizens of many civil liberties that Westerners assume to be their rights. The list of Soviet violations of civil liberties is long, extending from the silencing of dissident literary figures to the incarceration of political dissenters in mental institutions, a practice that reached serious dimensions during the Brezhnev era. Thus, although terror and mass violence as means of political control have become things of the past, the state has not ceased to use repressive measures against citizens who dare to criticize its policies openly.

Nor is it clear that the reforms championed by General Secretary Gorbachev will extend so far as to end political repression. That official policies toward dissenters had moderated became apparent late in 1986, when Andrei Sakharov was released from house arrest and allowed to return to Moscow, where he began speaking out publicly for some of the causes he had espoused before his internal exile. Other political prisoners have also been released, literary and artistic censorship has been significantly liberalized, and travel restrictions have been lessened. All of these changes bode positively for the cause of civil liberties in the Soviet Union, but none of them has been complete—and, significantly, the regime has persisted in denying that its policies violate international standards of human rights.

By their policies, Soviet leaders exhibit the belief that repression is vital to the survival of socialism or to the stability of party rule; whether or not it is could be determined only by its cessation. A Westerner might understandably ask why, if the Communist party truly represents the interests of the working class, the Soviet elite finds it necessary to deprive the workers of individual rights. Many of the USSR's ideological allies, including several of the largest West European Communist parties, have gone on record to disavow the Soviet human rights policies. From the Soviet leaders, one hears no clear answer.

As the USSR proceeds along the path of economic reform, it is likely that its leaders will hear increasing demands for political reforms as well. Indeed, if the economic reforms succeed in decentralizing management authority, they will in and of themselves go some distance toward decentralizing political control because of the multitude of far-reaching decisions that will have to be made by managers of plants and cartels. This does not mean that political democratization, or even liberalization, follows inevitably; as we have seen, the Soviet system already relies on the meaningful participation of many more people than surface appearances indicate, and it may very well be that the power system can be partially decentralized without radically changing the configuration of power—a broadening of the oligarchy, in other words. But to realize that objective, the Gorbachev government will be required to walk a line that might prove to be very narrow.

Despite the long history of Soviet rule and the extent to which it appears to have taken root, there are several potential sources of political instability. The least of them, though by no means insignificant, exists within the oligarchy itself. Consensus formation among the elites requires some measure of sensitivity on the part of the general secretary; should he fail to do his political spadework—that is, secure and maintain a broadly based agreement on all his policy initiatives—his authority could weaken.[15] The political system remains that of rule by a collective, and the Politburo functions as a committee, but whether in a democracy or in an oligarchy, committees work effectively only if they have strong leadership. A weakened general secretary, therefore, would cause instability in the governing system.

A second possible source of instability might be discontent brought on by economic reforms. For decades, Soviet workers and managers alike have grown accustomed to the accepted procedures; now, there is a likelihood that procedures will change. In particular, wage differentials are likely to increase according to efficiency and productivity, and occupa-

---

[15]During the autumn of 1987, for example, Gorbachev suffered what Westerners widely interpreted as a close call when one of his most trusted colleagues, Boris Yeltsin, was forced out of his powerful position as chief of the Moscow party committee. Yeltsin had come under fire by conservatives in the central party elite for his radical approach to economic reform. His fall was seen as a victory for those, presumed to be led by CPSU Second Secretary Yegor Ligachev, who urged caution in pursuing the Gorbachev reforms. The affair caused a momentary stir in the world press, but it apparently signaled no serious government instability.

Table 9.3 NATIVE CADRES IN SOVIET UNION REPUBLICS, 1976

Institution	Number	Percent of indigenous cadres
Party Central Committee bureaus and Presidium of Council of Ministers of all union republics	252	75.8
Top party-state executive cadres in		
Uzbekistan	176	76.0
Latvia	112	74.0
Georgia	134	94.0

Source: S. Bialer, *Stalin's Successors: Leadership, Stability, and Change in the Soviet Union* (1980), p. 214.

tional dislocations may result if inefficient plants are required to close down.[16] It is conceivable that the ensuing inequalities will lead to resentment among the work force, whose members have up until now been content—if not with their wages and living standards, at least in the knowledge that they are all in the same boat. Such resentment, if it persisted and spread, could erode the government's authority.

Probably the most serious potential for political instability lies among the non-Russian nationalities. Although the elites have largely been assimilated into the Soviet system, the underlying non-Russian populations remain less so. It remains to be seen what effect economic reforms will have on the poorer regions inhabited by non-Russian majorities, particularly in Central Asia and the Caucasus; if these regions fall further behind the more developed regions, anger and frustration might build and produce a serious conflict. Nor does the potential for trouble lie only in economic backwardness; it also exists in the communities with traditions (or at least aspirations) of national independence, particularly the Latvians, Lithuanians, Ukrainians, and Armenians. Whether a region is economically deprived or advanced, the basis for conflict is always present in the primordial sociocultural identities which many non-Russians consider to be their proud heritage.

These groups are generally not seething with rebelliousness, however. None of them is large enough to stand alone against the Soviet state in any circumstances, and the probability of an anti-Russian alliance or conspiracy between any two or more nationalities is negligible. Those that express discontent—the Armenians, for example—often aim their anger not at the Russians or the Soviet state, but at other, neighboring nationalities. Perhaps most important, the Soviet elite has been adept at co-opting ambitious non-Russians into positions of local and national responsibility, thereby forestalling the rise of discontented ethnic elites. (See Table 9.3.) Should this conscious policy of native co-optation fail, or

[16]Nor is such an event only hypothetical in socialist systems; Hungary, which has led the way in economic reforms among Soviet bloc countries, experienced its first bankruptcy in a state-owned enterprise in 1987.

should there come a time when the indigenous elites seriously outnumber the official posts available for them, then the ethnic situation could become dangerous.

Able for the time being to neutralize or control these potential trouble spots, the Soviet regime sits astride one of the most stable political systems in the world. Its institutions are strong and effective. The quality of Soviet political leadership, while by no means consistent across the many layers of party and government, is high at least among the top ranks, and since the accession of General Secretary Gorbachev, the regime has taken on a dynamic and businesslike image that distinguishes it, at least on the surface, from the torpor of the 1970s and the unpredictability of the Khrushchev years.

The Soviet political culture, rooted in centuries of tsarist absolutism and further conditioned by decades of communist oligarchy, provides a context of relative congruence between public assumptions about political power and the actual patterns of government. Among the populace, deference to authority prevails. Rebelliousness is rare; where and when it breaks out, it occurs on the basis of a limited grievance—protesting broken promises of human rights, for example, rather than challenging the regime's authority to govern—and is always easily checked by force.

Acceptance of authority, especially in these circumstances, does not necessarily mean affection for the system. Indeed, one commonly hears Soviet citizens refer to representatives of the state or party as "they," implying a conscious separation between "civilians" and politicians. Soviet citizens are probably not enamored of all their government's policies, and perhaps they do not even think of the regime as "theirs," but as far as we can judge, they do not seriously question its right to rule.

China: Stability Amid Revolutionary Change

From the middle of the nineteenth century through the communist revolution, China experienced political instability almost continuously. After 1949, the communist regime consolidated control of the polity and slowly, sporadically, evolved a set of institutions for the transaction of public business. The regime has endured, but its leadership has undergone frequent changes—often in the form of purges—that have been linked to radical policy shifts, which in turn have disturbed the system. Unlike the Soviet purges of the 1930s, those in China have been mostly bloodless; those purged have been removed from positions of power, sometimes subjected to "thought reform" sessions, and removed from the public eye. Nevertheless, the purges have been destabilizing events in China's political life.

Clearly, there is a strain of thinking in Chinese communism that values change and, along with it, appears to value turbulence as a constructive phenomenon in achieving socialism:

> Overthrowing the old social system and establishing a new one is a great strug-
> gle. . . . It must not be assumed that the new system can be completely consolidated
> the moment it is achieved, for that is impossible. It has to be consolidated step by
> step. To achieve its ultimate consolidation it is necessary to . . . persevere in the
> socialist revolution on the economic front and to carry on constant and arduous social
> revolutionary struggles.[17]

Mao's proposition that change and consolidation occur dialectically, that is, through conflict and struggle, is at the heart of the dilemma confronting the Chinese leadership since the communist revolution.[18] In the People's Republic of China, political stability as a value takes on an ambivalent character. The leadership desires stability to the extent that the ruling party maintains power, but nothing else is sacred. Social, economic, and political institutions all undergo change, and even the party may be subjected to major transformations—as, for example, when Mao attacked it during the Hundred Flowers campaign of 1957 and launched the Cultural Revolution in the 1960s.

The twin goals of stability and change often conflict, and when they do in China, social change usually prevails—not social change originating in the evolution of society itself, however, but social change as promulgated by the political leaders. The authoritarian presumption behind such a revolution-from-above poses its own curious dialectic, for authoritarianism is exactly what the revolution seeks ultimately to destroy in the pursuit of a democratic society. Mao believed that the ideal way to realize this goal was through mass participation, meaning the mobilization of the masses by the leaders. His approach was frequently challenged by critics within the party, and the resulting conflict created an undercurrent of deep political instability which has persisted to this day. The economic liberalization program of the 1980s has reaffirmed this underlying conflict, as the "modernizers" continue to struggle against their opponents.

Elite instability has always been associated with policy disputes, often in combination with factional power struggles. When the coalition headed by Gao Gang and Jao Shushi challenged Mao's leadership in the 1950s, it did so both on the basis of issues (the nature of Chinese-Soviet relations, the role of the party in the economy) and as the spokesmen for the power claims of the "red" party faction (those whose pre-1949 experience had primarily been in communist-controlled areas) as opposed to

---

[17]Mao Zedong, "Speech to Chinese Communist Party National Conference on Propaganda Work," in *On New Democracy* (Beijing: Foreign Language Press, 1967), p. 235.

[18]Mao's affinity for dialectical reasoning was drawn from Karl Marx, who argued that at the heart of historical change is the social law of opposites. Every object and every behavior has its direct opposites, called by Marx the thesis and the antithesis, which clash against one another and ultimately produce a synthesis. This, in turn, contains the seeds of a new conflict between opposing forces. The process through which the thesis, in conflict with its antithesis, is resolved in a synthesis recurs infinitely; this process is called the *dialectic.*

the "whites" (those whose communist activities had been carried out in Guomindang-controlled areas). A second instance of elite instability took place in 1957–1958, when many intellectuals, bureaucrats, and their supporters were purged following the Hundred Flowers movement. Further incidents, as we have seen, occurred in the 1960s and early 1970s, culminating in the Cultural Revolution and the Lin Biao affair. Once again, both before and after Mao's death in 1976, party factions fought for power on the basis of contrasting political and economic programs, resulting in the triumph (for the time being) of Deng's group.

Revolutionary change has its costs, and one of them is the high probability of social unrest. In the 1950s there was significant opposition to the Communists among groups that felt they had suffered from the post-1949 policy changes: landlords and rich peasants, members of the Mongolian and Tibetan minorities, merchants and industrialists of the former capitalist class. The opposition of these groups prompted a series of party-sponsored movements to "reform their thoughts." Dissent increased in the late 1950s, first with the Hundred Flowers movement and later with the Great Leap Forward. The Hundred Flowers movement ended in the abrupt suppression of the dissenters; the Great Leap led to a change in political leadership in favor of Liu Shaoqi's group.

It was during the late 1960s that China experienced its greatest communist-era social unrest. Table 9.4 chronicles the processes by which this particular movement emerged. Seen in its details, the Cultural Revolution illustrates the range of activities, both those instigated by the party elite and those which emerged among other groups, that have characterized Chinese politics at other times during the Communists' rule. Many of the ingredients that have made up the dialectic of stability and instability since 1949 were condensed into the period of the Cultural Revolution: leadership rivalries, the manipulation of mass groups for the purpose of resolving elite conflicts, the emergence of social forces that threatened the party's control, and the firm reassertion of central authority. Some of these events, as we have seen, repeated themselves in the struggle to succeed Mao Zedong.

Thus, the events of the Cultural Revolution—the factional infighting, the use of mass movements by one or another faction to support its claim to power, and so on—form parts of a complex model from which Chinese political actors can draw precedents as they jockey for power. The "Ching Ming" riots that broke out in Beijing in 1976 aided Hua Guofeng in his effort to remove Deng Xiaoping from the Politburo; two years later, the tables were turned as Deng utilized his support within the so-called Democracy Movement to aid his return to power. In yet another twist, Deng, on top as of early 1979, turned against the Democracy Movement and closed down its most famous symbol, the "Democracy Wall," where demonstrators had posted political statements, including calls for democratic reform.

The seeds of this movement did not die; in 1986 they germinated

Table 9.4 GREAT PROLETARIAN CULTURAL REVOLUTION: HIGHLIGHTS, 1967–1968

1967

January	A Shanghai faction in the CCP commences the January Revolution. Red Guards are told to organize throughout China and to win power.
February	"February Adverse Current." Zhou Enlai seeks to protect the State Council. An opposing faction in the Politburo seeks to defend its position.
March	The army is mobilized to support agriculture, thus attempting to isolate them from the political infighting.
April	The Red Guard faction in the Party leadership denounces Liu Xiaoqi. However, moderates in the Party ask the Red Guards to honor the veteran cadres.
May	Army "rectification" campaign commenced.
July	Political and labour violence erupts in Wu Han. Zhou Enlai intervenes to restore order.
August	Red Guards seize the foreign ministry, then lose it.
September	Mao travels to key points in China and urges the competing factions to compromise.
October	The Red Guard leadership seeks to accelerate the formation of the ruling tripartite Revolutionary Committees. These are composed of representatives from the Military, the Party, and the Red Guards.
November	Deng Xiaoping is denounced.
December	Editorials in *The People's Daily* call for unity among the competing factions.

1968

January	The Party leadership commences a campaign to back the army (a prelude to army intervention).
February	The Party leadership orders the army to support the left, but they do not designate a specific faction.
March	Red Guard activities against party cadres and intellectuals and government cadres continue. Army Chief of Staff Yang Jengwu is purged as the leftists gain momentum.
April	*The People's Daily* approves factionalism.
May	The ruling faction in the Party, government, and other organizations are attacked by the Red Guard.
June	The violence accelerates throughout the country.
July	Mao denounces Red Guard for lack of discipline.
August	Zhou Enlai attempts to pacify Red Guards by announcing the existence of Revolutionary Committees throughout country. Mao concedes to allow Zhou to use the army to restore order.
September	The two competing factions in the Party are at par. The military under Lin Biao and with Mao's blessing ascends.

again and began to grow into another major democratization movement. As in 1978–1979, the movement's proponents advocated the adoption of political reforms to parallel the ongoing economic changes; nor were their appeals modest in scope, for they expressed a clear desire for democracy as it is understood in the West. This movement, however, was nipped in the bud by party conservatives, who were already feeling threatened by the reforms under way in the economy; they agreed to support the economic program but drew the line at major political reform. Deng, apparently backtracking, sacrificed party leader Hu Yaobang to placate the conservatives.

Because the main political events have been kept ultimately under the control of the party, it has been hard to ascertain the level of public acceptance for the Chinese communist regime. Meaningful public opinion data are as scarce for the Soviet Union as they are for China, and the question of the government's legitimacy must be evaluated through other evidence. While there undoubtedly is continued trust in the party, it is also clear that the liberalization of the 1980s has brought with it a greater willingness to question the party's authority and competence. Students and intellectuals have been actively calling for a more open and competitive political system. Many others affected by the inflationary effects of the modernization drive are also skeptical of the party's performance capabilities. Minority groups such as Tibetans have risen in protest, most recently in 1987 before the cameras of Western journalists and tourists. Obviously, the question of the regime's legitimacy is complex; the "average" Chinese peasant or worker appears to show support through hard work and political quiescence, while groups of protesters await the proper moment to express their dissatisfaction.

Despite these recurrent signs of disquiet, and despite major mistakes which have undermined the system's stability, China's Communist party has survived in power for four decades. Since Mao's demise the party has increasingly come to share power with governmental institutions, thereby acknowledging the authority of governmental structures and procedures as long as they remain under party supervision. The party has skillfully maintained control over the army by merging top military leadership into the party's highest offices. Its support among the wide masses stems from its historic role and the revolutionary legends, as well as from the economic progress it has brought about. In all of this, the party has benefited from the leadership skills of its top personalities, who have created a successful organization with considerable internal discipline—no small achievement in the world's most populous country.

To be sure, China's huge population poses an ever-present political threat. Such a large number of people creates a perpetual strain on the

Liberalization in China has occasionally led to outright protest against the government. Here students burn copies of the *Peking Daily* in 1987, claiming it misreported their campaign for democracy. (Neal Ulevich / AP)

state's resources as well as on its ability to maintain order. Active programs to curb population growth have included campaigns to delay marriage, the promotion of contraception, free abortions, and restricted distribution of ration cards for those with more than two children. Most Chinese still live in rural areas, where public services are less readily available than in the cities. The uneven distribution of population has given rise to campaigns to return educated and aspiring urban migrant jobholders to the countryside. Their return has often been colored by resentment, and, whether resentful or not, they take with them the heightened consciousness and increased expectations of the city dweller.

Another factor, as yet indeterminate in its consequences for political stability, is the economic reforms. Economic liberalization may produce political effects quite apart from the Democracy Movement already seen, as a nascent class conflict takes shape between efficient and inefficient producers. The demise of the "iron rice bowl" (i.e., a guaranteed livelihood) has rendered the individual vulnerable to loss of job and income; indeed, there has already been a dramatic leap in unemployment. Many problems plaguing rapidly developing Third World countries—such as urban squalor, mounting unemployment, and labor unrest—could emerge to threaten political stability.

Our assessment of China's stability, therefore, concludes on a mixed note. On the one hand, there have been the purposeful disruptions of society in the Great Leap Forward and the Cultural Revolution, the recurrent instability in the party leadership as manifested in periodic top-level purges, and strained socioeconomic relations that might well be aggravated should population growth continue. On the other hand, China compares favorably with many other countries at similar stages of development. The party has weathered numerous crises, emerging as a strong instrument for political control and mass mobilization. Perhaps most important is the fact that, unlike so many other developing countries, China has successfully avoided military takeover. While other Asian and African states that achieved independence at about the time of China's communist takeover have fallen under military dictatorships, the principle of civilian rule has been maintained in China.

MEXICO AND NIGERIA: THE STRUGGLE FOR POLITICAL ORDER

Mexico and Nigeria have both modeled their democratic regimes on foreign examples, Mexico's on the constitution of the United States and Nigeria's first on the British parliamentary example and later on the U.S. model. In each case, the resulting political system has become very different from the one taken as an example, as both have been affected by their own political cultures. As we have seen, Mexico's political development has been shaped by authoritarianism and distrust and Nigeria's by ethnic conflict. The lesson is that Third World countries tend to follow their own political paths according to their own national conditions, despite the influences the developed countries may have had on them.

Thus, political stability in Third World countries inheres only partly in their institutional trappings. It took Mexico a hundred years of instability, including frequent military interventions, before a system evolved under PRI leadership to create the basis of a stable order. Nigeria, a country that is almost 150 years younger, began its independence with a parliamentary system which fell to a military coup within six years; its second attempt at democracy, a presidential regime, fell even more quickly. Long-term political stability, a hard-won achievement for Mexico which is now once again coming into question, has not yet been realized in Nigeria.

One obstacle to stability is that it is often seen as a negative value by segments of the society which favor change. In 1968, for example, Mexican students took to the streets declaring, "The revolution has brought stability; what we need is more revolution." One year earlier, rebel leaders in Nigeria's Eastern Region had seceded and declared the independent republic of Biafra. Both of these movements proved to be short-lived, but both demonstrated a sentiment that valued other objectives above political stability. Their proponents contended that if a regime is stable but neglects the people's needs, or is ineffectual in meeting them, the costs of stability outweigh the returns.

Mexico: Stability Under Challenge

Mexico since the 1910 revolution stands in direct political contrast with its nineteenth-century history. During Mexico's first half-century, governments averaged about one per year, and only three presidents (out of 30) served complete terms. There were even times when two or three groups claimed control of the government simultaneously. It has been calculated that, between 1821 and 1910, more than 1000 armed uprisings took place.[19]

Since the 1910 revolution, order has been achieved through consolidation of a one-party system. PRI rule, characterized by a strong executive and relatively weak legislative branches and local governments, has firmly planted roots. In the first place, the party was organized to incorporate key social groups, such as the unions and the peasantry, whose cooperation was important in achieving stability. In the second place, the evolution of the party into a powerful political force created a high level of elite stability, as the system of leadership recruitment through patronage and party service became standard. Further, the revolutionary ideology and its widely popular symbols have continued to appeal to the citizenry much more than any alternative ideology or symbol system to date, solidifying the government's claim to legitimacy.

These bases on which the state's stability is established may, however, have begun to erode in recent years. The support of poor people for the PRI, for example, is attributable as much to the party's ability to manipulate revolutionary symbols and promises as to its actual achievements, and given an attractive alternative, the poor might one day be as easily led to support an opposition force. Current trends are creating an

[19]Roger D. Hansen, "Mexican Economic Development: The Roots of Rapid Growth," in *Studies in Development,* no. 2 (Washington, D.C.: National Planning Association, 1971), p. 9.

increasingly large Mexican underclass, especially in the cities, and the more urban poverty grows, the likelier it is that the PRI's rhetoric will cease to persuade.

Signs of instability have appeared in frequent outbreaks of unrest among students, peasants, and workers. The violent student demonstrations of 1968 were not the first such expression of discontent; earlier in the 1960s some peasant leaders had found Fidel Castro's success in Cuba an appealing model, and the government spent much of the 1960s and early 1970s suppressing protests and even guerrilla movements. Frustrated peasants engaged in acts of violence against large landholders; labor discontent sometimes prompted individual unions to bolt temporarily from the control of the PRI; and, between 1968 and 1973, radical students challenged the government almost continuously. Often, the government resorted to force to restore order. Nor has the problem abated in the 1980s; with rising overall education levels and increasing economic difficulties, there are growing forces whose leaders dream of a change in the existing political formula.

Different kinds of unrest have emerged, moreover. In state and local elections held in 1985 and 1986, members of the opposition party PAN believed they had won, only to be overruled by PRI loyalists on the election commissions. The ensuing protests were often violent, especially along the border with the United States, and police were called in repeatedly as more elections yielded similar results and similar protests. In 1987 some 40,000 people marched in protest against the failure of the government to provide prompt assistance to the approximately 15,000 families left homeless by the 1985 Mexico City earthquake. As isolated manifestations of discontent, these protests were no threat to the government, but if future protests from dissatisfied groups—students, peasants, the urban poor—should coincide, then the PRI-dominated government could come under serious threat.

Even within the PRI-dominated system itself, there are weaknesses. The process of leadership selection for local government offices is not always above suspicion. There is evidence that the PRI has at other times overturned the results of mayoral and even gubernatorial ballots in order to maintain one-party rule. The aftermath of the 1988 elections saw several massive demonstrations, including one in Mexico City where over 300,000 gathered to denounce the government's "manipulation" of the election. Moreover, the alliance with key groups that has long made up the PRI has shown some cracks since the oil boom of the 1970s. Many capitalists, both state and private, came into great wealth as a result of that boom, and this has distanced them from the masses of workers and peasants even more than before. The disillusioned hopes of the 1980s have hit the lower and middle classes hard, especially as the government must squeeze society for the means to pay its own debts. Inflation has impoverished many who were once self-sufficient and has made survival, for those who were not, extremely difficult. The unity of the once-stable PRI coalition has thus been strained by hardening economic realities, engendered in part by factors like the price of oil or the level of international interest rates, which are beyond Mexico's control. They have raised what is probably the greatest threat to the system's stability since its consolidation.

Intensifying social problems signal further potentially destabilizing conditions. Rapid population growth has accelerated urbanization and created a vast subculture of people who have been uprooted from rural communities which, though poor, were familiar. If they find work in their new locations, organized groups such as unions may help to integrate them into the urban environment; if not, they become marginal squatters barely able to survive. Extended family ties often help provide subsistence and a sense of security—assuming the urban migrants have not removed themselves so far from their origins that they are out of contact with their families—but they do not counter all effects of poverty. Already during the 1970s the slums of Mexico City, Monterrey, and Guadalajara have erupted in violence.

The continuing growth of this marginal subculture obviously calls into question the regime's legitimacy, based as it is on the promises of the revolution. In the urban setting, poor people are exposed to life-styles other than their own, and they glimpse how the wealthy few live. They are also exposed to the mass media, a greater variety of consumer goods that they can rarely afford to purchase, and better educational opportunities. Their hopes for upward social mobility may be intensified, and their frustrations are often heightened. The urban slums understandably become fertile territory for radical political ideas.

Thus, there are forces pushing for reform in Mexico, both from within the ruling party and from the outside. The big question is whether the PRI will be able to co-opt all these continuing political elements or whether they will split off, seriously destabilizing the system. Another question mark is the army. Military leaders know they have a role in politics, historically and potentially. Aware of the power of their counterparts in neighboring countries and throughout Latin America, military leaders may very well yearn for a taste themselves; circumstances of extreme socioeconomic stress and the deterioration of PRI authority could conceivably open the door to military intervention.

Historically, the PRI has shown remarkable resilience and continuity. It remains in control of many crucial organizations and continues to enjoy the cooperation of most of those, like the church, that it does not control. Its continued domination of politics will depend on its ability to generate sound, innovative policies to deal with the current economic crisis, domestic and international, and to devise ways of integrating the marginal segments of society into the system. Whether the party can do all this is an open question, for the current problems are serious and will defy easy solutions.

Certainly, antigovernment sympathies have increased during the 1980s. In the past, the PRI has prevented political conflict through two tactics, co-optation and coercion. Co-optation, the preferred method, has traditionally been effective, but in recent years the use of coercion has been on the increase. The challenge of the immediate future is great, and the ruling party will have ample opportunity to test its mettle as it confronts the immensity of the economic crisis and the sharpness of its sociopolitical effects.

Nigeria: Democratic Instability and Military Order

Like Mexico in its first century, Nigeria since independence has gone through tremendous instability. The closest approximation to political stability has been provided by some of the military governments, but even these have been vulnerable to coups and coup attempts by other military leaders. The history of Nigerian independence, alas, is a succession of coups, with political assassinations, civilian violence, and a civil war in which more than 1 million people were killed. It is difficult to be optimistic about the chances for political stability in a country which has experienced the overthrow of two democratic regimes within its first 25 years.

The first place to look for explanations for this state of affairs is in the highly divided social constituency of modern-day Nigeria. As we have seen, Nigeria is composed of highly distinct ethnic groups, with their own languages, religions, and political and cultural traditions. Unlike many other new states, Nigeria was not led to independence by a charismatic leader who could overcome social divisions and unite the country behind a program of economic development and state-building. As a result, there has been, since independence, no enduring consensus on national political structures to make policy decisions, to select leaders, to transfer power, or to mediate political disputes. Government stability has eluded Nigerian aspirations, as conflicts between regions, ethnic communities, and religious groups have perennially sabotaged efforts to concoct a stable political formula.

The earliest structures, based on regions, nourished regional and ethnic distrust, intensified rivalries, and ultimately dissolved in civil war. When the Ironsi and Gowon regimes redivided the country into states and broke up the ethnically based political parties, they succeeded in giving a sense of security to the major groups—for the time being, at least. Gowon's reconciliation efforts with Biafra after the civil war also helped diminish ethnic and regional animosities. These divisions did not disappear, however; they just became less violent. Moreover, other forms of social cleavage such as religion have arisen to threaten the society's stability. Christians and Muslims come into conflict in the Northern and Western Regions, and in the north the Muslims fight against animists and other pagan groups as well. In the west, Christians and Muslims have battled to a draw, each converting about 40 percent of the Yorubas to their flag. Many of these conflicts have been heightened with the rise of Islamic fundamentalism in the late 1970s and 1980s, and, as in other parts of the world with strong Muslim communities, the potential for a major destabilizing conflict in Nigeria is ever present.

Another source of political instability, newer but just as salient, arises out of Nigeria's socioeconomic development. As in Mexico, the oil bonanza sharpened class cleavages, drew large number of peasants into urban industrial centers, and raised expectations of all groups exposed to the lure of petrodollars. A get-rich-at-all-costs mentality developed among many, only to be dashed in the economic crisis of the 1980s. In the city slums there emerged a large community of squatters, often criminal and violent, which has become a menace to order. Accompanying the growth of industry has been the development of a new and vociferous working class, as well as a politically active student culture, both affected by the economic disillusionment. In short, one finds in Nigeria all the potentially destabilizing socioeconomic factors that one expects to find in industrializing countries—on top of the underlying ethnic, religious, and regional cleavages.

Compounding the political situation in the early 1980s was widespread and flagrant corruption among the officials of civilian government. Although corruption has been common in Nigeria, the sudden infusion of oil money in the 1970s greatly aggravated the problem, and the revelations of high-level graft did much to undermine public confidence in the regime. For years there had been plans to build a new federal capital in Abuja, for example, but the project became mired in corruption.[20] Added to these issues were reports that the election of 1983 was marred by extensive vote-rigging.

Thus it was that the army, long imbued with a self-image as the savior and monitor of the country's affairs, saw its task in 1983 as a cleaning-up mission. The military leadership took it upon itself to interpret the public will following the disputed election and, under General Buhari's leadership, staged the fifth coup in Nigeria's short history. The sixth took place two years later, with the country sinking ever more deeply into economic crisis, amid continued official corruption and a widespread public distaste for the disciplinary character of Buhari's rule. Again, as was the case with Buhari, the promises of Babangida's new regime exceeded the government's capacity to deliver. One reason for this is that the army has not always been the bearer of constructive change. Incidents of public violence and police brutality in 1987 escalated into serious confrontations between citizens and authorities in several localities. These, combined with rampant incompetence, divisiveness, greed, and corruption that seem common to civilian and military regimes alike, only reinforce Nigeria's tendency to political instability.

Are there factors working for stability in Nigeria? At present, there

---

[20]Finally in 1987, under the military rule of General Babangida, the new capital was completed.

seem to be relatively few. The only effective unifying force apparent is the army; the fact that military recruitment takes place according to a system of regional quotas does help to neutralize sectional disputes over troop constitution. The military has taken certain other steps to overcome ethnic and regional divisiveness as well. One such step was the creation of the new states out of the larger regions, which was aimed at reducing the power of the larger ethnic groups over the smaller ones and undercutting the divisive regionalism that had led to civil war. Moving the capital to Abuja was also aimed at soothing some of the old irritations; Lagos, the former capital, is in the heart of Yorubaland, whereas Abuja, the new capital, lies in ethnically more neutral territory. The best of the military rulers have tried their utmost to govern on behalf of all Nigerians, whether Ibo, Hausa, Yoruba, Muslim, or Christian, but the general assumption—accepted even by the military rulers—is that their power is temporary, that it must and will one day be handed over to constitutionally elected civilian authorities.

In 1987 the military, mindful of the problems the First and Second Republics experienced, drew up a careful plan for a return to civilian rule. The plan calls for a five-year transitional phase, during which the military will supervise each step in the process, monitoring and eliminating abuses as they crop up. The first step is the introduction of local government elections, followed by the presentation of a new constitution to the electorate for ratification. Political parties will be free to organize, but the military will decide which two of them will be allowed to remain in existence and compete electorally. In this selection, emphasis will be placed on national parties as opposed to ethnic or regionally based parties. Following ratification of the constitution, elections will be held for state governments under the two-party format. This is to be followed by the final step, presidential and congressional elections for a revived House of Representatives and Senate (tentatively scheduled for 1992).

Despite the carefully crafted nature of the proposed return to democracy, any future civilian government will face the same problem that has underlain Nigerian politics ever since independence: how does a regime prove its legitimacy to a populace so riven with fundamental cleavages and so accustomed, by now, to the strong rule of the military? Tests of the previous civilian governments' legitimacy fail to demonstrate convincing evidence. During the First Republic, fewer than half of the eligible voters turned out for elections—hardly a ringing endorsement of the political process—and only an estimated 35 percent of the registered electorate voted in the first elections of the Second Republic.

One might, of course, argue that judging the government's legitimacy on the basis of low electoral turnout is unfair in a country where only 25 to 30 percent of the adult population is literate. And indeed, by other measures, the elections of the Second Republic showed impressive activity—in the number of political parties that appeared on the scene (as many as 40 in 1979, reduced to 5 by the electoral commission), the number of people who became involved in the campaigns, and the passions aroused by the elections (scattered violence was reported in connection with the 1983 voting). On the other hand, the violence of the 1983 elections was hardly something that connotes stability, and the widespread reports of dishonesty undermined the credibility of the civilian government that had organized the elections.

Clearly, the military rulers have stepped into a political vacuum, or at least what they have perceived as a vacuum. Their rule may indeed have been necessary, but it can hardly be called legitimate by any standard definition of the term, based as it is on the judgment of a small elite of officers who have proclaimed themselves the arbiters (for the time being) of the public will. And if the army itself represents the closest thing Nigeria has to a nationally unifying institution, it does so imperfectly, for even under military rule, northerners dominate the positions of power.

Dissent has been on the rise during the 1980s. Both civilian and military governments have taken firm stands with dissidents, whether they be students, workers, or Islamic fundamentalists, but the causes of conflict have not disappeared. Indeed, they have become more complicated and more widely disseminated. Class, ethnic, and religious antagonisms have been exacerbated by abusive authorities confronting citizens. The populace is becoming more and more sophisticated and sensitized politically, and it is increasingly unwilling to suffer mistreatment. The bases for a stable constitutional order—consensus on the rules of the game, tolerance of dissent, and respect for both public and private property—have not yet been laid, and thus the outlook for the 1990s cannot be optimistic. It takes time to build a sense of nationhood within any diverse community, and Nigeria must work against divisions that are long-standing, complex, and bitter.

CONCLUSIONS

Challenges to political stability come from a variety of sources; intense ethnic, religious, linguistic, or regional cleavages that divide a country's population, strains and dislocations engendered by economic development, and severe setbacks produced by changes in global commodity prices or interest rates are among the more prominent. For the world's older countries, centuries of collective existence have often facilitated the emergence of norms of tolerance and respect for others, standards of equal government treatment for all, and feelings of national unity that can carry them through difficult times. For many newer countries, these norms have had little chance to develop, and the processes of social, economic, and political change they are experiencing are more likely to exacerbate differences than to moderate them.

Political stability is not just a matter of norms; there must be political institutions capable of channeling demands, managing conflicts, and providing for the orderly and efficient administration of government. In regimes born of popular revolution, such as the Soviet Union, China, and Mexico, the emergence of a powerful political party has been an important step in this regard, especially when it articulates an ideology that can inspire widespread popular allegiance and thereby enlist support and cooperation for the regime. Where ideologies are taken very seriously, however, the result may be intense intraparty struggles or even totalitarian efforts to ensure complete popular conformity to the party's ideological pronouncements, which can be highly destabilizing. Both the Soviet Union and China have experienced episodes of these types. The Mexican case illustrates another means of establishing and maintaining party control: the co-option of major social sectors within the ruling party. The success of this strategy depends on the party's willingness and ability to deliver on at least some of the promises of the revolution. In Nigeria, the absence of strong, unifying parties has encouraged the one public institution capable of maintaining order, the military, to step in.

In today's world, external circumstances can also play an important role in undermining political stability. The ability of Mexico's PRI-led government to live up to the expectations created by the Mexican Revolution has been undermined, not just by corruption and patronage but also by events beyond its control, such as the collapse of oil prices in the early 1980s. Nigeria's efforts to institute a stable civilian regime may be threatened, in part at least, by an international Islamic revival that could fuel antagonisms between the country's Muslim and non-Muslim populations. Certain countries, such as Poland, do not have the freedom to introduce the types of political institutions that would satisfy popular demands for democracy and freedom; as a client state of the Soviet Union, Poland must conform to its patron's communist one-party model. These external influences are explored more fully in the next chapter, which considers the challenges of change in an era of increasing global interdependence.

chapter *10*

The Challenges of Change and the Future

INTRODUCTION

> We live in an age when problems are increasingly worldwide—the world food prob-
> lem, threat of world inflation, the world population problem, world environmental
> crisis, world drug problems, and so forth. . . . As rapid population growth in much of
> the world continues, mankind's backlog of unsolved problems is growing. . . . Each
> promises to worsen in the years ahead.[1]

Human beings as physical organisms are subject to continual
change. Societies, which are human creations, share this human property. The ways in which social and economic change affect, and are
affected by, the political process is a central concern of political scientists. For many countries, the interaction of politics with socioeconomic
change centers on the desire to develop economically, which involves not
only industrialization and the introduction of modern agricultural forms
and methods but also some measure of control over population growth.
In newer states particularly, the challenges of political development—
that is, of forging national unity and developing stable and effective
political institutions, such as parties, bureaucracies, and law courts—
must also be met. Most developed countries, in contrast, already possess
strong political institutions and enjoy acceptable levels of national unity
and population stability; their challenges concern the difficulties of

[1]Lester Brown, *World Without Borders* (New York: Random House, 1972), p. 11.

427

maintaining economic growth and prosperity in an increasingly competitive world economy.

A major obstacle to the achievement of these goals is that countries may not necessarily be free to pursue their own course of change because of increasing global interdependence. In Europe, economic development took place together with the development of the sovereign nation-state. It was essentially the competition for power and territory that stimulated the development of stronger, more efficient states, and political leaders were not slow to appreciate the connection between economic strength and military power. As a result, the modern state became a powerful tool for promoting and guiding economic development, and as economic development proceeded, the ability of states to maintain their sovereignty was enhanced. Today, national sovereignty has come increasingly into question.

Global interdependence and the waning of the ideal of the sovereign state can be seen in a number of domains, including the vulnerability of national economies to the world economy, the exercise of political influence and even interventionism by some states on others, and the grim reality that the possession of massive arsenals of nuclear weapons by the world's two superpowers makes possible the destruction of all human life. Global interdependence, moreover, does not affect all states in the same way: a country's vulnerability to the vicissitudes of the world economy and the possibility of political influence depends largely on its size and its level of economic and political development. The sovereignty each state enjoys is relative to the political, economic, and military resources it has at its disposal.

Another complicating factor is the degree of unpredictability or surprise inherent in change. Although change is often introduced in a deliberate or planned manner, as when political leaders expand the range of government services or limit the opportunities for popular participation, unforeseen circumstances may also affect the course and rate of change. For example, the downfall of the dictatorship of Anastasio Somoza in Nicaragua was abetted by his regime's inept handling of a totally unanticipated event, the devastating Managua earthquake of 1972. Similarly, the extent to which population growth and urban migration would undermine attempts at economic development in much of the Third World was unanticipated by experts in the 1950s and 1960s who predicted rapid economic growth and rising prosperity in what they optimistically labeled the "developing world."

In the next section, we outline four major levels or states of socioeconomic development, together with their associated political regime types, and indicate the principal kinds of economic and political challenge that are faced by each. This is followed by an examination of the principal ways in which increasing global interdependence affects these challenges and the ability of theoretically sovereign states to tackle them. Finally, we evaluate the viability of attempts by governments to plan or control change in light of the unpredictability of future events.

Developmental States and Change

The challenges that countries face differ profoundly according to their overall levels of political and economic development. In considering the very complicated issue of development, it is useful to distinguish four broad levels or states: (1) agrarian, (2) preindustrial, (3) industrial, and (4) postindustrial or advanced technological. These distinctions are not absolute; the boundaries between them tend to be fuzzy (partly because countries are often unequally developed across their regions). Moreover, certain challenges confront countries at very different levels of development. Industrial pollution, for example, affects both less developed and highly developed countries. Nevertheless, as long as we remember that these categories are ideal types or abstract categories rather than exact descriptions of reality, they will be useful in helping us understand the challenges of change. Table 10.1 summarizes these phases and their characteristics.

The Agrarian State   In the agrarian state, there is little planned change. Individuals and groups are integrated with their political institutions and their environments, and leaders tend to play both religious and secular roles: through them, the forces of nature (e.g., the sun and moon cycles) are invoked to explain human events. The family unit tends to be the "extended" family, in which many generations live in one household or a common residential compound. This familial unit is also the main economic and social unit, responsible for food, housing, clothing, education, entertainment, and the security of the young and elderly. The primary economic activity is subsistence agriculture.

The major challenges in this state concern adequate food production for a growing population, housing, basic educational opportunities, public amenities (potable water, streets, sewage), and, perhaps, the initial steps towards state-building and national integration. For liberal democracies such as Britain and France, which began these processes several centuries ago, economic development occurred gradually and largely of its own accord. Political order, national integration, and the establishment of state institutions, although more deliberately pursued, were also achieved over a very long period. By contrast, countries currently in this state are concerned with catching up, both politically and economically. Taking their cue from the developed world, most countries in this state of development seek to industrialize their economies and consolidate the institutions of a modern nation-state within decades rather than centuries.

Four types of political systems tend to characterize this state: traditional authoritarian monarchies, authoritarian military regimes, single-

Table 10.1 DEVELOPMENTAL PHASES

Characteristics	Agrarian	Preindustrial	Industrial	Advanced technological
Social	Communal; high integration; religiosecular elite; extended family; large rural population; ethnic-geographic cleavages; parochial loyalties	Mainly rural; extended and nuclear families; emerging urban migration; differentiation of religious and secular elites; regional, ethnic, class cleavages	Nuclear family; high mobility; atomistic; secular belief systems (rationality); high levels of education; multiple identifications	Lower nuclear family cohesion; high specialization; high mobility; widespread higher education; high suburban, low rural population; large professional/technocratic groups
Economic	Subsistence agriculture; village markets; high proportion of GNP in agriculture; high proportion of labor force in agriculture	Subsistence and commercial agriculture; monetarized economy; highly labor-intensive industry; integration into national markets; more blue-collar employees	Highly industrial; substantial service sector; capital-intensive industry; high use of credit; little or no subsistence agriculture	Service sector exceeds industrial sector; increasing emphasis on science and advanced technology in both sectors
Political	Leadership by traditional elites; patron-client networks; low participation; traditional legitimacy; inherited status; politics follows regional, class, ethnic cleavages	Authoritarian (single-party or military) government; patron-client networks; some ideologically mobilized parties; low participation (except in mobilized systems); traditional and modern (class) cleavages; legitimacy often charismatic	Pluralist single or competitive parties; class cleavages more important; high mobilization/participation; rational-legal authority	Pluralist single or competitive parties; high political awareness and participation; increased concern for postmaterial values and conflicts; decentralization of authority to specialized agencies

party systems, and personal dictatorships. For a variety of reasons, including a legacy of authoritarian rule, the absence of national unity or political consensus, and the strains generated by economic change, stable liberal democracy is likely to prove difficult to establish.

The Preindustrial State   In this state, the integration of authority in society tends to give way to specialization; for example, separate secular and religious leaders typically emerge. The economic elite—those with land and/or capital—has begun to eclipse the religious elite in major issue areas. Family production of food, clothes, tools, and other needs is in the process of being replaced by specialized economic units engaged in the production of goods in excess of those consumed by the producer. The savings from such enterprises in turn stimulate industrial and commercial expansion. Urban areas are increasing in importance. Mobility and technological advances enhance the process of change, though not always its scope. Change, save in communist countries, may affect only an incrementally increasing select few, and social disparities tend to increase markedly.

The major issues in this state include increased food production, population growth, national integration, education, industrialization, and increased demands for political participation. In communist countries, the tension between economic development and the realization of communist ideals of social justice emerges as a prominent issue. In noncommunist developing states, a typical problem is that indigenous capitalists find they are unable to compete with foreign multinational corporations and imports from the developed world. Political systems at this level tend to resemble those of the previous level, but it is not unusual for institutionalized single-party systems or even incipient competitive systems to gain supremacy over the military and traditional elites.

The Industrial State   The prime economic characteristic of this state is that industry contributes more than agriculture to the country's gross national product. As a result, a substantial and increasing population of the labor force is employed in higher-paying blue-collar and white-collar jobs. With urban populations expanding, pressure increases on urban public services (education, sanitation, roads, and water supplies) as well as on land. Widespread education, mass communication, and higher per capita incomes stimulate greater political participation. Governments are likely to be of the competitive-party representative type, rather than the inherited monarchies, single-party regimes, or military regimes characteristic of the earlier states. Exceptions to this generalization are communist and some Third World countries, which may pass through the industrial state with single-party systems. However, there is likely to be increased pluralism even within the single parties as the proliferation of professional and occupational groups and interests prompts a competition for positions and policy outcomes. The major issues in this state include unemployment, income distribution, working conditions, urban blight, and crime.

The Advanced Technological State   In this state, the service sector (e.g., public administration, finance, the liberal professions, leisure) has eclipsed the industrial sector as the largest employer of labor; more important, both sectors have become heavily influenced by advanced levels of science and technology.[2] The trend toward suburban living may well have reached the point where suburbs surpass cities as places of residence. The stability of the nuclear family is threatened by increasing geographic mobility and perhaps also by a greater emphasis on "postmaterial" or quality-of-life goals such as self-realization, or achieving one's full potential.[3] Where these values are not satisfied within the individual's present occupational and familial situations, the result is often a decision for change. This emphasis on quality-of-life issues translates politically as increased concern for environmental protection, greater responsiveness for political leaders, and greater control by citizens over decisions affecting their lives. Political awareness is relatively high because of high levels of education and greater responsiveness to the electronic media. Governments tend to be representative, and their principal challenge is to supply continued economic growth and quality-of-life benefits at the same time. Experiments in decentralization occur with increasing frequency in an attempt to increase government responsiveness. Specialized "private governments," such as large associations, increasingly make decisions formerly reserved for political units.

One of the principal frustrations facing Third World and to some extent communist countries is that progressing through these states is by no means automatic. While some countries—particularly East Asian countries such as Taiwan, South Korea, and Singapore—are undergoing rapid industrialization, the bulk of the Third World remains at levels below industrialization. This includes new countries, such as India, which are still overwhelmingly agrarian and older countries, including those in Latin America, that languish at a preindustrial or partially industrialized level. Although the developed world often sees the relative backwardness of other countries as their own fault, countries struggling to develop prefer to blame the predominant military and economic power of the developed world for their woes. In the next subsection, we consider some of the issues involved in the interdependence of rich and poor, powerful and not-so-powerful countries.

[2]While it is difficult to find a completely appropriate term for this state, it is this property which leads us to prefer the term "advanced technological" over the vaguer term "postindustrial."

[3]The theme of the rise of postmaterial values is explored in R. Inglehart, *The Silent Revolution* (Princeton, N.J.: Princeton University Press, 1977).

Global Interdependence

At the beginning of this book, we identified the emergence of the modern era in politics with the emergence of the sovereign state. Sovereignty means that the state is the ultimate source of public decisions within its territory. Although it has always been the case that stronger states have been able to influence the behavior of weaker ones, until relatively recently this influence was severely limited by geography: the farther a state was from the dominant powers of its day, the freer it was to set its own political and economic course. Today, electronic communications and motorized transportation have made it much easier for the world's superpowers to acquire "global reach," and the emergence of a truly world economy binds the economic futures of countries at opposite ends of the world much more closely to one another than was ever thought possible in the days of sailing ships.

Economic Interdependence The growth of economic interdependence, particularly since World War II, has generated a great deal of controversy. According to classical economic theory, an international division of labor in which each country specializes in the products that it is best capable of producing, and trades for the other goods that it needs or requires, should benefit all concerned. For underdeveloped countries which lack the industrial or technological basis for producing modern products, this thesis is bound to be attractive. By concentrating on producing the raw materials they possess in abundance or on agricultural products that their climate or soil conditions favor, these countries should be able to produce goods that can be sold in world markets at competitive prices; the income earned in this fashion can then be employed to purchase needed machinery and other products from more technologically advanced countries. However, as we saw in Chapter 9, specialization can also leave these countries dangerously dependent on the world markets. When a recession causes demand and therefore prices for their commodities to fall, these countries may find themselves unable to purchase even essential imports such as food or oil. The collapse of the world price for copper had a devastating effect on Chile's economy in the 1970s, for example, and both Nigeria and Mexico encountered serious foreign debt problems when the price of their principal export, oil, fell unexpectedly in the 1980s.

Many Marxist-oriented theorists, especially in Latin America, have argued that the world capitalist system is based on a system of "unequal exchange." They believe that commodities such as raw materials or agricultural products are undervalued relative to the manufactured goods of the industrialized world, thereby keeping the world's poorer countries in their present state. Mainstream economic theorists, in contrast, reject the concept of unequal exchange and insist that underdeveloped countries will develop if they simply remove restrictions, such as tariffs or import quotas, that prevent the free play of market forces. Whichever interpretation is accepted, it is undeniable that the prices of commodities fluctuate much more widely than do the prices of manufactured goods on the world market and that dependence on just one or two commodities can be disastrous. Many observers believe that only international agreements to raise the prices of the commodities produced by underdeveloped countries will alleviate the debt problem many of them face. In the meantime, indebtedness to the Western banks or to international agencies like the World Bank obliges these countries to alter their economic and fiscal policies; the result is often cutbacks in government subsidies or imports during periods of economic distress and high unemployment. The dilemma this poses for developing countries was poignantly expressed in Argentine President Raul Alfonsin's observation that his country's $53 billion debt is a "bloodletting that conspires against the consolidation of democracy."[4] However, to repudiate these debts would likely mean that these countries would be denied future loans and investments or even market access to the developed world, a consequence that would make future economic development much more difficult.

National Security and Political Sovereignty   The increasing technological sophistication of modern warfare and the possession of nuclear arms by a handful of countries have significantly undermined the extent to which states can provide for their own defense. States such as Cuba and Israel are highly dependent on their patron-states, the Soviet Union and the United States, respectively, to support their military operations. Cuba's policy of aiding revolutions in Latin America and Africa and Israel's ability to protect itself and maintain control of conquered Arab territories on its borders are largely contingent on this aid. A great deal of the foreign aid that flows from developed to underdeveloped countries takes the form of armaments, and the giving or selling of weapons almost inevitably brings with it a loss of political independence. The USSR and the United States compete for influence throughout the world, and their offers of military assistance are not likely to be extended to a country unless it is willing to structure its policies so as to support the overall aims of its would-be patron state. Occasionally, client countries break free of the influence of their patrons, but the price can be high. In the Iran-Iraq war which began in 1980, Iran's failure to crush its much smaller adversary easily and quickly is due in large measure to its inability to purchase either new aircraft or spare parts for its American-built aircraft, a direct consequence of the takeover of power by the anti-American regime of the Ayatollah Khomeini in 1979.[5]

The effect on political sovereignty of the possession of nuclear

[4]*Christian Science Monitor* (June 25, 1987), p. 1

[5]Iran was able to purchase some military supplies from the United States covertly in return for assistance in securing the release of U.S. hostages in Lebanon. The relevation of these dealings in 1986 led to a major scandal in U.S. politics.

weapons by a few countries is more difficult to assess. In one sense, the United States and the USSR can ensure their own survival because of the deterrent or dissuasive effect of their huge nuclear arsenals; no country could attack them and expect to survive. Moreover, even such developed and powerful states as West Germany, Britain, and Japan see their defense against the Soviet Union as dependent, in the final analysis, on the American nuclear deterrent. To that extent, they have abdicated the ultimate responsibility of any sovereign state—that of providing for its own defense—to another power. The influence which nuclear weapons give to the United States and the USSR does, however, have its limits. In the Vietnam War, the United States settled for defeat rather than unleash even a limited nuclear attack; the adverse reaction of world opinion and the risk of a Soviet retaliation made the nuclear option unpalatable. Similarly, the Soviet Union struggled for years against opponents of the Marxist regime in Afghanistan without significant success, but there was no likelihood that even its battlefield nuclear weapons would be put into use. The ultimate irony is that nuclear weapons have such destructive power that they cannot be used—except in the most dire circumstances.

The influence of the powerful on the less powerful is not confined to military aid or military force. The world's two superpowers have staked out areas of influence that infringe on the political sovereignty of many states. For the United States, Latin America is the principal area of influence. While larger countries like Mexico, Brazil, and Argentina are relatively free of direct involvement, smaller states such as Guatemala (1954), Cuba (1961), the Dominican Republic (1965), Chile (1973), and Nicaragua (since 1980) have experienced U.S. or U.S.-supported attempts to overthrow governments. For the Soviet Union, the main zone of influence is East Europe; revolts against their Soviet-backed regimes have been crushed with direct or indirect Soviet involvement in East Germany (1953), Hungary (1956), and Poland (1981–1982). Regimes which find themselves in one or the other sphere of influence not only must toe the line politically; they are also expected to structure their economies according to the economic model—command or free-market—favored by their patron states. It is not surprising, in these circumstances, if resentment against the superpowers occasionally flares up in these countries, for they face the challenges of political and economic development without the political freedom of choice to tackle them in any manner they see fit.

Controlling Change

It is often assumed that revolutionary change is invariably governmentally induced, yet marked changes in the social and economic spheres have occurred without direct governmental intervention. Nongovernmental factors that have accelerated change include population growth, dynamic entrepreneurship, and rapid technological innovation. Because both laissez-faire and interventionist approaches to social and economic transformation have their successes and their failures—and because they are associated with the ideologies and interests of the United States and the USSR, respectively—the issue of how much governments should become involved in attempts to plan or control social and economic change is highly controversial, as we saw in Chapter 8. Is planning really a faster or more effective means of achieving such goals as economic development than a free-market approach? If planning is better, can it be undertaken and successfully implemented in less developed societies, which lack such resources as skilled professional administrators and technology? In developed societies, will political cultures that place a high value on individualism and liberty allow greater centralized control and the massive information systems required for effective monitoring?

There are no easy answers to these questions, but two important aspects of the dynamics of change must be taken into account if the planning solution is chosen. The first consideration is that, in order to plan successfully, governments must be able to anticipate future developments. One traditional way of doing so is by studying history. For example, the experience of the older developing countries of Latin America may be useful in predicting future political, social, and economic developments in the more recently independent countries of Africa and Asia. At several points in our analysis of Mexico and Nigeria, we explicitly compared a given stage of development in the histories of both countries to suggest future trends in Nigeria. As valuable as this historical approach may be, it is limited by the fact that the same kind of social changes that occurred in a past era may lead to entirely different outcomes in the present. For example, during the eighteenth and nineteenth centuries the growing population of Western Europe produced mass migrations to urban areas and provided cheap labor for new labor-intensive industries in the early stages of the industrial revolution. Today, similar population movements in the Third World often lead instead to serious overcrowding of cities and potential political turmoil, since modern industry is more dependent on technology and skilled labor than on cheap labor.

A second complication concerns the rate at which change occurs. Many factors involved in development (e.g., population growth, demands for food and natural resources) have exponential growth patterns, which means that the period during which certain challenges can be anticipated narrows faster than one might expect. Table 10.2 lists the doubling times for some growth rates. With the present world population rate increasing at 2.0 percent per year, the doubling time is only 35 years. A French children's riddle illustrates another aspect of exponential growth, the suddenness with which it approaches a fixed limit:

Suppose you own a pond on which a water lily is growing. The lily plant doubles in size each day. If the lily were allowed to grow unchecked, it would completely cover

Table 10.2   DOUBLING TIMES

Growth rate (% per year)	Doubling time (years)
0.1	700
1.0	70
2.0	35
5.0	14
10.0	7

the pond in 30 days, choking off the other forms of life in the water. For a long time the lily plant seems small, and so you decide not to worry about cutting it back until it covers half the pond. On what day will that be? On the twenty-ninth day of course. You have one day to save your pond.[6]

It is not difficult to imagine the implications of this phenomenon for environmental quality, housing, family structures, crime, demand for jobs and welfare programs, and other needs and problems that are likely to crop up in the course of development. Nor need one be surprised that the challenges and frustrations of development so often lie at the root of violence and stability throughout much of the Third World today.

CHANGE IN LIBERAL DEMOCRACIES

Change in liberal democracies tends to come incrementally in response to social and economic problems rather than in anticipation of them. The limited vision of democratic governments is due partly to the inherent difficulties of planning amid the unforeseeable contingencies and conflicting pressures typical of pluralistic social systems, as discussed in Chapter 7. But it is due also to the nature of the political system itself. There is in liberal democracies no single vision of a better future; it is assumed that different groups and individuals will have different opinions about what should be attempted and how it should be achieved. In addition, political leaders must focus most of their attention on short-term problems and objectives if they are to remain in office. Policies that may show benefits in 10 or 20 years' time are of little importance to them; what counts for their careers is winning the next election.

Larger concerns cannot always be avoided, however. British governments, for example, have had to face the problem of the country's long-term economic decline. Together with France and other European countries, Britain must also confront the challenges posed by the rapid development in the United States and Japan of new techniques such as genetic engineering and microelectronics. Politically, both Britain and France are presented with the very difficult choices of either maintaining their own nuclear arsenals at levels sufficient to deter a Soviet attack—a very expensive proposition—or relying increasingly on U.S.

[6]Donella H. Meadows et al., *The Limits to Growth* (New York: Universe Books, 1972), p. 29.

conventional and nuclear forces. As states which were until recently considered great powers, the specter of second-rate status, either economically or politically, is unsettling.

Britain: Coping with Lost Rank

Britain emerged from World War II as one of the victorious "Big Three," a partner with the United States and the Soviet Union in the construction of the postwar political order. What Britain lacked in population size and natural resources, it made up for through its possession of the largest empire the world has ever known. Moreover, Britain had participated with the United States in the invention of the ultimate weapon, the atom bomb, which even the Soviet Union did not possess at that time. Victory over Germany, continental Europe's strongest state, together with the "special relationship" with the United States, seemed to provide the basis on which Britain's future greatness could be preserved.

The succeeding decades have been disillusioning for many Britons. The empire dissolved with unexpected rapidity; its "jewel," India, was lost in 1948, and by 1960 most of its other components had achieved their independence or were in the process of doing so. 1960 was also the date by which it had become apparent that the full employment and affluence of the 1950s masked an underlying lack of competitiveness in the British economy. Britain's inability to continue as one of the Big Three was easier to accept than the inability to keep pace economically with such middle-level powers as France and Germany. With slow economic growth came embarrassing balance-of-payment crises, devaluations of the pound sterling, and most important, an incapacity to play the global political and military role which Britain had been accustomed to playing since the eighteenth century. By the mid-1970s Britain had to submit to a situation usually observed only for Third World states: adopting expenditure cutbacks demanded by the International Monetary Fund in order to receive loans to bail out the hard-pressed national currency.

We have seen that many attempts were made by British governments to check and reverse economic decline, including efforts to curtail the powers of trade unions, the decision to seek membership in the European Community, and the commitment of large amounts of government money to high-technology projects such as the Concorde supersonic aircraft (developed in cooperation with France). In general, these policies have failed to achieve their objective. Unforeseen events are partly to blame for this failure: the Concorde aircraft, a technological triumph, became commercially unviable because of rising fuel prices generated by OPEC in the 1970s. However, the massive government expenditures on older, failing industries such as shipbuilding and automobiles indicate that the perceived need to curry public favor, in this case by preventing further unemployment, has been an important component of decision-making on these issues.

Since 1979, Britain has experienced an unusual confluence of factors that has permitted a major change in direction. The first factor was the arrival in office of a prime minister, Margaret Thatcher, dedicated to a fundamental and long-term transformation in the British economy and in British values. The laissez-faire course chosen by Thatcher as a remedy for economic decline involved tolerating very high rates of inflation in the early 1980s, a substantial decline in Britain's manufacturing output (overcome only in 1987), and levels of unemployment not experienced since the depression of the 1930s. Yet she has been returned to office in two subsequent elections—a feat no other twentieth-century prime minister has managed. This achievement was made possible in large part by a second factor, the division of the opposition between Labour and the Social Democratic-Liberal Alliance, which made it easier for the Conservatives to win parliamentary majorities with only minority support among the electorate. The third factor facilitating a break with the past was the discovery of North Sea oil, which has generated enough income to spare Britain the balance-of-payments crises that so often disrupted economic policy in the 1950s and the 1960s. It is not clear whether the improved growth rates of the 1980s indicate an end to Britain's economic woes or merely an end to the severe recession which began the decade, but there is no doubt that Britain is now launched on a longer-term strategy for economic regeneration that will not be reversed or subverted for short-term political advantage.

Another challenge that Britain must face is defining its future role in world affairs. Britain's relationship with the European Community amply illustrates the difficulties that this task involves. When the Common Market idea was first promoted in the late 1950s, Britain chose to preserve its independence rather than submit to the sacrifice in economic and political sovereignty that membership would have entailed. When economic difficulties forced a change of opinion in the 1960s, many British leaders saw Britain's role as one of leading Europe from within the European Community. However, the British soon found that even their participation was not desired by all members: President de Gaulle of France reckoned that Britain was still too tied to the United States and to the British Commonwealth to commit itself to the grand ambition of unifying Europe. Finally admitted in 1973, British governments have had to grapple with the fact that many Community policies—such as the Common Agricultural Policy—do not suit Britain's needs particularly well. Efforts to oppose these policies, or to demand special compensation for their adverse effects, have frequently been met with the accusation that Britain is a "bad European" because it is not willing to put Community interests above national advantage. Although these accusations are somewhat unfair—all member states seek their own advantage in the Community—it is nonetheless true that British politicians and the British public tend to see the European Community less as a vehicle for creating a united Europe and more as a device to improve Britain's own economic fortunes. As a result, leadership in the Community has remained by and large in the hands of the French and the West Germans.

A similar dilemma confronts Britain's ties with its former colonies. Most of these countries are now associated within the Commonwealth, headed symbolically by the British monarch. Although the leaders of Commonwealth countries meet every two years to exchange views on a variety of topics, it is clear that they have very little in common. For the majority of members who are Third World states, the Commonwealth is primarily useful as a means of soliciting foreign aid from the more developed member states. Britain's hope that its influence in the world could somehow be preserved through the Commonwealth has not been borne out; on some issues, such as economic sanctions against the white-dominated former British colony of South Africa, Britain's opposition to the measure has placed it in the uncomfortable position of being a much-criticized minority of one. Tellingly, the organization is no longer even known as the British Commonwealth; officially, it is just "the Commonwealth."

Britain's military role has experienced a similar diminution in size and importance since 1945. In the immediate aftermath of the war, Britain saw its role as one of sharing global responsibilities with the United States, albeit as a junior partner. British troops were active on a variety of fronts, fighting communist guerrillas in Greece and Malaya, attempting to keep the peace between Jews and Arabs in Palestine, and maintaining a major military presence in the Mediterranean and the Indian and Pacific oceans. The expense involved in maintaining this global posture was enormous; during the 1950s Britain was spending as much as 10 percent of its gross national product, one-third of government expenditures, on defense. Not surprisingly, this level of defense expenditures had an adverse effect on Britain's economic performance; without the overseas defense outlays, Britain would not have experienced the balance-of-payments deficits that caused economic crises in the 1950s and 1960s. In the end, the effort sustained at such a high cost proved futile. As early as 1947, Britain realized that it could no longer afford to maintain anticommunist activities in Greece and relinquished that role to the United States, which moved its Sixth Fleet into the Mediterranean. Thereafter, Britain gradually abandoned most of its global responsibilities in favor of concentrating on its role in NATO (the North Atlantic Treaty Organization), which is responsible for the defense of Western Europe.

Britain has been unwilling, however, to accept a reduced role in the field of nuclear weapons. As early as 1946, it received a stern lesson in the limits of its "special relationship" with the United States when the U.S. government decided not to share its nuclear secrets with Britain. The following year the Labour government decided to build an atomic bomb on its own, and in 1955 the Conservative government took the further step of undertaking the development of a hydrogen bomb. In 1958, following the first successful test of that weapon, the United States reversed its position. In the 1960s Britain was allowed to purchase U.S.-made Polaris nuclear submarines, and the Thatcher government has now committed itself to acquiring a fleet of U.S. Trident nuclear submarines in the 1990s.

The decision to purchase American nuclear armaments illustrates many of the dilemmas facing Britain's defense policy. The decision was taken primarily because the cost of developing its own nuclear submarine force would be staggering. But if Britain does not have the resources to build nuclear weapons, critics argue, why is it still attempting to play a strategic nuclear role at all? The cost just of purchasing Trident submarines is enormous, and they would give Britain a highly increased strategic nuclear capacity, far more than is required for the defense of Western Europe. Opinion has been growing that it would be better to spend that money instead on strengthening Britain's conventional (i.e., nonnuclear) military forces in Europe, where NATO faces much larger conventional forces under Soviet command.

Although both opposition parties oppose Trident, the Labour party has gone much further by adopting the position that Britain should abandon nuclear weapons entirely. Anger over Britain's nuclear dependence on the United States, together with fears that the United States has become dangerously militaristic since President Reagan's accession to the White House, has led Labour to advocate the removal of U.S.-controlled nuclear weapons located in Britain and the abandonment of the British nuclear deterrent. In addition, Labour is now in favor of creating jobs by erecting tariffs and other barriers to protect British industry from foreign imports, a direct violation of Britain's Common Market commitments. Both steps would have the effect of withdrawing Britain from its political and economic ties with both its continental European and American allies.

The two major parties in Britain thus have chosen very different courses for Britain's future. The Conservatives see Britain continuing to exercise a strategic nuclear role—even if the weapons are supplied by the United States—and believe that, through free access to the huge European market, private enterprise in Britain can be regenerated and economic strength restored. Labour sees Britain's future as within itself, unsullied by U.S. military and political influence and free of the need to submit to the policies of the European Community. Both parties wish to alter significantly the direction Britain has been following since 1945, but in very different ways. The consensus on basic issues that characterized British party politics in past decades is gone; Britons must now choose between two competing visions of the future.

France: Striking an Independent Course

France entered the postwar era at a starting point fundamentally different from Britain's: instead of being one of the victorious powers, France was one of the defeated ones. Although de Gaulle's Free French movement was ultimately admitted into the councils of the Big Three—France even shared in the Allied occupation of Germany—it was clear to all that French troops had been allowed to participate in Germany's defeat only as a courtesy and that their contribution was negligible. Great relief was experienced by most French men and women at the liberation of France in 1944, but the sense of national humiliation remained.

It was obvious to French leaders in 1945 that overcoming that humiliation would require a major effort. Concerning the economy, many concluded that France could no longer afford to modernize at its own slow pace; if France was to be able to defend itself, it had to be in the forefront, both industrially and technologically. In addition, to meet any future German challenge, the size of France's population would presumably have to approach Germany's; this, too, made economic growth imperative. Finally, economic weakness in the past had also led to a dangerous degree of political dependence: to meet the challenge of Nazi Germany in the 1930s, France had felt obliged to rely totally on the British, who encouraged France to declare war on Germany and then proved unable to defend it from invasion. Political and military independence therefore became a high priority in postwar France.

The economic challenge was the first one to be successfully addressed. The establishment of a system of national planning was an early indication that economic development was no longer going to be left to the private marketplace. Pioneered by Jean Monnet, the plan gave the state a major role in directing the course of economic development. Although the plan itself is now less influential and greater reliance is now placed on private initiative in economic matters, even by the Socialists, the French state continues to play an active role in developing economic sectors it regards as national priorities.

The European Community represents the second major thrust in France's postwar design for economic recovery. The origins of the European Community lay with the European Coal and Steel Community (ECSC), which Monnet played a leading role in establishing in 1951. The purpose of the ECSC was as much political as economic: by integrating or tying together the French and German coal and steel industries, which are essential to the manufacture of armaments, Monnet believed it would be much more difficult for the two countries to wage war against each other in the future. Despite the success of the ECSC, the decision to join the European Community was opposed by French business leaders, who feared German industrial competition; as it turned out, French industries proved just as capable of competing with the Germans over a broad range of industrial products as they were in coal and steel.

Although the French economy would undoubtedly have shared in the general economic growth of the 1950s and 1960s in any case, the decision to "take on Europe" in the Common Market (with the aid of state-led planning) clearly reflected a more aggressive and more ambitious French attitude, which has paid large dividends. However, France now faces an even greater challenge: competing not just with Germany but with the industrial superpowers of the United States and Japan as well. In many important areas of technological advance, such as semiconductors, biogenetics, and computers, Europe as a whole has tended to trail behind developments in the United States and East Asia. The French initiative to found Eureka, a program of inter-European government aid to promising industries, indicates that the seriousness of this challenge is appreciated; whether the project will succeed has yet to be determined.

The initiative to restore France's political standing began with the replacement of the ineffectual Fourth Republic with the Fifth Republic under de Gaulle in 1959. Essential to de Gaulle's vision was the building of a Europe that was independent of both the Soviet Union and the United States. Participation in the European Community, even though it involved some diminution of France's sovereignty, was therefore acceptable to de Gaulle. He realized that the Common Market could form a powerful economic force in its own right; moreover, given Germany's Nazi past, leadership of the European Community, he believed, would have to go to France.

On the military side, however, the picture was very different. France was a member of NATO, which included not just other European countries but the United States as well. Moreover, the United States clearly had the dominant position within the alliance: the NATO high command was always headed by an American general, and the alliance relied ultimately on the American nuclear deterrent to defend Western Europe. De Gaulle, who declared in his memoirs that "France cannot be France without greatness," was determined to rectify this situation of dependency. Shortly after his arrival in power in 1958, he proposed a joint U.S.-British-French directorate to govern Allied political and defense policies (including policies governing the use of nuclear weapons). The rejection of this proposal by the Americans opened the way for his decision to develop a French nuclear force. Determined to establish France's political independence from the United States, de Gaulle also launched a campaign of improving relations with the Soviet Union and its East European allies, opening diplomatic relations with the communist regime in China, and criticizing (American) interventionism in Latin America and Southeast Asia, including Vietnam. Finally, in 1966, de Gaulle took the ultimate step: withdrawal of French forces from the NATO high command. The new French nuclear deterrent, along with other aspects of French defense and foreign policy, now came under the exclusive control of the French government.

The decision to maintain an independent nuclear deterrent was designed to achieve three objectives. The first objective was to ensure that the Americans lived up to their commitment to defend Europe with nuclear weapons. If the Americans hesitated to use nuclear weapons in the face of a Soviet invasion, France could launch her own nuclear missiles; the Soviet Union would then retaliate, and at that point the Americans would presumably have to step in. The second objective was to ensure that France itself would be capable of inflicting enough damage on the Soviet Union to deter a Soviet attack, just in case the Soviets calculated that the Americans would not be willing to undertake a nuclear war in order to defend Europe. A final objective was to ensure that the two superpowers would not be able to confine their nuclear hostilities to a limited engagement that would destroy Europe but leave the Soviet Union and the United States unharmed. If both superpowers decided to use only battlefield nuclear weapons, France would still be able to retaliate by striking targets in the Soviet Union. All three objectives suggested an underlying French distrust of the American commitment to stake its own survival on the defense of Europe; de Gaulle remained wedded to the conviction that France must never count on any other country for defense.

The policy decisions de Gaulle took to establish French independence from the United States were enormously popular among French citizens at the time and have remained so to this day. Although subsequent French presidents have been more willing to cooperate militarily with NATO—by undertaking joint military exercises, for example—the fundamental lines of de Gaulle's policies have not been altered. Even the opposition parties of the Left, which committed themselves to eliminating France's nuclear arsenal in their 1972 Common Program, have come to accept France's nuclear profile. The policy does, however, present a major difficulty for the United States and its European allies. In the event of war or threat of war, France reserves for itself the right to decide whether and when to resort to nuclear weapons. This position preserves France's military independence from the United States, but it also means that France has the power to turn a nonnuclear conflict into a nuclear one, with or without the consent of its West European and American allies. If the French government decides that the moment has come to use the nuclear arsenal—which most likely would occur when it judges that the country is at imminent risk of invasion—the NATO countries and, indeed, the rest of the world may find themselves engulfed in a nuclear holocaust.

The French nuclear arsenal is not as large as those of the two superpowers, but it could still trigger a general conflagration. There are two basic reasons for this. First, the two superpowers are bound by the Anti-Ballistic Missile (ABM) Treaty of 1972, which limits each to just one anti-ballistic missile installation. This means that apart from the missile defenses surrounding Moscow, the Soviet Union has no defense against an incoming nuclear missile attack. The French nuclear deterrent, although small in comparison with that of the Soviet Union, is nevertheless capable of inflicting catastrophic damage on an unprotected Soviet Union. Second, the French have continued to devote large expenditures to the modernization of their nuclear forces. They have, for example, developed their own neutron bombs and cruise missiles and are currently engaged in building a new generation of powerful nuclear submarines. Unlike the British, the French have been prepared to undertake these enormously expensive tasks totally on their own. The high price of nuclear independence is one that French leaders, mindful of the disaster of 1940, are still willing to pay.

The French nuclear arms program has been a success in terms both of its technical achievements and of its popularity, but it nevertheless faces major challenges in the future. One of these is cost. France, with a population about one-fifth that of the United States or the Soviet Union, is much less able to afford the cost of nuclear competitiveness than are the two superpowers. To be sure, much will depend on France's ability to maintain levels of economic growth sufficient to generate enough tax revenues for the continued development of the nuclear weapons program; in an increasingly competitive technological and industrial environment, keeping up with Japan and the United States will not be easy. In addition, the problem of cost will be made much worse if the Soviet Union should decide to construct a system of defenses against strategic (i.e., intercontinental) nuclear missiles to match the United States' proposed Strategic Defense Initiative (popularly known as "Star Wars"). Building a system of nuclear missiles sophisticated enough to beat such a defensive system may well be beyond France's resources. A third challenge could ensue from arms limitation. If the superpowers make significant moves toward reducing their strategic nuclear weapons, pressure will undoubtedly increase on France to follow suit. It is one thing to justify huge expenditures on nuclear arms when the larger powers are arming themselves; it may be much more difficult to convince the public that the policy should be continued if strategic nuclear disarmament by the superpowers becomes a serious possibility—particularly if the French nuclear arsenal turns out to be an obstacle to that process. As memories of the 1940 debacle fade and worldwide concern over nuclear arms rises, French leaders may well have to entertain the prospect that maintaining both a prosperous economy and a credible nuclear deterrent may be beyond the resources of a middle-level power such as France and that it is the nuclear deterrent that has to be abandoned.

CHANGE IN COMMUNIST SYSTEMS

From their official ideology Communist states derive a vague but idealistically compelling design for the long-term development of their communities. According to the ideology, this design began to be realized with the violent overthrow of the preceding regime, the violent elimination of the former ruling class, and the establishment of a new social order aimed at pursuing the distant goal of a prosperous and egalitarian society. The violent phase of Soviet policy lasted through Stalin's rule, that is, until 1953; in China, violence as an official tactic diminished within a few years after the 1949 revolution, but it reappeared during the Cultural Revolution. Today, neither the Soviet nor the Chinese ruling party employs systematic violence in pursuit of social change; rather, both strive to manage and direct change through the orderly implementation of policy.

Of course, the party is unable to control all aspects of change; as the world becomes more complex, new and often obdurate problems arise both domestically and internationally. Bad harvests or bureaucratic miscalculation may cause five-year plans to be unfulfilled; conflicts elsewhere in the world may demand resources that would otherwise be devoted to domestic programs; a power struggle at home might disrupt the functioning of government.

Karl Marx, the nineteenth-century thinker whose political ideas laid the groundwork of communism, believed the revolution of the proletariat would occur in mature industrial societies. However, Russia in 1917 was only partially industrialized, and China in 1949 was even less so. It became one of the revolutionary governments' first priorities to propel the industrialization process forward, bypassing much of the experience undergone by the Western countries and Japan as their capitalist economies matured.

Assuming their state to be isolated in a hostile capitalist world, the leaders of the Soviet Union opted during the 1920s for going it alone; the Stalinist formula for industrialization was one of autarky, or economic self-sufficiency. The same principle guided economic policies in Eastern Europe after 1947 and China after 1949, albeit mixed with elements of mutual trade and aid with the Soviet Union. In time, however, the leaders of all these countries came to realize that their development beyond the basic industrial phase would be possible only on the establishment of working economic ties with the powerful technological societies of the capitalist world. Thus, the 1970s and 1980s have seen a movement toward the opening of trade and technology transfer between East and West, as the communist regimes acknowledge their membership in a world of global interdependence.

Soviet Union: The Growing Pains of a Young Superpower

Russia is old; the Soviet Union is relatively young. Younger still is this country's status as a global power. Nearly defeated by Nazi Germany during the first year of combat in World War II, the USSR emerged from that conflict battered but victorious. Within one year after the war's end, the battle line across Europe had been redrawn; not yet recovered from its wounds, the Soviet Union found itself in a hostile confrontation with the entire western half of the continent, and soon the ideological and diplomatic battle known as the "cold war" was joined. Even worse from the USSR's standpoint, the West was now led by the United States, the one major power that had been spared the ravages of war on its own territory.

Over the next three decades, the Soviet Union grew to be the military equal of the United States. How it did so is one of the most fascinating and controversy-ridden stories of the twentieth century. The story is long and complicated, but it essentially involved (1) the USSR's occupation of formerly independent countries in Eastern Europe (Bulgaria, Romania, Hungary, Czechoslovakia, and Poland), as well as nearly one-third of Germany, and the establishment among them of a Communist bloc; (2) the development of a nuclear weapons capacity and a delivery system to rival that of the United States; (3) the extension of Soviet interests, and the expression of Soviet power, in locations as far flung as Afghanistan, Cuba, Angola, and Vietnam; and (4) the grudging acknowledgement by Western leaders that the Soviet state is not a temporary aberration of world history but a reality that is here to stay.

The Soviet Union and its political ancestor, tsarist Russia, provide an example of how social, cultural, and economic change can be stimulated and conditioned by outside pressures. In emulation of the West, Peter the Great instigated the first sweeping changes in Russia nearly 300 years ago. Defeat at the hands of the Western powers in the Crimean War provoked the imperial soul-searching that led to the abolition of serfdom in 1861 and spurred the tsars of the late nineteenth century to begin the industrialization of their land; foreign capital made possible the first stage of that industrialization. Following defeat again in World War I, the new communist rulers sought to build a stronger state that could withstand what they perceived to be a mortal threat: their socialist country was alone in a world of capitalist powers. Far behind the industrial levels of Europe, the Soviet Union attempted during the 1930s to catch up—but found itself short of time. When the western regions of the USSR were quickly overrun by the German armies in 1941–1942, the nightmarish threat of military vulnerability became a reality. Unlike World War I, the outcome this time was victory, long and costly in its achievement; and facing the danger of another devastating conflict after 1945, Soviet decision-makers continued giving priority to heavy industry and military preparedness. By the 1980s the Soviet Union had amply demonstrated its ability to stand as the military equal of the United States, but it has not yet developed the capacity to satisfy its citizens' hunger for a modicum of consumer goods, much less address the more sophisticated quality-of-life issues that we associate with technologically advanced Western society.

Over the course of Soviet history, the government's perspective on the world has changed periodically. Lenin believed in 1917 that a revolt by the proletariat in backward Russia would ignite the flames of revolution among the working class of the more advanced West, and Russia would be one of many countries sharing the Marxist vision. By the mid-1920s it was obvious that he had been wrong; the industrialization program of the late twenties through the 1930s was inspired by the then-startling concept of "socialism in one country." The end of World War II found the Soviet army occupying the lands of East-Central Europe, and, fearful of any new military invasions coming from the West, the Soviets took steps to ensure the rule of friendly governments in the countries on the borderland.

While the Western powers looked on in horror, what began as a Soviet security zone turned into a bloc of client states whose political systems Stalin and his successors assumed the right to determine. Fearing that Soviet intentions after 1945 extended beyond the bloc and into the West, Western leaders in 1949 formed NATO as an institution of collective defense. The Soviet bloc responded by establishing the Warsaw Treaty Organization (WTO) in 1955. Like NATO, the WTO has persisted to this day as the institutional framework for its members' military unity. Unlike NATO, the WTO is held together by the might of its dominant member state; France was able to withdraw from NATO, despite the strong objections of the United States, but Hungary's attempt to leave the Soviet bloc in 1956 triggered a violent and overwhelming Soviet response that quickly ended the small country's revolt and erased any doubt that the USSR would resort to force if necessary to keep the WTO together.[7] Today, it is clear that the East European countries' membership in a Soviet-led alliance persists only in the face of popular resentment throughout the region; the only bloc country in which the Soviets appear to be popular is Bulgaria.

The Soviet Union pays a high price for its superpower status. In Eastern Europe the potential for public unrest creates instability; the armed forces of the Soviet allies bordering the West—Hungary, East Germany, and especially Czechoslovakia—cannot be relied on to defend the bloc against NATO, and therefore Soviet forces must be deployed in these lands. Economic relations within the bloc are a burden for all participants, including the Soviet Union; Western technology is greatly desired for the modernization of the Soviet and East European economies, but costly long-term commitments to each other make it difficult to reorient trade patterns toward the West.

Nor have the Soviets found it easy to deal with communist countries elsewhere in the world. Hardly more than a decade after Mao's revolution, the two communist giants broke with each other in a bitter conflict over ideology, economic relations, and nationalism, and to this day they remain distrustful of each other. The Vietnam War tested the Soviets' ability to aid a friendly government in a deadly conflict, and Moscow demonstrated its ambivalence: communist North Vietnam received Soviet military support, but not so much as to bring the USSR into a direct confrontation with the United States. During the 1980s another conflict closer to home pitted a Soviet-backed regime in Afghanistan against

---

[7]There has been one exception. Albania's communist leaders broke with Moscow in 1961 and subsequently withdrew their country from the Warsaw Treaty Organization. Albania, however, is tiny, remote, and of marginal strategic importance.

Islamic rebels; in a situation mirroring the American role in Vietnam, Soviet armed forces engaged in combat for a foreign government involved in a civil war that dragged on and on, costing many Soviet lives and billions of rubles in weapons and equipment. By the middle of 1988, the leaders in Moscow had begun to withdraw their country's forces from Afghanistan.

In other parts of the Third World, Soviet efforts at spreading their influence have had mixed results. Leftist movements, in and out of power, often look to Moscow for support and guidance. Many Third World leaders, on the other hand, distrust the Soviets and prefer to keep their diplomatic distance. Right-wing politicians in the West frequently point with concern to Soviet diplomatic "victories" in countries such as Angola, South Yemen, and (a highly debatable case) Nicaragua; what they overlook is the fact that the Soviets have also lost allies in places that include Egypt, Somalia, and China.

Ultimately, the cost of superpower status is paid by the consumer. Data on Soviet military expenditures are a closely guarded secret, and all Western estimates are highly controversial; nonetheless, it is clear that a consistently larger proportion of the country's gross national product has been devoted to military costs than is true in the United States—and the USSR's GNP is only approximately one-half that of the United States.

Even given this high cost, Soviet governments have consistently refused to skimp on the military budget, and the Gorbachev government is no exception. Almost as consistently, however, Soviet leaders have sought to reach agreements with the United States on methods of limiting or reducing armaments—particularly nuclear armaments—both in an effort to lower the risk of thermonuclear war and to release scarce national resources for nonmilitary purposes.

Under General Secretary Gorbachev's leadership, the Soviet government has worked particularly hard to reach accords with the United States on arms reduction. The first fruits of this effort were seen in the signing of the 1987 U.S.-Soviet treaty eliminating intermediate-range ballistic missiles. As before, the regime's motives are a mixture of security and economic interests, but the economic rationale has become ever more compelling. The Gorbachev economic reforms require increased investment in technology to modernize industry and consumer incentives to boost labor productivity. Facing the classical economic choice between guns and butter, the Soviet Union has always given guns its top priority; as the society stumbles toward the postindustrial era, Gorbachev and his colleagues have apparently decided that the balance between the two priorities needs to shift, and they hope they can bring about such a shift without jeopardizing their country's military security.

As a superpower, the Soviet Union has suffered far less loss of its sovereignty than smaller countries. Its leaders remain in charge of their country's defense—as well as that of their East European allies—and, while military policy is profoundly conditioned by the strength of the

United States, the converse is also true; that is, the strength of Soviet armed forces profoundly conditions American military policy.

As in the day of Peter the Great, the rulers look to the West with curiosity and sometimes envy; they are always ready to adopt technologies, products, and even (to a degree) management ideas "made in the West." However, the regime continues to resist outside influences on its political practices. The Soviet leadership is not completely deaf to world opinion on such questions as human rights—it did respond, for example, to American pressure during the 1970s when it allowed many dissatisfied Jews to emigrate—but neither is it ready to change its policies radically just because the president of the United States or anyone else demands that it do so.

On the other hand, the West permeates Soviet society in more subtle ways. For a long time, Soviet leaders tried to shield their citizens from what they considered decadent bourgeois influences. Increasingly in the past two decades, they have admitted there is little they can do to stop their citizens from mimicking Western fashions and popular culture, and the current regime seems to be concerned very little, if at all, about this issue. Western radio broadcasts, once jammed by Soviet interference, bring in alternative points of view and a taste of capitalist lifestyles. Larger numbers of citizens are meeting Westerners personally as the traffic across the borders picks up. Official representatives abroad no longer present a picture of stodgy apparatchiks who speak in slogans and through interpreters; they are mastering foreign languages and showing a sophisticated familiarity with the countries they visit. These are all signs of change within the USSR, subtle and gradual and—so far—still under the control of the party elite.

China: Transforming a Peasant Society

The development of China in the twentieth century fits the patterns noted at the beginning of this chapter remarkably well. Until the revolution of 1910, China was a classic example of an agrarian society untouched by industrialization and ruled by an authoritarian monarchy and a landed elite. The imperial system crumbled under the pressures generated by foreign ideas of economic growth and political democracy and the shame many felt at the extent of foreign control over China's affairs. While some leaders, such as Sun Yatsen, attempted to create an independent democratic regime, China experienced instead the rapacity of regional warlords, the single-party government of the Guomindang under Jiang Kaishek, and invasion and occupation of much of the country by the Japanese in the 1930s.

The communist takeover of power in 1949 opened a very different phase in China's development. The Communist party has managed to control the military and to maintain overall direction of the development of the country's economy, usually with the cooperation of a loyal, or at least acquiescent, population. However, the precise direction that development should take became a source of sharp divisions within the party and radical shifts in government policy. Although Mao at times was revered as a messianic leader on the scale of Stalin, he never achieved the unquestioning obedience to his program of development that Stalin did. In the "red versus expert" debate, Mao's call to be both red and expert resulted in an emphasis on ideological purity over technical expertise, a strong push to eradicate "bourgeois" or capitalist influences, and severe limits on popular involvement in decision-making. The profound disruptions in economic development that have followed from this course, such as during the Great Leap Forward and the Cultural Revolution, have given fodder to Mao's opponents.

Those who have opposed Mao, including Liu Shaoqi and more recently Deng Xiaoping, have stressed the importance of higher education and expertise and encouraged flexibility in determining solutions to problems. As Deng once put it, "practice is the only criterion for determining truth." In place of ideological purity determined from above, greater reliance is now placed on individuals. This is true in both the economic sphere, where private enterprise has been encouraged as a way of stimulating growth and efficiency, and the political sphere, where more choice in elections and a climate of greater freedom to express opinions are being fostered.

Although China is still predominantly a preindustrial society, great strides in development have been made despite the changes in official policy. Industrialization and urbanization have led to the emergence of a large sector of professionals, intellectuals, and technocrats who increasingly seek a major role in determining policy. Industrial managers frequently call for an end to political interference in their enterprises and for greater government attention to the development of roads, water supplies, and electricity, as well as to educational programs to enhance the skills of workers. What they do not want is to have party cadres telling them whom to hire or what decisions they should make concerning their enterprises. Politically, the rise of professional managers and technocrats is creating a new force seeking an input in the political arena. They increasingly seek to make their wishes known through both party and the government bureaucracies. Deng has handled these demands by recruiting people with these backgrounds to both bodies. The emphasis on practical experience is indicated by the fact that one of the key routes to the Politburo is through the provincial party first secretary positions. This has meant that leaders have had provincial administrative-developmental experience prior to moving to top party positions.

Among the issues emerging with these changes are demands for jobs by those affected by firms cutting back on labor in order to become more efficient, social security for the unemployed, and bonuses and other material incentives for workers. In addition, industrialization is leading to problems of environmental protection. Water and air are increasingly becoming polluted, causing serious threats to human health. These concerns are likely to receive more party and government attention in the future.

China's developmental objectives have involved greater exposure to foreign influences. China has purchased much advanced technology from the West, seeks foreign investment to assist in its industrialization, and is actively pursuing export markets in the United States and elsewhere. In many areas, future economic development will be dependent on international trade agreements and the openness of foreign markets, in particular those of the United States. Recessions and other adverse economic developments that take place in the capitalist world may therefore come to affect China more and more. Global economic interdependence will increasingly touch China in significant ways.

With the passing of most of the original revolutionary leaders who "wore two hats," those of party and military leadership, there has been an increase in the differentiation between the party and the military. This has meant a professionalization of both. However, if the present course of economic and political policy leads to further disturbances such as the student demonstrations for democratic reforms in 1986, or to major decreases in the central control of society, the military's role in society could increase. Given the extent of the deviation from strict socialist practice entailed by Deng's reforms, major political tensions between "hard-liners" and those favoring reform could lead to mass movements and demonstrations. Should matters appear to be getting out of hand, a military intervention is not out of the question. It is significant in this regard that although Deng resigned from the party's Central Committee in 1987 because of his advanced age (83), he did not relinquish control of military affairs.

China's future will also be marked by challenges related to the party's and the government's ability to control an immense population. China will continue to be torn by conflicts between communist purists, whose attitudes are strongly influenced by an essentially Confucian socialization which stresses norms of order and authority, and those who seek a more open and democratic political system. In addition, tensions could arise over foreign and defense policies. There are those within the party and government leadership who support closer association with the West because of its technological advantages. However, despite hard feelings that go back to Stalin's support of Jiang Kaishek in the 1920s and the rupture with the Soviet Union in the early 1960s, there are still many who see the Soviet Union as a natural ideological ally and the United States as the leading representative of the hated capitalist world. The Soviet example of devoting enormous resources to the military even at the expense of economic development is attractive to many, especially within the military itself. As military technology becomes more sophisticated and more expensive—particularly in the area of nuclear weapons, where China is actively involved—pressures to devote greater resources to the military will undoubtedly increase.

China is increasingly seen as the world's third major power, after the United States and the Soviet Union. However, the task of catching up technologically and industrially with these superpowers represents a daunting challenge, one that clearly demands major sacrifices and will provoke major disagreements. How much free enterprise is compatible with Marxist-Leninist ideology? With which side should China align itself—the Soviet Union, the homeland of Lenin but also a rival and adversary in many respects, or the United States, technologically more advanced than the Soviet Union (and geographically more distant) but also staunchly capitalist? Or should China pursue a path of maintaining distance from, while seeking economic and military parity with, both superpowers? How these questions are answered will determine China's course in the coming decades.

CHANGE AND INTERDEPENDENCE IN THE THIRD WORLD

Only two decades ago, a sensitive African author recorded the awe of a villager at his first impression of urban life:

"There is no darkness there," he told his admiring listeners, "because at night the electric light shines like the sun, and people are always walking about, that is, those who want to walk. If you don't want to walk, you only have to wave your hand and a pleasure car stops for you." His audience [villagers] made sounds of wonderment.[8]

This passage reflects the range of development spanned by many Third World countries. Most have built modernizing industrial centers, noisy and bustling cities whose inhabitants struggle to gain material wealth; and yet, when one leaves the cities, one commonly enters a world caught in the past—primitive villages remote from modern civilization, their inhabitants often engaged in subsistence agriculture (and, in too many cases, failing to produce even at a subsistence level).

The scope of Third World governments' objectives can be broad indeed: economic growth and industrialization without foreign economic domination, elimination of the traditional social structures that inhibit modernization, mass education and national systems of higher education, durable and effective political institutions. Often, however, a country does not have sufficient natural and human resources to meet these goals; worse, events in the international environment can threaten or destroy a government's ability to determine its own policies independently. The result is, in the first instance, uneven or frustrated socioeconomic development and, in the second, foreign political or economic penetration.

Mexico and Nigeria illustrate the transitional, mixed nature of the Third World—without, however, exemplifying the most undeveloped societies such as Bangladesh or Chad. Nigeria may perhaps be consid-

---

[8]Chinua Achebe, *No Longer at Ease* (New York: Fawcett, 1969), p. 20.

ered to have passed from the agrarian to the preindustrial phase of development, since it has both a growing industrial sector and a large village-based agricultural sector. Mexico has entered the industrial stage, though by no means uniformly, as rural areas lag far behind the material standards of cities and certain regions remain largely undeveloped. Neither country has suffered military invasion in this century or been pressured to yield its independence to a foreign power; both, however, have been forced by unfavorable economic circumstances to modify their policies to suit the interests of foreign creditors. Both, therefore, demonstrate the special vulnerability of sovereignty among Third World states.

Mexico: The PRI Under Challenge

In many ways Mexico's political evolution follows a pattern dominant throughout Latin America. That is, Mexico has maintained an authoritarian political system throughout much of its history, shifting from military caudillo leadership to single-party-dominant rule. Unlike many other Latin countries, Mexico experienced a revolution dedicated to sweeping reform, but with the "institutionalization" of the revolution through the PRI, the reforming drive ebbed quickly as the country settled into a stability that has lasted for half a century.

Mexico conforms quite closely to the categorization outlined in Table 10.1. Through its agrarian and preindustrial phases, it has maintained either personalist or single-party authoritarian regimes. With development, pressures for reform have grown, but even the intellectuals and students who oppose the regime tend to favor an authoritarian leftist solution to Mexico's problems.

Mexico today exhibits many features typical of the earlier stages of industrialization. The proportion of the labor force engaged in industry is now roughly equal to that of agriculture, and the population is more urban than rural. The urban areas display characteristics familiar to the developed world—modern factories, affluent life-styles, and thriving educational systems side by side with slums and late-twentieth-century problems including crime, pollution, inflation, and alienation. At the same time, in most of the nonurban localities preindustrial conditions can be found: traditional authoritarian power structures and near-feudal distinctions between the landholding few and the illiterate, landless population living on society's margins.

Change has often come to Mexico from the outside. The Spaniards brought a new religion, created a new social structure dominated by a landowning elite, and destroyed much of the traditional culture. When Mexicans ended Spanish control in the early nineteenth century, they adopted institutions inspired by another outside influence, the United States. Moreover, the failure of those institutions to function stably did not cause Mexicans to search out a different set of political institutions:

Rapid urbanization has turned Mexico City into one of the world's largest cities, but it has also created widespread poverty and homelessness. (B. Glinn/Magnum)

the constitutions of 1857 and 1917 both set out a presidential system of government.

Mexico's sovereignty, in fact, has always been conditioned by the proximity of the United States, a superpower neighbor whose influence extends, often intrusively, throughout the western hemisphere. The weight of the United States was felt especially in the middle of the nineteenth century, when Mexico lost Texas and the rest of what is now the American Southwest.

Allowing for the ever-present "Yanqui" influence, Mexico had grown to enjoy a relatively high degree of political and military independence in the decades following the U.S.-Mexican War (1846–1848). In international economic affairs, ironically, the first Mexican policies intentionally opened the door to outside penetration as the indigenous political elite of the late nineteenth century encouraged foreign investment to stimulate industrialization and spur the development of agriculture. The 1917 constitution, however, reversed this policy; nationalist pride prompted the new regime to limit foreign investment opportunities and landholding privileges. During the 1930s, as we have seen, President Cárdenas nationalized the oil industry—a very popular move—and steadfastly defended it against outside pressures. By the time of the great oil boom in the 1970s, it seemed as if Mexico was on its way to achieving full economic development.

The 1980s have seen a reversal of this trend. Fluctuations in the price of oil, Mexico's main export, have contributed to a general failure of economic performance. Skyrocketing population growth has caused a severe drain on national resources, and other countries' policies have harmed Mexico's interests. The combination of these forces has thrown Mexico's prospects for developing a well-rounded industrial base independent of foreign influence into doubt.

During the oil price boom, foreign creditors—banks in the United States, West Germany, Britain, and Canada—rushed to offer big loans at favorable interest rates. Mexico readily accepted and began to accumulate a rising debt. When export earnings from oil fell, the country could not repay these loans; indeed, it became difficult even to pay the annual interest without sacrificing funds needed for Mexico's development. Additional loans were required merely to make interest payments. Foreign lenders forced heavy Mexican concessions; President de la Madrid was obliged to inaugurate a program of austerity that bit sharply into social welfare expenditures. The concessions, moreover, spilled over into foreign policy as well, in particular with respect to Central America, as the U.S. government insisted that Mexico cease oil shipments to Nicaragua and back off from Central American peace proposals which Washington opposed.

Mexico's sovereignty was further compromised by U.S. legislation in 1987 that came down severely on the many Mexican emigrants who pass into the United States illegally—more than 1 million each year during the 1980s. Since 1983, de la Madrid's austerity programs have increased unemployment, driving record numbers of poor Mexicans northward in search of jobs. The effectiveness of the new U.S. law remains to be seen but, either way, Mexican economists anticipate an ever-increasing employment crisis in their own country; some believe that the Mexican economy will be doing well if it can provide jobs for even one-half of those reaching employment age between the years 1987 and 2005.

At the present time, the Mexican government confronts a situation in which unplanned changes, stemming from population growth at home and unfavorable economic conditions abroad, have greatly restricted its capacity to respond effectively. In such circumstances, the danger is that a vicious circle will be set in motion: unable to manage the domestic economy and unable to pay its foreign debts, the government may be forced to yield even further to pressures from its creditors, whose demands for more economic austerity may push Mexico into an ever greater crisis. Relief is likely to come only if oil prices rise spectacularly or if some other means of export income is developed. Barring a solution to this crisis, the long-running stability of the PRI's rule may very well undergo its most serious test yet.

Signs of the weakening of PRI control can be detected in a number of areas. As we have seen, mobilized peasants and workers have at various times pressed the government for changes and sometimes succeeded. Today, elements of the middle classes and students demand a more competitive democratic structure, and although they have not realized the changes they seek, their voices sound an alarm that future Mexican regimes must take seriously. In addition, the PRI is facing challenges from within its own ranks, especially between technocrats and the traditional party faithful. The main channel of leadership recruitment tends to go not through elective office or state government service but through the federal bureaucracy. Increasingly, those with expertise and experience in government administration are being recruited directly into cabinet positions, and this has led to growing resentment among those excluded from the process. In 1987 and 1988, there occurred two dramatic indications of these trends: the party chose as its 1988 presidential candidate a technocrat, Salinas de Gortari, who had never held elective office, and the leftist opposition united around Cuahtemoc Cárdenas, the grandson of former President Lázaro Cárdenas, who ran against him under the National Democratic Front banner. The seriousness of this challenge was indicated in the election's result: The PRI candidate won just 50 percent of the popular vote.

With the PRI declining in popularity, there is a possibility that the military will assume the role of monitor of the political system. The need to quell protests that have come in the wake of questionable electoral outcomes has increased the PRI's dependence on the military. This dependence most likely will last as long as the gap between rich and poor continues to widen and disenchantment with the lack of democracy under PRI rule grows. While Mexico is far from becoming a praetorian political system, a failure to maintain PRI control could lead the military to assume, once again, a direct political role.

Nigeria: The Quest for Unity and Growth

The British colonial rulers of Nigeria instigated processes of change that proved to have a profound and irreversible effect on the country's future. They brought numerous small communities together into one political-administrative entity, established a common language for official use (English), introduced European religion and European political rules, and left a legacy of European institutions—a parliament, elections, parties, bureaucracies, a modern army. Libertarian values bequeathed by the British political culture have dominated the outlooks of the Nigerian intelligentsia, and British legal norms have strongly influenced the development of Nigeria's judicial system.

If the Nigerians have not succeeded in realizing the high ideals of this inherited political culture, it is not for want of trying. Even the military elite, as we have pointed out, accepts the principle of civilian democracy. Military regimes have ruled for most of Nigeria's independent period so far, bringing the suspension of two democratic regimes. However, they always have ruled under the assumption that the constitution would eventually be restored. Thus, while Nigerian regimes have more often taken the form that one would expect of a basically agrarian society, the influence of Nigeria's more economically developed former colonial masters has been strongly felt.

The persistence of military rule overlying a liberal-democratic value system is only the most obvious of the inconsistencies between intent and actuality. As in so many Third World countries, Nigerian governments have continously struggled to impose their wills on conditions that are undergoing constant, and often rapid, change. Policies that have promoted industrial development have had both intended and unintended effects. As had been hoped, the beginnings of Nigerian industrialization succeeded in generating a dynamic process that brought parts of Nigerian society into the modern world. New social classes were created—blue-collar workers, white-collar workers, technocrats, expanded bureaucracies. Partly intended and partly not are the natural political cleavages produced by these new social identities. Wholly unintended are the psychological effects that appear to be the inevitable companions of change and modernization—the stress of being uprooted from family and village, the loneliness of urban life, the alienating sense of no longer being the master of one's own labor and no longer feeling connected to the product one creates.

For those who are able to take advantage of educational opportunities offered by the new society, the door may be open to upward mobility, perhaps wealth, and power. On the other hand, increasing numbers of educated people create a strain on the employment structures. If the economy does not provide enough jobs that utilize the skills of the educated, the result can be a growing stratum of unemployed or underemployed among people who now have access to the written media and understand the concepts of individualism and achievement—and whose frustrated ambition, therefore, is fertile soil for the seeds of protest.

As in Mexico, rapid demographic changes place an added pressure on policy. Here is an area in which an intended effect of modernization, improved standards of health and mortality, meets an underlying fact of traditional culture, the preference for large families, to produce an unwanted result: a population explosion. Population growth places increased demands on the land, reduces family and individual incomes, and prompts urban migration, which in turn puts further stress on the limited capacities of urban governments. Increasingly, the society is populated by children below the age of 15, who of course consume but do not produce for the economy.

The beginnings of development can be seen in the presence of electricity, cars, and bicycles in the traditional life of this Northern Nigerian town. (Carl Frank)

Even in strictly political matters, where policies have aimed at unambiguous results, one can see a mixture of intended and unintended effects. The reconciliation following the Biafran revolt, for example, was impressive, as the repartition of Nigeria into states effectively broke the power of old regional identities. However, new divisions sprang up to replace the old ones; the North-South division so evident today, moreover, tends to be reinforced by an underlying Muslim-Christian division.

This division has been affected by the rise of Islamic fundamentalism beyond the borders, especially in Libya. In 1986 the government decided to join the Islamic Conference, in effect throwing a spark on the kindling of Nigeria's North-South division. Localized violence ensued, and Libya was accused of involvement in it. Although this violence did not approach the levels leading up to the Biafran secession, the potential for future hostilities fanned by a world Islamic movement is evident.

The impact of Islamic fundamentalism is but one illustration of Nigeria's vulnerability to international forces. As in Mexico, the global markets for goods and financial services have held out the lure of enrichment but also demonstrated the risk of economic ruin. A pattern familiar elsewhere has repeated itself in Nigeria: the discovery of oil, rising prices on the world market, intensified exploitation of the oil reserves financed by large foreign loans, the collapse of world oil prices, drastically reduced export earnings, an inability to meet international loan payments. With foreign debts surpassing $20 billion, Nigeria has been pressured by the World Bank to devalue its currency, cut back its imports severely, and lower its subsidies on the domestic price of gasoline by 50 percent (thus increasing the price paid by Nigerian consumers). In return, Nigeria has been granted a restructuring of its debts—that is, further credits, which, of course, must also be repaid.

The decline in oil revenues forced Nigeria to curtail its industrial investment. Moreover, being compelled to reduce imports struck another blow to development efforts, since Nigeria had grown to depend on imports for 70 percent of its raw materials and a large proportion of its industrial technology as well. There has been an attempt to stimulate domestic production for import substitution of some goods, but this cannot be done overnight. Deprived of essential ingredients, Nigerian industry at one point in the mid-1980s was operating at only 30 percent of its capacity.

Thus Nigeria, at a level of development lower than Mexico's, faces problems that are of similar difficulty: rapid population growth and the attendant demographic changes, new social cleavages resulting from industrialization, the potential of a revolutionary stratum composed of frustrated members of a growing middle class, and severe vulnerability to foreign penetration, political and economic. In addition, Nigeria must wrestle with a problem Mexico does not have, serious cleavages resulting from ethnic, regional, and religious divisions. As the military regime attempts to prepare the way for a return to constitutional rule in the 1990s, there is little to indicate that conditions for the civilian leaders will be more propitious than they were before.

REFLECTIONS ON CHANGE AND INTERDEPENDENCE

At the basis of our era's greatest political debate is a question about the possibility of meaningful change in the absence of a violent revolution. The debate is illustrated in the following comment on the results of the 1920 Mexican election:

> To an observer, the Mexican government appeared no different from that of the Diaz period [1876–1911] with its politicians, demagogues, ambitious generals, big landowners (albeit new, uniformed owners who, as a rule, had seized their lands during the Revolution), small groups who disputed the executive power, and fraudulent elections. All this was too deeply embedded in Mexico by the thirty years of Porfiriate to be conjured away in an instant.[9]

Can fundamental changes in a society's political order be purposely effected without an upheaval of the existing socioeconomic structure? This is the heart of the issue. On one side we see the simple objectives

[9]Victor Alba, *The Mexicans* (New York: Pegasus, 1973), p. 147.

of the Mexican Revolution—land for the landless, improvement in the conditions of labor, and reforms of the political institutions. On the other side is the Marxian contention that altering the political "superstructure" will not bring meaningful change without a thoroughgoing revolution of society's socioeconomic "base." Were he still alive, Mao Zedong, a follower of Marx, could point to the shortcomings of Mexico and Nigeria to bolster his position that nothing short of a full-scale effort to reconstruct the economic base and refashion the political culture would suffice to achieve true democracy and realize full human dignity. Those who oppose this argument hold that change should not be sought at the price of individual liberties, including the right to own private property, the basis of the social order that Marx believed must be overturned.

The division of our contemporary world into capitalist, communist, and Third World states, though in some ways a convention that oversimplifies reality, is based on this very argument. The developed capitalist states of the "First World," including Great Britain and France, have held to the position that revolutionary changes of the type Marx predicted would simply be too high a price to pay for whatever political results might ensue. Their leaders and spokesmen point out that the communist states have failed to build democratic systems in the wake of their revolutions and, instead, hang on to the vanguard-elitism of Lenin's and Mao's oligarchies. The communist states of the "Second World" naturally reject the notion that their systems are undemocratic and insist that their way is the only route to an ultimate form of true democracy. Third World leaders are divided on this question. Some, such as those who govern in Cuba, Ethiopia, and Vietnam, accept the Marxist premise together with the oligarchical political corollary, that is, the need for an elite vanguard to guide society in its forward march. Many others, however, agree with the First World premise that individual rights are by no means incompatible with—and indeed may be important to—modernization and political development.

In the course of time it has become evident to many world leaders that reality is too complex to be explained by simplistic notions and superficial ideologies. Capitalist states have experimented with policies suggesting socialistic ideas (e.g., the nationalization of key industries, "socialized" medicine), while communist states have moved to privatize certain sectors of their economies. Third World leaders have realized that the conventional strategies for economic development based on increasing the GNP will not necessarily result in a more equitable distribution of wealth (the "trickle-down" theory central to free enterprise systems) and that economic progress does not necessarily mean political development.

Indeed, economic development itself is often elusive. It is clear today that certain countries face obstacles to development that are enormously difficult—lack of natural resources, forbidding climates, populations in excess of imaginable productive potential. Such countries—one thinks of Afghanistan, Bangladesh, the countries of the African Sahara, and some others—are now sometimes categorized as the "Fourth World," emphasizing the seeming intractability of their problems. And yet one should not give up hope for them; history points to a number of countries with limited natural resources or other obstacles which they have succeeded in overcoming, Japan being the most spectacular example.

Even the highly developed countries of the First World face the task of guiding and controlling continuous change. "The more you have, the more you want"—so goes the old saying—and modern societies involve themselves in a never-ending quest for enhanced standards of living, a more equitable distribution of wealth, improved systems of justice, and human dignity. Western governments must strive to foster economic stability, technological advancement, and many other goals which their citizens demand, at the same time as they provide for national security in an international environment over which the threat of nuclear annihilation constantly hangs. Bound together in an increasingly interdependent world, all governments confront challenges that demand the best of their capabilities.

Bibliography

BRITAIN

Ashford, Douglas E., *Policy and Politics in Britain: The Limits of Consensus* (Philadelphia: Temple University Press, 1981).

Beer, Samuel H., *Britain Against Itself: The Political Contradictions of Collectivism* (New York: Norton, 1982).

Butler, David E., and Anne Sloman, eds. *British Political Facts, 1900–1979* (New York: St. Martin's, 1980).

Kavanagh, Dennis, "Political Culture in Great Britain: Decline of the Civic Culture," in G. Almond and S. Verba, eds., *The Civic Culture Revisited* (Boston: Little Brown, 1980).

Kavanagh, Dennis, ed. *The Politics of the Labour Party.* (Boston: Allen and Unwin, 1982).

King, Anthony, ed., *The British Prime Minister* (London: Macmillan, 1985).

Kramnick, I., ed., *Is Britain Dying? Perspectives on the Current Crisis* (Ithaca, NY: Cornell University Press, 1979).

Norton, Philip, *The British Polity* (New York: Longman, 1984).

Norton, Philip, *The Commons in Perspective* (New York: Longman, 1981).

Norton, Philip, *The Constitution in Flux* (Oxford: Martin Robertson, 1982).

Rose, Richard, *Do Parties Make a Difference?* 2nd ed. (Chatham, NJ: Chatham House, 1984).

Rose, Richard, *Politics in Britain,* 4th ed. (Boston: Little, Brown, 1985).

Rose, Richard, *The Territorial Dimension in Government: Understanding the United Kingdom* (Chatham, NJ: Chatham House, 1982).

Sampson, Anthony, *The Changing Anatomy of Britain* (New York: Vintage, 1984).

Smith, Geoffrey, and Nelson W. Polsby, *British Government and Its Discontents* (New York: Basic Books, 1981).

Walkland, S. A., and M. Ryle. *The Commons Today* (London: Fontana, 1981).

FRANCE

Ambler, John S., ed., *The French Socialist Experiment* (Philadelphia: Institute for the Study of Human Issues, 1984).

Andrews, William G., and Stanley Hoffmann, eds. *The Fifth Republic at Twenty* (Albany: State University of New York Press, 1981).

Ardagh, John, *France in the 1980s* (Harmondsworth, England: Penguin Books, 1983).

Ashford, Douglas E., *Policy and Politics in France: Living With Uncertainty* (Philadelphia: Temple University Press, 1982).

Cerny, Philip G., and Martin A. Schain, eds., *French Politics and Public Policy* (New York: St. Martin's, 1980).

Crozier, Michel, *The Stalled Society* (New York: Viking, 1974).

Ehrmann, Henry W., *Politics in France,* 4th ed. (Boston: Little, Brown, 1983).

Hayward, Jack, *Governing France: The One and Indivisible Republic,* 2nd ed. (London: Weidenfeld and Nicholson, 1983).

Hoffmann, Stanley, *Decline of Renewal: France Since the 1930s* (New York: Viking, 1974).

Kesselman, Mark, ed., *The French Workers' Movement: Economic Crisis and Political Change* (London: George Allen & Unwin, 1984).

Peyrefitte, Alain. *The Trouble with France* (New York: Knopf, 1981).

Suleiman, Ezra N., *Elites in French Society: The Politics of Survival* (Princeton, NJ: Princeton University Press, 1978).

Suleiman, Ezra N., *Politics, Power and Bureaucracy in France: The Administrative Elite* (Princeton, NJ: Princeton University Press, 1974).

Thomson, David. *Democracy in France Since 1870* (New York: Oxford University Press, 1964).

Wilson, Frank L., *Political Parties Under the Fifth Republic* (New York: Praeger, 1982).

Wright, Vincent, *The Government and Politics of France,* 2nd ed. (New York: Holmes & Meier, 1983).

Wright, Vincent, ed., *Continuity and Change in France* (London: George Allen & Unwin, 1984).

Zeldin, Theodore, *The French* (New York: Vintage Books, 1984).

USSR

Barry, Donald D., and Carol Barner-Barry, *Contemporary Soviet Politics: An Introduction,* 2nd ed. (Englewood Cliffs, NJ: Prentice-Hall, 1982).

Bergson, Abram, and Herbert S. Levine, eds., *The Soviet Economy: Toward the Year 2000* (London: George Allen & Unwin, 1983).

Bialer, Seweryn, *Stalin's Successors: Leadership, Stability, and Change in the Soviet Union* (Cambridge: Cambridge University Press, 1981).

Bialer, Seweryn, and Thane Gustafson, eds., *Russia at the Crossroads: The 26th Congress of the CPSU* (London: George Allen & Unwin, 1982).

Brown, Archie, and Michael Kaser, eds. *Soviet Policy for the 1980s* (Bloomington: Indiana University Press, 1982).

Breslauer, George, *Khrushchev and Brezhnev as Leaders: Building Authority in Soviet Politics* (London: George Allen & Unwin, 1982).

Byrnes, Robert F., ed., *After Brezhnev: Sources of Soviet Conduct in the 1980s* (Bloomington: Indiana University Press, 1983).

d'Encausse, Hélène Carrère, *Confiscated Power: How Soviet Russia Really Works.* Translated from the French by George Holoch (New York: Harper & Row, 1982).

Goldman, Marshall I., *USSR in Crisis: The Failure of an Economic System* (New York: Norton, 1983).

Harasymiw, Bohdan, *Political Elite Recruitment in the Soviet Union* (London: Macmillan, 1984).

Hill, Ronald J., *The Soviet Union: Politics, Economics and Society from Lenin to Gorbachev* (London: Frances Pinter, 1985).

Hill, Ronald J., and Peter Frank, *The Soviet Communist Party.* (London: George Allen & Unwin, 1981).

Hoffmann, Erik P., and Robin F. Laird, eds., *The Soviet Polity in the Modern Era* (New York: Aldine, 1984).

Löwenhardt, John, *Decision Making in Soviet Politics* (London: Macmillan, with St. Martin's, New York, 1985).

Matthews, Mervyn, *Privilege in the Soviet Union: A Study of Elite Life-Styles Under Communism* (London: George Allen & Unwin, 1978).

Shipler, David K., *Russia: Broken Idols, Solemn Dreams* (New York: Times Books, 1983).

Simis, Konstantin, *USSR: The Corrupt Society, The Secret World of Soviet Capitalism* (New York: Simon & Schuster, 1982).

White, Stephen, *Political Culture and Soviet Politics* (London: Macmillan, 1979).

CHINA

Bennet, Gordon, and Ronald Montaperto, *Red Guard: The Political Biography of Dai Hsaio-ai* (New York: Doubleday, 1971).

Barnett, A. Doak, *China's Economy in Global Perspective* (Washington, DC: Brookings Institution, 1981).

Baum, Richard, ed., *China's Four Modernizations: The New Technological Revolution* (Boulder, CO: Westview, 1980).

Bonavia, David, *The Chinese,* rev. ed. (New York: Pelican, 1982).

Bush, Richard C., and James R. Townsend, comp. *The People's Republic of China: A Basic Handbook,* 3rd ed. (New York: Learning Resources in International Studies, 1982).

Camilleri, Joseph, *Chinese Foreign Policy: The Maoist Era and Its Aftermath* (Seattle: University of Washington Press, 1980).

Dittmer, Lowell, *Liu Shao-Ch'i and the Chinese Cultural Revolution* (Berkeley: University of California Press, 1974).

Fairbank, John King, *The United States and China,* 4th ed. (Cambridge: Harvard University Press, 1979).

Freedman, Maurice, *The Study of Chinese Society* (Stanford, CA: Stanford University Press, 1979).

Harding, Harry, *Organizing China: The Problem of Bureaucracy,* 1949–1976 (Stanford, CA: Stanford University Press, 1981).

Hinton, Harold C., ed., *The People's Republic of China: A Handbook* (Boulder, CO: Westview, 1979).

Lee, Hong Yung, *The Politics of the Chinese Cultural Revolution: A Case Study* (Berkeley: University of California Press, 1978).

Liu, Alan P. L., *Political Culture and Group Conflict in China* (Santa Barbara, CA: Clio Books, 1976).

Meisner, Maurice, *Mao's China: A History of the People's Republic* (New York: Free Press, 1977).

Mozingo, David, *State and Society in Contemporary China* (Ithaca, NY: Cornell University Press, 1983).

Pye, Lucian, *The Dynamics of Chinese Politics* (Cambridge, MA: Oelgeschlager, Gunn and Hain, 1981).

Snow, Edgar, *Red Star over China* (New York: Grove, 1944).

Spence, Jonathan D., *The Gate of Heavenly Peace: The Chinese and Their Revolution, 1895–1980* (New York: Viking, 1981).

Starr, John Bryan, *Continuing the Revolution: The Political Thought of Mao* (Princeton, NJ: Princeton University Press, 1979).

Townsend, James R., *Politics in China,* 3rd ed. (Boston: Little, Brown, 1986).

Wang, James C. F., *Contemporary Chinese Politics: An Introduction,* 2nd ed. (Englewood Cliffs, NJ: Prentice-Hall, 1985).

Wolf, Margery, *Revolution Postponed: Women in Contemporary China* (Stanford, CA: Stanford University Press, 1985).

MEXICO

Alba, Victor, *The Mexicans* (New York: Pegasus, 1970).

Cornelius, Wayne A., *Politics and the Migrant Poor in Mexico City* (Stanford, CA: Stanford University Press, 1975).

Craig, Ann L., *The First Agraristas: An Oral History of a Mexican Agrarian Reform Movement* (Berkeley: University of California Press, 1983).

Craig, Ann L., and Wayne Cornelius, "Political Culture in Mexico: Continuities and Revisionist Interpretations." In G. Almond and S. Verba, eds., *The Civic Culture Revisited* (Boston: Little, Brown, 1980).

Fagen, Richard R., and William S. Tuohy, *Politics and Privilege in a Mexican Community* (Stanford, CA: Stanford University Press, 1972).

From, E., and M. Maccoby, *Social Character in a Mexican Village* (Englewood Cliffs, NJ: Prentice-Hall, 1970).

González Casanova, Pablo, *Democracy in Mexico* (London: Oxford University Press, 1970).

Grindle, Merilee S., *Bureaucrats, Politicians, and Peasants in Mexico: A Case Study in Public Policy* (Berkeley: University of California Press, 1977).

Hamilton, Nora, *The Limits of State Autonomy: Post-Revolutionary Mexico* (Princeton, NJ: Princeton University Press, 1982).

Hewlett, Sylvia A., and Richard S. Weinert, eds., *Brazil and Mexico: Patterns in Late Development* (Philadelphia: Institute for the Study of Human Issues, 1982).

Levy, Daniel, and Gabriel Székely, *Mexico: Paradoxes of Stability and Change* (Boulder, CO: Westview, 1983).

Lewis, Oscar, *Pedro Martinez* (New York: Random House, 1964).

Lieuwen, Edwin, *Mexican Militarism: The Political Rise and Fall of the Revolutionary Army* (Albuquerque: University of New Mexico Press, 1968).

McBride, Robert H., ed., *Mexico and the United States* (Englewood Cliffs, NJ: American Assembly–Prentice-Hall, 1981).

Purcell, Susan Kaufman, ed., *Mexico–United States Relations* (New York: Academy of Political Science, Columbia University, 1981).

Reyna, José Luis, and Richard S. Weinert, eds., *Authoritarianism in Mexico* (Philadelphia: Institute for the Study of Human Issues, 1977).

Smith, Peter H., *Labyrinths of Power: Political Recruitment in Twentieth-Century Mexico* (Princeton, NJ: Princeton University Press, 1979).

Stevens, Evelyn P., *Protest and Response in Mexico* (Cambridge: Massachusetts Institute of Technology Press, 1974).

Wyman, Donald L., ed., *Mexico's Economic Crisis and Stabilization Policies* (La Jolla, CA: Center for U.S.-Mexican Studies, University of California, San Diego, 1983).

NIGERIA

Adamolekun, Ladipo, *The Fall of the Second Republic* (Ibadan: Spectrum Books, 1985).

Arnold, Guy, *Modern Nigeria* (London: Longman, 1977).

Bienen, Henry, "Military Rule and Political Process: Nigerian Examples," *Comparative Politics* 10 (January 1978): 205–226.

Bienen, Henry, and V. J. Diejomaoh, eds., *The Political Economy of Income Distribution in Nigeria* (New York: Holmes & Meier, 1981).

Coleman, James S., *Nigeria: Background to Nationalism* (Berkeley, CA: University of California Press, 1960).

Crowder, Michael, *The Story of Nigeria,* 4th ed. (London: Faber and Faber, 1978).

Dent, Martin, and D. Austin, eds., *Implementing Civil Rule: The First Two Years* (Manchester, England: Manchester University Press, 1981).

Diamond, Larry, "Nigeria In Search of Democracy," *Foreign Affairs* 62 (Spring 1984): 905–928.

Diamond, Larry, "Nigeria Update," *Foreign Affairs* 64, No. 2 (Winter 1985–1986).

Dudley, Billy, *An Introduction to Nigerian Government and Politics* (Bloomington: Indiana University Press, 1982).

Frank, Lawrence P., "Two Responses to the Oil Boom: Iranian and Nigerian Politics after 1973," *Comparative Politics* 16 (April 1984): 295–314.

Gibbs, J. L., ed., *Peoples of Africa* (New York: Holt, Rinehart and Winston, 1965).

Joseph, Richard A., "Democracy Under Military Tutelage: Crisis and Consensus in the Nigerian 1979 Election," *Comparative Politics* 14 (October 1981): 75–100.

Nwabuzor, Elone, ed., *State and Society in Nigeria* (Benin City: Nigerian Political Science Association, 1985).

Ostheimer, John M., *Nigerian Politics* (New York: Harper & Row, 1973).

Oyediran, Oyeleye, ed., *Nigerian Government and Politics Under Military Rule, 1966–1979.* (New York: St. Martin's, 1979).

Panter-Brick, Keith, ed., *Soldiers and Oil: The Political Transformation of Nigeria* (London: Frank Cass, 1978).

Peil, Margaret, *Nigerian Politics: The People's View* (London: Cassell, 1976).

Whitaker, C. S., *The Politics of Tradition: Continuity and Change in Northern Nigeria* (Princeton, NJ: Princeton University Press, 1970).

Wolpe, Howard, *Urban Politics in Nigeria* (Berkeley: University of California Press, 1974).

Index

Afghanistan, 435
Aleman, Miguel, 110, 246
Alfonsin, Raul, 434
Allende, Salvador, 263
Andropov, Yuri, 278, 283, 367
Argentina, 393, 434
Aristotle, 124
Austria, 126–127
Authoritarianism. *See* Political
    culture

Belgium, 126–127
Bill of Rights (1689), 36, 85
Bolshevik Revolution, 31, 47, 50, 80,
    97, 145, 237, 322, 363, 407, 408
Brazil, 393
Brezhnev, Leonid, 278, 282–283, 366,
    367, 408, 409
Britain, 34ff, 178
    comparison with France, 33–34,
        45, 74–75, 85, 136, 179, 181,
        183–184, 221–222, 254, 267–268,
        312, 353, 398, 437–438
    comparison with United States,
        82, 83, 84, 132–133, 175–176
    Conservative Party, 40, 131–133,
        168, 223, 224, 225, 268, 313, 315,
        353, 355, 356–358, 440, 441

economic development, 35–36, 37,
    343–347, 353–358
economic policy, 35, 222
elections, 135, 168, 174–176, 226,
    227
forces of change, 437–441
foreign relations, 435, 437, 438,
    439–441
historical development, 30, 33–40,
    74–75
human rights, 173, 179
Industrial Relations Act (1971),
    313, 355
interest groups, 131–132, 223,
    268–269, 313, 354, 355
Labour Party, 40, 130–133, 168,
    214, 223–225, 227, 268–269, 313,
    315, 353, 354, 357, 358, 439, 440,
    441
leadership, 267–273, 299–300, 355
military, 272–273
Northern Ireland, 40, 125, 133–134,
    135, 179, 207, 262, 389, 390,
    401–402
political culture, 38, 40, 116, 129,
    174–179, 183–184, 221–222,
    254
political development, 85, 136, 179

Britain (*Continued*)
  political participation, 179–181,
    206–207
  political parties, 83, 88, 175–176,
    214, 221–222, 225, 226–227, 439
  political stability, 398–402
  political structure, 82, 83, 85–90,
    99, 173–174, 270, 271–272, 273,
    313–314, 315, 389, 398, 399
  public policy formulation, 304,
    306, 312–317
  social cleavages, 130–131, 132–133,
    135–136, 161, 171, 401
  trade unions, 131–132, 135, 178,
    222, 223, 268–269, 313, 354, 355
Bulgaria, 448
Bureaucracies. *See* Public policy

Cambodia, 389
Canada, 79, 80, 122, 373
Carranza, 294
Castro, Fidel, 259, 420
Chernenko, Konstantin, 278, 283,
  367
Chile, 263, 397
China
  comparison with the Soviet
    Union, 45–46, 75, 277–278, 407,
    445–446
  comparison with the West,
    198–199, 321–322
  Cultural Revolution, Great
    Proletarian, 58, 103, 107, 148,
    149, 150, 151, 185, 194, 219, 239,
    284, 288, 289, 300, 328, 330, 369,
    371, 373, 374, 392, 409, 423, 414,
    418, 451
  Democracy Movement, 106–107,
    197, 198, 240, 284, 414, 418
  economic policy, 362–363, 369–375
  elections, 106
  forces of change, 445–446, 450–453
  foreign relations, 452
  Four Modernizations, 59, 286, 371
  Great Leap Forward, 58, 103, 194,
    239, 242, 284, 328, 330, 414, 418,
    451
  historical development, 54–61, 242,
    286, 330, 450, 452
  human rights, 198–199
  Hundred Flowers Campaign, 185,
    194, 240, 284, 328
  interest groups/mass
    organizations, 185, 194–197, 213,
    232–233, 239–240

  leadership, 58, 148, 197, 198, 240,
    242, 277–278, 283–289, 299–300,
    330, 331, 413, 414, 416, 451
  military, 242, 287–289, 307
  political culture, 51, 54–57, 59–60,
    84, 198
  political participation, 171,
    184–185, 192–199, 206–207, 240,
    285, 289, 331, 413, 414
  political stability, 389, 390, 407,
    412–418, 426
  political structure, 81, 83, 84,
    103–107, 108, 192, 193, 239, 240,
    241–242, 243–244, 286, 414, 451
  public policy formulation, 307,
    321–322, 328–333, 341
  social cleavages, 116, 146, 148–150,
    151, 414, 416
  social mobilization, 56–57, 128,
    185, 194–197, 213, 232–233, 418
  trade unions, 239
Chinese Communist Party, 104, 107,
  193, 197, 214, 240–243, 255, 332.
  See also China
Chirac, Jacques, 230, 318, 361
Churchill, Winston, 89, 365
Civil liberties. *See* Human rights
Civil rights. *See* Human rights
Class. *See* Social cleavages
Colonialism, 77–78, 80, 220
  Mexico in, 61–62, 66
  Nigeria in, 61–62, 68, 69, 71, 73,
    112
Communism
  China's version, 59–60
  class differences, 145, 186
  compared to parliamentary
    system, 83, 84
  democratic centralism, 218–219
  dictatorship of the proletariat, 186
  function of, 95–96, 217–219
  general will, 186
  legitimacy, 219
  liberty, 167–168
  New Economic Policy (NEP), 51
  political participation, 184–185
  role of judiciary, 84
  war communism, 51, 322
Confederalism, 77–78
Constitutions, 76–77. *See also specific
  countries*
Communist Party of the Soviet
  Union (CPSU), 49, 254. *See also*
  Communism; Marxism-
  Leninism; Soviet Union

apparatchiki, 235
Central Committee, 101, 171, 188,
    279
class privileges, 144–145
elections, 99–100
function and role, 235–238,
    324–325
Gulag, 238
KOMSOMOL, 234, 279
mass organizations, 233–235
membership, 145, 186, 188, 235,
    281
nomenklatura, 101, 101ff, 237, 326
Politburo, 81, 83, 101, 188, 234, 278,
    279, 324–326
political participation, 186–188
rules of, 96
Secretariat, 324
structure of, 235–238
succession, 84, 101, 102–103
Courts, 29. *See also specific*
    countries
  in communist systems, 84
  in parliamentary systems, 82, 83
Cromwell, Oliver, 36, 272
Cuba, 420, 434
Czechoslavakia, 367, 448

Dalai Lama, 149
DeGaulle, Charles, 43, 92, 94, 138,
    229–230, 273, 274, 276–277, 319,
    356, 405, 406, 439, 441, 443, 444.
    See also Fifth Republic; France
Democracy, 165–171
  corporatism, 212
  liberal democratic systems,
    206–207, 215
  stability of, 220, 395–396
  theory of, 129
Deng Xiaoping, 58, 103, 194, 197,
    240, 242, 285, 286, 328, 331, 414,
    451
Disraeli, Benjamin, 131, 132
Division of power
  horizontal, 81
  vertical, 77–78
Douglas-Home, Alex, 271
Duvalier, 397

East Germany, 215, 448
Echeverria, 201, 377
Eckstein, H., congruence theory, 396
Economic interdependence, 433–434.
    See also specific countries
Economic development, 31, 171, 212,

262, 263, 264–265, 428. *See also*
    Economic policy making;
    specific countries
Economic policy making, 343–345,
    387–388. *See also specific*
    countries
  in communist systems, 348–349,
    362–363
  in liberal democracies, 345–348,
    353
  in Third World systems, 349–353,
    375
England. *See* Britain
Ethnicity, 119–129. *See also* Social
    cleavages; *specific countries*
European Common Market. *See also*
    DeGaulle
  and Britain, 355–356, 358, 400, 438,
    439
  Common Agricultural Policy
    (CAP), 355–356, 361, 439
  as a confederal system, 78
  and France, 229, 356, 358, 360, 362,
    442, 443

Federalism, 77–80, 109, 112–113, 114,
    142
Fifth Republic. *See also* DeGaulle;
    France
  constituency's interest, 274–275
  executive power, 318
  function and structure of, 92–95,
    179, 318
  initiation of, 43, 273–274
  and labor, 228
  and party politics, 232
  political stability, 403, 404, 405, 406
  support of, 183–184
Forces of change, 427–437, 460–462.
    See also specific countries
  agrarian state, 429–431
  channelling of, 427–429
  in communist systems, 445–446
  controlling change, 435–437
  economic interdependence,
    433–434
  industrial state, 431
  interdependence, 460–462
  interdependence in the Third
    World, 453–454
  interdependence of security and
    sovereignty, 434–435
  in liberal democracies, 437–438
  postindustrial state, 432–433
  preindustrial state, 431

Fourth Republic, 43, 91–92, 183, 273, 390, 404, 443. *See also* France
France
   comparison with Britain, 33–34, 74–75, 85, 136, 179, 181, 221–222, 254, 267–268, 353, 398, 437–438
   comparison with the United States, 94
   economic policy, 137, 306, 343–347, 353, 358–362, 442–443
   elections, 179–181, 180ff, 216
   forces of change, 437–438, 441–445, 461
   foreign relations, 443–445
   historical development, 30, 31, 40–45, 75, 80, 129, 136, 182, 402
   human rights, 184
   interest groups, 227, 229
   leadership, 90, 94, 230, 231, 273–277, 299–230, 318, 319, 356, 360, 361, 406
   military, 276–277
   political culture, 80, 90, 137, 184, 221–222, 229, 267
   political participation, 179–181, 206–207
   political parties, 44, 90, 94, 95, 137, 138, 182, 214, 221, 228, 229–232, 275, 318, 319, 360, 361, 362, 405, 406
   political stability, 44, 83, 92, 138, 182, 228, 230, 273, 276–277, 300, 390, 398, 402–407
   political structure, 92–95, 275–276, 299, 317–318, 359, 361, 404, 405, 406
   public policy formulation, 307, 312, 317–321, 342, 359
   social cleavages, 32, 42–45, 95, 116, 129, 136, 137–138, 181, 231, 232, 319
   trade unions, 228–229, 231

Gang of Four, 285
Germany, 28, 32, 51, 92, 129, 166, 306
Gorbachev, Mikhail, 101, 141, 191, 278, 280, 281, 283, 324–325, 367, 368, 409, 410, 412, 448
Greece
   ancient, 165–166, 166ff, 168, 208, 209
   modern, 263

Haiti, 397
Heath, Edward, 271, 355

Hitler, Adolf, 259
Hua Guofong, 197, 240, 285, 289, 331, 414
Human Rights, 173. *See also specific countries*
   Amnnesty International, 173, 198, 202
   citizens' rights, 173
   Helsinki Accord, 173, 190, 191
   Marxism-Leninism, 173
   Rights of Man and the Citizen, 184
   Sakharov, Andrei, 190, 409
   Solzhenitsyn, Alexander, 190, 238
Hungary, 349, 367, 448
Huntington, Samuel, 393
Hu Yaobang, 285, 416

Ibarra, Rosario, 202
India, 120
Inglehart, Ronald, 124
Interdependence, 428, 433. *See also specific countries*
Interest groups/mass organizations. *See also specific countries;* Trade unions
   in authoritarian settings, 212–214
   in pluralistic settings, 210–212
International Monetary Fund, 393, 438
Iran, 128, 143, 151, 391, 392, 434
Iraq, 434
Israel, 434
Italy, 390

Japan, 56–57, 347, 361, 373, 435
Jiang Kaishek, 57
Johnson, Lyndon B., 346

Keynes, R. J., 345–346, 354, 360
Khomeini, Ayatollah, 392, 434
Khrushchev, Nikita, 53, 102
Kitto, H. D., 165–166, 165ff

Legitimacy, 76, 260
   of communist parties, 219
   and military takeover, 263
   and political stability, 396–397
   revolutionary mythology, 185
   succession, 84–85
Lenin, V. I., 49, 50–51, 97, 139, 141, 185, 188, 278, 363, 364, 367, 447. *See also* Communism; Communist Party of the Soviet Union; Marxism-Leninism; Soviet Union

Li Peng, 287
Lijphart, Arendt, 126
Lin Biao, 285, 288, 414
Liu Shaoqi, 148, 242, 285, 451

Madrid, Miguel de la, 292, 337, 375, 377, 378, 379, 456
Mao Zedong, 57–58, 369, 392, 407, 413, 414, 451. *See also* China; Chinese Communist Party; Communism
    and class, 146, 147–148
    and Cultural Revolution, 58, 332
    and Great Leap Forward, 242, 332
    leadership, 259, 285
    and the military, 289
Marshall Plan, 359
Marx, Karl, 119, 141
Marxism-Leninism, 49, 95, 97, 185–186, 217. *See also* China; Chinese Communist Party; Communism; Communist Party of the Soviet Union; Lenin; Marx; Soviet Union
    cleavages, 119–120, 122–123, 128, 139, 142
    dictatorship of the proletariat, 186
    false consciousness, 122–123, 135
    human rights, 173
    industrial revolution and class, 131
    liberty, 167
    party function, 185
    pluralism, 129
    political parties, 217
    possessive individualism, 122–123
    revolutionary mythology, 185
    theory of capitalism, 119–120, 122–124, 348
    views on religion, 140
Maslow, Abraham, 124
Mateos, Lopez, 110, 334–335
Maurras, Charles, 404
McLuhan, Marshall, 120
Mexico
    comparison with China, 75
    comparison with Nigeria, 75, 107–108, 151–152, 157, 161, 205, 243–244, 333, 375, 418–419, 453–457
    comparison with Soviet Union, 75
    economic policy, 152, 156–157, 161, 221, 337, 375–382
    elections, 109–111, 200
    forces of change, 453–457, 461

foreign relations, 454, 455, 456, 461
historical development, 61, 65, 68, 110, 153, 156, 161, 199, 246, 294, 334–335, 375, 419, 426, 454, 456
human rights, 202–203, 246
interest groups, 243–246, 254
leadership, 201, 203, 289–294, 299–300, 337, 375, 377, 378, 379, 456
military, 65, 293–294
political culture, 63, 65–66, 67–68, 201, 291, 397, 418, 421
political participation, 199, 201–202, 206–207, 248
political parties, 65, 151, 202, 203, 221, 245, 246, 248–249, 420
political stability, 393, 395, 397, 418–422, 426
political structure, 64, 107–111, 247, 248, 249, 456
PRI, 65, 108, 109–111, 153–154, 199, 200, 202, 215, 221, 244–249, 254, 261, 290, 292, 334, 335, 337, 382, 418, 419, 420, 421, 426, 454, 457
public policy formulation, 307, 333–338
social cleavages, 62, 66, 109, 116, 152–156, 199–200, 244
Meyer, Alfred, 326–327
Mitterrand, François, 90, 94, 231, 318, 360, 406
Monarchy
    absolute, 30, 137, 166
    limits to authority, 29, 35–37, 81–82, 85, 166–167
    monarchs, 35–36, 41, 81, 87, 166
Mongolia, 150
Monnet, Jean, 442

Napoleon, 31, 90, 136, 273, 403
National integration. *See specific countries*
NATO, 440–441. *See also specific countries*
Netherlands, 126–127
Nicaragua, 428
Nigeria
    Biafra, 72, 160, 419, 422
    civil war, 72, 128, 158, 160, 204, 295, 422
    comparison with China, 75
    comparison with Mexico, 75, 107–108, 151–152, 157, 161, 199, 243–244, 289–290, 297, 333, 338, 375, 418–419, 453–454, 460

Nigeria (*Continued*)
  comparison with Soviet Union, 75
  economic policy, 71, 160, 375,
    382–387, 423
  elections, 69, 251–254
  forces of change, 453–454, 457–460,
    461
  foreign relations, 456–460
  historical development, 61–62,
    68–74, 112–114, 115, 157–158, 199,
    204, 249–251, 252, 253, 254, 295,
    296, 338, 339–340, 424–425
  human rights, 205–206
  interest groups, 249–251, 254–255
  leadership, 72, 113, 114, 115, 158,
    159, 160, 252, 253, 256, 289–290,
    295–299, 300, 422, 423
  military, 71–72, 113, 114, 115, 160,
    203, 206, 252, 338, 424–425, 458
  political culture, 72–74, 458
  political participation, 199,
    203–207, 251–254
  political parties, 70, 71, 113, 214,
    221, 250, 251–255
  political stability, 390, 391,
    418–419, 422–425, 426
  political structure, 69, 70, 71, 72,
    112–115, 338, 339–340
  public policy formulation, 307,
    333, 338–341, 342
  social cleavages, 68–74, 112–114,
    116–117, 157–162, 203–204,
    249–254, 295–296, 299, 300, 340,
    422, 424, 457, 459

OPEC, 346, 356, 438
Orwell, George, 27–28

Parliaments. *See also* Britain;
    France
  parliamentary system of
    government, 81–83
Patron-client relations
  China, 196
  Mexico, 201, 291, 292, 293, 335
  Nigeria, 297
Peru, 395
Pétain, Henri (marshal), 43
Pinochet, General, 397
Pluralism, 31–33, 129, 210, 215, 312
Poland, 215, 219, 262, 409, 426
Political culture. *See also* specific
    countries
  authoritarian and, 30, 31–33,
    212–214
  constraints on leaders, 259–260

  definition of, 32
  pluralist, 31, 32–33, 38, 210–212,
    215
Political development, 28–32, 74–75
  in communist systems, 45–46
  definition of, 28–29
  in liberal democracy, 33–34
  and political culture, 32–33
  in Third World systems, 61–62
Political frameworks, 76–85,
    115–117. *See also specific*
    countries
  in communist systems, 95–96
  in liberal democratic systems, 85
  in Third World systems, 107–108
Political leadership, 256–267,
    299–300. *See also specific*
    countries
  civilian, 256–261
  in communist systems, 277–278
  in liberal democracies, 267–268
  military, 262–267
  in Third World systems, 289–
    290
Political participation, 165–173,
    206–207. *See also specific*
    countries
  in communist systems, 184–185
  in liberal democracies, 173–174
  in Third World systems, 199
Political parties, 214–221. *See also*
    Chinese Communist Party;
    Communist Party of the Soviet
    Union; *specific countries*
  in communist systems, 217–219
  in liberal democracies, 215–217
  in Third World systems, 219–221
Political stability, 389–397, 425–426.
    See also Legitimacy; *specific*
    countries
  causes of, 391–395
  in communist systems, 407
  definition of, 390–391
  in force, 396–397
  in liberal democracies, 398
  in Third World, 418–419
Political succession, 83–85, 102–103,
    111
Pompidou, Georges, 230, 356, 406
Portillo, Jose Lopez, 203, 292, 378,
    379
Praetorianism, 263, 263ff, 267
Public policy, 303–312, 341–342. *See*
    also specific countries
  bureaucracy and, 310–312
  in communist systems, 321–322

in liberal democracies, 312
origin of issues, 303–306
styles of, 305–310
in Third World systems, 333

Red Guards. *See* China
Religion. *See also* Northern Ireland;
      specific countries
   Catholicism, 29, 30–31, 41, 42, 63,
      122, 137, 155–156
   Islam, 69–70, 74, 120, 160, 204, 389,
      422, 423, 424, 426
   Protestantism, 30–31, 41, 42, 122
   Russian Orthodox Church, 30, 52,
      140
Republic of Ireland, 401
Revolutions
   China. *See specific revolution*
   England, 272
   France, 31, 42, 75, 80, 129, 136, 182,
      184
   Mexico, 63, 64
   Soviet Union, 47, 50. *See also*
      Bolshevik Revolution
Richelieu, 41
Rigby, T. H., 234
Rousseau, Jean-Jacques, 124,
      166–167, 168–169, 221, 227–228

Sakharov, Andrei, 190, 409
Scargill, Arthur, 132
Scotland, 40, 86, 121, 136, 402
Snow, Edgar, 145
Social cleavages, 118–129, 161–162.
      See also Ethnicity; Religion;
      specific countries
   class and cleavage, 124
   in communist systems, 139
   and consociationalism, 126–127,
      134, 136, 143, 161
   cross-cutting, 125–126, 132,
      133–134, 136
   and electoral systems, 216–217
   liberal democratic view, 121–122,
      129–130
   Marxist view of, 119–120, 122–123
   and political parties, 215–216
   possessive individualism, 122–123
   in Third World, 151–152
   types, 119
Social mobilization, 31–32, 128
Solzhenitsyn, Aleksandr, 190, 238
Somoza, Anastasio, 428
South Africa, 125, 397, 440
South Korea, 81, 390, 393
Sovereignty, 29–30, 76, 428, 433

Soviet Union
   comparison with Britain, 101
   comparison with China, 45–46, 75,
      277–278, 407
   comparison with the West, 192,
      321–322
   economic policy, 48–49, 51, 81,
      143–144, 322–327, 362–368, 409
   elections, 187–188
   forces of change, 141, 324, 445–450
   foreign relations, 30, 434, 448–449
   historical development, 47, 50, 51,
      322
   human rights, 173, 190–192, 238,
      408, 409
   mass organizations, 50, 98,
      186–187, 213, 232–235, 254, 279
   KGB, 190, 238, 279, 305, 326
   leadership, 277–283, 299–300, 366,
      367, 408, 409, 411–412
   military, 279
   political culture, 47–49, 80, 185
   political participation, 171–173,
      185–192, 207
   political stability, 84, 101, 102–103,
      390, 397, 407–412, 426
   political structure, 80, 81, 83, 96,
      97–103, 186, 191, 278, 279,
      324–325, 364, 367, 410
   public policy formulation, 307,
      309, 321–321, 341
   social cleavages, 47–48, 49, 80, 98,
      116, 120–121, 140–143, 144, 149,
      161, 189–190, 409, 411–412, 450
Spain, 63
Sri Lanka, 390
Stalin, Joseph, 28, 51–54, 57, 102,
      143, 185, 219, 238, 259, 281, 322,
      363, 364, 407, 408, 451. *See also*
      Soviet Union
State building, 29–32. *See also*
      Political development
Switzerland, 126–127

Taiwan, 81, 393
Thailand, 389
Thatcher, Margaret, 86, 132, 225,
      270, 355, 356–358, 402, 439. *See
      also* Britain
Tibet, 149–150, 414, 416
Tsars, 47, 50, 185, 363, 447, 450

Unitary system, 77, 79, 86, 103–104,
      113
United Kingdom. *See* Britain
United Nations, 32

United States
  comparison with Britain, 132–133, 175–176, 183–184
  comparison with France, 183–184
  economic policy, 358, 359, 361, 362, 364, 373, 400
  elections, 216
  foreign relations, 434–435, 452
  historical development, 83
  human rights, 78, 79, 262, 409
  interest groups, 210
  political parties, 216
  political structure, 78, 79, 80, 81, 82, 83–84, 271
  public policy formulation, 304
  social cleavages, 121, 132, 409

Vietnam, 346, 389, 435, 448

Wai Jingsheng, 198
Wales, 40, 86, 121, 136
Watergate, 44
Weber, Max, 31, 76, 260
West Germany, 347, 435
World Bank, 434, 460

Yugoslavia, 349

Zhao Ziyang, 285, 287
Zhou Enlai, 58, 242, 286, 330